LANGUAGES AND LINGUISTICS

STUDIES AND EXERCISES IN FORMAL LOGIC

LANGUAGES AND LINGUISTICS

Additional books and e-books in this series can be found
on Nova's website under the Series tab.

LANGUAGES AND LINGUISTICS

STUDIES AND EXERCISES IN FORMAL LOGIC

JOHN NEVILLE KEYNES

Copyright © 2019 by Nova Science Publishers, Inc.

All rights reserved. No part of this book may be reproduced, stored in a retrieval system or transmitted in any form or by any means: electronic, electrostatic, magnetic, tape, mechanical photocopying, recording or otherwise without the written permission of the Publisher.

We have partnered with Copyright Clearance Center to make it easy for you to obtain permissions to reuse content from this publication. Simply navigate to this publication's page on Nova's website and locate the "Get Permission" button below the title description. This button is linked directly to the title's permission page on copyright.com. Alternatively, you can visit copyright.com and search by title, ISBN, or ISSN.

For further questions about using the service on copyright.com, please contact:
Copyright Clearance Center
Phone: +1-(978) 750-8400   Fax: +1-(978) 750-4470   E-mail: info@copyright.com.

NOTICE TO THE READER

The Publisher has taken reasonable care in the preparation of this book, but makes no expressed or implied warranty of any kind and assumes no responsibility for any errors or omissions. No liability is assumed for incidental or consequential damages in connection with or arising out of information contained in this book. The Publisher shall not be liable for any special, consequential, or exemplary damages resulting, in whole or in part, from the readers' use of, or reliance upon, this material. Any parts of this book based on government reports are so indicated and copyright is claimed for those parts to the extent applicable to compilations of such works.

Independent verification should be sought for any data, advice or recommendations contained in this book. In addition, no responsibility is assumed by the Publisher for any injury and/or damage to persons or property arising from any methods, products, instructions, ideas or otherwise contained in this publication.

This publication is designed to provide accurate and authoritative information with regard to the subject matter covered herein. It is sold with the clear understanding that the Publisher is not engaged in rendering legal or any other professional services. If legal or any other expert assistance is required, the services of a competent person should be sought. FROM A DECLARATION OF PARTICIPANTS JOINTLY ADOPTED BY A COMMITTEE OF THE AMERICAN BAR ASSOCIATION AND A COMMITTEE OF PUBLISHERS.

Additional color graphics may be available in the e-book version of this book.

Library of Congress Cataloging-in-Publication Data

ISBN: 978-1-53616-195-3

Published by Nova Science Publishers, Inc. † New York

Contents

Preface to the Fourth Edition		vii
Preface to the Third Edition		ix
Preface to the Second Edition		xi
Preface to the First Edition		xiii
Reference List of Initial Letters Shewing the Authorship or Source of Questions and Problems		xv
Introduction		xvii
Part I.	Terms	1
Chapter 1	The Logic of Terms	3
Chapter 2	Extension and Intension	11
Chapter 3	Real, Verbal, and Formal Propositions	27
Chapter 4	Negative Names and Relative Names	33
Part II.	Propositions	39
Chapter 5	Import of Judgments and Propositions	41
Chapter 6	Kinds of Judgments and Propositions	49
Chapter 7	The Opposition of Propositions	69
Chapter 8	Immediate Inferences	81
Chapter 9	The Diagrammatic Representation of Propositions	101
Chapter 10	Propositions in Extension and in Intension	117
Chapter 11	Logical Equations and the Quantification of the Predicate	125
Chapter 12	The Existential Import of Categorical Propositions	139
Chapter 13	Conditional and Hypothetical Propositions	163
Chapter 14	Disjunctive (or Alternative) Propositions	179

Part III.	**Syllogisms**	**187**
Chapter 15	The Rules of the Syllogism	189
Chapter 16	The Figures and Moods of the Syllogism	207
Chapter 17	The Reduction of Syllogisms	215
Chapter 18	The Diagrammatic Representation of Syllogisms	233
Chapter 19	Conditional and Hypothetical Syllogisms	241
Chapter 20	Disjunctive Syllogisms	251
Chapter 21	Irregular and Compound Syllogisms	259
Chapter 22	Problems on the Syllogism	275
Chapter 23	The Characteristics of Inference	293
Chapter 24	Examples of Arguments and Fallacies	305
Appendix A.	**The Doctrine of Division**	313
Appendix B.	**The Three Fundamental Laws of Thought**	319
Appendix C.	**A Generalization of Logical Processes in Their Application to Complex Propositions**	331
Index		385
Related Nova Publications		393

Preface to the Fourth Edition[*]

In this edition many of the sections have been re-written and a good deal of new matter has been introduced. The following are some of the more important modifications.

In Part I a new definition of "connotative name" is proposed, in the hope that some misunderstanding may thereby be avoided; and the treatment of negative names has been revised.

In Part II the problem of the import of judgments and propositions in its various aspects is dealt with in much more detail than before, and greater importance is attached to distinctions of modality. Partly in consequence of this, the treatment of conditional and hypothetical propositions has been modified. I have partially re-written the chapter on the existential import of propositions in order to meet some recent criticisms and to explain my position more clearly. Many other minor changes in Part II have been made.

Amongst the changes in Part III are a more systematic treatment of the process of the indirect reduction of syllogisms, and the introduction of a chapter on the characteristics of inference.

An appendix on the fundamental laws of thought has been added; and the treatment of complex propositions which previously constituted Part IV of the book has now been placed in an appendix.

The reader of this edition will perceive my indebtedness to Sigwart's *Logic*. I have received valuable help from Professor J. S. Mackenzie and from my son, Mr. J. M. Keynes; and I cannot express too strongly the debt I once more owe to Mr. W. E. Johnson, who by his criticisms has enabled me to improve my exposition in many parts of the book, and also to avoid some errors.

J. N. Keynes.
6, Harvey Road, Cambridge,
4 September 1906.

---

[*] This is an edited, augmented and reformatted version of the fourth edition of "Studies and Exercises in Formal Logic" by John Neville Keynes, originally published by Macmillan and Co., dated 1906. The views, opinions, and nomenclature expressed in this book are those of the authors and do not reflect the views of Nova Science Publishers, Inc.

PREFACE TO THE THIRD EDITION

This edition has been in great part re-written and the book is again considerably enlarged.

In Part I the mutual relations between the extension and the intension of names are examined from a new point of view, and the distinction between real and verbal propositions is treated more fully than in the two earlier editions. In Part II more attention is paid to tables of equivalent propositions, certain developments of Euler's and Lambert's diagrams are introduced, the interpretation of propositions in extension and intension is discussed in more detail, and a brief explanation is given of the nature of logical equations. The chapters on the existential import of propositions and on conditional, hypothetical, and disjunctive (or, as I now prefer to call them, alternative) propositions have also been expanded, and the position which I take on the various questions raised in these chapters is I hope more clearly explained. In Parts III and IV there is less absolutely new matter, but the minor modifications are numerous. An appendix is added containing a brief account of the doctrine of division.

In the preface to earlier editions I was glad to have the opportunity of acknowledging my indebtedness to Professor Caldecott, to Mr. W. E. Johnson, to Professor Henry Laurie, to Dr. Venn, and to Mrs. Ward. In the present edition my indebtedness to Mr. Johnson is again very great. Many new developments are due to his suggestion, and in every important discussion in the book I have been most materially helped by his criticism and advice.

Cambridge,
25 July 1894.

Preface to the Second Edition

This edition has been carefully revised, and numerous sections have been almost entirely re-written.

In addition to the introduction of some brief prefatory sections, the following are among the more important modifications. In Part I an attempt has been made to differentiate the meanings of the three terms connotation, intension, comprehension, with the hope that such differentiation of meaning may help to remove an ambiguity which is the source of much of the current controversy on the subject of connotation. In Part II a distinction between conditional and hypothetical propositions is adopted for which I am indebted to Mr W. E. Johnson; and the treatment of the existential import of propositions has been both expanded and systematised. In Part IV particular propositions, which in the first edition were practically neglected, are treated in detail; and, while the number of mere exercises has been diminished, many points of theory have received considerable development. Throughout the book the unanswered exercises are now separated from the expository matter and placed together at the end of the several chapters in which they occur. An index has been added.

I have to thank several friends and correspondents, amongst whom I must especially mention Mr. Henry Laurie of the University of Melbourne and Mr. W. E. Johnson of King's College, Cambridge, for suggestions and criticisms from which I have derived the greatest assistance. Mr. Johnson has kindly read the proof sheets throughout; and I am particularly indebted to him for the generous manner in which he has placed at my disposal not only his time but also the results of his own work on various points of formal logic.

Cambridge,
22 June 1887.

Preface to the First Edition[1]

In addition to a somewhat detailed exposition of certain portions of what may be called the book-work of formal logic, the following pages contain a number of problems worked out in detail and unsolved problems, by means of which the student may test his command over logical processes.

In the expository portions of Parts I, II, and III, dealing respectively with terms, propositions, and syllogisms, the traditional lines are in the main followed, though with certain modifications; e.g., in the systematisation of immediate inferences, and in several points of detail in connection with the syllogism. For purposes of illustration Euler's diagrams are employed to a greater extent than is usual in English manuals.

In Part IV, which contains a generalisation of logical processes in their application to complex inferences, a somewhat new departure is taken. So far as I am aware this part constitutes the first systematic attempt that has been made to deal with formal reasonings of the most complicated character without the aid of mathematical or other symbols of operation, and without abandoning the ordinary non-equational or predicative form of proposition. This attempt has on the whole met with greater success than I had anticipated; and I believe that the methods formulated will be found to be both as easy and as effective as the symbolical methods of Boole and his followers. The book concludes with a general and sure method of solution of what Professor Jevons called the inverse problem, and which he himself seemed to regard as soluble only by a series of guesses.

The writers on logic to whom I have been chiefly indebted are De Morgan, Jevons, and Venn. To Mr. Venn I am peculiarly indebted, not merely by reason of his published writings, vii especially his *Symbolic Logic*, but also for most valuable suggestions and criticisms while this book was in progress. I am glad to have this opportunity of expressing to him my thanks for the ungrudging help he has afforded me. I am also under great obligation to Miss Martin of Newnham College, and to Mr. Caldecott of St John's College, for criticisms which I have found extremely helpful.

Cambridge,
19 January 1884.

---

[1] With some omissions.

Reference List of Initial Letters Shewing the Authorship or Source of Questions and Problems

B = Professor J. I. Beare, Trinity College, Dublin;
C = University of Cambridge;
J = Mr. W. E. Johnson, King's College, Cambridge;
K = Dr. J. N. Keynes, Pembroke College, Cambridge;
L = University of London;
M = University of Melbourne;
N = Professor J. S. Nicholson, University of Edinburgh;
O = University of Oxford;
O'S = Mr. C. A. O'Sullivan, Trinity College, Dublin;
R = the late Professor G. Croom Robertson;
RR = Mr. R. A. P. Rogers, Trinity College, Dublin;
T = Dr. F. A. Tarleton, Trinity College, Dublin;
V = Dr. J. Venn, Gonville and Caius College, Cambridge;
W = Professor J. Ward, Trinity College, Cambridge.

Note. A few problems have been selected from the published writings of Boole, De Morgan, Jevons, Solly, Venn, and Whately, from the Port Royal Logic, and from the Johns Hopkins Studies in Logic. In these cases the source of the problem is appended in full.

INTRODUCTION

1. *The General Character of Logic.*—Logic may be defined as the science which investigates the general principles of valid thought. Its object is to discuss the characteristics of judgments, regarded not as psychological phenomena but as expressing our knowledge and beliefs; and, in particular, it seeks to determine the conditions under which we are justified in passing from given judgments to other judgments that follow from them.

As thus defined, logic has in view an ideal; it is concerned fundamentally with how we ought to think, and only indirectly and as a means to an end with how we actually think. It may accordingly be described as a normative or regulative science. This character it possesses in common with ethics and aesthetics. These three branches of knowledge—all of them based on psychology—form a unique trio, to be distinguished from positive sciences on the one hand, and from practical arts on the other. It may be said roughly that they are concerned with the ideal in the domains of thought, action, and feeling respectively. Logic seeks to determine the general principles of valid thought, ethics the general principles of right conduct, aesthetics the general principles of correct taste.

2. *Formal Logic.*—As regards the scope of logic, one of the principal questions ordinarily raised is whether the science is *formal* or *material*, subjective or objective, concerned with thoughts or with things. It is usual to say that logic is *formal*, in so far as it is concerned merely with the form of thought, that is, with our manner of thinking irrespective of the particular objects about which we are thinking; and that it is *material*, in so far as it regards as fundamental the objective reference of our thought, and recognises as of essential importance the differences existing in the objects themselves about which we think.

Logic is certainly formal, or at any rate non-material, in the sense that it cannot guarantee the actual objective or material truth of any particular conclusions. Moreover any valid reasoning whatsoever must conform to some definite type, or—in other words—must be reducible to some determinate form; and one of the main objects of logic is by abstraction to discover what are the various types or forms to which all valid reasoning may be reduced.

But, on the other hand, it is essential that logic should recognise an objective reference in every judgment, that is, a reference outside the state of mind which constitutes the judgment itself: apart from this, as we shall endeavour to shew in more detail later on, the true nature of judgment cannot be understood. It is, moreover, possible for logic to examine and formulate certain general conditions which must be satisfied if our thoughts and judgments are to have objective validity; and the science may recognise and discuss certain general presuppositions relating to external nature which are involved in passing from the particular facts of observation to general laws.

Logic fully treated has then both a formal and a material side. The question may indeed be raised whether the distinction between form and matter is not a relative, rather than an absolute, distinction. All sciences are in a sense formal, since they abstract to some extent from the matter of thought. Thus physics abstracts in the main from the chemical properties of bodies, while geometry abstracts also from their physical properties, considering their figure only. In this way we become more and more formal as we become more and more general; and logic may be said to be more abstract, more general, more formal, than any other science, except perhaps pure mathematics.

It is to be added that, within the domain of logic itself, the answer to the question whether two given propositions have or have not the same form may depend upon the particular system of propositions in connection with which they are considered. Thus, if we carry our analysis no further than is usual in ordinary formal logic, the two propositions, *Every angle in a semi-circle is equal to a right angle*, *Any two sides of a triangle are together greater than the third side*, may be considered to be identical in form. Each is universal, and each is affirmative; they differ only in matter. But it will be found that in the logic of relatives, to which further reference will subsequently be made, the two propositions (one expressing an equality and the other an inequality) may be regarded as differing in form as well as in matter; and, moreover, that the difference between them in form is capable of being symbolically expressed.

The difficulty of assigning a distinctive scope to formal logic *par excellence* is increased by the fact that certain problems falling naturally into the domain of material logic—for example, the inductive methods—admit up to a certain point of a purely formal treatment.

It is not possible then to draw a hard and fast line and to say that a certain determinate portion of logic is formal, and that the rest is not formal. We must content ourselves with the statement that when we speak of formal logic in a distinctive sense we mean the most abstract parts of the science, in which no presuppositions are made relating to external nature, and in which—beyond the recognition of the necessary objective reference contained in all judgments—there is an abstraction from the matter of thought. Because they are so abstract, the problems of formal logic as thus conceived admit usually of symbolic treatment; and it is with problems admitting of such treatment that we shall more particularly concern ourselves in the following pages.

3. *Logic and Language.*—Some logicians, in their treatment of the problems of formal logic, endeavour to abstract not merely from the matter of thought but also from the language which is the instrument of thought. This method of treatment is not adopted in the following pages. In order to justify the adoption of the alternative method, it is not necessary to maintain that thought is altogether impossible without language. It is enough that all thought-processes of any degree of complexity are as a matter of fact carried on by the aid of language, and that thought-products are normally expressed in language. That language is in this sense the universal instrument of thought will not be denied; and it seems a fair corollary that the principles by which valid thought is regulated, and more especially the application of these principles to the criticism of thought-products, cannot be adequately discussed, unless account is taken of the way in which this instrument actually performs its functions.

Language is full of ambiguities, and it is impossible to proceed far with the problems with which logic is concerned until a precise interpretation has been placed upon certain forms of words as representing thought. In ordinary discourse, to take a simple example, the word *some* may or may not be used in a sense in which it is exclusive of *all*; it may be understood to mean *not-all* as well as *not-none*, or its full meaning may be taken to be *not-none*. The logician must decide in which of these senses the word is to be understood in any given scheme of propositional forms. Now, if thought were considered exclusively in itself, such a question as this could not arise; it has to do with the expression of thought in language. The fact that such questions do arise and cannot help arising shews that actually to eliminate all consideration of language from logic is an impossibility. A not infrequent result of attempting to rise above mere considerations of language is needless prolixity and dogmatism in regard to what are really verbal questions, though they are not recognised as such.

The method of treating logic here advocated is sometimes called *nominalist*, and the opposed method *conceptualist*. A word or two of explanation is, however, desirable in order that this use of terms may not prove misleading. Nominalism and conceptualism usually denote certain doctrines concerning the nature of general notions. Nominalism is understood to involve the assertion that generality belongs to language alone and that there is nothing general in thought. But a so-called nominalist treatment of logic does not involve this. It involves no more than a clear recognition of the importance of language as the instrument of thought; and this is a circumstance upon which modern advocates of conceptualism have themselves insisted.

It is perhaps necessary to add that on the view here taken logic in no way becomes a mere branch of grammar, nor does it cease to have a place amongst the mental sciences. Whatever may be the aid derived from language, it remains true that the validity of formal reasonings depends ultimately on laws of thought. Formal logic is, therefore, still concerned primarily with thought, and only secondarily with language as the instrument of thought.

In our subsequent discussion of the relation of *terms* to *concepts*, and of *propositions* to *judgments*, we shall return to a consideration of the question raised in this section.[2]

4. *Logic and Psychology*.—Since processes of reasoning are mental processes depending upon the constitution of our minds, they fall within the cognizance of psychology as well as of logic. But laws of reasoning are regarded from different points of view by these two sciences. Psychology deals with such laws in the sense of uniformities, that is, as laws in accordance with which men are found by experience normally to think and reason. Logic, on the other hand, deals with laws of reasoning as regulative and authoritative, as affording criteria by the aid of which valid and invalid reasonings may be discriminated, and as determining the formal relations in which different products of thought stand to one another.

Looking at the relations between logic and psychology from a slightly different standpoint, we observe that while the latter is concerned with the actual, the former is concerned with the ideal. Logic does not, like psychology, treat of all the ways in which men actually reach conclusions, or of all the various modes in which, through the association of ideas or otherwise, one belief actually generates another. It is concerned with reasonings only as regards their cogency, and with the dependence of one judgment upon another only in so far as it is a dependence in respect of proof.

---

[2] See sections 7 and 46.

There are various other ways in which the contrast between the two sciences may be expressed. We may, for example, say that psychology is concerned with thought-processes, logic with thought-products; or that psychology is concerned with the origin of our beliefs, logic with their validity.

Logic has thus a unique character of its own, and is not a mere branch of psychology. Psychological and logical discussions are no doubt apt to overlap one another at certain points, in connection, for example, with theories of conception and judgment. In the following pages, however, the psychological side of logic is comparatively little touched upon. The metaphysical questions also to which logic tends to give rise are as far as possible avoided.

5. *The Utility of Logic.*—We have seen that logic has in view an ideal and treats of what ought to be. Its object is, however, to investigate general principles, and it puts forward no claim to be a practical art. Its utility is accordingly not to be measured by any direct help that it may afford towards the attainment of particular scientific truths. No doubt the procedure in all sciences is subject to the general principles formulated by logic; but, in details, the weighing of evidence will often be better performed by the judgment of the expert than by any formal or systematic observance of logical rules.

It is important to bear in mind that, in the study of logic, our immediate aim is the scientific investigation of general principles recognised as authoritative in relation to thought-products, not the formulation of a system of rules and precepts. It may be said that the art of dealing with particular concrete arguments, with the object of determining their validity, is related to the science of logic in the same way as the art of casuistry (that is, the art of deciding what it is right to do in particular concrete circumstances) is related to the science of ethics. Moreover, just as in the art of casuistry we meet with problems which are elusive and difficult to decide because in the concrete they cannot be brought exactly under the abstract formulae of ethical science, so in the art of detecting fallacies we meet with arguments which cannot easily be brought under the abstract formulae of logical science. As it would be a mistake to subordinate ethics to the treatment of casuistical questions, so it would be a mistake to mould the science of logic with constant reference to concrete arguments which, either because of the ambiguity of the terms employed, or because of the uncertain bearing of the context in which they occur, elude any attempt to reduce them to a form to which general principles are directly applicable.

Wherein then consists the utility of logic? In answer to this question, it may be observed primarily that if logic determines truly the principles of valid thought, then its study is of value simply in that it adds to our knowledge. To justify the study of logic it is, as Mansel has observed, sufficient to shew that what it teaches is true, and that by its aid we advance in the knowledge of ourselves and of our capacities.

To this it must be added (in qualification of what has been said previously) that, while logic is not to be regarded as an art of attaining truth, it still does possess utility as propaedeutic to other studies and independently of the addition that it makes to our knowledge. Fallacious arguments can no doubt usually be recognised as such by an acute intellect apart from any logical study; and, as we have seen, it is not the primary function of logic to deal with particular concrete arguments. At the same time, it is only by the aid of logic that we can analyse a reasoning, explain precisely why a fallacious argument is faulty, and give the fallacy a name. In other words, while logic is not to be identified with the criticism of particular concrete arguments, such criticism when systematically undertaken must be based on logic.

Greater, however, than the indirect value of logic in its subsequent application to the examination of particular reasonings is its value as a general intellectual discipline. The study of logic cultivates the power of abstract thought; and it is not too much to say that, when undertaken with thoroughness, it affords a unique mental training.

PART I. TERMS

Chapter 1

THE LOGIC OF TERMS

6. *The Three Parts of Logical Doctrine*—It has been usual to divide logical doctrine into three parts, dealing with terms (or concepts), propositions (or judgments), and reasonings respectively; and it will be convenient to adopt this arrangement in the present treatise. At the same time, we may in passing touch upon certain objections that have been raised to this mode of treating the subject.

Mr. Bosanquet treats of logic in two parts, not in three, giving no separate discussion of names (or concepts). His main ground for taking up this position is that "the name or concept has no reality in living language or living thought, except when referred to its place in a proposition or judgment" (*Essentials of Logic*, p. 87). He urges that "we ought not to think of propositions as built up by putting words or names together, but of words or names as distinguished though not separable elements in propositions." There is undoubted force in this argument, and attention should be called to the points raised by Mr. Bosanquet, even though we may not be led to quite the same conclusion.

Logic is essentially concerned with truth and falsity as characteristics of thought, and truth and falsity are embodied in judgments and in judgments only. Hence the judgment (or the proposition as expressing the judgment) may be regarded as fundamentally the logical unit. It would, moreover, now be generally agreed that the concept is not by itself a complete mental state, but is realised only as occurring in a context. Correspondingly the name does not by itself express any mental state. If a mere name is pronounced it leaves us in a state of expectancy, except in so far as it is the abbreviated expression of a proposition, as it may be when spoken in answer to a question or when the special circumstances or manner of its utterance connect it with a context that gives it predicative force.

At the same time, in ideal analysis the developed judgment yields the concept as at any rate a distinguishable element of which it is composed, while the proposition similarly yields the term; and in order that the import of judgments and propositions may be properly understood some discussion of concepts and terms is necessary.

The question as to the proper order of treatment remains. In dealing with this question we need not trouble ourselves with the enquiry as to whether the concept or the judgment has psychological priority, that is to say, as to whether in the first instance the process of forming judgments requires that concepts should have been already formed, or whether on the other hand the process of forming conceptions itself involves the formation of judgments, or whether the two processes go on *pari passu*. It is enough that the developed judgment and the proposition, as we are concerned with them in logic, yield respectively the concept, and the term as elements out of which they are constituted.

We shall then give a separate discussion of terms, and shall enter upon this part of the subject before discussing propositions. But in doing this we shall endeavour constantly to bear in mind that the proposition is the true logical unit, and that the logical import of terms cannot be properly understood except with reference to their employment in propositions.[3]

7. *Names and Concepts.*—We have in the preceding section spoken more or less indiscriminately of *names* (or terms) and of *concepts*, and this has been intentional. We have already expressed our disagreement with those who would exclude from logic all consideration of language. Our judgments cannot have certainty and universal validity unless the ideas which enter into them are fixed and determined; and, apart from the aid that we derive from language, our ideas cannot be thus fixed and determined.

It is, therefore, a mistake to treat of concepts to the exclusion of names. But, on the other hand, we must not forget that the logician is concerned with names only as representative of ideas. His real aim is to treat of ideas, though he may think it wiser to do so not directly, but indirectly by considering the names by which ideas are represented. For this reason it is well, now and then at any rate, to refer explicitly to the concept.

The so-called conceptualist school of logicians are apt in their treatment of the first part of logical doctrine to discuss problems of a markedly psychological character, as, for example, the mode of formation of concepts and the controversy between conceptualism and nominalism. Apart, however, from the fact that the conceptualist logicians do not draw so clear a line of distinction as do the nominalists between logic and psychology, the difference between the two schools is to a large extent a mere difference of phraseology. Practically the same points, for example, are raised whether we discuss the extension and intension of concepts or the denotation and connotation of names. At the same time, it must be said that the attempt to deal with the intension of concepts to the entire exclusion of any consideration of the connotation of names appears to be responsible for a good deal of confusion.

8. *The Logic of Terms.*—Attention has already been called to the relation of dependence that exists between the logic of terms and the logic of propositions. It will be found that we cannot in general fully determine the logical characteristics of a given name without explicit reference to its employment as a constituent of a proposition. We cannot again properly discuss or understand the import of so-called negative names without reference to negative judgments.

It must be added that in dealing with distinctions between names, it is particularly difficult for the logician who follows at all on the traditional lines to avoid discussing

---

[3] In this connection attention may be called to Mill's well known dictum that "names are names of things, not of our ideas," Apart from its context, the force of this antithesis may easily be misunderstood. It is clear that every name that is employed in an intelligible sense must have some mental equivalent, must call up some idea or other to our minds, and must therefore in this sense be the name of an idea. It is not, however, Mill's intention to deny this. Nor, on the other hand, does he intend to assert that things actually exist corresponding to all the names we employ. His dictum really has reference to *predication*. What he means is that when any name appears as the subject of a proposition, an assertion is made not about the corresponding idea, but about something which is distinct both from the name and the idea, though both are related to it. He is in fact affirming the objective reference that is essential to the conception of truth or falsity. The discussion may, therefore, be said to be properly part of the discussion of the import of propositions rather than of names, and it would certainly be less puzzling if it were introduced in that connection. Our special object, however, in referring to the matter here is not to criticise Mill, but to illustrate the difficulty of discussing names logically apart from the use that may be made of them for purposes of predication.

problems that belong more appropriately to psychology, metaphysics, or grammar; and to some of the questions which arise it may hardly be possible to give a completely satisfactory answer from the purely logical point of view. This remark applies especially to the distinction between *abstract* and *concrete* terms, a distinction, moreover, which is of little further logical utility or significance. It is introduced in the following pages in accordance with custom; but adequately to discriminate between things and their attributes is the function of metaphysics rather than of logic. The portion of the logic of terms (or concepts) to which by far the greatest importance attaches is that which is concerned with the distinction between extension and intension.

9. *General and Singular Names.*—A *general* name is a name which is actually or potentially predicable in the same sense of each of an indefinite number of units; a *singular* or *individual* name is a name which is understood in the particular circumstances in which it is employed to denote someone determinate unit only.

The nature and logical importance of this distinction may be illustrated by considering names as the subjects of propositions. A general name is the name of a divisible class, and predication is possible in respect of the whole or a part of the class; a singular name is the name of a unit indivisible. Hence we may take as the test or criterion of a general name, the possibility of prefixing *all* or *some* to it with any meaning.

Thus, *prime minister of England* is a general name, since it is applicable to more than one individual, and statements may be made which are true of all prime ministers of England or only of some. The name *God* is singular to a monotheist as the name of the Deity, general to a polytheist, or as the name of any object of worship. *Universe* is general in so far as we distinguish different kinds of universes, e.g., the material universe, the terrestrial universe, &c.; it is singular if we mean the totality of all things. *Space* is general if we mean any portion of space, singular if we mean space as a whole. *Water* is general. Professor Bain takes a different view here; he says, "Names of material—earth, atone, salt, mercury, water, flame—are singular. They each denote the entire collection of one species of material" (*Logic, Deduction*, pp. 48, 49). But when we predicate anything of these terms it is generally of *any portion* (or of some particular portion) of the material in question, and not of the entire collection of it *considered as one aggregate*; thus, if we say, "Water is composed of oxygen and hydrogen," we mean any and every particle of water, and the name has all the distinctive characters of the general name. Again, we can distinguish *this* water from *that* water, and we can say, "*some* water is not fit to drink"; but the word *some* cannot, as we have seen above, be attached to a really singular name. Similarly with regard to the other terms in question. It is also to be observed that we distinguish between different kinds of stone, salt, &c.[4]

A name is to be regarded as general if it is *potentially* predicable of more than one object, although as a matter of fact it happens that it can be truly affirmed of only one, e.g., *an English sovereign six times married*. A really singular name is not even potentially applicable to more than one individual; e.g., *the last of the Mohicans, the eldest son of King Edward the First*. This may be differently expressed by saying that a really singular name implies in its signification the uniqueness of the corresponding object. We may take as examples *the summum bonum, the centre of gravity of the material universe*. It is not easy to find such

---

[4] Terms of the kind here under discussion are called by Jevons *substantial terms*. (See *Principles of Science*, 2, § 4.) Their peculiarity is that, although they are concrete, the things denoted by them possess a peculiar homogeneity or uniformity of structure; also we do not as a rule use the indefinite article with them as we do with other general names.

names except in cases where uniqueness results from some explicit or implicit limitation in time or space or from some relation to an object denoted by a proper name. Even in such a case as *the centre of gravity of the material universe* some limitation in time appears to be necessary, for the centre of gravity of the universe may be differently situated at different periods.

Any general name may be transformed into a singular name by means of an individualising prefix, such as a demonstrative pronoun (e.g., *this book*), or by the use of the definite article, which usually indicates a restriction to someone determinate person or thing (e.g., *the Queen, the pole star*). Such restriction by means of the definite article may sometimes need to be interpreted by the context, e.g., *the garden, the river*; in other cases some limitation of place or time or circumstance is introduced which unequivocally defines the individual reference, e.g., *the first man, the present Lord Chancellor, the author of Paradise Lost*.

On the other hand, propositions with singular names as subjects may sometimes admit of subdivision into universal and particular. This is the case when, with reference to different times or different conditions, a distinction is made or implied in regard to the manner of existence, actual or potential, of the object denoted by the name: for example, "Homer sometimes nods," "The present Pope always dwells in the Vatican," "This country is sometimes subject to earthquakes."[5]

10. *Proper Names.*—A *proper* name is a name assigned as a mark to distinguish an individual person or thing from others, without implying in its signification the possession by the individual in question of any specific attributes. Such names are given to objects which possess interest in respect of their individuality and independently of their specific nature. For the most part they are confined to persons and places; but they are also given to domestic animals, and sometimes to inanimate objects to which affection-value is attached, as, for example, by children to their dolls. Proper names form a sub-class of singular names, being distinguished from the singular names of which examples were given in the preceding section in that they denote individual objects without at the same time necessarily conveying any information as to particular properties belonging to those objects.[6]

Many proper names, e.g., *John, Victoria*, are as a matter of fact assigned to more than one individual; but they are not therefore general names, since on each particular occasion of their use, with the exception noted below, there is an understood reference to someone determinate individual only. There is, moreover, no implication that different individuals who may happen to be called by the same proper name have this name assigned to them on account of properties which they possess in common.[7] The exception above referred to occurs when we speak of the class composed of those who bear the name, and who are constituted a distinct class by this common feature alone: e.g., "All Victorias are honoured in their name," "Some Johns are not of Anglo-Saxon origin, but are negroes." The subjects of such propositions as these must, however, be regarded as elliptical; written out more fully, they become *all persons called Victoria, some individuals named John*.

11. *Collective Names.*—A *collective* name is one which is applied to a group of similar things regarded as constituting a single whole; e.g., *regiment, nation, army*. A *non-collective*

---

[5] Compare sections 70 and 82.
[6] Proper names are farther discussed in section 25 in connection with the connotation of names.
[7] Professor Bain brings out this distinction in his definition of a general name: "A general name is applicable to a number of things in virtue of their being similar, or having something in common."

name, e.g., *stone*, may also be the name of something which is composed of a number of precisely similar parts, but this is not in the same way present to the mind in the use of the name.[8]

A collective name may be singular or general. It is the name of a group or collection of things, and so far as it is capable of being correctly affirmed in the same sense of only one such group, it is singular; e.g., *the 29th regiment of foot, the English nation, the Bodleian Library*, But if it is capable of being correctly affirmed in the same sense of each of several such groups it is to be regarded as general; e.g., *regiment, nation, library*.[9]

Some logicians imply an antithesis between collective and general names, either regarding collectives as a sub-class of singulars, or else recognising a threefold division into singular, collective, and general. There is, properly speaking, no such antithesis; and both the above alternatives must be regarded as misleading, if not actually erroneous; for, as we have just seen, the class of collective names overlaps each of the other classes.

The correct and really important logical antithesis is between the *collective* and the *distributive* use of names. A collective name such as *nation*, or any name in the plural number, is the name of a collection or group of similar things. These we may regard as one whole, and something may be predicated of them that is true of them only as a whole; in this case the name is used *collectively*. On the other hand, the group may be regarded as a series of units, and something may be predicated of these which is true of them taken individually; in this case the name is used *distributively*.[10]

The above distinction may be illustrated by the propositions, "All the angles of a triangle are equal to two right angles," "All the angles of a triangle are less than two right angles." In the first case the predication is true only of the angles all taken together, while in the second it is true only of each of them taken separately; in the first case, therefore, the term is used collectively, in the second distributively. Compare again the propositions, "The people filled the church," "The people all fell on their knees."[11]

12. *Concrete and Abstract Names.*—The distinction between concrete and abstract names, as ordinarily recognised, may be most briefly expressed by saying that a *concrete* name is the name of a *thing*, whilst an *abstract* name is the name of an *attribute*. The

---

[8] To *collective* name as above defined there is no distinctive antithetical term in ordinary use. The antithesis between the *collective* and the *distributive* use of names arises, as we shall see, in connection with predication only.

[9] It is pointed out by Dr Venn that certain proper names may be regarded as collective, though such names are not common. "One instance of them is exhibited in the case of geographical groups. For instance, the Seychelles, and the Pyrenees, are distinctly, in their present usage, proper names, denoting respectively two groups of things. They simply denote these groups, and give us no information whatever about any of their characteristics" (*Empirical Logic*, p. 172).

[10] It is held by Dr Venn (*Empirical Logic*, p. 170) that *substantial terms* are always used collectively when they appear as subjects of general propositions. If, however, we take such a proposition as "Oil is lighter than water" it seems clear that the subject is used not collectively, but distributively; for the assertion is made of each and every portion of oil, whereas if we used the term collectively our assertion would apply only to all the portions taken together. The same is clearly true in other instances; for example, in the propositions, "Water is composed of oxygen and hydrogen," "Ice melts when the temperature rises above 32° Fahr."

[11] When in an argument we pass from the collective to the distributive use of a term, or *vice versâ*, we have what is technically called a *fallacy of division* or *of composition* as the case may be. The following are examples: The people who attended Great St Mary's contributed more than those who attended Little St Mary's, therefore, A (who attended the former) gave more than B (who attended the latter); All the angles of a triangle are less than two right angles, therefore A, B, and C, which are all the angles of a triangle, are together less than two right angles. The point of the old riddle, "Why do white sheep eat more than black?" consists in the unexpected use of terms collectively instead of distributively.

question, however, at once arises as to what is meant by a *thing* as distinguished from an *attribute*; and the only answer to be given is that by a thing we mean whatever is regarded as possessing attributes. It would appear, therefore, that our definitions may be made more explicit by saying that a *concrete* name is the name of anything which is regarded as possessing attributes, i.e., as a *subject of attributes*; while an *abstract* name is the name of anything which is regarded as an attribute of something else, i.e., as an *attribute of subjects*.[12]

This distinction is in most cases easy of application; for example, *plane triangle* is the name of all figures that possess the attribute of being bounded by three straight lines, and is a concrete name; *triangularity* is the name of this distinctive attribute of triangles, and is an abstract name. Similarly, *man, living being, generous* are concretes; *humanity, life, generosity* are the corresponding abstracts.[13]

Abstract and concrete names usually go in pairs as in the above illustrations. A concrete general name is the name of a class of things grouped together in virtue of some quality or set of qualities which they possess in common; the name given to the quality or qualities themselves apart from the individuals to which they belong is the corresponding abstract.[14] Using the terms *connote* and *denote* in their technical senses, as defined in the following chapter, an abstract name *denotes* the qualities which are *connoted* by the corresponding concrete name. This relation between concretes and the corresponding abstracts is the one point in connection with abstract and concrete names that is of real logical importance, and it may be observed that it does not in itself give rise to the somewhat fruitless subtleties with which the distinction is apt to be associated. For when two names are given which are thus related, there will never be any difficulty in determining which is concrete and which is abstract in relation to the other.

But whilst the distinction is absolute and unmistakeable when names are thus given in pairs, the application of our definitions is by no means always easy when we consider names in themselves and not in this definite relation to other names. We shall find indeed that if we adopt the definitions given above, then the division of names into abstract and concrete is not an exclusive one in the sense that every name can once and for all be assigned exclusively to one or other of the two categories.

We are at any rate driven to this if we once admit that attributes may themselves be the subjects of attributes, and it is difficult to see how this admission can be avoided. If, for example, we say that "unpunctuality is irritating," we ascribe the attribute of being irritating

---

[12] The distinction is sometimes expressed by saying that an abstract name is the name of an attribute, a concrete name the name of a *substance*. If by *substance* is merely meant whatever possesses attributes, then this distinction is equivalent to that given in the text; but if, as would ordinarily be the case, a fuller meaning is given to the term, then the division of names into abstract and concrete is no longer an exhaustive one. Take such names as *astronomy, proposition, triangle*: these names certainly do not denote attributes; but, on the other hand, it seems paradoxical to regard them as names of substances. On the whole, therefore, it is best to avoid the term *substance* in this connection.

[13] It will be observed that, according to the above definitions, a name is not called abstract, simply because the corresponding idea is the result of abstraction, i.e., attending to some qualities of a thing or class of things to the exclusion as far as possible of others. In this sense all general names, such as *man, living being*, &c., would be abstract.

[14] Thus, in the case of every general concrete name there is or may be constructed a corresponding abstract. But this is not true of proper names or other singular names regarded strictly as such. We may indeed have such abstracts as *Caesarism* and *Bismarckism*. These names, however, do not denote all the differentiating attributes of Caesar and Bismarck respectively, but only certain qualities supposed to be specially characteristic of these individuals. In forming the above abstracts we generalise, and contemplate a certain type of character and conduct that may possibly be common to a whole class.

to unpunctuality, which is itself an attribute. *Unpunctuality*, therefore, although primarily an abstract name, can also be used in such a way that it is, according to our definition, concrete.

Similarly when we consider that an attribute may appear in different forms or in different degrees, we must regard it as something which can itself be modified by the addition of a further attribute; as, for example, when we distinguish physical courage from moral courage, or the whiteness of snow from the whiteness of smoke, or when we observe that the beauty of a diamond differs in its characteristics from the beauty of a landscape.

Hence, if the definitions under discussion are adopted, we arrive at the conclusion that while some names are concrete and never anything but concrete, names which are primarily formed as abstracts and continue to be used as such are apt also to be used as concretes, that is to say, they are names of attributes which can themselves be regarded as possessing attributes. They are abstract names when viewed in one relation, concrete when viewed in another.[15]

It must be admitted that this result is paradoxical. As yielding a division of names that is non-exclusive, it is also unscientific. There are two ways of avoiding this difficulty.

In the first place, we may further modify our definitions and say that an *abstract* name is the name of anything which *can* be regarded as an attribute of something else (whether it is or is not itself a subject of attributes), while a *concrete* name is the name of that which *cannot* be regarded as an attribute of something else. This distinction is simple and easy of application, it is in accordance with popular usage, and it satisfies the condition that the members of a division shall be mutually exclusive. But it may be doubted whether it has any logical value.

A second way of avoiding the difficulty is to give up for logical purposes the distinction between concrete and abstract names, and to substitute for it a distinction between the concrete and the abstract use of names. A name is then used in a concrete sense when the thing called by the name is contemplated as a subject of attributes, and in an abstract sense when the thing called by the name is contemplated as an attribute of subjects. It follows from what has been already said that some names can be used as concrete only, while others can be used either as abstract or as concrete. This solution is satisfactory from the logical point of view, since logic is concerned not with names as such, but with the use of names in propositions. It may be added that as logicians we have very little to do with the abstract use of names, A consideration of the import of propositions will shew that when a name appears either as the subject or as the predicate of a non-verbal proposition its use is always concrete.

13. *Can Abstract Names be subdivided into General and Singular?*—The question whether any abstract names can be considered general has given rise to much difference of opinion amongst logicians. On the one hand, it is argued that all abstract names must necessarily be singular, since an attribute considered purely as such and apart from its concrete manifestations is one and indivisible, and cannot admit of numerical distinction.[16] On the other hand, it is urged that some abstracts must certainly be considered general since they are names of attributes of which there are various kinds or subdivisions; and in confirmation of this view it is pointed out that we frequently write abstracts in the plural

---

[15] The use of the same term as both abstract and concrete in the manner above described must be distinguished from the not unfrequent case of quite another kind in which a name originally abstract changes its meaning and comes to be used in the sense of the corresponding concrete; as, for example, when we talk of *the Deity* meaning thereby God, not the qualities of God. Compare Jevons, *Elementary Lessons in Logic*, pp. 21, 22.

[16] This represents the view taken by Jevons. See *Principles of Science*, 2, § 3.

number, as when we say, "Redness and yellowness are *colours*," "Patience and meekness are *virtues*."[17]

The solution of the question really depends upon our use of the term *abstract*.

If we adopt the definition given in the last paragraph but one of the preceding section, and include under abstract names the names of attributes which are themselves the subjects of attributes, these latter attributes possibly varying in different instances, then there can be no doubt that some abstracts are general; for they are the names of a class of things which, while having something in common, are also distinguishable *inter se*.

So far, however, as the question is raised in regard to the abstract (as distinguished from the concrete) use of names in the manner indicated in the last paragraph of the preceding section, we are led to the conclusion that it is only when names are used in a concrete sense that they can be considered general. For it is clear that the name of an attribute can be described as general only in so far as the attribute is regarded as exhibiting characteristics which vary in different instances, only in so far, that is to say, as it is itself a subject of attributes; and when the attribute is so regarded, the name is used in a concrete, not an abstract, sense.

Take the propositions, "Some colours are painfully vivid," "All yellows are agreeable," "Some courage is the result of ignorance," "Some cruelty is the result of fear," "All cruelty is detestable." The subjects of these propositions are certainly general. According to the definition given in the last paragraph but one of the preceding section they are also abstract. If, however, in place of distinguishing between abstract and concrete names *per se*, we distinguish between the abstract and the concrete use of names as proposed in the last paragraph of the preceding section, then the terms in question are all used in a concrete, not an abstract, sense.

EXERCISES

14. Discuss Mill's statement that "names are names of things, not of our ideas," with special reference to the following names: *dodo, mermaid, chimaera, toothache, jealousy, idea*. [C.]

15. Discuss the logical characteristics of adjectives. [K.]

---

[17] Compare Mill, *Logic*, i. 2, § 4.

Chapter 2

EXTENSION AND INTENSION

16. *The Extension and the Intension of Names.*[18]—Every concrete general name is the name of a real or imaginary class of objects which possess in common certain attributes; and there are, therefore, two aspects under which it may be regarded. We may consider the name (i) in relation to the objects which are called by it; or (ii) in relation to the qualities belonging to those objects. It is desirable to have terms by which to refer to this broad distinction without regard to further refinements of meaning; and the terms *extension* and *intension* will accordingly be employed to express in the most general way these two aspects of names respectively.[19]

The *extension* of a name then consists of objects of which the name can be predicated; its *intension* consists of properties which can be predicated of it. For example, by the extension of *plane triangle* we mean a certain class of geometrical figures, and by its intension certain qualities belonging to such figures. Similarly, by the extension of *man* is meant a certain class of material objects, and by its intension the qualities of rationality, animality, &c., belonging to these objects.

17. *Connotation, Subjective Intension, and Comprehension.*—The term *intension* has been used in the preceding section to express in the most general way that aspect of general names under which we consider not the objects called by the names but the qualities belonging to those objects. Taking any general name, however, there are at least three different points of view from which the qualities of the corresponding class may be regarded; and it is to a want of discrimination between these points of view that we may attribute many of the controversies and misunderstandings to which the problem of the connotation of names has given rise.

(1) There are those qualities which are essential to the class in the sense that the name implies them in its definition. Were any of this set of qualities absent the name would not be applicable; and any individual thing lacking them would accordingly not be regarded as a

---

[18] We may speak also of the extension and the intension of concepts. In the discussion, however, of questions concerning extension and intension, it is essential to recognise the part played by language as the instrument of thought. Hence it seems better to start from names rather than from concepts. Neglect to consider names explicitly in this connection has been responsible for much confusion.

[19] It is usual to employ the terms *comprehension* and *connotation* as simply synonymous with *intension*, and *denotation* as synonymous with *extension*. We shall, however, presently find it convenient to differentiate the meanings of these terms. The force of the terms *extension* and *intension* in the most general sense might perhaps also be expressed by the pair of terms *application* and *implication*.

member of the class. The standpoint here taken may be said to be *conventional*, since we are concerned with the set of characteristics which are supposed to have been conventionally agreed upon as determining the application of the name.

(2) There are those qualities which in the mind of any given individual are associated with the name in such a way that they are normally called up in idea when the name is used. These qualities will include the marks by which the individual in question usually recognises or identifies an object as belonging to the class. They may not exhaust the essential qualities of the class in the sense indicated in the preceding paragraph, but on the other hand they will probably include some that are not essential to it. The standpoint here taken is *subjective* and relative. Even when there is agreement as to the actual meaning of a name, the qualities that we naturally think of in connection with it may vary both from individual to individual, and, in the case of any given individual, from time to time.

We may consider as a special case under this head the complete group of attributes *known* at any given time to belong to the class. All these attributes can be called up in idea by any person whose knowledge of the class is fully up to date; and this group may, therefore, be regarded as constituting the most scientific form of intension from the subjective point of view.

(3) There is the sum-total of qualities actually possessed in common by all members of the class. These will include all the qualities included under the two preceding heads,[20] and usually many others in addition. The standpoint here taken is *objective*.[21]

In seeking to give a precise meaning to *connotation*, we may start from the above classification. It suggests three distinct senses in which the term might possibly be used, and as a matter of fact all three of these senses have been selected by different logicians, sometimes without any clear recognition of divergence from the usage of other writers. It is desirable that we should be quite clear in our own minds in which sense we intend to employ the term.

(i) According to Mill's usage, which is that adopted in the following pages, the conventional standpoint is taken when we speak of the *connotation* of a name. On this view, we do not mean by the connotation of a class-name all the qualities possessed in common by the class; nor do we necessarily mean those particular qualities which may be mentally associated with the name; but we mean just those qualities on account of the possession of which any individual is placed in the class and called by the name. In other words, we include in the connotation of a class-name only those attributes upon which the classification is based, and in the absence of any of which the name would not be regarded as applicable. For example, although all equilateral triangles are equiangular, equiangularity is not on this view included in the connotation of equilateral triangle, since it is not a property upon which the classification of triangles into equilateral and non-equilateral is based; although all kangaroos may happen to be *Australian* kangaroos, this is not part of what is necessarily implied by the use of the name, for an animal subsequently found in the interior of New Guinea, but otherwise possessing all the properties of kangaroos, would not have the name kangaroo denied to it; although all ruminant animals are cloven-hoofed, we cannot regard cloven-

---

[20] It is here assumed, as regards the qualities mentally associated with the name, that our knowledge of the class, so far as it extends, is correct.

[21] When the objective standpoint is taken, there is an implied reference to some particular universe of discourse, within which the class denoted by the name is supposed to be included. The force of this remark will be made clearer at a subsequent stage.

hoofed as part of the meaning of ruminant, and (as Mill observes) if an animal were to be discovered which chewed the cud, but had its feet undivided, it would certainly still be called ruminant.

(ii) Some writers who regard proper names as connotative appear to include in the connotation of a name all those attributes which the name suggests to the mind, whether or not they are actually implied by it. And it is to be observed in this connection that a name may in the mind of any given individual be closely associated with properties which even the same individual would in no way regard as implied in the meaning of the name, as, for instance, "Trinity undergraduate" with a blue gown. This interpretation of connotation is, therefore, clearly to be distinguished from that given in the preceding paragraph.

We may further distinguish the view, apparently taken by some writers, according to which the connotation of a class-name at any given time would include all the properties *known* at that time to belong to the class.

(iii) Other writers use the term in still another sense and would include in the connotation of a class-name all the properties, known and unknown, which are possessed in common by all members of the class. Thus, Mr. E. C. Benecke writes,—"Just as the word 'man' denotes every creature, or class of creatures, having the attributes of humanity, whether we know him or not, so does the word properly connote the *whole* of the properties common to the class, whether we know them or not. Many of the facts, known to physiologists and anatomists about the constitution of man's brain, for example, are not involved in most men's idea of the brain; the possession of a brain precisely so constituted does not, therefore, form any part of their meaning of the word 'man.' Yet surely this is properly connoted by the word…. We have thus the denotation of the concrete name on the one side and its connotation on the other, occupying perfectly analogous positions. Given the connotation,—the denotation is all the objects that possess the whole of the properties so connoted. Given the denotation,—the connotation is the whole of the properties possessed in common by all the objects so denoted" (*Mind*, 1881, p. 532). Jevons uses the term in the same sense. "A term taken in intent (connotation) has for its meaning the whole infinite series of qualities and circumstances which a thing possesses. Of these qualities or circumstances some may be known and form the description or definition of the meaning; the infinite remainder are unknown" (*Pure Logic*, p. 6).[22]

While rejecting the use of the term *connotation* in any but the first of the above mentioned senses, we shall find it convenient to have distinctive terms which can be used with the other meanings that have been indicated. The three terms connotation, intension, and comprehension are commonly employed almost synonymously, and there will certainly be a gain in endeavouring to differentiate their meanings. *Intension*, as already suggested, may be used to indicate in the most general way what may be called the implicational aspect of names; the complex terms *conventional intension*, *subjective intension*, and *objective intension* will then explain themselves. *Connotation* may be used as equivalent to *conventional intension*; and *comprehension* as equivalent to *objective intension*. *Subjective*

---

[22] Bain appears to use the term in an intermediate sense, including in the connotation of a class-name not *all* the attributes common to the class but all the *independent* attributes, that is, all that cannot be derived or inferred from others.

intension is less important from the logical standpoint, and we need not seek to invent a single term to be used as its equivalent.[23]

Conventional intension or *connotation* will then include only those attributes which constitute the meaning of a name;[24] *subjective intension* will include those that are mentally associated with it, whether or not they are actually signified by it; *objective intension* or *comprehension* will include all the attributes possessed in common by all members of the class denoted by the name. We might perhaps speak more strictly of the *connotation* of the *name* itself, the *subjective intension* of the *notion* which is the mental equivalent of the name, and the *comprehension* of the *class* which is denoted by the name.[25]

18. *Sigwart's distinction between Empirical, Metaphysical, and Logical Concepts.*—Sigwart observes that in speaking of concepts we ought to distinguish between three meanings of the word. These three meanings of "concept" he describes as follows.[26]

(1) By a concept may be meant a natural psychological production,—the general idea which has been developed in the natural course of thought. Such ideas are different for different people, and are continually in process of formation; even for the individual himself they change, so that a word does not always keep the same meaning even for the same person. Strictly speaking, it is only by a fiction which neglects individual peculiarities that we can speak of the concepts corresponding to the terms used in ordinary language.

(2) In contrast with this empirical meaning the concept may be viewed as an ideal; it is then the mark at which we aim in our endeavour to attain knowledge, for we seek to find in it an *adequate copy of the essence of things*.

(3) Between these two meanings of the word, which may be called the *empirical* and the *metaphysical*, there lies the *logical*. This has its origin in the logical demand for certainty and universal validity in our judgments. All that is required is that our ideas should be absolutely fixed and determined, and that all who make use of the same system of denotation should have the same ideas.

This threefold distinction may be usefully compared with that drawn in the preceding section. Sigwart is approaching the question from a different point of view, but it will be observed that his three "meanings of concept" correspond broadly with subjective intension, objective intension, and conventional intension respectively.

It may be added that Mr. Bosanquet's distinction (*Logic*, I. pp. 41 to 46) between the objective reference of a name (its *logical meaning*) and its content for the individual mind (the *psychical idea*) appears to some extent to correspond to the distinction between connotation and subjective intension.

19. *Connotation and Etymology.*—The connotation of a name must not be confused with its etymology. In dealing with names from the etymological or historical point of view we consider the circumstances in which they were first imposed and the reasons for their

---

[23] For anyone who is given the meaning of a name but knows nothing of the objects denoted by the name, subjective intension coincides with connotation. Were the ideal of knowledge to be reached, subjective intension would coincide with comprehension.

[24] It is to be observed that in speaking of the connotation of a name we may have in view either the signification that the name bears in common acceptation, or some special meaning assigned to it by explicit definition for some scientific or other specific purpose.

[25] The distinctions of meaning indicated in this section will be found essential for clearness of view in discussing certain questions to which we shall pass on immediately; in particular, the questions whether connotation and denotation necessarily vary inversely, and whether proper names are connotative.

[26] *Logic*, I. p. 245. This and future references to Sigwart are to the English translation of his work by Mrs Bosanquet.

adoption; also the successive changes, if any, in their meaning that have subsequently occurred. In making precise the connotation to be attached to a name we may be helped by considering its etymology. But we must clearly distinguish between the two; in finally deciding upon the connotation to be assigned to a name for any particular scientific purpose, we may indeed find it necessary to depart not merely from its original meaning, but also from its current meaning in everyday discourse.

20. *Fixity of Connotation.*—It has been already pointed out that subjective intension is variable. A given name will almost certainly call up in the minds of different persons different ideas; and even in the case of the same person it will probably do so at different times. The question may be raised how far the same is true of connotation. It has been implied in the preceding section that the scientific use of a name may differ from its use in everyday discourse; and there can be no doubt that as a matter of fact different people may by the same name intend to signify different things, that is to say, they would include different attributes in the connotation of the name. It is, moreover, not unfrequently the case that some of us may be unable to say precisely what is the meaning that we ourselves attach to the words we use.

At the same time a clear distinction ought to be drawn between subjective intension and connotation in respect of their variability. Subjective intension is necessarily variable; it can never be otherwise. Connotation, on the other hand, is only variable by accident; and in so far as there is variation language fails of its purpose. "Identical reference," as Mr. Bosanquet puts it, "is the root and essence of the system of signs which we call language" (*Logic*, I. p. 16). It is only by some conventional agreement which shall make language fixed that scientific discussions can be satisfactorily carried on; and there would be no variation in the connotation of names in the case of an ideal language properly employed. In dealing with reasonings from the point of view of logical doctrine, it is, therefore, no unreasonable assumption to make that in any given argument the connotation of the names employed is fixed and definite; in other words, that every name employed is either used in its ordinary sense and that this is precisely determined, or else that, the name being used with a special meaning, such meaning is adhered to consistently and without equivocation.

21. *Extension and Denotation.*—The terms *extension* and *denotation* are usually employed as synonymous, but there will be some advantage in drawing a certain distinction between them. We shall find that when names are regarded as the subjects of propositions there is an implied reference to some *universe of discourse*, which may be more or less limited. For example, we should naturally understand such propositions as *all men are mortal*, *no men are perfect*, to refer to all men who have actually existed on the earth, or are now existing, or will exist hereafter, but we should not understand them to refer to all fictitious persons or all beings possessing the essential characteristics of men whom we are able to conceive or imagine. The meaning of *universe of discourse* will be further illustrated subsequently. The only reason for introducing the conception at this point is that we propose to use the term *denotation* or *objective extension* rather than the term extension simply when there is an explicit or implicit limitation to the objects actually to be found in some restricted universe. By the *subjective extension* of a general name, on the other hand, we shall understand the whole range of objects real or imaginary to which the name can be correctly applied, the only limitation being that of logical conceivability. Every name, therefore, which can be used in an intelligible sense will have a positive subjective extension, but its denotation in a universe which is in some way restricted by time, place, or circumstance may be zero.[27]

In the sense here indicated, *denotation* is in certain respects the correlative of *comprehension* rather than of *connotation*. For in speaking of denotation we are, as in the case of comprehension, taking an objective standpoint; and there is, moreover, in the case of comprehension, as in that of denotation, a tacit reference to some particular universe of discourse. Since, however, denotation is generally speaking determined by connotation, there is one very important respect in which connotation and denotation are still correlatives.

22. *Dependence of Extension and Intension upon one another.*[28]—Taking any class-name X, let us first suppose that there has been a conventional agreement to use it wherever a certain selected set of properties P_1, P_2, ... P_m, are present. This set of properties will constitute the *connotation* of X, and will, with reference to a given universe of discourse,[29] determine the *denotation* of the name, say, Q_1, Q_2, ... Q_y; that is, Q_1, Q_2, ... Q_y, are all the individuals possessing in common the properties P_1, P_2, ... P_m.

These properties may not, and almost certainly will not, exhaust the properties common to Q_1, Q_2, ... Q_y. Let all the common properties be P_1, P_2, ... P_x; they will include P_1, P_2, ... P_m, and in all probability more besides, and will constitute the *comprehension* of the class-name.

Now it will always be possible in one or more ways to make out of Q_1, Q_2, ... Q_y, a selection Q_1, Q_2, ... Q_n, which shall be precisely typical of the whole class;[30] that is to say, Q_1, Q_2, ... Q_n will possess in common those attributes and only those attributes (namely, P_1, P_2, ... P_x) which are possessed in common by Q_1, Q_2, ... Q_y.[31] Q_1, Q_2, ... Q_n may be called

---

[27] The value of the above distinction may be illustrated by reference to the divergence of view indicated in the following quotation from Mr Monck, who uses the terms *denotation* and *extension* as synonymous: "It is a matter of accident whether a general name will have any extension (or denotation) or not. *Unicorn, griffin,* and *dragon* are general names because they have a meaning, and we can suppose another world in which such beings exist; but the terms have no extension, because there are no such animals in this world. Some logicians speak of these terms as having an extension, because we can *suppose* individuals corresponding to them. In this way every general term would have an extension which might be either real or imaginary. It is, however, more convenient to use the word *extension* for a real extension (past, present, or future) only" (*Introduction to Logic*, p. 10). It should be added, in order to prevent possible misapprehension, that by *universe of discourse*, as used in the text, we do not necessarily mean the material universe; we may, for example, mean the universe of fairy-land, or of heraldry, and in such a case, *unicorn, griffin,* and *dragon* may have denotation (in our special sense), as well as subjective extension, greater than zero. What is the particular universe of reference in any given proposition will generally be determined by the context. For logical purposes we may assume that it is conventionally understood and agreed upon, and that it remains the same throughout the course of any given argument. As Dr Venn remarks, "We might include amongst the assumptions of logic that the speaker and hearer should be in agreement, not only as to the meaning of the words they use, but also as to the conventional limitations under which they apply them in the circumstances of the case" (*Empirical Logic*, p. 180).

[28] This section may be omitted on a first reading.

[29] It will be assumed in the remainder of this section that we are throughout speaking with reference to a given universe of discourse.

[30] It may chance to be necessary to make Q_1, Q_2, ... Q_n coincide with Q_1, Q_2, ... Q_y. But this must be regarded as the limiting case; usually a smaller number of individuals will be sufficient.

[31] Mr Johnson points out to me that in pursuing this line of argument certain restrictions of a somewhat subtle kind are necessary in regard to what may be called our "universe of attributes." The "universe of objects" which is what we mean by the "universe of discourse," implies *individuality of object* and *limitation of range of objects*; and if we are to work out a thoroughgoing reciprocity between attributes and objects, we must recognise in our "universe of attributes" restrictions analogous to the above, namely, *simplicity of attribute* and *limitation of range of attributes*. By "simplicity of attribute" is meant that the universe of attributes must not contain any attribute which is a *logical function* of any other attribute or set of attributes. Thus, if A, B are two attributes recognised in our universe, we must not admit such attributes as X (= A and B), or Y (= A or B), or Z

the *exemplification* or *extensive definition* of X. The reason for selecting the name *extensive definition* will appear in a moment. It will sometimes be convenient correspondingly to speak of the connotation of a name as its *intensive definition*.

We have then, with reference to X,

(1) *Connotation*: $P_1 \ldots P_m$;
(2) *Denotation*: $Q_1 \ldots Q_n \ldots Q_y$;
(3) *Comprehension*: $P_1 \ldots P_m \ldots P_x$;
(4) *Exemplification*: $Q_1 \ldots Q_n$.

Of these, either the connotation or the exemplification will suffice to mark out or completely identify the class, although they do not exhaust either all its common properties or all the individuals contained in it. In other words, whether we start from the connotation or from the exemplification, the denotation and the comprehension will be the same.[32]

For a concrete illustration of the above, the term *metal* may be taken. From the chemical point of view a metal may be defined as an element which can replace hydrogen in an acid and thus form a salt. This then is the *connotation* of the name. Its *denotation* consists of the complete list of elements fulfilling the above condition now known to chemists, and possibly of others not yet discovered.[33] The members of the whole class thus constituted are, however, found to possess other properties in common besides those contained in the definition of the name, for example, fusibility, the characteristic lustre termed metallic, a high degree of opacity, and the property of being good conductors of heat and electricity. The complete list of these properties forms the *comprehension* of the name. Now a chemist would no doubt be able from the full denotation of metal to make a selection of a limited number of metals which would be precisely typical of the whole class;[34] that is to say, his selected list would

---

(= *not-A*). We may indeed have a negatively defined attribute, but it must not be the formal contradictory of another or formally involve the contradictory of another. The following example will shew the necessity of this restriction. Let P_1, P_2, P_3, be selected as typical of the whole class $P_1, P_2, P_3 P_4, P_5, P_6$; and let A_1 be an attribute possessed by P_1 alone, A_2 an attribute possessed by P_2 alone, and so on. Then if we recognise A_1 *or* A_2 *or* A_3 as a distinct attribute, it is at once clear that P_1, P_2, P_3 will no longer be typical of the whole class; and the same result follows if *not-A*$_4$ is recognised as a distinct attribute. Similarly, without the restriction in question *any* selection (short of the whole) would necessarily fail to be typical of the whole class. As a concrete example, suppose that we select from the class of *professional men* a set of examples that have in common no attribute except those that are common to the whole class. It may turn out that our examples are all *barristers* or *doctors*, but none of them *solicitors*. Now if we recognise as a distinct attribute being "either a barrister or a doctor," our selected group will thereby have an extra common attribute not possessed by every professional man. The same result will follow if we recognise the attribute "non-solicitor." Not much need be added as regards the necessity of some limitation in the range of attributes which are recognised. The mere fact of our having selected a certain group would indeed constitute an additional attribute, which would at once cause the selection to fail in its purpose, unless this were excluded as inessential. Similarly, such attributes as position in space or in time &c. must in general be regarded as inessential. For example, I might draw on a sheet of paper a number of triangles sufficiently typical of the whole class of triangles, but for this it would be necessary to reject as inessential the common property which they would possess of all being drawn on a particular sheet of paper.

[32] It will be observed that connotation and exemplification are distinguished from comprehension and denotation in that they are *selective*, while the latter pair are *exhaustive*. In making our selection our aim will usually be to find the *minimum* list which will suffice for our purpose.

[33] It is necessary to distinguish between the *known* extension of a term and its full denotation, just as we distinguish between the *known* intension of a term and its full comprehension.

[34] He would take metals as different from one another as possible, such as aluminium, antimony, copper, gold, iron, mercury, sodium, zinc.

possess in common only such properties as are common to the whole class. This selected class would constitute the *exemplification* of the name.

We have so far assumed that (1) connotation or *intensive definition* has first been arbitrarily fixed, and that this has successively determined (2) denotation, (3) comprehension, and—with a certain range of choice—(4) exemplification. But it is clear that theoretically we might start by arbitrarily fixing (i) the exemplification or *extensive definition*; and that this would successively determine (ii) comprehension, (iii) denotation, and then—again with a certain range of choice[35]—(iv) connotation.

It is interesting from a theoretical point of view to note the possibility of this second order of procedure; and this order may, moreover, be said to represent what actually occurs—at any rate in the first instance—in certain cases, as, for example, in the case of natural groups in the animal, vegetable, and mineral kingdoms. Men form classes out of vaguely recognised resemblances long before they are able to give an intensive definition of the class-name, and in such a case if they are asked to explain their use of the name, their reply will be to enumerate typical examples of the class. This would no doubt ordinarily be done in an unscientific manner, but it would be possible to work it out scientifically. The extensive definition of a name will take the form: *X is the name of the class of which Q_1, Q_2, ... Q_n are typical*. This primitive form of definition may also be called *definition by type*.[36]

In this connection the names of simple feelings which are incapable of analysis may be specially considered. For the names of ultimate elements, there is, says Sigwart,[37] no definition; we must assume that everyone attaches the same meaning to them. To such names we may indeed be able to assign a proximate genus, as when we say "red is a colour"; but we cannot add a specific difference. It is, however, only an *intensive definition* that is wanting in these cases; and the deficiency is supplied by means of an *extensive definition*. The way in which we make clear to others our use of such a term as "red" is by pointing out or otherwise indicating various objects which give rise in us to the feeling. Thus "red" is the colour of field poppies, hips and haws, ordinary sealing-wax, bricks made from certain kinds of clay, &c. This is nothing more or less than an extensive definition as above defined.

In the case of most names, however, where formal definition is attempted, it is more usual, as well as really simpler, to start from an intensive definition, and this in general

---

[35] It is ordinarily said that "of the denotation and connotation of a term one may, both cannot, be arbitrary," and this is broadly true. It is possible, however, to make the statement rather more exact. Given either intensive or extensive definition, then both denotation and comprehension are, with reference to any assigned universe of discourse, absolutely fixed. But different intensive definitions, and also different extensive definitions, may sometimes yield the same results; and it is therefore possible that, everything else being given, connotation or exemplification may still be *within certain limits indeterminate*. For example, given the class of *parallel straight lines*, the connotation may be determined in two or three different ways; or, given the class of *equilateral equiangular triangles*, we may select as connotation either having three equal sides or having three equal angles. Again, given the connotation of *metal*, it would no doubt be possible to select in more ways than one a limited number of metals not possessing in common any attributes which are not also possessed by the remaining members of the class.

[36] It is not of course meant that when we start from an extensive definition, we are classing things together at random without any guiding principle of selection. No doubt we shall be guided by a resemblance between the objects which we place in the same class, and in this sense intension may be said always to have the priority. But the resemblance may be unanalysed, so that we may be far more familiar with the application of the class-name than with its implication; and even when a connotation has been assigned to the name, it may be extensively controlled, and constantly subject to modification, just because we are much more concerned to keep the denotation fixed than the connotation.

[37] Logic, I. p. 289.

corresponds with the ultimate procedure of science. For logical purposes, it is accordingly best to assume this order of procedure, unless an explicit statement is made to the contrary.[38]

23. *Inverse Variation of Extension and Intension*.[39]—In general, as intension is increased or diminished, extension is diminished or increased accordingly, and *vice versâ*. If, for example, *rational* is added to the connotation of animal, the denotation is diminished, since all non-rational animals are now excluded, whereas they were previously included. On the other hand, if the denotation of *animal* is to be extended so as to include the vegetable kingdom, it can only be by omitting *sensitive* from the connotation. Hence the following law has been formulated: "In a series of common terms standing to one another in a relation of subordination[40] *the extension and the intension vary inversely.*" Is this law to be accepted? It must be observed at the outset that the notion of inverse variation is at any rate not to be interpreted in any strict mathematical or numerical sense. It is certainly not true that whenever the number of attributes included in the intension is altered in any manner, then the number of individuals included in the extension will be altered in some assigned numerical proportion. If, for example, to the connotation of a given name different single attributes are added, the denotation will be affected in very different degrees in different cases. Thus, the addition of *resident* to the connotation of *member of the Senate of the University of Cambridge* will reduce its denotation in a much greater degree than the addition of *non-resident*. There is in short no *regular* law of variation. The statement must not then be understood to mean more than that any increase or diminution of the intension of a name will necessarily be accompanied by *some* diminution or increase of the extension as the case may be, and *vice versâ*.[41] We will discuss the alleged law in this form, considering, first, connotation and denotation, exemplification and comprehension; and, secondly, denotation and comprehension.[42]

A. (1) Let connotation be supposed arbitrarily fixed, and used to determine denotation in some assigned universe of discourse. Then it will not be true that connotation and denotation will necessarily vary inversely. For suppose the connotation of a name, i.e., the attributes signified by it, to be *a, b, c*. It may happen that in fact wherever the attributes *a* and *b* are present, the attributes *c* and *d* are also present. In this case, if *c* is dropped from the connotation, or *d* added to it, the denotation of the name will remain unaffected. We have

---

[38] It is worth noticing that in practice an intensive definition is often followed by an enumeration of typical examples, which, if well selected, may themselves almost amount to an extensive definition. In this case, we may be said to have the two kinds of definition supplementing one another.

[39] This section may be omitted on a first reading.

[40] As in the *Tree of Porphyry*: Substance, Corporeal Substance (Body), Animate Body (Living Being), Sensitive Living Being (Animal), Rational Animal (Man). In this series of terms the intension is at each step increased, and the extension diminished.

[41] It has been said that while the extension of a term is capable of quantitative measurement, the same is not equally true of intension. "The parts of extension may be counted, but it is inept to count the parts in intension. For they are not external to each other, and they form a whole such as cannot be divided into units except by the most arbitrary dilaceration. And if it were so divided, all its parts would vary in value, and there would be no reason to expect that ten of them (that is, ten attributes) should have twice the amount or value of five" (Bosanquet, *Logic*, I. p. 59). There is some force in this, and it is decisive against interpreting *inverse variation* in the present connection in any strict numerical sense. But, at the same time, no error is committed and no difficulty of interpretation arises, if we content ourselves with speaking merely of the enlargement or restriction of the intension of a term. There can be no doubt that intension is increased when we pass from animal to man, or from man to negro; or again when we pass from triangle to isosceles triangle, or from isosceles triangle to right-angled isosceles triangle.

[42] The discussion is purposely made as formal and exact as possible. If indeed the doctrine of inverse variation cannot be treated with precision, it is better not to attempt to deal with it at all.

concrete examples of this, if we suppose *equiangularity* added to the connotation of *equilateral triangle*, or *cloven-hoofed* to that of *ruminant*, or *having jaws opening up and down* to that of *vertebrate*, or if we suppose *invalid* dropped from the connotation of *invalid syllogism with undistributed middle*. It is clear, however, that *if* any alteration in denotation takes place when connotation is altered, it must necessarily be in the opposite direction. Some individuals possessing the attributes *a* and *b* may lack the attribute *c* or the attribute *d*; but no individuals possessing the attributes *a*, *b*, *c*, or *a*, *b*, *c*, *d* can fail to possess the attributes *a*, *b*, or *a*, *b*, *c*. For example, if to the connotation of *metal* we add *fusible*, it makes no difference to the denotation; but if we add *having great weight*, we exclude potassium, sodium, &c.

The *law of variation of denotation with connotation* may then be stated as follows:—If the connotation of a term is arbitrarily enlarged or restricted, the denotation in an assigned universe of discourse will either remain unaltered or will change in the opposite direction.[43]

(2) Let exemplification be supposed arbitrarily fixed, and used to determine comprehension. It is unnecessary to shew in detail that a corresponding *law of variation of comprehension with exemplification* will hold good, namely:—If the exemplification (extensive definition) of a term is arbitrarily enlarged or restricted, the comprehension in an assigned universe of discourse will either remain unaltered or will change in the opposite direction.

B. We may now consider the relation between the *comprehension* and the *denotation* of a term. Let $P_1, P_2, \ldots P_x$ be the totality of attributes possessed by the class X, and $Q_1, Q_2, \ldots Q_y$ the totality of objects included in the class X. Both these groups are objectively, not arbitrarily,[44] determined; and the relation between them is reciprocal. $P_1, P_2, \ldots P_x$ are the only attributes possessed in common by the objects $Q_1, Q_2, \ldots Q_y$; and $Q_1, Q_2, \ldots Q_y$ are the only objects possessing all the attributes $P_1, P_2, \ldots P_x$.

We cannot suppose any direct arbitrary alteration either in comprehension or in denotation. We can, however, establish the following law of inverse variation, namely, that *any arbitrary alteration in either intensive definition or extensive definition which results in an alteration of either denotation or comprehension will also result in an alteration in the opposite direction of the other.*

Let X and Y be two terms which are so related that the definition (either intensive or extensive, as the case may be) of Y includes all that is included in the definition of X and more besides. We have to shew that either the denotations and comprehensions of X and Y will be identical or if the denotation of one includes more than the denotation of the other then its comprehension will include less, and *vice versâ*.

(a) Let X and Y be determined by connotation or intensive definition. Thus, let X be determined by the set of properties $P_1 \ldots P_m$ and Y by the set $P_1 \ldots P_{m+1}$, which includes the additional property P_{m+1}.

---

[43] Since reference is here made to the actual denotation of a term in some assigned universe of discourse, the above law may be said to turn partly on material, and not on purely formal, considerations. It should, therefore, be added that although an alteration in the connotation of a term will not always alter its actual denotation in an assigned universe of discourse, it will always affect potentially its subjective extension. If, for example, the connotation of a term X is a, b, c, and we add d; then the (real or imaginary) class of X's that are not d is necessarily excluded from, while it was previously included in, the subjective extension of the term X. Hence, if the connotation of a term is arbitrarily enlarged or restricted, the *subjective extension* will be potentially restricted or enlarged accordingly. Cf. Jevons, *Principles of Science*, 30, § 13.

[44] What may be arbitrary is the intensive definition ($P_1, P_2, \ldots P_m$) or the extensive definition ($Q_1, Q_2, \ldots Q_n$) which determines them both.

Then P_{m+1} either does or does not always accompany $P_1 \ldots P_m$.

If the former, no object included in the denotation of X is excluded from that of Y, so that the denotations of X and Y are the same; and it follows that the comprehensions of X and Y are also the same.

If the latter, then the denotation of Y is less than that of X by all those objects that possess $P_1 \ldots P_m$ without also possessing P_{m+1}. At the same time, the comprehension of Y includes at least P_{m+1} in addition to the properties included in the comprehension of X.

(*b*) Let X and Y be determined by exemplification or extensive definition. Thus, let X be determined by the set of examples $Q_1 \ldots Q_n$, and Y by the set $Q_1 \ldots Q_{n+1}$ which includes the additional object Q_{n+1}.

Then Q_{n+1} either does or does not possess all the properties common to $Q_1 \ldots Q_n$.

If the former, no property included in the comprehension of X is excluded from that of Y, so that the comprehensions of X and Y are the same; and it follows that the denotations of X and Y are also the same.

If the latter, then the comprehension of Y is less than that of X by all those properties that belong to $Q_1 \ldots Q_n$ without also belonging to Q_{n+1}. At the same time, the denotation of Y includes at least Q_{n+1} in addition to the objects included in the denotation of X.

All cases have now been considered, and it has been shown that the law above formulated holds good universally. This law and the two laws given on page 37 must together be substituted for the law of inverse relation between extension and intension in its usual form if full precision of statement is desired.

It should be observed that in speaking of variations in comprehension or denotation, no reference is intended to changes in things or in our knowledge of them. The variation is always supposed to have originated in some arbitrary alteration in the intensive or extensive definition of a given term, or in passing from the consideration of one term to that of another with a different extensive or intensive definition. Thus fresh things may be discovered to belong to a class, and the comprehension of the class-name may not thereby be affected. But in this case the denotation has not itself varied; only our knowledge of it has varied. Or we may discover fresh attributes previously overlooked; in which case similar remarks will apply. Again, new things may be brought into existence which come under the denotation of the name, and still its comprehension may remain unchanged. Or possibly new qualities may be developed by the whole of the class. In these cases, however, there is no *arbitrary* alteration in the application or implication of the name, and hence no real exception to what has been laid down above.

24. *Connotative Names.*—Mill's use of the word *connotative*, which is that generally adopted in modern works on logic, is as follows: "A non-connotative term is one which signifies a subject only, or an attribute only. A connotative term is one which denotes a subject, and implies an attribute" (*Logic*, I. 2, § 5). According to this definition, a connotative name must not only possess extension, but must also have a conventional intension assigned to it.

Mill considers that the following kinds of names are connotative in the above sense:—(1) All concrete general names. (2) Some singular names. For example, *city* is a general name, and as such no one would deny it to be connotative. Now if we say *the largest city in the world*, we have individualised the name, but it does not thereby cease to be connotative. Proper names are, however, according to Mill, non-connotative, since they merely denote a subject and do not imply any attributes. To this point, which is a subject of controversy, we shall return in the following section. (3) While admitting that most abstract names are non-connotative, since they merely signify an attribute and do not denote a subject, Mill maintains that some abstracts may justly be "considered as connotative; for attributes themselves may have attributes ascribed to them; and a word which denotes attributes may connote an attribute of those attributes" (*Logic*, I. 2, § 5).

The wording of Mill's definition is unfortunate and is probably responsible for a good deal of the controversy that has centred round the question as to whether certain classes of names are or are not connotative.

All names that we are able to use in an intelligible sense must have subjective intension for us. For we must know to what objects or what kinds of objects the names are applicable, and we cannot but associate some properties with these objects and therefore with the names.

Moreover all names that have denotation in any given universe of discourse must have comprehension also; for no object can exist without possessing properties of some kind.

If then any name can properly be described as non-connotative, it cannot be in the sense that it has no subjective intension or no comprehension. This is at least obscured when Mill speaks of non-connotative names as not implying any attributes; and if misunderstanding is to be avoided, his definitions must be amended, so as to make it quite clear that in a non-connotative name it is connotation only that is lacking, and not either subjective intension or comprehension.

A *connotative name* may be defined as a name whose application is determined by connotation or *intensive definition*, that is, by a conventionally assigned attribute or set of attributes. A *non-connotative name* is an *exemplificative name*, a name whose application is determined by exemplification or *extensive definition* in the sense explained in section 22; in other words, it is a name whose application is determined by pointing out or indicating, by means of a description or otherwise, the particular individual (if the name is singular), or typical individuals (if the name is general), to which the name is attached.

If it is allowed that the application of any names can be determined in the latter way, as distinguished from the former, then it must be allowed that some names are non-connotative.

25. *Are proper names connotative?*—To this question absolutely contradictory answers are given by ordinarily clear thinkers as being obviously correct. To some extent, however, the divergence is merely verbal, the terms "connotation" and "connotative name" being used in different senses.

It is necessary at the outset to guard against a misconception which quite obscures the real point at issue. Thus, with reference to Mill, Jevons says, "Logicians have erroneously asserted, as it seems to me, that singular terms are devoid of meaning in intension, the fact being that they exceed all other terms in that kind of meaning" (*Principles of Science*, 2, § 2, with a reference to Mill in a foot-note). But Mill distinctly states that some singular names are connotative, e.g., *the sun*,[45] *the first emperor of Rome* (*Logic*, I. 2, § 5). We may certainly narrow down the extension of a term till it becomes individualised without destroying its

---

[45] The question has been asked on what grounds *the sun* can be regarded as connotative, while *John* is considered non-connotative; compare T. H. Green, *Philosophical Works*, ii. p. 204. The answer is that *sun* is a general name with a definite signification which determines its application, and that it does not lose its connotation when individualised by the prefix *the*; while *John*, on the other hand, is a name given to an object merely as a mark for purposes of future reference, and without signifying the possession by that object of any conventionally selected attributes.

connotation; "the present Professor of Pure Mathematics in University College, London" is a singular term—its extension cannot be further diminished—but it is certainly connotative.

It must then be understood that only one class of singular names, namely, *proper names*, are affirmed to be non-connotative; and that no more is meant by this than that their application is not determined by a conventionally assigned set of attributes.[46] The ground may be further cleared by our explicitly recognising that, although proper names have no connotation, they nevertheless have both subjective intension and comprehension. An individual object can be recognised only through its attributes; and a proper name when understood by me to be a mark of a certain individual undoubtedly suggests to my mind certain qualities.[47] The qualities thus suggested by the name constitute its subjective intension. The comprehension of the name will include a good deal more than its subjective intension, namely, the whole of the properties that belong to the individual denoted.

It will be found that most writers who regard proper names as possessing connotation really mean thereby either subjective intension or comprehension. Thus Jevons puts his case as follows:—"Any proper name such as John Smith, is almost without meaning until we know the John Smith in question. It is true that the name alone connotes the fact that he is a Teuton, and is a male; but, so soon as we know the exact individual it denotes the name surely implies, also, the peculiar features, form, and character, of that individual. In fact, as it is only by the peculiar qualities, features, or circumstances of a thing, that we can ever recognise it, no name could have any fixed meaning unless we attached to it, mentally at least, such a definition of the kind of thing denoted by it, that we should know whether any given thing was denoted by it or not. If the name John Smith does not suggest to my mind the qualities of John Smith, how shall I know him when I meet him? For he certainly does not bear his name written upon his brow" (*Elementary Lessons in Logic*, p. 43). A wrong criterion of connotation in Mill's sense is here taken. The connotation of a name is not the quality or qualities by which I or anyone else may happen to recognise the class which it denotes. For example, I may recognise an Englishman abroad by the cut of his clothes, or a Frenchman by his pronunciation, or a proctor by his bands, or a barrister by his wig; but I do not mean any of these things by these names, nor do they (in Mill's sense) form any part of the connotation of the names. Compare two such names as *Henry Montagu Butler* and *the Master of Trinity College, Cambridge*. At the present time they denote the same person; but the names are not equivalent,—the one is given to a certain individual as a mark to distinguish him from others, and has no further signification; the other is given because of the performance of certain functions, on the cessation of which the name would cease to apply. Surely there is a distinction here, and one which it is important that we should not overlook.

It may indeed fairly be said that many, if not most, proper names do signify something, in the sense that they were chosen in the first instance for a special reason. For example,

---

[46] The treatment of the question adopted in this work has been criticised on the ground that it is question-begging, since in section 10 proper names have really been *defined* as non-connotative. This criticism cannot, however, be pressed unless it is at the same time maintained that the definition given in section 10 yields a denotation different from that ordinarily understood to belong to proper names.

[47] A proper name may have suggestive force even for those who are not actually acquainted with the person or thing denoted by it. Thus *William Stanley Jevons* may suggest any or all of the following to one who never heard the name before: an organised being, a human being, a male, an Anglo-Saxon, having some relative named Stanley, having parents named Jevons. But at the same time, the name cannot be said necessarily to signify any of these things, in the sense that if they were wanting it would be misapplied. Consider, for example, such a name as *Victoria Nyanza*. Some further remarks bearing on this point will be found later on in this section.

Strongi'th'arm, Smith, Jungfrau. But such names even if in a certain sense connotative when first imposed soon cease to be so, since their subsequent application to the persons or things designated is not dependent on the continuance of the attribute with reference to which they were originally given. As Mill puts it, *the name once given is independent of the reason*. In other words, we ought carefully to distinguish between the *connotation* of a name and its *history*. Thus, a man may in his youth have been strong, but we should not continue to calling strong in his dotage; whilst the name *Strongi'th'arm* once given would not be taken from him. Again, the name *Smith* may in the first instance have been given because a man plied a certain handicraft, but he would still be called by the same name if he changed his trade, and his descendants continue to be called Smith whatever their occupations may be.[48]

It has been argued that proper names must be connotative because the use of a proper name conveys more information than the use of a general name. "Few persons," says Mr Benecke,[49] "will deny that if I say *the principal speaker was Mr. Gladstone*, I am giving not less but more information than if, instead of *Mr. Gladstone*, I say either *a member of Parliament*, or *an eminent man*, or *a statesman*, or *a Liberal leader*. It will be admitted that the predicate *Mr. Gladstone* tells us all that is told us by all these other connotative predicates put together, and more; and, if so, I cannot see how it can be denied that it also connotes more." It is clear, however, that the information given when a thing is called by any name depends not on the connotation of the name, but on its intension for the person addressed. To anyone who knows that Mr. Gladstone was Prime Minister in 1892 the same information is afforded whether a speaker is referred to as *Mr. Gladstone* or as *Prime Minister of Great Britain and Ireland in* 1892. But it certainly cannot be maintained that the connotation of these two names is identical.

In criticism of the position that the application of a proper name such as *Gladstone* is determined by some attribute or set of attributes, we may naturally ask, *what* attribute or set of attributes? The answer cannot be that the connotation consists of the complete group of attributes possessed by the individual designated; for it is absurd to require any such enumeration as this in order to determine the application of the name. It is, however, impossible to select some particular attributes of the individual in question, and point to them as a group that would be accepted as constituting the definition of the name; and if it is said that the application of the name is determined by *any* set of attributes that will suffice for identification, the case is given up. For this amounts to identifying the individual by a description (that is, practically by exemplification), not by a particular set of attributes conventionally attached to the name as such. The truth is that no one would ever propose to give an *intensive definition* of a proper name. All names, however, that are connotative must necessarily admit of intensive definition.[50]

Proper names of course become connotative when they are used to designate a certain type of person; for example, a Diogenes, a Thomas, a Don Quixote, a Paul Pry, a Benedick, a

---

[48] It cannot, however, be said that the name necessarily implies ancestors of the same name. As Dr Venn remarks, "he who changes his family name may grossly deceive genealogists, but he does not tell a falsehood" (*Empirical Logic*, p. 185).

[49] In a paper on *the Connotation of Proper Names* read before the Aristotelian Society.

[50] Mr. Bosanquet arrives at the conclusion that "a proper name has a connotation, but not a fixed general connotation. It is attached to a unique individual, and connotes whatever may be involved in his identity, or is instrumental in bringing it before the mind" (*Essentials of Logic*, p. 93). So far as I can understand this statement, it amounts to saying that proper names have comprehension and subjective intension, but not connotation, in the senses in which I have defined these terms.

Socrates. But, when so used, such names have really ceased to be proper names at all; they have come to possess all the characteristics of general names.[51]

Attention may be called to a class of singular names, such as *Miss Smith*, *Captain Jones*, *President Roosevelt*, *the Lake of Lucerne*, *the Falls of Niagara*, which may be said to be partially but only partially connotative. Their peculiarity is that they are partly made up of elements that have a general and permanent signification, and that consequently some change in the object denoted might render them no longer applicable, as, for example, if Captain Jones received promotion and were made a major; while, at the same time, such connotation as they possess is by itself insufficient to determine completely their application. It may be said that their application is *limited*, but not *determined*, by reference to specific assignable attributes. They occupy an intermediate position, therefore, between connotative singular names, such as *the first man*, and strictly proper names.

We may in this connection touch upon Jevons's argument that such a name as "John Smith" connotes at any rate "Teuton" and "male." This is not strictly the case, since "John Smith" might be a dahlia, or a racehorse, or a negro, or the pseudonym of a woman, as in the case of George Eliot. In none of these cases could the name be said to be misapplied as it would be if a dahlia or a horse were called a man, or a negro a Teuton, or a woman a male. At the same time, it cannot be denied that certain proper names are in practice so much limited to certain classes of objects, that some incongruity would be felt if they were applied to objects belonging to any other class. It is, for example, unlikely that a parent would deliberately have his daughter christened "John Richard." So far as this is the case, the names in question may be said to be partially connotative in the same way as the names referred to in the preceding paragraph, though to a less extent; that is to say, their application is limited, though not determined, by reference to specific attributes. We should have a still clearer case of a similar kind if the right to bear a certain name carried with it specific legal or social privileges.[52]

The position has been taken that every proper name is at least partially connotative inasmuch as it necessarily implies individuality and the property of being called by the name in question. If we refer to anything by any name whatsoever, it must at any rate have the quality of being called by that name. If we call a man John when he really passes by the name of James, we make a mistake; we attribute to him a quality which he does not possess,—that of passing by the name of John. This argument, although it does not appear to establish the conclusion that proper names are in any degree connotative, nevertheless calls attention to a distinctive peculiarity of proper names that is worthy of notice. The denotation of connotative names may, and usually does, vary from time to time; and this is true of connotative singular names as well as of general names. But it is clearly essential in the case of a proper name that (in any given use) the name shall be consistently affixed to the same individual object. It is, however, one thing to say that the identity of the object called by the name with that to which the name has previously been assigned is a condition essential to the correct use of a proper name, and another thing to say that this is connoted by a proper name. If indeed by connotation we mean the attributes by reason of the possession of which by any object the

---

[51] Compare Gray's lines,—
"Some village Hampden, that, with dauntless breast,
 The little tyrant of his fields withstood,
 Some mute inglorious Milton here may rest,
 Some Cromwell guiltless of his country's blood."
[52] Compare Bosanquet, *Logic*, i. p. 53.

name is applicable to that object, it seems a case of ὕστερον πρότερον to include in the connotation the property of being called by the name.

EXERCISES

26. Are such concepts as "equilateral triangle" and "equiangular triangle" identical or different? [K.]

[This question should be considered with reference to the discussion in sections 17 and 18.]

27. Let X_1, X_2, X_3, X_4, and X_5 constitute the whole of a certain universe of discourse: also let a, b, c, d, e, f exhaust the properties of X_1; a, b, c, d, e, g, those of X_2; b, c, d, f, g, those of X_3; a, b, d, e, f, those of X_4; and a, c, e, f, g those of X_5.

(i) Given that, under these conditions, a term has the connotation a, b, find its denotation and its comprehension, and determine an exemplification that would yield the same result.

(ii) Given that, under the same conditions, a term has the exemplification X_4, X_5, find its comprehension and its denotation, and determine a connotation that would yield the same result. [K.]

28. On what grounds may it be held that names may possess (*a*) denotation without connotation, (*b*) connotation without denotation?

Give illustrations shewing that the denotation of a term of which the connotation is known must be regarded as relative to the proposition in which it is used as subject and to the context in which the proposition occurs. [J.]

29. What do you consider to be the question really at issue when it is asked whether proper names are connotative?

Enquire whether the following names are respectively connotative or non-connotative: *Caesar, Czar, Lord Beaconsfield, the highest mountain in Europe, Mont Blanc, the Weisshorn, Greenland, the Claimant, the pole star, Homer, a Daniel come to judgment.* [K.]

30. Bring out any special points that arise in the discussion of the extensional and intensional aspects of the following terms respectively: *the Rosaceae, equilateral triangle, colour, giant.* [C.]

Chapter 3

REAL, VERBAL, AND FORMAL PROPOSITIONS

31. *Real (Synthetic), Verbal (Analytic or Synonymous), and Formal Propositions.*—(1) A *real proposition* is one which gives information of something more than the meaning or application of the term which constitutes its subject; as when a proposition predicates of a connotative subject some attribute not included in its connotation, or when a connotative term is predicated of a non-connotative subject. For example, *All bodies have weight, The angles of any triangle are together equal to two right angles, Negative propositions distribute their predicates, Wordsworth is a great poet.*

Real propositions are also described as *synthetic, ampliative, accidental.*

(2) A *verbal proposition* is one which gives information only in regard to the meaning or application of the term which constitutes its subject.[53]

Two classes of verbal propositions are to be distinguished, which may be called respectively *analytic* and *synonymous.* In the former the predicate gives a partial or complete analysis of the connotation of the subject; e.g., *Bodies are extended, An equilateral triangle is a triangle having three equal sides, A negative proposition has a negative copula.*[54] *Definitions* are included under this division of verbal propositions; and the importance of definitions is so great, that it is clearly erroneous to speak of verbal propositions as being in all cases trivial. In general they are trivial only in so far as their true nature is misunderstood; when, for example, people waste time in pretending to prove what has been already assumed in the meaning assigned to the terms employed.[55]

---

[53] Although verbal propositions may be distinguished from real propositions in accordance with the above definitions, it may be argued that every verbal proposition implies a real proposition of a certain sort behind it. For the question as to what meaning is attached to a given term in ordinary discourse, or by a given individual, is a question of matter of fact, and a statement respecting it may be true or false. Thus, *X means abc* is a verbal proposition; but such propositions as *The meaning commonly attached to the term X is abc, The meaning attached in this work to the term X is abc, The meaning with which it would be most convenient to employ the term X is abc,* are real. Looked at from this point of view the distinction between verbal and real propositions may perhaps be thought to be a rather subtle one. It remains true, however, that the proposition *X means abc* is verbal relatively to its subject X. Out of the given material we cannot by any manipulation obtain a real predication about X, that is, about *the thing signified by the term X,* but only about *the meaning of the term X.* The real proposition involved can thus only be obtained by substituting for the original subject another subject.

[54] Since we do not here really advance beyond an analysis of the subject-notion, Dr Bain describes the verbal proposition as the "notion under the guise of the proposition." Hence the appropriateness of treating verbal propositions under the general head of Terms.

[55] By a *verbal dispute* is meant a dispute that turns on the meaning of words. Dr Venn observes that purely verbal disputes are very rare, since "a different usage of words almost necessarily entails different convictions as to

Besides propositions giving a more or less complete analysis of the connotation of names, the following—which we may speak of as *synonymous* propositions—are to be included under the head of verbal propositions: (*a*) where the subject and predicate are both proper names, e.g., *Tully is Cicero*; (*b*) where they are dictionary synonyms, e.g., *Wealth is riches*, *A story is a tale*, *Charity is love*. In these cases information is given only in regard to the application or meaning of the terms which appear as the subjects of the propositions.

Analytic propositions are also described as *explicative* and as *essential*. Very nearly the same distinction, therefore, as that between *verbal* and *real* propositions is expressed by the pairs of terms—*analytic* and *synthetic*, *explicative* and *ampliative*, *essential* and *accidental*. These terms do not, however, cover quite the same ground as verbal and real, since they leave out of account *synonymous* propositions, which cannot, for example, be properly described as either analytic or synthetic.[56]

The distinction between real and verbal propositions as above given assumes that the use of terms is fixed by their connotation and that this connotation is determinate.[57] Whether any given proposition is as a matter of fact verbal or real will depend on the meaning attached to the terms which it contains; and it is clear that logic cannot lay down any rule for determining under which category any given proposition should be placed.[58] Still, while we cannot with certainty distinguish a real proposition by its form, it may be observed that the attachment of a sign of quantity, such as *all*, *every*, *some*, &c., to the subject of a proposition may in general be regarded as an indication that in the view of the person laying down the proposition a fact is being stated and not merely a term explained. Verbal propositions, on the other hand, are usually unquantified or indesignate (see section 69). For example, in order to give a partially correct idea of the meaning of such a name as *square*, we should not say "all squares are four-sided figures," or "every square is a four-sided figure," but "a square is a four-sided figure."[59]

(3) There are propositions usually classed as verbal which ought rather to be placed in a class by themselves, namely, those which are valid whatever may be the meaning of the terms

---

facts" (*Empirical Logic*, p. 296). This is true and important; it ought indeed always to be borne in mind that the problem of scientific definition is not a mere question of words, but a question of things. At the same time, disputes which are *partly* verbal are exceedingly common, and it is also very common for their true character in this respect to be unrecognised. When this is the case, the controversy is more likely than not to be fruitless. The questions whether proper names are connotative, and whether every syllogism involves a *petitio principii*, may be taken as examples. We certainly go a long way towards the solution of these questions by clearly differentiating between different meanings which may be attached to the terms employed.

[56] Thus, Mansel calls attention to "a class of propositions which are not, in the strict sense of the word, analytical, *viz.*, those in which the predicate is a single term synonymous with the subject" (Mansel's *Aldrich*, p. 170).

[57] We can, however, adapt the distinction to the case in which the use of terms is fixed by extensive definition. We may say that whilst a proposition (expressed affirmatively and with a copula of inclusion) is *intensively verbal* when the connotation of the predicate is a part or the whole of the connotation of the subject, it is *extensively verbal* when the subject taken in extension is a part or the whole of the extensive definition of the predicate. Thus, if the use of the term *metal* is fixed by an extensive definition, that is to say, by the enumeration of certain typical metals, of which we may suppose *iron* to be one, then it is a verbal proposition to say that *iron is a metal*. If, however, *tin* is not included amongst the typical metals, then it is a real proposition to say that *tin is a metal*.

[58] It does not follow from this that the distinction between verbal and real propositions is of no logical importance. Although the logician cannot *quâ* logician determine in doubtful cases to which category a given proposition belongs, he can point out what are the conditions upon which this depends, and he can shew that in any discussion or argument no progress is possible until it is clearly understood by all who are taking part whether the propositions laid down are to be interpreted as being real or merely verbal. To refer to an analogous case, it will not be said that the distinction between truth and falsity is of no logical importance because the logician cannot *quâ* logician determine whether a given proposition is true or false.

[59] It should be added that we may formally distinguish a full definition from a real proposition by connecting the subject and the predicate by the word "means" instead of the word "is."

involved; e.g., *All A is A, No A is not-A, All Z is either B or not-B, If all A is B then no not-B is A, If all A is B and all B is C then all A is C*. These may be called *formal propositions*, since their validity is determined by their bare form.[60]

Formal propositions are the only propositions whose validity is examined and guaranteed by logic itself irrespective of other sources of knowledge, and many of the results reached in formal logic may be summed up in such propositions; for any formally valid reasoning can be expressed by a formal hypothetical proposition as in the last two of the examples given above.

A formal proposition as here defined must not be confused with a proposition expressed in symbols. A formal proposition need not indeed be expressed in symbols at all. Thus, the proposition *An animal is an animal* is a formal proposition; *All S is P* is not. Strictly speaking, a symbolic expression, such as *All S is P*, is to be regarded as a *propositional form*, rather than as a proposition *per se*. For it cannot be described as in itself either true or false. What we are largely concerned with in logic are relations between propositional forms; because these involve corresponding relations between all propositions falling into the forms in question.

We have then three classes of propositions—*formal, verbal*, and *real*—the validity or invalidity of which is determined respectively by their bare form, by the mere meaning or application of the terms involved, by questions of fact concerning the things denoted by these terms.[61]

32. *Nature of the Analysis involved in Analytic Propositions.*—Confusion is not unfrequently introduced into discussions relating to analytic propositions by a want of agreement as to the nature of the analysis involved. If identified, as above, with a division of the verbal proposition, an analytic proposition gives an analysis, partial or complete, of the *connotation* of the subject-term. Some writers, however, appear to have in view an analysis of the *subjective intension* of the subject-term. There is of course nothing absolutely incorrect in this interpretation, if consistently adhered to, but it makes the distinction between analytic and synthetic propositions logically valueless and for all practical purposes nugatory. "Both intension and extension," says Mr. Bradley, "are relative to our knowledge. And the perception of this truth is fatal to a well-known Kantian distinction. A judgment is not fixed as 'synthetic' or 'analytic': its character varies with the knowledge possessed by various persons and at different times. If the meaning of a word were confined to that attribute or

---

[60] Propositions which are in appearance purely tautologous have sometimes an epigrammatic force and are used for rhetorical purposes, e.g., *A man's a man (for a' that)*. In such cases, however, there is usually an implication which gives the proposition the character of a real proposition; thus, in the above instance the true force of the proposition is that *Every man is as such entitled to respect*. "In the proposition, *Children are children*, the subject-term means only the age characteristic of childhood; the predicate-term the other characteristics which are connected with it. By the proposition, *War is war*, we mean to say that when once a state of warfare has arisen, we need not be surprised that all the consequences usually connected with it appear also. Thus the **predicate adds new determinations to the meaning in which the subject was first taken**" (Sigwart, *Logic*, I. p. 86).

[61] Real propositions are divided into true and false according as they do or do not accurately correspond with facts. By verbal and formal propositions we usually mean propositions which from the point of view taken are valid. A proposition which from either of these points of view is invalid is spoken of as a *contradiction in terms*. Properly speaking we ought to distinguish between a *verbal* contradiction in terms and a *formal* contradiction in terms, the contradiction depending in the first case upon the force of the terms employed and in the second case upon the mere form of the proposition; e.g., *Some men are not animals*, *A is not-A*. Any purely formal fallacy may be said to resolve itself into a formal contradiction in terms. It should be added that a mere term, if it is complex, may involve a contradiction in terms; e.g., *Roman Catholic* (if the separate terms are interpreted literally), *A not-A*.

group of attributes with which it set out, we could distinguish those judgments which assert within the whole one part of its contents from those which add an element from outside; and the distinction thus made would remain valid for ever. But in actual practice the meaning itself is enlarged by synthesis. What is added to-day is implied to-morrow. We may even say that a synthetic judgment, so soon as it is made, is at once analytic."[62]

If by intension is meant subjective intension, and by an analytic judgment one which analyses the intension of the subject, the above statements are unimpeachable. It is indeed so obviously true that in this sense synthetic judgments are only analytic judgments in the making, that to dwell upon the distinction itself at any length would be only waste of time. It is, however, misleading to identify subjective intension with *meaning*;[63] and this is especially the case in the present connection, since it may be maintained with a certain degree of plausibility that *some* synthetic judgments are only analytic judgments in the making, even when by an analytic judgment is meant one which analyses the *connotation* of the subject. For undoubtedly the connotation of names is not in practice unalterably fixed. As our knowledge progresses, many of our definitions are modified, and hence a form of words which is synthetic at one period may become analytic at another.

But, in the first place, it is very far indeed from being a universal rule that newly-discovered properties of a class are taken ultimately into the connotation or intensive definition of the class-name. Dr Bain (*Logic, Deduction*, pp. 69 to 73) seems to imply the contrary; but his doctrine on this point is not defensible on the ground either of logical expediency or of actual practice. As to logical expediency, it is a generally recognised principle of definition that we ought to aim at including in a definition the minimum number of properties necessary for identification rather than the maximum which it is possible to include.[64] And as to what actually occurs, it is easy to find cases where we are able to say with confidence that certain common properties of a class never will as a matter of fact be included in the definition of the class-name; for example, *equiangularity* will never be included in the definition of *equilateral triangle*, or *having cloven hoofs* in the definition of *ruminant animal*.

In the second place, even when freshly discovered properties of things come ultimately to be included in the connotation of their names, the process is at any rate gradual, and it would, therefore, be incorrect to say—in the sense in which we are now using the terms—that a synthetic judgment becomes in the very process of its formation analytic. On the other hand, it may reasonably be assumed that in any given discussion the meaning of our terms is fixed,

---

[62] *Principles of Logic*, p. 172. Professor Veitch expresses himself somewhat similarly. "Logically all judgments are analytic, for judgment is an assertion by the person judging of what he knows of the subject spoken of. To the person addressed, real or imaginary, the judgment may contain a predicate new—a new knowledge. But the person making the judgment speaks analytically, and analytically only; for he sets forth a part of what he knows belongs to the subject spoken of. In fact, it is impossible anyone can judge otherwise. We must judge by our real or supposed knowledge of the thing already in the mind" (*Institutes of Logic*, p. 237).

[63] Compare the following criticism of Mill's distinction between real and verbal propositions: "If every proposition is merely verbal which asserts something of a thing under a name that already presupposes what is about to be asserted, then every statement by a scientific man is *for him* merely verbal" (T. H. Green, *Works*, ii. p. 233). This criticism seems to lose its force if we bear in mind the distinction between connotation and subjective intension.

[64] If we include in the definition of a class-name all the common properties of the class, how are we to make any universal statement of fact about the class at all? Given that the property P belongs to the whole of the class S, then by hypothesis P becomes part of the meaning of S, and the proposition *All S is P* merely makes this verbal statement, and is no assertion of any matter of fact at all. We are, therefore, involved in a kind of vicious circle.

and the distinction between analytic and synthetic propositions then becomes highly significant and important. It may be added that when a name changes its meaning, any proposition in which it occurs does not strictly speaking remain the same proposition as before. We ought rather to say that the same form of words now expresses a different proposition.[65]

EXERCISES

33. State which of the following propositions you consider real, and which verbal, giving your reasons in each case:

(i) All proper names are singular;
(ii) A syllogism contains three and only three terms;
(iii) Men are vertebrates;
(iv) All is not gold that glitters;
(v) The dodo is an extinct bird;
(vi) Logic is the science of reasoning;
(vii) Two and two are four;
(viii) All equilateral triangles are equiangular;
(ix) Between any two points one, and only one, straight line can be drawn;
(x) Any two sides of a triangle are together greater than the third side.

[C.]

34. Enquire whether the following propositions are real or verbal: (*a*) Homer wrote the *Iliad*, (*b*) Milton wrote *Paradise Lost*. [C.]

35. How would you characterise a proposition which is *formally* inferred from the conjunction of a *verbal* proposition with a *real material* proposition? Explain your view by the aid of an illustration. [J.]

36. If all x is y, and some x is z, and p is the name of those z's which are x; is it a verbal proposition to say that all p is y? [V.]

37. Is it possible to make any term whatever the subject (*a*) of a verbal proposition, (*b*) of a real proposition? [J.]

---

[65] This point is brought out by Mr Monck in the admirable discussion of the above question contained in his *Introduction to Logic*, pp. 130 to 134.

Chapter 4

NEGATIVE NAMES AND RELATIVE NAMES

38. *Positive and Negative Names.*—A pair of names of the forms *A* and *not-A* are commonly described as positive and negative respectively. The true import of the negative name *not-A*, including the question whether it really has any signification at all, has, however, given rise to much discussion.

Strictly speaking neither affirmation nor negation has any meaning except in reference to judgments or propositions. A concept or a term cannot be itself either affirmed or denied. If I affirm, it must be a judgment or a proposition that I affirm; if I deny, it must be a judgment or a proposition that I deny.

Starting from this position, Sigwart is led to the conclusion that, "taken literally, the formula *not-A*, where *A* denotes any idea, has no meaning whatever" (*Logic*, I. p. 134). Apart from the fact that the mere absence of an idea is not itself an idea, *not-A* cannot be interpreted to mean the *absence* of *A* in thought; for, on the contrary, it implies the *presence* of *A* in thought. We cannot, for instance, think of *not-white* except by thinking of *white*. Nor again can we interpret *not-A* as denoting whatever does not necessarily accompany *A* in thought. For, if so, *A* and *not-A* would not as a rule be exclusive or incompatible. For example, *square*, *solid*, do not necessarily accompany *white* in thought; but there is no opposition between these ideas and the idea of *white*. In order to interpret *not-A* as a real negation we must, says Sigwart, tacitly introduce a judgment or rather a series of judgments, meaning by *not-A* "whatever is not *A*," that is, everything whatsoever of which *A* must be denied. "I must review in thought all possible things in order to deny *A* of them, and these would be the positive objects denoted by *not-A*. But even if there were any use in this, it would be an impossible task" (p. 135).

Whilst agreeing with much that Sigwart says in this connection, I cannot altogether accept his conclusion. We shall return to the question from the more controversial point of view in the following section. In the meantime we may indicate the result to which Sigwart's general argument really seems to lead us.

We must agree that *not-A* cannot be regarded as representing any independent concept; that is to say, we cannot form any idea of *not-A* that negates the notion *A*. It is, therefore, true that, taken literally (that is, as representing an idea which is the pure negation of the idea *A*), the formula *not-A* is unintelligible. Regarding *not-A*, however, as equivalent to *whatever is not A*, we may say that its justification and explanation is to be found primarily by reference to the *extension* of the name. The thinking of anything as *A* involves its being distinguished from that which is not *A*. Thus on the extensive side every concept divides the universe with reference to which it is thought (whatever that may be) into two mutually exclusive subdivisions, namely, a portion of which *A* can be predicated and a portion of which *A* cannot be predicated. These we designate *A* and *not-A* respectively. While it may be said that *A* and *not-A* involve *intensively* only one concept, they are *extensively* mutually exclusive.

Confining ourselves to connotative names, we may express the distinction between positive and negative names somewhat differently by saying that a *positive* name implies the *presence* in the things called by the name of a certain specified attribute or set of attributes, while a *negative* name implies the *absence* of one or other of certain specified attributes. A negative name, therefore, has its denotation determined indirectly. The class denoted by the positive name is determined positively, and then the negative name denotes what is left.

39. *Indefinite Character of Negative Names.*—*Infinite* and *indefinite* are designations that have been applied to negative names when interpreted in such a way as not to involve restriction to a limited universe of discourse. For without such restriction (explicit or implicit) a negative name, for example, *not-white*, must be understood to denote the whole infinite or indefinite class of things of which *white* cannot truly be affirmed, including such entities as virtue, a dream, time, a soliloquy, New Guinea, the Seven Ages of Man.

Many logicians hold that no significant term can be really infinite or indefinite in this way.[66] They say that if a term like *not-white* is to have any meaning at all, it must be understood as denoting, not all things whatsoever except white things, but only things that are black, red, green, yellow, etc., that is, all *coloured* things except such as are white. In other words, the universe of discourse which any pair of contradictory terms *A* and *not-A* between them exhaust is considered to be necessarily limited to the proximate genus of which *A* is a species; as, for example, in the case of *white* and *not-white*, the universe of colour.

It is doubtless the case that we seldom or never make use of negative names except with reference to some proximate genus. For instance, in speaking of *non-voters* we are probably referring to the inhabitants of some town or locality whom we subdivide into those who have votes and those who have not. In a similar way we ordinarily deny *red* only of things that are coloured, *squareness* only of things that have some figure, etc., so that there is an implicit limitation of sphere. It may be granted further that a proposition containing a negative name interpreted as infinite can have little or no practical value. But it does not follow that some limitation of sphere is necessary in order that a negative term may have *meaning*. The argument is used that it is an utterly impossible feat to hold together in any one idea a chaotic mass of the most different things. But the answer to this argument is that we do not profess to hold together the things denoted by a negative name by reference to any positive elements which they may have in common: they are held together simply by the fact that they all lack someone or other of certain determinate elements. In other words, the argument only shews that a *negative* name has no *positive* concept corresponding to it.[67] It may be added that if this argument had force, it would apply also to the subdivision of a genus with reference to the presence or absence of a certain quality. If we divide coloured objects into *red* and *not-red*,

---

[66] This is at the root of Sigwart's final difficulty with regard to negative names, as indicated in the preceding section. Later on he points out that in division we are justified in including negative characteristics of the form *not-A* in a concept, although we cannot regard *not-A* itself as an independent concept. Thus we may divide the concept *organic being* into *feeling* and *not-feeling*, a specific difference being here constituted by the absence of a characteristic which is compatible with the remaining characteristics, but is not necessarily connected with them (*Logic*, I. p. 278). Compare also Lotze, *Logic*, § 40.

[67] For a good statement of the counter-argument, compare Mrs Ladd Franklin in *Mind*, January, 1892, pp. 130, 1.

we may say equally that we cannot hold together coloured objects other than red by any positive element that they have in common: the fact that they are all coloured is obviously insufficient for the purpose.

A somewhat different argument is implied by Sigwart when he says, "If A = *mortal*, where will justice, virtue, law, order, distance find a place? They are neither *mortal beings*, nor yet *not-mortal* beings, for they are not beings at all." The answer seems clear. They are *not-(mortal beings)*, and therefore *not-A*. As a rule, it is needless to exclude explicitly from a species what does not even belong to some higher genus. But the fact of the exclusion remains.

Granting then that in practice we rarely, if ever, employ a negative name except with reference to some proximate genus, we nevertheless hold that *not-A* is perfectly intelligible whatever the universe of discourse may be and however wide it may be. For it denotes in that universe whatever is not denoted by the corresponding positive name. Moreover in formal processes we should be unnecessarily hampered if not allowed to pass unreservedly from *X is not A* to *X is not-A*.[68]

From this point of view attention may be called to the difference in ordinary use between such forms as *unholy, immoral, discourteous* and such forms as *non-holy, non-moral, non-courteous*. The latter *may* be used with reference to any universe of discourse, however extensive. But not so the former; in their case there is undoubtedly a restriction to some universe of discourse that is more or less limited in its range. We can, for example, speak of a *table* as *non-moral*, although we cannot speak of it as *immoral*. A want of recognition of this distinction may be partly responsible for the denial that any terms can properly be described as infinite or indefinite.[69]

40. *Contradictory Terms.*—A positive name and the corresponding negative are spoken of as *contradictory*. We may define contradictory terms as a pair of terms so related that between them they exhaust the entire universe to which reference is made, whilst in that universe there is no individual of which both can be affirmed at the same time. It is desirable to repeat here that contradiction can exist primarily between judgments or propositions only, so that as applied to terms or ideas the notion of contradiction must be interpreted with reference to predication. *A* and *not-A* are spoken of as contradictory because they cannot without contradiction be predicated together of the same subject. Thus it is in their exclusive

---

[68] Writers who take the view which we are here criticising must in consistency deny the universal validity of the process of immediate inference called obversion. Thus Lotze, rightly on his own view, will not allow us to pass from *spirit is not matter* to *spirit is not-matter*; in fact he rejects altogether the form of judgment *S is not-P* (*Logic*, § 40). Some writers, who follow Lotze on the general question here raised, appear to go a good deal further than he does, not merely disallowing such a proposition as *virtue is not-blue* but also such a proposition as *virtue is not blue*, on the ground that if we say "virtue is not blue," there is no real predication, since the notion of colour is absolutely foreign to an unextended and abstract concept such as "virtue." Lotze, however, expressly draws a distinction between the two forms *S is non-Q* and *S is not Q*, and tells us that "everything which it is wished to secure by the affirmative predicate *non-Q* is secured by the intelligible negation of *Q*" (*Logic*, § 72; cf. § 40). On the more extreme view it is wrong to say that *Virtue is either blue or it is not blue*; but Lotze himself does not thus deny the universality of the law of excluded middle.

[69] It should be added that in the ordinary use of language the negative prefix does not always make a term negative as here defined. Thus, as Mill points out, "the word *unpleasant*, notwithstanding its negative form, does not connote the mere absence of pleasantness, but a less degree of what is signified by the word *painful*, which, it is hardly necessary to say, is positive." On the other hand, some names positive in form may, with reference to a limited universe of discourse, be negative in force; e.g., *alien, foreign*. Another example is the term *Turanian*, as employed in the science of language. This term has been used to denote groups lying outside the Aryan and Semitic groups, but not distinguished by any positive characteristics which they possess in common.

character that they are termed contradictory; as between them exhausting the universe of discourse they might rather be called *complementary*.[70]

41. *Contrary Terms.*—Two terms are usually spoken of as *contrary*[71] to one another when they denote things which can be regarded as standing at opposite ends of some definite scale in the universe to which reference is made; e.g., *first* and *last*, *black* and *white*, *wise* and *foolish*, *pleasant* and *painful*.[72] Contraries differ from contradictories in that they admit of a mean, and therefore do not between them exhaust the entire universe of discourse. It follows that, although two contraries cannot both be true of the same thing at the same time, they may both be false. Thus, a colour may be neither black nor white, but blue; a feeling may be neither pleasant nor painful, but indifferent.

It will be observed that not every term has a contrary as above defined, for the thing denoted by a term may not be capable of being regarded as representing the extreme in any definite scale. Thus *blue* can hardly be said to have a contrary in the universe of colour, or *indifferent* in the universe of feeling.

By some writers, the term *contrary* is used in a wider sense than the above, contrariety being identified with simple incompatibility (a mean between the two incompatibles being possible); thus, *blue* and *yellow* equally with *black*, would in this sense be called *contraries* of *white*.[73] Other writers use the term *repugnant* to express the mere relation of incompatibility; thus *red*, *blue*, *yellow* are in this sense *repugnant* to one another.[74]

42. *Relative Names.*—A name is said to be *relative*, when, over and above the object that it denotes, it implies in its signification another object, to which in explaining its meaning reference must be made. The name of this other object is called the *correlative* of the first. Non-relative names are sometimes called *absolute*.

Jevons considers that in certain respects all names are relative. "The fact is that everything must really have relations to something else, the water to the elements of which it is composed, the gas to the coal from which it is manufactured, the tree to the soil in which it is rooted" (*Elementary Lessons in Logic*, p. 26). Again, by the law of relativity, consciousness is possible only in circumstances of change. We cannot think of any object except as

---

[70] Dr Venn (*Empirical Logic*, p. 191) distinguishes between *formal contradictories* and *material contradictories*, according as the relation in which the pair of terms stand to one another is or is not apparent from their mere form. Thus *A* and *not-A* are formal contradictories; so are *human* and *non-human*. Material contradictories, on the other hand, are not constructed "for the express purpose of indicating their mutual relation." No formal contradiction, for example, is apparent between *British* and *Foreign*, or between *British* and *Alien*; and yet "within their range of appropriate application—which in the latter case includes persons only, and in the former case is extended to produce of most kinds—these two pairs of terms fulfil tolerably well the conditions of mutual exclusion and collective exhaustion."

[71] De Morgan uses the terms contrary and contradictory as equivalent, his definition of them corresponding to that given in the preceding section.

[72] It has been already pointed out that the negative prefix does not always make a term really negative in force. Thus *pleasant* and *unpleasant* are not contradictories, for they admit of a mean; when we say that anything is unpleasant, we intend something more than the mere denial that it is *pleasant*. It should be added that a pair of terms of this kind may also fail to be contraries as above defined, since while admitting of a mean they may at the same time not denote extremes. *Unpleasant*, for example, denotes only that which is mildly painful: unless intended ironically, it would be a misuse of terms to speak of the tortures of the Inquisition as merely unpleasant. Compare Carveth Read, *Logic*, p. 49.

[73] There is much to be said in favour of this wider use of the term *contrary*. Compare the discussion of contrary propositions in section 81.

[74] So long as we are confined to simple terms the relations of contrariety and repugnancy cannot be expressed *formally* or in mere symbols. But it is otherwise when we pass on to the consideration of complex terms. Thus, while *XY* and *not-X or not-Y* are formal contradictories, *XY* and *X not-Y* may be said to be formal repugnants, *XY* and *not-X not-Y* formal contraries (in the narrower of the two senses indicated above).

distinguished from something else. Every term, therefore, implies its negative as an object of thought. Take the term *man*. It is an ambiguous term, and in many of its meanings is clearly relative,—for example, as opposed to master, to officer, to wife. If in any sense it is absolute it is when opposed to not-man; but even in this case it may be said to be relative to not-man. To avoid this difficulty, Jevons remarks, "Logicians have been content to consider as relative terms those only which imply some peculiar and striking kind of relation arising from position in time or space, from connection of cause and effect, &c.; and it is in this special sense, therefore, that the student must use the distinction."

A more satisfactory solution of the difficulty may be found by calling attention to the distinction already drawn between the point of view of connotation (which has to do with the signification of names) and the subjective and objective points of view respectively. From the subjective point of view all notions are relative by the law of relativity above referred to. Again, from the objective point of view all things, at any rate in the phenomenal world, are relative in the sense that they could not exist without the existence of something else; e.g., man without oxygen, or a tree without soil. But when we say that a *name* is relative, we do not mean that what it denotes cannot exist or be thought about without something else also existing or being thought about; we mean that its signification cannot be explained without reference to something else which is called by a correlative name, e.g., *husband*, *parent*. It cannot be said that in this sense all names are relative.

The fact or facts constituting the ground of both correlative names is called the *fundamentum relationis*. For example, in the case of partner, the fact of partnership; in the case of husband and wife, the facts which constitute the marriage tie; in the case of ruler and subject, the control which the former exercises over the latter.

Sometimes the relation which each correlative bears to the other is the same; for example, in the case of partner, where the correlative name is the same name over again. Sometimes it is not the same; for example, father and son, slave-owner and slave.

The consideration of relative names is not of importance except in connection with the logic of relatives, to which further reference will be made subsequently.

EXERCISES

43. Give one example of each of the following,—(i) a collective general name, (ii) a singular abstract name, (iii) a connotative singular name, (iv) a connotative abstract name. Add reasons justifying your example in each case. [K.]

44. Discuss the logical characteristics of the following names:—*beauty*, *fault*, *Mrs Grundy*, *immortal*, *nobility*, *slave*, *sovereign*, *the Times*, *truth*, *ungenerous*. [K.]

[In discussing the character of any name it is necessary first of all to determine whether it is *univocal*, that is, used in one definite sense only, or *equivocal* (or *ambiguous*), that is, used in more senses than one. In the latter case, its logical characteristics may vary according to the sense in which it is used.]

45. It has been maintained that the doctrine of terms is extra-logical. Justify or controvert this position. [J.]

Part II. Propositions

Chapter 5

IMPORT OF JUDGMENTS AND PROPOSITIONS

46. *Judgments and Propositions.*—In passing to the next division of our subject we are confronted, first of all, with a question which is partly, but not entirely, a question of phraseology. Shall we speak of the *judgment* or of the *proposition*? The usage of logicians differs widely. Some treat almost exclusively of judgments; others almost exclusively of propositions. It will be found that for the most part the former are those who tend to emphasise the psychological or the metaphysical aspects of logic, while the latter are those who are more inclined to develop the symbolic or the material aspects.

To a certain extent it is a matter of little importance which of the alternatives is ostensively adopted. Those who deal with judgments from the logical standpoint must when pressed admit that they can deal with them only as expressed in language, and all their illustrations necessarily consist of judgments expressed in language. But a *judgment expressed in language* is precisely what is meant by a *proposition*. Hence in treating of judgments it is impossible not to treat also of propositions.

On the other hand, so far as we treat of propositions in logic, we treat of them not as grammatical sentences, but as assertions, as verbal expressions of judgments. The logical proposition is the proposition as understood; and a *proposition as understood* is a *judgment*. Hence in treating of propositions in logic we necessarily treat also of judgments.

In a large degree, then, the problem does resolve itself into a merely verbal question. At the same time, reasons and counter-reasons may be adduced in favour of the one alternative and in favour of the other.

On the one side, it is said that the use of the term *proposition* tends to confuse the sentence as a grammatical combination of words with the proposition as apprehended and intellectually affirmed; and it is urged that in treating of propositions the logician tends to become a mere grammarian.

On the other side, it is submitted that the logician is primarily concerned, not with the *process* of judgment, the discussion of which belongs to the sphere of psychology, but with judgment as a *product*, and moreover that he is concerned with this product only in so far as it assumes a fixed and definite form, which it cannot do until it receives verbal expression; and it is urged that if we concentrate our attention on judgments without explicit regard to their expression in language, our treatment tends to become too psychological.

It has been said above that logically we can deal with judgments only as expressed in propositions; and no doubt all judgments can with more or less effort be so expressed. But as a matter of fact we constantly judge in a vague sort of way without the precision that is necessary even in loose modes of expression, and we find that to give expression to our judgments may sometimes require very considerable effort. It must be remembered that logic has in view an ideal. Its object is to determine the conditions to which valid judgments must conform, and it is concerned with the characteristics of actual judgments only in subordination to this end. From this point of view it is especially important that we should deal with judgments in the only form in which it is possible for them to attain precision; and this consideration appears to be conclusive in favour of our treating explicitly of propositions in some part at any rate of a logical course.

No doubt in dealing with propositions we have to raise certain questions that relate to the usage of language. Unfortunately the same propositional form may be understood as expressing very different judgments. It is therefore requisite that in any scientific treatment of logic we should discuss the interpretation of the propositional forms that we recognise. This problem is akin to the problem of definition which has to be faced sooner or later in every science; and, as is also true of a definition, the solution in any particular case is largely of the nature of a convention. But this does not detract from its importance as conducing to clearness of thought.

The question of the interpretation of propositional forms is as a matter of fact one that cannot be altogether avoided on any treatment of logic; and it is of importance to recognise explicitly that in discussing this question we are not dealing with judgments pure and simple. Words are like mathematical symbols, and the meaning of a given form of words is not something inherent either in the words themselves or in the thoughts that they may represent, but is dependent on a convention established by those who employ the words. In the force of a given judgment, however, there can be nothing that is dependent on convention. This distinction is not always remembered by those who confine their attention mainly to judgments, and they are consequently sometimes led to express themselves with an appearance of dogmatism on questions that do not really admit of dogmatic treatment.

But while in certain aspects of logical enquiry it is requisite to deal explicitly with *propositions*, it must never be forgotten that as logicians we are concerned with propositions only as the expressions of judgments; and there are numerous occasions when we have to go behind propositional forms and ask what are the fundamental characteristics of the judgments that they express.

47. *The Abstract Character of Logic.*—Reference has been made in the preceding section to the necessity for logical purposes of making our judgments precise. For only if they are precise is it possible to determine with accuracy what are their logical implications considered either individually or in conjunction with one another. It has also been pointed out that we can make our judgments precise only by expressing them in propositional forms, the interpretation of which has been agreed upon.

But this is not without its disadvantages. Sometimes the full force of an actual judgment hardly admits of being expressed in words, and even the force of a proposition as understood may not be found exclusively in the words of which it composed, but may depend partly on the context in which it is placed. Hence the isolated proposition must frequently be regarded as in a sense an abstraction, leaving behind it some portion of the actual judgment for which it stands.

This is indeed much less true of the propositions of science than of those of everyday life; and the more fully a statement is independent of context the more fully may it be regarded as fulfilling its purpose from the scientific standpoint. Still the abstract character of logic must be frankly recognised. "Just as thought is abstract in its dealings with reality, so logic is abstract in its dealings with ordinary thought."[75]

That they are in some degree abstractions is true not only of propositions, but also of inferences, as we have to deal with them in logic. Much of the reasoning of everyday life does not admit of expression in the form of definite premisses and conclusions such as would satisfy the canons of logic. The grounds upon which our conclusions are based are often so complex, and the influence which some of them exert upon our beliefs is so subtle and delicate, that they cannot be completely set forth. This will be realised at once if an attempt is made to apply the rules of logic to any ordinary inference; and an explanation is herein found why the illustrations given in logical text-books frequently appear so artificial and unreal.

It must be admitted that the abstract character of logic detracts to some extent from its utility as an art, though the extent of this drawback may easily be exaggerated. Regarded as a science, however, the value, of logic remains unimpaired. Other sciences besides logic have to proceed by abstractions and separations that do not fully correspond to the complexities of nature; and this often becomes the more true the higher the stage that the science has reached. Its necessary abstractness does not prevent logic from analysing successfully the characteristics of the developed judgment or from determining the principles of valid reasoning. If we were to seek to treat logical problems without abstraction we should be in danger of destroying the scientific character of logic without achieving any valuable result even from the purely utilitarian point of view. It is of little value to criticise received systems without providing any new constructive system in their place.

48. *Nature of the Enquiry into the Import of Propositions.*—Under the general head of the *import of propositions* it is usual to include problems that are really very different in character.[76]

(1) There is, in the first place, the fundamental problem or series of problems as to what are the *essential characteristics of judgments*, and therefore of propositions as expressing judgments. The discussion of questions of this character must be based directly on psychological or philosophical considerations, and in the solutions nothing arbitrary or conventional can find a place.

Under this head are to be included such problems as the following: Do all judgments contain a reference to reality? In what sense, if any, can all judgments claim to possess universality or necessity? What is the nature of significant denial? Are distinctions of modality subjective or objective?

(2) In the *interpretation of propositional forms* we have an enquiry of a very different character, an enquiry which relates distinctively to propositions, and not to judgments considered apart from their expression. The problem is indeed to determine what is the precise judgment that a given proposition shall be understood to express; and, in consequence of the uncertainty and ambiguity of ordinary language, the solution of the problem includes an optional or selective element.

As a simple illustration of the kind of problem that we here have in view, we may note that in the traditional scheme of propositions, *All S is P, No S is P, Some S is P, Some S is not*

---

[75] Hobhouse, *Theory of Knowledge*, p. 7.
[76] Compare Mr. W. E. Johnson in *Mind*, April, 1895, p. 242.

P, the signs of quantity have to be interpreted. The existential and modal import of these propositions is also partly a question of interpretation.

In connection with the interpretation of propositions, the distinction between *meaning* and *implication* has to be considered. What we do in interpreting propositions is to assign to them a meaning; and when the meaning has once been fixed, the implications are determined in accordance with logical principles.

The dividing line between meaning and implication is not in practice always easy to draw, and some writers seek to ignore it by including within the scope of meaning all the implications of a proposition. But this is a fatal error. The assignment of meaning is within certain limits arbitrary and selective. But if element a necessarily involves element b, then a having been assigned as part of the meaning of a given propositional form, it is no question of meaning as to whether the form in question does or does not imply b, and there is nothing arbitrary or selective in the solution of this question.

Sometimes the elements a and b mutually involve one another. It may then be a question of interpretation whether a shall be included in meaning, b thus becoming an implication, or whether b shall be included in meaning, a becoming an implication.

A failure to recognise what is really the point at issue in a case like this has sometimes caused discussions to take a wrong turn. Thus the question is raised whether the import of the proposition *All S is P* is that the class S is included in the class P, or that the set of attributes S is invariably accompanied by the set of attributes P; and these are regarded as antagonistic theories. If the implications of a proposition are regarded as part of its import, then the proposition may be said to import both these things. But if by the import of a proposition we intend to signify its meaning only, then we may adopt an interpretation that will make either of them (but not both) part of its import, or our interpretation may be such that the proposition imports neither of them. The question here raised is dealt with in more detail later on.

(3) A third problem, distinct from both those described above, arises in connection with the expression of judgments in propositional form.

In ordinary discourse we meet with an infinite variety of forms of statement. To recognise and deal separately with all these forms in our treatment of logical problems would, however, be impracticable. We have, therefore, in some at any rate of our discussions, to limit ourselves to a certain number of selected forms; and in such discussions we have to assume that the judgments with which we are dealing are at the outset expressed in one or other or a combination of these selected forms.

This reduction of a statement to some canonical form has been called by Mr Johnson its *formulation*.

A given statement, since it involves many different relations which mutually implicate one another, may be formulated in a number of different ways; and it is needless to say that there is no one scheme of formulating propositions that we are bound to accept to the exclusion of others. Different schemes are useful for different purposes, and several schedules of propositions (for example, equational and existential schedules) will presently be considered in addition to the traditional fourfold schedule. It should be added that a given scheme may profess to cover part only of the field. Thus the traditional schedule (*All S is P*, etc.) professes to be a scheme for categorical judgments only, and (as traditionally interpreted) for assertoric judgments only.

With reference to the reduction of a statement to a form in which it belongs to a given schedule two points call for notice.

(*a*) There is danger lest some part of the force of the original statement may be lost.

To a certain extent this is inevitable, especially if the original statement contains suggestion or innuendo in addition to what it definitely affirms; and this must be taken in connection with what has already been said about the abstract character of logic. If, however, there is any substantial loss of import, the scheme stands condemned so far as it professes to be a complete scheme of formulation. It may, as we have seen, not profess to be a complete scheme, but only to formulate statements falling within a certain category, for example, assertoric statements or categorical statements.

It is to be added that a statement which does not admit of being translated into any one of the simple forms included in a given scheme may still be capable of being expressed by a conjunctive or disjunctive combination of such simple forms. Thus, if the statement *Some S is P* is made with an emphasis on *some*, implying *not all*, then the statement cannot be expressed in any one of the forms of the traditional schedule of propositions, but it is equivalent to *Some S is P and some S is not P*.

(*b*) In the reduction of a statement to a form in which it belongs to a given schedule there may be involved what must be admitted to be *inference*. As, for instance, if statements are given in the ordinary predicative form and have to be expressed in an equational scheme.

It may perhaps be urged that this is legitimate, simply on the ground that one of the postulates of logic is that we be allowed to substitute for any given form of words the technical form (and in an equational system this will be an equation) which is equivalent to it. Have we not, however, in reality a vicious circle if a process which involves inference is to be regarded as a *postulate* of logic?

The difficulty here raised is a serious one only if we suppose ourselves rigidly limited in logic to a single scheme of formulation; and the solution is to be found in our not confining ourselves to any one scheme, but in our recognising several and investigating the logical relations between them. We can then refuse to regard any substitution of one set of words for another as pre-logical except in so far as it consists of a merely verbal transformation: and our postulate will merely be that we are free to make verbal changes as we please; it will not by itself authorise any change of an inferential character. For a change of this kind, appeal must be made to logical principles.

We have then in this section distinguished between three problems any or all of which may be involved in discussions concerning the import of propositions. We have

(1) the discussion of the essential nature of judgments and of the fundamental distinctions between judgments;
(2) the interpretation of propositional forms;
(3) the discussion and comparison of logical schedules or schemes of propositions, drawn up with a view to the expression of judgments in a limited number of propositional forms.

These problems are inter-related and do not admit of being discussed in complete isolation. It is clear, for instance, that the drawing up of a schedule of propositions needs to be supplemented by the exact interpretation of the different forms which it is proposed to recognise; and both in the drawing up of the schedule and in the interpretation we shall be guided and controlled by a consideration of fundamental distinctions between judgments.

The problems are, however, in themselves distinct; and some misunderstanding may be avoided if we can make it clear what is the actual problem that we are discussing at any given point.

In particular, it is important to recognise that in the formulation and interpretation of propositions there is an arbitrary and selective element which is absent from the more fundamental problem. Systems of formulation and interpretation, therefore, if only they are intelligible and self-consistent, can hardly be condemned as radically wrong, though they may be rejected as inconvenient or unsuitable. When, however, we are dealing with the fundamental import of judgments, the questions raised do become questions of absolute right or wrong.

It should be added that in the present treatise, since it is concerned with logic in its more formal aspects, questions of interpretation and formulation occupy a position of greater relative importance than they would in a treatment of the science more fully developed on the philosophical side.

49. *The Objective Reference in Judgments.*—A judgment can be formed or understood only through the occurrence of certain psychical events in the minds of those who form or understand it; and in this sense it may be included amongst subjective states. It is, however, distinguished from all other subjective states by the fact that it *claims to be true*.

This claim to be true implies an objective reference. For a merely subjective state is not, as such, either true or false; it is simply an occurrence. Thus, the distinction between truth and falsity is inapplicable to an emotion or a volition. An emotion may be pleasurable or painful; it may be strong or weak; it may or may not impel to action; but we cannot describe it as true or false.

And the same applies to a judgment regarded as no more than a subjective connection of ideas. The claim to truth necessarily involves more than this, namely, a reference to something external to the psychical occurrence involved in the formation of the judgment. Every judgment implies, therefore, on the part of the judging mind, the recognition of an objective system of reality of some sort. The validity that is claimed for judgment is an *objective validity*.

The word "objective" is always a dangerous word to use, and some further explanation may be given of the meaning to be attached to it here. When we say that a judgment refers to an *objective* system, we mean a system that subsists independently of the act of judgment itself, and that is not dependent on the passing fancy of the person who forms the judgment. An objective system of reality in this sense may, however, include subjective states, that is, states of consciousness. A body of psychological doctrine consists of judgments relating to states of mind. But such judgments have an external reference (that is, external to the judgments themselves) just as much as a body of judgments relating to material phenomena. Indeed the doctrine of judgment here laid down is not inconsistent with the theory of subjective idealism that resolves all phenomena into states of consciousness.

Even when a judgment relates to purely fictitious objects there is still an external reference,—in this case, to the world of convention.

The particular aspect or portion of the total system of reality referred to in any judgment may sometimes be conveniently spoken of as the *universe of discourse*. The limits, if any, intended to be placed upon the universe of discourse in any given proposition are usually not explicitly stated; but they must be considered to be implicit in the judgment which the proposition is meant to express, and to be capable of being themselves expressed should there be any danger of misunderstanding. At the same time, it is only fair to add that attempts to define the universe of discourse are likely to raise metaphysical difficulties as to the ultimate nature of reality. What is of main importance from the logical standpoint is the recognition that there is a reference to *some* system of reality which is to be distinguished from the uncontrolled course of our own ideas. And so far as a distinction can be drawn between different systems of reality, there is need of the assumption that, when we combine judgments or view them in their mutual relations, the universe of discourse is the same throughout.

50. *The Universality of Judgments.*—The fundamental characteristic then of judgments is their objective reference, their claim to objective validity. It follows that all judgments claim *universality*, that is to say, they claim to be acknowledged as true not for a given person only, or for a limited number of persons, but for everyone; and again, not for a given time only, or for a limited time, but for all time. In other words, the import of a judgment is not merely to express some connection of ideas in my own mind; but to express something that claims to be *true*. And truth is not relative to the individual, nor is it when fully set forth limited by considerations of time.

We shall have subsequently to deal with the ordinary distinction between universal and particular propositions; but it will be clear that the claim to universality which we are now considering is one that must be made on behalf of so-called particular, as well as of so-called universal, propositions. The judgment that *some men are six feet in height* claims universal acceptance just as much as the judgment that *all men are mortal*.

Some judgments again contain an explicit or implicit reference to time. But this is really part of the judgment. As soon as the judgment is fully stated it becomes independent of time. It may perhaps be said that the judgment *France is under Bourbon rule* was true two centuries ago, but is not true now. But the judgment as it stands, without context, is incompletely stated. That France is (or was) under Bourbon rule in the year 1906 A.D. is for all time false; that France is (or was) under Bourbon rule in the year 1706 A.D. is for all time true.

In regard to the nature and significance of the reference to time in judgments, Mr Bosanquet draws a useful distinction between the time *of* predication and the time *in* predication.[77] By the time *of* predication is meant the time at which some thinking being makes the judgment; and this in no way affects the truth of the judgment. But, as Sigwart points out, everything which exists as a particular thing occupies a definite position in time. Hence all judgments relating to particular things, including singular judgments and so-called narrative judgments, relate to some definite time, past, present, or future, with reference to which alone the statements made are valid. This is the time *in* predication, and the reference to it must be regarded as an intrinsic part of the judgment itself, although it is not always explicitly mentioned.

It will be seen that the recognition of the universality of all judgments in the sense here indicated is but the recognition in another aspect of their objective character.

51. *The Necessity of Judgments.*—A further characteristic that has been ascribed to all judgments, when considered in relation to the judging mind, is *necessity*. This too is connected with the claim to objective validity. When we judge, we are not free to judge as we will. No doubt by controlling the intellectual influences to which we subject ourselves we may indirectly and in the long run modify within certain limits our beliefs. This is a question belonging to psychology into which we need not now enter. But at any given moment the

---

[77] *Logic*, I. p. 215. Compare Sigwart, *Logic*, § 15.

judgments we form are determined by our mental history and the circumstances in which we are placed. We are bound to judge as we do judge; so far as we feel a question to be an open one our judgment regarding it is suspended. It must be granted that we not unfrequently make statements which do not betray the doubts which as a matter of fact we feel with regard to the point at issue; but such statements do not represent our real judgments. The propositions we utter are the expressions of possible judgments, but not of *our* judgments.

In any discussion of the modality of judgments, other senses in which the term "necessary" may be applied to judgments have to be considered. In here affirming necessity as a characteristic of *all* judgments, we are merely declaring over again in another aspect their objective character. The merely subjective sequence of ideas in our minds is more or less under our own control. At any rate we can at will bring given ideas together in our mind. But a judgment is more than a relation between ideas. It claims to be true of some system of reality; and hence it is not so much determined *by* us, as *for* us by the knowledge which we have come to possess or think we have come to possess about that system of reality.

EXERCISE

52. "What is once true is always true."
"What is true to-day may be false to-morrow."
Examine these statements. [L.]

Chapter 6

KINDS OF JUDGMENTS AND PROPOSITIONS

53. *The Classification of Judgments.*—It is customary for logicians to offer a classification of judgments or propositions. There is, however, so much variation in the objects they have in view in drawing up their classifications, that very often their results are not really comparable.

(1) Our object in classifying propositions may, in the first place, be to produce a working scheme for the formulation of judgments. An illustration of this is afforded by the traditional scheme of propositions (*All S is P*, *No S is P*, etc.), or by the Hamiltonian scheme based upon the quantification of the predicate. A classification of this kind is essentially formal. The different propositional forms that are recognised must receive clearly defined interpretations; and the resulting scheme, if it is worth anything at all, will be orderly and compact. On the other hand, it is not likely to be comprehensive or exhaustive; for many natural modes of judgment will not find a place in it, at any rate until they have been expressed in a modified, though as nearly as possible equivalent, form.

There are many ways of formulating judgments, each of which has its special merits and is from some particular point of view specially appropriate. We must, however, give up the idea that any one of these ways can hold the field as a fundamental and essentially suitable classification of judgments looked at from the psychological point of view.

(2) From the psychological standpoint our endeavour must be to give rather what may be called a natural history classification of judgments. Primitive types of judgment, which in a logical scheme of formulation are not likely to find a place at all, will now be regarded as of equal importance with more developed and scientific types. Our object may indeed be (as with Mr. Bosanquet) to sketch the development of judgments from the most primitive types to those which give expression to the ideal of knowledge.

In a classification of this kind the dividing lines are not so clear and sharply defined as in a scheme framed for the logical formulation of judgments. The different types, moreover, do not stand out in marked distinction from one another, and it is difficult to arrange the different classes in due subordination, and with complete avoidance of cross divisions. The underlying plan is indeed apt to be obscured by details, so that the whole discussion tends to become somewhat cumbrous.

(3) A classification of propositions of still another kind is given by Mill in the later part of his chapter on the Import of Propositions. The conclusion at which he arrives is that every proposition affirms, or denies, either simple existence, or else some sequence, coexistence,

causation, or resemblance. This classification is certainly not a formal one; it is not a scheme for the logical formulation of judgments. Nor, on the other hand, can it be regarded as a psychological classification of types of judgment, designed to illustrate the nature and growth of thought. Mill's point of view is objective and material. In one place he describes his scheme as a classification of matters of fact, of all things that can be believed; and the main use that he subsequently makes of it is in connection with the enquiry as to the methods of proof that are appropriate according to the nature of the matter of fact that is asserted.

In the pages that follow various schemes for formulating judgments will be considered. For reasons already stated, however, no scheme of this kind can be regarded as constituting an exhaustive classification of judgments. The traditional scheme, for example, is ludicrously unsatisfactory and incomplete if put forward as affording such a classification.

We shall not attempt to give what has been spoken of above as a natural history classification of judgments. The really important distinctions involved in such a classification can be raised independently, and the general plan of this work is to dwell principally on the more formal aspects of logic. It may be added that even from a broader point of view the problem of the evolution of thought is hardly to be regarded as primarily a logical problem.

Again, such a classification as Mill's involves material considerations that are outside the scope of this treatise.

Without, however, professing to give any complete scheme of classification, we shall endeavour to touch upon the most fundamental differences that may exist between judgments.

54. *Kant's Classification of Judgments.*—Kant classified judgments according to four different principles (*Quantity*, *Quality*, *Relation*, and *Modality*) each yielding three subdivisions, as follows:

(1)	Quantity.	(i)	Singular	This S is P.
		(ii)	Particular	Some S is P.
		(iii)	Universal	All S is P.
(2)	Quality.	(i)	Affirmative	All S is P.
		(ii)	Negative	No S is P.
		(iii)	Infinite	All S is not-P.
(3)	Relation.	(i)	Categorical	S is P.
		(ii)	Hypothetical	If S is P then Q is R.
		(iii)	Disjunctive	Either S is P or Q is R.
(4)	Modality.	(i)	Problematic	S may be P.
		(ii)	Assertoric	S is P.
		(iii)	Apodeictic	S must be P.

This arrangement is open to criticism from several points of view; and its symmetry, although attractive, is not really defensible. At the same time it has the great merit of making prominent what really are the fundamental distinctions between judgments.

The first distinction that we shall consider is that between simple and compound judgments (replacing Kant's distinction according to relation). We shall then consider in turn distinctions of modality, of quantity, and of quality.

55. *Simple Judgments and Compound Judgments.*—Under the head of *relation*, Kant gave the well-known threefold division of judgments into *categorical*, where the affirmation or denial is absolute (*S is P*); *hypothetical* (or *conditional*), where the affirmation or denial is made under a condition (*If A is B then S is P*); and *disjunctive*, where the affirmation or denial is made with an alternative (*Either S is P or Q is R*).

These three kinds of judgment cannot, however, properly be co-ordinated as on an equality with one another in a threefold division. For the categorical judgment appears as an element in both the others, and hence the distinction between the categorical, on the one hand, and the hypothetical and the disjunctive, on the other, appears to be on a different level from that between the two latter. Moreover, the hypothetical and the disjunctive do not exhaust the modes in which categorical judgments may be combined so as to form further judgments. It is, therefore, better not to start from the above threefold division, but from a twofold, namely, into *simple* and *compound*.

A *compound judgment* may be defined as a judgment into the composition of which other judgments enter as elements.[78] There are three principal ways in which judgments may be combined, and in each case the denial of the validity of the combination yields a further form of judgment, so that there are six kinds of compound judgments to be considered.

(1) We may affirm two or more simple judgments together. Thus, given that *P* and *Q* stand separately for judgments, we may affirm "*P and Q*."

It has been held that a synthesis of two independent judgments in this way does not really yield any fresh judgment distinct from the two judgments themselves.[79] In a sense this is true. Anyone may, however, be challenged for holding two judgments together on grounds which would have no application to either taken separately. Hence it is convenient to regard the combination as constituting a distinct logical whole, which demands some kind of separate treatment; and on this ground the description of "*P and Q*" as a compound judgment may be justified.

The synthesis involved is conjunctive. Hence *P and Q* may be spoken of more distinctively as a *conjunctive judgment*. Its denial yields "*Not both P and Q*" and this form is more truly disjunctive than the form (*P or Q*) to which that designation is more commonly applied.

(2) Without committing ourselves to the affirmation of either *P* or *Q* we may hold them to be so related that the truth of the former involves that of the latter. This yields the hypothetical judgment, "*If P then Q*."

It has been held that to regard this as a combination of judgments, and to speak of it as in this sense a compound judgment, is misleading, since P and Q are here not judgments at all, that is to say, they are not at the moment intended as statements. Neither *P* nor *Q* is affirmed to be true. What is affirmed to be true is a certain relation between them.[80]

It is certainly the case that when I judge "*If P then Q*," P need not be *my* judgment, nor need *Q*; my object may even be to establish the falsity of *P* on the ground of the known falsity of *Q*. A more impersonal view, however, being taken, *P* and *Q* are suppositions, that is, possible judgments, so that they have meaning as judgments; and *If P then Q* may fairly be said to express a relation between judgments in the sense of its force being that the acceptance

---

[78] The distinction here implied has been criticised on the ground that (*a*) if the so-called elements are really judgments, the combination of them yields no fresh judgment; while (*b*) if the combination is really an independent judgment, the elements into which it can be analysed are not themselves judgments. It will be seen that (*a*) is intended to apply to conjunctive syntheses, and (*b*) to hypotheticals and disjunctives. We shall consider the argument under these heads severally.
[79] Compare Sigwart, *Logic*, i. p. 214.
[80] Compare Sigwart, *Logic*, i. p. 219.

of *P* as a true judgment involves the acceptance of *Q* as a true judgment also. The description of the hypothetical judgment as compound appears therefore to be in this sense justified. Such a judgment as *If P then Q* cannot be interpreted except on the supposition that *P* and *Q* taken separately have meaning as judgments.

As we get a compound judgment when we declare two judgments to be so related that if one is accepted the other must be accepted also, so we get a compound judgment when we deny that this relation subsists between them. Thus in addition to the judgment "*If P then Q*," we have its denial, namely, "*If P then not necessarily Q*."[81] The best mode of describing this form of proposition will be considered in a subsequent chapter.

(3) We have another form of compound judgment when we affirm that *one or other* of two given judgments is true. This form of judgment, "*P or Q*," is usually called *disjunctive*, though *alternative* would be a better name. It has been already pointed out that *Not both P and Q* is the more distinctively disjunctive form.

It may be denied that *P or Q* is a compound judgment on the same grounds as those on which this is denied of *If P then Q*. Since, however, the points at issue are practically the same as before, the discussion need not be repeated.

The denial of "*P or Q*" yields "*Neither P nor Q*." This may be called a *remotive* judgment if a distinctive name is wanted for it.

It should be added that not all forms of proposition which would ordinarily be described as hypothetical or disjunctive are really the expressions of compound judgments as above described. Thus the forms *If any S is P it is Q* (*If a triangle is isosceles the angles at its base are equal*). *Every S is either P or Q* (*Every blood vessel is either a vein or an artery*), do not—like the forms *If P is true Q is true* (*If there is a righteous God the wicked will not escape their just punishment*), *Either P or Q is true* (*Either free will is a fact or the sense of obligation is an illusion*)—express any relation between two independent judgments or propositions. This point will be developed subsequently in a distinction that will be drawn between the true hypothetical (*If P is true Q is true*) and the conditional (*If any S is P it is Q*).

56. *The Modality of Judgments.*—Very different accounts of the modality of judgments or propositions are given by different writers, and the problems to which distinctions of modality give rise are as a rule not easy of solution. At the same time such distinctions are of a fundamental character, and they are apt to present themselves in a disguised form, thus obscuring many questions that at first sight appear to have no connection with modality at all. It is a drawback to have to deal with so difficult a problem nearly at the commencement of our treatment of judgments, and the space at our disposal will not admit of our dealing with it in great detail. Moreover, it can hardly be hoped that the solution offered will be accepted by all readers. Still a brief consideration of modal distinctions at this stage will help to make some subsequent discussions easier.

The main point at issue is whether distinctions of modality are subjective or objective. In attempting to decide this question it will be convenient to deal separately with simple judgments and compound judgments.

57. *Modality in relation to Simple Judgments.*—The Aristotelian doctrine of modals, which was also the scholastic doctrine, gave a fourfold division into (*a*) *necessary*, (*b*) *contingent*, (*c*) *possible*, and (*d*) *impossible*, according as a proposition expresses (*a*) that

---

[81] In giving this as the contradictory of *If P then Q*, we are assuming a particular doctrine of the import of the hypothetical judgment. The question will be discussed more fully later on.

which is necessary and unchangeable, and which cannot therefore be otherwise; or (*b*) that which happens to be at any given time, but might have been otherwise; or (*c*) that which is not at any given time, but may be at some other time; or (*d*) that which cannot be. The point of view here taken is objective, not subjective; that is to say, the distinctions indicated depend upon material considerations, and do not relate to the varying degrees of belief with which different propositions are accepted.[82]

Kant's doctrine of modality is distinguished from the scholastic doctrine in that the point of view taken is subjective, not objective, according to one of the senses in which Kant uses these terms. Kant divides judgments according to modality into (*a*) *apodeictic* judgments—*S must be P*, (*b*) *assertoric* judgments—*S is P*, and (*c*) *problematic* judgments—*S may be P*; and the distinctions between these three classes have come to be interpreted as depending upon the character of the belief with which the judgments are accepted.

The distinction between these two doctrines is fundamental; for, as Sigwart puts it,[83] the statement that a judgment is possible or necessary is not the same as the statement that it is possible or necessary for a predicate to belong to a subject. The former (which is the Kantian doctrine) refers to the subjective possibility or necessity of judgment; the latter (which is the Aristotelian doctrine) refers to the objective possibility or necessity of what is stated in the judgment.

58. *Subjective Distinctions of Modality.*—We must reject the view that subjective distinctions of modality can be drawn in relation to simple judgments.[84] For all judgments, as we have seen, possess the characteristic of necessity, and hence this characteristic cannot be made the distinguishing mark of a particular class of judgments, the apodeictic.

We may touch on two ways in which it has been attempted to draw a distinction, from the subjective point of view, between assertoric and apodeictic judgments.

The assertoric judgment has been regarded as expressing what has only subjective validity, that is, what can be affirmed to be true only for the person forming the judgment, while the apodeictic judgment expresses what has universal validity and can be affirmed to be true for everyone.

This again conflicts with the general doctrine of judgment already laid down. We hold that every judgment claims to be true, and that truth cannot be relative to the individual. The assertoric judgment, therefore, as thus defined is no true judgment at all, and we find that all judgments are really apodeictic.

Another suggested ground of distinction is that between immediate knowledge and knowledge that is based on inference, the former being expressed by the assertoric judgment, and the latter by the apodeictic.

There is no doubt that we often say a thing *is* so and so when this is a matter of direct perception, while we say it *must be* so and so when we cannot otherwise account for certain

---

[82] The consideration of modality as above conceived has sometimes been regarded as extra-logical on the ground that necessity, contingency, possibility, and impossibility depend upon matters of fact with which the logician as such has no concern. But it also depends upon matters of fact whether any given predicate can rightly be predicated affirmatively or negatively, universally or particularly, of any given subject. Distinctions of quality and quantity can nevertheless be formally expressed, and if distinctions of modality can also be formally expressed, there is no initial reason why they should not be recognised by the logician, even though he is not competent to determine the validity of any given modal. In so far, however, as the modality of a proposition is something that does not admit of formal expression, so that propositions of the same form may have a different modality, then the argument that the doctrine of modals is extra-logical is more worthy of consideration.

[83] *Logic*, i. p. 176.

[84] What follows in this section is based mainly on Sigwart's treatment of the subject (*Logic*, § 31).

perceived facts. Thus, if I have been out in the rain, I say *it has rained*; if, without having observed any rain fall, I notice that the roads and roofs are wet, I say *it must have rained*.

It is obvious, however, that this distinction is quite inconsistent with the ascription of any superior certainty to the apodeictic judgment. For that which we know mediately must always be based on that which we know immediately; and, since in the process of inference error may be committed, it follows that that which we know mediately must have inferior certainty to that of which we have immediate knowledge. Accordingly in ordinary discourse the statement that anything *must be* so and so would generally be understood as expressing a certain degree of doubt.

We cannot then justify the recognition of the apodeictic judgment as expressing a higher degree of certainty than the merely assertoric.

On the other hand, the so-called problematic judgment, interpreted as expressing mere uncertainty,[85] cannot be regarded as in itself expressing a judgment at all. It may imply a judgment in regard to the validity of arguments brought forward in support or in disproof of a given thesis; and it implies also a judgment as to the state of mind of the person who is in a state of uncertainty; but it is in itself a mere suspension of judgment.

59. *Objective Distinctions of Modality.*—We have next to consider whether, having regard not to the judgment as a subjective product, but to the objective fact expressed in a judgment, any valid distinction can be drawn between the *necessary*, the actual (or *contingent*), and the *possible*; and our answer must be in the affirmative, provided that we are prepared to admit the conception of the operation of law.

Thus the judgment *Planets move in elliptic orbits* is in this sense a *judgment of necessity*. It expresses something which we regard as the manifestation of a law, and it has an indefinitely wide application. For we believe it to hold good not only of the planets with which we are acquainted, but also of other planets (if such there be) which have not yet been discovered.

Now take the judgment, *All the kings who ruled in France in the eighteenth century were named Louis*. This is a statement of fact, but clearly is not the expression of any law. The proposition relates to a limited number of individuals who happened to have the same name given to them; but we recognise that their names might have been different, and that their being kings of France was not dependent on their possessing the name in question. This then we may call a *judgment of actuality*.

We have a *judgment of possibility* when we make such a statement as that *a seedling rose may be produced different in colour from any roses with which we are at present acquainted*, meaning that there is nothing in the inherent nature of roses (or in the laws regulating the production of roses) to render this impossible.

We have then a *judgment of necessity* (an *apodeictic* judgment) when the intention is to give expression to some law relating to the class of objects denoted by the subject-term; we have a *judgment of actuality* (an *assertoric* judgment) when the intention is to state a fact, as distinguished from the affirmation or denial of a law; we have a *judgment of possibility* (a *problematic* judgment) when the intention is to deny the operation of any law rendering some complex of properties impossible.[86]

---

[85] The problematic judgment as interpreted in the following section does more than express mere uncertainty. The form of proposition *S may be P* is no doubt ambiguous.

[86] The case of a proposition which may be regarded as expressing a particular instance of the operation of a law needs to be specially considered. Granting, for instance, that the proposition *Every triangle has its angles*

I shall not attempt to give here any adequate philosophic analysis of the conception of objective necessity. It must suffice to say that we all have the conception of the operation of law, and that for our present purpose the validity of this conception is assumed.

With regard to this treatment of modality the objection may perhaps be raised that, whatever their value in themselves, the distinctions involved are not of a kind with which formal logic has any concern. It is true that, in a sense, judgments of necessity are the peculiar concern of inductive, as distinguished from formal, logic. The main function of inductive logic is indeed to determine how apodeictic judgments (as above defined) are to be established on the basis of individual observations; for what we mean by induction is the process of passing from particulars to the laws by which they are governed. Granting this, however, there are also many problems, with which logic in its more formal aspects has to deal, in the solution of which some recognition of the distinctions under discussion is desirable, if not essential.

But it will be said that the distinctions cannot be applied formally: that, for example, given a proposition in the bare form *S is P*, or given an ordinary universal affirmative proposition *All S is P*, it cannot be determined, apart from the matter of the proposition, whether it is apodeictic (in the sense in which that term is used in this section) or merely assertoric. This is true if we are limited to the traditional schedule of propositions. But it is to be remembered that the formulation and the interpretation of propositions are within certain limits under our own control, and that it is within our power so to interpret propositional forms for logical purposes as to bring out distinctions that are not made clear in ordinary discourse or in the traditional logic. Thus, the form *S as such is P* might be used for giving formal expression to the apodeictic judgment, *S is P* being interpreted as merely assertoric.

Another solution, however, and one that may be made to yield a symmetrical scheme, is to utilise the conditional (as distinguished from the true hypothetical,[87]) proposition, and to differentiate it from the categorical, by interpreting it as modal,[88] while the categorical remains merely assertoric.

Thus, we should have,—

If anything is S it is P,—apodeictic;
All S is P,—assertoric;
If anything is S it may be P,—problematic.[89]

It is of course not pretended that the differentiation here proposed is adopted in the ordinary use of the propositional forms in question; we shall, for example, have presently to point out that in the customary usage of categoricals the universal affirmative has frequently an apodeictic force. We shall return to a discussion of the suggested scheme later on.

---

equal to two right angles is apodeictic, are we to describe the proposition *This triangle has its angles equal to two right angles* as apodeictic or as assertoric? The right answer seems to be that, as thus barely stated, the proposition may be merely assertoric; for it may do no more than express a fact that has been ascertained by measurement. If, however, the proposition is interpreted as meaning *This figure, being a triangle, has its angles equal to two right angles*, then it is apodeictic.

[87] See section 173.
[88] Here and elsewhere in speaking of a proposition as modal (in contradistinction to assertoric) we mean a proposition that is either apodeictic or problematic.
[89] It will be observed that in this scheme (leaving on one side the question of existential import) the categorical proposition *All S is P* is inferable from the conditional *If anything is S it is P*, but not *vice versâ*.

60. *Modality in relation to Compound Judgments.*—We may now consider the application of distinctions of modality to compound judgments, that is, to judgments which express a relation in which simple judgments stand one to another. It is one thing to say that as a matter of fact two judgments are not both true; it is another thing to say that two judgments are so related to one another that they cannot both be true. We may describe the one statement as assertoric, the other as apodeictic. An apodeictic judgment thus conceived expresses a relation of ground and consequence; an obligation, therefore, to affirm the truth of a certain proposition when the truth of a certain other proposition or combination of propositions is admitted. The obligation may sometimes depend upon the assistance of certain other propositions which are left unexpressed.[90]

In section 55 a threefold classification of compound judgments was given; the distinction now under consideration points, however, to a more fundamental twofold classification. From this point of view a scheme may be suggested in which conjunctives (*P and Q*) and so-called disjunctives (*P or Q*) would be regarded as assertoric, while hypotheticals (*If P then Q*) would be regarded as modal. The enquiry as to how far this is in accordance with the ordinary usage of the propositional forms in question must be deferred. It may, however, be desirable to point out at once that, if this scheme is adopted, certain ordinarily recognised logical relations are not valid. For the hypothetical *If P then Q* is ordinarily regarded as equivalent to the disjunctive *Either not-P or Q*, and this as equivalent to the denial of the conjunctive *Both P and not-Q*. If, however, the conjunctive (and, therefore, its denial) and also the disjunctive are merely assertoric, while the hypothetical is apodeictic, it is clear that this equivalence no longer holds good. The disjunctive can indeed still be inferred from the hypothetical, but not the hypothetical from the disjunctive. This result will be considered further at a later stage.

So far we have spoken only of the *apodeictic* form, *If P then Q*. The corresponding *problematic* form is, *If P then possibly Q*; for example, *If all S is P it is still possible that some P is not S*. This denies the obligation to admit that *all P is S* when it has been admitted that *all S is P*. It is to be observed that in any treatment of modality, the apodeictic and the problematic involve one another, since the one form is always required to express the contradictory of the other.

61. *The Quantity and the Quality of Propositions.*—Propositions are commonly divided into *universal* and *particular*, according as the predication is made of the whole or of a part of the subject. This division of propositions is said to be according to their *quantity*.

Kant added a third subdivision, namely, *singular*; and other logicians have added a fourth, namely, *indefinite*. Under the head of quantity there have also to be considered what are called *plurative* and *numerically definite* propositions; and the possibility of *multiple quantification* has to be recognised. The question may also be raised whether there are not some propositions, e.g., hypothetical propositions, which do not admit of division according to quantity at all. The discussion of the various points here indicated may, however, conveniently be deferred until the traditional scheme of categorical propositions, which is based on the definitive division into universal and particular, has been briefly touched upon.

---

[90] In an apodeictic compound judgment, the necessity may (at any rate in certain cases) be described as *subjective*. This is so in the case of a formal hypothetical; as, for example, in the proposition *If all S is P then all not-P is not-S*, or in the proposition *If all S is M and all M is P then all S is P*.

Another primary division of propositions is into *affirmative* and *negative*, according as the predicate is affirmed or denied of the subject. This division of propositions is said to be according to their *quality*.

Here, again, Kant added a third subdivision, namely, *infinite*. This threefold division and the more fundamental question as to the true significance of logical denial, will also be deferred until some account has been given of the traditional scheme of propositions.

62. *The traditional Scheme of Propositions.*—The traditional scheme of formulating propositions is intended primarily for categoricals, and it is based on distinctions of quantity and quality only, distinctions of modality not being taken into account. For the purposes of the traditional scheme the following analysis of the categorical proposition may be given.

A categorical proposition consists of two terms (which are respectively the *subject* and the *predicate*), united by a *copula*, and usually preceded by a *sign of quantity*. It thus contains four elements, two of which—the subject and the predicate—constitute its *matter*, while the remaining two—the copula and the sign of quantity—constitute its *form*.[91]

The *subject* is that term about which affirmation or denial is made. The *predicate* is that term which is affirmed or denied of the subject.

When propositions are brought into one of the forms recognised in the traditional scheme the subject precedes the predicate. In ordinary discourse, however, this order is sometimes inverted for the sake of literary effect, for example, in the proposition—*Sweet are the uses of adversity*.

The *sign of quantity* attached to the subject indicates the extent to which the individuals denoted by the subject-term are referred to. Thus, in the proposition *All S is P* the sign of quantity is *all*, and the affirmation is understood to be made of each and every individual denoted by the term *S*.

The *copula* is the link of connection between the subject and the predicate, and indicates whether the latter is *affirmed* or *denied* of the former.

The different elements of the proposition as here distinguished are by no means always separately expressed in the propositions of ordinary discourse; but by analysis and expansion they may be made to appear without any change of meaning. Some grammatical change of form is, therefore, often necessary before propositions can be dealt with in the traditional scheme. Thus in such a proposition as "All that love virtue love angling," the copula is not separately expressed. The proposition may, however, be written—

sign of quantity	subject	copula	predicate
All	*lovers of virtue*	*are*	*lovers of angling*;

and in this form the four different elements are made distinct. The older logicians distinguished between propositions *secundi adjacentis* and propositions *tertii adjacentis*. In the former, the copula and the predicate are not separated, e.g., The man runs, All that love virtue love angling; in the latter, they are made distinct, e.g., The man is running, All lovers of virtue are lovers of angling.

---

[91] The *logical* analysis of a proposition must be distinguished from its *grammatical* analysis. Grammatically only two elements are recognised, namely, the subject and the predicate. Logically we further analyse the grammatical subject into quantity and logical subject, and the grammatical predicate into copula and logical predicate.

The traditional scheme of propositions is obtained by a combination of the division (according to quantity) into universal and particular, and the division (according to quality) into affirmative and negative. This combination yields four fundamental forms of proposition as follows:—

(1) the *universal affirmative*—*All S is P* (or *Every S is P*, or *Any S is P*, or *All S's are P's*)—usually denoted by the symbol **A**;

(2) the *particular affirmative*—*Some S is P* (or *Some S's are P's*)—usually denoted by the symbol **I**;

(3) the *universal negative*—*No S is P* (or *No S's are P's*)—usually denoted by the symbol **E**;

(4) the *particular negative*—*Some S is not P* (or *Not all S is P*, or *Some S's are not P's*, or *Not all S's are P's*)—usually denoted by the symbol **O**.

These symbols **A, I, E, O**, are taken from the Latin words *affirmo* and *nego*, the affirmative symbols being the first two vowels of the former, and the negative symbols the two vowels of the latter.

Besides these symbols, it will sometimes be found convenient to use the following,—

SaP = All S is P;
SiP = Some S is P;
SeP = No S is P;
SoP = Some S is not P.

These forms are useful when it is desired that the symbol which is used to denote the proposition as a whole should also indicate what symbols have been chosen for the subject and the predicate respectively. Thus,

MaP = All M is P;
PoQ = Some P is not Q.

It will further be found convenient sometimes to denote *not-S* by *S'*, *not-P* by *P'*, and so on. Thus we shall have

S'aP' = All not-S is not-P;
PiQ' = Some P is not-Q.

It is better not to write the universal negative in the form *All S is not P*;[92] for this form is ambiguous and would usually be interpreted as being merely particular, the *not* being taken to qualify the *all*, so that we have *All S is not P = Not-all S is P*. Thus, "All that glitters is not gold" is intended for an **O** proposition, and is equivalent to "Some things that glitter are not gold."

The traditional scheme of formulation is somewhat limited in its scope, and from more points of view than one it is open to criticism. It has, however, the merit of simplicity, and it

---

[92] Similar remarks apply to the form *Every S is not P*.

has met with wide acceptance. For these reasons it is as a rule convenient to adopt it as a basis of discussion, though it is also not infrequently necessary to look beyond it.

63. *The Distribution of Terms in a Proposition.*—A term is said to be distributed when reference is made to *all* the individuals denoted by it; it is said to be undistributed when they are only referred to *partially*, that is, when information is given with regard to a portion of the class denoted by the term, but we are left in ignorance with regard to the remainder of the class. It follows immediately from this definition that the subject is distributed in a universal, and undistributed in a particular,[93] proposition. It can further be shown that the predicate is distributed in a negative, and undistributed in an affirmative proposition. Thus, if I say *All S is P*, I identify every member of the class *S* with some member of the class *P*, and I therefore imply that at any rate *some P* is *S*, but I make no implication with regard to the whole of *P*. It is left an open question whether there is or is not any *P* outside the class *S*. Similarly if I say *Some S is P*. But if I say *No S is P*, in excluding the whole of *S* from *P*, I am also excluding the whole of *P* from *S*, and therefore *P* as well as *S* is distributed. Again, if I say *Some S is not P*, although I make an assertion with regard to a part only of *S*, I exclude this part from the whole of *P*, and therefore the whole of *P* from it. In this case, then, the predicate is distributed, although the subject is not.[94]

Summing up our results, we find that

A distributes its subject only,
I distributes neither its subject nor its predicate,
E distributes both its subject and its predicate,
O distributes its predicate only.

64. *The Distinction between Subject and Predicate in the traditional Scheme of Propositions.*—The nature of the distinction ordinarily drawn between the subject and the predicate of a proposition may be expressed by saying that the subject is that of which something is affirmed or denied, the predicate that which is affirmed or denied of the subject; or we may say that the subject is that which we regard as the determined or qualified notion, while the predicate is that which we regard as the determining or qualifying notion.

It follows that the subject must be given first in idea, since we cannot assert a predicate until we have something about which to assert it. Can it, however, be said that because the subject logically comes first in order of thought, it must necessarily do so in order of statement, the subject always preceding the copula, and the predicate always following it? In other words, can we consider the order of the terms in a proposition to suffice as a criterion? If the subject and the predicate are pure synonyms[95] or if the proposition is practically reduced to an equation, as in the doctrine of the quantification of the predicate, it is difficult

---

[93] *Some* being used in the sense of *some, it may be all*. If by *some* we understand *some, but not all*, then we are not really left in ignorance with regard to the remainder of the class which forms the subject of our proposition.

[94] Hence we may say that the quantity of a proposition, so far as its predicate is concerned, is determined by its quality. The above results, however, no longer hold good if we explicitly quantify the predicate as in Hamilton's doctrine of the quantification of the predicate. According to this doctrine, the predicate of an affirmative proposition is sometimes expressly distributed, while the predicate of a negative proposition is sometimes given undistributed. For example, such forms are introduced as *Some S is all P, No S is some P*. This doctrine will be discussed in chapter 7.

[95] For illustrations of this point, and on the general question raised in this section, compare Venn, *Empirical Logic*, pp. 208 to 214.

to see what other criterion can be taken; or it may rather be said that in these cases the distinction between subject and predicate loses all importance. The two are placed on an equality, and nothing is left by which to distinguish them except the order in which they are stated. This view is indicated by Professor Baynes in his *Essay on the New Analytic of Logical Forms*. In such a proposition, for example, as "Great is Diana of the Ephesians," he would call "great" the subject, reading the proposition, "(Some) great is (all) Diana of the Ephesians."

With reference to the traditional scheme of propositions, however, it cannot be said that the order of terms is always a sufficient criterion. In the proposition just quoted, "Diana of the Ephesians" would generally be accepted as the subject. What further criterion then can be given? In the case of **E** and **I** propositions (propositions, as will be shewn, which can be simply converted) we must appeal to the context or to the question to which the proposition is an answer. If one term clearly conveys information regarding the other term, it is the predicate. It will be shewn also that it is more usual for the subject to be read in extension and the predicate in intension.[96] If these considerations are not decisive, then the order of the terms must suffice. In the case of **A** and **O** propositions (propositions, as will be shewn, which cannot be simply converted) a further criterion may be added. From the rules relating to the distribution of terms in a proposition it follows that in affirmative propositions the distributed term (if either term is distributed) is the subject; whilst in negative propositions, if only one term is distributed, it is the predicate. It is doubtful if the inversion of terms ever occurs in the case of an **O** proposition; but in **A** propositions it is not infrequent. Applying the above considerations to such a proposition as "Workers of miracles were the Apostles," it is clear that the latter term is distributed while the former is not; the latter term is, therefore, the subject. Since a singular term is equivalent to a distributed term, it follows further as a corollary that in an affirmative proposition if one and only one term is singular it is the subject. This decides such a case as "Great is Diana of the Ephesians."

65. *Universal Propositions.*—In discussing the import of the universal proposition *All S is P*, attention must first be called to a certain ambiguity resulting from the fact that the word *all* may be used either distributively or collectively. In the proposition, *All the angles of a triangle are less than two right angles*, it is used distributively, the predicate applying to each and every angle of a triangle taken separately. In the proposition. *All the angles of a triangle are equal to two right angles*, it is used collectively, the predicate applying to all the angles taken together, and not to each separately. This ambiguity attaches to the symbolic form *All S is P*, but not to the form *All S's are P's*. Ambiguity may also be avoided by using *every* instead of *all*, as the sign of quantity. In any case the ambiguity is not of a dangerous character, and it may be assumed that *all* is to be interpreted distributively, unless by the context or in some other way an indication is given to the contrary.

A more important distinction between propositions expressed in the form *All S is P* remains to be considered. For such propositions may be merely assertoric or they may be apodeictic, in the sense given to these terms in section 59.

It will be convenient here to commence with a threefold distinction.

(1) The proposition *All S is P* may, in the first place, make a predication of a limited number of particular objects which admit of being enumerated: e.g., *All the books on that shelf are novels*, *All my sons are in the army*, *All the men in this year's eleven were at public*

---

[96] The subject is often a substantive and the predicate an adjective. Compare section 135.

schools. A proposition of this kind may be called distinctively an *enumerative universal*. It is clear that such a proposition cannot claim to be apodeictic.

(2) The proposition *All S is P* may, in the second place, express what is usually described as an empirical law or uniformity: e.g., *All lions are tawny*, *All scarlet flowers are without sweet scent*, *All violets are white or yellow or have a tinge of blue in them*. Many propositions relating to the use of drugs, to the succession of certain kinds of weather to certain appearances of sky, and so on, fall into this class. A proposition of this kind expresses a uniformity which has been found to hold good within the range of our experience, but which we should hesitate to extend much beyond that range either in space or in time. The predication which it makes is not limited to a definite number of objects which can be enumerated, but at the same time it cannot be regarded as expressing a necessary relation between subject and predicate. Such a proposition is, therefore, assertoric, not apodeictic.

(3) The proposition *All S is P* may, in the third place, express a law in the strict sense, that is to say, a uniformity that we believe to hold good universally and unconditionally: e.g., *All equilateral triangles are equiangular*, *All bodies have weight*, *All arsenic is poisonous*. A proposition of this kind is to be regarded as expressing a necessary relation between subject and predicate, and it is, therefore, apodeictic.

Propositions falling under the first two of the above categories may be described as *empirically universal*, and those falling under the third as *unconditionally universal*.[97]

Lotze (*Logic*, § 68) indicates the distinction we are discussing by the terms *universal* and *general*. But again there seems some uncertainty as to which term he would apply to judgments belonging to our second class. In the universal judgment, he says, we have merely a summation of what is found to be true in every individual instance of the subject; in the general judgment the predication is of the whole of an indefinite class, including both examined and unexamined cases. From this it would appear that the universal judgment corresponds to (1) only, while the general judgment includes both (2) and (3). Lotze, however, continues, "The universal judgment is only a collection of many singular judgments, the sum of whose subjects does as a matter of fact fill up the whole extent of the universal concept; ... the universal proposition, *All men are mortal*, leaves it still an open question whether, strictly speaking, they might not all live forever, and whether it is not merely a remarkable concatenation of circumstances, different in every different case, which finally results in the fact that no one remains alive. The general judgment, on the other hand, *Man is mortal*, asserts by its form that it lies in the character of mankind that mortality is inseparable from everyone who partakes in it." The illustration here given seems to imply that a judgment may be regarded as universal, though it relates to a class of objects, not all of which can be enumerated.

If this distinction is regarded merely as a distinction between different ways in which judgments may be obtained (for example, by enumeration or empirical generalisation on the one hand, or by abstract reasoning or the aid of the principle of causality on the other hand),

---

[97] I have borrowed these terms from Sigwart, *Logic*, § 27; but I cannot be sure that my usage of them corresponds exactly with his. In section 27 he appears to include under empirically universal judgments only such judgments as belong to the first of the three classes distinguished from one another above. At the same time, his description of the unconditionally universal judgment applies to the third class only: such a judgment, he says, expresses a necessary connection between the predicate *P* and the subject *S*; it means, *If anything is S it must also be P*. And it seems clear from his subsequent treatment (in § 96) of judgments belonging to the second class that he does not regard them as unconditionally universal.

without any real difference of content, it becomes merely genetic and can hardly be retained as a distinction between judgments considered in and by themselves. If we are so to retain it, it must be as a distinction between the merely assertoric and the apodeictic in the sense already explained. In order to be able to deal with it as a *formal* distinction, we must further be prepared to assign distinctive forms of expression to the two kinds of universal judgments respectively. Lotze appears to regard the forms *All S is P* and *S is P* as sufficiently serving this purpose. But this is hardly borne out by the current usage of these forms. *All the S's are P* might serve for the enumerative universal and *S as such is P* for the unconditionally universal. These forms do not, however, fit into any generally recognised schedules; and our second class of universal would be left out. Another solution, which has been already indicated in section 59, would be to use the categorical form for the empirically universal judgment only, adopting the conditional form for the unconditionally universal judgment.

The most important outcome of the above discussion is that a proposition ordinarily expressed in the form *All S is P* may be either assertoric or apodeictic. It will be found that this distinction has an important bearing on several questions subsequently to be raised.

66. *Particular Propositions.*—In dealing with particular propositions it is necessary to assign a precise signification to the sign of quantity *some*.

In its ordinary use, the word *some* is always understood to be exclusive of *none*, but in its relation to *all* there is ambiguity. For it is sometimes interpreted as excluding *all* as well as *none*, while sometimes it is not regarded as carrying this further implication. The word may, therefore, be defined in two conflicting senses: *first*, as equivalent simply to *one at least*, that is, as the pure contradictory of *none*, and hence as covering every case (including *all*) which is inconsistent with *none*; *secondly*, as any quantity intermediate between *none* and *all* and hence carrying with it the implication *not all* as well as *not none*. In ordinary speech the latter of these two meanings is probably the more usual.[98] It has, however, been customary with logicians in interpreting the traditional scheme to adopt the other meaning, so that *Some S is P* is not inconsistent with *All S is P*. Using the word in this sense, if we want to express *Some, but not all, S is P*, we must make use of two propositions—*Some S is P, Some S is not P*. The particular proposition as thus interpreted is *indefinite*, though with a certain limit; that is, it is indefinite in so far that it may apply to any number from a single one up to all, but on the other hand it is definite in so far as it excludes *none*. We shall henceforth interpret *some* in this indefinite sense unless an explicit indication is given to the contrary.

Mr. Bosanquet regards the particular proposition as unscientific, on the ground that it always depends either upon imperfect description or upon incomplete enumeration.[99] I may, for instance, know that all *S*'s of some particular description are *P*, but not caring or not troubling to define them I content myself with saying *Some S is P*, for example, *Some truth is better kept to oneself*.[100] Contrasted with this, we have the particular proposition of

---

[98] We might indeed go further and say that in ordinary speech *some* usually means *considerably less than all*, so that it becomes still more limited in its signification. In common language, as is remarked by De Morgan, "*some* usually means a rather small fraction of the whole; a larger fraction would be expressed by *a good many*; and somewhat more than half by *most*; while a still larger proportion would be *a great majority* or *nearly all*" (*Formal Logic*, p. 58).

[99] *Essentials of Logic*, pp. 116, 117.

[100] It is implied that a proposition of this kind might be expanded into the proposition *All S that is A is P*, that is, *All AS is P*. Mr Bosanquet gives, as an example, *Some engines can drag a train at a mile a minute for a long distance*. "This does not mean a certain number of engines, though of course there are a certain number. It means certain engines of a particular make, not specified in the judgment."

incomplete enumeration where our ground for asserting it is simply the observation of individual instances in which the proposition is found to hold good.

It is true that the particular proposition is not in itself of much scientific importance; and its indefinite character naturally limits its practical utility. It seems, however, hardly correct to describe it as unscientific, since—as will subsequently be shown in more detail—it may be regarded as possessing distinctive functions. Two such functions may be distinguished, though they are often implicated the one in the other. In the first place, the utility of the particular proposition often depends rather on what it denies than on what it affirms, and the proposition that it denies is not indefinite. One of the principal functions of the particular affirmative is to deny the universal negative, and of the particular negative to deny the universal affirmative. In the second place, the distinctive purpose of the particular proposition may be to affirm existence; and this is probably as a rule the case with propositions which are described as resulting from incomplete description. If, for example, we say that "some engines can drag a train at a mile a minute for a long distance," our object is primarily to affirm that there *are* such engines; and this would not be so clearly expressed in the universal proposition of which the particular is said to be the incomplete and imperfect expression.

The relation of the particular proposition, *Some S is P*, to the problematic proposition, *S may be P*, will be considered subsequently.

67. *Singular Propositions.*—By a *singular* or *individual* proposition is meant a proposition in which the affirmation or denial is made of a single individual only: for example, *Brutus is an honourable man*; *Much Ado about Nothing is a play of Shakespeare's*; *My boat is on the shore*.

Singular propositions may be regarded as forming a sub-class of universals, since in every singular proposition the affirmation or denial is of the *whole* of the subject.[101] More definitely, the singular proposition may be said to fall into line, as a rule, with the enumerative universal proposition.

Hamilton distinguishes between universal and singular propositions, the predication being in the former case of a *whole undivided*, and in the latter case of a *unit indivisible*. The distinction here indicated is sometimes useful; but it can with advantage be expressed somewhat differently. A singular proposition may generally without risk of confusion be denoted by one of the symbols **A** or **E**; and in syllogistic inferences a singular may ordinarily be treated as equivalent to a universal proposition. The use of independent symbols for singular propositions (affirmative and negative) would introduce considerable additional complexity into the treatment of the syllogism; and for this reason it seems desirable as a rule to include singulars under universals. Universal propositions may, however, be divided into *general* and *singular*, and there will then be terms whereby to call attention to the distinction whenever it may be necessary or useful to do so.

There is also a certain class of propositions which, while *singular*, inasmuch as they relate but to a single individual, possess also the indefinite character which belongs to the

---

[101] It is argued by Father Clarke that singulars ought to be included under particulars, on the ground that when a predicate is asserted of one member only of a class, it is asserted of a portion only of the class. "Now if I say, *This Hottentot is a great rascal*, my assertion has reference to a smaller portion of the Hottentot nation than the proposition *Some Hottentots are great rascals*. The same is the case even if the subject be a proper name. *London is a large city* must necessarily be a more restricted proposition than *Some cities are large cities*; and if the latter should be reckoned under particulars, much more the former" (*Logic*, p. 274). This view fails to recognise that what is really characteristic of the particular proposition is not its *restricted* character—since the particular is not inconsistent with the universal—but its *indefinite* character.

particular proposition: for example, *A certain man had two sons*; *A great statesman was present*; *An English officer was killed*. Having two such propositions in the same discourse we cannot, apart from the context, be sure that the same individual is referred to in both cases. Carrying the distinction indicated in the preceding paragraph a little further, we have a fourfold division of propositions:—*general definite*, "All *S* is *P*"; *general indefinite*, "Some *S* is *P*"; *singular definite*, "This *S* is *P*"; *singular indefinite*, "A certain *S* is *P*." This classification admits of our working with the ordinary twofold distinction into universal and particular—or, as it is here expressed, definite and indefinite—wherever this is adequate, as in the traditional doctrine of the syllogism; while at the same time it introduces a further distinction which may in certain connections be of importance.

68. *Plurative Propositions and Numerically Definite Propositions*.—Other signs of quantity besides *all* and *some* are sometimes recognised by logicians. Thus, propositions of the forms *Most S's are P's*, *Few S's are P's*, are called *plurative* propositions. *Most* may be interpreted as equivalent to *at least one more than half*. *Few* has a negative force; and *Few S's are P's* may be regarded as equivalent to *Most S's are not P's*.[102] Formal logicians (excepting De Morgan and Hamilton) have not as a rule recognised these additional signs of quantity; and it is true that in many logical combinations they cannot be regarded as yielding more than particular propositions, *Most S's are P's* being reduced to *Some S's are P's*, and *Few S's are P's* to *Some S's are not P's*. Sometimes, however, we are able to make use of the extra knowledge given us; e.g., from *Most M's are P's*, *Most M's are S's*, we can infer *Some S's are P's*, although from *Some M's are P's*, *Some M's are S's*, we can infer nothing.

Numerically definite propositions are those in which a predication is made of some definite proportion of a class; e.g., *Two-thirds of S are P*. A certain ambiguity may lurk in numerically definite propositions; e.g., in the above proposition is it meant that *exactly two-thirds of S neither more nor less are P*, so that we are also given implicitly *one-third of S are not P*, or is it merely meant that *at least two-thirds of S but perhaps more are P*? In ordinary discourse we should no doubt mean sometimes the one and sometimes the other. If we are to fix our interpretation, it will probably be best to adopt the first alternative, on the ground that if figures are introduced at all we should aim at being quite determinate.[103] Some such words as *at least* can then be used when it is not professed to state more than the minimum proportion of *S's* that are *P's*.

---

[102] With perhaps the further implication "although *some S's* are *P's*"; thus, *Few S's are P's* is given by Kant as an example of the *exponible* proposition (that is, a proposition which, though not compound in form, can nevertheless be resolved into a conjunction of two or more simpler propositions, which are independent of one another), on the ground that it contains both an affirmation and a negation, though one of them in a concealed way. It should be added that *a few* has not the same signification as *few*, but must be regarded as affirmative, and generally, as simply equivalent to *some*; e.g., *A few S's are P's* = *Some S's are P's*. Sometimes, however, it means *a small number*, and in this case the proposition is perhaps best regarded as singular, the subject being collective. Thus, "a few peasants successfully defended the citadel" may be rendered "a small band of peasants successfully defended the citadel," rather than "some peasants successfully defended the citadel," since the stress is intended to be laid at least as much on the paucity of their numbers as on the fact that they were peasants. Whilst the proposition interpreted in this way is singular, not general, it is *singular indefinite*, not singular definite; for what small band is alluded to is left indeterminate.

[103] De Morgan remarks that "a perfectly *definite particular*, as to quantity, would express how many X's are in existence, how many Y's, and how many of the X's are or are not Y's; as in 70 *of the* 100 *X's are among the* 200 *Y's*" (*Formal Logic*, p. 58). He contrasts the *definite particular* with the *indefinite particular* which is of the form *Some X's are Y's*. It will be noticed that De Morgan's *definite particular*, as here defined, is still more explicit than the *numerically definite* proposition, as defined in the text.

69. *Indefinite Propositions.*—According to quantity, propositions have by some logicians been divided into (1) Universal, (2) Particular, (3) Singular, (4) Indefinite. Singular propositions have already been discussed.

By an *indefinite* proposition is meant one "in which the quantity is not explicitly declared by one of the designatory terms *all, every, some, many,* &c."; e.g., *S is P, Cretans are liars.* We may perhaps say with Hamilton, that *indesignate* would be a better term to employ. At any rate the so-called *indefinite proposition* is not the expression of a distinct form of *judgment*. It is a form of proposition which is the imperfect expression of a judgment. For reasons already stated, the particular has more claim to be regarded as an *indefinite judgment*.

When a proposition is given in the indesignate form, we can generally tell from our knowledge of the subject-matter or from the context whether it is meant to be universal or particular. Probably in the majority of cases indesignate propositions are intended to be understood as universals, e.g., "Comets are subject to the law of gravitation"; but if we are really in doubt with regard to the quantity of the proposition, it must logically be regarded as particular.[104]

70. *Multiple Quantification.*—The application of a predicate to a subject is sometimes limited with reference to times or conditions, and this may be treated as yielding a *secondary* quantification of the proposition; for example, *All men are sometimes unhappy, In some countries all foreigners are unpopular.* This differentiation may be carried further so as to yield triple or any higher order of quantification. Thus, we have triple quantification in the proposition, *In all countries all foreigners are sometimes unpopular.*[105]

In this way a proposition with a singular term for subject may, with reference to some secondary quantification, be classified as universal or particular as the case may be; for example, *Gladstone is always eloquent, Browning is sometimes obscure.*

71. *Infinite or Limitative Propositions.*—In place of the ordinary twofold division of propositions in respect of quality, Kant gave a *threefold* division, recognising a class of *infinite* (or *limitative*) judgments, which are neither affirmative nor negative. Thus, *S is P* being affirmative, and *S is not P* negative, *S is not-P* is spoken of as infinite or limitative.[106] It is, however, difficult to justify the separate recognition of this third class, whether we take the purely formal stand-point, or have regard to the real content of the propositions. From the formal stand-point we might substitute some other symbol, say *Q*, for *not-P*, and from this point of view *Some S is not-P* must be regarded as simply affirmative. On the other hand, *Some S is not-P* is equivalent in meaning to *Some S is not P*, and (assuming *P* to be a positive

---

[104] In the *Port Royal Logic* a distinction is drawn between *metaphysical universality* and *moral universality.* "We call metaphysical universality that which is perfect and without exception; and moral universality that which admits of some exception, since in moral things it is sufficient that things are generally such" (*Port Royal Logic*, Professor Baynes's translation, p. 150). The following are given as examples of moral universals: *All women love to talk*; *All young people are inconstant*; *All old people praise past times.* Indesignate propositions may almost without exception be regarded as universals either metaphysical or moral. But it seems clear that moral universals have in reality no valid claim to be called universals at all. Logically they ought not to be treated as more than particulars, or at any rate pluratives.

[105] For a further development of the notion of multiple quantification see Mr Johnson's articles on *The Logical Calculus* in *Mind*, 1892.

[106] An *infinite* judgment, in the sense in which the term is here used, may be described as the affirmative predication of a negative. Some writers, however, include under *propositiones infinitae* those whose subject, as well as those whose predicate, is negative. Thus Father Clarke defines *propositiones infinitae* as propositions in which "the subject or predicate is indefinite in extent, being limited only in its exclusion from some definite class or idea: as, *Not to advance is to recede*" (*Logic*, p. 268).

term) these two propositions must, having regard to their real content, be equally negative in force.

Some writers go further and appear to deny that the so-called infinite judgment has any meaning at all. This point is closely connected with a question that we have already discussed, namely, whether the negative term *not-P* has any meaning. If we recognise the negative term—and we have endeavoured to shew that we ought to do so—then the proposition *S is not-P* is equivalent to the proposition *S is not P*, and the former proposition must, therefore, have just as much meaning as the latter.

The question of the utility of so called infinite propositions has been further mixed up with the question as to the nature of significant denial. But it is better to keep the two questions distinct. Whatever the true character of denial may be, it is not dependent on the use of negative terms.

EXERCISES

72. Determine the quality of each of the following propositions, and the distribution of its terms: (*a*) A few distinguished men have had undistinguished sons; (*b*) Few very distinguished men have had very distinguished sons; (*c*) Not a few distinguished men have had distinguished sons. [J.]

73. Examine the significance of *few*, *a few*, *most*, *any*, in the following propositions; *Few* artists are exempt from vanity; *A few* facts are better than a great deal of rhetoric; *Most* men are selfish; If *any* philosophers have been wise, Socrates and Plato must be numbered among them. [M.]

74. *Everything is either X or Y*; *X and Y are coextensive*; *Only X is Y*; *The class X comprises the class Y and something more*. Express each of these statements by means of ordinary *A, I, E, O* categorical propositions. [C.]

75. Express each of the following statements in one or more of the forms recognised in the traditional scheme of categorical propositions: (i) No one can be rich and happy unless he is also temperate and prudent, and not always then; (ii) No child ever fails to be troublesome if ill taught and spoilt; (iii) It would be equally false to assert that the rich alone are happy, or that they alone are not. [V.]

76. Express, as nearly as you can, each of the following statements in the form of an ordinary categorical proposition, and determine its quality and the distribution of its terms:

(*a*) It cannot be maintained that pleasure is the sole good;

(*b*) The trade of a country does not always suffer, if its exports are hampered by foreign duties;

(*c*) The man who shews fear cannot be presumed to be guilty;

(*d*) One or other of the members of the committee must have divulged the secret. [C.]

77. Find the categorical propositions, expressed in terms of cases of *Q* or *non-Q* and of *R* or *non-R*, which are directly or indirectly implied by each of the following statements:

(*a*) The presence of *Q* is a necessary, but not a sufficient, condition for the presence of *R*;
(*b*) The absence of *Q* is a necessary, but not a sufficient, condition for the presence of *R*;
(*c*) The presence of *Q* is a necessary, but not a sufficient, condition for the absence of *R*.

In what respects, if any, does the categorical form fail to express the full significance of such propositions as the above? [J.]

78. "Honesty of purpose is perfectly compatible with blundering ignorance."

"The affair might have turned out otherwise than it did."
"It may be that *Hamlet* was not written by the actor known by his contemporaries as Shakespeare."
Employ the above propositions to illustrate your views in regard to the modality of propositions; and examine the relations between each of the propositions and any assertoric proposition which may be taken to be its ground or to be partially equivalent to it. [C.]

Chapter 7

THE OPPOSITION OF PROPOSITIONS[107]

79. *The Square of Opposition.*—In dealing with the subject of this chapter it will be convenient to begin with the ancient square of opposition which relates exclusively to the traditional schedule of propositions. It will, however, ultimately be found desirable to give more general accounts of what is to be understood by the terms *contradictory*, *contrary*, &c., so that they may be adapted to other schedules of propositions.

Two propositions are technically said to be *opposed* to each other when they have the same subject and predicate respectively, but differ in quantity or quality or both.[108]

Taking the propositions *SaP, SiP, SeP, SoP*, in pairs, we find that there are four possible kinds of relation between them.

(1) The pair of propositions may be such that they can neither both be true nor both false. This is called *contradictory* opposition, and subsists between *SaP* and *SoP*, and between *SeP* and *SiP*.

(2) They may be such that whilst both cannot be true, both may be false. This is called *contrary* opposition. *SaP* and *SeP*.

(3) They may be such that they cannot both be false, but may both be true. *Subcontrary* opposition. *SiP* and *SoP*.

(4) From a given universal proposition, the truth of the particular having the same quality follows, but not *vice versâ*.[109] This is *subaltern* opposition, the universal being called the *subalternant*, and the particular the *subalternate* or *subaltern*. *SaP* and *SiP*. *SeP* and *SoP*.

---

[107] This chapter will be mainly concerned with the opposition of *categorical* propositions; and, as regards categoricals, complications arising in connection with their existential interpretation will for the present be postponed.

[108] This definition, according to which opposed propositions are not necessarily incompatible with one another, is given by Aldrich (p. 53 in Mansel's edition). Ueberweg (*Logic*, § 97) defines opposition in such a way as to include only contradiction and contrariety; and Mansel remarks that "subalterns are improperly classed as *opposed* propositions" (*Aldrich*, p. 59). Modern logicians, however, usually adopt Aldrich's definition, and this seems on the whole the best course. Some term is wanted to signify the above general relation between propositions; and though it might be possible to find a more convenient term, no confusion is likely to result from the use of the term *opposition* if the student is careful to notice that it is here employed in a technical sense.

[109] This result and some of our other results may need to be modified when, later on, account is taken of the existential interpretation of propositions. But, as stated in the note at the beginning of the chapter, all complications resulting from considerations of this kind are for the present put on one side.

All the above relations are indicated in the ancient square of opposition.

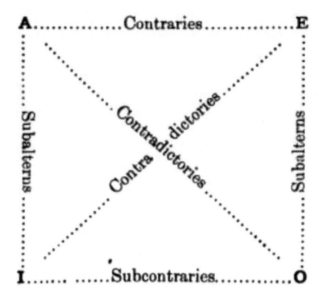

The doctrine of opposition may be regarded from two different points of view, namely, as a relation between two given propositions; and, secondly, as a process of inference by which one proposition being given either as true or as false, the truth or falsity of certain other propositions may be determined. Taking the second of these points of view, we have the following table:—

A being given *true*, E is *false*, I *true*, O *false*;
E being given *true*, A is *false*, I *false*, O *true*;
I being given *true*, A is unknown, E *false*, O unknown;
O being given *true*, A is *false*, E unknown, I unknown;
A being given *false*, E is unknown, I unknown, O *true*;
E being given *false*, A is unknown, I *true*, O unknown;
I being given *false*, A is *false*, E *true*, O *true*;
O being given *false*, A is *true*, E *false*, I *true*.

80. *Contradictory Opposition.*—The doctrine of opposition in the preceding section is primarily applicable only to the fourfold schedule of propositions ordinarily recognised. We must, however, look at the question from a wider point of view. It is, in particular, important that we should understand clearly the nature of contradictory opposition whatever may be the schedule of propositions with which we are dealing.

The nature of significant denial will be considered in some detail in the concluding section of this chapter. At this point it will suffice to say that to deny the truth of a proposition is equivalent to affirming the truth of its *contradictory*; and *vice versâ*. The criterion of contradictory opposition is that *of the two propositions, one must be true and the other must be false*; they cannot be true together, but on the other hand no mean is possible between them. The relation between two contradictories is mutual; it does not matter which is given true or false, we know that the other is false or true accordingly. Every proposition has its contradictory, which may however be more or less complicated in form.

It will be found that attention is almost inevitably called to any ambiguity in a proposition when an attempt is made to determine its contradictory. It has been truly said that we can never fully understand the meaning of a proposition until we know precisely what it denies; and indeed the problem of the import of propositions sometimes resolves itself at least partly into the question how propositions of a given form are to be contradicted.

The nature of contradictory opposition may be illustrated by reference to a discussion entered into by Jevons (*Studies in Deductive Logic*, p. 116) as to the precise meaning of the assertion that a proposition—say, *All grasses are edible*—is false. After raising this question, Jevons begins by giving an answer, which may be called the orthodox one, and which, in spite of what he goes on to say, must also be considered the correct one. When I assert that a proposition is false, I mean that its contradictory is true. The given proposition is of the form **A**, and its contradictory is the corresponding **O** proposition—*Some grasses are not edible*. When, therefore, I say that it is false that all grasses are edible, I mean that some grasses are not edible. Jevons, however, continues, "But it does not seem to have occurred to logicians in general to enquire how far similar relations could be detected in the case of disjunctive and other more complicated kinds of propositions. Take, for instance, the assertion that 'all endogens are *all* parallel-leaved plants.' If this be false, what is true? Apparently that one or more endogens are not parallel-leaved plants, or else that one or more parallel-leaved plants are not endogens. But it may also happen that no endogen is a parallel-leaved plant at all. There are three alternatives, and the simple falsity of the original does not shew which of the possible contradictories is true."

This statement is open to criticism in two respects. In the first place, in saying that one or more endogens are not parallel-leaved plants, we do not mean to exclude the possibility that no endogen is a parallel-leaved plant at all. Symbolically, *Some S is not P* does not exclude *No S is P*. The three alternatives are, therefore, at any rate reduced to the two first given. But in the second place, it is incorrect to speak of either of these alternatives as being by itself a contradictory of the original proposition. The true contradictory is the affirmation of the truth of *one or other* of these alternatives. If the original proposition is false, we certainly know that the new proposition limiting us to such alternatives is true, and *vice versâ*.

The point at issue may be made clearer by taking the proposition in question in a symbolic form. *All S is all P* is a condensed expression, resolvable into the form, *All S is P and all P is S*. It has but one contradictory, namely, *Either some S is not P or some P is not S*.[110] If either of these alternatives holds good, the original statement must in its entirety be false; and, on the other hand, if the latter is false, one at least of these alternatives must be true. *Some S is not P* is not by itself a contradictory of *All S is all P*. These two propositions are indeed inconsistent with one another; but they may both be false.

It follows that we must reject Jevons's further statement that "a proposition of moderate complexity has an almost unlimited number of contradictory propositions, which are more or less in conflict with the original. The truth of any one or more of these contradictories establishes the falsity of the original, but the falsity of the original does not establish the truth

---

[110] The contradictory of *All S is all P* may indeed be expressed in a different form, namely, *S and P are not coextensive*, but this has precisely the same force as the contradictory given in the text. We go on to shew that two different forms of the contradictory of the same proposition must necessarily be equivalent to one another.

of any one or more of its contradictories."[111] No doubt a proposition which is complicated in form may yield an indefinite number of other non-equivalent propositions the truth of any one of which is *inconsistent with* its own. It will also be true that its contradictory can be expressed in more than one form. But these forms will necessarily be equivalent to one another, since it is impossible for a proposition to have two or more non-equivalent contradictories. This position may be formally established as follows. Let Q and R be both contradictories of P. They will be equivalent if it can be shewn that *if Q then R*, and *if R then Q*. Since P and Q are contradictories, we have *If Q then not P*, and since P and R are contradictories we have *If not P then R*. Combining these two propositions we have the conclusion *If Q then R*. *If R then Q* follows similarly. Hence we have established the desired result.

In connection with the same point, Jevons raises another question, in regard to which his view is also open to criticism. He says, "But the question arises whether there is not confusion of ideas in the usual treatment of this ancient doctrine of opposition, and whether a contradictory of a proposition is not any proposition which involves the falsity of the original, but is not the sole condition of it. I apprehend that any assertion is false which is made without sufficient grounds. It is false to assert that the hidden side of the moon is covered with mountains, not because we can prove the contradictory, but because we know that the assertor must have made the assertion without evidence. If a person ignorant of mathematics were to assert that 'all involutes are transcendental curves,' he would be making a false assertion, because, whether they are so or not, he cannot know it." We should, however, involve ourselves in hopeless confusion were we to consider the truth or falsity of a proposition to depend upon the knowledge of the person affirming it, so that the same proposition would be now true, now false. It will be observed further that on Jevons's view both the propositions *S is P* and *S is not P* would be false to a person quite ignorant of the nature of *S*. This would mean that we could not pass from the falsity of a proposition to the truth of its contradictory; and such a result as this would render any progress in thought impossible.

81. *Contrary Opposition.*—Seeking to generalise the relation between **A** and **E**, we might naturally be led to characterize the contrary of a given proposition by saying that it goes beyond mere denial, and sets up a further assertion as far as possible removed from the original assertion; so that, whilst the contradictory of a proposition denies its entire truth, its contrary may be said to assert its entire falsehood. A pair of contraries as thus defined may be regarded as standing at the opposite ends of a scale on which there are a number of intermediate positions.

On this definition, however, the notion of contrariety cannot very satisfactorily be extended much beyond the particular case contemplated in the ordinary square of opposition. For if we have a proposition which cannot itself be regarded as standing at one end of a scale, but only as occupying an intermediate position, such proposition cannot be regarded as

---

[111] It must be admitted that it has not been uncommon for logicians to use the word *contradict* somewhat loosely. For example, in the *Port Royal Logic*, we find the following: "*Except the wise man* (said the Stoics) *all men are truly fools*. This may be contradicted (1) by maintaining that the wise man of the Stoics was a fool as well as other men; (2) by maintaining that there were others, besides their wise man, who were not fools; (3) by affirming that the wise man of the Stoics was a fool, and that other men were not" (p. 140). The affirmation of any one of these three propositions certainly renders it necessary to deny the truth of the given proposition, but no one of them is by itself the *contradictory* of the given proposition. The true contradictory is the alternative proposition: *Either the wise man of the Stoics is a fool or some other men are not fools.*

forming one of a pair of contraries. Plurative and numerically definite propositions may be taken as illustrations.

Hence if it is desired to define contrariety so that the conception may be generally applicable, the idea of two propositions standing, as it were, furthest apart from each other must be given up, and any two propositions may be described as contraries if they are inconsistent with one another without at the same time exhausting all possibilities. Contraries must on this definition always admit of a mean, but they may not always be what we should speak of as diametrical opposites, and any given proposition is not limited to a single contrary, but may have an indefinite number of non-equivalent contraries. At the same time, it will be observed that this definition still suffices to identify **A** and **E** as a pair of contraries, and as the only pair in the traditional scheme of opposition.

82. *The Opposition of Singular Propositions.*—Taking the proposition *Socrates is wise*, its contradictory is *Socrates is not wise*;[112] and so long as we keep to the same terms, we cannot go beyond this simple denial. The proposition has, therefore, no formal contrary.[113] This opposition of singulars has been called *secondary opposition* (Mansel's *Aldrich*, p. 56).

If, however, there is secondary quantification in a proposition having a singular subject, then we may obtain the ordinary square of opposition. Thus, if our original proposition is *Socrates is always* (or *in all respects*) *wise*, it is contradicted by the statement that *Socrates is sometimes* (or *in some respects*) *not wise*, while it has for its contrary, *Socrates is never* (or *in no respects*) *wise*, and for its subaltern, *Socrates is sometimes* (or *in some respects*) *wise*. It may be said that when we thus regard Socrates as having different characteristics at different times or under different conditions, our subject is not strictly singular, since it is no longer a whole indivisible. This is in a sense true, and we might no doubt replace our proposition by one having for its subject "the judgments or the acts of Socrates." But it does not appear that this resolution of the proposition is necessary for its logical treatment.

The possibility of implicit secondary quantification, although no such quantification is explicitly indicated, is a not unfruitful source of fallacy in the employment of propositions having singular subjects. If we take such propositions as *Browning is obscure*, *Epimenides is a liar*, *This flower is blue*, and give as their contradictories *Browning is not obscure*, *Epimenides is not a liar*, *This flower is not blue*, shall we say that the original proposition or its contradictory is true in case Browning is sometimes (but not always) obscure, or in case Epimenides sometimes (but not often) speaks the truth, or in case the flower is partly (but not wholly) blue? There is certainly a considerable risk in such instances as these of confusing contradictory and contrary opposition, and this will be avoided if we make the secondary quantification of the propositions explicit at the outset by writing them in the form *Browning is always* (or *sometimes*) *obscure*, &c.[114] The contradictory will then be particular or universal accordingly.

---

[112] This must be regarded as the correct contradictory from the point of view reached in the present chapter. The question becomes a little more difficult when the existential interpretation of propositions is taken into account.

[113] We can obtain what may be called a *material* contrary of the given proposition by making use of the contrary of the predicate instead of its mere contradictory; thus, *Socrates has not a grain of sense*. This is spoken of as *material* contrariety because it necessitates the introduction of a fresh term that could not be formally obtained out of the given proposition. It should be added that the distinction between formal and material contrariety might also be applied in the case of general propositions.

[114] Or we might reduce them to the forms,—All (or some) of the poems of Browning are obscure, All (or some) of the statements of Epimenides are false, All (or some) of the surface of this flower is blue.

83. *The Opposition of Modal Propositions.*—So far in this chapter our attention has been confined to assertoric propositions. For the present, a very brief reference to the opposition of modals will suffice. The main points involved will come up for further consideration later on.

We have seen that the unconditionally universal proposition, whether expressed in the ordinary categorical form *All S is P*, or as a conditional *If anything is S it is P*, affirms a necessary connection, by which is meant not merely that all the *S*'s are as a matter of fact *P*'s, but that it is inherent in their nature that they should be so. The statement that some *S*'s *are not P*'s is *inconsistent* with this proposition, but is not its contradictory, since both the propositions might be false: the *S*'s might all happen to be *P*'s, and yet there might be no law of connection between *S* and *P*. The proposition in question being *apodeictic* will have for its contradictory a modal of another description, namely, a *problematic* proposition; and this may be written in the form *S need not be P*, or *If anything is S still it need not be P*, according as our original proposition is expressed as a categorical or as a conditional.

Similarly, the contradictory of the hypothetical *If P is true then Q is true*, this proposition being interpreted modally, is *If P is true still Q need not be true*.

84. *Extension of the Doctrine of Opposition.*[115]—If we do not confine ourselves to the ordinary square of opposition, but consider any pair of propositions (whatever may be the schedule to which they belong), it becomes necessary to amplify the list of formal relations recognised in the square of opposition, and also to extend the meaning of certain terms. We may give the following classification:

(1) Two propositions may be *equivalent* or *equipollent*, each proposition being formally inferable from the other. Hence if either one of the propositions is true, the other is also true; and if either is false, the other is also false. For example, as will presently be shewn, *All S is P* and *All not-P is not-S* stand to each other in this relation.

(2) and (3) One of the two propositions may be formally inferable from the other, but not *vice versâ*. If we are considering two given propositions *Q* and *R*, this yields two cases: for *Q* may carry with it the truth of *R*, but not conversely; or *R* may carry with it the truth of *Q*, but not conversely. Ordinary subaltern propositions with their subalternants fall into this class; and it will be convenient to extend the meaning of the term *subaltern*, so as to apply it to any pair of propositions thus related, whether they belong to the ordinary square of opposition or not. It will indeed be found that any pair of simple propositions of the forms **A, E, I, O**, that are subaltern in the extended sense, are equivalent to some pair that are subaltern in the more limited sense.[116] Thus *All S is P* and *Some P is S*, which are subaltern in the extended sense, are equivalent to *All S is P* and *Some S is P*. *All S is P* and *Some not-S is not P* are another pair of subalterns. Here it is not so immediately obvious in what direction we are to look for a pair of equivalent propositions belonging to the ordinary square of opposition. *No not-P is S* and *Some not-P is not S* will, however, be found to satisfy the required conditions.

(4) The propositions may be such that they can both be true together, or both false, or either one true and the other false. For example, *All S is P* and *All P is S*. Such propositions may be called *independent* in their relation to one another.

(5) The propositions may be such that *one or other* of them *must be* true while *both may be* true. A pair of propositions which are thus related—for example, *Some S is P* and *Some*

---

[115] The illustrations given in this section presuppose a knowledge of immediate inferences. The section may accordingly on a first reading be postponed until part of the following chapter has been read.

[116] This will of course not hold good when we apply the term subaltern to compound propositions, e.g., to the pair *Some S is not P and some P is not S*, *Some S is not P or some P is not S*.

not-S is P—may, by an extension of meaning as in the case of the term *subaltern*, be said to be *subcontrary*. It can be shewn that any pair of subcontraries of the forms **A, E, I, O** are equivalent to some pair of subcontraries belonging to the ordinary square of opposition; thus, the above pair are equivalent to *Some P is S* and *Some P is not S*.

(6) The two propositions may be *contrary* to one another, in the sense that they cannot both be true, but can both be false. It can as before be shewn that any pair of contraries of the forms **A, E, I, O** are equivalent to some pair of contraries in the more ordinary sense. For example, the contraries *All S is P* and *All not-S is P* are equivalent to *No not-P is S* and *All not-P is S*.

(7) The two propositions may be *contradictory* to one another according to the definition given in section 80, that is, they can neither both be true nor both false. *All S is P* and *Some not-P is S* afford an example outside the ordinary square of opposition. It will be observed that these two propositions are equivalent to the pair *All S is P* and *Some S is not P*.

Two propositions, then, may, in respect of inferability, consistency, or inconsistency, be formally (1) equivalent, (2) and (3) subaltern, (4) independent, (5) subcontrary, (6) contrary, (7) contradictory, the terms *subaltern*, &c., being used in the most extended sense. What pairs of categorical propositions (into which only the same terms or their contradictories enter) actually fall into these categories respectively will be shown in sections 106 and 107.

These seven possible relations between propositions (taken in pairs) will be found to be precisely analogous to the seven possible relations between classes (taken in pairs) as brought out in a subsequent chapter (section 130).

85. *The Nature of Significant Denial.*—It is desirable that, before concluding this chapter, we should briefly discuss a more fundamental question than any that has yet been raised, namely, the meaning and nature of negation and denial.

We observe, in the first place, that negation always finds expression in a judgment, and that it always involves the denial of some other judgment. The question therefore arises whether negation always presupposes an antecedent affirmation. This question must be answered in the negative if it is understood to mean that in order to be able to deny a proposition we must begin by regarding it as true. The proposition which we deny may be asserted or suggested by someone else; or it may occur to us as one of several possible alternatives; or it may be put in the form of a question.

It is, however, to be added that if a denial is to have any value as a statement of matter of fact, the corresponding affirmation must be consistent with the meaning of the terms employed. Thus if A connotes m, n, p, and B connotes *not-p*, q, r, then the denial that A is B gives no real information respecting A. For the affirmation that A is B cannot be made by anyone who knows what is meant by A and B respectively. The same point may be otherwise expressed by saying that just as the affirmation of a verbal proposition is insignificant regarded as a real affirmation concerning the subject (and not merely as an affirmation concerning the meaning to be attached to the subject-term), so the denial of a contradiction in terms is insignificant from the same point of view. Such a denial yields merely what is tautologous and practically useless.

For example, the denial that *the soul is a ship in full sail* is insignificant regarded as a statement of matter of fact; for such denial gives no information to anyone who is already acquainted with the meaning of the terms involved.

The nature of logical negation is of so fundamental and ultimate a character that any attempt to explain it is apt to obscure rather than to illumine. It cannot be expressed more simply and clearly than by the laws of contradiction and excluded middle: *a judgment and its contradictory cannot both be true; nor can they both be false.*

Because every negative judgment involves the denial of some other judgment, it has been argued that a negative judgment such as *S is not P* is primarily a judgment concerning the positive judgment *S is P*, not concerning the subject *S*; and hence that a negative judgment is not co-ordinate with a positive judgment, but dependent upon it.[117]

Passing by the point that a positive judgment also involves the denial of some other judgment, we may observe that a distinction must be drawn between "*S is P*" *is not true* (which is a judgment about *S is P*), and *S is not P* (which is a judgment about *S*). Denial no doubt presents itself to the mind most simply in the first of these two forms. But in contradicting a given judgment our method usually is to establish another judgment involving the same terms which stands to the given judgment in the relation expressed by the laws of contradiction and excluded middle; and when we oppose the judgment *S is not P* to the judgment *S is P* we have reached the less direct mode of denial in which we have again a judgment concerning our original subject.

The example here taken tends perhaps to obscure the point at issue because the distinction between "*S is P*" *is not true* and *S is not P* may appear to be so slight as to be immaterial. That there is a real distinction will, however, appear clear if we take such pairs of propositions as "*All S is P*" *is not true, Some S is not P*; "*All S is all P*" *is not true, Either some S is not P or some P is not S*; "*If any P is Q it is R*" *is not true, P might be Q without being R*.

It will be convenient if in general we understand by the *contradictory* of a proposition *P* not its simple denial "*P is not true*," but the proposition *Q* involving the same terms, which is formally so related to *P*, that *P* and *Q* cannot both be true or both false.

Sigwart observes that the ground of a denial may be either (*a*) a deficiency, or (*b*) an opposition.[118] I may, for example, pronounce that a certain thing does not possess a given attribute either (*a*) because I fail to discover the presence of the attribute, or (*b*) because I recognise the presence of some other attribute which I know to be incompatible with the one suggested.

This distinction may be illustrated by one or two further examples. Thus, I may deny that a man travelled by a certain train either (*a*) because I searched the train through just before it started and found he was not there, or (*b*) because I know he was elsewhere when the train started,—I may, for instance, have seen him leave the station at the same moment in another train in the opposite direction. Similarly, I may deny a universal proposition either (*a*) because I have discovered certain instances of its not holding good, or (*b*) because I accept another universal proposition which is inconsistent with it. Again, I may deny that a given metal, or the metal contained in a certain salt, is copper (*a*) on the ground of deficiency, namely, that it does not answer to a certain test, or (*b*) on the ground of opposition, namely, that I recognise it to be another metal, say, zinc.

The ground of denial always involves something positive, for example, the search through the train, or the discovery of individual exceptions. But it is clear that when we establish an opposition we get a result that is itself positive in a way that is not the case when

---

[117] Compare Sigwart, *Logic*, i. pp. 121, 2.
[118] *Logic*, i. p. 127.

we merely establish a deficiency. This may lead up to a brief examination of a doctrine of the nature of significant denial that is laid down by Mr Bosanquet.

Mr Bosanquet holds that *bare* denial has in itself no significance, and he apparently denies that the *contradictory* of a judgment, apart from the grounds on which it is based, conveys any information.[119] For the meaning of significant negation we must, he says, look to the grounds of the negation; or else for *contradictory* denial we must substitute *contrary* denial. As a consequence, a judgment can, strictly and properly, "only be denied by another judgment of the same nature; a singular by a singular judgment, a generic by a generic, a hypothetical by a hypothetical";[120] and, presumably, a particular by a particular, an apodeictic by an apodeictic.

It is of course true that every denial must have some kind of positive basis, but it is also necessary that a judgment should be distinguished from the grounds on which it is based. We cannot say that a judgment of given content is different for two people because they accept it on different grounds; and if it is said that this is to beg the question, since a difference in ground constitutes in itself a difference in content, the reply is that such a doctrine must render the content of every judgment so elusive and uncertain as to make it impossible of analysis.

The view that identifies the denial of a judgment with its contrary not only mixes up a judgment with its grounds, but also overlooks one of the two principal grounds of denial. When the ground of negation is an opposition, we may no doubt be said to reach denial through the contrary, though we should still hold that the denial is in itself something less than the contrary; but when the ground of denial is a deficiency, even this cannot be allowed. If, for example, I have arrived at the conclusion that a man did not start by a given train because I searched the train through before its departure and did not find him there; or if I conclude that a given metal is not copper because it does not satisfy a given test; I have obtained no contrary judgment, and yet my denial is justified.

These would be cases of *bare* denial. I have gained no positive knowledge of the whereabouts of the man in question, nor can I identify the given metal. But surely it cannot be seriously maintained that the denial is meaningless or useless, say, to a detective in the first instance, or to an analytical chemist in the second.

Of course we seldom or never rest content with bare denial. The contrary rather than the contradictory represents our ultimate aim. But it is often the case that, temporarily at any rate, we cannot get beyond bare denial; and we ought not to consider that we have altogether failed to make progress when all that we have achieved is the exclusion of a possible alternative or the overthrow of a false theory. Recent researches, for example, into the origin of cancer have led to no positive results; but it is claimed for them that by destroying preconceived ideas on the subject they have cleared the way for future advance. Will anyone affirm that this was not worth doing or that the time spent on the researches was wasted?

Looking at the question from another point of view, it is surely absurd to say that we cannot deny a universal unless we are able to substitute another universal in its place. Various algebraical formulae have from time to time been suggested as necessarily yielding a prime number. They have all been overthrown, and no valid formula has been established in their

---

[119] *Logic*, i. p. 305.
[120] *Ibid*, p. 383.

place. But knowledge that these formulae are false is not quite appropriately described as ignorance.

Elsewhere Mr. Bosanquet says that mere enumerative exceptions are futile and cannot touch the essence of the unconditionally universal judgments they apparently oppose.[121] He appears to have in view cases where nothing more than some modification of the original judgment is shewn to be necessary. But even so the enumerative exceptions *have* overthrown the original judgment. No doubt a scientific law which has had a great amount of evidence in its favour is likely to contain elements of truth even if it is not altogether true; and the object of a man of science who overthrows a law will be to set up some other law in its place. But, says Mr. Bosanquet, even if the first generic judgment were a sheer blunder and confusion, as has been the case from time to time with judgments propounded in science, it is scarcely possible to rectify the confusion except by substituting for it the true positive conceptions that arise out of the cases which overthrew it." Here it is admitted that the exceptions do overthrow the law, and the rest of the argument is surely an instance of *ignoratio elenchi*. It is moreover a pure, and in many cases an unjustifiable, assumption that the cases which suffice to overthrow a false law will also suffice as the basis for the establishment of a true law in its place.

Exercises

86. Examine the nature of the opposition between each pair of the following propositions:—None but Liberals voted against the motion; Amongst those who voted against the motion were some Liberals; It is untrue that those who voted against the motion were all Liberals. [K.]

87. If *some* were used in its ordinary colloquial sense, how would the scheme of opposition between propositions have to be modified? [J.]

88. Explain the technical terms "contradictory" and "contrary" applying them to the following propositions: *Few S are P*; *He was not the only one who cheated*; *Two-thirds of the army are abroad*. [V.]

89. Give the contradictory of each of the following propositions:—*Some but not all S is P*; *All S is P and some P is not R*; *Either all S is P or some P is not R*; *Wherever the property A is found, either the property B or the property C will be found with it, but not both of them together*. [K.]

90. Give the contradictory, and also a contrary, of each of the following propositions:

Half the candidates failed;
Wellington was always successful both in beating the enemy and in utilising his victory;
All men are either not knaves or not fools;
All but he had fled;
Few of them are honest;
Sometimes all our efforts fail;
Some of our efforts always fail. [L.]

---

[121] *Logic*, i. p. 313.

91. Give the contradictory, and also a contrary, of each of the following propositions:

I am certain you are wrong;
Sometimes when it rains I find myself without an umbrella;
Whatever you say, I shall not believe you. [C.]

92. Define the terms *subaltern, subcontrary, contrary, contradictory*, in such a way that they may be applicable to pairs of propositions generally, and not merely to those included in the ordinary square of opposition. Do the above exhaust the formal relations (in respect of inferability, consistency, or inconsistency) that are possible between pairs of propositions?

Illustrate your answer by considering the relation (in respect of inferability, consistency, or inconsistency) between each of the following propositions and each of the remainder: *S and P are coincident*; *Some S is P*; *Not all S is P*; *Either some S is not P or some P is not S*; *Anything that is not P is S*. [K.]

93. Given that the propositions X and Z are contradictory, Y and V contradictory, and X and Y contrary, shew (without assuming that X, Y, V, Z belong to the ordinary schedule of propositions) that the relations of V to X, Z to Y, V to Z are thereby deducible. [J.]

94. Prove formally that if two propositions are equivalent, their contradictories will also be equivalent. [K.]

95. Examine the doctrine that a judgment can properly be denied only by another judgment of the same type. Illustrate by reference to (*a*) universal judgments, (*b*) particular judgments (*c*) disjunctive judgments, (*d*) apodeictic judgments. [K.]

Chapter 8

IMMEDIATE INFERENCES[122]

96. *The Conversion of Categorical Propositions.*—By *conversion*, in a broad sense, is meant a change in the position of the terms of a proposition.[123] Logic, however, is concerned with conversion only in so far as the truth of the new proposition obtained by the process is a legitimate inference from the truth of the original proposition. For example, the change from *All S is P* to *All P is S* is not a legitimate logical conversion, since the truth of the latter proposition does not follow from the truth of the former. In other words, logical conversion is a case of *immediate inference*, which may be defined as the inference of a proposition from a single other proposition.[124]

The simplest form of logical conversion, and that which is understood in logic when we speak of conversion without further qualification, may be defined as *a process of immediate inference in which from a given proposition we infer another, having the predicate of the original proposition for subject, and its subject for predicate.* Thus, given a proposition having *S* for its subject and *P* for its predicate, our object in the process of conversion is to obtain by immediate inference a new proposition having *P* for its subject and *S* for its predicate. The original proposition may be called the *convertend*, and the inferred proposition the *converse*.

The process will be valid if the two following rules are observed:

(1) The converse must be the same in quality as the convertend (*Rule of Quality*);

---

[122] In this chapter we concern ourselves mainly with the traditional scheme of propositions, and except where an explicit statement is made to the contrary we proceed on the assumption that each class represented by a simple term exists in the universe of discourse, while at the same time it does not exhaust that universe. This assumption appears to have been made implicitly in the traditional treatment of logic.

[123] Ueberweg (*Logic*, § 84) defines conversion thus. Compare also De Morgan, *Formal Logic*, p. 58. In geometry, *all equiangular triangles are equilateral* would be regarded as the converse of *all equilateral triangles are equiangular*. In this sense of the term conversion, which is its ordinary non-technical sense, we may say—as we frequently do say—"Yes, such and such a proposition is true; but its converse is not true."

[124] In discussing immediate inferences we "pursue the content of an enunciated judgment into its relations to judgments not yet uttered" (Lotze). Instead of "immediate inferences" Professor Bain prefers to speak of "equivalent propositional forms." It will be found, however, that the new propositions obtained by immediate inference are not always equivalent to the original proposition, e.g., in conversion *per accidens*. Miss Jones suggests the term *eduction* as a synonym for *immediate inference* (*General Logic*, p. 79); and she then distinguishes between *eversions* and *transversions*, an *eversion* being an eduction from categorical form to categorical, or from hypothetical to hypothetical, &c., and *transversion* an eduction from categorical form to conditional, or from conditional to categorical, &c. For the present we shall be concerned with eversions only.

(2) No term must be distributed in the converse unless it was distributed in the convertend (*Rule of Distribution*).

Applying these rules to the four fundamental forms of proposition, we have the following table:—

Convertend.	Converse.
All *S* is *P*. **A**.	Some *P* is *S*. **I**.
Some *S* is *P*. **I**.	Some *P* is *S*. **I**.
No *S* is *P*. **E**.	No *P* is *S*. **E**.
Some *S* is not *P*. **O**.	(None)

It is desirable at this stage briefly to call attention to a point which will receive fuller consideration later on in connection with the reading of propositions in extension and intension, namely, that, generally speaking, in any judgment we have naturally before the mind the objects denoted by the subject, but the qualities connoted by the predicate. In the process of converting a proposition, however, the extensive force of the predicate is made prominent, and an import is given to the predicate similar to that of the subject. At the same time the distribution of the predicate has to be made explicit in thought. It is in passing from the *predicative* to the *class* reading (e.g., from *all men are mortal* to *all men are mortals*), that the difficulty sometimes found in correctly converting propositions probably consists. We shall at any rate do well to recognise that conversion and other immediate inferences usually involve a distinct mental act of the above nature.

It follows from what has been said above that some propositions lend themselves to the process of conversion much more readily than others. When the predicate of a proposition is a substantive little or no effort is required in order to convert the proposition; more effort is necessary when the predicate is an adjective; and still more when in the original proposition the logical predicate is not expressed separately at all, as in propositions *secundi adjacentis*. Compare for purposes of conversion the propositions, *Whales are mammals*, *Lions are carnivorous*, *A stitch in time saves nine*. In some cases, in consequence of the awkwardness of changing adjectives and verbal predicates into substantives, the conversion of a proposition appears to be a very artificial production.[125]

97. *Simple Conversion and Conversion per accidens.*—It will be observed that in the case of **I** and **E**, the converse is of the same form as the original proposition; moreover we do not lose any part of the information given us by the convertend, and we can pass back to it by re-conversion of the converse. The convertend and its converse are accordingly *equivalent* propositions. The conversion under these conditions is said to be *simple*.

In the case of **A**, it is different; we cannot pass by immediate inference from *All S is P* to *All P is S*, inasmuch as *P* is distributed in the latter of these propositions but undistributed in the former. Hence, although we start with a universal proposition, we obtain by conversion a particular proposition only,[126] and by no means of operating upon the converse can we regain the original proposition. The convertend and its converse are accordingly non-equivalent

---

[125] Compare Sigwart, *Logic*, i. p. 340.
[126] The failure to recognise or to remember that universal affirmative propositions are not simply convertible is a fertile source of fallacy.

propositions. The conversion in this case is called conversion *per accidens*,[127] or conversion *by limitation*.[128]

For concrete illustrations of the process of conversion we may take the propositions,—A stitch in time saves nine; None but the brave deserve the fair. The first of these may be written in the form,—All stitches in time are things that save nine stitches. This, being an **A** proposition, is only convertible *per accidens*, and we have for our converse,—Some things that save nine stitches are stitches in time. The second of the given propositions may be written,—No one who is not brave is deserving of the fair. This, being an **E** proposition, may be converted simply, giving, No one deserving of the fair is not brave. Our results may be expressed in a more natural form as follows: One way of saving nine stitches is by a stitch in time; No one deserving of the fair can fail to be brave.

No difficulty ought ever to be found in converting or performing other immediate inferences upon any given proposition when once it has been brought into the traditional logical form, its quantity and quality being determined, its subject, copula, and predicate being definitely distinguished from one another, and its predicate as well as its subject being read in extension. If, however, this rule is neglected, mistakes are pretty sure to follow.

98. *Inconvertibility of Particular Negative Propositions.*—It follows immediately from the rules of conversion given in section 96 that *Some S is not P* does not admit of ordinary conversion; for *S* which is undistributed in the convertend would become the predicate of a negative proposition in the converse, and would therefore be distributed.[129] It will be shewn presently, however, that although we are unable to infer anything about *P* in this case, we are able to draw an inference concerning *not-P*.

Jevons considers that the fact that the particular negative proposition is incapable of ordinary conversion "constitutes a blot in the ancient logic" (*Studies in Deductive Logic*, p. 37). There is, however, no sufficient justification for this criticism. We shall find subsequently that just as much can be inferred from the particular negative as from the particular affirmative (since the latter unlike the former does not admit of contraposition). No logic, symbolic or other, can actually obtain more from the given information than the ancient logic does. It has been suggested that what Jevons means is that the inconvertibility of **O** results in a want of symmetry and that logicians ought specially to aim at symmetry. With this last contention we may heartily agree. The want of symmetry, however, in the case before us is apparent only and results from taking an incomplete view. It will be found that symmetry reappears later on.[130]

99. *Legitimacy of Conversion.*—Aristotle proves the conversion of **E** *indirectly*, as follows;[131] *No S is P*, therefore, *No P is S*; for if not, *Some individual P, say Q, is S*; and hence *Q is both S and P*; but this is inconsistent with the original proposition.

---

[127] The conversion of **A** is said by Mansel to be called conversion *per accidens* 'because it is not a conversion of the universal *per se*, but by reason of its containing the particular. For the proposition 'Some B is A' is *primarily* the converse of 'Some A is B,' *secondarily* of 'All A is B'" (Mansel's *Aldrich*, p. 61). Professor Baynes seems to deny that this is the correct explanation of the use of the term (*New Analytic of Logical Forms*, p. 29); but however this may be, we certainly need not regard the converse of **A** as necessarily obtained through its subaltern. It is possible to proceed directly from *All A is B* to *Some B is A* without the intervention of *Some A is B*.

[128] Simple conversion and conversion *per accidens* are also called respectively *conversio pura* and *conversio impura*. Compare Lotze, *Logic*, § 79.

[129] As regards the inconvertibility of **O** see also sections 99 and 126.

[130] See sections 105, 106.

[131] "By the method called ἔκθεσις, i.e., by the *exhibition* of an individual instance." See Mansel's *Aldrich*, pp. 61, 2.

Having shewn that the simple conversion of **E** is legitimate, we can prove that the conversion *per accidens* of **A** is also legitimate. *All S is P*, therefore, *Some P is S*; for, if not, *No P is S*, and therefore (by conversion) *No S is P*; but this is inconsistent with the original supposition. The legitimacy of the simple conversion of **I** follows similarly.

The above proof appears to involve nothing beyond the principles of contradiction and excluded middle. The proof itself, however, is not satisfactory; for it practically assumes the validity of the very process that it seeks to justify, that is to say, it assumes the equivalence of the propositions *S is Q* and *Q is S*.

A better justification of the process of conversion may be obtained by considering the class relations involved in the propositions concerned. Thus, taking an **E** proposition, it is self-evident that if one class is entirely excluded from another class, this second class is entirely excluded from the first.[132] In the case of an **A** proposition it is clear on reflection that the statement *All S is P* is consistent with either of two relations of the classes *S* and *P*, namely, *S* and *P* coincident, or *P* containing *S* and more besides, and further that these are the only two possible relations with which it is consistent. It is self-evident that in each of these cases *Some P is S*; and hence the inference by conversion from an **A** proposition is shewn to be justified.[133] In the case of an **O** proposition, if we consider all the relationships of classes in which it holds good, we find that nothing is true of *P* in terms of *S* in *all* of them. Hence **O** is inconvertible.[134] The inconvertibility of **O** can also be established by shewing that *Some S is not P* is compatible with every one of the following propositions—*All P is S*, *Some P is S*, *No P is S*, *Some P is not S*.

100. *Table of Propositions connecting any two terms.*—There are—connecting any two terms *S* and *P*—eight propositions of the forms **A**, **E**, **I**, **O**, namely, four with *S* as subject, and four with *P* as subject. The results at which we have arrived concerning the conversion of propositions shew that of these eight, the two **E** propositions are equivalent to one another, and that the same is true of the two **I** propositions, **E** and **I** being simply convertible; also that these are the only equivalences obtainable. We have, therefore, the following table of propositions connecting any two terms *S* and *P*:—

SaP,
PaS,
SeP = PeS,
SiP = PiS,
SoP,
PoS.

---

[132] It is impossible to agree with Professor Bain, who would establish the rules of conversion by a kind of inductive proof. He writes as follows:—"When we examine carefully the various processes in Logic, we find them to be material to the very core. Take *Conversion*. How do we know that, if No *X* is *Y*, No *Y* is *X*? By examining cases in detail, and finding the equivalence to be true. Obvious as the inference seems on the mere formal ground, we do not content ourselves with the formal aspect. If we did, we should be as likely to say, All *X* is *Y* gives All *Y* is *X*; we are prevented from this leap merely by the examination of cases" (*Logic, Deduction*, p. 251). But no one would on reflection maintain it to be self-evident that the simple conversion of **A** is legitimate; for when the case is put to us we recognise immediately that the contradictory of *All P is S* is compatible with *All S is P*. On the other hand, no one can deny that in the case of **E** the legitimacy of the process of conversion is self-evident.

[133] Compare section 126, where this and other similar inferences are illustrated by the aid of the Eulerian diagrams.

[134] Again, compare section 126.

The pair of propositions *SaP* and *PaS* are independent (see section 84); and the same is true of the pairs *SoP* and *PoS*, *SaP* and *PoS*, *PaS* and *SoP*. The first pair taken together indicate that the classes *S* and *P* are coextensive, and they may be called *complementary* propositions. The second pair taken together indicate that the classes *S* and *P* are neither coextensive nor either included within the other; they may be called *sub-complementary* propositions. The third pair taken together indicate that the class *S* is included within the class *P* but that it does not exhaust that class; they may be called *contra-complementary* propositions. The fourth pair taken together indicate that the class *P* is included within the class *S* but that it does not exhaust that class; they are, therefore, also *contra-complementary*.[135]

The above table will be supplemented in section 106 by a table of propositions connecting any two terms and their contradictories, *S*, *P*, *not-S*, *not-P*. It will then be found that we have a symmetry that is at present wanting.

101. *The Obversion of Categorical Propositions.*[136]—Obversion is *a process of immediate inference in which the inferred proposition* (or *obverse*), *whilst retaining the original subject, has for its predicate the contradictory of the predicate of the original proposition* (or *obvertend*). This process is legitimate for a proposition of any form if at the same time the quality of the proposition is changed. The inferred proposition is, moreover, in all cases equivalent to the original proposition, so that we can always pass back from the obverse to the obvertend.

We have the following table:—

Obvertend.	Obverse.
All *S* is *P*. **A.**	No *S* is not-*P*. **E**
Some *S* is *P*. **I.**	Some *S* is not not-*P*. **O.**
No *S* is *P*. **E.**	All *S* is not-*P*. **A.**
Some *S* is not *P*. **O.**	Some *S* is not-*P*. **I.**

It will be observed that the obversion of *All S is P* depends upon the principle of contradiction, which tells us that if anything is *P* then it is not *not-P*; but that we pass back from *No S is not-P* to *All S is P* by the principle of excluded middle, which tells us that if anything is not *not-P* then it is *P*. The remaining inferences by obversion also depend upon one or other of these two principles.

---

[135] The new technical terms here introduced have been suggested by Mr Johnson.
[136] The process of immediate inference discussed in this section has been called by a good many different names. The term *obversion*, which is used by Professor Bain, is the most convenient. Other names which have been used are *permutation* (Fowler), *aequipollence* (Ueberweg), *infinitation* (Bowen), *immediate inference by private conception* (Jevons), *contraversion* (De Morgan), *contraposition* (Spalding). Professor Bain distinguishes between *formal obversion* and *material obversion*. By *formal obversion* is meant the kind of obversion discussed in the above section, and this is the only kind of obversion that can properly be recognised by the formal logician. *Material obversion* is described as the process of making "obverse inferences which are justified only on an examination of the matter of the proposition" (*Logic*, vol. i., p. 111); and the following are given as examples—"Warmth is agreeable; therefore, cold is disagreeable. War is productive of evil; therefore, peace is productive of good. Knowledge is good; therefore, ignorance is bad." It is very doubtful if these are legitimate inferences, formal or otherwise. The conclusions appear to require quite independent investigations to establish them. Apart from this, however, it is a mistake to regard the process as analogous to formal obversion. In the latter, the inferred proposition has the same subject as the original proposition, whilst its quality is different; but neither of these conditions is fulfilled in the above examples. The process is really more akin to the immediate inference presently to be discussed under the name of *inversion*.

102. *The Contraposition of Categorical Propositions.*[137]—Contraposition may be defined as *a process of immediate inference in which from a given proposition another proposition is inferred having for its subject the contradictory of the original predicate.* Thus, given a proposition having *S* for its subject and *P* for its predicate, we seek to obtain by immediate inference a new proposition having *not-P* for its subject.

It will be observed that in the above definition it is left an open question whether the contrapositive of a proposition has the original subject or the contradictory of the original subject for its predicate; and every proposition which admits of contraposition will accordingly have two contrapositives, each of which is the obverse of the other. For example, in the case of *All S is P* there are the two forms *No not-P is S* and *All not-P is not-S*. For many purposes the distinction may be practically neglected without risk of confusion. It will be observed, however, that when *not-S* is taken as the predicate of the contrapositive, the quality of the original proposition is preserved and there is greater symmetry.[138] On the other hand, if we regard contraposition as compounded out of obversion and conversion in the manner indicated in the following paragraph, the form with *S* as predicate is the more readily obtained. Perhaps the best solution (in cases in which it is necessary to mark the distinction) is to speak of the form with *not-S* as predicate as the full contrapositive, and the form with *S* as predicate as the partial contrapositive.[139]

The following rule may be adopted for obtaining the full contrapositive of a given proposition:—Obvert the original proposition, then convert the proposition thus obtained, and then once more obvert. For given a proposition with *S* as subject and *P* as predicate, obversion will yield an equivalent proposition with *S* as subject and *not-P* as predicate; the conversion of this will make *not-P* the subject and *S* the predicate; and a repetition of the process of obversion will yield a proposition with *not-P* as subject and *not-S* as predicate.

Applying this rule, we have the following table:—

Original Proposition	*Obverse*	*Partial Contrapositive*	*Full Contrapositive*
All *S* is *P*. **A.**	No *S* is not-*P*. **E.**	No *not-P* is *S*. **E.**	All not-*P* is not-*S* **A.**
Some *S* is *P*. **I.**	Some *S* is not not-*P*. **O.**	(None.)	(None.)
No *S* is *P*. **E.**	All *S* is not-*P*. **A.**	Some not-*P* is *S*. **I.**	Some not-*P* is not not-*S*. **O.**
Some *S* is not *P*. **O.**	Some *S* is not-*P*. **I.**	Some not-*P* is *S*. **I.**	Some not-*P* is not not-*S*. **O.**

---

[137] This form of immediate inference is called by some logicians *conversion by negation*; Miss Jones suggests the name *contraversion*. More strictly we might speak of *conversion by contraposition*. The word *contrapositive* was used by Boethius for the opposite of a term (e.g., *not-A*), the word *contradictory* being confined to propositional forms; and the passage from *All S is P* to *All not-P is not-S* was called *Conversio per contrapositionem terminorum*. In this usage Boethius was followed by the medieval logicians. Compare Minto, *Logic*, pp. 151, 153.

[138] The following is from Mansel's *Aldrich*, p. 61,—"Conversion by contraposition, which is not employed by Aristotle, is given by Boethius in his first book, *De Syllogismo Categorico*. He is followed by Petrus Hispanus. It should be observed, that the old logicians, following Boethius, maintain that in conversion by contraposition, as well as in the others, the *quality* should remain unchanged. Consequently the converse of 'All *A* is *B*' is 'All not-*B* is not-*A*,' and of 'Some *A* is not *B*,' 'Some not-*B* is not not-*A*.' It is simpler, however, to convert **A** into **E**, and **O** into **I**, ('No not-*B* is *A*,' 'Some not-*B* is *A*'), as is done by Wallis and Archbishop Whately; and before Boethius by Apuleius and Capella, who notice the conversion, but do not give it a name. The principle of this conversion may be found in Aristotle, *Top*. II. 8. 1, though he does not employ it for logical purposes."

[139] In previous editions the form with *S* as predicate was called the contrapositive, and the form with *not-S* as predicate was called the obverted contrapositive.

It will be observed that in the case of **A** and **O**, the contrapositive is equivalent to the original proposition, the quantity being unchanged, whereas in the case of **E** we pass from a universal to a particular.[140] In order to emphasize this difference, and following the analogy of ordinary conversion, the contraposition of **A** and **O** has been called *simple contraposition*, and that of **E** *contraposition per accidens*.[141]

That **I** has no contrapositive follows from the inconvertibility of **O**. For when *Some S is P* is obverted it becomes a particular negative, and the conversion of this proposition would be necessary in order to render the contraposition of the original proposition possible.

As regards the utility of the investigation as to the inferences that can be drawn from given propositions by the aid of contraposition, De Morgan[142] points out that the recognition that *Every not-P is not-S* follows from *Every S is P*, whatever *S* and *P* may stand for, renders unnecessary the special proofs that Euclid gives of certain of his theorems.[143]

In consequence of his dislike of negative terms Sigwart regards the passage from *All S is P* to *No not-P is S* as an artificial perversion. But he recognises the value of the inference from *If anything is S it is P* to *If anything is not P it is not S*. This distinction seems to be little more than verbal. It is to be observed that we can avoid the use of negative terms without having recourse to the conditional form of proposition: for example, *Whatever is S is P*, therefore, *Whatever is not P is not S*; *Anything that is S is P*, therefore, *Anything that is not P is not S*.

103. *The Inversion of Categorical Propositions.*—In discussing conversion and contraposition we have enquired in what cases it is possible, having given a proposition with *S* as subject and *P* as predicate, to infer (*a*) a proposition with *P* as subject, (*b*) a proposition with *not-P* as subject. We may now enquire further in what cases it is possible to infer (*c*) a proposition with *not-S* as subject.

If such a proposition can be inferred at all, it will be obtainable by a certain combination of the more elementary processes of ordinary conversion and obversion.[144] We will, therefore, take each of the fundamental forms of proposition and see what can be inferred (1) by first converting it, and then performing alternately the operations of obversion and conversion; (2) by first obverting it, and then performing alternately the operations of conversion and obversion. It will be found that in each case the process can be continued until a particular negative proposition is reached whose turn it is to be converted.

(1) The results of performing alternately the processes of conversion and obversion, commencing with the *former*, are as follows:—

---

[140] In most text-books, no *definition* of contraposition is given at all, and it may be pointed out that, in the attempt to generalise from special examples, Jevons in his *Elementary Lessons in Logic* involves himself in difficulties. For the contrapositive of **A** he gives *All not-P is not-S*; **O** he says has no contrapositive (but only a converse by negation, *Some not-P is S*); and for the contrapositive of **E** he gives *No P is S*. It is impossible to discover any definition of contraposition that can yield these results. Assuming that in contraposition the quality of the proposition is to remain unchanged as in Jevons's contrapositive of **A**, then the contrapositive of both **E** and **O** is *Some not-P is not not-S*.

[141] Compare Ueberweg, *Logic*, § 90.

[142] *Syllabus of Logic*, p. 32.

[143] It will be found that, taking Euclid's first book, proposition 6 is obtainable by contraposition from proposition 18, and 19 from 5 and 18 combined; or that 5 can be obtained by contraposition from 19, and 18 from 6 and 19. Similar relations subsist between propositions 4, 8, 24, and 25; and, again, between axiom 12 and propositions 16, 28, and 29. Other examples might be taken from Euclid's later books. In some of the cases the logical relations in which the propositions stand to one another are obvious; in other cases some supplementary steps are necessary.

[144] It might also be obtained directly; by the aid, for example, of Euler's circles. See the following chapter.

(i) All *S* is *P*,
therefore (by conversion), Some *P* is *S*,
therefore (by obversion), Some *P* is not not-*S*.

Here comes the turn for conversion; but as we have to deal with an **O** proposition, we can proceed no further.

(ii) Some *S* is *P*,
therefore (by conversion), Some *P* is *S*,
therefore (by obversion), Some *P* is not not-*S*;
and again we can go no further.

(iii) No *S* is *P*,
therefore (by conversion), No *P* is *S*,
therefore (by obversion), All *P* is not-*S*,
therefore (by conversion), *Some not-S is P*,
therefore (by obversion), *Some not-S is not not-P*.

In this case either of the propositions in italics is the immediate inference that was sought.

(iv) Some *S* is not *P*.

In this case we are not able even to commence our series of operations.

(2) The results of performing alternately the processes of conversion and obversion, commencing with the *latter*, are as follows:—
(i) All *S* is *P*,
therefore (by obversion), No *S* is not-*P*,
therefore (by conversion), No not-*P* is *S*,
therefore (by obversion), All not-*P* is not-*S*,
therefore (by conversion), *Some not-S is not-P*,
therefore (by obversion), *Some not-S is not P*.

Here again we have obtained the desired form.

(ii) Some *S* is *P*,

therefore (by obversion), Some *S* is not not-*P*.

(iii) No *S* is *P*,
therefore (by obversion), All *S* is not-*P*,
therefore (by conversion), Some not-*P* is *S*,
therefore (by obversion), Some not-*P* is not not-*S*.

(iv) Some *S* is not *P*,
therefore (by obversion), Some *S* is not-*P*,

therefore (by conversion), Some not-*P* is *S*,
therefore (by obversion), Some not-*P* is not not-*S*.

We can now answer the question with which we commenced this enquiry. The required proposition can be obtained only if the given proposition is universal; we then have, according as it is affirmative or negative,—

All S is P, therefore, *Some not-S is not P* (= *Some not-S is not-P*);
No S is P, therefore, *Some not-S is P* (= *Some not-S is not not-P*).

This form of immediate inference has been more or less casually recognised by various logicians, without receiving any distinctive name. Sometimes it has been vaguely classed under contraposition (compare Jevons, *Elementary Lessons in Logic*, pp. 185, 6), but it is really as far removed from the process to which that designation has been given as the latter is from ordinary conversion. The term *inversion* was suggested in an earlier edition of this work, and has since been adopted by some other writers. Inversion may be defined as *a process of immediate inference in which from a given proposition another proposition is inferred having for its subject the contradictory of the original subject*. Thus, given a proposition with *S* as subject and *P* as predicate, we obtain by inversion a new proposition with *not-S* as subject. The original proposition may be called the *invertend*, and the inferred proposition the *inverse*.

In the above definition it is not specified whether the inverse is to have for its predicate *P* or *not-P*. Hence two forms (each being the obverse of the other) have been obtained as in the case of contraposition. So far as it is necessary to mark the distinction, we may speak of the form in which *P* is the predicate as the partial inverse, and of that in which *not-P* is the predicate as the full inverse.

104. *The Validity of Inversion.*—It will be remembered that we are at present working on the assumption that each class represented by a simple term exists in the universe of discourse, while at the same time it does not exhaust that universe; in other words, we assume that *S*, *not-S*, *P*, *not-P*, all represent existing classes. This assumption is perhaps specially important in the case of inversion, and it is connected with certain difficulties that may have already occurred to the reader. In passing from *All S is P* to its inverse *Some not-S is not P* there is an apparent illicit process, which it is not quite easy either to account for or explain away. For the term *P*, which is undistributed in the premiss, is distributed in the conclusion, and yet if the universal validity of obversion and conversion is granted, it is impossible to detect any flaw in the argument by which the conclusion is reached. It is in the assumption of the existence of the contradictory of the original predicate that an explanation of the apparent anomaly may be found. That assumption may be expressed in the form *Some things are not P*. The conclusion *Some not-S is not P* may accordingly be regarded as based on this premiss combined with the explicit premiss *All S is P*; and it will be observed that, in the additional premiss, *P* is distributed.[145]

105. *Summary of Results.*—The results obtained in the preceding sections are summed up in the following table:—

---

[145] The question of the validity of inversion under other assumptions will be considered in chapter 8.

		A.	E.	I.	O.
i	Original proposition	SaP	SiP	SeP	SoP
ii	Obverse	SeP'	SoP'	SaP'	SiP'
iii	Converse	PiS	PiS	PeS	
iv	Obverted Converse	PoS'	PoS'	PaS'	
v	Partial Contrapositive[146]	P'eS		P'iS	P'iS
vi	Full Contrapositive[146]	P'aS'		P'oS'	P'oS'
vii	Partial Inverse[146]	S'oP		S'iP	
viii	Full Inverse[146]	S'iP'		S'oP'	

It may be pointed out that the following rules apply to all the above immediate inferences:—

Rule of Quality.—The total number of negatives admitted or omitted in subject, predicate, or copula must be even.

Rules of Quantity.—If the new subject is S, the quantity may remain unchanged; if S', the quantity must be depressed;[147] if P, the quantity must be depressed in **A** and **O**; if P', the quantity must be depressed in **E** and **I**.

106. *Table of Propositions connecting any two terms and their contradictories.*—Taking any two terms and their contradictories, S, P, *not-S*, *not-P*, and combining them in pairs, we obtain thirty-two propositions of the forms **A, E, I, O**. The following table, however, shews that only eight of these thirty-two propositions are non-equivalent.

	(i)		(ii)		(iii)		(iv)
			Universals				
A	**SaP**	=	SeP'	=	P'eS	=	P'aS'
A'	S'aP'	=	S'eP	=	PeS'	=	PaS
E	SaP'	=	**SeP**	=	PeS	=	PaS'
E'	S'aP	=	**S'eP'**	=	P'eS'	=	P'aS
			Particulars				
O	SoP	=	SiP'	=	P'iS	=	P'oS'
O'	S'oP'	=	S'iP	=	PiS'	=	PoS
I	SoP'	=	**SiP**	=	PiS	=	PoS'
I'	S'oP	=	**S'iP'**	=	P'iS'	=	P'oS

In this table, columns (i) and (ii) contain the propositions in which S or S' is subject, and columns (iii) and (iv) the propositions in which P or P' is subject. In columns (i) and (iv) we have the forms which admit of simple contraposition (i.e., **A** and **O**), and in columns (ii) and (iii) those which admit of simple conversion (i.e., **E** and **I**). Contradictories are shewn by identical places in the universal and particular rows. We pass from column (i) to column (ii) by obversion; from column (ii) to column (iii) by simple conversion; and from column (iii) to column (iv) by obversion.

---

[146] In previous editions what are here called the partial contrapositive and the full contrapositive respectively were called the contrapositive and the obverted contrapositive; and what are here called the partial inverse and the full inverse were called the inverse and the obverted inverse.

[147] In speaking of the quantity as depressed, it is meant that a universal yields a particular, and a particular yields nothing.

The forms in black type shew that we may take for our eight non-equivalent propositions the four propositions connecting *S* and *P*, and a similar set connecting *not-S* and *not-P*.[148] To establish their non-equivalence we may proceed as follows: *SaP* and *SeP* are already known to be non-equivalent, and the same is true of *S'aP'* and *S'eP'*; but no universal proposition can yield a universal inverse; therefore, no one of these four propositions is equivalent to any other. Again, *SiP* and *SoP* are already known to be non-equivalent, and the same is true of *S'iP'* and *S'oP'*; but no particular proposition has any inverse; therefore, no one of these propositions is equivalent to any other. Finally, no universal proposition can be equivalent to a particular proposition.[149]

107. *Mutual Relations of the non-equivalent Propositions connecting any two terms and their contradictories.*[150]—We may now investigate the mutual relations of our eight non-equivalent propositions. *SaP, SeP, SiP, SoP* form an ordinary square of opposition; and so do *S'aP', S'eP', S'iP', S'oP'*. Reference to columns (iii) and (iv) in the table will shew further that *SaP, S'eP', S'iP', SoP* are equivalent to another square of opposition; and that the same is true of *S'aP', SeP, SiP, S'oP'*. This leaves only the following pairs unaccounted for: *SaP, S'aP'*; *SeP, S'eP'*; *SoP, S'oP'*; *SiP, S'iP'*; *SaP, S'oP', S'aP', SoP*; *SeP, S'iP'*; *S'eP', SiP*; and it will be found that in each of these cases we have an independent pair.

SaP and *S'aP'* (which are equivalent to *SaP, PaS*, and also to *P'aS', S'aP'*) taken together serve to identify the classes *S* and *P*, and also the classes *S'* and *P'*. They are therefore *complementary* propositions, in accordance with the definition given in section 100. Similarly, *SeP* and *S'eP'* (which are equivalent to *SaP', P'aS*, and also to *PaS', S'aP*) are complementary; they serve to identify the classes *S* and *P'*, and also the classes *S'* and *P*. It will be observed that the complementary of any universal proposition may be obtained by replacing the subject and predicate respectively by their contradictories. A not uncommon fallacy is the tacit substitution of the complementary of a proposition for the proposition itself.

The complementary relation holds only between universals. Particulars between which there is an analogous relation (the subject and predicate of the one being respectively the contradictories of the subject and predicate of the other) will be found to be *sub-complementary* in accordance with the definition in section 100; this relation holds between *SoP* and *S'oP'*, and between *SiP* and *S'iP'*. *SoP* and *S'oP'* (which are equivalent to *SoP, PoS*, and also to *P'oS', S'oP'*) indicate that the classes *S* and *P* are neither coextensive nor either included within the other, and also that the same is true of *S'* and *P'*; *SiP* and *S'iP'* (which are

---

[148] The former set being denoted by **A, E, I, O**, the latter set may be denoted by **A', E', I', O'**.

[149] Mrs Ladd Franklin, in an article on *The Proposition* in *Baldwin's Dictionary of Philosophy and Psychology*, reaches the result arrived at in this section from a different point of view. Mrs Franklin shews that, if we express everything that can be said in the form of existential propositions (that is, propositions affirming or denying existence), it is at once evident that the actual number of different statements possible in terms of *X* and *Y* and their contradictories *x* and *y* is eight. For the combinations of *X* and *Y* and their contradictories are *XY, Xy, xY, xy*, and we can affirm each of these combinations to exist or to be non-existent. Hence it is clear that eight different statements of fact are possible, and that these eight must remain different, no matter what the form in which they may be expressed.

It may be worth adding that the conditional and disjunctive forms as well as the categorical may here be included on the understanding that all the propositions are interpreted assertorically. Thus, the four following propositions are, on the above understanding, equivalent to one another: *All X is Y* (categorical); *If anything is X, it is Y* (conditional); *Nothing is Xy* (existential); *Everything is x or Y* (disjunctive).

[150] This section may be omitted on a first reading.

equivalent to *SoP'*, *P'oS*, and also to *PoS'*, *S'oP*) indicate the same thing as regards *S* and *P'*, *S'* and *P*.

The four remaining pairs are *contra-complementary*, each pair serving conjointly to *subordinate* a certain class to a certain other class; or, rather, since each such subordination implies a supplementary subordination, we may say that each pair subordinates two classes to two other classes. Thus, *SaP* and *S'oP'* (which are equivalent to *SaP*, *PoS*, and also to *P'aS'*, *S'oP'*) taken together shew that the class *S* is contained in but does not exhaust the class *P*, and also that the class *P'* is contained in but does not exhaust the class *S'*; *S'aP'* and *SoP* (which are equivalent to *S'aP'*, *P'oS'*, and also to *PaS*, *SoP*) yield the same results as regards the classes *S'* and *P'*, and the classes *P* and *S*; *SeP* and *S'iP'* (which are equivalent to *SaP'*, *P'oS*, and also to *PaS'*, *S'oP*) as regards *S* and *P'*, and *P* and *S'*; and *S'eP'* and *SiP* (which are equivalent to *S'aP*, *PoS'*, and also to *P'aS*, *SoP'*) as regards *S'* and *P*, *P'* and *S*.

Denoting the complementaries of **A** and **E** by **A'** and **E'**, and the sub-complementaries of **I** and **O** by **I'** and **O'**, the various relations between the non-equivalent propositions connecting any two terms and their contradictories may be exhibited in the following *octagon* of opposition:

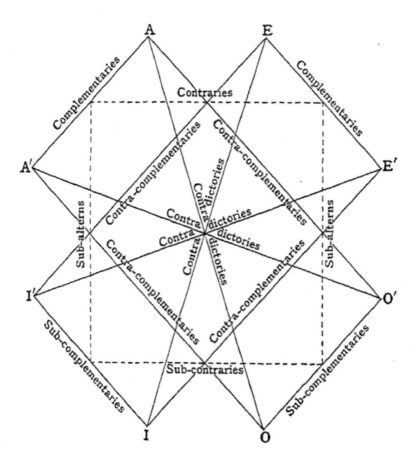

Each of the *dotted* lines in the above takes the place of *four* connecting lines which are not filled in; for example, the dotted line marked as connecting contraries indicates the relation between **A** and **E**, **A** and **E'**, **A'** and **E**, **A'** and **E'**.[151]

108. *The Elimination of Negative Terms.*[152]—The process of obversion enables us by the aid of negative terms to reduce all propositions to the affirmative form; and the question may be raised whether the various processes of immediate inference and the use, where necessary, of negative propositions will not equally enable us to eliminate negative terms.

It is of course clear that by means of obversion we can get rid of a negative term occurring as the predicate of a proposition. The problem is more difficult when the negative term occurs as subject, but in this case elimination may still be possible; for example, $S'iP = PoS$. We may even be able to get rid of two negative terms; for example, $S'aP' = PaS$. So long, however, as we are limited to categorical propositions of the ordinary type we cannot eliminate a negative term (without introducing another in its place) where such a term occurs as subject either (*a*) in a universal affirmative or a particular negative with a positive term as predicate, or (*b*) in a universal negative or a particular affirmative with a negative term as predicate.

The validity of the above results is at once shewn by reference to the table of equivalences given in section 106. At least one proposition in which there is no negative term will be found in each line of equivalences except the fourth and the eighth, which are as follows:

$S'aP$	=	$S'eP'$	=	$P'eS'$	=	$P'aS$;
$S'oP$	=	$S'iP'$	=	$P'iS'$	=	$P'oS$.

In these cases we may indeed get rid of S' (as, for example, from $S'aP$), but it is only by introducing P' (thus, $S'aP = P'aS$); there is no getting rid of negative terms altogether. We may here refer back to the results obtained in sections 100 and 106; with two terms *six* non-equivalent propositions were obtained, with two terms and their contradictories *eight* non-equivalent propositions. The ground of this difference is now made clear.

If, however, we are allowed to enlarge our scheme of propositions by recognising certain additional types, and if we work on the assumption that universal propositions are existentially negative while particular propositions are existentially affirmative,[153] then negative terms may always be eliminated. Thus, *No not-S is not-P* is equivalent to the statement *Nothing is both not-S and not-P*, and this becomes by obversion *Everything is either S or P*. Again, *Some not-S is not-P* is equivalent to the statement *Something is both not-S and not-P*, and this becomes by obversion *Something is not either S or P*, or, as this proposition may also be written, *There is something besides S and P*. The elimination of negative terms has now been accomplished in all cases. It will be observed further that we now have *eight* non-equivalent propositions containing only *S* and *P*—namely, *All S is P, No S is P, Some S is P, Some S is not P, All P is S, Some P is not S, Everything is either S or P, There is something besides S and P*.

---

[151] For the octagon of opposition in the form in which it is here given I am indebted to Mr Johnson.
[152] This section may be omitted on a first reading.
[153] It is necessary here to anticipate the results of a discussion that will come at a later stage. See chapter 8.

Following out this line of treatment, the table of equivalences given in section 106 may be rewritten as follows [columns (ii) and (iii) being omitted, and columns (v) and (vi) taking their places]:

(i)		(iv)		(v)		(vi)
SaP	=	*P'aS'*	=	*Nothing is SP'*	=	*Everything is S' or P.*
S'aP'	=	*PaS*	=	*Nothing is S'P*	=	*Everything is S or P'.*
SaP'	=	*PaS'*	=	*Nothing is SP*	=	*Everything is S' or P'.*
S'aP	=	*P'aS*	=	*Nothing is S'P'*	=	*Everything is S or P.*
SoP	=	*P'oS'*	=	*Something is SP'*	=	*There is something besides S' and P.*
S'oP'	=	*PoS*	=	*Something is S'P*	=	*There is something besides S and P'.*
SoP'	=	*PoS'*	=	*Something is SP*	=	*There is something besides S' and P'.*
S'oP	=	*P'oS*	=	*Something is S'P'*	=	*There is something besides S and P.*

Taking the propositions in two divisions of four sets each, the two diagonals from left to right give propositions containing S and P only.[154]

The scheme of propositions given in this section may be brought into interesting relation with the three fundamental laws of thought.[155] The scheme is based upon the recognition of the following propositional forms and their contradictories:

Every S is P;
Every not-P is not-S;
Nothing is both S and not-P;
Everything is either P or not-S;

and these four propositions have been shewn to be equivalent to one another. If in the above propositions we now write S for P, we have the following:

Every S is S;
Every not-S is not-S;
Nothing is both S and not-S;
Everything is either S or not-S.

But the first two of these propositions express the law of identity, with positive and negative terms respectively, the third is an expression of the law of contradiction, and the fourth of the law of excluded middle. The scheme of propositions with which we have been dealing may, therefore, be said to be based upon the recognition of just those propositional forms which are required in order to express the fundamental laws of thought.

Since the propositional forms in question have been shown to be mutually equivalent to one another, the further argument may suggest itself that if the validity of the immediate inferences involved be granted, then it follows that the fundamental laws of thought have

---

[154] The first four propositions in column (v) may be expressed symbolically $SP' = 0$, &c.; the second four $SP' > 0$, &c.; the first four in column (vi) $S' + P = 1$, &c.; and the second four $S' + P < 1$, &c.; where 1 = the universe of discourse, and 0 = nonentity, i.e., the contradictory of the universe of discourse. Compare section 138.

[155] Compare Mrs Ladd Franklin in *Mind*, January, 1890, p. 87.

been shown to be mutually inferable from one another. But it may, on the other hand, be held that this argument is open to the charge of involving a *circulus in probando* on the ground that the validity of the immediate inferences themselves requires that the laws of thought be first postulated as an antecedent condition.

109. *Other Immediate Inferences.*—Some other commonly recognised forms of immediate inference may be briefly touched upon.

(1) *Immediate inferences based on the square of opposition* have been discussed in the preceding chapter.

(2) *Immediate inference by change of relation* is the process whereby we pass from a categorical proposition to a conditional or a disjunctive, or from a conditional to a disjunctive or a categorical, or from a disjunctive to a categorical or a conditional.[156] For example, *All S is P*, therefore, *If anything is S it is P*; *Every S is P or Q*, therefore, *Any S that is not P is Q*. References have been already made to inferences such as these, and they will be further discussed later on.

(3) *Immediate inference by added determinants* is a process of immediate inference which consists in limiting both the subject and the predicate of the original proposition by means of the same determinant. For example,—*All P is Q*, therefore, *All AP is AQ*; A negro is a fellow creature, therefore, A suffering negro is a suffering fellow creature. The formal validity of the reasoning may be shewn as follows: *AP* is a subdivision of the class *P*, namely, that part of it which also belongs to the class *A*; and, therefore, whatever is true of the whole of *P* must be true of *AP*; hence, given that *All P is Q*, we can infer that *All AP is Q*; moreover, by the law of identity, *All AP is A*; therefore, *All AP is AQ*.[157]

The formal validity of immediate inference by added determinants has been denied on the ground of the obvious fallacy of arguing from such a premiss as *an elephant is an animal* to the conclusion *a small elephant is a small animal*, or from such a premiss as *cricketers are men* to the conclusion *poor cricketers are poor men*. In these cases, however, the fallacy really results from the ambiguity of language, the added determinant receiving a different interpretation when it qualifies the subject from that which it has when it qualifies the predicate. A term of comparison like *small* can indeed hardly be said to have an independent interpretation, its force always being relative to some other term with which it is conjoined. While then the inference in its symbolic form (*P is Q*, therefore, *AP is AQ*) is perfectly valid, it is especially necessary to guard against fallacy in its use when significant terms are employed. All that we have to insist upon is that the added determinant shall receive the same interpretation in both subject and predicate. There is, for example, no fallacy in the following: An elephant is an animal, therefore, A small elephant is an animal which is small compared with elephants generally; Cricketers are men, therefore, Poor cricketers are men who in their capacity as cricketers are poor.

(4) *Immediate inference by complex conception* is a process of immediate inference which consists in employing the subject and the predicate of the original proposition as parts

---

[156] Miss Jones speaks of an inference of this kind as a *transversion*. See note 3 on page 126.
[157] It must be observed, however, that the validity of this argument requires an assumption in regard to the existential import of propositions, which differs from that which we have for the most part adopted up to this point. It has to be assumed that universals do not imply the existence of their subjects. Otherwise this inference would not be valid in the case of no *P* being *A*. *P* might exist, and all *P* might be *Q*, but we could not pass to *AP is AQ*, since this would imply the existence of *AP*, which would be incorrect. It is necessary briefly to call attention to the above at this point, but our aim through all these earlier chapters has been to avoid as far as possible the various complications that arise in connection with the difficult problem of existential import.

of a more complex conception. Symbolically we can only express it somewhat as follows: *P is Q*, therefore, *Whatever stands in a certain relation to P stands in the same relation to Q*. The following is a concrete example: An elephant is an animal, therefore, the ear of an elephant is the ear of an animal. A systematic treatment of this kind of inference belongs to the special branch of formal logic known as the *logic of relatives*, any detailed consideration of which is beyond the scope of the present work. Attention may, however, be called to the danger of our committing a fallacy, if we perform the process carelessly. For example, Protestants are Christians, therefore, A majority of Protestants are a majority of Christians; A negro is a man, therefore, the best of negroes is the best of men. The former of these fallacies is akin to the fallacy of composition (see section 11), since we pass from the distributive to the collective use of a term.

(5) *Immediate inference by converse relation* is a process of immediate inference analogous to ordinary conversion but belonging to the logic of relatives. It consists in passing from a statement of the relation in which *P* stands to *Q* to a statement of the relation in which *Q* consequently stands to *P*. The two terms are transposed and the word by which their relation is expressed is replaced by its correlative. For example, *A* is greater than *B*, therefore, *B* is less than *A*; Alexander was the son of Philip, therefore, Philip was the father of Alexander; Freedom is synonymous with liberty, therefore, Liberty is synonymous with freedom.

Mansel gives the first two of the above as examples of *material consequence* as distinguished from *formal consequence*. "A Material Consequence is defined by Aldrich to be one in which the conclusion follows from the premisses solely by the force of the terms. This in fact means from some understood Proposition or Propositions, connecting the terms, by the addition of which the mind is enabled to reduce the Consequence to logical form...... The failure of a Material Consequence takes place when no such connection exists between the terms as will warrant us in supplying the premisses required; i.e., when one or more of the premisses so supplied would be *false*. But to determine this point is obviously beyond the province of the Logician. For this reason, Material Consequence is rightly excluded from Logic...... Among these material, and therefore extralogical, Consequences, are to be classed those which Reid adduces as cases for which Logic does not provide; e.g., 'Alexander was the son of Philip, therefore, Philip was the father of Alexander'; '*A* is greater than *B*, therefore, *B* is less than *A*.' In both these it is our material knowledge of the relations 'father and son,' 'greater and less,' that enables us to make the inference" (*Aldrich*, p. 199).

The distinction between what is formal and what is material is not in reality so simple or so absolute as is here implied.[158] It is usual to recognise as formal only those relations which can be expressed by the ordinary copula *is* or *is not*; and there is very good reason for proceeding upon this basis in the greater part of our logical discussions. No other relation is of the same fundamental importance or admits of an equally developed logical superstructure. But it is important to recognise that there are other relations which may remain the same while the things related vary; and wherever this is the case we may regard the relation as constituting the form and the things related the matter. Accordingly with each such relation we may have a different formal system. The logic of relatives deals with such systems as are outside the one ordinarily recognised. Each immediate inference by converse relation will, therefore, be formal in its own particular system. This point is admirably put by Miss Jones:

---

[158] Compare section 2.

"A proposition containing a relative term furnishes—besides the ordinary immediate inferences—other immediate inferences to any one acquainted with the system to which it refers. These inferences cannot be educed except by a person knowing the 'system'; on the other hand, no knowledge is needed of the objects referred to, except a knowledge of their place in the system, and this knowledge is in many cases coextensive with ordinary intelligence; consider, e.g., the relations of magnitude of objects in space, of the successive parts of time, of family connections, of number" (*General Logic*, p. 34).

(6) *Immediate inference by modal consequence* or, as it is also called, inference by change of modality, is somewhat analogous to subaltern inference. It consists in nothing more than weakening a statement in respect of its modality; and hence it is never possible to pass back from the inferred to the original proposition. Thus, from the *validity* of the apodeictic judgment we can pass to the validity of the assertoric, and from that to the validity of the problematic; but not *vice versâ*. On the other hand, from the *invalidity* of the problematic judgment we can pass to the invalidity of the assertoric, and from that to the invalidity of the apodeictic; but again not *vice versâ*.[159]

110. *Reduction of immediate inferences to the mediate form*[160]—Immediate inference has been defined as the inference of a proposition from a single other proposition; mediate inference, on the other hand, is the inference of a proposition from at least two other propositions.

We may briefly consider various ways of establishing the validity of immediate inferences by means of mediate inferences.

(1) One of the old Greek logicians, Alexander of Aphrodisias, establishes the conversion of **E** by means of a syllogism in *Ferio*.

	No S is P,
therefore,	*No P is S*;

for, if not, then by the law of contradiction, *Some P is S*; and we have this syllogism,—

	No S is P,
	Some P is S,
therefore,	*Some P is not P*,

a *reductio ad absurdum*.[161]

(2) It may be plausibly maintaisned that in Aristotle's proof of the conversion of **E** (given in section 99), there is an implicit syllogism: namely,—*Q is P, Q is S*, therefore, *Some S is P*.

(3) The contraposition of **A** may be established by means of a syllogism in *Camestres* as follows:—

Given	*All S is P*,	
we have also	*No not-P is P*,	by the law of contradiction,
therefore,	*No not-P is S*.[162]	

---

[159] Compare Ueberweg, *Logic*, § 98.
[160] Students who have not already a technical knowledge of the syllogism may omit this section until they have read the earlier chapters of Part III.
[161] Compare Mansel's *Aldrich*, p. 62. The conversion of **A** and the conversion of **I** may be established similarly.

(4) We might also obtain the contrapositive of *All S is P* as follows:—
By the law of excluded middle, *All not-P is S or not-S*, and, by hypothesis, *All S is P*,

therefore,	*All not-P is P or not-S*;
but, by the law of contradiction,	*No not-P is P*,
therefore,	*All not-P is not-S*.[163]

(5) The contraposition of **A** may also be established indirectly by means of a syllogism in *Darii*:—

| | *All S is P*, |
| therefore, | *No not-P is S*; |

for, if not, *Some not-P is S*; and we have the following syllogism,—

	All S is P,
	Some not-P is S,
therefore,	*Some not-P is P*,

which is absurd.[164]

All the above are interesting, as illustrating the processes of immediate inference; but regarded as proofs they labour under the disadvantage of deducing the less complex by means of the more complex.

EXERCISES

111. Give all the logical opposites of the proposition,—Some rich men are virtuous; and also the converse of the contrary of its contradictory. How is the latter directly related to the given proposition?

Does it follow that a proposition admits of simple conversion because its predicate is distributed? [K.]

112. Point out any ambiguities in the following propositions, and give the contradictory and (where possible) the converse of each of them:—(i) Some of the candidates have been successful; (ii) All are not happy that seem so; (iii) All the fish weighed five pounds. [K.]

---

[162] Similarly, granting the validity of obversion, the contraposition of **O** may be established by a syllogism in *Datisi* as follows:—
Given *Some S is not P*, then we have

	All S is S,	by the law of identity,
and	*Some S is not-P*,	by obversion of the given proposition,
therefore,	*Some not-P is S*.	

It will be found that, adopting the same method, the contraposition of **E** is yielded by a syllogism in *Darapti*.

[163] Compare Jevons, *Principles of Science*, chapter 6, § 2; and *Studies in Deductive Logic*, p. 44.

[164] Compare De Morgan, *Formal Logic*, p. 25. Granting the validity of obversion, the contraposition of **E** and the contraposition of **O** may be established similarly.

113. State in logical form and convert the following propositions:—(*a*) He jests at scars who never felt a wound; (*b*) Axioms are self-evident; (*c*) Natives alone can stand the climate of Africa; (*d*) Not one of the Greeks at Thermopylae escaped; (*e*) All that glitters is not gold.
[O.]

114. "The angles at the base of an isosceles triangle are equal." What can be inferred from this proposition by obversion, conversion, and contraposition respectively? [L.]

115. Give the obverse, the contrapositive, and the inverse of each of the following propositions:—The virtuous alone are truly noble; No Athenians are Helots. [M.]

116. Give the contrapositive and (where possible) the inverse of the following propositions:—(i) A stitch in time saves nine; (ii) None but the brave deserve the fair; (iii) Blessed are the peacemakers; (iv) Things equal to the same thing are equal to one another; (v) Not every tale we hear is to be believed. [K.]

117. If it is false that "Not only the virtuous are happy," what can we infer (*a*) with regard to the non-virtuous, (*b*) with regard to the non-happy? [J.]

118. Write down the contradictory, and also—where possible—the converse, the contrapositive, and the inverse of each of the following propositions:

A bird in the hand is worth two in the bush;
No unjust acts are expedient;
All are not saints that go to church. [K.]

119. Give the contrapositive and the inverse of each of the following propositions,—They never fail who die in a great cause; Whom the Gods love die young. If *A* is either *B* or else both *C* and *D*, what do we know about that which is not *D*? [K.]

120. Take the following propositions in pairs, and in regard to each pair state whether the two propositions are consistent or inconsistent with each other; in the former case, state further whether either proposition can be inferred from the other, and, if it can be, point out the nature of the inference; in the latter case, state whether it is possible for both the propositions to be false:—(*a*) *All S is P*; (*b*) *All not-S is P*; (*c*) *No P is S*; (*d*) *Some not-P is S*.
[K.]

121. Transform the following propositions in such a way that, without losing any of their force, they may all have the same subject and the same predicate:—*No not-P is S*; *All P is not-S*; *Some P is S*; *Some not-P is not not-S*. [K.]

122. Describe the logical relations, if any, between each of the following propositions, and each of the others:—

(i) There are no inorganic substances which do not contain carbon;
(ii) All organic substances contain carbon;
(iii) Some substances not containing carbon are organic;
(iv) Some inorganic substances do not contain carbon. [C.]

123. "All that love virtue love angling."
Arrange the following propositions in the three following groups:—(α) those which can be inferred from the above proposition; (β) those which are consistent with it, but which cannot be inferred from it; (γ) those which are inconsistent with it.

(i) None that love not virtue love angling.
(ii) All that love angling love virtue.
(iii) All that love not angling love virtue.
(iv) None that love not angling love virtue.
(v) Some that love not virtue love angling.
(vi) Some that love not virtue love not angling
(vii) Some that love not angling love virtue.
(viii) Some that love not angling love not virtue. [K.]

124. Determine the logical relation between each pair of the following propositions:—

(1) All crystals are solids.
(2) Some solids are not crystals.
(3) Some not crystals are not solids.
(4) No crystals are not solids.
(5) Some solids are crystals.
(6) Some not solids are not crystals.
(7) All solids are crystals. [L.]

Chapter 9

THE DIAGRAMMATIC REPRESENTATION OF PROPOSITIONS

125. *The use of Diagrams in Logic.*—In representing propositions by geometrical diagrams, our object is not that we may have a new set of symbols, but that the relation between the subject and predicate of a proposition may be exhibited by means of a sensible representation, the signification of which is clear at a glance. Hence the first requirement that ought to be satisfied by any diagrammatic scheme is that the interpretation of the diagrams should be intuitively obvious, as soon as the principle upon which they are based has been explained.[165]

A second essential requirement is that the diagrams should be adequate; that is to say, they should give a complete, and not a partial, representation of the relations which they are intended to indicate. Hamilton's use of Euler's diagrams, as described in the following section, will serve to illustrate the failure to satisfy this requirement.

In the third place, the diagrams should be capable of representing all the propositional forms recognised in the schedule of propositions which are to be illustrated, e.g., particulars as well as universal. One scheme of diagrams may, however, be better suited for one purpose, and another scheme for another purpose. It will be found that Dr. Venn's diagrams, to be described presently, are not quite so well adapted to the representation of particulars as of universals.

Lastly, it is advantageous that a diagrammatic scheme should be as little cumbrous as possible when it is desired to represent two or more propositions in combination with one another. This is the weak point of Euler's method. A scheme of diagrams may, however,

---

[165] Hamilton's "geometric scheme," which he himself describes as "easy, simple, compendious, all-sufficient, consistent, manifest, precise, complete" (*Logic*, II. p. 475), fails to satisfy this condition. He represents an affirmative copula by a horizontal tapering line (▬), the broad end of which is towards the subject. Negation is marked by a perpendicular line crossing the horizontal one (✦). A colon (:) placed at either end of the copula indicates that the corresponding term is distributed; a comma (,) that it is undistributed. Thus, for *All S is P* we have,—
S : ▬ , P;
and similarly for the other propositions.
Dr Venn rightly observes that this scheme is purely symbolical, and does not deserve to rank as a diagrammatic scheme at all. There is clearly nothing in the two ends of a wedge to suggest subjects and predicates, or in a colon and comma to suggest distribution and non-distribution" (*Symbolic Logic*, p. 432). Hamilton's scheme may certainly be rejected as valueless. The schemes of Euler and Lambert belong to an altogether different category.

serve a very useful function in making clear the full force of individual propositions, even when it is not well adapted for the representation of combined propositions.

A further requirement is sometimes added, namely, that each propositional form should be represented by a single diagram, not by a set of alternative diagrams. This is, however, by no means essential. For if we adopt a schedule of propositions some of which yield only an indeterminate relation in respect of extension between the terms involved, it is important that this should be clearly brought out, and a set of alternative diagrams may be specially helpful for the purpose. This point will be illustrated, with reference to Euler's diagrams, in the following section.[166]

126. *Euler's Diagrams.*—We may begin with the well-known scheme of diagrams, which was first expounded by the Swiss mathematician and logician, Leonhard Euler, and which is usually called after his name.[167]

Representing the individuals included in any class, or denoted by any name, by a circle, it will be obvious that the five following diagrams represent all possible relations between any two classes:—

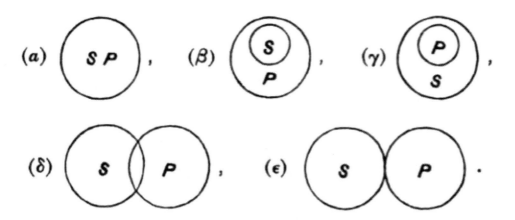

The force of the different propositional forms is to exclude one or more of these possibilities.

All S is P limits us to one of the two α, β;

Some S is P to one of the four $\alpha, \beta, \gamma, \delta$;

No S is P to ε;

Some S is not P to one of the three $\gamma, \delta, \varepsilon$.

It will be observed that there is great want of symmetry in the number of circles corresponding to the different propositional forms; also that there is an apparent inequality in the amount of information given by **A** and by **E**, and again by **I** and by **O**. We shall find that these anomalies disappear when account is taken of negative terms.

It is most misleading to attempt to represent *All S is P* by a single pair of circles, thus

---

[166] It must be borne in mind that in all the schemes described in this chapter the terms of the propositions which are represented diagrammatically are taken in extension, not in intension.

[167] Euler lived from 1707 to 1783. His diagrammatic scheme is given in his *Lettres à une Princesse d'Allemagne* (Letters 102 to 105).

or *Some S is P* by a single pair, thus

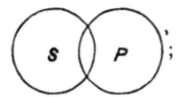

for in each case the proposition really leaves us with other alternatives. This method of employing the diagrams has, however, been adopted by a good many logicians who have used them, including Sir William Hamilton (*Logic*, I. p. 255), and Professor Jevons (*Elementary Lessons in Logic*, pp. 72 to 75); and the attempt at such simplification has brought their use into undeserved disrepute. Thus, Dr Venn remarks, "The common practice, adopted in so many manuals, of appealing to these diagrams—Eulerian diagrams as they are often called—seems to me very questionable. The old four propositions **A, E, I, O**, do not exactly correspond to the five diagrams, and consequently none of the moods in the syllogism can in strict propriety be represented by these diagrams" (*Symbolic Logic*, pp. 15, 16; compare also pp. 424, 425). This criticism, while perfectly sound as regards the use of Euler's circles by Hamilton and Jevons, loses most of its force if the diagrams are employed with due precautions. It is true that the diagrams become somewhat cumbrous in relation to the syllogism; but the logical force of propositions and the logical relations between propositions can in many respects be well illustrated by their aid. Thus, they may be employed:—

(1) To illustrate the distribution of the predicate in a proposition. In the case of each of the four fundamental propositions we may shade the part of the predicate concerning which information is given us.

We then have,—

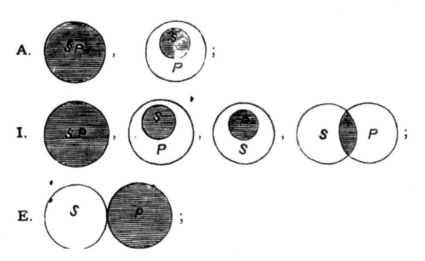

We see that with **A** and **I**, only part of *P* is in some of the cases shaded; whereas with **E** and **O**, the whole of *P* is in every case shaded; and it is thus made clear that negative propositions distribute, while affirmative propositions do not distribute, their predicates.

(2) To illustrate the opposition of propositions. Comparing two contradictory propositions, e.g., **A** and **O**, we see that they have no case in common, but that between them they exhaust all possible cases. Hence the truth, that two contradictory propositions cannot be true together but that one of them must be true, is brought home to us under a new aspect. Again, comparing two subaltern propositions, e.g., **A** and **I**, we notice that the former gives us all the information given by the latter and something more, since it still further limits the possibilities. The other relations involved in the doctrine of opposition may be illustrated similarly.

(3) To illustrate the conversion of propositions. Thus it is made clear by the diagrams how it is that **A** admits only of conversion *per accidens*. *All S is P* limits us to one or other of the following,—

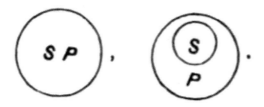

What then do we know of *P*? In the first case we have *All P is S*, in the second *Some P is S*; and since we are ignorant as to which of the two cases holds good, we can only state what is common to them both, namely, *Some P is S*.

Again, it is made clear how it is that **O** is inconvertible. *Some S is not P* limits us to one or other of the following,—

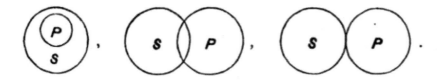

What then do we know concerning *P*? The three cases give us respectively,—(i) *All P is S*; (ii) *Some P is S* and *Some P is not S*; (iii) *No P is S*. But (i) and (iii) are inconsistent with one another. Hence nothing can be affirmed of *P* that is true in all three cases indifferently.

(4) To illustrate the more complicated forms of immediate inference. Taking, for example, the proposition *All S is P*, we may ask, What does this enable us to assert about *not-P* and *not-S* respectively? We have one or other of these cases,—

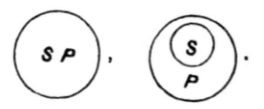

As regards *not-P*, these yield respectively (i) *No not-P is S*; (ii) *No not-P is S*. And thus we obtain the contrapositive of the given proposition.

As regards *not-S*, we have (i) *No not-S is P*, (ii) *Some not-S is P* and *some not-S is not P*.[168] Hence in either case we may infer *Some not-S is not P*.

E, I, O may be dealt with similarly.

(5) To illustrate the joint force of a pair of complementary or contra-complementary or sub-complementary propositions (compare section 100). Thus, the pair of complementary propositions, *SaP* and *PaS*, taken together, limit us to

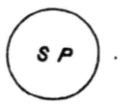

Similarly the pair of contra-complementary propositions, *SaP* and *PoS*, limit us to the relation marked β on page 158; and the pair of contra-complementary propositions, *SoP* and *PaS*, to γ; while the pair of sub-complementary propositions, *SoP* and *PoS*, give us a choice between δ and ε.

The application of the diagrams to syllogistic reasonings will be considered in a subsequent chapter.

With regard to all the above, it may be said that the use of the circles gives us nothing that could not easily have been obtained independently. This is of course true; but no one, who has had experience of the difficulty that is sometimes found by students in properly understanding the elementary principles of formal logic, and especially in dealing with immediate inferences, will despise any means of illustrating afresh the old truths, and presenting them under a new aspect.

The fact that we have not a single pair of circles corresponding to each fundamental form of proposition is fatal if we wish to illustrate any complicated train of reasoning in this way; but in indicating the real nature of the information given by the propositions themselves, it is rather an advantage than otherwise, inasmuch as it shews how limited in some cases this information actually is.[169]

---

[168] It is assumed in the use of Euler's diagrams that *S* and *P* both exist in the universe of discourse, while neither of them exhausts that universe. This assumption is the same as that upon which our treatment of immediate inferences in the preceding chapter has been based.

[169] Dr Venn writes in criticism of Euler's scheme, "A fourfold scheme of propositions will not very conveniently fit in with a fivefold scheme of diagrams... What the five diagrams are competent to illustrate is the actual relation of the classes, not our possibly imperfect knowledge of that relation" (*Empirical Logic*, p. 229). The reply to this criticism is that inasmuch as the fourfold scheme of propositions gives but an imperfect knowledge of the actual relation of the classes denoted by the terms, the Eulerian diagrams are specially valuable in making this clear and unmistakeable. By the aid of dotted lines it is indeed possible to represent each proposition by a single Eulerian figure; but the diagrams then become so much more difficult to interpret that the loss is considerably greater than the gain. The first and second of the following diagrams are borrowed from Ueberweg (*Logic*, § 71). In the case of **O**, Ueberweg's diagram is rather complicated; and I have substituted a simpler one.

127. *Lambert's Diagrams.*—A scheme of diagrams was employed by Lambert[170] in which horizontal straight lines take the place of Euler's circles. The extension of a term is represented by a horizontal straight line, and so far as two such lines overlap it is indicated that the corresponding classes are coincident, while so far as they do not overlap these classes are shewn to be mutually exclusive. Both the absolute and the relative length of the lines is of course arbitrary and immaterial.

We may first shew how Lambert's lines may be used in such a manner as to be precisely analogous to Euler's circles. Thus, the four fundamental propositions may be represented as follows:—

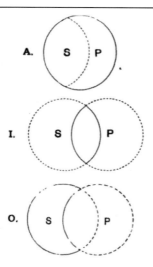

In the last of these diagrams we get the three cases yielded by an **O** proposition by (1) filling in the dotted line to the left and striking out the other, (2) filling in both dotted lines, (3) filling in the dotted line to the right and striking out the other. These three cases are respectively those marked γ, δ, ε.

[170] Johann Heinrich Lambert was a German philosopher and mathematician who lived from 1728 to 1777. His *Neues Organon* was published at Leipzig in 1768. Lambert's own diagrammatic scheme differs somewhat from both of those given in the text; but it very closely resembles the one in which portions of the lines are dotted. The modifications in the text have been introduced in order to obviate certain difficulties involved in Lambert's own diagrams. See note 2.

These diagrams occupy less space than Euler's circles. But they seem also to be less intuitively clear and less suggestive. The different cases too are less markedly distinct from one another. It is probable that one would in consequence be more liable to error in employing them.

The different cases may, however, be combined by the use of dotted lines so as to yield but a single diagram for each proposition much more satisfactorily than in Euler's scheme. Thus, *All S is P* may be represented by the diagram

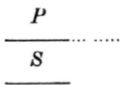

where the dotted line indicates that we are uncertain as to whether there is or is not any *P* which is not *S*. We obviously get two cases according as we strike out the dots or fill them in, and these are the two cases previously shewn to be compatible with an **A** proposition.

Again, *Some S is P* may be represented by the diagram

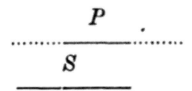

and here we get the four cases previously given for an **I** proposition by (*a*) filling in the dots to the left and striking out those to the right, (*b*) filling in all the dots, (*c*) striking them all out, (*d*) filling in those to the right and striking out those to the left.

Two complete schemes of diagrams may be constructed on this plan, in one of which no part of any *S* line, and in the other no part of any *P* line, is dotted.[171] These two schemes are given below to the left and right respectively of the propositional forms themselves.

It must be understood that the two diagrams given above in the cases of **A**, **I**, and **O** are alternative in the sense that we may select which we please to represent our proposition; but either represents it completely.

We shall find later on that for the purpose of illustrating the syllogistic moods, Lambert's method is a good deal less cumbrous than Euler's.[172] An adaptation of Lambert's diagrams in

---

[171] It is important to give both these schemes as it will be found that neither one of them will by itself suffice when this method is used for illustrating the syllogism. For obvious reasons the **E** diagram is the same in both schemes.

[172] Dr Venn (*Symbolic Logic*, p. 432) remarks, "As a whole Lambert's scheme seems to me distinctly inferior to the scheme of Euler, and has in consequence been very little employed by other logicians." The criticism offered in support of this statement is directed chiefly against Lambert's own representation of the particular affirmative proposition, namely,

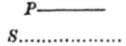

which the contradictories of S and P are introduced as well as S and P themselves will be given in section 131. This more elaborated scheme will be found useful for illustrating the various processes of immediate inference.

$$
\begin{array}{c}
\left.\begin{array}{c} \dfrac{P}{} \\ \dfrac{}{S} \\ \underline{} \end{array}\right\} \text{All } S \text{ is } P \qquad \left\{\begin{array}{c} \dfrac{P}{} \\ \dfrac{}{S} \\ \underline{} \cdots \end{array}\right. \\[2em]
\left.\begin{array}{c} \dfrac{P}{} \\ \cdots \dfrac{}{S} \cdots \\ \underline{} \end{array}\right\} \text{Some } S \text{ is } P \qquad \left\{\begin{array}{c} \dfrac{P}{} \\ \dfrac{}{S} \\ \cdots \underline{} \end{array}\right. \\[2em]
\left.\begin{array}{c} \dfrac{P}{} \\ \dfrac{}{S} \\ \underline{} \end{array}\right\} \text{No } S \text{ is } P \qquad \left\{\begin{array}{c} \dfrac{P}{} \\ \dfrac{}{S} \\ \underline{} \end{array}\right. \\[2em]
\left.\begin{array}{c} \dfrac{P}{} \\ \cdots \dfrac{}{S} \\ \underline{} \end{array}\right\} \text{Some } S \text{ is not } P \qquad \left\{\begin{array}{c} \dfrac{P}{} \\ \dfrac{}{S} \\ \underline{} \cdots \end{array}\right.
\end{array}
$$

128. *Dr Venn's Diagrams*.—In the diagrammatic scheme employed by Dr Venn (*Symbolic Logic*, chapter 5) the diagram

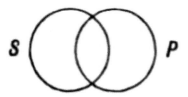

does not itself represent any proposition, but the framework into which propositions may be fitted. Denoting *not-S* by *S'* and what is both *S* and *P* by *SP*, &c., it is clear that everything must be contained in one or other of the four classes *SP*, *SP'*, *S'P*, *S'P'*; and the above diagram shews four compartments (one being that which lies outside both the circles) corresponding to these four classes. Every universal proposition denies the existence of one or more of such classes, and it may therefore be diagrammatically represented by shading out the corresponding compartment or compartments. Thus, *All S is P*, which denies the existence of *SP'*, is represented by

---

This diagram certainly seems as appropriate to **O** as it does to **I**; but the modification introduced in the text, and indeed suggested by Dr Venn himself, is not open to a similar objection.

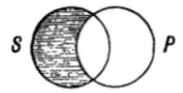

No S is P by

With three terms we have three circles and eight compartments, thus,—

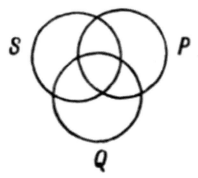

All S is P or Q is represented by

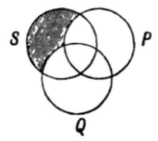

All S is P and Q by

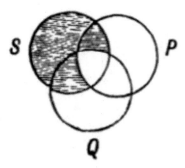

It is in cases involving three or more terms that the advantage of this scheme over the Eulerian scheme is most manifest. The diagrams are not, however, quite so well adapted to the case of particular propositions. Dr Venn (in *Mind*, 1883, pp. 599, 600) suggests that we might draw a bar across the compartment declared to be saved by a particular proposition;[173] thus, *Some S is P* would be represented by drawing a bar across the *SP* compartment. This plan can be worked out satisfactorily; but in representing a combination of propositions in this way special care is needed in the interpretation of the diagrams. For example, if we have the diagram for three terms *S, P, Q*, and are given *Some S is P*, we do not know that *both* the compartments *SPQ*, *SPQ'*, are to be saved, and in a case like this a bar drawn across the *SP* compartment is in some danger of misinterpretation.

129. *Expression of the possible relations between any two classes by means of the propositional forms* **A, E, I, O.**—Any information given with respect to two classes limits the possible relations between them to something less than the five *à priori* possibilities indicated diagrammatically by Euler's circles as given at the beginning of section 126. It will be useful to enquire how such information may in all cases be expressed by means of the propositional forms **A, E, I, O**.

The five relations may, as before, be designated respectively $\alpha, \beta, \gamma, \delta, \varepsilon$.[174] Information is given when the possibility of one or more of these is denied; in other words, when we are limited to one, two, three, or four of them. Let limitation to α, or β, the exclusion of $\gamma, \delta, \varepsilon$ be denoted by α, β; limitation to α, β, or γ (i.e., the exclusion of δ and ε) by α, β, γ; and so on.

In seeking to express our information by means of the four ordinary propositional forms, we find that sometimes a single proposition will suffice for our purpose; thus α, β is expressed by *All S is P*. Sometimes we require a combination of propositions; thus α is expressed by the pair of complementary propositions *All S is P and all P is S*, (since *all S is P* excludes $\gamma, \delta, \varepsilon$, and *all P is S* further excludes β). Some other cases are more complicated; thus the fact that we are limited to α or δ cannot be expressed more simply than by saying, *Either All S is P and all P is S, or else Some S is P, some S is not P, and some P is not S*.

Let **A** = *All S is P*, **A**$_1$ = *All P is S*, and similarly for the other propositions. Also let **AA**$_1$ = *All S is P and all P is S*, &c. Then the following is a scheme for all possible cases:—

---

[173] Dr Venn's scheme differs from the schemes of Euler and Lambert, in that it is not based upon the assumption that our terms and their contradictories all represent existing classes. It involves, however, the doctrine that particulars are existentially affirmative, while universals are existentially negative.

[174] Thus, the classes being *S* and *P*, α denotes that *S* and *P* are wholly coincident; β that *P* contains *S* and more besides; β that *S* contains *P* and more besides; δ that *S* and *P* overlap each other, but that each includes something not included by the other; ε that *S* and *P* have nothing whatever in common.

Limitation to	Denoted By	Limitation To	Denoted By
α	AA_1	α, β, γ	A or A_1
β	AO_1	α, β, δ	A or IO_1
γ	A_1O	$\alpha, \beta, \varepsilon$	A or E
δ	IOO_1	α, γ, δ	A_1 or IO
ε	E	$\alpha, \gamma, \varepsilon$	A_1 or E
α, β	A	$\alpha, \delta, \varepsilon$	AA_1 or OO_1
α, γ	A_1	β, γ, δ	IO or IO_1
α, δ	AA_1 or IOO_1	$\beta, \gamma, \varepsilon$	AO_1 or A_1O or E
α, ε	AA_1 or E	$\beta, \delta, \varepsilon$	O_1
β, γ	AO_1 or A_1O	$\gamma, \delta, \varepsilon$	O
β, δ	IO_1	$\alpha, \beta, \gamma, \delta$	I
β, ε	AO_1 or E	$\alpha, \beta, \gamma, \varepsilon$	A or A_1 or E
γ, δ	IO	$\alpha, \beta, \delta, \varepsilon$	A or O_1
γ, ε	A_1O or E	$\alpha, \gamma, \delta, \varepsilon$	A_1 or O
δ, ε	OO_1	$\beta, \gamma, \delta, \varepsilon$	O or O_1

It will be found that any combinations of propositions other than those given above either involve contradictions or redundancies, or else give no information because all the five relations that are *à priori* possible still remain possible.

For example, **AI** is clearly redundant; **AO** is self-contradictory; **A** or **A₁O** is redundant (since the same information is given by **A** or **A₁**); **A** or **O** gives no information (since it excludes no possible case). The student is recommended to test other combinations similarly. It must be remembered that $I_1 = I$, and $E_1 = E$.

It should be noticed that if we read the first column downwards and the second column upwards we get pairs of contradictories.

130. *Euler's diagrams and the class relations between S, not-S, P, not-P.*—In Euler's diagrams, as ordinarily given, there is no explicit recognition of *not-S* and *not-P*; but it is of course understood that whatever part of the universe lies outside *S* is *not-S*, and similarly for *P*, and it may be thought that no further account of negative terms need be taken. Further consideration, however, will shew that this is not the case; and, assuming that *S, not-S, P, not-P* all represent existing classes, we shall find that *seven*, not five, determinate class relations between them are possible.

Taking the diagrams given in section 126, the above assumption clearly requires that in the cases of α, β, and γ, there should be some part of the universe lying outside both the circles, since otherwise either *not-S* or *not-P* or both of them would no longer be contained in the universe. But in the cases of δ and ε it is different. S, not-S, P, not-P are now all of them represented within the circles; and in each of these cases, therefore, the pair of circles may or may not between them exhaust the universe.

Our results may also be expressed by saying that in the cases of α, β, and γ, there must be something which is both *not-S* and *not-P*; whereas in the cases of δ and ε, there may or may not be something which is both *not-S* and *not-P*. Euler's circles, as ordinarily used, are no doubt a little apt to lead us to overlook the latter of these alternatives. If, indeed, there were always part of the universe outside the circles, every proposition, whether its form were **A**, **E**, **I**, or **O**, would have an inverse and the same inverse, namely, *Some not-S is not-P*; also, every proposition, including **I**, would have a contrapositive. These are erroneous results against which we have to be on our guard in the use of Euler's fivefold scheme.

We find then that the explicit recognition of *not-S* and *not-P* practically leaves α, β, and γ unaffected, but causes δ and ε each to subdivide into two cases according as there is or is not anything that is both *not-S* and *not-P*; and the Eulerian fivefold division has accordingly to give place to a sevenfold division.

In the diagrammatic representation of these seven relations, the entire universe of discourse may be indicated by a larger circle in which the ordinary Eulerian diagrams (with some slight necessary modifications) are included. We shall then have the following scheme:—

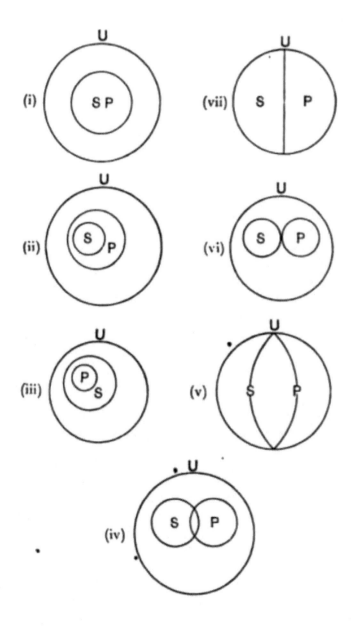

It may be useful to repeat these diagrams with an explicit indication in regard to each subdivision of the universe as to whether it is *S* or *not-S*, *P* or *not-P*.[175] The scheme will then appear as follows:—

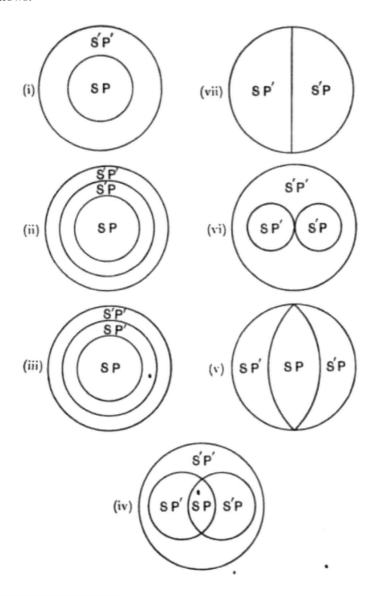

---

[175] We might also represent the universe of discourse by a long rectangle divided into compartments, shewing which of the four possible combinations *SP*, *SP'*, *S'P*, *S'P'* are to be found. This plan will give the following which precisely correspond, as numbered, with those in the text:—

(i)	*SP*		*S'P'*	
(ii)	*SP*	*S'P*		*S'P'*
(iii)	*SP*	*SP'*		*S'P*
(iv)	*SP*	*SP'*	*S'P*	*S'P'*
(v)	*SP*	*SP'*		*S'P*
(vi)	*SP'*	*S'P*		*S'P'*
(vii)	*SP'*		*S'P*	

Comparing the above with the five ordinary Eulerian diagrams (which may be designated α, β &c. as in section 126), it will be seen that (i) corresponds to α; (ii) to β; (iii) to γ; (iv) and (v) represent the two cases now yielded by δ; (vi) and (vii) the two yielded by ε.

Our seven diagrams might also be arrived at as follows:—Every part of the universe must be either S or S', and also P or P'; and hence the mutually exclusive combinations SP, SP', $S'P$, $S'P'$ must between them exhaust the universe. The case in which these combinations are all to be found is represented by diagram (iv); if one but one only is absent we obviously have four cases which are represented respectively by (ii), (iii), (v), and (vi); if only two are to be found it will be seen that we are limited to the cases represented by (i) and (vii) or we should not fulfil the condition that neither S nor S', P nor P', is to be altogether non-existent; for the same reason the universe cannot contain less than two of the four combinations. We thus have the seven cases represented by the diagrams, and these are shewn to exhaust the possibilities.

The four traditional propositions are related to the new scheme as follows:—

A limits us to (i) or (ii);
I to (i), (ii), (iii), (iv), or (v);
E to (vi) or (vii);
O to (iii), (iv), (v), (vi), or (vii).

Working out the further question how each diagram taken by itself is to be expressed propositionally we get the following results:

(i) SaP and $S'aP'$;
(ii) SaP and $S'oP'$;
(iii) $S'aP'$ and SoP;
(iv) SoP, SoP', $S'oP$, and $S'oP'$;
(v) $S'aP$ and SoP';
(vi) SaP' and $S'oP$;
(vii) SaP' and $S'aP$.

It will be observed that the new scheme is in itself more symmetrical than Euler's, and also that it succeeds better in bringing out the symmetry of the fourfold schedule of propositions.[176] **A** and **E** give two alternatives each, **I** and **O** give five each; whereas with Euler's scheme **E** gives only one alternative, **A** two, **O** three, **I** four, and it might, therefore, seem as if **E** afforded more definite and unambiguous information than **A**, and **O** than **I**, which is not really the case. Further, the problem of expressing each diagram propositionally yields a more symmetrical result than the corresponding problem in the case of Euler's diagrams.

This sevenfold scheme of class relations should be compared with the sevenfold scheme of relations between propositions given in section 84.

131. *Lambert's diagram and the class-relations between S, not-S, P, not-P.*—The following is a compact diagrammatic representation of the seven possible class-relations between *S, not-S, P, not-P*, based upon Lambert's scheme.

---

[176] We have seen that, similarly, in the case of immediate inferences symmetry can be gained only by the recognition of negative terms.

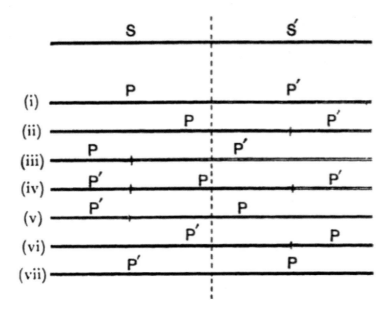

In this scheme each line represents the entire universe of discourse, and the first line must be taken in connection with each of the others in turn. Further explanation will be unnecessary for the student who clearly understands the Lambertian method.

On the same principle and with the aid of dotted lines the four fundamental propositional forms may be represented as follows:

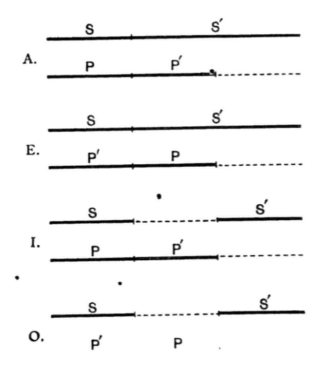

In each case the full extent of a line represents the entire universe of discourse; any portion of a line that is dotted may be either S or S' (or P or P', as the case may be).

This last scheme of diagrams is perhaps more useful than any of the others in shewing at a glance what immediate inferences are obtainable from each proposition by conversion, contraposition, and inversion (on the assumption that S, S', P, and P' all represent existing classes). Thus, from the first diagram we can read off at a glance *SaP*, *PiS*, *P'aS'*, *S'iP'*; from the second *SeP*, *PeS*, *P'oS'*, *S'oP'*; from the third *SiP* and *PiS*; and from the fourth *SoP* and *P'oS'*. The last two diagrams are also seen at a glance to be indeterminate in respect to P' and S', P and S', respectively (that is to say, **I** has no contrapositive and no inverse, **O** has no converse and no inverse).

EXERCISES

132. Illustrate by means of the Eulerian diagrams (1) the relation between **A** and **E**, (2) the relation between **I** and **O**, (3) the conversion of **I**, (4) the contraposition of **O**, (5) the inversion of **E**.   [K.]

133. *A* denies that none but *X* are *Y*; *B* denies that none but *Y* are *X*. Which of the five class relations between *X* and *Y* (1) must they agree in rejecting, (2) may they agree in accepting?   [C.]

134. Take all the ordinary propositions connecting any two terms, combine them in pairs so far as is possible without contradiction, and represent each combination diagrammatically.
                                                                                                                                                                    [J.]

Chapter 10

PROPOSITIONS IN EXTENSION AND IN INTENSION

135. *Fourfold Implication of Propositions in Connotation and Denotation.*—In dealing with the question whether propositions assert a relation between objects or between attributes or between objects and attributes, logicians have been apt to commit the fallacy of exclusiveness, selecting some one of the given alternatives, and treating the others as necessarily excluded thereby. It follows, however, from the double aspect of names—in extension and intension—that the different relations really involve one another, so that all of them are implied in any categorical proposition whose subject and predicate are both general names.[177] If any one of the relations is selected as constituting the *meaning* of the proposition, the other relations are at any rate involved as *implications*.

The problem will be made more definite if we confine ourselves to a consideration of *connotation* and *denotation* in the strict sense, as distinguished from comprehension and exemplification, our terms being supposed to be defined intensively.[178] Both subject and predicate will then have a denotation determined by their connotation, and hence our proposition may be considered from four different points of view, which are not indeed really independent of one another, but which serve to bring different aspects of the proposition into prominence. (1) The subject may be read in denotation and the predicate in connotation; (2) both terms may be read in denotation; (3) both terms may be read in connotation; (4) the subject may be read in connotation and the predicate in denotation.

As an example, we may take the proposition, *All men are mortal.*[179] According to our point of view, this proposition may be read in any of the following ways:

(1) The objects denoted by *man* possess the attributes connoted by *mortal*;

(2) The objects denoted by *man* are included within the class of objects denoted by *mortal*;

---

[177] In the discussion that follows we limit ourselves to the traditional scheme of propositions.

[178] With extensive definitions we might similarly work out the relations between the terms of a proposition in exemplification and comprehension; and with either intensive or extensive definitions, we might consider them in denotation and comprehension. The discussion in the text will, however, be limited to connotation and denotation, except that a separate section will be devoted to the case in which both subject and predicate are read in comprehension.

[179] A distinction may perhaps be drawn between the four following types of propositions; (*a*) *All men are mortal*; (*b*) *All men are mortals*; (*c*) *Man is mortal*; (*d*) *Man is a mortal*. Of these, (*a*) naturally suggests the reading of subject in denotation and predicate in connotation as *meaning*, the three other readings being *implications*; (*b*) is similarly related to the reading numbered (2) above; (*c*) to (3); and (*d*) to (4).

(3) The attributes connoted by *man* are accompanied by the attributes connoted by *mortal*;

(4) The attributes connoted by *man* indicate the presence of an object belonging to the class denoted by *mortal*.

It should be specially noticed that a different relation between subject and predicate is brought out in each of these four modes of analysing the proposition, the relations being respectively (i) *possession*, (ii) *inclusion*, (iii) *concomitance*, (iv) *indication*.

It may very reasonably be argued that a certain one of the above ways of regarding the proposition is (*a*) psychologically the most prominent in the mind in predication; or (*b*) the most fundamental in the sense of making explicit that relation which ultimately determines the other relations; or (*c*) the most convenient for a given purpose, e.g., for dealing with the problems of formal logic. We need not, however, select the same mode of interpretation in each case. There would, for example, be nothing inconsistent in holding that to read the subject in denotation and the predicate in connotation is most correct from the psychological standpoint; to read both terms in connotation the most ultimate, inasmuch as connotation determines denotation and not *vice versâ*, and to read both terms in denotation the most serviceable for purposes of logical manipulation. To say, however, that a certain one of the four readings alone can be regarded as constituting the import of the proposition to the exclusion of the others cannot but be erroneous. They are in truth so much implicated in one another, that the difficulty may rather be to justify a treatment which distinguishes between them.[180]

(1) *Subject in denotation, predicate in connotation.*

If we read the subject of a proposition in denotation and the predicate in connotation, we have what is sometimes called the *predicative mode* of interpreting the proposition. This way of regarding propositions most nearly corresponds in the great majority of cases with the course of ordinary thought;[181] that is to say, we naturally contemplate the subject as a class of objects of which a certain attribute or complex of attributes is predicated. Such propositions as *All men are mortal, Some violets are white, All diamonds are combustible*, may be taken as examples. Dr Venn puts the point very clearly with reference to the last of these three propositions: "If I say that 'all diamonds are combustible,' I am joining together two connotative terms, each of which, therefore, implies an attribute and denotes a class; but is there not a broad distinction in respect of the prominence with which the notion of a class is presented to the mind in the two cases? As regards the diamond, we think at once, or think very speedily, of a class of things, the distinctive attributes of the subject being mainly used to carry the mind on to the contemplation of the objects referred to by them. But as regards the combustibility, the attribute itself is the prominent thing ... Combustible *things*, other than the diamond itself, come scarcely, if at all, under contemplation. The assertion in itself does not cause us to raise a thought whether there be other combustible things than these in existence" (*Empirical Logic*, p. 219).

---

[180] The true doctrine is excellently stated by Mrs Ladd Franklin in an article in *Mind*, October, 1890, pp. 561, 2.

[181] Though perhaps what is actually present to the mind is usually rather more complex than what is represented by any one of the four readings taken by itself.

Two points may be noticed as serving to confirm the view that generally speaking the predicative mode of interpreting propositions is psychologically the most prominent:

(*a*) The most striking difference between a substantive and an attributive (i.e., an adjective or a participle) from the logical point of view is that in the former the denotation is usually more prominent than the connotation, even though it may be ultimately determined by the connotation, whilst in the latter the connotation is the more prominent, even though the name must be regarded as the name of a class of objects if it is entitled to be called a *name* in the strict logical sense at all. Corresponding to this we find that the subject of a proposition is almost always a substantive, whereas the predicate is more often an attributive.

(*b*) It is always the denotation of a term that we quantify, never the connotation. Whether we talk of *all men* or of *some men*, the complex of attributes connoted by *man* is taken in its totality; the distinction of quantity relates entirely to the denotation of the term. Corresponding to this, we find that we naturally regard the *quantity* of a proposition as pertaining to its *subject*, and not to its predicate. It will be shown in the following chapter that the doctrine of the quantification of the predicate has at any rate no psychological justification.

There are, however, numerous exceptions to the statement that the subject of a proposition is naturally read in denotation and the predicate in connotation; for example, in the classificatory sciences. The following propositions may be taken as instances: *All palms are endogens, All daisies are compositae, None but solid bodies are crystals, Hindoos are Aryans, Tartars are Turanians*. In such cases as these most of us would naturally think of a certain class of objects as included in or excluded from another class rather than as possessing or not possessing certain definite attributes; in other words, as Dr Venn puts it, "the class-reference of the predicate is no less definite than that of the subject" (*Empirical Logic*, p. 220). In the case of such a proposition as *No plants with opposite leaves are orchids*, the position is even reversed, that is to say, it is the subject rather than the predicate that we should more naturally read in connotation. We may pass on then to other ways of regarding the categorical proposition.

(2) *Subject in denotation, predicate in denotation.*

If we read both the subject and the predicate of a proposition in denotation, we have a relation between two classes, and hence this is called the *class mode* of interpreting the proposition. It must be particularly observed that the relation between the subject and the predicate is now one of *inclusion in* or *exclusion from*, not one of *possession*. It may at once be admitted that the class mode of interpreting the categorical proposition is neither the most ultimate, nor—generally speaking—that which we naturally or spontaneously adopt. It is, however, extremely convenient for manipulative purposes, and hence is the mode of interpretation usually selected, either explicitly or implicitly, by the formal logician. Attention may be specially called to the following points:

(*a*) When subject and predicate are both read in denotation, they are *homogeneous*.

(*b*) In the *diagrammatic* illustration of propositions both subject and predicate are necessarily read in denotation, since it is the denotation—not the connotation—of a term that we represent by means of a diagram.

(*c*) The predicate of a proposition must be read in denotation in order to give a meaning to the question whether it is or is not *distributed*.

(*d*) The predicate as well as the subject must be read in denotation before such a process as *conversion* is possible.

(*e*) In the treatment of the *syllogism* both subject and predicate must be read in denotation (or else both in connotation), since either the middle term (first and fourth figures) or the major term (second and fourth figures) or the minor term (third and fourth figures) is subject in one of the propositions in which it occurs and predicate in the other.

The class mode of interpreting categorical propositions is nevertheless treated by some writers as being positively erroneous. But the arguments used in support of this view will not bear examination.

(i) It is said that to read both subject and predicate in denotation is psychologically false. It has indeed been pointed out already that the class mode of interpretation is not that which as a rule first presents itself to our mind when a proposition is given us; but we have also seen that there are exceptions to this, as, for example, in the propositions *All daisies are compositae. All Hindoos are Aryan, All Tartars are Turanians.* It is, therefore, clearly wrong to describe the reading in question as in all cases psychologically false. On the same shewing, any other reading would equally be psychologically false, for what is immediately present to the mind in judgment varies very much in different cases. Undoubtedly there are many judgments in regard to which we do not spontaneously adopt the class reading. Still, analysis shews that in these judgments, as in others, inclusion in or exclusion from a class is really implicated along with other things, although this relation may be neither that which first impresses itself upon us nor that which is most important or characteristic.

(ii) It is asked what we mean by a class, by the class of birds, for example, when we say *All owls are birds.* "It is nothing existing in space; the birds of the world are nowhere collected together so that we can go and pick out the owls from amongst them. The classification is a mental abstraction of our own, founded upon the possession of certain definite attributes. The class is not definite and fixed, and we do not find out whether any individual belongs to it by going over a list of its members, but by enquiring whether it possesses the necessary attributes."[182] In so far as this argument applies against reading the predicate in denotation, it applies equally against reading the subject in denotation. It is in effect the argument used by Mill (*Logic*, i. 5, § 3) in order to lead up to his position that the *ultimate* interpretation of the categorical proposition requires us to read both subject and predicate in connotation, since denotation is determined by connotation. But if this be granted, it does not prove the class reading of the proposition erroneous; it only proves that in the class reading, the analysis of the import of the proposition has not been carried as far as it admits of being carried.

(iii) It is argued that when we regard a proposition as expressing the inclusion of one class within another, even then the predicate is only apparently read in denotation. "On this view, we do not really assert *P* but 'inclusion in *P*,' and this is therefore the true predicate. For example, in the proposition 'All owls are birds,' the real predicate is, on this view, not 'birds' but 'included in the class birds.' But this inclusion is an attribute of the subject, and the real predicate, therefore, asserts an attribute. It is meaningless to say 'Every owl *is* the class birds,' and it is false to say 'The class owls *is* the class birds.'"[183] This argument simply begs the question in favour of the predicative mode of interpretation. It overlooks the fact that the precise kind of relation brought out in the analysis of a proposition will vary according to the way in which we read the subject and the predicate. An analogous argument might also be

---

[182] Welton, *Logic*.
[183] Welton, *Logic*.

used against the predicative reading itself. Take the proposition, "All men are mortal." It is absurd to say that "Every man *is* the attribute mortality," or that "The class men *is* the attribute mortality."

(iv) It is said that a class interpretation of both *S* and *P* would lead properly to a fivefold, not a fourfold, scheme of propositions, since there are just five relations possible between any two classes, as is shewn by the Eulerian diagrams. This contention has force, however, only upon the assumption that we must have quite determinate knowledge of the class relation between *S* and *P* before being able to make any statement on the subject; and this assumption is neither justifiable in itself nor necessarily involved in the interpretation in question. It may be added that if a similar view were taken on the adoption of the predicative mode of interpretation, we should have a threefold, not a fourfold scheme. For then the quantity of our subject at any rate would have to be perfectly determinate, and with *S* and *P* for subject and predicate, the three possible statements would be—*All S is P, Some S is P and some is not, No S is P*. The point here raised will presently be considered further in connection with the quantification of the predicate.

(3) *Subject in connotation, predicate in connotation.*

If we read both the subject and the predicate of a proposition in connotation, we have what may be called the *connotative mode* of interpreting the proposition. In the proposition *All S is P*, the relation expressed between the attributes connoted by *S* and those connoted by *P* is one of *concomitance*—"the attributes which constitute the connotation of *S* are always found accompanied by those which constitute the connotation of *P*."[184] Similarly, in the case of *Some S is P*,—"the attributes which constitute the connotation of *S* are sometimes found accompanied by those which constitute the connotation of *P*"; *No S is P*,—"the attributes which constitute the connotation of *S* are never found along with those which constitute the connotation of *P*"; *Some S is not P*,—"the attributes which constitute the connotation of *S* are sometimes found unaccompanied by those which constitute the connotation of *P*."

---

[184] This is the only possible reading in connotation, so far as real propositions are concerned, if the term connotation is used in the strict sense as distinguished both from subjective intension and from comprehension. Unfortunately confusion is apt to be introduced into discussions concerning the intensive rendering of propositions simply because no clear distinction is drawn between the different points of view which may be taken when terms are regarded from the intensive side. Hamilton distinguished between judgments in extension and judgments in intension, the relation between the subject and the predicate in the one case being just the reverse of the relation between them in the other. Thus, taking the proposition *All S is P*, we have in extension *S is contained under P*, and in intension *S comprehends P*. On this view the intensive reading of *All men are mortal* is "mortality is part of humanity" (the extensive reading being "the class man is part of the class mortal"). This reading may be accepted if the term intension is used in the objective sense which we have given to *comprehension*, so that by *humanity* is meant the totality of attributes common to all men, and by *mortality* the totality of attributes common to all mortals. To this point of view we shall return in the next section. Leaving it for the present on one side, it is clear that if by *humanity* we mean only what may be called the distinctive or essential attributes of man, then in order that the above reading may be correct, the given proposition must be regarded as analytical. In other words, if *humanity* signifies only those attributes which are included in the connotation of *man*, then, if mortality is included in humanity, we shall merely have to analyse the connotation of the name *man*, in order to obtain our proposition. Hence on this view it must either be maintained that all universal affirmative propositions are analytical, or else that some universal affirmatives cannot be read in intension. But obviously the first of these alternatives must be rejected, and the second practically means that the reading in question breaks down so far as universal affirmatives are concerned.

Hamilton's reading breaks down even more completely in the case of particulars and negatives. *The attributes constituting the intensions of S and P partly coincide* is clearly not equivalent to *Some S is P*; for example, the intension (in any sense) of *Englishman* has something in common with the intension of *Frenchman*, but it does not follow that *Some Englishmen are Frenchmen*. Again, from the fact that the intension of *S* has nothing in common with the intension of *P*, we cannot infer that *No S is P*; suppose, for example, that *S* stands for "ruminant," and *P* for "cloven-hoofed." Compare Venn, *Symbolic Logic*, pp. 391–5.

It will be noticed that in the connotative reading we have always to take the attributes which constitute the connotation *collectively*. In other words, by the attributes constituting the connotation of a term we mean those attributes regarded as a whole. Thus, *No S is P* does not imply that none of the attributes connoted by *S* are ever accompanied by any of those connoted by *P*. This is apparent if we take such a proposition as *No oxygen is hydrogen*. It follows that when the subject is read in connotation the quantity of the proposition must appear as a separate element, being expressed by the word "always" or "sometimes," and must not be interpreted as meaning "all" or "some" of the attributes included in the connotation of the subject.

It is argued by those who deny the possibility of the connotative mode of interpreting propositions, that this is not really reading the subject in connotation at all; *always* and *sometimes* are said to reduce us to denotation at once. In reply to this, it must of course be allowed that real propositions affirm no relation between attributes independently of the objects to which they belong. The connotative reading implies the denotative, and we must not exaggerate the nature of the distinction between them. Still the connotative reading presents the import of the proposition in a new aspect, and there is at any rate a *prima facie* difference between regarding one class as included within another, and regarding one attribute as always accompanied by another, even though a little consideration may shew that the two things mutually involve one another.[185]

(4) *Subject in connotation, predicate in denotation.*

Taking the proposition *All S is P*, and reading the subject in connotation and the predicate in denotation, we have, "The attributes connoted by *S* are an indication of the presence of an individual belonging to the class *P*." This mode of interpretation is always a possible one, but it must be granted that only rarely does the import of a proposition naturally present itself to our minds in this form. There are, however, exceptional cases in which this reading is not unnatural. The proposition *No plants with opposite leaves are orchids* has already been given as an example. Another example is afforded by the proposition *All that glitters is not gold*. Taking the subject in connotation and the predicate in denotation we have, *The attribute of glitter does not always indicate the presence of a gold object*; and it will be found that this reading of the proverb serves to bring out its meaning really better than any of the three other readings which we have been discussing.

It is worth while noticing here by way of anticipation that on any view of the existential interpretation of propositions, as discussed in chapter 8, we shall still have a fourfold reading of categorical propositions in connotation and denotation. The universal negative and the particular affirmative may be taken as examples, on the supposition that the former is interpreted as existentially negative and the latter as existentially affirmative. The universal negative yields the following: (1) There is no individual belonging to the class *S* and possessing the attributes connoted by *P*; (2) There is no individual common to the two classes *S* and *P*; (3) The attributes connoted by *S* and *P* respectively are never found conjoined; (4)

---

[185] Mill attaches great importance to the connotative mode of interpreting propositions as compared with the class mode or the predicative mode, on the ground that it carries the analysis a stage further; and this must be granted, at any rate so far as we consider the application of the terms involved to be determined by connotation and not by exemplification. Mill is, however, sometimes open to the charge of exaggerating the difference between the various modes of interpretation. This is apparent, for example, in his rejection of the *Dictum de omni et nullo* as the axiom of the syllogism, and his acceptance of the *Nota notae est nota rei ipsius* in its place.

There is no individual possessing the attributes connoted by *S* and belonging to the class *P*. Similarly the particular affirmative yields: (1) There are individuals belonging to the class *S* and possessing the attributes connoted by *P*; (2) There are individuals common to the two classes *S* and *P*; (3) The attributes connoted by *S* and *P* respectively are sometimes found conjoined; (4) There are individuals possessing the attributes connoted by *S* and belonging to the class *P*. We see, therefore, that the question discussed in this section is independent of that which will be raised in chapter 8; and that for this reason, if for no other, no solution of the general problem raised in the present chapter can afford a complete solution of the problem of the import of categorical propositions.

136. *The Reading of Propositions in Comprehension.*—If, in taking the intensional standpoint, we consider comprehension instead of connotation, our problem is to determine what relation is implied in any proposition between the comprehension of the subject and the comprehension of the predicate. This question being asked with reference to the universal affirmative proposition *All S is P*, the solution clearly is that *the comprehension of S includes the comprehension of P*. The interpretation in comprehension is thus precisely the reverse of that in denotation (*the denotation of S is included in the denotation of P*); and we might be led to think that, taking the different propositional forms, we should have a scheme in comprehension, analogous throughout to that in denotation. But this is not the case, for the simple reason that in our ordinary statements we do not distributively quantify comprehension in the way in which we do denotation; in other words, comprehension is always taken in its totality. Thus, reading an **I** proposition in denotation we have—*the classes S and P partly coincide*; and corresponding to this we should have—*the comprehensions of S and P partly coincide*. But this is clearly not what we express by *Some S is P*; for the partial coincidence of the comprehensions of *S* and *P* is quite compatible with *No S is P*, that is to say, the classes *S* and *P* may be mutually exclusive, and yet some attributes may be common to the whole of *S* and also to the whole of *P*; for example, *No Pembroke undergraduates are also Trinity undergraduates*. Again, given an **E** proposition, we have in denotation—*the classes S and P have no part in common*; but for the reason just given, it does not follow that *the comprehension of S and the comprehension of P have nothing in common*.

It is indeed necessary to obvert **I** and **E** in order to obtain a correct reading in comprehension. We then have the following scheme, in which the relation of contradiction between **A** and **O** and between **E** and **I** is made clearly manifest:

All S is P, The comprehension of *S* includes the comprehension of *P*;
No S is P, The comprehension of *S* includes the comprehension of *not-P*;
Some S is P, The comprehension of *S* does not include the comprehension of *not-P*;
Some S is not P, The comprehension of *S* does not include the comprehension of *P*.

Chapter 11

LOGICAL EQUATIONS AND THE QUANTIFICATION OF THE PREDICATE

137. *The employment of the symbol of Equality in Logic.*—The symbol of equality (=) is frequently used in logic to express the identity of two classes. For example,

Equilateral triangles = equiangular triangles;
Exogens = dicotyledons;
Men = mortal men.

It is, however, important to recognise that in thus borrowing a symbol from mathematics we do not retain its meaning unaltered, and that a so-called *logical equation* is, therefore, something very different from a mathematical equation. In mathematics the symbol of equality generally means numerical or quantitative equivalence. But clearly we do not mean to express mere numerical equality when we write *equilateral triangles = equiangular triangles*. Whatever this so-called equation signifies, it is certainly something more than that there are precisely as many triangles with three equal sides as there are triangles with three equal angles. It is further clear that we do not intend to express mere similarity. Our meaning is that the denotations of the terms which are equated are absolutely identical; in other words, that the class of objects denoted by the term *equilateral triangle* is absolutely identical with the class of objects denoted by the term *equiangular triangle*.[186] It may, however, be objected that, if this is what our equation comes to, then inasmuch as a statement of mere identity is empty and meaningless, it strictly speaking leaves us with nothing at all; it contains no assertion and can represent no judgment. The answer to this objection is that whilst we have identity in a certain respect, it is erroneous to say that we have *mere* identity. We have *identity of denotation* combined with *diversity of connotation*, and, therefore, with *diversity of determination* (meaning thereby diversity in the ways in which the application of the two terms identified is determined).[187] The meaning of this will be made clearer by the aid of one

---

[186] It follows that the comprehensions (but of course not the connotations) of the terms will also be identical; this cannot, however, be regarded as the primary signification of the equation.
[187] I have practically borrowed the above mode of expression from Miss Jones, who describes an affirmative categorical proposition as "a proposition which asserts identity of application in diversity of signification" (*General Logic*, p. 20). Miss Jones's meaning may, however, be slightly different from that intended in the text, and I am unable to agree with her general treatment of the import of categorical propositions, as she does

or two illustrations. Taking, then, as examples the logical equations already given, we may analyse their meaning as follows. If out of all triangles we select those which possess the property of having three equal sides, and if again out of all triangles we select those which possess the property of having three equal angles, we shall find that in either case we are left with precisely the same set of triangles. Thus, each side of our equation denotes precisely the same class of objects, but the class is determined or arrived at in two different ways. Similarly, if we select all plants that are exogenous and again all plants that are dicotyledonous, our results are precisely the same although our mode of arriving at them has been different. Once more, if we simply take the class of objects which possess the attribute of humanity, and again the class which possess both this attribute and also the attribute of mortality, the objects selected will be the same; none will be excluded by our second method of selection although an additional attribute is taken into account.

Since the identity primarily signified by a logical equation is an identity in respect of denotation, any equational mode of reading propositions must be regarded as a modification of the "class" mode. What has been said above, however, will make it clear that here as elsewhere denotation is considered not to the exclusion of connotation but as dependent upon it; and we again see how denotative and connotative readings of propositions are really involved in one another, although one side or the other may be made the more prominent according to the point of view which is taken.

Another point to which attention may be called before we pass on to consider different types of logical equations is that in so far as a proposition is regarded as expressing an identity between its terms the distinction between subject and predicate practically disappears. We have seen that when we have the ordinary logical copula *is*, propositions cannot always be simply converted, the reason being that the relation of the subject to the predicate is not the same as the relation of the predicate to the subject. But when two terms are connected by the sign of equality, they are similarly, and not diversely, related to each other; in other words, the relation is symmetrical. Such an equation, for example, as $S = P$ can be read either forwards or backwards without any alteration of meaning. There can accordingly be no distinction between subject and predicate except the mere order of statement, and that may be regarded as for most practical purposes immaterial.

138. *Types of Logical Equations*[188]—Jevons (*Principles of Science*, chapter 3) recognises three types of logical equations, which he calls respectively *simple identities, partial identities,* and *limited identities*.

Simple identities are of the form $S = P$; for example, *Exogens = dicotyledons*. Whilst this is the simplest case equationally, the information given by the equation requires two propositions in order that it may be expressed in ordinary predicative form. Thus, *All S is P* and *All P is S*; *All exogens are dicotyledons* and *All dicotyledons are exogens*. If, however, we are allowed to quantify the predicate as well as the subject, a single proposition will suffice. Thus, *All S is all P*, *All exogens are all dicotyledons*. We shall return presently to a consideration of this type of proposition.

Partial identities are of the form $S = SP$, and are the expression equationally of ordinary universal affirmative propositions. If we take the proposition *All S is P*, it is clear that we

---

 not appear to allow that before we can regard a proposition as asserting identity of application we must implicitly, if not explicitly, have quantified the predicate.
[188] This section may be omitted on a first reading.

cannot write it $S = P$, since the class P, instead of being coextensive with the class S, may include it and a good deal more besides. Since, however, by the law of identity *All S is S*, it follows from *All S is P* that *All S is SP*. We can also pass back from the latter of these propositions to the former. Hence the two propositions are equivalent. But *All S is SP* may at once be reduced to the equational form $S = SP$. For this breaks up into the two propositions *All S is SP* and *All SP is S*, and since the second of these is a mere formal proposition based on the law of identity, the equation must necessarily hold good if *All S is SP* is given. To take a concrete example, the proposition *All men are mortal* becomes equationally *Men = mortal men*. Similarly the universal negative proposition *SeP* may be expressed in the equational form $S = Sp$ (where $p = $ *not-P*).

Limited identities are of the form $VS = VP$, which may be interpreted "Within the sphere of the class V, all S is P and all P is S," or "The S's and P's, which are V's, are identical." So far as V represents a determinate class, there is little difference between these limited identities and simple identities. This is shewn by the fact that Jevons himself gives *Equilateral triangles = equiangular triangles* as an instance of a simple identity, whereas its proper place in his classification would appear to be amongst the limited identities, for its interpretation is that "*within the sphere of triangles*—all the equilaterals are all the equiangulars."

The equation $VS = VP$ is, however, used by Boole—and also by Jevons subsequently—as the expression equationally of the particular proposition, and if it can really suffice for this, its recognition as a distinct type is justified. If we take the proposition *Some S is P*, we find that the classes S and P are affirmed to have some part in common, but no indication is given whereby this part can be identified. Boole accordingly indicates it by the arbitrary symbol V. It is then clear that *All VS is VP* and also that *All VP is VS*, and we have the above equation.

It is no part of our present purpose to discuss systems of symbolic logic; but it may be briefly pointed out that the above representation of the particular proposition is far from satisfactory. In order to justify it, limitations have to be placed upon the interpretation of V which altogether differentiate it from other class-symbols. Thus, the equation $VS = VP$ is consistent with *No S is P* (and, therefore, cannot be equivalent to *Some S is P*) provided that no V is either S or P, for in this case we have $VS = 0$ and $VP = 0$. V must, therefore, be limited by the antecedent condition that it represents an existing class and a class that contains either S or P, and it is in this condition quite as much as in the equation itself that the real force of the particular proposition is expressed.[189]

If particular propositions are true contradictories of universal propositions, then it would seem to follow that in a system in which universals are expressed as equalities, particulars should be expressed as inequalities. This would mean the introduction of the symbols > and <, related to the corresponding mathematical symbols in just the same way as the logical symbol of equality is related to the mathematical symbol of equality; that is to say, $S > SP$ would imply logically more than mere numerical inequality, it would imply that the class S includes the whole of the class SP and more besides. Thus interpreted, $S > SP$ expresses the particular negative proposition, *Some S is not P*.[190] If we further introduce the symbol 0 as

---

[189] Compare Venn, *Symbolic Logic*, pp. 161, 2.
[190] Similarly $X > Y$ expresses the two statements "All Y is X, but Some X is not Y," just as $X = Y$ expresses the two statements "All Y is X and All X is Y."

expressing nonentity, *No S is P* may be written $SP = 0$, and its contradictory, i.e., *Some S is P*, may be written $SP > 0$. We shall then have the following scheme (where $p = $ *not-P*):

All S is P	expressed by $S = SP$ or by $Sp = 0$;
Some S is not P	" " $S > SP$ " $Sp > 0$;
No S is P	" " $SP = 0$ " $S = Sp$;
Some S is P	" " $SP > 0$ " $S > Sp$.

This scheme, it will be observed, is based on the assumption that particulars are existentially affirmative while universals are existentially negative. This introduces a question which will be discussed in detail in the following chapter. The object of the present section is merely to illustrate the expression of propositions equationally, and the symbolism involved has, therefore, been treated as briefly as has seemed compatible with a clear explanation of its purport. Any more detailed treatment would involve a discussion of problems belonging to symbolic logic.

139. *The expression of Propositions as Equations.*—There are rare cases in which propositions fall naturally into what is practically an equational form; for example, *Civilization and Christianity are co-extensive.* But, speaking generally, the equational relation, as implicated in ordinary propositions, is not one that is spontaneously, or even easily, grasped by the mind. Hence as a psychological account of the process of judgment the equational rendering may be rejected. It is, moreover, not desirable that equations should supersede the generally recognised propositional forms in ordinary logical doctrine, for such doctrine should not depart more than can be helped from the forms of ordinary speech. But, on the other hand, the equational treatment of propositions must not be simply put on one side as erroneous or unworkable. It has been shewn in the preceding section that it is at any rate possible to reduce all categorical propositions to a form in which they express equalities or inequalities; and such reduction is of the greatest importance in systems of symbolic logic. Even for purposes of ordinary logical doctrine, the enquiry how far propositions may be expressed equationally serves to afford a more complete insight into their full import, or at any rate their full implication. Hence while ordinary formal logic should not be entirely based upon an equational reading of propositions, it cannot afford altogether to neglect this way of regarding them.

We may pass on to consider in somewhat more detail a special equational or semi-equational system—open also to special criticisms—by which Hamilton and others sought to revolutionise ordinary logical doctrine.

140. *The eight propositional forms resulting from the explicit Quantification of the Predicate.*—We have seen that in the ordinary fourfold schedule of propositions, the quantity of the predicate is determined by the quality of the proposition, negatives distributing their predicates, while affirmatives do not. It seems a plausible view, however, that by explicit quantification the quantity of the predicate may be made independent of the quality of the proposition, and Sir William Hamilton was thus led to recognise eight distinct propositional forms instead of the customary four:—

All S is all P,	U.
All S is some P,	A.
Some S is all P,	Y.
Some S is some P,	I.
No S is any P,	E.
No S is some P,	η.
Some S is not any P,	O.
Some S is not some P,	ω.

The symbols attached to the different propositions in the above schedule are those employed by Archbishop Thomson,[191] and they are those now commonly adopted so far as the quantification of the predicate is recognised in modern text-books.

The symbols used by Hamilton were *Afa, Afi, Ifa, Ifi, Ana, Ani, Ina, Ini*. Here *f* indicates an affirmative proposition, *n* a negative; *a* means that the corresponding term is distributed, *i* that it is undistributed.

For the new forms we might also use the symbols *SuP, SyP, SηP, SωP*, on the principle explained in section 62.

141. *Sir William Hamilton's fundamental Postulate of Logic.*—The fundamental postulate of logic, according to Sir William Hamilton, is "that we be allowed to state explicitly in language all that is implicitly contained in thought"; and we may briefly consider the meaning to be attached to this postulate before going on to discuss the use that is made of it in connection with the doctrine of the quantification of the predicate.

Giving the natural interpretation to the phrase "implicitly contained in thought," the postulate might at first sight appear to be a broad statement of the general principle underlying the logician's treatment of formal inferences. In all such inferences the conclusion is implicitly contained in the premises; and since logic has to determine what inferences follow legitimately from given premises, it may in this sense be said to be part of the function of logic to make *explicit in language* what is *implicitly contained in thought*.

It seems clear, however, from the use made of the postulate by Hamilton and his school that he is not thinking of this, and indeed that he is not intending any reference to *discursive thought* at all. His meaning rather is that we should make *explicit in language* not what is implicit in thought, but what is *explicit in thought*, or, as it may be otherwise expressed, that we should make explicit in language all that is really present in thought in the act of judgment.

Adopting this interpretation, we may come to the conclusion that the postulate is obscurely expressed, but we can have no hesitation in admitting its validity. It is obviously of importance to the logician to clear up ambiguities and ellipses of language. For this reason it is, amongst other things, desirable that we should avoid condensed and elliptical modes of expression. But whether Hamilton's postulate, as thus interpreted, supports the doctrine of the quantification of the predicate is another question. This point will be considered in the next two sections.

142. *Advantages claimed for the Quantification of the Predicate.*—Hamilton maintains that "in thought the predicate is always quantified," and hence he makes it follow immediately from the postulate discussed in the preceding section that "in logic the quantity

---

[191] Thomson himself, however, ultimately rejects the forms η and ω.

of the predicate must be expressed, on demand, in language." "The quantity of the predicate," says Dr Baynes in the authorised exposition of Hamilton's doctrine contained in his *New Analytic of Logical Forms*, "is not expressed in common language because common language is elliptical. Whatever is not really necessary to the clear comprehension of what is contained in thought, is usually elided in expression. But we must distinguish between the ends which are sought by common language and logic respectively. Whilst the former seeks to exhibit with clearness the matter of thought, the latter seeks to exhibit with exactness the form of thought. Therefore in logic the predicate must always be quantified." It is further maintained that the quantification of the predicate is necessary for intelligible predication. "Predication is nothing more or less than the expression of the relation of quantity in which a notion stands to an individual, or two notions to each other. If this relation were indeterminate—if we were uncertain whether it was of part, or whole, or none—there could be no predication."

Amongst the practical advantages said to result from quantifying the predicate are the reduction of all species of the conversion of propositions to one, namely, simple conversion; and the simplification of the laws of syllogism. As regards the first of these points, it may be observed that if the doctrine of the quantification of the predicate is adopted, the distinction between subject and predicate resolves itself into a difference in order of statement alone. Each propositional form can without any alteration in meaning be read either forwards or backwards, and every proposition may, therefore, rightly be said to be simply convertible.

It is further argued that the new propositional forms resulting from the quantification of the predicate are required in order to express relations that cannot otherwise be so simply expressed. Thus, U alone serves to express the fact that two classes are co-extensive; and even ω is said to be needed in logical divisions, since if we divide (say) Europeans into Englishmen, Frenchmen, &c., this requires us to think that some Europeans are not some Europeans (e.g., Englishmen are not Frenchmen).

143. *Objections urged against the Quantification of the Predicate.*—Those who reject Hamilton's doctrine of the quantification of the predicate deny at the outset the fundamental premiss upon which it is based, namely, that the predicate of a proposition is always thought of as a determinate quantity. They go further and deny that it is as a rule thought of as a quantity, that is, as an aggregate of objects, at all. We have already in section 135 indicated grounds for the view that, while in the great majority of instances the subject of a proposition is in ordinary thought naturally interpreted in denotation, the predicate is naturally interpreted in connotation. This psychological argument is valid against Hamilton, inasmuch as he really bases his doctrine upon a psychological consideration; and it seems unanswerable.

Mill (in his *Examination of Hamilton*, pp. 495-7) puts the point as follows: "I repeat the appeal which I have already made to every reader's consciousness: Does he, when he judges that all oxen ruminate, advert even in the minutest degree to the question, whether there is anything else which ruminates? Is this consideration at all in his thoughts, any more than any other consideration foreign to the immediate subject? One person may know that there are other ruminating animals, another may think that there are none, a third may be without any opinion on the subject: but if they all know what is meant by ruminating, they all, when they judge that every ox ruminates, mean exactly the same thing. The mental process they go through, so far as that one judgment is concerned, is precisely identical; though some of them may go on further, and add other judgments to it. The fact, that the proposition 'Every A is B' only means 'Every A is *some B*,' so far from being always present in thought, is not at first seized without some difficulty by the tyro in logic. It requires a certain effort of thought to perceive that when we say, 'All *A*'s are *B*'s,' we only identify *A* with a portion of the class *B*. When the learner is first told that the proposition 'All *A*'s are *B*'s' can only be converted in the form 'Some *B*'s are *A*'s,' I apprehend that this strikes him as a new idea; and that the truth of the statement is not quite obvious to him, until verified by a particular example in which he already knows that the simple converse would be false, such as, 'All men are animals, therefore, all animals are men.' So far is it from being true that the proposition 'All *A*'s are *B*'s' is spontaneously quantified in thought as 'All *A* is some *B*.'"

A word may be added in reply to the argument that if the quantity of the predicate were indeterminate—if we were uncertain whether the reference was to the whole or part or none—there could be no predication. This is perfectly true so long as we are left with all three of these alternatives; but we may have predication which involves the elimination of only one of them, so that there is still indeterminateness as regards the other two. To argue that unless we are definitely limited to one of the three we are left with all of them is practically to confuse contradictory with contrary opposition.

A further objection raised to the doctrine of the quantification of the predicate is that some of the quantified forms are composite not simple predications. Thus *All S is all P* is a condensed mode of expression, which may be analysed into the two propositions *All S is P* and *All P is S*. Similarly, if we interpret *some* as exclusive of *all*, a point to which we shall presently return, *All S is some P* is an exponible proposition resolvable into *All S is P* and *Some P is not S*. As a rule, however, the use of exponible forms tends to make the detection of fallacy the more difficult, and this general consideration applies with undoubted force to the particular case of the quantification of the predicate. The bearing of the quantification doctrine upon the syllogism will be briefly touched upon subsequently, and it will be found that the problem of discriminating between valid and invalid moods is rendered more complex and difficult. It may indeed be doubted whether any logical problem, with the one exception of conversion, is really simplified by the introduction of quantified predicates.

Even apart from the above objections, the Hamiltonian doctrine of quantification is sufficiently condemned by its want of internal consistency. Its unphilosophical character in this respect will be shewn in the following sections.

144. *The meaning to be attached to the word "some" in the eight propositional forms recognised by Sir William Hamilton.*—Professor Baynes, in his authorised exposition of Sir William Hamilton's doctrine, would at the outset lead us to suppose that we have no longer to do with the indeterminate *some* of the Aristotelian Logic, but that this word is now to be used in the more definite sense of *some, but not all*. He argues, as we have seen, that intelligible predication requires an absolutely determinate relation in respect of quantity between subject and predicate, and that this ought to be clearly expressed in language. Thus, "if the objects comprised under the subject be some part, but not the whole, of those comprised under the predicate, we write *All X is some P*, and similarly with other forms."

But if it is true that we know definitely the relative extent of subject and predicate, and if *some* is used strictly in the sense of *some but not all*, we should have but *five* propositional forms instead of eight, namely,—*All S is all P, All S is some P, Some S is all P, Some S is some P*,[192] *No S is any P*.

---

[192] Using *some* in the sense here indicated, the interpretation of the proposition *Some S is some P* is not altogether free from ambiguity. The interpretation I am adopting is to regard it as equivalent to the two following propositions with unquantified predicates, namely, *Some but not all S is P* and *Some but not all P is S*. It then necessarily implies the Hamiltonian propositions *Some S is not any P* and *No S is some P*.

We have already seen (in section 126) that the only possible relations between two terms in respect of their extension are given by the following five diagrams,—

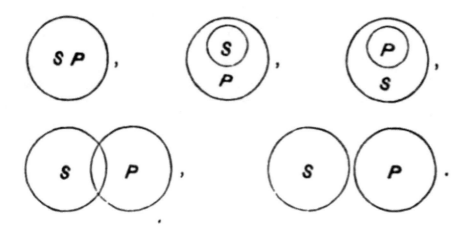

These correspond respectively to the five propositional forms given above;[193] and it is clear that on the view indicated by Dr Baynes the eight forms are redundant.[194]

It is altogether doubtful whether writers who have adopted the eightfold scheme have themselves recognised the pitfalls surrounding the use of the word *some*. Many passages might be quoted in which they distinctly adopt the meaning—*some but not all*. Thus, Thomson (*Laws of Thought*, p. 150) makes **U** and **A** inconsistent. Bowen (*Logic*, pp. 169, 170) would pass from **I** to **O** by immediate inference.[195] Hamilton himself agrees with Thomson and Bowen on these points; but he is curiously indecisive on the general question here raised. He remarks (*Logic*, II. p. 282) that *some* "is held to be a definite *some* when the other term is definite," i.e., in **A** and **Y**, η and **O**: but "on the other hand, when both terms are indefinite or particular, the *some* of each is left wholly indefinite," i.e., in **I** and ω.[196] This is very confusing, and it would be most difficult to apply the distinction consistently. Hamilton himself certainly does not so apply it. For example, on his view it should no longer be the case that two affirmative premisses necessitate an affirmative conclusion; or that two negative premisses invalidate a syllogism.[197] Thus, the following should be regarded as valid:

---

[193] Namely **U, A, Y, I, E. O** and η cannot be interpreted as giving precisely determinate information; **O** allows an alternative between **Y** and **I**, and η between **A** and **I**. For the interpretation of ω see note 2 on page 206.

[194] Compare Venn, *Symbolic Logic*, chapter I.

[195] "This sort of inference," he remarks, "Hamilton would call *integration*, as its effect is, after determining one part, to reconstitute the whole by bringing into view the remaining part."

[196] Compare Veitch, *Institutes of Logic*, pp. 307 to 310, and 367, 8. "Hamilton would introduce *some only* into the theory of propositions, without, however, discarding the meaning of *some at least*. It is not correct to say that Hamilton discarded the ordinary logical meaning of *some*. He simply supplemented it by introducing into the propositional forms that of *some only*." "*Some*, according to Hamilton, is always thought as semi-definite (*some only*) where the other term of the judgment is universal." Mr Lindsay, however, in expounding Hamilton's doctrine (*Appendix to Ueberweg's System of Logic*, p. 580) says more decisively,—"Since the subject must be equal to the predicate, vagueness in the predesignations must be as far as possible removed. *Some* is taken as equivalent to *some but not all*." Spalding (*Logic*, p. 184) definitely chooses the other alternative. He remarks that in his own treatise "the received interpretation *some at least* is steadily adhered to."

[197] The anticipation of syllogistic doctrine which follows is necessary in order to illustrate the point which we are just now discussing.

	All P is some M,
	All M is some S,
therefore,	*Some S is not any P.*
	No M is any P,
	Some S is not any M,
therefore,	*Some or all S is not any P.*

Such syllogisms as these, however, are not admitted by Hamilton and Thomson; and, on the other hand, Thomson admits as valid certain combinations which on the above interpretation are not valid. Hamilton's supreme canon of the categorical syllogism is:— "What worse relation[198] of subject and predicate subsists between either of two terms and a common third term, with which one, at least, is positively related; that relation subsists between the two terms themselves" (*Logic*, II. p. 357). This clearly provides that one premiss at least shall be affirmative, and that an affirmative conclusion shall follow from two affirmative premises. Thomson (*Laws of Thought*, p. 165) explicitly lays down the same rules; and his table of valid moods (given on p. 188) is (with the exception of one obvious misprint) correct and correct only if *some* means "some, it may be all."

145. *The use of "some" in the sense of "some only."*—Jevons, in reply to the question, "What results would follow if we were to interpret 'Some A's are B's' as implying that 'Some other A's are not B's'?" writes, "The proposition 'Some A's are B's' is in the form **I**, and according to the table of opposition **I** is true if **A** is true; but **A** is the contradictory of **O**, which would be the form of 'Some other A's are not B's.' Under such circumstances **A** could never be true at all, because its truth would involve the truth of its own contradictory, which is absurd" (*Studies in Deductive Logic*, 151). It is not, however, the case that we necessarily involve ourselves in self-contradiction if we use *some* in the sense of *some only*. What should be pointed out is that, if we use the word in this sense, the truth of **I** no longer follows from the truth of **A**; and that, so far from this being the case, these two propositions are inconsistent with each other.

Taking the five propositional forms, *All S is all P, All S is some P, Some S is all P, Some S is some P, No S is P*, and interpreting *some* in the sense of *some only*, it is to be observed that each one of them is inconsistent with each of the others, whilst at the same time no one is the contradictory of any one of the others. If, for example, on this scheme we wish to express the contradictory of **U**, we can do so only by affirming an alternative between **Y**, **A**, **I**, and **E**. Nothing of all this appears to have been noticed by the Hamiltonian writers. Thus, Thomson (*Laws of Thought*, p. 149) gives a scheme of opposition in which **E** and **I** appear as contradictories, but **A** and **O** as contraries.

One of the strongest arguments against the use of *some* in the sense of *some only* is very well put by Professor Veitch, himself a disciple of Sir William Hamilton. *Some only*, he remarks, is not so fundamental as *some at least*. The former implies the latter; but I can speak of *some at least* without advancing to the more definite stage of *some only*. "Before I can speak of *some only*, must I not have formed two judgments—the one that *some are*, the other that others of the same class *are not*? ...... The *some only* would thus appear as the composite of two propositions already formed...... It seems to me that we must, first of all, work out

---

[198] The negative relation is here considered "worse" than the affirmative, and the particular than the universal.

logical principles on the indefinite meaning of *some at least*...... *Some only* is a secondary and derivative judgment." (*Institutes of Logic*, p. 308).

If *some* is used in the sense of *some only*, the further difficulty arises how we are to express any knowledge that we may happen to possess about a part of a class when we are in ignorance in regard to the remainder. Supposing for example, that all the *S*'s of which I happen to have had experience are *P*'s, I am not justified in saying either that *all S's are P's* or that *some S's are P's*. The only solution of the difficulty is to say that *all or some S's are P's*. The complexity that this would introduce is obvious.

146. *The interpretation of the eight Hamiltonian forms of proposition, "some" being used in its ordinary logical sense.*[199]—Taking the five possible relations between two terms, as illustrated by the Eulerian diagrams, and denoting them respectively by α, β, γ, δ, ε, as in section 126, we may write against each of the propositional forms the relations which are compatible with it, on the supposition that *some* is used in its ordinary logical sense, that is, as exclusive of *none* but not of *all*:— [200]

U	α
A	α, β
Y	α, γ
I	$\alpha, \beta, \gamma, \delta$
E	ε
η	$\beta, \delta, \varepsilon$
O	$\gamma, \delta, \varepsilon$
ω	$\alpha, \beta, \gamma, \delta, \varepsilon$

We have then the following pairs of contradictories—**A, O; Y, η; I, E**. The contradictory of **U** is obtained by affirming an alternative between η and **O**.

Without the use of quantified predicates, the same information may be expressed as follows:—

| U = *SaP, PaS*; |
| A = *SaP*; |
| Y = *PaS*; |
| I = *SiP*; |
| E = *SeP*; |
| η = *PoS*; |
| O = *SoP*. |

What information, if any, is given by ω will be discussed in section 149.

147. *The propositions* **U** *and* **Y**.—It must be admitted that these propositions are met with in ordinary discourse. We may not indeed find propositions which are actually written in the form *All S is all P*; but we have to all intents and purposes **U**, whenever there is an

---

[199] The corresponding interpretation when *some* is used in the sense of *some only* is given in notes 1 and 2 on page 200, and in note 2 on page 206.

[200] If the Hamiltonian writers had attempted to illustrate their doctrine by means of the Eulerian diagrams, they would I think either have found it to be unworkable, or they would have worked it out to a more distinct and consistent issue.

unmistakeable affirmation that the subject and the predicate of a proposition are co-extensive. Thus, all definitions are practically **U** propositions; so are all affirmative propositions of which both the subject and the predicate are singular terms.[201] Take also such propositions as the following: Christianity and civilization are co-extensive; Europe, Asia, Africa, America, and Australia are all the continents;[202] The three whom I have mentioned are all who have ever ascended the mountain by that route; Common salt is the same thing as sodium chloride.[203]

Such propositions as the following, sometimes known as *exclusive* propositions, may be given as examples of *Y*: *Only S is P*; Graduates alone are eligible for the appointment; Some passengers are the only survivors. These propositions may be interpreted as being equivalent to the following: *Some S is all P*; Some graduates are all who are eligible for the appointment; Some passengers are all the survivors.[204] This is, indeed, the only way of treating the propositions which will enable us to retain the original subjects as subjects and the original predicates as predicates.

We cannot then agree with Professor Fowler that the additional forms "are not merely unusual, but are such as we never do use" (*Deductive Logic*, p. 31). Still in treating the syllogism &c. on the traditional lines, it is better to retain the traditional schedule of propositions. The addition of the forms **U** and **Y** does not tend towards simplification, but the reverse; and their full force can be expressed in other ways. On this view, when we meet with a **U** proposition, *All S is all P*, we may resolve it into the two **A** propositions, *All S is P* and *All P is S*, which taken together are equivalent to it; and when we meet with a **Y** proposition, *Some S is all P* or *S alone is P*, we may replace it by the **A** proposition *All P is S*, which it yields by conversion.

148. *The proposition* η.—This proposition in the form *No S is some P* is not I think ever found in ordinary use. We may, however, recognise its possibility; and it must be pointed out that a form of proposition which we do meet with, namely. *Not only S is P* or *Not S alone is P*, is practically η, provided that we do not regard this proposition as implying that any *S* is certainly *P*.

Archbishop Thomson remarks that η "has the semblance only, and not the power of a denial. True though it is, it does not prevent our making another judgment of the affirmative kind, from the same terms" (*Laws of Thought*, § 79). This is erroneous; for although **A** and η may be true together, **U** and η cannot, and **Y** and η are strictly contradictories.[205] The relation of contradiction in which **Y** and η stand to each other is perhaps brought out more clearly if they are written in the forms *Only S is P*, *Not only S is P*, or *S alone is P, Not S alone is P*. It will be observed, moreover, that η is the converse of **O**, and *vice versâ*. If, therefore, η has no power of denial, the same will be true of **O** also. But it certainly is not true of **O**.

---

[201] Take the proposition, "Mr Gladstone is the present Prime Minister." If any one denies that this is **U**, then he must deny that the proposition "Mr Gladstone is an Englishman" is **A**. We have at an earlier stage discussed the question how far singular propositions may rightly be regarded as constituting a sub-class of universals.

[202] In this and the example that follows the predicate is clearly quantified universally; so that if these are not **U** propositions, they must be **Y** propositions. But it is equally clear that the subject denotes the whole of a certain class, however limited that class may be.

[203] These are all examples of what Jevons would call *simple identities* as distinguished from *partial identities*. Compare section 138.

[204] In these propositions, *some* is to be interpreted in the indefinite sense, and not as exclusive of *all*.

[205] We are again interpreting *some* as indefinite. If it means *some at most*, then the power of denial possessed by η is increased.

149. *The proposition* ω.—The proposition ω, *Some S is not some P*, is not inconsistent with any of the other propositional forms, not even with **U**, *All S is all P*. For example, granting that "all equilateral triangles are all equiangular triangles," still "this equilateral triangle is not that equiangular triangle," which is all that ω asserts. *Some S is not some P* is indeed always true except when both the subject and the predicate are the name of an individual and the same individual.[206] De Morgan[207] (*Syllabus*, p. 24) observes that its contradictory is—"*S* and *P* are singular and identical; there is but one *S*, there is but one *P*, and *S* is *P*."[208] It may be said without hesitation that the proposition ω is of absolutely no logical importance.

150. *Sixfold Schedule of Propositions obtained by recognising* **Y** *and* η, *in addition to* **A, E, I, O**.[209]—The schedule of propositions obtained by adding **Y** and η to the ordinary schedule presents some interesting features, and is worthy of incidental recognition and discussion.[210] It has been shewn in section 100 that in the ordinary scheme there are six and only six independent propositions connecting any two terms, namely, *SaP*, *PaS*, *SeP* (= *PeS*), *SiP* (= *PiS*), *PoS*, *SoP*. If we write the second and the last but one of these in forms in which *S* and *P* are respectively subject and predicate, we have the schedule which we are now considering, namely,

SaP	=	All S is P;
SyP	=	Only S is P;
SeP	=	No S is P;
SiP	=	Some S is P;
SηP	=	Not only S is P;
Sop	=	Some S is not P.

It will be observed that the pair of propositions, *SyP* and *SηP*, are contradictories; so that we now have three pairs of contradictories. There are of course other additions to the

---

[206] *Some* being again interpreted in its ordinary logical sense. Mr Johnson points out that if *some* means *some but not all*, we are led to the paradoxical conclusion that ω is equivalent to **U**. We may regard a statement involving a reference to *some but not all* as a statement relating to *some at least*, combined with a denial of the corresponding statement in which *all* is substituted for *some*. On this interpretation, *Some S is not some P* affirms that "*S* and *P* are not identically one," but also denies that "some *S* is not any *P*" and that "some *P* is not *any S*"; that is, it affirms *SaP* and *PaS*.

[207] De Morgan in several passages criticizes with great acuteness the Hamiltonian scheme of propositions.

[208] Professor Veitch remarks that in ω "we assert parts, and that these can be divided, or that there are parts and parts. If we deny this statement, we assert that the thing spoken of is indivisible or a unity...... We may say that there are men and men. We say, as we do every day, there are politicians and politicians, there are ecclesiastics and ecclesiastics, there are sermons and sermons. These are but covert forms of the *some are not some*...... 'Some vivisection is not some vivisection' is true and important; for the one may be with an anaesthetic, the other without it" (*Institutes of Logic*, pp. 320, 1). It will be observed that the proposition *There are politicians and politicians* is here given as a typical example of ω. The appropriateness of this is denied by Mr Monck. "Again, can it be said that the proposition *There are patriots and patriots* is adequately rendered by *Some patriots are not some patriots*? The latter proposition simply asserts non-identity: the former is intended to imply also a certain degree of dissimilarity [i.e., in the characteristics or consequences of the patriotism of different individuals]. But two non-identical objects may be perfectly alike" (*Introduction to Logic*, p. xiv).

[209] In this schedule *some* is interpreted throughout in its ordinary logical sense. **U** is omitted on account of its composite character; its inclusion would also destroy the symmetry of the scheme.

[210] It is not intended that this sixfold schedule should supersede the fourfold schedule in the main body of logical doctrine. It is, however, important to remember that the selection of any one schedule is more or less arbitrary, and that no schedule should be set up as authoritative to the exclusion of all others.

traditional table of opposition, and some new relations will need to be recognised, e.g., between *SaP* and *SyP*. With the help, however, of the discussion contained in section 107, the reader will have no difficulty in working out the required hexagon of opposition for himself.

As regards immediate inferences, we cannot in this scheme obtain any satisfactory obverse of either **Y** or η, the reason being that they have quantified predicates, and that, therefore, the negation cannot in these propositions be simply attached to the predicate. We have, however, the following interesting table of other immediate inferences:—[211]

		Converse.		Contrapositive.		Inverse.
SaP	=	*PyS*	=	*P'aS'*	=	*S'yP'*
SyP	=	*PaS*	=	*P'yS'*	=	*S'aP'*
SeP	=	*PeS*	=	*P'yS*	=	*S'yP*
SiP	=	*PiS*	=	*P'ηS*	=	*S'ηP*
SηP	=	*PoS*	=	*P'ηS'*	=	*S'oP'*
SoP	=	*PηS*	=	*P'oS'*	=	*S'ηP'*

The main points to notice here are (1) that each proposition now admits of conversion, contraposition, and inversion; and (2) that the inferred proposition is in every case equivalent to the original proposition, so that there is not in any of the inferences any loss of logical force. In other words, we obtain in each case a simple converse, a simple contrapositive, and a simple inverse.

EXERCISES

151. Explain precisely how it is that **O** admits of ordinary conversion if the principle of the quantification of the predicate is adopted, although not otherwise. [K.]

152. Draw out a table, corresponding to the ordinary Aristotelian table of opposition, for the six propositions, **A, Y, E, I, η, O** (some being interpreted in the sense of *some at least*). [K.]

---

[211] It will be observed that the impracticability of obverting **Y** and η leads to a certain want of symmetry in the third and fourth columns.

Chapter 12

THE EXISTENTIAL IMPORT OF CATEGORICAL PROPOSITIONS[212]

153. *Existence and the Universe of Discourse.*—It has been shewn in section 49 that every judgment involves an objective reference, or—as it may otherwise be expressed—a reference to some system of reality distinct from the act of judgment itself. The reference may be to the total system of reality without limitation, or it may be to some particular aspect or portion of that system. Whatever it may be, we may speak of it as the *universe of discourse.*[213] The universe of discourse may be limited in various ways; for example, to physical objects, or to psychical events, or again with reference to time or space. But in all cases it is a universe of reality in the sense in which that term has been used in section 49. The nature of the reference in propositions relating to fictitious objects, for example, to the characters and occurrences in a play or a novel, may be specially considered. We may say that in a case of this kind the universe of discourse consists of a series of statements about persons and events made by a certain author; and it is clear that such statements have objective reality, although the persons and events themselves are fictitious. It follows that, as regards the reference to reality, such a proposition as "Hamlet killed Polonius" must be considered elliptical. For the reference is not to real persons or to the actual course of events in the past history of the world, as it is when we say "Mary Stuart was beheaded," but to a series of descriptions given by Shakespeare in a particular play. These descriptions have, however, a reality of their own, and (the different nature of the reference being clearly understood) I am no more free to say that Hamlet did not kill Polonius (that is, that Shakespeare did not describe Hamlet as killing Polonius) than I am to say that Mary Stuart was not beheaded.

The substance of the above has been expressed by saying that reality is the ultimate subject of every proposition. Every proposition makes an affirmation about a certain universe of discourse, and the universe of discourse (whatever it may be) has some real content. In this sense then every proposition has an existent subject.[214] A further question may, however, be raised, namely, whether—using the word "subject" in its ordinary logical signification—all or

---

[212] It will be advisable for students, on a first reading, to omit this chapter.
[213] "The universe of discourse is sometimes limited to a small portion of the actual universe of things, and is sometimes co-extensive with that universe" (Boole, *Laws of Thought*, p. 166). On the conception of a limited universe of discourse, compare also De Morgan, *Syllabus of a Proposed System of Logic*, §§ 122, 3, and *Formal Logic*, p. 55; Venn, *Symbolic Logic*, pp. 127, 8; and Jevons, *Principles of Science*, chapter 3, § 4.
[214] Compare Bradley, *Principles of Logic*, p. 41.

any propositions should be interpreted as implying the existence (or occurrence) of their subjects within the universe of discourse (or particular portion of reality) to which reference is made. It is mainly with this problem, and the ways in which ordinary logical doctrines are affected by its solution, that we shall be concerned in the present chapter.

In our discussion of existential import it will not be necessary that we should make any attempt to determine the ultimate nature of reality. The questions at issue are, however, not exactly easy of solution, and various sources of misunderstanding are apt to arise.

There is one sense in which the existence of something corresponding to the terms employed must be postulated in all predication. For in order to make use of any term in an intelligible sense we must mentally attach some meaning to it. Hence there must be something in the mind corresponding to every term we use. Even in cases where there cannot be said to be any corresponding mental product, there must at any rate be some corresponding mental process. This applies even to such terms as *round square* or *non-human man* or *root of minus one*. We are not indeed able to form an image of a round square or an idea of a non-human man, nor can we evaluate the root of minus one. But we attach a meaning to these terms, and they must therefore have a mental equivalent of some sort. In the case of "round square" or "non-human man" this is not the actual combination in imagination or idea of "round" with "square" or "non-human" with "man," for such combinations are impossible. But it is the idea of the combination, regarded as a problem presented for solution, and perhaps involving an unsuccessful effort to effect the combination in thought. It is apparently of existence of this kind that some writers are thinking when they maintain that of necessity every proposition implies logically the existence of its subject. But our meaning is something quite different when we speak of existence in the universe of discourse. The nature of the distinction may be made more clear by the following considerations.

It will be admitted that whatever else is included in the full implication of a universal proposition, it at least denies the existence of a certain class of objects. *No S is P* denies the existence of objects that are both S and P; *All S is P* denies the existence of objects that are S without also being P. In these propositions, however, we do not intend to deny the existence of SP (or SP') as objects of thought. For example, in the proposition *No roses are blue* it is not our intention to deny that we can form an idea of *blue roses*; nor in the proposition *All ruminant animals are cloven-hoofed* is it our intention to deny that *ruminant animals without cloven hoofs* can exist as objects of thought. These illustrations may help us to understand more clearly what is meant by existence in the universe of discourse. *The universe of discourse in the case of the proposition No S is P is the universe* (whatever it may be) *in which the existence of SP is denied.* The universe of discourse in the case of a universal affirmative proposition may be defined similarly. As regards particulars it may be best to seek an interpretation through the universals by which the particulars are contradicted. Thus, the universe of discourse in the case of the proposition *Some S is P* may be defined as the universe (whatever it may be) in which the existence of SP would be understood to be denied in the corresponding universal negative. The proposition *Some S is not P* may be dealt with similarly.

The question whether a categorical proposition is to be interpreted as formally implying that its terms are the names of existing things may then be interpreted as follows: *Given a categorical proposition with S and P as subject and predicate, is the existence of S or of P formally implied in that sphere* (whatever it may be) *in which the existence of SP* (or *SP'*) *is denied by the proposition* (or *by its contradictory*)?

The question may be somewhat differently expressed as follows. Such a proposition as *No S is P* denies the existence of a certain complex of attributes, namely, *SP*. But with rare exceptions, *S* itself signifies a certain complex of attributes; and so does *P*. Does the proposition affirm the existence of these latter complexes in the same sense as that in which it denies the existence of the former complex?

No general criterion can be laid down for determining what is actually the universe of discourse in any particular case. It may, however, be said that knowledge as to what is the universe referred to is involved in understanding the meaning of any given proposition; and cases in which there can be any practical doubt are exceptional.[215] Thus, in the propositions *No roses are blue, All men are mortal, All ruminant animals are cloven-hoofed*, the reference clearly is to the actual physical universe; in *The wrath of the Olympian gods is very terrible* to the universe of the Greek mythology;[216] in *Fairies are able to assume different forms* to the universe of folk-lore;[217] in *Two straight lines cannot enclose a space* to the universe of spatial intuitions.

With respect to the existential import of propositions the following questions offer themselves for consideration:

(i) Is the problem one with which logic, and more particularly formal logic, is properly concerned?
(ii) How should the propositions belonging to the traditional schedule be interpreted as regards their existential implications?
(iii) Can we formulate a schedule of propositions which directly affirm or deny existence, and how will such a schedule be related to the traditional schedule?
(iv) How are ordinary logical doctrines affected by the answer given to the second of these questions?

It is clear that the first and fourth of these questions are connected, since if the fourth admits of any positive answer at all, the first is thereby answered in the affirmative. Since, however, the first question blocks the way and seems to demand an answer before we carry the discussion further, it will be well to deal with it briefly at the outset.

The second and third questions are also closely connected together.

Between the second and fourth questions an important distinction must be drawn. The second question is one of interpretation, and within certain limits the answer to it is a matter of convention. Hence a given solution may be preferred on grounds that would not justify the rejection of other solutions as altogether erroneous, although they may be considered inconvenient or unsuitable. But the answer to the fourth question is not similarly a matter of

---

[215] It must at the same time be admitted that controversies sometimes turn upon an unrecognised want of agreement between the controversialists as to the universe of discourse to which reference is made.
[216] The universe of the Greek mythology does not consist of gods, heroes, centaurs, &c., but of accounts of such beings currently accepted in ancient Greece, and handed down to us by Homer and other authors. As regards the reference to reality, therefore, such a proposition as *The wrath of the Olympian gods is very terrible* is elliptical in a sense already explained.
[217] Here again there is an ellipsis. The universe of folk-lore does not consist of fairies, elves, &c., but of descriptions of them, based on popular beliefs, and conventionally accepted when such beings are referred to. Of course for anyone who really believed in the existence of fairies there would be no ellipsis, and the universe of discourse would be different.

convention. On the basis of any given interpretation of propositional forms, the manner in which logical doctrines are affected can admit of only one correct solution.

It is to be observed further that the fourth question can be dealt with hypothetically, that is to say, we can work out the consequences of interpretations which we have no intention of adopting; and it is desirable that we should work out such consequences before deciding upon the adoption of any given interpretation. Hence we propose to deal with the fourth question before discussing the second. The third question may conveniently be taken after the first.

154. *Formal Logic and the Existential Import of Propositions.*—We have then, in the first place, briefly to consider the question whether the problem of existential import is one with which logic has any proper concern. It may be urged that formal logic, at any rate, cannot from its very nature be concerned with questions relating to existence in any other sphere than that of thought. The function of the formal logician, it may be said, is to distinguish between that which is self-consistent and that which is self-contradictory; it is his business to distinguish between what can and what cannot exist in the world of thought. But beyond this he cannot go. Any considerations relating to objective existence are beyond the scope of formal logic.

We may meet the above argument by clearly defining our position. It is of course no function of logic to determine whether or not certain classes actually exist in any given universe of discourse, any more than it is the function of logic to determine whether given propositions are true or false. But it does not follow that logic has, therefore, no concern with any questions relating to objective existence. For, just as, certain propositions being given true, logic determines what other propositions will as a consequence also be true, so given an assertion or a set of assertions to the effect that certain combinations do or do not exist in a given universe of discourse, it can determine what other assertions about existence in the same universe of discourse follow therefrom.[218] As a matter of fact, the premisses in any argument necessarily contain certain implications in regard to existence in the particular universe of discourse to which reference is made, and the same is true of the conclusion; it is accordingly essential that the logician should make sure that the latter implications are clearly warranted by the former.

Without at present going into any detail we may very briefly indicate one or two existential questions that cannot be altogether excluded from consideration in formal logic. Universal propositions, as we have seen, assert non-existence in some sphere of reality; and it is not possible to bring out their full import without calling attention to this fact. Again, the proposition *All S is P* at least involves that if there are any *S*'s in the universe of discourse, there must also be some *P*'s, while it does not seem necessarily to involve that if there are any *P*'s there must be some *S*'s. But now convert the proposition. The result is *Some P is S*, and this does involve that if there are any *P*'s there must be some *S*'s.[219] How then can the process

---

[218] The latter part of this statement is indeed nothing more than a repetition of the former part from a rather different point of view. The doctrine that the conclusions reached by the aid of formal logic can never do more than relate to what is merely conceivable is a very mischievous error. The material truth of the conclusion of a formal reasoning is only limited by the material truth of the premisses.

[219] Dr Wolf denies this. His argument is, however, based mainly on the misinterpretation of a single concrete example. "Let us," he says, "take a concrete example. *Some things that children fear are ghosts*. Does this proposition imply that if there is anything that children fear then there are also ghosts? Surely one may legitimately make such an assertion while believing that there are things that children fear, and yet absolutely disbelieving in the existence of ghosts. In fact the above proposition might very well be used in conjunction with an express denial of the existence of ghosts in order to prove that, while some things that children fear are

of conversion be shewn to be valid without some assumption which will serve to justify this latter implication? Similarly, in passing from *All S is P* to *Some not-S is not-P*, it must at least be assumed that if *S* does not constitute the entire universe of discourse, neither does *P* do so. It is indeed quite impossible to justify the process of inversion in any case without having some regard to the existential interpretation of the propositions concerned.[220]

155. *The Existential Formulation of Propositions.*—We may define an *existential proposition* as one that directly affirms or denies existence (or occurrence) in the universe of discourse (or portion of reality) to which reference is made. Such propositions are of course met with in ordinary forms of speech: for example, *God exists, It rains, There are white hares, It does not rain, Unicorns are non-existent. There is no rose without a thorn.* Sometimes the affirmation or denial of existence takes a less simple form, but is none the less direct: for example, *The assassination of Caesar is an historical event, D'Artagnan is not an imaginary person, The centaur is a fiction of the poets, The large copper butterfly is extinct.*

In the formal expression of existential propositions it will be convenient to make use of certain symbols described in the preceding chapter. Thus, the affirmation of the existence of *S*

---

real, they are also afraid of things that do not exist, but are merely imaginary" (*Studies in Logic*, p. 144). Any speciousness that this argument may possess arises from the ambiguity of the words "thing" and "real." It is clear that in order to make the proposition in question intelligible the word "things" must be interpreted to mean "things, real or imaginary." Moreover "imaginary things" have a reality of their own, though it is not a physical, material reality. Ghosts, therefore, do exist in the universe of discourse to which reference is made. The objects denoted by the predicate of the proposition have in fact just the same kind of existence as certain of the objects denoted by the subject. Looking at the matter from a slightly different point of view, it is clear that if by "things" in the subject we mean things having material existence, then unless ghosts have a similar existence the proposition is not true.

Bearing in mind the constant ambiguity of language, and the ways in which verbal forms may fail to represent adequately the judgments they are intended to express, it would in any case be unsatisfactory to allow a question of the kind we are here discussing to be decided by a single concrete example. Dr Wolf's view is that *Some S is P* does not imply that if there are any *S*'s there are also some *P*'s. Suppose then that there are some *S*'s and that there are no *P*'s. It follows that there are *S*'s but not a single one of them is *P*. What in these circumstances the proposition *Some S is P* can mean it is difficult to understand.

So far as Dr Wolf's argument is independent of the above concrete example, it appears to depend upon an identification of the proposition *Some S is P* with the proposition *S may be P*. The latter is a modal form, and is undoubtedly consistent with the existence of *S* and the non-existence of *P*. But I venture to think that the identification of the two forms runs entirely counter to the current use of language. I am quite prepared to admit that if *All S is P* is interpreted as an unconditional universal, meaning *S as such is P*, its true contradictory is *S may be P*, not *Some S is P*. But this is just because I do not think that *Some S is P* would be understood to express merely the abstract compatibility of *S* and *P*. Certainly Dr Wolf's own concrete example, referred to above, cannot bear this interpretation. For some further observations on modals in connection with existential import, see sections 160 and 163.

[220] Jevons remarks that he does not see how there can be in deductive logic any question about existence, and observes, with reference to the opposite view taken by De Morgan, that "this is one of the few points in which it is possible to suspect him of unsoundness " (*Studies in Deductive Logic*, p. 141). It is, however, impossible to attach any meaning to Jevons's own "Criterion of Consistency," unless it has some reference to "existence." "It is assumed as a necessary law that every term must have its negative. Thence arises what I propose to call the *Criterion of Consistency*, stated as follows:—*Any two or more propositions are contradictory when, and only when, after all possible substitutions are made, they occasion the total disappearance of any term, positive or negative, from the Logical Alphabet*" (p. 181). What can this mean but that although we may deny the existence of the combination *AB*, we cannot without contradiction deny the existence of *A* itself, or *not-A*, or *B*, or *not-B*? This assumption regarding the existential implication of propositions runs through the whole of Jevons's equational logic. The following passage, for example, is taken almost at random: "There remain four combinations, *ABC, aBC, abC, abc*. But these do not stand on the same logical footing, because if we were to remove *ABC*, there would be no such thing as *A* left; and if we were to remove *abc* there would be no such thing as *c* left. Now it is the criterion or condition of logical consistency that every separate term and its negative shall remain. Hence there must exist some things which are described by *ABC*, and other things described by *abc*" (p. 216).

may be written in the form $S > 0$, and the denial of the existence of S in the form $S = 0$. We shall then have an existential schedule of propositions if we reduce our statements to one or other of these forms or to a conjunctive or disjunctive combination of them. The relation between the traditional schedule and an existential schedule of this kind will be discussed in the next section but one.

It may here be pointed out that since the universe of discourse is itself assumed to be real and hence cannot be entirely emptied of content, any denial of existence involves also an affirmation of existence. For if we deny the existence of S, we thereby implicitly affirm the existence of *not-S*, since by the law of excluded middle everything in the universe of discourse must be either S or *not-S*. It follows that every proposition contains directly or indirectly an affirmation of existence.[221]

156. *Various Suppositions concerning the Existential Import of Categorical Propositions.*—Several different views may be taken as to what implication with regard to existence, if any, is involved in categorical propositions of the traditional type. The following may be formulated for special discussion:—[222]

(1) It may be held that every categorical proposition should be interpreted as implying the existence both of objects denoted by the terms directly involved and also of objects denoted by their contradictories; that, for example, *All S is P* should be regarded as implying the existence of S, *not-S*, P, *not-P*. This view is implied in Jevons's Criterion of Consistency mentioned in the note on page 217. It is also practically adopted by De Morgan.[223]

(2) It may be held that every proposition should be interpreted as implying simply the existence of its subject. This is Mill's view (as regards real propositions); for he holds that we cannot give information about a non-existent subject.[224] This is no doubt the view that, at any rate on a first consideration of the subject, appears to be at once the most reasonable and the most simple.

(3) It may be held that we should not regard propositions as necessarily implying the existence either of their subjects or of their predicates. On this view, the full implication of *All*

---

[221] In an article in Baldwin's *Dictionary of Philosophy and Psychology*, Mrs Ladd Franklin points out that the proposition *All S is P* is equivalent to the proposition *Everything is P or not-S*, and hence necessarily implies the existence of either P or *not-S*. Write x for *not-S* and y for P, so that the original proposition becomes *All but x is y*; it then implies, as its minimum existential import, the existence of *either x or y*.

[222] The suppositions that follow are not intended to be exhaustive. We might, for instance, regard propositions as implying the existence both of their subjects and their predicates, but not of the contradictories of these; or we might regard universals as always implying the existence of their subjects, but particulars as not necessarily implying the existence of theirs (see note 3 on p. 241); or affirmatives as always implying the existence of their subjects, but negatives as not necessarily implying the existence of theirs. This last supposition represents the view of Ueberweg. Still another view is taken by Lewis Carroll, who regards all categorical propositions, except universal negatives, as implying the existence of their subjects. "In every proposition beginning with *some* or *all*, the actual existence of the subject is asserted. If, for instance, I say 'all misers are selfish,' I mean that misers *actually exist*. If I wished to avoid making this assertion, and merely to state the *law* that miserliness necessarily involves *selfishness*, I should say 'no misers are unselfish,' which does not assert that any misers exist at all, but merely that, if any *did* exist, they would be selfish" (*Game of Logic*, p. 19). It would take too much space, however, to give a separate discussion to suppositions other than those mentioned in the text.

[223] "By the *universe* (of a proposition) is meant the collection of all objects which are contemplated as objects about which assertion or denial may take place. *Let every name which belongs to the whole universe be excluded as needless*: this must be particularly remembered. Let every object which has not the name X (*of which there are always some*) be conceived as therefore marked with the name x meaning *not-X*" (*Syllabus*, pp. 12, 13). Compare, also, De Morgan's *Formal Logic*, p. 55.

[224] "An accidental or non-essential affirmation does imply the real existence of the subject, because in the case of a non-existent subject there is nothing for the proposition to assert" (*Logic*, I. 6, § 2).

S is P may be expressed by saying that it denies the existence of anything that is at the same time *S* and *not-P*. Similarly *No S is P* implies the existence neither of *S* nor of *P*, but merely denies the existence of anything that is both *S* and *P*. *Some S is P* (or *is not P*) may be read *Some S, if there is any S, is P* (or *is not P*). Here we neither affirm nor deny the existence of any class absolutely;[225] the sum total of what we affirm is that *if any S* exists, then something which is both *S* and *P* (or *S* and *not-P*) also exists. On this interpretation, therefore, particular propositions have a hypothetical and not a purely categorical character.

(4) It may be held that universal propositions should not be interpreted as implying the existence of their subjects, but that particular propositions should be interpreted as doing so.[226] On this view *All S is P* merely denies the existence of anything that is both *S* and *not-P*; *No S is P* denies the existence of anything that is both *S* and *P*; *Some S is P* affirms the existence of something that is both *S* and *P*; *Some S is not P* affirms the existence of something that is both *S* and *not-P*. Thus, *universals* are interpreted as having existentially a *negative* force, while *particulars* have an *affirmative* force. This hypothesis will be found to lead to certain paradoxical results, but it will also be shewn to lead to a more satisfactory and symmetrical treatment of logical problems than is otherwise possible.[227]

157. *Reduction of the traditional forms of proposition to the form of Existential Propositions.*—Without at present attempting to decide between the different possible suppositions as to the existential import of the traditional forms of proposition, we may enquire how on the different suppositions they may be reduced to existential form. It will be assumed throughout that both the traditional forms and the existential forms are interpreted assertorically. In the case of each of the traditional forms it will suffice to deal with the two fundamental suppositions, namely, that it does and that it does not imply the existence of its subject.

The universal affirmative. (1) If *SaP* is interpreted as not carrying with it any existential implication in regard to its separate terms, it is equivalent to the existential proposition $SP' = 0$. Dr Wolf denies this on the ground that *SaP* contains further the implication "If there are any *S*'s, they must all be *P*'s"; and hence that, while on the supposition in question $SP' = 0$ is an *inference* from *SaP*, it is *not equivalent* to it. It is of course a very elementary truth that inferences are not always the exact equivalents of their premisses. But in the above argument Dr Wolf has apparently overlooked the fact that $SP' = 0$, equally with *SaP*, contains the implication "If there are any *S*'s they are all *P*'s."[228] By the law of excluded middle, every *S*

---

[225] Jevons lays down the *dictum* that "we cannot make any statement except a truism without implying that certain combinations of terms are contradictory and excluded from thought" (*Principles of Science*, 2nd edition, p. 32). This is true of universals (though somewhat loosely expressed), but it does not seem to be true of particular propositions, whatever view may be taken of them.

[226] Dr Venn advocates this doctrine with special reference to the operations of symbolic logic; but there is no reason why it should not be extended to ordinary formal logic.

[227] The hypothesis in question has been already provisionally adopted in the scheme of logical equivalences given in section 108, and also in the symbolic scheme of propositions given on page 193.

[228] Dr Wolf perhaps draws a distinction between the proposition "If there are any *S*'s they must all be *P*'s" and the proposition "If there are any *S*'s they are all *P*'s," giving to the former an apodeictic, and to the latter a merely assertoric, force. But if so, then the former is implied by *All S is P*, only if this proposition is apodeictic, not if it is merely assertoric. The argument is in this case irrelevant so far as the position which I take is concerned, since it is only the assertoric *SaP* that I regard as equivalent to $SP' = 0$. Dr Wolf can hardly maintain that all propositions of the form *All S is P* are apodeictic. His whole treatment of the subject with which we are now dealing appears, however, to be valid only if it relates to a modal schedule of propositions. At the same time he nowhere clearly indicates a limitation of this kind, and many of the doctrines which he criticises are intended by those who adopt them to apply only to an assertoric schedule.

(if there are any S's) must be P or *not P*, and since $SP' = 0$, the above inference clearly follows. $SP' = 0$ carries with it in fact the two implications *If $S > 0$ then $P > 0$, If $P > 0$ then $S' > 0$*. These may also be written in the forms *Either $S = 0$ or $P > 0$, Either $P' = 0$ or $S' > 0$*.

(2) If *SaP* is interpreted as implying the existence of S, then it may be expressed existentially $S > 0$ and $SP' = 0$. These existential forms carry with them the implications $P > 0$, *Either $P' = 0$ or $S' > 0$*.

The universal negative. Taking the same two suppositions the corresponding existentials will be:—

(1) $SP = 0$ (carrying with it the implications *Either $S = 0$ or $P' > 0$, Either $P = 0$ or $S' > 0$*);

(2) $S > 0$ and $SP = 0$ (with the implications $P' > 0$, *Either $P = 0$ or $S' > 0$*).

These results need no separate discussion.

The particular affirmative. (1) On the supposition that *SiP* does not carry with it any implication as to the separate existence of its terms, it can be expressed existentially *Either $S = 0$ or $SP > 0$*. It might also be written in the form *If $S > 0$ then $SP > 0$*. Complications resulting from the introduction of considerations of modality will, however, be more easily avoided if the hypothetical form is not made use of.

(2) On the supposition that the existence of S is implied, *SiP* is reducible to the form $SP > 0$.

The particular negative. Here the corresponding results are (1) *Either $S = 0$ or $SP' > 0$*; (2) $SP' > 0$.

We may sum up our results with reference to the third and fourth of the suppositions formulated in the preceding section.

Let no proposition be interpreted as implying the existence of its separate terms. Then corresponding to the traditional schedule we have the following existential schedule:—

| A,—$SP' = 0$; |
| E,—$SP = 0$; |
| I,—*Either $S = 0$ or $SP > 0$*; |
| O,—*Either $S = 0$ or $SP' > 0$*. |

This represents what may be regarded as the *minimum* existential import of each of the traditional propositions (interpreted assertorically).

It must be remembered that $SP' = 0$ carries with it the implications *Either $S = 0$ or $P > 0$, Either $P' = 0$ or $S' > 0$*.

Let particulars be interpreted as implying, while universals are not interpreted as implying, the existence of their subjects. We then have:—

| A,—$SP' = 0$; |
| E,—$SP = 0$; |
| I,—$SP > 0$; |
| O,—$SP' > 0$. |

158. *Immediate Inferences and the Existential Import of Propositions.*—It has been already suggested that before coming to any decision in regard to the existential import of propositions, it will be well to enquire how certain logical doctrines are affected by the different existential assumptions upon which we may proceed. This discussion will as far as possible be kept distinct from the enquiry as to which of the assumptions ought normally to be adopted. The latter question is of a highly controversial nature, but the logical consequences of the various suppositions ought to be capable of demonstration, so as to leave no room for differences of opinion.

We shall in the present section enquire how far different hypotheses regarding the existential import of propositions affect the validity of obversion and conversion and the other immediate inferences based upon these. In the next section we shall consider inferences connected with the square of opposition.

We may take in order the suppositions formulated in section 156.

(1) *Let every proposition he understood to imply the existence of both its subject and its predicate and also of their contradictories.*

It is clear that on this hypothesis the validity of conversion, obversion, contraposition, and inversion will not be affected by existential considerations. The terms of the original proposition together with their contradictories being in each case identical with the terms of the inferred proposition together with their contradictories, the latter cannot possibly contain any existential implication that is not already contained in the original proposition.[229]

(2) *Let every proposition he understood to imply simply the existence of its subject.*

(*a*) The validity of obversion is not affected.

(*b*) The conversion of **A** is valid, and also that of **I**. If *All S is P* and *Some S is P* imply directly the existence of *S*, then they clearly imply indirectly the existence of *P*; and this is all that is required in order that their conversion may be legitimate. The conversion of **E** is not valid; for *No S is P* implies neither directly nor indirectly the existence of *P*, whilst its converse does imply this.

(*c*) The contraposition of **E** is valid, and also that of **O**. *No S is P* and *Some S is not P* both imply on our present supposition the existence of *S*, and since by the law of excluded middle every *S* is either *P* or *not-P*, it follows that they imply indirectly the existence of *not-P*. The contraposition of **A** is not valid; for it involves the conversion of **E**, which we have already seen not to be valid.[230]

(*d*) The process of inversion is not valid; for it involves in the case of both **A** and **E** the conversion of an **E** proposition.[231]

If along with an **E** proposition we are specially given the information that *P* exists, or if this is implied in some other proposition given us at the same time, then the **E** proposition may of course be converted. In corresponding circumstances the contraposition and inversion

---

[229] The reader may be reminded that in our first working out of these immediate inferences we provisionally assumed, apart from any implication contained in the propositions themselves, that the terms involved and also their contradictories represented existing classes.

[230] Or we might argue directly that the contraposition of **A** is not valid, since *All S is P* does not imply the existence of *not-P*, whilst its contrapositive does imply this.

[231] Or again we might argue directly from the fact that neither *All S is P* nor *No S is P* implies the existence of *not-S*.

of **A** and the inversion of **E** may be valid.[232] Or again, given simply *No S is P*, we may infer *Either P is non-existent or no P is S*; and similarly in other cases.

(3) *Let no proposition he understood to imply the existence either of its subject or of its predicate.*

Having now got rid of the implication of the existence either of subject or predicate in the case of all propositions, we might naturally suppose that in no case in which we make an immediate inference need we trouble ourselves with any question of existence at all. As already indicated, however, this conclusion would be erroneous.

(*a*) The process of obversion is still valid. Take, for example, the obversion of *No S is P*. The obverse *All S is not-P* implies that if there is any *S* there is also some *not-P*. But this is necessarily implied in the proposition *No S is P* itself. If there is any *S* it is by the law of excluded middle either *P* or *not-P*; therefore, given that *No S is P*, it follows immediately that if there is any *S* there is some *not-P*.

(*b*) The conversion of **E** is valid. Since *No S is P* denies the existence of anything that is both *S* and *P*, it implies that if there is any *S* there is some *not-P* and that if there is any *P* there is some *not-S*; and these are the only implications with regard to existence involved in its converse. The conversion of **A**, however, is not valid; nor is that of **I**. For *Some P is S* implies that if there is any *P* there is also some *S*; but this is not implied either in *All S is P* or in *Some S is P*.

(*c*) That the contraposition of **A** is valid follows from the fact that the obversion of **A** and the conversion of **E** are both valid.[233] That the contraposition of **E** and that of **O** are invalid follows from the fact that the conversion of **A** and that of **I** are both invalid.

(*d*) That inversion is invalid follows similarly.

On our present supposition then the following are valid: the obversion and contraposition of **A**, the obversion of **I**, the obversion and conversion of **E**, the obversion of **O**; the following are invalid: the conversion and inversion of **A**, the conversion of **I**, the contraposition and inversion of **E**, the contraposition of **O**.[234]

(4) *Let particulars be understood to imply, while universals are not understood to imply, the existence of their subjects.*

---

[232] For example, given (α) *No S is P*, (β) *All R is P*, we may under our present supposition convert (α), since (β) implies indirectly the existence of *P*; and we may contraposit (β), since (α) implies indirectly the existence of *not-P*. It will also he found that, given these two propositions together, they both admit of inversion.

[233] Or we might argue directly as follows; since the proposition *All S is P* denies the existence of anything that is both *S* and *not-P*, it implies that if there is any *S* there is some *P* and that if there is any *not-P* there is some *not-S*; and these are the only implications with regard to existence involved in its contrapositive.

[234] Dr Wolf holds in opposition to the view here expressed that on the supposition in question all the ordinary immediate inferences remain valid. This conclusion is based on the doctrine that *Some S is P* does not imply that if there is any *S* there is also some *P*. "*All S is P* and *Some S is P*, it is true, do not imply that 'if there is any *P* there is also some *S*.' But then *Some P is S* does not necessarily imply that either. There can, therefore, be no objection, on that score, against inferring, by conversion, *Some P is S* from *All S is P* or *Some S is P*. With the vindication of conversion all the remaining supposed illegitimate inferences connected with it are also vindicated. We may, therefore, conclude that to let no propositional form as such necessarily imply the existence of either its subject or its predicate in no way affects the validity of any of the traditional inferences of logic" (*Studies in Logic*, p. 147). I have dealt with Dr Wolf's position in the note on page 216; and it is unnecessary to repeat the argument here. If importance is attached to concrete examples, I may suggest, as an example for conversion, *All blue roses are blue* (a formal proposition which must be regarded as valid on the existential supposition under discussion); and, as an example for inversion, *All human actions are foreseen by the Deity*. There are, moreover, certain difficulties connected with syllogistic and more complex reasonings that need a brief separate discussion, even when the case of conversion has been disposed of.

(*a*) The validity of obversion is again obviously unaffected.[235]
(*b*) The conversion of **E** is valid, and also that of **I**, but not that of **A**.[236]
(*c*) The contraposition of **A** is valid, and also that of **O**, but not that of **E**.
(*d*) The process of inversion is not valid.

These results are obvious; and the final outcome is—as might have been anticipated—that we may infer a universal from a universal, or a particular from a particular, but not a particular from a universal.[237]

An important point to notice is that in the immediate inferences which remain valid on this supposition (namely, obversion, simple conversion, and simple contraposition) there is no loss of logical force; while at the best the reverse would be the case in those that are no longer valid (namely, conversion *per accidens*, contraposition *per accidens*, and inversion).

159. *The Doctrine of Opposition and the Existential Import of Propositions.*—The ordinary doctrine of opposition, in its application to the traditional schedule of propositions, is as follows: (*a*) The truth of *Some S is P* follows from that of *All S is P*, and the truth of *Some S is not P* from that of *No S is P* (doctrine of subalternation); (*b*) *All S is P* and *Some S is not P* cannot both be true and they cannot both be false, similarly for *Some S is P* and *No S is P* (doctrine of contradiction); (*c*) *All S is P* and *No S is P* cannot both be true but they may both be false (doctrine of contrariety); (*d*) *Some S is P* and *Some S is not P* may both be true but they cannot both be false (doctrine of sub-contrariety). We will now examine how far these several doctrines hold good under various suppositions respecting the existential import of propositions.[238]

It should be added that, throughout the discussion, the propositions are supposed to be interpreted assertorically, as has always been the custom with the traditional schedule. The necessity for this proviso will from time to time be pointed out.

(1) *Let every proposition be interpreted as implying the existence both of its subject and of its predicate and also of their contradictories.*[239]

---

[235] Obversion thus remains valid on all the suppositions which have been specially discussed above. If, however, affirmatives are interpreted as implying the existence of their subjects while negatives are not so interpreted, then of course we cannot pass by obversion from **E** to **A**, or from **O** to **I**.

[236] But from the two propositions, *All S is P, Some R is S*, we can infer *Some P is S*; and similarly in other cases.

[237] On the assumption, however, that the universe of discourse can never be entirely emptied of content, *Something is P* may be inferred from *Everything is P*, and *Something is not P* may be inferred from *Nothing is P*. Again, as is shewn by Dr Venn (*Symbolic Logic*, pp. 142–9), the three universals *All S is P, No not-S is P, All not-S is P*, together establish the particular *Some S is P*. Any universe of discourse contains *à priori* four classes—(1) SP, (2) S not-P, (3) not-S P, (4) not-S not-P. *All S is P* negatives (2); *No not-S is P* negatives (3); *All not-S is P* negatives (4). Given these three propositions, therefore, we are able to infer that there is some SP, for this is all that we have left in the universe of discourse. As already pointed out, the assumption that the universe of discourse can never be entirely emptied of content is a necessary assumption, since it is an essential condition of a significant judgment that it relate to reality. If the universe of discourse is entirely emptied of content we must either fail to satisfy this condition, or else unconsciously transcend the assumed universe of discourse and refer to some other and wider one in which the former is affirmed not to exist.

[238] Of course the doctrine of contradiction always holds good in the sense that a pair of real contradictories cannot both be true or both false; and similarly with the other doctrines. The doctrines that we have to consider are not these, but whether *SaP* and *SoP* are really contradictories irrespective of the existential interpretation of the propositions, whether *SaP* and *SeP* are really contraries, and so on.

[239] It would be quite a different problem if we were to assume the existence of *S* and *P* independently of the affirmation of the given proposition. A failure to distinguish between these problems is probably responsible for a good deal of the confusion and misunderstanding that has arisen in connection with the present discussion. But it is clearly one thing to say (*a*) "All *S* is *P* and *S* is assumed to exist," and another to say (*b*) "all *S* is *P*," meaning thereby "*S* exists and is always *P*." In case (*a*) it is futile to go on to make the supposition

On this supposition, if either the subject or the predicate of a proposition is the name of a class which is unrepresented in the universe of discourse or which exhausts that universe, then that proposition is false; for it implies what is inconsistent with fact. It follows that a pair of contradictories as usually stated, and also a pair of sub-contraries, may both be false. For example, *All S is P* and *Some S is not P* both imply the existence of *S* in the universe of discourse. In the case then in which *S* does not exist in that universe, these propositions would both be false.

If a concrete illustration is desired, we may take the propositions, *None of the answers to the question shewed originality*, *Some of the answers to the question shewed originality*, and assume that each of these propositions includes as part of its implication the actual occurrence of its subject in the universe of discourse. Then our position is that if there were no answers to the question at all, the truth of both the propositions must be denied. The fact of there having been no answers does not render the propositions meaningless; but it renders them false, their full import being assumed to be, respectively, *There were answers to the question but none of them shewed originality*, *There were answers to the question and some of them shewed originality*.

We must not of course say that under our present supposition true contradictories cannot be found; for this is always possible. The true contradictory of *All S is P* is *Either some S is not P, or else either S or not-S or P or not-P is non-existent*. Similarly in other cases. The ordinary doctrines of subalternation and contrariety remain unaffected.

(2) *Let every proposition be interpreted as implying the existence of its subject*.

For reasons similar to those stated above, the ordinary doctrines of contradiction and sub-contrariety again fail to hold good. The true contradictory of *All S is P* now becomes *Either some S is not P, or S is non-existent*. The ordinary doctrines of subalternation and contrariety again remain unaffected.

(3) *Let no proposition be interpreted as implying the existence either of its subject or of its predicate*.

(*a*) The ordinary doctrine of subalternation holds good.

(*b*) The ordinary doctrine of contradiction does not hold good. *All S is P*, for example, merely denies the existence of any *S*'s that are not *P*'s; *Some S is not P* merely asserts that *if* there are any *S*'s some of them are not *P*'s. In the case in which *S* does not exist in the universe of discourse we cannot affirm the falsity of either of these propositions.[240]

---

that *S* is non-existent; in case (*b*), on the other hand, there is nothing to prevent our making the supposition, and we find that, if it holds good, the given proposition is false.

[240] Dr Wolf (*Studies in Logic*, p. 132) denies the validity of this reasoning. He admits apparently that the existential propositions $SP' = 0$ and *Either $S = 0$ or $SP' > 0$* are not contradictories; but he denies that on the supposition under discussion *SaP* and $SP' = 0$ are equivalent. His main ground for taking this view is that *SaP* carries with it the implication *If there are any S's they are all P's*, while $SP' = 0$ does not carry with it any such implication. This position has been already criticized in section 157. Dr Wolf relies partly upon concrete examples, but in so doing he complicates the discussion by introducing modal forms of expression. Thus for the proposition "Some successful candidates do not receive scholarships," we find substituted in the course of his argument "If there are any successful candidates then some of them do not (or *need not*) receive scholarships," and the insertion of the words in brackets yields a proposition which, although an inference from the original proposition, is not really equivalent to it, unless the original proposition is itself interpreted modally. Later on Dr Wolf explicitly alters the whole problem by assuming that what is under consideration is a modal schedule of propositions. Thus he goes on to say, "What *SaP* and *SeP* really express severally is the *necessity* and the *impossibility* of *S* being *P*"; and for the purpose of contradicting *SaP* and *SeP*, "*SiP* and *SoP* need mean no more than *S may be P* and *S need not be P*." The question how far *SaP* and *SeP* should be interpreted modally is discussed elsewhere. All I would point out here is that it is a distinct question from that

(*c*) The ordinary doctrine of contrariety does not hold good. For if there is no implication of the existence of the subject in universal propositions we are not actually precluded from asserting together two propositions that are ordinarily given as contraries. *All S is P* merely denies that there are any *S not-P*'s, *No S is P* that there are any *SP*'s. We may, therefore, without inconsistency affirm both *All S is P* and *No S is P*; but this is virtually to deny the existence of *S*.[241]

(*d*) The ordinary doctrine of sub-contrariety remains unaffected.

(4) *Let particulars be interpreted as implying, while universals are not interpreted as implying, the existence of their subjects.*

(*a*) The ordinary doctrine of subalternation does not hold good. *Some S is P*, for example, implies the existence of *S*, while this is not implied by *All S is P*.

(*b*) The ordinary doctrine of contradiction holds good. *All S is P* denies that there is any *S* that is *not-P*; *Some S is not P* affirms that there is some *S* that is *not-P*. It is clear that these propositions cannot both be true; it is also clear that they cannot both be false. Similarly for *No S is P* and *Some S is P*.

(*c*) The ordinary doctrine of contrariety does not hold good. *All S is P* and *No S is P* are not inconsistent with one another, but the force of asserting both of them is to deny that there are any *S*'s.[242] This follows just as in the case of our third supposition.[243]

(*d*) The ordinary doctrine of sub-contrariety does not hold good.[244] *Some S is P* and *Some S is not P* are both false in the case in which *S* does not exist in the universe of discourse.

Another example is contained in the following quotation from Mrs Ladd Franklin: "*All x is y, No x is y*, assert together that *x* is neither *y* nor *not-y*, and hence that there is no *x*. It is common among logicians to say that two such propositions are incompatible; but that is not true, they are simply together incompatible with the existence of *x*. When the schoolboy has proved that the meeting point of two lines is not on the right of a certain transversal and that it is not on the left of it, we do not tell him that his propositions are incompatible and that one or other of them must be false, but we allow him to draw the natural conclusion that there is no meeting point, or that the lines are parallel" (*Mind*, 1890, p. 77 *n*.).

Dr Wolf (*Studies in Logic*, p. 140), criticizing Mrs Ladd Franklin's concrete example, maintains that the two propositions given by her are sub-contraries (**I** and **O**), not contraries

---

raised in the text, which is a question relating to the traditional schedule of propositions interpreted assertorically. The whole question of existential import is indeed one that cannot be discussed to any purpose until the character of the schedule of propositions under consideration has been defined. From the mixing up of schedules and interpretations nothing but confusion can result. In the following section the opposition of modals will be briefly considered in connection with their existential import.

[241] Of course on the view under consideration we ought not to continue to speak of these two propositions as contraries.

[242] If, however, we are given *No S is P* and also *Some S is P*, then we are able to infer that *All S is P* is false. The second of these propositions affirms the existence of *S*, and therefore destroys the hypothesis on which alone the first and third can be treated as compatible.

[243] The above doctrine has been criticized on the ground that it practically amounts to saying that neither of the given propositions has any meaning whatever, but that each is a mere sham and pretence of predication; and a request is made for concrete examples. The following example may perhaps suffice to illustrate the particular point now at issue: "An honest miller has a golden thumb"; "Well, I am sure that no miller, honest or otherwise, has a golden thumb." These two propositions are in the form of what would ordinarily be called contraries; but taken together they may quite naturally be interpreted as meaning that no such person can be found as an honest miller. The former proposition would indeed probably be intended to be supplemented by the latter or by some proposition involving the latter, and so to carry inferentially the denial of the existence of its subject.

[244] It may be worth observing that, given (*b*), (*d*) might be deduced from (*c*) or *vice versâ*.

(**A** and **E**). A moment's consideration will, however, shew that this is not the case since neither of the propositions is particular. At the same time it is true that a little manipulation is required to bring them to the forms **A** and **E**. There is also the assumption that "on the right" and "on the left" exhaust the possibilities and are therefore contradictory terms. Granting this assumption, the two propositions may be expressed symbolically in the forms *No S is P, No S is not P*, and it then needs only the obversion of one of them to bring them to the forms **A** and **E**.

The relation between contradictories is by far the most important relation with which we are concerned in dealing with the opposition of propositions, and it will be observed that the last of the above suppositions is the only one under which the ordinary doctrine of contradiction holds good.

160. *The Opposition of Modal Propositions considered in connection with their Existential Import.*—The propositions discussed in the preceding sections have been the propositions belonging to the traditional schedule interpreted assertorically. Turning now to the corresponding modal schedule, we may briefly consider how the doctrine of opposition is affected, if at all, on the supposition that the propositions included in the schedule are not interpreted as implying the existence of their subjects. We find that on this supposition *S as such is P* and *S need not be P* are true contradictories.

S as such is P (interpreted as not necessarily implying the existence of *S*) does more than deny the actual occurrence of the conjunction *S not-P*, it denies the possibility of such a conjunction; and all that is necessary in order to contradict this is to affirm the possibility of the conjunction. This is done by the proposition *S need not be P* (also interpreted as not necessarily implying the existence of *S*). On the same supposition, *S as such is P, S as such is other than P*, are true contraries.

Here, however, another problem suggests itself. Leaving on one side the question as to any implication of *actuality*, are modal propositions to be interpreted as containing any implication in regard to the *possibility* of their antecedents? And, further, how does our answer to this question affect the opposition of modals? The consideration of this problem may be deferred until we come to deal with the opposition of conditional propositions (see section 176).

161. *Jevons's Criterion of Consistency.*—In passing to the explicit discussion of the existential import of categorical propositions, we may consider first the Criterion of Consistency, which is laid down by Jevons (following De Morgan):—Any two or more propositions are contradictory when, and only when, after all possible substitutions are made, they occasion the total disappearance of any term, positive or negative, from the Logical Alphabet. The criterion amounts to this, that every proposition must be understood to imply the existence of things denoted by every simple term contained in it, and also of things denoted by the contradictories of such terms. If, for example, we have the proposition *All S is P*, this implies that among the members of the universe of discourse are to be found *S*'s and *P*'s, *not-S*'s, and *not-P*'s. In defence of this doctrine Jevons appears to rely mainly upon the psychological law of relativity, namely, that we cannot think at all without separating what we think about from other things. Hence if either a term or its contradictory represents nonentity, that term cannot be either subject or predicate in a significant proposition.[245] It is

---

[245] This point is put somewhat tentatively in a passage in Jevons's *Principles of Science* (chapter 6, § 5) where he remarks: "If *A* were identical with '*B* or not-*B*,' its negative not-*A* would be non-existent. This result would

clear, however, that this psychological argument falls away as soon as it is allowed that we may be confining ourselves to a limited universe of discourse, or indeed if we confine ourselves to any universe less extensive than that which covers the whole realm of the conceivable. Of course the more limited the universe to which our proposition is supposed to relate the more easily may S or P either exhaust it or be absent from it; but with very complex subjects and predicates the contradictory of one or both of our terms may easily exhaust even an extended universe. Take, for example, the proposition, *No satisfactory solution of the problem of squaring the circle has ever been published by Mr A.* Here the subject is non-existent; and it may happen also that Mr A. has never published anything at all.[246] Further, if I am not allowed to negative X, why should I be allowed to negative AB? There is nothing to prevent X from representing a class formed by taking the part common to two other classes. In certain combinations indeed it may be convenient to substitute X for AB, or *vice versâ*. It would appear then that what is contradictory when we use a certain set of symbols may not be contradictory when we use another set of symbols. This argument has a special bearing on the complex propositions which are usually relegated to symbolic logic, but to which Jevons's criterion is intended particularly to apply.

No doubt Jevons's criterion is sometimes a convenient assumption to make; provisionally, for example, in working out the doctrine of immediate inferences on the traditional lines. But it is an assumption that should always be explicitly referred to when made; and it ought not to be regarded as having an axiomatic and binding force, so as to make it necessary to base the whole of logic upon it.

162. *The Existential Import of the Propositions included in the Traditional Schedule.*— We may now turn to the consideration of the question whether the propositions *SaP, SeP, SiP, SoP* should or should not be interpreted as implying the existence of their subjects in the universe of discourse to which reference is made. In this section it will be assumed that the import of all the propositions under discussion is assertoric, not modal.

A brief reference may be made to two sources of misunderstanding to which attention has already been called.

(*a*) All propositions contain affirmations relating to some system of reality; and by analysis every proposition may be made to yield an "ultimate subject" which is real, namely, the system of reality to which the proposition relates. This system of reality is what we mean by the universe of discourse; and, as we have seen, the universe of discourse can never be entirely emptied of content. It must then be understood that if we decide that certain propositional forms are not to be interpreted as containing as part of their import the affirmation of the existence of their subjects, it is far from being thereby intended that propositions falling into these forms contain no affirmation relating to reality.[247]

(*b*) We must put on one side a very summary solution of our problem, which, if it were correct, would render any further discussion needless. How, it may be asked, can we possibly speak about anything and at the same time exclude it from the universe of discourse? This

---

generally be an absurd one, and I see much reason to think that in a strictly logical point of view it would always be absurd. In all probability we ought to assume as a fundamental logical axiom that every term has its negative in thought. We cannot think at all without separating what we think about from other things, and these things necessarily form the negative notion. If so, it follows that any term of the form '*B* or not-*B*' is just as self-contradictory as one of the form '*B* and not-*B*'."

[246] Other examples will be given in the following section.
[247] Compare Sigwart, *Logic*, i. p. 97 *n*.

question suggests a certain ambiguity which may attach to the phrase *universe of discourse*, but which can hardly remain an ambiguity after the explanations already given. The answer is that we can certainly think and speak about a thing *with reference to* a given universe of discourse without implying, or even believing in, its existence in that universe. Suppose, for example, that I say there are no such things as unicorns. If this statement is to be accepted, it must be interpreted literally (not elliptically); and it is clear that the universe of discourse referred to is the material universe.[248] I speak then of unicorns *with reference to* the material universe, but deny that such creatures are to be found (or exist) in it.

The question we have to discuss is one of the *interpretation of propositional forms*,[249] and the solution will therefore be to some extent a matter of convention. We shall be guided in our solution partly by the ordinary usage of language, and partly by considerations of logical convenience and suitability.

As regards the ordinary usage of language there can be no doubt that we seldom do as a matter of fact make predications about non-existent subjects. For such predications would in general have little utility or interest for us. "The practical exigencies of life," as Dr Venn remarks, "confine most of our discussions to what does exist, rather than to what might exist" (*Symbolic Logic*, p. 131). We must, however, consider whether there are not exceptional cases; and if we can find any in which it is clear that the speaker would not necessarily intend to imply the existence of the subject, we may draw the conclusion that the propositional form of which he makes use is not in popular usage uniformly intended to convey such an implication.

Universal Affirmatives. If a universal affirmative proposition is obtained by a process of exhaustive enumeration (e.g., *All the Apostles were Jews, All the books on that shelf are bound in morocco*), or if it is obtained by empirical generalisation based on the examination of individual instances (e.g., *All ruminant animals are cloven-hoofed*), then it is clear that the existence of the subject is a presupposition of the affirmation. We may, however, note certain other classes of cases in which such a presupposition is not necessary.

(*a*) We may affirm an abstract connection of attributes, based on considerations of a deductive character or at any rate not obtained by direct generalisation from observed instances of the subject, and the existence of the subject is then not essential. For example, *The impact of two perfectly elastic bodies leads to no diminution of kinetic energy*; *Every body, not compelled by impressed forces to change its state, continues in a state of rest or of uniform motion in a straight line*.

It may perhaps be said that all propositions falling within this category will be really apodeictic, and that our present discussion has been limited to assertoric propositions. There is some force in this criticism. It is, however, to be remembered that the assertoric *SaP* can be inferred from the apodeictic *SaP*, so that if we can have the latter without any implication as to the existence of *S* we may have the former also, unless indeed we decide to differentiate between them in regard to their existential implication. The examples that we have given are moreover expressed in ordinary assertoric form, and not in any distinctive apodeictic form, such as *S as such is P, It is inherent in the nature of S to be P*.

---

[248] It is hardly necessary to point out that ideas of unicorns exist in imagination, and that statements about unicorns are to be met with in fairy tales.
[249] See section 48.

(*b*) The proposition *SaP* may express a rule laid down, and remaining in force, without any actual instance of its application having arisen. For example, *All candidates arriving five minutes late are fined one shilling*, *All candidates who stammer are excused reading aloud*, *All trespassers are prosecuted*.

If it is argued that, in such cases as these,[250] the propositions ought properly to be written in the conditional and not in the categorical form (e.g., *If any candidate arrives five minutes late, that candidate is fined one shilling*), the reply is that this is to misunderstand the point just now at issue, which is whether we meet with propositions in ordinary discourse which are categorical in form and yet are hypothetical so far as the existence of their subjects is concerned. It is of course open to us to decide that for logical purposes we will so interpret categorical propositions that in such cases as the above the categorical form can no longer be used. But for the present we are merely discussing popular usage.

(*c*) Assertions in regard to possible future events are sometimes thrown into the form *SaP*. For example, *Who steals my purse steals trash*, *Those who pass this examination an lucky men*. The first of these propositions would not be invalidated supposing my purse never to be stolen, and the latter, as Dr Venn remarks,[251] would be tacitly supplemented by the clause "if any such there be."

(*d*) There are cases in which the intended implication of a proposition of the form *All S is P* is to deny that there are any *S*'s; for example, *An honest miller has a golden thumb*, *All the carts that come to Crowland are shod with silver*.[252]

Universal Negatives. It is still easier to find instances from common speech in which universal negative propositions, that is, propositions of the form *No S is P*, are not to be regarded as necessarily implying the existence of their subjects.

(*a*) There are again cases in which the proposition is reached by a process of abstract reasoning about a subject the actual existence or occurrence of which is not presupposed; for example, *A planet moving in a hyperbolic orbit can never return to any position it once occupied*.[253]

(*b*) The import of the proposition may be distinctly to imply, if not definitely to affirm, the non-existence of the subject; for example, *No ghosts have troubled me*, *No unicorns have ever been seen*.[254]

---

[250] This argument might be used with, reference to cases coming under (*a*) or (*c*) as well as with reference to those coming under (*b*).

[251] *Symbolic Logic*, p. 132.

[252] Both these propositions are naturally to be interpreted as containing an indirect denial of the existence of their subjects. "Crowland is situated in such moorish rotten ground in the Fens, that scarce a horse, much less a cart, can come to it" (Bohn's *Handbook of Proverbs*, p. 211). It would appear, however, that this proverb has now lost its force, inasmuch as "since the draining, in summer time, carts may go thither."

[253] This example is taken from Dixon, *Essay on Reasoning*, p. 62.

[254] The universe of discourse must here be taken to be the material universe. With reference to this example, however, a critic writes, "But surely the universe of imagination is the only one applicable; for unicorns have long been known not to belong to the actual material universe." The universe of imagination may be required in order to sustain the position that the subject of the proposition exists in the universe of discourse; but any person making the statement would certainly not be referring to the world of imagination or the universe of heraldry, for the simple reason that in either of these cases the proposition (which must then be interpreted elliptically) would obviously not be true. On the other hand, we can quite well suppose the statement made with reference to the material universe: "Whether unicorns exist or not, at any rate they have never been seen." Again, to take another example of a similar kind where the reference is also to the phenomenal universe, we can quite well suppose the statement made: "Whether there are ghosts or not, at any rate none have ever troubled me." In order to avoid misapprehension, it is important to distinguish the above examples from such (elliptical) propositions as the following: "The wrath of the Homeric gods is very terrible," "Fairies are able to

(*c*) A denial of the conjunction ABC may be expressed in the form *No AB is C* without any intention of thereby affirming the conjunction *AB*; for example, *No satisfactory solution of the problem of squaring the circle has been published, No woman candidate for the Theological Tripos has been educated at Newnham College, No Advanced Student in Law is on the boards of Trinity College.*[255]

Particulars. In the case of particular propositions, it is far less easy to give examples, such as might be met with in ordinary discourse, in which there is no implication of the existence of the subjects of the propositions. There may be exceptions, but at any rate the cases are exceedingly rare in which in ordinary speech we predicate anything of a non-existent subject without doing so universally. The main reason for this is, as Dr Venn points out, that "an assertion confined to 'some' of a class generally rests upon observation or testimony rather than on reasoning or imagination, and therefore almost necessarily postulates existent data, though the nature of this observation and consequent existence is, as already remarked, a perfectly open question. 'Some twining plants turn from left to right,' 'Some griffins have long claws,' both imply that we have looked in the right quarters to assure ourselves of the fact. In one case I may have observed in my own garden, and in the other on crests or in the works of the poets, but according to the appropriate tests of verification, we are in each case talking of what *is*."[256] If we look at the question from the other side, we find that when our primary object is to affirm the existence of a class of objects, our assertion very naturally takes the form of a particular proposition. If, for example, we desire to affirm the existence of black swans, we say *Some swans are black*. The existential implication of a proposition of this kind in ordinary discourse is one of its most fundamental characteristics.

On the whole it cannot be said that the usages of ordinary speech afford a decisive solution of the problem under discussion. It has, however, been shewn (1) that we seldom or never make statements about non-existent subjects in the form *Some S is P* or the form *Some S is not P*; (2) that, although it is also true that we do not as a rule do so in the form *All S is P* or the form *No S is P*, still there are several classes of cases in which the use of these latter forms is not to be understood as necessarily carrying with it the implication that *S* is existent. Hence we should be departing very little from ordinary usage if we were to decide to interpret particulars as implying the existence of their subjects, but universals as not doing so (that is, as not doing so by their bare form).

I do not, however, regard this solution as necessitated by popular usage. It is, for instance, still open to anyone to adopt the convention that, for logical purposes, the categorical form shall only be used when the implication of the existence of the subject is intended. On this interpretation, the conditional or hypothetical form must be adopted whenever the existence of the subject is left an open question. Thus, if we are doubtful about the existence of *S* (or, at any rate, do not wish to affirm its existence), we must be careful to say, *If there is any S, then all S is P*, instead of simply *All S is P*; in other words, the hypothetical character of the proposition so far as the existence of its subject is concerned must be made explicit.

---

assume different forms." In each of these cases, the subject of the proposition (properly interpreted) exists in the particular universe to which reference is made. See notes 2 and 3 on page 213.

[255] "As an instance of a possibly non-existent subject of a negative proposition, take the following: 'No person condemned for witchcraft in the reign of Queen Anne was executed.'" (Venn, *Symbolic Logic*, p. 132).

[256] *Symbolic Logic*, p. 131. Again, in such a proposition as "Some sea-serpents are not half a mile long" (meaning *your so-called* sea-serpents), the subject of the proposition exists in the universe to which reference is made, namely, the universe which may be described as the universe of travellers' tales. We are here regarding the proposition as elliptical in a sense that has been already explained.

The problem then not being decided by considerations of popular usage alone, we must go on to enquire how the question is affected by considerations of logical convenience and suitability. Here again there is no one solution that is inevitable. Reasons can, however, be urged in favour of interpreting particulars as implying, but universals as not implying, the existence of their subjects;[257] and this, as we have seen, is a solution that derives some sanction from popular usage.

(1) A consideration of the manner in which the validity of immediate inferences is affected by the existential import of propositions affords reasons for the adoption of this interpretation.[258] The most important immediate inferences are simple conversion (i.e., the conversion of **E** and of **I**) and simple contraposition (i.e., the contraposition of **A** and of **O**). If, however, universals are regarded as implying the existence of their subjects, then, as shewn in section 158, neither the conversion of **E** nor the contraposition of **A** is valid, irrespective of some farther assumption; whereas, if universals are not regarded as implying the existence of their subjects, then both these operations are legitimate without qualification. On the other hand, the conversion of **I** and the contraposition of **O** are valid only if particulars *do* imply the existence of their subjects.[259]

Turning to immediate inferences of another kind, it is clear that if universal propositions formally imply the existence of their subjects, we cannot legitimately pass from *All X is Y* to *All AX is Y*.[260] For it is possible that there may be *X*'s and yet no *AX*'s, and in this case the former proposition may be true, while the latter will certainly be false. Again, given that *A is X, B is Y, C is Z*, we cannot infer that *ABC is XYZ*. Such restrictions as these would constitute an almost insurmountable bar to progress in inference as soon as we have to do with complex propositions.[261]

(2) We may next consider the existential import of propositions with reference to the doctrine of opposition. It has been shewn in section 159 that if particulars are interpreted as implying the existence of their subjects, while universals are not so interpreted, then **A** and **O**, **E** and **I**, are true contradictories; but that this is not the case under any of the other

---

[257] On this view whenever it is desired specially to affirm the existence in the universe of discourse of the subject of a universal proposition, a separate statement to this effect must be made. For example, *There are S's, and all of them are P's*. If, on the other hand, it is ever desired to affirm a particular proposition without implying the existence of the subject, then recourse must be had to the hypothetical or conditional form of statement. Thus, if we do not intend to imply the existence of *S*, instead of writing *Some S's are P's*, we must write, *If there are any S's, then in some such cases they are also P's*.

[258] It has been objected that to base our view of the existential import of propositions upon the validity or invalidity of immediate inferences is to argue in a circle. "Whether," it is said, "the immediate inferences are valid or not must be a consequence of the view taken of the existential import of the proposition and should not, therefore, be made a portion of the ground on which that view is based." This objection involves a confusion between different points of view from which the problem of the relation between the existential import of propositions and the validity of logical operations may be regarded. In section 158 the logical consequences of various assumptions were worked out without any attempt being made to decide between these assumptions. Our point of view is now different; we are investigating the grounds on which one of the assumptions may be preferred to the others, and there is no reason why the consequences previously deduced should not form part of our data for deciding this question. The argument contains nothing that is of the nature of a *circulus in probando*.

[259] Thus, the table of equivalences given in section 106 is valid on the interpretation with which we are now dealing. The dependence of the table given in section 108 upon the same supposition is still more obvious. It has been already pointed out that the remaining immediate inferences based on conversion and obversion are of much less importance; see page 227.

[260] It will be observed further that upon the same assumption we cannot even affirm the formal validity of the proposition *All X is X*. For *X* might be non-existent, and the proposition would then be false.

[261] Hence Mrs Ladd Franklin is led to the conclusion that "no consistent logic of universal propositions is possible except with the convention that they do not imply the existence of their terms" (*Mind*, 1890, p. 88).

suppositions discussed in the same section.[262] There can, however, be no doubt that one of the most important functions of particular propositions is to contradict the universal propositions of opposite quality; and hence we have a strong argument in favour of a view of the existential import of propositions which will leave the ordinary doctrine of contradiction unaffected.

As regards the doctrines of subalternation, contrariety, and subcontrariety, our results (namely, that **I** does not follow from **A**, or **O** from **E**, that **A** and **E** may both be true, and that **I** and **O** may both be false) are no doubt paradoxical. But this objection is far more than counterbalanced by the fact that the doctrine of contradiction is saved. For as compared with the relation between contradictories, these other relations are of little importance. We may specially consider the relation between **A** and **I**. *Some S is P* cannot now without qualification be inferred from *All S is P*, since the former of these propositions implies the existence of *S*, while the latter does not. But as a matter of fact this is an inference which we never have occasion to make. If their existential import is the same why should we ever lay down a particular proposition when the corresponding universal is at our service? On the other hand, the view that we are advocating gives *Some S is P* a status relatively to *All S is P* as well as relatively to *No S is P* which it could not otherwise possess; and similarly for *Some S is not P*. Our result as regards the relation between *SaP* and *SiP* has been described as equivalent to saying "that a statement of partial knowledge carries more real information than a statement of full knowledge; since if we only possess limited information, and so can only assert *SiP*, we thereby affirm the existence of *S*; but if we have sufficient knowledge to speak of *all S* (*S* remaining the same) the statement of that full knowledge immediately casts a doubt upon that existence." This way of putting it is, however, misleading if not positively erroneous. On the view in question it is incorrect to say simply that *SiP* and *SaP* give "partial" and "full" knowledge respectively, for *SiP* while giving less knowledge than *SaP* in one direction gives more in another. In other words, the knowledge which is "full" relatively to *SiP* is not expressed by *SaP* by itself, but by *SaP* together with the statement that there are such things as *S*.[263]

(3) There is one further point of importance to be noted, and that is, that the interpretation of **A**, **E**, **I**, **O** propositions under consideration is the only interpretation according to which each one of these propositions is resolved into a *single categorical statement*. For if **A** and **E** imply the existence of their subjects they express *double*, not single, judgments, being equivalent respectively to the statements: *There are S's, but there are no SP"s*; *There are S's, but there are no SP's*; whereas on the interpretation here proposed they simply express

---

[262] **A** and **O**, **E** and **I**, will also be true contradictories if universals are interpreted as implying the existence of their subjects, while particulars are not so interpreted. It would be interesting, if space permitted, to work out the results of this supposition in detail. If the student does this for himself, he will find that this is the *only* supposition, under which the ordinary doctrine of opposition holds good throughout. All other considerations, however, are opposed to its adoption. It altogether conflicts with popular usage; it renders the processes of simple conversion and simple contraposition illegitimate; and whilst making universals double judgments, it destroys the categorical character of particulars altogether. In regard to this last point see page 220.

[263] The position taken above in regard to subalternation is very well expressed by Mrs Ladd Franklin. "Nothing of course is now illogical that was ever logical before. It is merely a question of what convention in regard to the existence of terms we adopt before we admit the warm-blooded sentences of real life into the iron moulds of logical manipulation. With the old convention (which was never explicitly stated) subalternation ran thus: *No x's are y's* (and we hereby mean to imply that there are *x's*, whatever *x* may be), therefore, *Some x's are non-y's*. With the new convention the requirement is simply that if it is known that there are *x's* (as it is known, of course, in by far the greater number of sentences that it interests us to form) that fact must be expressly stated. The argument then is: *No x's are y's, There are x's,* therefore, *There are x's which are non-y's.*"

respectively the single judgments: *There are no SP"s*; *There are no SP's*. On the other hand, if **I** and **O** do not imply the existence of their subjects, instead of expressing categorical judgments, they express somewhat complex hypothetical ones, being equivalent respectively to the statement: *If there are any S's then there are some SP's*; *If there are any S's then there are some SP"s*; whereas on our interpretation they express respectively the categorical judgments: *There are SP's*; *There are SP"s*.[264]

On the whole, there is a strong cumulative argument in favour of interpreting particulars, but not universals, as implying formally the existence of their subjects.[265] This solution is to be regarded as partly of the nature of a convention. We arrive, however, at the conclusion that no other solution can equally well suffice as the basis of a scientific treatment of the traditional schedule of propositions, so long, at any rate, as the propositions included in the schedule are regarded as assertoric and not modal.

(*a*) Mill argues that a synthetical proposition necessarily implies "the real existence of the subject, because in the case of a non-existent subject there is nothing for the proposition to assert" (*Logic*, i. 6, § 2). In answer to this it is sufficient to point out that a non-existent thing will be described as possessing attributes which are separately attributes of existing things, although that particular combination of them may not anywhere be found, and if we know (as we may do) that certain of these attributes are always accompanied by other attributes we may predicate the latter of the non-existent thing, thereby obtaining a real proposition which does not involve the actual existence of its subject. As an argument *ad hominem* it may further be pointed out that Mill inclines to deny the existence of perfect straight lines or perfect circles. Would he therefore affirm that we can make no real assertions about such things?

(*b*) Mr. Welton repeats several times that a proposition which relates to a non-existent subject must be a mere jumble of words, a predication in appearance only. "That the meaning of a universal proposition can be expressed as a denial is true, but this is not its primary import. And this denial itself must rest upon what the proposition affirms. Unless *SaP* implies the existence of *S*, and asserts that it possesses *P*, we have no data for denying the existence of *SP'*. For if *S* is non-existent the denial that it is non-*P* can have no intelligible meaning" (*Logic*, p. 241). The examples which we have already given are sufficient to dispose of this objection; but it may be worthwhile to add a further argument. According to Mr. Welton, an **E** proposition implies the existence of its subject but not of its predicate. We cannot then infer *PeS* from *SeP* because we have no assurance of the existence of *P*. But in accordance with the position taken by Mr Welton, we ought to go further and say that *PeS* must be a mere jumble of words unless we are assured of the existence of *P*. It is impossible, however, to regard *PeS* as a mere unmeaning jumble of words, a predication in appearance only, when *SeP* is a significant and true proposition. *PeS* may be false, or it may be an unnatural form of statement, but it cannot be meaningless if *SeP* has a meaning. Take, for example, the propositions—*No woman is now hanged for theft in England*, *No person now hanged for theft in England is a woman*. The second of these propositions is false if it is taken to imply that there are at the present time persons who are hanged for theft in England, but how it can possibly be regarded as meaningless I cannot understand.

---

[264] Compare sections 156, 157.
[265] We may briefly discuss in a note one or two objections to this view which have not yet been explicitly considered.

(*c*) Miss Jones argues that if *some* carries with it an implication of existence, when used with a subject-term, it must do so equally when used with a predicate-term; but the predicate of an **A** proposition being undistributed is practically qualified by *some*; hence, if *Some S is P* implies the existence of *S* and therefore of *P*, *All S is P* must imply the existence of *P* and therefore of *S*. In reply to this argument it may be pointed out, first, that a distinction may fairly be drawn without any risk of confusion between a term explicitly quantified by the word *some* and a term which we can shew to be undistributed but which is not explicitly quantified at all; and, secondly, that the position which we have taken is based upon a consideration of the import of propositions as a whole, not upon the force of signs of quantity considered in the abstract. The irrelevancy of the argument will be apparent if it is taken in connection with the reasons which we have urged for holding that particulars should be interpreted as implying the existence of their subjects.

163. *The Existential Import of Modal Propositions.*—Of apodeictic propositions it may be said still more emphatically than of assertoric universals that they do not necessarily imply the existence of their subjects. For they assert a necessary relation between attributes, the ground of which is frequently to be sought in abstract reasoning rather than in concrete experiences. And the same is true of the denial of apodeictic propositions. We may on abstract grounds assert the possibility of a certain concomitance (or non-concomitance) of attributes without having had actual experience of that concomitance (or non-concomitance), and without intending to imply its actuality. Hence we should not interpret the proposition *S may be P*, any more than the proposition *S must be P*, as by its bare form affirming the existence of *S*.

It has been shewn that in order that the propositions *All S is P* and *Some S is not P* may be true contradictories, one or other of them must be interpreted as implying the existence of *S*. It follows, however, from what has been said above that the same condition need not be fulfilled in order that *S must be P* and *S need not be P* may be true contradictories.[266]

But to this it has to be added that, in order that these two propositions may be true contradictories, one or other of them must be interpreted as implying the *possible existence* of *S*. This line of thought has been suggested in section 160, and it will be pursued farther in sections 176 and 179.

EXERCISES

164. The *particular* judgment has, from different stand-points, been identified (*a*) with the *existential* judgment, (*b*) with the *problematic* judgment, (*c*) with the *narrative* judgment. Comment on each of these views. [C.]

The student may find that to write a detailed answer to this question will help to clear up his views respecting the particular proposition. No detailed answer will here be given; but attention may be called to one or two points.

---

[266] It is because Dr Wolf identifies the ordinary particular proposition with the problematic proposition that he is led to the conclusion that *SaP* and *SoP* are true contradictories although neither of them is interpreted as implying the existence of *S*.

(*a*) Two kinds of existential judgments may be distinguished.

(i) Those which affirm existence indefinitely, that is, somewhere in the universe of discourse; for example, *There are white hares, There is a devil.*

(ii) Those which affirm existence with reference to some definite time and place; for example, *It rains, I am hungry.*

The particular may perhaps be identified with (i), hardly with (ii).

(*b*) We may be justified in affirming the problematical *S may be P*, when we cannot affirm the particular *Some S is P*. There are reasons for interpreting the latter judgment existentially as regards its subject, which do not apply to the former judgment.

(*c*) The narrative judgment need not have the indefinite character of the particular. We may, however, hold that the two kinds of judgment have this in common that there are grounds for interpreting both existentially as regards their subjects.

165. Discuss the relation between the propositions *All S is P* and *All not-S is P*.

This is an interesting case to notice in connection with the discussion raised in sections 158 and 159.

We have

$$SaP = SeP' = P'eS;$$
$$S'aP = S'eP' = P'eS' = P'aS.$$

The given propositions come out, therefore, as contraries.

On the view that we ought not to enter into any discussion concerning existence in connection with immediate inference, we must, I suppose, rest content with this statement of the case. It seems, however, sufficiently curious to demand further investigation and explanation. We may as before take different suppositions with regard to the existential import of propositions.

(1) If every proposition implies the existence of both subject and predicate and their contradictories, then it is at once clear that the two propositions cannot both be true together; for between them they deny the existence of *not-P*.

(2) On the view that propositions imply simply the existence of their subjects, it has been shewn in section 158 that we are not justified in passing from *All not-S is P* to *All not-P is S* unless we are given independently the existence of *not-P*. But it will be observed that in the case before us the given propositions make this impossible. Since *all S is P* and *all not-S is P*, and everything is either *S* or *not-S* by the law of excluded middle, it follows that nothing is *not-P*. In order, therefore, to reduce the given propositions to such a form that they appear as contraries (and consequently[267] as inconsistent with each other) we have to assume the very thing that taken together they really deny.

(3) and (4). On the view that at any rate universal propositions do not imply the existence of their subjects, we have found in section 159 that the propositions *No not-P is S, All not-P is S*, are not necessarily inconsistent, for they may express the fact that *P* constitutes the entire

---

[267] It will be remembered that under suppositions (1) and (2) the ordinary doctrine of contrariety holds good.

universe of discourse. But this fact is just what is given us by the propositions in their original form.

Under each hypothesis, then, the result obtained is satisfactorily accounted for and explained.

166. "The boy is in the garden."

"The centaur is a creation of the poets."

"A square circle is a contradiction."

Discuss the above propositions as illustrating different functions of the verb "to be"; or as bearing upon the logical conception of different universes of discourse or of different kinds of existence. [C.]

167. Discuss the existential import of singular propositions.

"The King of Utopia did not die on Tuesday last." Examine carefully the meaning to be attached to the denial of this proposition. [K.]

168. Some logicians hold that from *All S is P* we may infer *Some not-S is not-P*. Take as an illustration, *All human actions are foreseen by the Deity*. [C.]

169. Discuss the validity of the following inference:—All trespassers will be prosecuted, No trespassers have been prosecuted, therefore, There have been no trespassers. [C.]

170. On the assumption that particulars are interpreted as implying while universals are not interpreted as implying the existence of their subjects in the universe of discourse, examine (stating your reasons) the validity of the following inferences; *All S is P* and *Some R is not S* therefore, *Some not-S is not P*; *All S is P* and *Some R is not P*, therefore, *Some not-S is not P*; *All S is P* and *Some R is S*, it is, therefore, false that *No P is S*; *All S is P* and *Some R is P*, it is, therefore, false that *No P is S*. [K.]

171. Discuss the formal validity of the following arguments, (i) on the supposition that all categorical propositions are to be interpreted as implying the existence of their subjects in the universe of discourse, (ii) on the supposition that no categorical propositions are to be so interpreted:

(*a*) All P is Q, therefore, All AP is AQ;
(*b*) All AP is AQ, therefore, Some P is Q. [K.]

172. Work out the doctrine of Opposition and the doctrine of Immediate Inferences on the hypothesis that universals are to be interpreted as implying, while particulars are not to be interpreted as implying, the existence of their subjects in the universe of discourse. [K.]

Chapter 13

CONDITIONAL AND HYPOTHETICAL PROPOSITIONS

173. *The distinction between Conditional Propositions and Hypothetical Propositions*[268]—Propositions commonly written in the form *If A is B, C is D* belong to two very different types. For they may be the expression either of simple judgments or of compound judgments (as distinguished in section 55).

In the first place, *A being B* and *C being D* may be two events or two combinations of properties, concerning which it is affirmed that whenever or wherever the first occurs the second will occur also. For example, *If an import duty is a source of revenue, it does not afford protection*; *If a child is spoilt, his parents suffer*; *If a straight line falling upon two other straight lines makes the alternate angles equal to one another, the two straight lines are parallel to one another*; *If a lighted match is applied to gunpowder, there will be an explosion*; *Where the carcase is, there shall the eagles be gathered together*. What is affirmed in all such cases as these is a connection between phenomena; it may be either a co-inherence of attributes in a common subject, or a relation in time or space between certain occurrences. Propositions belonging to this type may be called distinctively *conditional*.

But again, *A is B* and *C is D* may be two propositions of independent import, the relation between which cannot be directly resolved into any time or space relation or into an affirmation of the co-inherence of attributes in a common subject. In other words, a relation may be affirmed between the truth of two judgments as holding good once and for all without distinction of place or time or circumstance. For example, *If it be a sin to covet honour, I am the most offending soul alive*; *If patience is a virtue, there are painful virtues*; *If there is a righteous God, the wicked will not escape their just punishment*; *If virtue is involuntary, so is vice*; *If the earth is immoveable, the sun moves round the earth*. Propositions belonging to this type may be called *hypothetical* as distinguished from conditional, or they may be spoken of still more distinctively as *true hypotheticals* or *pure hypotheticals*.[269]

The parts of the conditional and also of the true hypothetical are called the *antecedent* and the *consequent*. Thus, in the proposition *If A is B, C is D*, the antecedent is *A is B*, the consequent is *C is D*.

---

[268] For the distinction indicated in the present section I was in the first instance indebted to an essay, written in 1884, by Mr W. E. Johnson. This essay has not been published in its original form; but the substance of it has been included in some papers on *The Logical Calculus* by Mr Johnson which appeared in *Mind* in 1892.

[269] The above distinction has been adopted in some recent treatises on Logic, but it must be borne in mind that most logicians use the terms *conditional* and *hypothetical* as synonymous or else draw a distinction between them different from the above.

It is impossible formally to distinguish between conditionals and hypotheticals so long as we keep to the expression *If A is B, C is D*, since this may be either the one or the other. The following forms, however, are unmistakeably conditional: *Whenever A is B, C is D*; *In all cases in which A is B, C is D*; *If any P is Q then that P is R*.[270] The form *If A is true then C is true* is, on the other hand, distinctively hypothetical. *A* and *C* here stand for *propositions* or *judgments*, not terms, and the words "is true" are introduced in order to make this explicit. It is quite sufficient, however, to write the true hypothetical in the form *If A then C*.

Since a conditional proposition usually contains a reference to some concurrence in time or space, the *if* of the antecedent may as a rule be replaced either by *when* or by *where*, as the case may be, without any change in the significance of the proposition; but the same cannot be said in the case of the true hypothetical. This consideration will often suffice to resolve any doubt that may arise in concrete cases as to the particular type to which any given proposition belongs. Another and more fundamental criterion may be found in the answer to the question whether or not the antecedent and consequent are propositions of independent import, whose meaning will not be impaired if they are considered apart from one another. If the answer is in the affirmative, then the proposition is hypothetical. Thus, taking examples of hypotheticals already given, we find that the antecedents, *It is a sin to covet honour*, *Patience is a virtue*, *Virtue is involuntary*, and the consequents, *I am the most offending soul alive*, *There are painful virtues*, *Vice is involuntary*, all retain their full meaning though separated from one another. If, on the other hand, the consequent necessarily refers us back to the antecedent in order that it may be fully intelligible, then the proposition is conditional. Thus, taking by itself the consequent in the first conditional given on page 249, namely, *it does not afford protection*, we are at once led to ask what is here meant by *it*. The answer is—*that import duty*. But *what* import duty? An adequate answer can be given only by introducing into the consequent the whole of the antecedent,—*an import duty which is a source of revenue does not afford protection*. We now have the full force of our original conditional proposition in the form of a single categorical. It will be found that if other conditionals are treated in the same way, they resolve themselves similarly into categoricals of the form *All PQ is R*.[271] The problem of the reduction of conditionals and hypotheticals to categorical form will be considered in more detail later on in this chapter, and it will be shewn that whilst such reduction is always possible, and generally simple and natural, in the case of conditionals, it is not possible at all (with terms corresponding to the original antecedent and consequent) in the case of hypotheticals.[272]

---

[270] Conditionals can generally be reduced to the last of these three forms without much difficulty, and such reduction is sometimes useful. A consideration of the concrete examples already given will, however, shew that a certain amount of manipulation may be required in order to effect the reduction. The following are examples: *If any child is spoilt, then that child will have suffering parents*; *If any two straight lines are such that another straight line falling upon them makes the alternate angles equal to one another, then those two straight lines are parallel to one another*.

[271] As another example, we may take the conditional proposition, *If the weather is dry, the British root-crops are light*. Here it may at first sight appear that the consequent is a proposition of independent import. The proposition, *The British root-crops are light*, is, however, a judgment incompletely stated. For it contains a time-reference that needs to be made explicit. The conditional really means, *If in any year the weather is dry, the British root-crops in that year are light*; and this is equivalent to the categorical, *Any year in which the weather is dry is a year in which the British root-crops are light*. By looking at the conditional in this way, we see the necessity of referring back to the antecedent in order that the consequent may be fully expressed.

[272] The question may be raised whether a proposition of the form, *If this P is Q, it is R*, is properly to be described as a singular conditional or as a hypothetical. The answer is that a proposition of this form affords a kind of junction between the conditional and the hypothetical; it is derivable from the conditional, *If any P is Q, it is*

174. *The Import of Conditional Propositions.*—It is sometimes held that the real *differentia* of all propositions of the form *If A is B, C is D* is "to express human doubt." Clearly, however, there is no intention to express doubt as regards the relation between the antecedent and the consequent; and the doubt must, therefore, be supposed to relate to the actual occurrence of the antecedent. But so far at any rate as *conditionals* are concerned, the doubt which they may thus imply must be considered incidental rather than the fundamental or differentiating characteristic belonging to them. The *if* of the conditional may, as we have seen, usually be replaced by *when* without altering the significance of the proposition, and in this case the element of doubt is no more prominent than in the categorical proposition. From the *material* standpoint, conditionals may or may not involve the actual occurrence of their antecedents. Whenever the connection between the antecedent and the consequent can be inferred from the nature of the antecedent independently of specific experience (and this may be the more usual case), then the actual happening of the antecedent is not involved; but if our knowledge of the connection does depend on specific experience (as it sometimes may), then such actual happening is materially involved. For example, the statement, "If we descend into the earth, the temperature increases at a nearly uniform rate of 1° Fahr. for every fifty feet of descent down to almost a mile," is based upon knowledge gained by actual descents into the earth having been made, and apart from such experience the truth of the statement would not have been known.

The question of main importance in regard to the import of conditional propositions is whether such propositions are to be interpreted as modal or as merely assertoric. Confining ourselves for the present to the universal affirmative, that is, to the form *If any P is Q then it is R*, are we affirming a necessary relation between *P* being *Q* and its being *R*, or are we merely affirming that it so happens that every *P* that is *Q* is also *R*? This is really in another form the distinction already drawn between unconditionally universal propositions and empirically universal propositions, and our answer must again be that the same form of words may express the one judgment or the other. There can be no doubt that the proposition, *If the angles at the base of a triangle are equal to one another, that triangle is isosceles*, is intended to be interpreted modally as expressing a necessary connection, while the proposition, *If any book is taken down from that shelf, it will be found to be a novel*, would be intended to be interpreted merely assertorically.

In ordinary discourse conditionals are as a rule modal; but this is not universally the case. Unless, therefore, we are prepared to depart from ordinary usage (and there is a good deal to be said for such departure), we must recognise both *assertoric conditionals* and *modal conditionals*, and this distinction must be borne in mind in all that follows. We shall find that practically the same problem arises in regard to true hypotheticals, and we shall have to consider it further in that connection.

175. *Conditional Propositions and Categorical Propositions.*—We may go on to consider what is the essential nature of the distinction between conditional propositions and categorical propositions, and in particular whether the distinction is one of verbal form only or one that corresponds to a real distinction between judgments.

R; but it is itself hypothetical. The antecedent and the consequent are propositions of independent import; and the proposition as a whole is not directly reducible (as is the conditional, *If any P is Q, it is P*) to categorical form. Thus, the proposition, *If any P is Q, it is R*, may *prima facie* be reduced to the form *Any P that is Q is R*; but the proposition, *If this P is Q, it is R*, certainly cannot be identified with the singular categorical, *This P which is Q is R*.

If a vital distinction is to be drawn between the two forms, it must be on one or other of the two following grounds, namely, either (i) that the categorical is to be interpreted assertorically while the conditional is to be interpreted modally, or (ii) that the categorical is to be interpreted as implying the existence of its subject while the conditional is not to be interpreted as implying the occurrence of its antecedent.

(i) There is much to be said for adopting a convention by which the categorical form would be interpreted assertorically and the conditional form modally. The adoption of this convention would, however, necessitate some modification of the forms of ordinary speech, for, as we have already seen, the proposition *All S is P* is in current use sometimes apodeictic, while the proposition *If any S is P then it is Q* may (though perhaps rarely) be merely assertoric. Whether the one form or the other is used really depends a good deal on linguistic considerations. Consider, for instance, the propositions, *All isosceles triangles have the angles at their base equal to one another, If the angles at the base of a triangle are equal to one another, that triangle is isosceles*. These propositions fall naturally into the categorical and conditional forms respectively, simply because there happens to be no single adjective (like "isosceles") which connotes "having two equal angles." It is clear, however, that the use of the one form rather than the other is not intended to imply any fundamental difference in the character of the relation asserted. If either of the propositions in its ordinary use is apodeictic, so is the other; if either is merely assertoric, so is the other.

It is to be added that if we adopt the convention under consideration then the universal categorical is inferable from the universal conditional, but not *vice versâ*; while, on the other hand, the problematic conditional (which corresponds to the particular) is inferable from the particular categorical, but not *vice versâ*. Thus, *All PQ is R* is subaltern to *If any P is Q it is R*, while *If any P is Q it may be R* is subaltern to *Some PQ is R*.

(ii) We may pass on to consider whether categoricals and conditionals are to be differentiated in respect of their existential import.

We have seen in section 163 that if categoricals are interpreted modally they are not to be regarded as necessarily implying the existence of their subjects; and certainly conditionals, interpreted modally, are not to be regarded as necessarily implying the occurrence of their antecedents. Hence if both propositional forms are interpreted modally, we have no differentiation as regards their existential import.

It further seems clear that, so far as universal are concerned, a conditional proposition—even though interpreted as merely assertoric—is not to be regarded as necessarily implying the actual occurrence of its antecedent. Hence, whether, on the assertoric interpretation of both, the two forms are to be existentially differentiated depends upon our existential interpretation of the categorical.

(*a*) If a universal categorical is interpreted as necessarily implying the actual existence of its subject, then we have a marked distinction between the two forms.[273] *If any P is Q then it is also R* cannot be resolved into *All PQ is R*, since the latter implies the existence of *PQ*, while the former does not.

(*b*) If, on the other hand, universal categoricals are not interpreted as necessarily implying the existence of their subjects, then universal conditionals and universal categoricals (both being interpreted assertorically) may be resolved into one another. We may say indifferently

---

[273] This is Ueberweg's view, "The categorical judgment, in distinction from the hypothetical, always includes the pre-supposition of the existence of the subject" (*Logic*, § 122).

All S is P or *If anything is S it is P*; *If ever A is B then on all such occasions C is B* or *All occasions of A being B are occasions of C being D*.

Particular conditionals, so far as they are merely assertoric, are almost without exception based upon specific experience. Hence they may not unreasonably be interpreted as implying the occurrence of their antecedents, as, for example, in the proposition, "Sometimes when Parliament meets, it is opened by the Sovereign in person." The existential interpretation of categoricals for which a preference was expressed in the preceding chapter may therefore be adopted for conditionals also, so far as they are merely assertoric; and the two forms become mutually interchangeable.

On the whole, except in so far as we adopt the convention indicated under (i) above, there seems no reason for drawing a vital distinction between judgments according as they are expressed in the conditional or the categorical form.[274] Many of the conditionals of ordinary discourse are indeed so obviously equivalent to categoricals that they hardly seem to require a separate consideration.[275] At the same time, as we have seen, some statements fall more naturally into the one form and some into the other. The more complex the subject-term, the greater is the probability that the natural form of the proposition will be conditional.

176. *The Opposition of Conditional Propositions.*—This question needs a separate discussion according as conditionals are interpreted (*a*) assertorically, or (*b*) modally.

(*a*) If conditionals are interpreted assertorically, then the ordinary distinctions both of quality and of quantity can be applied to them in just the same way as to categoricals. We may regard the quality of a conditional as determined by the quality of its consequent; thus, the proposition *If any P is Q then that P is not R* may be treated as negative.[276] As regards quantity, conditionals are to be regarded as universal or particular, according as the consequent is affirmed to accompany the antecedent in all or merely in some cases.

We have then the four types included in the ordinary four-fold schedule:—

If any P is Q, it is also R; **A**
If any P is Q, it is not also R; **E**
Sometimes if a P is Q, it is also R; **I**
Sometimes if a P is Q, it is not also R. **O**

---

[274] It has been argued that, starting from the categorical form, we cannot pass to the conditional, if the subject of the proposition is a simple term. The basis of this argument is that the antecedent of a conditional requires two terms, and that in the case supposed these are not provided by the categorical. Thus, Miss Jones (*Elements of Logic*, p. 112) takes the example, "All lions are quadrupeds." It will not do, she says, to reduce this to the form, "If any creatures are lions, they are quadrupeds," since this involves the introduction of a new term, and passing back again to the categorical form, we should have "All creatures which are lions are quadrupeds," a proposition not equivalent to our original proposition. If, however, "creature" is regarded as part of the connotation of "lion," there is no reason for refusing to allow that the two propositions are equivalent to one another. Similarly, in any concrete instance, by taking some part of the connotation of the subject of our categorical proposition, we can obtain the additional term required for its reduction to the conditional form. Where we are dealing with purely symbolic expressions, and this particular solution of the difficulty is not open to us, we may have recourse to the all-embracing term "anything," such a proposition as *All S is P* being reduced to the form *If anything is S it is P*.

[275] The examples given at the commencement of section 173 are reducible to the following categoricals: *Import duties which are sources of revenue do not afford protection*; *All spoilt children have suffering parents*; *All pairs of straight lines which are such that another straight line falling upon them makes the alternate angles equal to one another are parallel*; *All occasions of the application of a lighted match to gunpowder are occasions of an explosion*; *Any place where there is a carcase is a place where the eagles will gather together*.

[276] The negative force of this proposition would be more clearly brought out if it were written in the form *If any P is Q then it is not the case that it is also R*. The categorical equivalent is *No PQ is R*.

These propositions constitute the ordinary square of opposition, and if conditionals are assimilated to categoricals so far as their existential import is concerned, then the opposition of conditionals on the assertoric interpretation seems to require no separate discussion.[277] It may, however, be pointed out that there is more danger of contradictories being confused with contraries in the case of conditionals than in the case of categoricals. *If A is B then C is not D* is very liable to be given as the contradictory of *If A is B then C is D*. But it is clear on consideration that both these propositions may be false. For example, the two statements—If the Times says one thing, the Westminster Gazette says another; If the Times says one thing, the Westminster Gazette says the same, i.e., does not say another—might be, and as a matter of fact are, both false; the two papers are sometimes in agreement and sometimes not.

(*b*) On the modal interpretation, the distinction between apodeictic and problematic takes the place of that between universal and particular; and if we maintain the distinction between affirmative and negative, we have the four following propositions corresponding to the ordinary square of opposition:

If any P is Q, that P must be R; $\mathbf{A}_m$
If any P is Q, that P cannot be R; $\mathbf{E}_m$
If any P is Q, that P may be R; $\mathbf{I}_m$
If any P is Q, that P need not be R. $\mathbf{O}_m$

It will be convenient to have distinctive symbols to denote modal propositions, and those that we have here introduced will serve to bring out the analogies between modals and the ordinary assertoric forms.

In the above schedule, subject to a certain condition mentioned below, $\mathbf{A}_m$ and $\mathbf{O}_m$, and also $\mathbf{E}_m$ and $\mathbf{I}_m$, are contradictories according to the definition given in section 84; $\mathbf{A}_m$ and $\mathbf{E}_m$ are contraries; $\mathbf{A}_m$ and $\mathbf{I}_m$, and also $\mathbf{E}_m$ and $\mathbf{O}_m$, are subalterns; and $\mathbf{I}_m$ and $\mathbf{O}_m$ are subcontraries.

The condition referred to relates to the interpretation of the propositions as regards the implication of the possibility of their antecedents. Thus, in order that $\mathbf{A}_m$ and $\mathbf{O}_m$ (or $\mathbf{E}_m$ and $\mathbf{I}_m$) may be true contradictories it is necessary that apodeictic and problematic propositions shall be interpreted *differently* in this respect. If, for example, $\mathbf{A}_m$ is interpreted as not implying the possibility of its antecedent then its full import is to deny the possibility of the combination *P* and *Q* without *R*. Its contradictory must affirm this possibility. $\mathbf{O}_m$ will not, however, do this unless it is interpreted as implying the possibility of the combination *P, Q*.

It is necessary to call attention to this complication, but hardly necessary to work out in detail the results which follow from the various principles of interpretation that might be adopted. If the student will do this for himself, he will find that the results correspond broadly with those obtained in section 159.[278]

---

[277] The four propositions are precisely equivalent to the four categoricals,—*All PQ is R, No PQ is R, Some PQ is R, Some PQ is not R*.

[278] In connection with the problem of opposition we may touch briefly on the relation between the apodeictic proposition *If any P is Q that P must be R* and the assertoric proposition *Some PQ is not R*. These propositions are not contradictories, for they may both be false. They cannot, however, both be true; and the latter, if it can be established, affords a valid ground for the denial of the former. Mr Bosanquet appears not to admit this, but to maintain, in opposition to it, that the enumerative particular is of no value as overthrowing the abstract universal. "When we have said that *If* (i.e., *in so far as*) *a man is good, he is wise*, it is idle to reply that *Some good men are not wise*. This is to attach an abstract principle with unanalysed examples. What we must say in

177. *Immediate Inferences from Conditional Propositions.*—In a conditional proposition the antecedent and the consequent correspond respectively to the subject and the predicate of a categorical proposition. In conversion, therefore, the old consequent must be the new antecedent, and in contraposition the negation of the old consequent must be the new antecedent.

(*a*) On the assertoric interpretation, the analogy with categoricals is so close that it is unnecessary to treat immediate inferences from conditionals in any detail. One or two examples may suffice. Taking the **A** proposition, *If any P is Q then it is R*, we have for its converse *Sometimes if a P is R it is also Q*, and for its contrapositive *If any P is not R then it is not Q*. Taking the **E** proposition *If any P is Q then it is not R*, we have for its converse *If any P is R then it is not Q*, and for its contrapositive *Sometimes if a P is not R it is Q*. The validity of these inferences is of course affected by the existential interpretation of the propositions just as in the case of the categoricals. It will be noticed that in some immediate inferences (for example, the contraposition of **A**) the conditional form has an advantage over the ordinary categorical form inasmuch as it avoids the use of negative terms, the employment of which is so strongly objected to by Sigwart and some other logicians.[279]

(*b*) If conditionals are interpreted modally, then the apodeictic form takes the place of the universal, and the problematic takes the place of the particular. On this basis, the converse of *If any P is Q that P must be R* would be *If any P is R that P may be Q*, and the contrapositive would be *If any P is not R that P cannot be Q*.

Are these inferences legitimate? On the interpretation that a modal proposition implies nothing as to the possibility of its antecedent, then our answer must be in the affirmative, as regards the contraposition of $\mathbf{A}_m$. The full import both of the original proposition and of the contrapositive is to deny the possibility of the combination *P* and *Q* without *R*. On the same interpretation, however, the conversion of $\mathbf{A}_m$ is not valid. For the converse implies that if *PR* is possible then *PQ* is possible, while the possibility of *PR* combined with the impossibility of *PQ* is compatible with the truth of the original proposition. It can be shewn similarly that, while the conversion of $\mathbf{E}_m$ is valid, its contraposition is invalid.

If we were to vary the interpretation, the results would be different.

The correspondence between the results shewn above and our results respecting the conversion and contraposition of the assertoric **A** and **E** propositions, on the interpretation that no proposition implies the existence of its subject (see page 225), is obvious. The truth is that the interpretation of modals in respect to the *possibility* of their antecedents gives rise to problems precisely analogous to those arising out of the interpretation of assertoric propositions in respect to the *actuality* of their subjects. It is unnecessary that we should work out the different cases in detail.

Amongst immediate inferences from a conditional proposition, its reduction to categorical form, so far as this is valid, is generally included. This is a case of what has been called *change of relation*, meaning thereby an immediate inference in which we pass from a given proposition to another which belongs to a different category in the division of

---

order to deny the above-mentioned abstract judgment is something of this kind: *If or Though a man is good, yet it does not follow that he is wise*, that is, *Though a man is good, yet he need not be wise*" (*Logic*, i. p. 316). But surely if we find that some good men are not wise, we are justified in saying that though a man is good yet he need not be wise. Of course the converse does not hold. We might be able to shew that wisdom does not necessarily accompany goodness by some other method than that of producing instances. But if we can produce undoubted instances, that amply suffices to confute the apodeictic conditional.

[279] Compare page 136.

propositions according to relation (see section 54). The more convenient term *transversion* is used by Miss Jones for this process.

How far conditionals can be inferred from categoricals and *vice versâ* depends on their interpretation. If both types of propositions are interpreted assertorically or both modally, and if they are interpreted similarly as regards the implication of the existence (or possibility) of their subjects (or antecedents), then the validity of passing from either type to the other cannot be called in question. Some doubt may, however, be raised as to whether in this case we have an inference at all or merely a verbal change. This is a distinction to which attention will be called later on.

If conditionals are interpreted modally and categoricals assertorically then (apart from any complications that may arise from existential implications) **A** can be inferred from $\mathbf{A}_m$ or **E** from $\mathbf{E}_m$, but not *vice versâ*. On the other hand, $\mathbf{I}_m$ can be inferred from **I**, or $\mathbf{O}_m$ from **O**, but not *vice versâ*.

We have another case of transversion when we pass from conditional to disjunctive, or from disjunctive to conditional. The consideration of this case must be deferred until we have discussed disjunctives.

178. *The Import of Hypothetical Propositions.*—The pure hypothetical may be written symbolically in the form *If A is true then C is true*, or more briefly, *If A then C*, where *A* and *C* stand for propositions of independent import. It is clear that this proposition affirms nothing as regards the truth or falsity of either *A* or *C* taken separately. We may indeed frame the proposition, knowing that *C* is false, with the express object of showing that *A* is false also. What we have is of course a judgment not about either *A* or *C* taken separately, but about *A* and *C* in relation to one another.

The main question at issue in regard to the import of the hypothetical proposition is whether it is merely assertoric or is modal. The contrast may be simply put by asking whether, when we say *If A then C*, our intention is merely *to deny the actuality of the conjunction of A true with C false* or is *to declare this conjunction to be an impossibility*.

The contrast between these two interpretations can be brought out most clearly by asking how the proposition *If A then C* is to be contradicted. If our intention is merely to deny the actuality of the conjunction of *A* true with *C* false, then the contradictory must assert the actuality of this conjunction; if our intention is to deny the possibility of the conjunction, then the contradictory will merely assert its possibility. In other words, on the assertoric interpretation the contradictory will be *A is true but C is false*;[280] on the modal interpretation it will be *If A is true C may be false*.[281]

Hypotheticals intended to be interpreted assertorically are to be met with in ordinary discourse, but they are unusual. There appear to be two cases: (*a*) When we know that one or other of two propositions is true but do not know (or do not remember) which, we may express our knowledge in the form of a hypothetical, *If X is not true then Y is true*, and such hypothetical will be merely assertoric. For example, *If the flowers I planted in this bed were*

---

[280] We may look at it in this way. Let *AC* denote the truth of both *A* and *C*, *AC'* the truth of *A* and the falsity of *C*, and so on. Then there are four *à priori* possibilities, namely, *AC*, *AC'*, *A'C*, *A'C'*, one or other of which must hold good, but any pair of which are mutually inconsistent. The proposition *If A then C* merely excludes *AC'*, and still leaves *AC*, *A'C*, *A'C'*, as possible alternatives. In denying it, therefore, we must definitely affirm *AC'*, and exclude the three other alternatives. Hence the contradictory as above stated.

[281] A certain assumption is necessary, in order that this result may be correct. The opposition of hypotheticals on the modal interpretation will be discussed in more detail in section 179.

not pansies they were violets. Here the intention is merely to deny the actuality of the flowers being neither pansies nor violets. (*b*) We may deny a proposition emphatically by a hypothetical in which the proposition in question is combined as antecedent with a manifestly false consequent; and such hypothetical will again be merely assertoric. For example, *If what you say is true, I'm a Dutchman*; *If that boy comes back, I'll eat my head* (vide *Oliver Twist*); *I'm hanged if I know what you mean*. In these examples the intention is to deny the actuality (not the possibility) of the conjunctions,—What you say is true and *I am not a Dutchman*; That boy will come back and *I shall not eat my head*; *I am not hanged* and I know what you mean; and since the elements of the conjunctions printed in italics are admittedly true, the force of the propositions is to deny the truth of the other elements, that is to say, to affirm,— What you say is not true, That boy will not come back, I do not know what you mean. Similarly we may sometimes employ the hypothetical form of expression as an emphatic way of declaring the truth of the consequent (an antecedent being chosen which is admittedly true); for example, *If he cannot act, at any rate he can sing*. Here once more the hypothetical is merely assertoric.

It cannot, however, be maintained that any of the above are typical hypotheticals; and the claim that our natural interpretation of hypotheticals is ordinarily modal may be justified on the ground that we do not usually consider it to be necessary to affirm the antecedent in order to be able to deny a hypothetical. We have seen that, in order to deny the assertoric hypothetical *If A then C*, we must affirm *A* and deny *C*; but we should usually regard it as sufficient for denial if we can shew that there is no necessary connection between the truth of *A* and that of *C*, whether *A* is actually true or not.

We shall then in the main be in agreement with ordinary usage if we interpret hypotheticals modally, and the adoption of such an interpretation will also give hypotheticals a more distinctive character. In what follows the hypothetical form will accordingly be regarded as modal, except in so far as an explicit statement is made to the contrary.[282]

Some writers who adopt the modal interpretation of hypotheticals speak of the consequent as being an *inference* from the antecedent. There are no doubt some hypotheticals to which this description accurately applies. Thus, we may have hypotheticals which are *formal* in the sense in which that term has been used in section 31, the consequent being, for

---

[282] *Either C is true or A is not true* is usually regarded as the disjunctive equivalent of the hypothetical *If A is true then C is true*. The relation between these two propositions will be discussed further later on. It is, however, desirable to point out at once that, if the equivalence is to hold good, both the propositions must be interpreted assertorically or both modally. There is a good deal to be said for differentiating the two forms by regarding the hypothetical as modal and the disjunctive as merely assertoric. This method of treatment is explicitly adopted by Mr McColl. He writes (using the symbolism, *a* : *b* for *If a then b*, *a* + *b* for *a or b*, *a'* for the denial of *a*)—"The expression *a* : *b* may be read *a* implies *b* or *If a is true, b must be true*. The statement *a* : *b* implies *a'* + *b*. But it may be asked are not the two statements really equivalent; ought we not therefore to write *a* : *b* = *a'* + *b*? Now if the two statements are really equivalent their denials will also be equivalent. Let us see if this will be the case, taking as concrete examples: 'If he persists in his extravagance he will be ruined'; 'He will either discontinue his extravagance or he will be ruined.' The denial of *a* : *b* is (*a* : *b*)' and this denial may be read—'He may persist in his extravagance without necessarily being ruined.' The denial of *a'* + *b* is *ab'* which may be read—'He will persist in his extravagance and he will not be ruined.' Now it is quite evident that the second denial is a much stronger and more positive statement than the first. The first only asserts the *possibility* of the combination *ab'*; the second asserts the *certainty* of the same combination. The denials of the statements *a* : *b* and *a'* + *b* having thus been proved to be not equivalent, it follows that the statements *a* : *b* and *a'* + *b* are themselves not equivalent, and that, though *a'* + *b* is a necessary consequence of *a* : *b*, yet *a* : *b* is not a necessary consequence of *a'* + *b*" (see *Mind*, 1880, pp. 50 to 54; one or two slight verbal changes have been made in this quotation).

instance, an immediate inference from the antecedent, or being the conclusion of a syllogism of which the premisses constitute the antecedent. The following are examples,—*If all isosceles triangles have the angles at the base equal to one another, then no triangle the angles at whose base are unequal can be isosceles*; *If all men are mortal and the Pope is a man, then the Pope must be mortal.*

But more usually the consequent of a hypothetical proposition cannot be inferred from the antecedent alone. The aid is required of suppressed premisses which are taken for granted, the premiss which alone is expressed being perhaps the only one as to the truth of which any doubt is regarded as admissible. It would, therefore, be better to speak of the consequent as being the *necessary consequence* of the antecedent, than as being an *inference* from it. When we speak of *C* as being an inference from *A*, there is a suggestion that *A* affords the complete justification of *C*, whereas when we speak of it as a necessary consequence, this suggestion is at any rate less prominent.[283]

179. *The Opposition of Hypothetical Propositions.*—Regarding hypotheticals as always affirming a necessary consequence, it may reasonably be held that they do not admit of distinctions of *quality*. Sigwart accordingly lays it down that all hypotheticals are affirmative. "Passing to hypothetical judgments containing negations, we find that the form 'If *A* is, *B* is not' represents the negation of a proposition as the necessary consequence of an affirmation, thus affirming that the hypotheses *A* and *B* are incompatible."[284] The force of this argument must be admitted. There is, however, some convenience in distinguishing between hypotheticals according as they lead up, in the consequent, to an affirmation or a denial; and in the formal treatment of hypotheticals, we shall be better able to preserve an analogy with categoricals and conditionals if we denote the proposition *If X is true then Y is true* by the symbol $\mathbf{A}_m$, and the proposition *If X is true then Y is not true* by the symbol $\mathbf{E}_m$.

Whether or not we decide thus to recognise distinctions of quality in the case of hypotheticals, we certainly cannot recognise distinctions of *quantity*. The antecedent of a hypothetical is not an event which may recur an indefinite number of times, but a proposition which is simply true or false. We have already seen that the same proposition cannot be sometimes true and sometimes false, since propositions referring to different times are different propositions.[285]

Do not distinctions of *modality*, however, take the place of distinctions of quantity? Up to this point, we have practically confined our attention to the *apodeictic* hypothetical, *If A then C*. This proposition is denied by the proposition *If A is true still C need not be true* (that is to say, *The truth of C is not a necessary consequence of the truth of A*). Can this latter proposition be described as a *problematic* hypothetical? Clearly it is not a hypothetical at all if we begin by defining a hypothetical as the affirmation of a necessary consequence. There

---

[283] Miss Jones (*General Logic*, p. 45) divides hypotheticals into *formal* or *self-contained hypotheticals* and *referential hypotheticals*. In the former, "the consequent is an inference from the antecedent alone"; in the latter, "the consequent is inferred not from the antecedent alone, but from the antecedent taken in conjunction with some other unexpressed proposition or propositions."

[284] *Logic*, i. p. 226.

[285] This, as Mr Johnson has pointed out, must be taken in connection with the recognition of propositions as involving *multiple quantification*. "Thus we may indicate a series of propositions involving single, double, triple ... quantification, which may reach any order of multiplicity: (1) 'All luxuries are taxed'; (2) 'In some countries all luxuries are taxed'; (3) 'At some periods it is true that in all countries all luxuries are taxed'.... with respect to each of the types of proposition (1), (2), (3).... I contend that, when made explicit with respect to time or place, etc., it is absurd to speak of them as sometimes true and sometimes false" (*Mind*, 1892, p. 30 n.).

seems, however, no need for this limitation. We may define a hypothetical as a proposition which starting from the hypothesis of the truth (or falsity) of a given proposition affirms (or denies) that the truth (or falsity) of another proposition is a necessary consequence thereof. But, whether or not we adopt this definition, there can be no doubt that the proposition *If A then possibly C* appropriately finds a place in the same schedule of propositions as *If A then necessarily C*. In such a schedule we have the four forms,—

If A is true then C is true; $\mathbf{A}_m$
If A is true then C is not true; $\mathbf{E}_m$
If A is true still C may be true; $\mathbf{I}_m$
If A is true still C need not be true. $\mathbf{O}_m$

These four propositions correspond to those included in the ordinary square of opposition; and, if we start with the assumption that A is possibly true,[286] the ordinary relations of opposition hold good between them. $\mathbf{A}_m$ and $\mathbf{O}_m$, $\mathbf{E}_m$ and $\mathbf{I}_m$ are pairs of contradictories; $\mathbf{A}_m$ and $\mathbf{E}_m$ are contraries; $\mathbf{A}_m$ and $\mathbf{I}_m$, $\mathbf{E}_m$ and $\mathbf{O}_m$, are pairs of subalterns; $\mathbf{I}_m$ and $\mathbf{O}_m$ are subcontraries.

If, however, it is *not* assumed that A is possibly true, then the problem is more complicated, since the character of the relations is affected by the manner in which the propositions are interpreted in respect to the possibility of their antecedents. The results are substantially the same as in the case of modal conditionals (section 176), and correspond with those obtained in section 159, where the analogous problem in regard to categoricals (assertorically interpreted) is discussed. Thus, in order that $\mathbf{A}_m$, and $\mathbf{O}_m$, $\mathbf{E}_m$ and $\mathbf{I}_m$, may be contradictories, apodeictic and problematic propositions must be interpreted *differently* as regards the implication or non-implication of the possible truth of their antecedents; while, on the other hand, in order that $\mathbf{A}_m$ and $\mathbf{I}_m$, $\mathbf{E}_m$ and $\mathbf{O}_m$, may be subalterns, problematic propositions must not be interpreted as implying the possible truth of their antecedents unless apodeictic propositions are interpreted *similarly* in this respect. If we interpret neither apodeictic nor problematic hypotheticals as implying the possible truth of their antecedents, then the contradictory of *If A, then C* may be expressed in the form *Possibly A, but not C* (or, as it may also be formulated, *A is possibly true, and if it is true, still C need not be true*).

It would occupy too much space to discuss in detail all the problems that might be raised in this connection. The principles involved have been sufficiently indicated; and the reader will find no difficulty in working out other cases for himself. We may, however, touch briefly on the relation between the propositions *If A then C* and *If A then not C*, shewing in particular that on no supposition are they true contradictories.

If these two propositions are interpreted assertorically, then so far from being contradictories, they are subcontraries. For, supposing A happens not to be true, then it cannot be said that either of them is false: the statement *If A then C* merely excludes AC', and *If A then C'* merely excludes AC; hence two possibilities are left, $A'C$ or $A'C'$, neither of which is

---

[286] By this is meant that we start with the assumption that A is possibly true *independently of the affirmation of any one of the propositions in question*. The reader must particularly notice that this assumption is quite different from the assumption that each of the propositional forms implies as part of its import that A is possibly true; otherwise the results reached in this paragraph may appear to be inconsistent with those reached in the following paragraph.

inconsistent with either of the propositions.[287] On the other hand, the propositions cannot both be false, since this would mean the truth of both AC' and AC.

Returning to the modal interpretation of the propositions, then if interpreted as implying the possible truth of their antecedents, they are contraries. They cannot both be true, but may both be false. It may be that neither the truth nor the falsity of C is a necessary consequence of the truth of A.[288]

Once more, if interpreted modally but not as implying the possible truth of their antecedents, the propositions may both be true as well as both false. This case is realised when we establish the impossibility of the truth of a proposition by shewing that, if it were true, inconsistent results would follow.

180. *Immediate Inferences from Hypothetical Propositions.*—The most important immediate inference from the proposition *If A then C* is *If C' then A'*. This inference is analogous to *contraposition* in the case of categoricals, and may without any risk of confusion be called by the same name. We may accordingly define the term *contraposition* as applied to hypotheticals as *a process of immediate inference by which we obtain a new hypothetical having for its antecedent the contradictory of the old consequent, and for its consequent the contradictory of the old antecedent.* If we recognise distinctions of quality in hypotheticals, then (as regards apodeictic hypotheticals) this process is valid in the case of affirmatives only. It will be observed that from the contrapositive we can pass back to the original proposition; and from this it follows that the original proposition and its contrapositive are equivalents.[289] The following are examples: "If patience is a virtue, there are painful virtues" = "If there are no painful virtues, patience is not a virtue"; "If there is a righteous God, the wicked will not escape their just punishment" = "If the wicked escape their just punishment, there is no righteous God."

From the negative hypothetical *If A is true then C is not true* we can infer *If C is true then A is not true*. This is analogous to *conversion* in the case of categoricals.

From the affirmative *If A then C*, we may obtain by conversion *If C then possibly A*; but this is only on the interpretation that both propositions imply the possibility of the truth of their antecedents.[290] The reader will notice that to pass from *If A then C* to *If C then A* would

---

[287] The validity of the above result will perhaps be more clearly seen by substituting for the hypotheticals their (assertoric) disjunctive equivalents, namely, *Either A is not true or C is true, Either A is not true or C is not true*. As a concrete example, we may take the propositions, "If this pen is not cross-nibbed, it is corroded by the ink," "If this pen is not cross-nibbed, it is not corroded by the ink." Supposing that the pen happens to be cross-nibbed, we cannot regard either of these propositions as false. It will be observed that their disjunctive equivalents are, "This pen is either cross-nibbed or corroded by the ink," "This pen is either cross-nibbed or not corroded by the ink." Take again the propositions, "If the sun moves round the earth, some astronomers are fallible." "If the sun moves round the earth, all astronomers are infallible." The truth of the first of these propositions will not be denied, and on the interpretation of hypotheticals with which we are here concerned the second cannot be said to be false. It may be taken as an emphatic way of denying that the sun does move round the earth.

[288] It has been argued that *If A then C* must have for its contradictory *If A then not C*, since the consequent must either follow or not follow from the antecedent. But to say that *C* does not follow from *A* is obviously not the same thing as to say that *not-C* follows from *A*.

[289] This holds good whether we adopt the assertoric or the modal interpretation. On the former interpretation, the import of both the propositions *If A then C* and *If C' then A'* is to negative AC'; on the latter interpretation, the import of both is to deny the possibility of the conjunction AC'.

[290] Compare section 158. The various results obtained in section 158 may be applied *mutatis mutandis* to modal hypotheticals. The reader may consider for himself the contraposition of $\mathbf{E}_m$.

be to commit a fallacy analogous to simply converting a categorical **A** proposition; and this is perhaps the most dangerous fallacy to be guarded against in the use of hypotheticals.[291]

A consideration of immediate inferences enables us to shew from another point of view that *If A then C* and *If A then C'* are not true contradictories. For the contrapositives *If A then C'*, *If C then A'*, are equivalent to one another; and whenever two propositions are equivalent, their contradictories must also be equivalent. But *If A then C* is not equivalent to *If C then A*.

If distinctions of quality are admitted, then the process of *obversion* is applicable to hypotheticals. For example, *If A is true then C is not true* = *If A is true then C' is true*. It is nearly always more natural and more convenient to take hypotheticals in their affirmative rather than in their negative form; and hence in the case of hypotheticals more importance attaches to the process of *contraposition* than to that of *conversion*.

If the falsity of C is assumed to be possible, then we may pass by inversion from *If A then C* to *It is possible for both A and C not to be true*; or, putting the same thing in a different way, we may by inversion pass from *If A then C* to *If the falsity of C is possible then the falsity of both A and C is possible*.[292] It is of course a fallacy to argue from *If A then C* to *If A' then C'*.

Turning to problematic hypotheticals, we find that from the proposition *If A is true C may be true*, we obtain by conversion *If C is true A may be true*; and from the proposition *If A is true C need not be true* we obtain by contraposition *If C is true A need not be true*. Here the analogy with categoricals is again very close.

181. *Hypothetical Propositions and Categorical Propositions.*—A true hypothetical proposition has been defined as a proposition expressing a relation between two other propositions of independent import, not between two terms; and it follows that a true hypothetical is not, like a conditional, easily reducible to categorical form. So far as we can obtain an equivalent categorical, its subject and predicate will not correspond with the antecedent and consequent of the hypothetical. Thus, the proposition *If A then C* may, according to our interpretation of it, be expressed in one or other of the following forms; *A is a proposition the truth of which is incompatible with the falsity of C*; *A is a proposition from the truth of which the truth of C necessarily follows*. It will be observed that, apart from the fact that these propositions are not of the ordinary categorical type,[293] the predicate is not in either of them equivalent to the consequent of the hypothetical.[294] No doubt a hypothetical proposition may be based on a categorical proposition of the ordinary type. But that is quite a different thing from saying that the two propositions are equivalent to one another.

---

[291] On the assertoric interpretation *If A then C* merely negatives *AC'*, while *If C then A* merely negatives *A'C*, and hence it is clear that neither of these propositions involves the other; on the modal interpretation the result is the same, for the truth of C may be a necessary consequence of the truth of A, while the converse does not hold good.

[292] The inversion of E_m may be worked out similarly. Here, as elsewhere, the process of inversion, although of little or no practical importance, raises problems that are of considerable theoretical interest.

[293] Since they are *compound*, not simple, propositions. The expression of compound propositions in categorical form is not convenient, and it is better to reserve the hypothetical and disjunctive forms for such propositions, the categorical and conditional forms being used for simple propositions.

[294] Amongst other differences the contrapositives of both these propositions differ from the contrapositive of the hypothetical. For, on either interpretation of the hypothetical, its contrapositive is *If C is not true then A is not true*, whilst the contrapositives of the above propositions are respectively,—*A proposition whose truth is compatible with the falsity of the proposition C is not the proposition A*, *A proposition from which the proposition C is not a necessary consequence is not the proposition A*.

The relation between hypothetical and disjunctive propositions will be discussed in the following chapter.

182. *Alleged Reciprocal Character of Conditional and Hypothetical Judgments.*—Mr Bosanquet argues that the hypothetical judgment (and under this designation he would include the conditional as well as what we have called the true hypothetical) "when ideally complete must be a reciprocal judgment. *If A is B, it is C* must justify the inference *If A is C, it is B*. We are of course in the habit of dealing with hypothetical judgments which will not admit of any such conversion, and the rules of logic accept this limitation ... If in actual fact ... *AB* is found to involve *AC* while *AC* does not involve *AB*, it is plain that what was relevant to *AC* was not really *AB* but some element $\alpha\beta$ within it ... Apart from time on the one hand and irrelevant elements on the other, I cannot see how the relation of conditioning differs from that of being conditioned ... In other words, if there is nothing in *A* beyond what is necessary to *B*, then *B* involves *A* just as much as *A* involves *B*. But if *A* contains irrelevant elements, then of course the relation becomes one-sided ... The relation of Ground is thus essentially reciprocal, and it is only because the 'grounds' alleged in every-day life are burdened with irrelevant matter or confused with causation in time, that we consider the Hypothetical Judgment to be in its nature not reversible" (*Logic*, I. pp. 261–3).

The question here raised is analogous to that of the possibility of plurality of causes which is discussed in inductive logic. It may perhaps be described as a wider aspect of the same question. So long as a given consequence has a plurality of grounds, it is clear that the hypothetical proposition affirming it to be a consequence of a particular one of these grounds cannot admit of simple conversion, for the converted proposition would hold good only if the ground in question were the sole ground.

Mr Bosanquet urges that the relation between ground and consequence will become reciprocal by the elimination from the antecedent of all irrelevant elements. It should be added that we can also secure reciprocity by the expansion of the consequent so that what follows from the antecedent is fully expressed. Thus, if we have the hypothetical *If A then γ*, which is not reciprocal, it is possible that *A* may be capable of analysis into $\alpha\beta$, and γ of expansion into $\gamma\delta$, so that either of the hypotheticals *If α then γ, If $\alpha\beta$ then $\gamma\delta$*, is reciprocal. In the former case we have a more exact statement of the ground, all extraneous elements being eliminated; in the latter case we have a more complete statement of the consequence. Sometimes, moreover, the latter of these alternatives may be practicable while the former is not.

This may be tested by reference to a formal hypothetical. The proposition *If all S is M and all M is P, then all S is P* is not reciprocal. We may make it so by expanding the consequent so that the proposition becomes *If all S is M and all M is P, then whatever is either S or M is P and is also M or not S*. But how in this case it would be possible to eliminate the irrelevant from the antecedent it is difficult to see. Our object is to eliminate *M* from the consequent, and if in advance we were to eliminate it from the antecedent the whole force of the proposition would be lost. And the same is true of non-formal hypotheticals, at any rate in many cases. Instances of reciprocal conditionals may be given without difficulty, for example, *If any triangle is equilateral, it is equiangular*. Such propositions are practically U propositions. We may also find instances of pure hypotheticals that are reciprocal; but, on the whole, while agreeing with a good deal that Mr Bosanquet says on the subject, I am disposed to demur to his view that the reciprocal hypothetical represents an ideal at which we should always aim. We have seen that there are two possible ways of securing reciprocity, whether or not they are always practicable; but the expansion of the consequent would generally speaking be extremely cumbrous and worse than useless, while the elimination from the antecedent of everything not absolutely essential for the realisation of the consequent would sometimes empty the judgment of all practical content for a given purpose. With reference to the case where *AB* involves *AC*, while *AC* does not involve *AB*, Mr. Bosanquet himself notes the objection,—"But may not the irrelevant element be just the element which made *AB* into *AB* as distinct from *AC*, so that by abstracting from it *AB* is reduced to *AC*, and the judgment is made a tautology, that is, destroyed?" (p. 261). This argument, although somewhat overstated, deserves consideration. The point upon which I should be inclined to lay stress is that in criticising a judgment we ought to have regard to the special object with which it has been framed. Our object may be to connect *AC* with *AB*, including whatever may be irrelevant in *AB*. Consider the argument,—*If anything is P it is Q*, *If anything is Q it is R*, therefore, *If anything is P it is R*. It is clear that if we compare the conclusion with the second premiss, the antecedent of the conclusion contains irrelevancies from which the antecedent of the premiss is free. Yet the conclusion may be of the greatest value to us while the premiss is by itself of no value. If our aim were always to get down to first principles, there would be a good deal to be said for Mr. Bosanquet's view, though it might still present some difficulties; but there is no reason why we should identify the conditional or the hypothetical proposition with the expression of first principles.

It is to be added that, if Mr. Bosanquet's view is sound, we ought to say equally that the **A** categorical proposition is imperfect, and that in categoricals the **U** proposition is the ideal at which we should aim. In categoricals, however, we clearly distinguish between **A** and **U**; and so far as we give prominence to the reciprocal modal, whether conditional or hypothetical, we ought to recognise its distinctive character. We may at the same time assign to it the distinctive symbol **U**$_m$.

EXERCISES

183. Give the contrapositive of the following proposition: If either no *P* is *R* or no *Q* is *R*, then nothing that is both *P* and *Q* is *R*. [K.]

184. There are three men in a house, Allen, Brown, and Carr, who may go in and out, provided that (1) they never go out all at once, and that (2) Allen never goes out without Brown.

Can Carr ever go out? [Lewis Carroll.]

185. There are two propositions, *A* and *B*.

Let it be granted that

If *A* is true, *B* is true. (i)

Let there be another proposition *C*, such that

If *C* is true, then if *A* is true *B* is not true. (ii)

(ii) amounts to this,—

If *C* is true, then (i) is not true.

But, *ex hypothesi*, (i) is true.

Therefore, *C* cannot be true; for the assumption of *C* involves an absurdity.

Examine this argument. [Lewis Carroll.]

[If the problem in section is regarded as a problem in conditionals, this is the corresponding problem in hypotheticals.]

186. Assuming that rain never falls in Upper Egypt, are the following genuine pairs of contradictories?

(*a*) The occurrence of rain in Upper Egypt is always succeeded by an earthquake; the occurrence of rain in Upper Egypt is sometimes not succeeded by an earthquake.

(*b*) If it is true that it rained in Upper Egypt on the 1st of July, it is also true that an earthquake followed on the same day; if it is true that it rained in Upper Egypt on the 1st of July, it is not also true that an earthquake followed on the same day.

If the above are not true contradictories, suggest what should be substituted. [B.]

187. Give the contrapositive and the contradictory of each of the following propositions:

(1) If any nation prospers under a Protective System, its citizens reject all arguments in favour of free-trade;

(2) If any nation prospers under a Protective System, we ought to reject all arguments in favour of free-trade. [J.]

188. Examine the logical relation between the two following propositions; and enquire whether it is logically possible to hold (*a*) that both are true, (*b*) that both are false: (i) If volitions are undetermined, then punishments cannot rightly be inflicted; (ii) If punishments can rightly be inflicted, then volitions are undetermined. [J.]

Chapter 14

DISJUNCTIVE (OR ALTERNATIVE) PROPOSITIONS

189. *The terms Disjunctive and Alternative as applied to Propositions.*—Propositions of the form *Either X or Y is true* are ordinarily called *disjunctive*. It has been pointed out, however, that two propositions are really *dis*joined when it is denied that they are both true rather than when it is asserted that one or other of them is true; and the term *alternative*, as suggested by Miss Jones (*Elements of Logic*, p. 115), is obviously appropriate to express the latter assertion. We should then use the terms *conjunctive, disjunctive, alternative, remotive*, for the four following combinations respectively: *X and Y are both true, X and Y are not both true, Either X or Y is true,*[295] *Neither X nor Y is true.*

Whilst, however, the name *alternative* is preferable to *disjunctive* for the proposition *Either X or Y is true*, the latter name has such an established position in logical nomenclature that it seems inadvisable altogether to discontinue its use in the old sense. It may be pointed out further that an alternative contains a veiled disjunction (namely, between *not-X* and *not-Y*) even in the stricter sense; for the statement that *Either X or Y is true* is equivalent to the statement that *Not-X and not-Y are not both true*. Hence, although generally using the term *alternative*, I shall not entirely discard the term *disjunctive* as synonymous with it.

190. *Two types of Alternative Propositions.*—In the case of propositions which are ordinarily described as simply disjunctive a distinction must be drawn similar to that drawn in the preceding chapter between conditionals and true hypotheticals. For the alternatives may be events or combinations of properties one or other of which it is affirmed will (always or sometimes) occur, e.g., *Every blood vessel is either a vein or an artery, Every prosperous nation has either abundant natural resources or a good government*; or they may be propositions of independent import whose truth or falsity cannot be affected by varying conditions of time, space, or circumstance, and which must therefore be simply true or false, e.g., *Either there is a future life or many cruelties go unpunished, Either it is no sin to covet honour or I am the most offending soul alive.*

Any proposition belonging to the first of the above types may be brought under the symbolic form *All (or some) S is either P or Q*, and may, therefore, be regarded as an ordinary categorical proposition with an *alternative term* as predicate. It is usual and for some

---

[295] Some writers indeed regard the proposition *Either X or Y is true* as expressing a relation between *X* and *Y* which is disjunctive in the above sense as well as alternative; but the disjunctive character of this proposition as regards *X* and *Y* is at any rate open to dispute, whilst its alternative character is unquestionable (see section 191).

reasons convenient to defer the discussion of the import of alternative terms until propositions of this type are being dealt with. Such propositions might otherwise be dismissed after a very brief consideration.[296]

Corresponding to this, we may note that an affirmative categorical proposition with a *conjunctive* predicate is equivalent to a conjunction of propositions if it is singular or universal, but not if it is particular. Thus, *This S is P and Q = This S is P and this S is Q*; *All S is P and Q = All S is P and all S is Q*. From the proposition *Some S is P and Q* we may indeed infer *Some S is P and some S is Q*; but we cannot pass back from this conclusion to the premiss, and hence the two are not equivalent to one another.

It may be added that a negative categorical proposition with an alternative predicate cannot be said to state an alternative at all, since to deny an alternation is the same thing as to affirm a conjunction. Thus the proposition *No S is either P or Q* can only be resolved into a *conjunctive* synthesis of propositions, namely, *No S is P and no S is Q*.

Alternative propositions of the second type are compound (as defined in section 55). They contain an alternative combination of propositions of independent import: and they have for their typical symbolic form *Either X is true or Y is true*, or more briefly, *Either X or Y*, where *X* and *Y* are symbols representing *propositions* (not terms). So far as it is necessary to give them a distinctive name, they have a claim to be called *true* alternative propositions, since they involve a true alternative synthesis of *propositions*, and not merely an alternative synthesis of terms.

It will be convenient to speak of *P* and *Q* as the *alternants* of the alternative term *P or Q*, and of *X* and *Y* as the *alternants* of the alternative proposition *Either X or Y*.

191. *The Import of Disjunctive (Alternative) Propositions.*—The two main questions that arise in regard to the import of alternative propositions are (1) whether the alternants of such propositions are necessarily to be regarded as mutually exclusive, (2) whether the propositions are to be interpreted as assertoric or modal.

(1) We ask then, in the first place, whether in an alternative proposition the alternants are to be interpreted as formally exclusive of one another; in other words, whether in the proposition *All S is either A or B* it is necessarily (or formally) implied that no *S* is both *A* and *B*,[297] and whether in the proposition *X is true or Y is true* it is necessarily (or formally) implied that *X* and *Y* are not both true. It is desirable to notice at the outset that the question is one of the interpretation of a propositional form, and one that does not arise except in

---

[296] It should be particularly observed that although the proposition *Every S is P or Q* may be said to state an alternative, it cannot be resolved into a true alternative combination of *propositions*. Such a resolution is, however, possible if the proposition (while remaining affirmative and still having an alternative predicate) is *singular* or *particular*: for example, *This S is P or Q = This S is P or this S is Q*; *Some S is P or Q = Some S is P or some S is Q*.

[297] This is an alternative proposition of the first type, and the same question is raised by asking whether the term *A or B* includes *AB* under its denotation or excludes it; in other words, whether the denotation of *A or B* is represented by the shaded portion of the first or of the second of the following diagrams:

 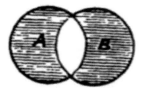

connection with the expression of judgments in language. Hence the solution will be, at any rate partly, a matter of convention.

The following considerations may help to make this point clearer. Let X and Y represent two judgments. Then the following are two possible states of mind in which we may be with regard to X and Y:

(*a*) we may know that one or other of them is true, and that they are not both true;

(*b*) we may know that one or other of them is true, but may be ignorant as to whether they are or are not both true.

Now whichever interpretation (exclusive or non-exclusive) of the propositional form X or Y is adopted, there will be no difficulty in expressing alternatively either state of mind. On the exclusive interpretation, (*a*) will be expressed in the form X or Y, (*b*) in the form XY or XY' or $X'Y$ (X' representing the falsity of X, and Y' the falsity of Y). On the non-exclusive interpretation, (*a*) will be expressed in the form XY' or $X'Y$, (*b*) in the form X or Y. There can, therefore, be no intrinsic ground based on the nature of judgment itself why X or Y must be interpreted in one of the two ways to the exclusion of the other.

As then we are dealing with a question of the interpretation of a certain form of expression, we must look for our solution partly in the usages of ordinary language. We ask, therefore, whether in ordinary speech we intend that the alternants in an alternative proposition should necessarily be understood as excluding one another?[298] A very few instances will enable us to decide in the negative. Take, for example, the proposition, "He has either used bad text-books or he has been badly taught." No one would naturally understand this to exclude the possibility of a combination of bad teaching and the use of bad text-books. Or suppose it laid down as a condition of eligibility for some appointment that every candidate must be a member either of the University of Oxford, or of the University of Cambridge, or of the University of London. Would anyone regard this as implying the ineligibility of persons who happened to be members of more than one of these Universities? Jevons (*Pure Logic*, p. 68) instances the following proposition: "A peer is either a duke, or a marquis, or an earl, or a viscount, or a baron." We do not consider this statement incorrect because many peers as a matter of fact possess two or more titles. Take, again, the proposition, "Either the witness is perjured or the prisoner is guilty." The import of this proposition, as it would naturally be interpreted, is that the evidence given by the witness is sufficient, supposing it is true, to establish the guilt of the prisoner; but clearly there is no implication that the falsity of this particular piece of evidence would suffice to establish the prisoner's innocence.

But it may be urged that this does not definitely settle the question of the best way of interpreting alternative propositions. Granted that in common speech the alternants may or may not be mutually exclusive, it may nevertheless be argued that in the use of language for logical purposes we should be more precise, and that an alternative statement should

---

[298] There are no doubt many cases in which as a matter of fact we understand alternants to be mutually exclusive. But this is not conclusive as shewing that even in these cases the mutual exclusiveness is *intended to be expressed* by the alternative proposition. For it will generally speaking be found that in such cases the fact that the alternants exclude one another is a matter of common knowledge quite independently of the alternative proposition; as, for example, in the proposition, *He was first or second in the race*. This point is further touched upon in Part III, Chapter 6.

accordingly not be admitted as a recognised logical proposition except on the condition that the alternants mutually exclude one another.

We may admit that the argument from the ordinary use of speech is not final. But at any rate the burden of proof lies with those who advocate a divergence from the usage of everyday language; for it will not be denied that, other things being equal, the less logical forms diverge from those of ordinary speech the better. Moreover, condensed forms of expression do not conduce to clearness, or even ultimately to conciseness.[299] For where our information is meagre, a condensed form is likely to express more than we intend, and in order to keep within the mark we must indicate additional alternatives. On this ground, quite apart from considerations of the ordinary use of language, I should support the non-exclusive interpretation of alternatives. The adoption of the exclusive interpretation would certainly render the manipulation of complex propositions much more complicated.

A further paradoxical result is pointed out by Mr G. R. T. Ross in an article on the Disjunctive Judgment in *Mind* (1903, p. 492), namely, that on the exclusive interpretation the disjunctives *A is either B or C* and *A is either not B or not C* are identical in their import; for in each case the real alternants are *B but not C* and *C but not B*. Thus, to take an illustration borrowed from Mr. Ross, the two following propositions are (on the interpretation in question) identical in their import,—"Anyone who affirms that he has seen his own ghost is either not sane or not telling what he believes to be the truth," "Anyone who affirms that he has seen his own ghost is either sane or truthful."

Mr. Bosanquet and other writers who advocate the exclusive interpretation of disjunctives appear to have chiefly in view the expression in disjunctive form of a logical division or scientific classification. I should of course agree that such a division or classification is imperfect if the members of which it consists are not mutually exclusive as well as collectively exhaustive. This condition must also be satisfied when we make use of the disjunctive judgment in connection with the doctrine of probability.[300] It will, however, hardly be proposed to confine the disjunctive judgment to these uses. We frequently have occasion to state alternatives independently of any scientific classification or any calculation of probability; and we must not regard the bare form of the disjunctive judgment as expressing anything that we are not prepared to recognise as universally involved in its use.

It is of course always possible to express an alternative statement in such a way that the alternants are *formally* incompatible or exclusive. Thus, not wishing to exclude the case of *A* being both *B* and *C* we may write *A is B or bC*;[301] or, wishing to exclude that case, *A is Bc or bC*. But in neither of these instances can we say that the incompatibility of the alternants is really given by the alternative proposition. It is a merely formal proposition that *No A is both*

---

[299] Obviously a disjunctive proposition is a more condensed form of expression on the exclusive than on the non-exclusive interpretation. Compare Mansel's *Aldrich*, p. 242, and *Prolegomena Logica*, p. 288. "Let us grant for a moment the opposite view, and allow that the proposition *All C is either A or B* implies as a condition of its truth *No C can be both*. Thus viewed, it is in reality a complex proposition, containing two distinct assertions, each of which may be the ground of two distinct processes of reasoning, governed by two opposite laws. Surely it is essential to all clear thinking that the two should be separated from each other, and not confounded under one form by assuming the Law of Excluded Middle to be, what it is not, a complex of those of Identity and Contradiction" (*Aldrich*, p. 242). It may be added that one paradoxical result of the exclusive interpretation of alternatives is that *not either P or Q* is not equivalent to *neither P nor Q*.

[300] In this connection the further condition of the "equality" in a certain sense of the alternants has in addition to be satisfied.

[301] Where *b = not-B*, and *c = not-C*. What is contained in this paragraph is to some extent a repetition of what is given on page 278.

B and *bC* or that *No A is both Bc and bC*. The proposition *Every A is Bc or bC* does, however, tell us that no *A* is both *B* and *C*; and when from our knowledge of the subject-matter it is obvious that we are dealing with alternants that are mutually exclusive (and no doubt this is a very frequent case), we have in the above form a means of correctly and unambiguously expressing the fact. Where it is inconvenient to use this form, it is open to us to make a separate statement to the effect that *No A is both B and C*. All that is here contended for is that the bare symbolic form *A is either B or C* should not be interpreted as being equivalent to *A is either Bc or bC*.

(2) We may pass on to consider the second main question that arises in connection with the import of disjunctive (alternative) propositions, namely, whether such propositions are to be interpreted as modal or as merely assertoric.

In chapter 9 it was urged that the modal interpretation of the typical hypothetical proposition *If A then C* must be regarded as the more natural one, on the ground that we should not ordinarily think it necessary to affirm the truth of *A* in order to contradict the proposition, as would be necessary if it were interpreted assertorically.[302] Similarly the enquiry as to how we should naturally contradict the typical alternative propositions *Every S is either P or Q, Either X or Y is true*, may help us in deciding upon the interpretation of these propositions.

On the assertoric interpretation, the contradictories of the propositions in question are *Some S is neither P nor Q, Neither X nor Y is true*; on the modal interpretation, they are *An S need not be either P or Q, Possibly neither X nor Y is true*. There can be no doubt that this last pair of propositions would not as a rule be regarded as adequate to contradict the pair of alternatives; and on this ground we may regard the assertoric interpretation of alternatives as most in accordance with ordinary usage. There is also some advantage in differentiating between hypotheticals and alternatives by interpreting the former modally and the latter assertorically, except in so far as a clear indication is given to the contrary. It is not of course meant that modal alternatives are never as a matter of fact to be met with or that they cannot receive formal recognition; they can always be expressed in the distinctive forms *Every S must be either P or Q, Either X or Y is necessarily true*.

192. *Scheme of Assertoric and Modal Propositions.*—By differentiating between forms of propositions in the manner indicated in preceding sections we have a scheme by which distinctive expression can be given to assertoric and modal propositions respectively, whether they are simple or compound.

Thus the *categorical* form of proposition might be restricted to the expression of *simple assertoric* judgments; the *conditional* form to that of *simple modal* judgments; the *disjunctive* (*alternative*)[303] form to that of *compound assertoric* judgments; and the *hypothetical* form to that of *compound modal* judgments.

I have not in the present treatise attempted to adopt this scheme to the exclusion of other interpretations of the different propositional forms; but I have had it in view throughout, and I put it forward as a scheme the adoption of which might afford an escape from some ambiguities and misunderstandings.

---

[302] See page 263.
[303] We are of course referring here to disjunctive (alternative) propositions of the second type only, alternative propositions of the first type being treated as categoricals with alternative predicates. See section 190.

193. *The Relation of Disjunctive (Alternative) Propositions to Conditionals and Hypotheticals*.—It may be convenient if we briefly consider this question independently of the distinctions indicated in the preceding section, the assumption being made that these different types of propositions are interpreted either all assertorically or all modally. On this assumption, alternative propositions are reducible to the conditional or the true hypothetical form according to the type to which they belong. Thus, the proposition, "Every blood vessel is either a vein or an artery," yields the conditional, "If any blood vessel is not a vein then it is an artery"; the true compound alternative proposition, "Either there is a future life or many cruelties go unpunished," yields the true hypothetical, "If there is no future life then many cruelties go unpunished."

It may be asked whether an alternative proposition does not require a conjunction of *two* conditionals or hypotheticals in order fully to express its import. This is not the case, however, on the view that the alternants are not to be interpreted as necessarily exclusive. It is true that even on this view an alternative proposition, such as *Either X or Y*, is primarily reducible to two hypotheticals, namely, *If not X then Y* and *If not Y then X*. But these are contrapositives the one of the other, and therefore mutually inferable. Hence the full meaning of the alternative proposition is expressed by means of either of them.

On the exclusive interpretation, the alternative proposition *Either X or Y* yields primarily four hypotheticals, namely, *If X then not Y* and *If Y then not X* in addition to the two given above. But these again are contrapositives the one of the other. Hence the full import of the alternative proposition will now be expressed by a conjunction of the two hypotheticals, *If X then not Y* and *If not X then Y*.

This is denied by Mr. Bosanquet, who holds that the disjunctive proposition yields a positive assertion not contained in either of the hypotheticals. "'This signal light shews either red or green.' Here we have the categorical element, 'This signal light shews some colour,' and on the top of this the two hypothetical judgments, 'If it shews red it does not shew green,' 'If it does not shew red it does shew green.' You cannot make it up out of the two hypothetical judgments alone; they do not give you the assertion that 'it shews some colour.'"[304] But surely the second of the two hypotheticals contains this implication quite as clearly and definitely as the disjunctive does.[305]

Returning to the distinctions indicated in the preceding section, it is hardly necessary to add that if the hypothetical *If not X then Y* is interpreted modally, while the alternative *Either X or Y* is interpreted assertorically, then the alternative can be inferred from the hypothetical, but not *vice versâ*.

---

[304] *Essentials of Logic*, p. 124.

[305] Mr Bosanquet's opinion that "the disjunction seems to complete the system of judgments," and that in some way it rises superior to other forms of judgment, is apparently based on the view that it is by the aid of the disjunctive judgment that we set forth the exposition of a system with its various subdivisions. Apart, however, from the fact that a disjunctive judgment does not necessarily contain such an exposition, Mr Bosanquet's doctrine appears to regard a classification of some kind as representing the ideal of knowledge; and this can hardly be allowed. We cannot, for example, regard the classifications of such a science as botany as of equal importance with the expressions of laws of nature, such as the law of universal gravitation. And the ultimate laws on which all the sciences are based are not expressed in the form of disjunctive propositions.

EXERCISES

194. Shew how an alternative proposition in which the alternants are not known to be mutually exclusive (e.g., *Either X or Y or Z is true*) may be reduced to a form in which they necessarily are so. Write the new proposition in as simple a form as possible. [K.]

195. Shew why the following propositions are not contradictories: *Wherever A is present, B is present and either C or B is also present*; *In some cases where A is present, either B or C or B is absent*. How must each of these propositions in turn be amended in order that it may become the true contradictory of the other? [K.]

196. *No P is both Q and R.* Reduce this proposition (*a*) to the form of a conditional proposition, (*b*) to the form of an alternative proposition. Give the contradictory of the original proposition, of its conditional equivalent, and of its alternative equivalent; and test your results by enquiring whether the three contradictories thus obtained are equivalent to one another. [K.]

Part III. Syllogisms

Chapter 15

THE RULES OF THE SYLLOGISM

197. *The Terms of the Syllogism.*—A reasoning which consists of three propositions of the traditional categorical form, and which contains three and only three terms, is called a *categorical syllogism*.

Of the three terms contained in a categorical syllogism, two appear in the conclusion and also in one or other of the premisses, while the third appears in the premisses only. That which appears as the predicate of the conclusion, and in one of the premisses, is called the *major term*; that which appears as the subject of the conclusion, and in one of the premisses, is called the *minor term*;[306] and that which appears in both the premisses, but not in the conclusion (being that term by their relations to which the mutual relation of the two other terms is determined), is called the *middle term*.

Thus, in the syllogism,—

	All M is P,
	All S is M,
therefore,	All S is P;

S is the minor term, M the middle term, and P the major term.

These respective designations of the terms of a syllogism resulted from such a syllogism as that just given being regarded as typical. With the exception of the somewhat rare case in which the terms of a proposition are coextensive, the above syllogism may be represented by the following diagram. Here

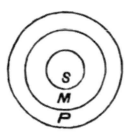

---

[306] The major and minor terms are also sometimes called the *extremes* of the syllogism.

clearly the major term is the largest in extent, and the minor the smallest, while the middle occupies an intermediate position.

But we have no guarantee that the same relation between the terms of a syllogism will hold, when one of the premisses is negative or particular. Thus, the syllogism—*No M is P, All S is M*, therefore, *No S is P*—yields as one case

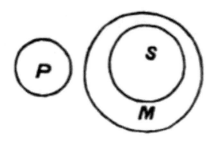

where the major term may be the smallest in extent, and the middle the largest. Again, the syllogism—*No M is P, Some S is M*, therefore, *Some S is not P*—yields as one case

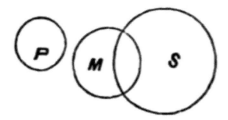

where the major term may be the smallest in extent and the minor the largest.

Whilst, however, the middle term is not always a middle term in extent, it is always a middle term in the sense that by its means the two other terms are connected, and their mutual relation determined.

198. *The Propositions of the Syllogism.*—Every categorical syllogism consists of three propositions. Of these one is the *conclusion*. The premisses are called the *major premiss* and the *minor premiss* according as they contain the major term or the minor term respectively.

Thus,	All M is P	(major premiss),
	All S is M	(minor premiss),
therefore,	All S is P	(conclusion).

It is usual (as in the above syllogism) to state the major premiss first and the conclusion last. This is, however, nothing more than a convention. The order of the premisses in no way affects the validity of a syllogism, and has indeed no logical significance, though in certain cases it may be of some rhetorical importance. Jevons (*Principles of Science*, 6, § 14) argues that the cogency of a syllogism is more clearly recognisable when the minor premiss is stated first. But it is doubtful whether any general rule of this kind can be laid down. In favour of the traditional order, it is to be said that in what is usually regarded as the typical syllogism (*All M is P, All S is M*, therefore, *All S is P*) there is a philosophical ground for stating the major premiss first, since that premiss gives the general rule, of which the minor premiss enables us to make a particular application.

199. *The Rules of the Syllogism.*—The rules of the categorical syllogism as usually stated are as follows:—

(1) *Every syllogism contains three and only three terms.*
(2) *Every syllogism consists of three and only three propositions.*

These two so-called rules are not properly speaking rules for the validity of an argument. They simply serve to *define* the syllogism as a particular *form* of argument. A reasoning which does not fulfil these conditions may be formally valid, but we do not call it a syllogism.[307] The four rules that follow are really rules in the sense that if, when we have got the reasoning into the form of a syllogism, they are not fulfilled, then the reasoning is invalid.[308]

Here is a valid reasoning which consists of three propositions. But it contains more than three terms; for the predicate of the second premiss is "greater than B," while the subject of the first premiss is "B." It is, therefore, as it stands, not a syllogism. Whether reasonings of this kind admit of being reduced to syllogistic form is a problem which will be discussed subsequently.

(3) *No one of the three terms of a syllogism may be used ambiguously; and the middle term must be distributed once at least in the premisses.*

This rule is frequently given in the form: "The middle term must be distributed once at least, and must not be ambiguous." But it is obvious that we have to guard against ambiguous major and ambiguous minor as well as against ambiguous middle. The fallacy resulting from the ambiguity of one of the terms of a syllogism is a case of *quaternio terminorum*, that is, a fallacy of four terms.

The necessity of distributing the middle term may be illustrated by the aid of the Eulerian diagrams. Given, for instance. *All P is M* and *All S is M*, we may have any one of the five following cases:—

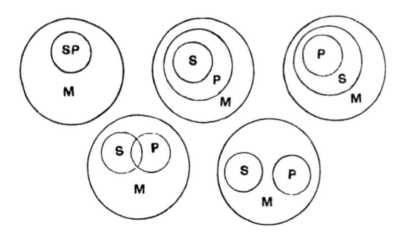

---

[307] For example, *B is greater than C, A is greater than B*, therefore, *A is greater than C*.
[308] Apparent exceptions to these rules will be shewn in sections 205 and 206 to result from the attempt to apply them to reasonings which have not first been reduced to syllogistic form.

Here all the five relations that are *à priori* possible between *S* and *P* are still possible. We have, therefore, no conclusion.

If in a syllogism the middle term is distributed in neither premiss, we are said to have a fallacy of *undistributed middle*.

(4) *No term may be distributed in the conclusion which was not distributed in one of the premisses.*

The breach of this rule is called *illicit process of the major*, or *illicit process of the minor*, as the case may be; or, more briefly, *illicit major* or *illicit minor*.

(5) *From two negative premisses nothing can be inferred.*

This rule may, like rule 3, be very well illustrated by means of the Eulerian diagrams.

(6) *If one premiss is negative, the conclusion must be negative; and to prove a negative conclusion, one of the premisses must be negative.*[309]

200. *Corollaries from the Rules of the Syllogism.*—From the rules given in the preceding section, three corollaries may be deduced:—[310]

(i) *From two particular premisses nothing can be inferred.*

Two particular premisses must be either

(α) both negative,

or (β) both affirmative,

or (γ) one negative and one affirmative.

But in case (α), no conclusion follows by rule 5.

In case (β), since no term can be distributed in two particular affirmative propositions, the middle term cannot be distributed, and therefore by rule 3 no conclusion follows.

In case (γ), if any valid conclusion is possible, it must be negative (rule 6). The major term, therefore, will be distributed in the conclusion; and hence we must have two terms distributed in the premisses, namely, the middle and the major (rules 3, 4). But a particular negative proposition and a particular affirmative proposition between them distribute only one term. Therefore, no conclusion can be obtained.

(ii) *If one premiss is particular, the conclusion must be particular.*

We must have either

(α) two negative premisses, but this case is rejected by rule 5;

or (β) two affirmative premisses;

or (γ) one affirmative and one negative.

In case (β) the premisses, being both affirmative and one of them particular, can distribute but one term between them. This must be the middle term by rule 3. The minor term is, therefore, undistributed in the premisses, and the conclusion must be particular by rule 4.

In case (γ) the premisses will between them distribute two and only two terms. These must be the middle by rule 3, and the major by rule 4 (since we have a negative premiss, necessitating by rule 6 a negative conclusion, and therefore the distribution of the major term in the conclusion). Again, therefore, the minor cannot be distributed in the premisses, and the conclusion must be particular by rule 4.

---

[309] This rule and the second corollary given in the following section are sometimes combined into the one rule, *Conclusio sequitur partem deteriorem*; i.e., the conclusion follows the worse or weaker premiss both in quality and in quantity, a negative being considered weaker than an affirmative and a particular than a universal.

[310] The formulation of these corollaries may in some cases help towards the more immediate detection of unsound syllogisms.

De Morgan (*Formal Logic*, p. 14) gives the following proof of this corollary:—"If two propositions P and Q together prove a third R, it is plain that P and the denial of R prove the denial of Q. For P and Q cannot be true together without R. Now, if possible, let P (a particular) and Q (a universal) prove R (a universal). Then P (particular) and the denial of R (particular) prove the denial of Q. But two particulars can prove nothing."[311]

(iii) *From a particular major and a negative minor nothing can be inferred.* Since the minor premiss is negative, the major premiss must by rule 5 be affirmative. But it is also particular, and it therefore follows that the major term cannot be distributed in it. Hence, by rule 4, it must be undistributed in the conclusion, i.e., the conclusion must be *affirmative*. But also, by rule 6, since we have a negative premiss, it must be *negative*. This contradiction establishes the corollary that from the given premisses no conclusion can be drawn.

The following mnemonic lines, attributed to Petrus Hispanus, afterwards Pope John XXI., sum up the rules of the syllogism and the first two corollaries:

Distribuas medium: nec quartus terminus adsit:
Utraque nec praemissa negans, nec particularis:
Sectetur partem conclusio deteriorem;
Et non distribuat, nisi cum praemissa, negetve.

201. *Restatement of the Rules of the Syllogism.*—It has been already pointed out that the first two of the rules given in section 199 are to be regarded as a description of the syllogism rather than as rules for its validity. Again, the part of rule 3 relating to ambiguity may be regarded as contained in the proviso that there shall be only three terms; for, if one of the terms is ambiguous, there are really four terms, and hence no syllogism according to our definition of syllogism. The rules may, therefore, be reduced to four; and they may be restated as follows:—

A. *Two rules of distribution*:

(1) The middle term must be distributed once at least in the premisses;

(2) No term may be distributed in the conclusion which was not distributed in one of the premisses;

B. *Two rules of quality*:

(3) From two negative premisses no conclusion follows;

(4) If one premiss is negative, the conclusion must be negative; and to prove a negative conclusion, one of the premisses must be negative.[312]

202. *Dependence of the Rules of the Syllogism upon one another.*—The four rules just given are not ultimately independent of one another. It may be shewn that a breach of the second, or of the third, or of the first part of the fourth involves indirectly a breach of the first; or, again, that a breach of the first, or of the third, or of the first part of the fourth involves indirectly a breach of the second.

(i) *The rule that two negative premisses yield no conclusion may be deduced from the rule that the middle term must be distributed once at least in the premisses.*

---

[311] Further attention will be called in a later chapter to the general principle upon which this proof is based. See section 264.

[312] The rules of quality might also be stated as follows; To prove an affirmative conclusion, both premisses must be affirmative; To prove a negative conclusion, one premiss must be affirmative and the other negative.

This is shewn by De Morgan (*Formal Logic*, p. 13). He takes two universal negative premisses E, E. In whatever figure they may be, they can be reduced by conversion to

No P is M,
No S is M.

Then by obversion they become (without losing any of their force),—

All P is not-M,
All S is not-M;

and we have undistributed middle. Hence rule 3 is exhibited as a corollary from rule 1. For if any connection between *S* and *P* can be inferred from the first pair of premisses, it must also be inferable from the second pair.

The case in which one of the premisses is particular is dealt with by De Morgan as follows;—"Again, *No Y is X, Some Ys are not Zs*, may be converted into

Every X is (*a thing which is not Y*),
Some (*things which are not Zs*) *are Ys,*

in which there is no middle term."

This is not satisfactory, since we may often exhibit a valid syllogism in such a form that there appear to be four terms; e.g., *All M is P, All S is M*, may be reduced to *All M is P, No S is not-M*, and there is now no middle term.

The case in question may, however, be disposed of by saying that if we cannot infer anything from two negative premisses both of which are universal, *à fortiori* we cannot from two negative premisses one of which is particular.[313]

(ii) *The rules that from two negative premisses nothing can be inferred and that if one premiss is negative the conclusion must be negative are mutually deducible from one another.*

The following proof that the second of these rules is deducible from the first is suggested by De Morgan's deduction of the second corollary as given in section 200. If two propositions *P* and *Q* together prove a third *R*, it is plain that *P* and the denial of *R* prove the denial of *Q*. For *P* and *Q* cannot be true together without *R*. Now, if possible, let *P* (a negative) and *Q* (an affirmative) prove *R* (an affirmative). Then *P* (a negative) and the denial of *R* (a negative) prove the denial of *Q*. But by hypothesis two negatives prove nothing.

It may be shewn similarly that if we start by assuming the second of the rules then the first is deducible from it.

(iii) *Any syllogism involving directly an illicit process of major or minor involves indirectly a fallacy of undistributed middle, and vice versâ.*[314]

Let *P* and *Q* be the premisses and *R* the conclusion of a syllogism involving illicit major or minor, a term *X* which is undistributed in *P* being distributed in *R*. Then the contradictory

---

[313] This argument holds good in the special case under consideration even if we interpret particulars, but not universals, as implying the existence of their subjects. For the validity of the above proof that two universal negatives yield no conclusion remains unaffected even if we allow to universals the maximum of existential import.

[314] For this theorem and its proof I am indebted to Mr Johnson.

of *R* combined with *P* must prove the contradictory of *Q*. But any term distributed in a proposition is undistributed in its contradictory. *X* is therefore undistributed in the contradictory of *R*, and by hypothesis it is undistributed in *P*. But *X* is the middle term of the new syllogism, which is therefore guilty of the fallacy of undistributed middle. It is thus shewn that any syllogism involving directly a fallacy of illicit major or minor involves indirectly a fallacy of undistributed middle.

Adopting a similar line of argument, we might also proceed in the opposite direction, and exhibit the rule relating to the distribution of the middle term as a corollary from the rule relating to the distribution of the major and minor terms.

203. *Statement of the independent Rules of the Syllogism*.—The theorems established in the preceding section shew that the first part of rule 4 (as given in section 201) is a corollary from rule 3, and that rule 3 is in its turn a corollary from rule 1; also that rules 1 and 2 mutually involve one another, so that either one of them may be regarded as a corollary from the other. We are, therefore, left with either rule 1 or rule 2 and also with the second part of rule 4; and the independent rules of the syllogism may accordingly be stated as follows:

(*α*) *Rule of Distribution*:—The middle term must be distributed once at least in the premisses [or, as alternative with this, No term may be distributed in the conclusion which was not distributed in one of the premisses];

(*β*) *Rule of Quality*:—To prove a negative conclusion one of the premisses must be negative.[315]

It should be clearly understood that it is not meant that every invalid syllogism will offend *directly* against one of these two rules. As a direct test for the detection of invalid syllogisms we must still fall back upon the *four* rules given in section 201.[316] All that we have succeeded in shewing is that ultimately these four rules are not independent of one another.

204. *Proof of the Rule of Quality*.—For the following very interesting and ingenious proof of the Rule of Quality (as stated in the preceding section) I am indebted to Mr R. A. P.

---

[315] On examination it will be found that the only syllogism rejected by this rule and not also rejected directly or indirectly by the preceding rule is the following:—*All P is M, All M is S*, therefore, *Some S is not P*. In the technical language explained in the following chapter, this is AAO in Figure 4. So far, therefore, as the first three figures are concerned, we are left with a single rule, namely, a rule of distribution, which may be stated in either of the alternative forms given above.

[316] If, for example, for our rule of distribution we select the rule relating to the distribution of the middle term, then the invalid syllogism,

	All M is P,
	No S is M,
therefore,	*No S is P*,

does not directly involve a breach of either of our two independent rules. But if this syllogism is valid, then must also the following syllogism be valid:

	All M is P (original major),
	Some S is P (contradictory of original conclusion),
therefore	*Some S is M* (contradictory of original minor);

and here we have undistributed middle. Hence the rule relating to the distribution of the middle term establishes *indirectly* the invalidity of the syllogism in question. The principle involved is the same as that on which we shall find the process of indirect reduction to be based.

Take, again, the syllogism: *PaM, SeM, ∴ SaP*. This does not directly offend against the rules given above; but the reader will find that its validity involves the validity of another syllogism in which a direct transgression of these rules occurs.

Rogers, of Trinity College, Dublin. In this proof the symbol $f_n(\ )$ is used to denote the form of a proposition, the terms which the proposition contains in any given case being inserted within the brackets. Thus, if $f_x(P, M)$ symbolises *All M is P*, then $f_x(B, A)$ will symbolise *All A is B*: or, again, if $f_y(S, M)$ symbolises *Some S is not M*, then $f_y(B, A)$ will symbolise *Some B is not A*. It will be observed that the order in which the terms are given does not necessarily correspond with the order of subject and predicate.

Let $f_1(\ )$, $f_2(\ )$, $f_3(\ )$ be propositions belonging to the traditional schedule. Then "$f_1(P, M)$, $f_2(S, M)$, $\therefore f_3(S, P)$" will be the expression of a syllogism; and, since the syllogism is a process of formal reasoning, if the above syllogism is valid in any case, it will hold good if other terms are substituted for S, M, P (or any of them). Thus, substituting S for M, and S for P, if "$f_1(P, M)$, $f_2(S, M)$, $\therefore f_3(S, P)$" is a valid syllogism, then "$f_1(S, S)$, $f_2(S, S)$, $\therefore f_3(S, S)$" will be a valid syllogism.

It follows, by contraposition, that if "$f_1(S, S)$, $f_2(S, S)$, $\therefore f_3(S, S)$" is an invalid syllogism, then "$f_1(P, M)$, $f_2(S, M)$, $\therefore f_3(S, P)$" will be an invalid syllogism.

If possible, let $f_1(\ )$ and $f_2(\ )$ be affirmative, while $f_3(\ )$ is negative. Then $f_1(S, S)$ and $f_2(S, S)$ will be formally true propositions, while $f_3(S, S)$ is formally false. Hence $f_3(S, S)$ cannot be a valid inference from $f_1(S, S)$ and $f_2(S, S)$; in other words, "$f_1(S, S)$, $f_2(S, S)$, $\therefore f_3(S, S)$" must be an invalid syllogism. Consequently, "$f_1(P. M)$, $f_2(S, M)$, $\therefore f_3(S, P)$" cannot be a valid syllogism; that is, we cannot have a valid syllogism in which both premisses are affirmative and the conclusion negative.

205. *Two negative premisses may yield a valid conclusion; but not syllogistically.*— Jevons remarks: "The old rules of logic informed us that from two negative premisses no conclusion could be drawn, but it is a fact that the rule in this bare form does not hold universally true; and I am not aware that any precise explanation has been given of the conditions under which it is or is not imperative. Consider the following example,—*Whatever is not metallic is not capable of powerful magnetic influence*, *Carbon is not metallic*, therefore, *Carbon is not capable of powerful magnetic influence*. Here we have two distinctly negative premisses, and yet they yield a perfectly valid negative conclusion. The syllogistic rule is actually falsified in its bare and general statement" (*Principles of Science*, 4, § 10).[317]

This apparent exception is, however, no real exception. The reasoning (which may be expressed symbolically in the form, *No not-M is P*, *No S is M*, therefore, *No S is P*) is certainly valid; but if we regard the premisses as negative it has four terms S, P, M, and *not-M*, and is therefore no syllogism. Reducing it to syllogistic form, the minor becomes by obversion *All S is not-M*, an affirmative proposition.[318] It is not the case, therefore, that we have succeeded in finding a valid *syllogism* with two negative premisses. In other words, while we must not say that from two negative premisses nothing follows, it remains true that

---

[317] Lotze (*Logic*, § 89; *Outlines of Logic*, §§ 40-42) holds that two negative premisses invalidate a syllogism in Figure 1 or Figure 2, but not necessarily in Figure 3. The example upon which he relies is this,—*No M is P, No M is S*, therefore, *Some not-S is not P*. The argument in the text may be applied to this example as well as to the one given by Jevons.

[318] It may be added that it is in this form that the cogency of the argument is most easily to be recognised. Of course every affirmation involves a denial and *vice versâ*; but it may fairly be said that in Jevons's example the primary force of the minor premiss, considered in connection with the major premiss, is to affirm that carbon belongs to the class of non-metallic substances, rather than to deny that it belongs to the class of metallic substances.

if a syllogism regularly expressed has two negative premises it is invalid.[319] It must not be considered that this is a mere technicality, and that Jevons's example shews that the rule is at any rate of no practical value. It is not possible to formulate specific rules at all except with reference to some defined form of reasoning; and no given rule is vitiated either theoretically or for practical purposes because it does not apply outside the form to which alone it professes to apply.[320]

206. *Other apparent exceptions to the Rules of the Syllogism.*—It is curious that the logicians who have laid so much stress on the case considered in the preceding section do not appear to have observed that, as soon as we admit more than three terms, other apparent breaches of the syllogistic rules may occur in what are perfectly valid reasonings. Thus, the premisses *All P is M* and *All S is M*, in which *M* is not distributed, yield the conclusion *Some not-S is not-P*;[321] and hence we might argue that undistributed middle does not invalidate an argument. Again, from the premisses *All M is P, All not-M is S*, we may infer *Some S is not P*,[322] although there is apparently an illicit process of the major. It is unnecessary after what has been said in the preceding section to give examples of valid reasonings in which we have a negative premiss with an affirmative conclusion, or two affirmative premisses with a negative conclusion, or a particular major with a negative minor. Any valid syllogism which is affirmative throughout will yield the first and, if it has a particular major, also the last of these by the obversion of the minor premiss, and the second by the obversion of the

---

[319] By a syllogism regularly expressed we mean a reasoning consisting of three propositions, which not only contain between them three and only three terms, but which are also expressed in the traditional categorical forms. Attention must be called to this because, if we introduce additional propositional forms of the kind indicated on page 146, we may have a valid reasoning with two negative premisses, which satisfies the condition of containing only three terms; for example,

	No M is P,
	Some M is not S,
therefore,	*There is something besides S and P.*

It will be found that this reasoning is easily reducible to a valid syllogism in *Ferison*.

[320] A case similar to that adduced by Jevons is dealt with in the *Port Royal Logic* (Professor Baynes's translation, p. 211) as follows:—"There are many reasonings, of which all the propositions appear negative, and which are, nevertheless, very good, because there is in them one which is negative only in appearance, and in reality affirmative, as we have already shewn, and as we may still further see by this example: *That which has no parts cannot perish by the dissolution of its parts; The soul has no parts; therefore, The soul cannot perish by the dissolution of its parts.* There are several who advance such syllogisms to shew that we have no right to maintain unconditionally this axiom of logic, *Nothing can be inferred from pure negatives*; but they have not observed that, in sense, the minor of this and such other syllogisms is affirmative, since the middle, which is the subject of the major, is in it the attribute. Now the subject of the major is not that which has parts, but that which has not parts, and thus the sense of the minor is, *The soul is a thing without parts*, which is a proposition affirmative of a negative attribute." Ueberweg also, who himself gives a clear explanation of the case, shews that it was not overlooked by the older logicians; and he thinks it not improbable that the doctrine of qualitative aequipollence between two judgments (i.e., obversion) resulted from the consideration of this very question (*System of Logic*, § 106). Compare, further, Whately's treatment of the syllogism, "No man is happy who is not secure; no tyrant is secure; therefore, no tyrant is happy" (*Logic*, II. 4, § 7).

The truth is that by the aid of the process of obversion the premisses of *every* valid syllogism may be expressed as negatives, though the reasoning will then no longer be technically in the form of a syllogism; for example, the propositions which constitute the premisses of a syllogism in *Barbara*—*All M is P, All S is M, therefore, All S is P*—may be written in a negative form, thus, *No M is not-P, No S is not-M*, and the conclusion *All S is P* still follows.

[321] By the contraposition of both premisses this reasoning is reduced to the valid syllogistic form, *All not-M is not-P, All not-M is not-S, therefore, Some not-S is not-P*.

[322] By the inversion of the first premiss, this reasoning is reduced to the valid syllogistic form, *Some not-M is not P, All not-M is S, therefore, Some S is not P*. Compare section 104.

conclusion. The only syllogistic rules, indeed, which still hold good when more than three terms are admitted are the rule providing against illicit minor and the first two corollaries.

But of course none of the above examples really invalidate the syllogistic rules; for these rules have been formulated solely with reference to reasonings of a certain form, namely, those which contain three and only three terms. In every case the reasoning inevitably conforms to the rule which it appears to violate, as soon as, by the aid of immediate inferences, the superfluous number of terms has been eliminated.

207. *Syllogisms with two singular premisses.*—Bain (*Logic, Deduction*, p. 159) argues that an apparent syllogism with two singular premisses cannot be regarded as a genuine syllogistic or deductive inference; and he illustrates his view by reference to the following syllogism:

	Socrates fought at Delium,
	Socrates was the master of Plato,
therefore,	*The master of Plato fought at Delium.*

The argument is that "the proposition 'Socrates was the master of Plato and fought at Delium,' compounded out of the two premisses, is nothing more than a grammatical abbreviation," whilst the step hence to the conclusion is a mere omission of something that had previously been said. "Now, we never consider that we have made a real inference, a step in advance, when we repeat *less* than we are entitled to say, or drop from a complex statement some portion not desired at the moment. Such an operation keeps strictly within the domain of Equivalence or Immediate Inference. In no way, therefore, can a syllogism with two singular premisses be viewed as a genuine syllogistic or deductive inference."

This argument leads up to some interesting considerations, but it proves too much. In the following syllogisms the premisses may be similarly compounded together:

All men are mortal,	*All men are mortal and rational;*
All men are rational,	
therefore, *Some rational beings are mortal.*	
All men are mortal,	*All men including kings are mortal;*
All kings are men,	
therefore, *All kings are mortal.*[323]	

Do not Bain's criticisms apply to these syllogisms as much as to the syllogism with two singular premisses? The method of treatment adopted is indeed particularly applicable to syllogisms in which the middle term is subject in both premisses. But we may always combine the two premisses of a syllogism in a single statement, and it is always true that the conclusion of a syllogism contains a part of, and only a part of, the information contained in

---

[323] Compare with the above the following syllogism which has two singular premisses:—The Lord Chancellor receives a higher salary than the Prime Minister; Lord Herschell is the Lord Chancellor; therefore, Lord Herschell receives a higher salary than the Prime Minister. These premisses would presumably be compounded by Bain into the single proposition, "The Lord Chancellor, Lord Herschell, receives a higher salary than the Prime Minister."

the two premisses taken together; hence we may always get Bain's result.[324] In other words, in the conclusion of every syllogism "we repeat less than we are entitled to say," or, if we care to put it so, "drop from a complex statement some portion not desired at the moment."

208. *Charge of incompleteness brought against the ordinary syllogistic conclusion.*—This charge (a consideration of which will appropriately supplement the discussion contained in the preceding section) is brought by Jevons (*Principles of Science*, 4, § 8) against the ordinary syllogistic conclusion. The premisses *Potassium floats on water, Potassium is a metal* yield, according to him, the conclusion *Potassium metal is potassium floating on water*. But "Aristotle would have inferred that *some metals float on water*. Hence Aristotle's conclusion simply *leaves out some of the information afforded in the premisses*; it even leaves us open to interpret the *some metals* in a wider sense than we are warranted in doing."

In reply to this it may be remarked: first, that the Aristotelian conclusion does not profess to sum up the whole of the information contained in the premisses of the syllogism; secondly, that *some* must here be interpreted to mean merely "not none," "one at least." The conclusion of the above syllogism might perhaps better be written "some metal floats on water," or "some metal or metals &c." Lotze remarks in criticism of Jevons: "His whole procedure is simply a repetition or at the outside an addition of his two premisses; thus it merely adheres to the given facts, and such a process has never been taken for a *Syllogism*, which always means a movement of thought that uses what is given for the purpose of advancing beyond it...... The meaning of the Syllogism, as Aristotle framed it, would in this case be that the occurrence of a floating metal Potassium proves that the property of being so light is not incompatible with the character of metal in general" (*Logic*, II. 3, note). This criticism is perhaps pushed a little too far. It is hardly a fair description of Jevons's conclusion to say that it is the mere sum of the premisses; for it brings out a relation between two terms which was not immediately apparent in the premisses as they originally stood. Still there can be no doubt that the elimination of the middle term is the very gist of syllogistic reasoning as ordinarily understood.

It may be added, as an *argumentum ad hominem* against Jevons, that his own conclusion also leaves out some of the information afforded in the premisses. For we cannot pass back from the proposition *Potassium metal is potassium floating on water* to either of the original premisses.

209. *The connection between the Dictum de omni et nullo and the ordinary Rules of the Syllogism.*—The *dictum de omni et nullo* was given by Aristotle as the axiom on which all syllogistic inference is based. It applies directly, however, to those syllogisms only in which the major term is predicate in the major premiss, and the minor term subject in the minor premiss (i.e., to what are called syllogisms in Figure 1). The rules of the syllogism, on the other hand, apply independently of the position of the terms in the premisses. Nevertheless, it is interesting to trace the connection between them. It will be found that all the rules are involved in the *dictum*, but some of them in a less general form, in consequence of the distinction just pointed out.

---

[324] It may be pointed out that the general method adopted by Boole in his *Laws of Thought* is to sum up all his given propositions in a single proposition, and then eliminate the terms that are not required. Compare also the methods employed in Appendix C of the present work.

The *dictum* may be stated as follows:—"Whatever is predicated, whether affirmatively or negatively, of a term distributed may be predicated in like manner of everything contained under it."

(1) The *dictum* provides for three and only three terms; namely, (i) a certain term which must be distributed, (ii) something predicated of this term, (iii) something contained under it. These terms are respectively the middle, major, and minor. We may consider the rule relating to the ambiguity of terms to be also contained here, since if any term is ambiguous we have practically more than three terms.

(2) The *dictum* provides for three and only three propositions; namely, (i) a proposition predicating something of a term distributed, (ii) a proposition declaring something to be contained under this term, (iii) a proposition making the original predication of the contained term. These propositions constitute respectively the major premiss, the minor premiss, and the conclusion, of the syllogism.

(3) The *dictum* prescribes not merely that the middle term shall be distributed once at least in the premisses, but more definitely that it shall be distributed in the *major* premiss,— "Whatever is predicated of a term *distributed*."[325]

(4) Illicit process of the major is provided against indirectly. This fallacy can be committed only when the conclusion is negative; but the words "in like manner" declare that if there is a negative conclusion, the major premiss must also be negative; and since in any syllogism to which the *dictum* directly applies, the major term is predicate of this premiss, it will be distributed in its premiss as well as in the conclusion. Illicit process of the minor is provided against inasmuch as the *dictum* warrants us in making our predication in the conclusion only of what has been shewn in the minor premiss to be contained under the middle term.

(5) The proposition declaring that something is contained under the term distributed must necessarily be an affirmative proposition. The *dictum* provides, therefore, that the premisses shall not both be negative.[326]

(6) The words "in like manner" clearly provide against a breach of the rule that if one premiss is negative, the conclusion must be negative, and *vice versâ*.

EXERCISES[327]

210. If *P* is a mark of the presence of *Q*, and *R* of that of *S*, and if *P* and *R* are never found together, am I right in inferring that *Q* and *S* sometimes exist separately? [V.]

The premisses may be stated as follows:

All P is Q,
All R is S,
No P is R;

---

[325] This is another form of what will be found to be a special rule of Figure 1, namely, that the major premiss must be universal. Compare section 244.
[326] It really provides that the *minor* premiss shall be affirmative, which again is one of the special rules of Figure 1.
[327] The following exercises may be solved without any knowledge beyond what is contained in the preceding chapter, the assumption however being made that if no rule of the syllogism as given in section 199 or section 201 is broken, then the syllogism is valid.

and in order to establish the desired conclusion we must be able to infer at least one of the following,—*Some Q is not S, Some S is not Q*. But neither of these propositions can be inferred; for they distribute respectively *S* and *Q*, and neither of these terms is distributed in the given premises. The question is, therefore, to be answered in the negative.

211. If it be known concerning a syllogism in the Aristotelian system that the middle term is distributed in both premisses, what can we infer as to the conclusion? [C.]

If both premisses are affirmative, they can between them distribute only two terms, and by hypothesis the middle term is distributed twice in the premisses; hence the minor term cannot be distributed in the premisses, and it follows that the conclusion must be particular.

If one of the premisses is negative, there may be three distributed terms in the premisses; these must, however, be the middle term twice (by hypothesis) and the major term (since the conclusion must now be negative and will therefore distribute the major term); hence the minor term cannot be distributed in the premisses, and it again follows that the conclusion must be particular.

But either both premisses will be affirmative, or one affirmative and the other negative; in any case, therefore, we can infer that the conclusion will be particular.

212. Shew *directly* in how many ways it is possible to prove the conclusions *SaP, SeP*; point out those that conform immediately to the *Dictum de omni et nullo*; and exhibit the equivalence between these and the remainder. [W.]

(1) To prove *All S is P*.

Both premisses must be affirmative, and both must be universal.

S being distributed in the conclusion must be distributed in the minor premiss, which must therefore be *All S is M*.

M not being distributed in the minor must be distributed in the major, which must therefore be *All M is P*.

SaP can therefore be proved in only one way, namely,

	All M is P,
	All S is M,
therefore,	*All S is P;*

and this syllogism conforms immediately to the *Dictum*.

(2) To prove *No S is P*.

Both premisses must be universal, and one must be negative while the other is affirmative; i.e., one premiss must be *E* and the other *A*.

First, let the major be *E*, i.e., either *No M is P* or *No P is M*. In each case the minor must be affirmative and must distribute *S*; therefore, it will be *All S is M*.

Secondly, let the minor be *E*, i.e., either *No S is M* or *No M is S*. In each case the major must be affirmative and must distribute *P*; therefore, it will be *All P is M*.

We can then prove *SeP* in four ways, thus,—

(i)	*MeP,*	(ii)	*PeM,*	(iii)	*PaM,*	(iv)	*PaM,*
	SaM,		*SaM,*		*SeM,*		*MeS,*
	—		—		—		—
	SeP.		*SeP.*		*SeP.*		*SeP.*

Of these, (i) only conforms immediately to the *dictum*, and we have to shew the equivalence between it and the others.

The only difference between (i) and (ii) is that the major premiss of the one is the simple converse of the major premiss of the other; they are, therefore, equivalent. Similarly the only difference between (iii) and (iv) is that the minor premiss of the one is the simple converse of the minor premiss of the other; they are, therefore, equivalent.

Finally, we may shew that (iv) is equivalent to (i) by transposing the premisses and converting the conclusion.

213. Given that the major term is distributed in the premisses and undistributed in the conclusion of a valid syllogism, determine the syllogism. [C.]

Since the major term is undistributed in the conclusion, the conclusion—and, therefore, both premisses—must be affirmative. Hence, in order to distribute P, the major premiss must be *PaM*; and in order to distribute M (which is not distributed in the major premiss), the minor premiss must be *MaS*. It follows that the syllogism must be

	All P is M,
	All M is S,
therefore,	Some S is P.

214. Prove that if three propositions involving three terms (each of which occurs in two of the propositions) are together incompatible, then (*a*) each term is distributed at least once, and (*b*) one and only one of the propositions is negative.

Shew that these rules are equivalent to the rules of the syllogism. [J.]

No two of the propositions can be formally incompatible with one another, since they do not contain the same terms. But each pair must be incompatible with the third, i.e., the contradictory of any one must be deducible from the other two. It follows that we shall have three valid syllogisms, in which the given propositions taken in pairs are the premisses, whilst the contradictory of the third proposition is in each case the conclusion.[328]

Then (*a*) *each term must be distributed once at least*. For if any one of the terms failed to be distributed at least once, we should obviously have undistributed middle in one of our syllogisms; and (since a term undistributed in a proposition is distributed in its contradictory) illicit major or minor in the two others. If, however, the above condition is fulfilled, it is clear that we cannot have either undistributed middle, or illicit major or minor. Hence rule (*a*) is equivalent to the syllogistic rules relating to the distribution of terms.

Again, (*b*) *one of the propositions must be negative, but not more than one of them can be negative*. For if all three were affirmative, then (since the contradictory of an affirmative is negative) we should in each of our syllogisms infer a negative from two affirmatives; and if two were negative, we should have two negative premisses in one of our syllogisms, and (since the contradictory of a negative is affirmative) an affirmative conclusion with a negative premiss in each of the others. If, however, the above condition is fulfilled, it is clear that we cannot have either two negative premisses, or two affirmative premisses with a negative

---

[328] Every syllogism involves two others, in each of which one of the original premisses combined with the contradictory of the conclusion proves the contradictory of the other original premiss. Hence the three syllogisms referred to in the text mutually involve one another. Compare sections 264, 265.

conclusion, or a negative premiss with an affirmative conclusion. Hence rule (*b*) is equivalent to the syllogistic rules relating to quality.

215. Explain what is meant by a *syllogism*; and put the following argument into syllogistic form:—"We have no right to treat heat as a substance, for it may be transformed into something which is not heat, and is certainly not a substance at all, namely, mechanical work." [N.]

216. Put the following argument into syllogistic form:—How can anyone maintain that pain is always an evil, who admits that remorse involves pain, and yet may sometimes be a real good? [V.]

217. It has been pointed out by Ohm that reasoning to the following effect occurs in some works on mathematics:—"A magnitude required for the solution of a problem must satisfy a particular equation, and as the magnitude x satisfies this equation, it is therefore the magnitude required." Examine the logical validity of this argument. [C.]

218. Obtain a conclusion from the two negative premisses,—*No P is M, No S is M*. [K.]

219. If it is false that the attribute B is ever found coexisting with A, and not less false that the attribute C is sometimes found absent from A, can you assert anything about B in terms of C? [C.]

220. Give examples (in symbols—taking S, M, P, as minor, middle, and major terms, respectively) in which, attempting to infer a universal conclusion where we have a particular premiss, we commit respectively one but one only of the following fallacies,—(*a*) undistributed middle, (*b*) illicit major, (*c*) illicit minor. Give also an example in which, making the same attempt, we commit none of the above fallacies. [K.]

221. Can an apparent syllogism break directly all the rules of the syllogism at once? [K.]

222. Can you give an instance of an invalid syllogism in which the major premiss is universal negative, the minor premiss affirmative, and the conclusion particular negative? If not, why not? [K.]

223. Shew that

(i) If both premisses of a syllogism are affirmative, and one but only one of them universal, they will between them distribute only one term;

(ii) If both premisses are affirmative and both universal, they will between them distribute two terms;

(iii) If one but only one premiss is negative, and one but only one premiss universal, they will between them distribute two terms;

(iv) If one but only one premiss is negative, and both premisses are universal, they will between them distribute three terms. [K.]

224. Ascertain how many distributed terms there may be in the premisses of a syllogism more than in the conclusion. [L.]

225. If the minor premiss of a syllogism is negative, what do you know about the position of the terms in the major? [O'S.]

226. If the major term of a syllogism is the predicate of the major premiss, what do you know about the minor premiss? [L.]

227. How much can you tell about a valid syllogism if you know (1) that only the middle term is distributed;

(2) that only the middle and minor terms are distributed;

(3) that all three terms are distributed? [W.]

228. What can be determined respecting a valid syllogism under each of the following conditions: (1) that only one term is distributed, and that only once; (2) that only one term is distributed, and that twice; (3) that two terms only are distributed, each only once; (4) that two terms only are distributed, each twice? [L.]

229. Two propositions are given having a term in common. If they are I and A, shew that either no conclusion or two can be deduced; but if I and E, always and only one. [T.]

230. Find out, from the rules of the syllogism, what are the valid forms of syllogism in which the major premiss is particular affirmative. [J.]

231. Given (*a*) that the major premiss, (*b*) that the minor premiss, of a valid syllogism is particular negative, determine in each case the syllogism. [K.]

232. Given that the major premiss of a valid syllogism is affirmative, and that the major term is distributed both in premisses and conclusion, while the minor term is undistributed in both, determine the syllogism. [N.]

233. Shew *directly* in how many ways it is possible to prove the conclusions *SiP*, *SoP*. [W.]

234. Shew that if the rule that a negative conclusion requires a negative premiss be omitted from the general rules of the syllogism, the only invalid syllogism thereby admitted is such that, if its conclusion be false whilst its premisses are true, the three terms of the syllogism must be absolutely coextensive. [O'S.]

235. Find, by direct application of the fundamental rules of syllogism, what are the valid forms of syllogism in which neither of the premisses is a universal proposition having the same quality as the conclusion. [J.]

236. In what cases will contradictory major premisses both yield conclusions when combined with the same minor?

How are the conclusions related?

Shew that in no case will contradictory minor premisses both yield conclusions when combined with the same major. [O'S.]

237. (*a*) All just actions are praiseworthy; (*b*) No unjust actions are expedient; (*c*) Some inexpedient actions are not praiseworthy; (*d*) Not all praiseworthy actions are inexpedient.

Do (*c*) and (*d*) follow from (*a*) and (*b*)? [K.]

238. Reduce the following arguments to ordinary syllogistic form:

(i) *No M is S, Whatever is not M is P, therefore, All S is P*;

(ii) *It cannot be that no not-S is P*, for *some M is P* and *no M is S*;

(iii) It is impossible for the three propositions, *All M is P, Anything that is not M is not S, Some things that are not P are S*, all to be true together;

(iv) *Everything is M or P, Nothing is both S and M, therefore, All S is P*. [K.]

239. Shew that the following syllogisms break directly or indirectly all the rules of the syllogism:

(1) *All P is M, All S is M, therefore, Some S is not P*;

(2) *All M is P, All M is S, therefore, No S is P*. [K.]

[The so-called rules that every syllogism contains three and only three terms, and that every syllogism consists of three and only three propositions, are not here included under the rules of the syllogism.]

240. In a circular argument involving two valid syllogisms, *Q* and *U* are used as premisses to prove *R*, while *R* and *V* are used as premisses to prove *Q*; shew that *U* and *V* must be a pair of complementary propositions, i.e., of the forms *All M is N* and *All N is M* respectively. [J.]

241. Shew that if two valid syllogisms have a common premiss while the other premisses are contradictories, both the conclusions must be particular. [K.]

242. Given the premisses of a valid syllogism, examine in what cases it is (*a*) possible, (*b*) impossible, to determine which is the minor term and which the major term. [J.]

Chapter 16

THE FIGURES AND MOODS OF THE SYLLOGISM

243. *Figure and Mood.*—By the *figure* of a syllogism is meant the position of the terms in the premisses. Denoting the major, middle, and minor terms by the letters *P*, *M*, *S* respectively, and stating the major premiss first, we have four figures of the syllogism as shewn in the following table:—

Figure 1.	Figure 2.	Figure 3.	Figure 4.
M – *P*	*P* – *M*	*M* – *P*	*P* – *M*
S – *M*	*S* – *M*	*M* – *S*	*M* – *S*
—	—	—	—
S – *P*	*S* – *P*	*S* – *P*	*S* – *P*

By the *mood* of a syllogism is meant the quantity and quality of the premisses and conclusion. For example, *AAA* is a mood in which both the premisses and also the conclusion are universal affirmatives; *EIO* is a mood in which the major is a universal negative, the minor a particular affirmative, and the conclusion a particular negative. It is clear that if figure and mood are both given, the syllogism is given.

244. *The Special Rules of the Figures; and the Determination of the Legitimate Moods in each Figure.*[329]—It may first of all be shewn that certain combinations of premisses are incapable of yielding a valid conclusion in any figure. *A priori*, there are possible the following sixteen different combinations of premisses, the major premiss being always stated first:—*AA, AI, AE, AO, IA, II, IE, IO, EA, EI, EE, EO, OA, OI, OE, OO*. Referring back, however, to the syllogistic rules and corollaries (as given in sections 199, 200), we find that *EE, EO, OE, OO* (being combinations of negative premisses) yield no conclusion by rule 5; that *II, IO, OI* (being combinations of particular premisses) are excluded by corollary i.; and that *IE* is excluded by corollary iii., which tells us that nothing follows from a particular major and a negative minor.

We are left then with the following eight possible combinations:—*AA, AI, AE, AO, IA, EA, EI, OA*; and we may go on to enquire in which figures these will yield conclusions. In pursuing this enquiry, special rules of the various figures may be determined, which, taken together with the three corollaries established in section 200, replace the general rules of

---

[329] The method of determination here adopted is only one amongst several possible methods. Another is suggested, for example, in sections 212, 233.

distribution. These special rules, supplemented by the general rules of quality and the corollaries,[330] will enable the validity of the different moods to be tested by a mere inspection of the form of the propositions of which they consist.

The special rules[331] and the legitimate moods of Figure 1.

The position of the terms in Figure 1 is shewn thus,—

$M - P$
$S - M$
———
$S - P$

and it can be deduced from the general rules of the syllogism that in this figure:—

(1) *The minor premiss must be affirmative.* For if it were negative, the major premiss would have to be affirmative by rule 5, and the conclusion negative by rule 6. The major term would therefore be distributed in the conclusion, and undistributed in its premiss; and the syllogism would be invalid by rule 4.

(2) *The major premiss must be universal.* For the middle term, being undistributed in the affirmative minor premiss, must be distributed in the major premiss.

Rule (1) shews that *AE* and *AO* and rule (2) that *IA* and *OA*, yield no conclusions in this figure. We are accordingly left with only four combinations, namely, *AA, AI, EA, EI.* From the rules that a particular premiss cannot yield a universal conclusion or a negative premiss an affirmative conclusion, while conversely a negative conclusion requires a negative premiss, it follows further that *AA* will justify either of the conclusions *A* or *I, EA* either *E* or *O, AI* only *I, EI* only *O*. There are then six moods in Figure 1 which do not offend against any of the rules of the syllogism,[332] namely, *AAA, AAI, AII, EAE, EAO, EIO.*

The actual validity of these moods may be established by shewing that the axiom of the syllogism, the *dictum de omni et nullo*, applies to them; or by taking them severally and shewing that in each case the cogency of the reasoning is self-evident.

The special rules and the legitimate moods of Figure 2.

The position of the terms in Figure 2 is shewn thus,—

---

[330] The general rules of quality and the corollaries can be directly applied without reference to the position of the terms in the premisses of a syllogism. This is not the case with the general rules of distribution. The object of the special rules is, in the case of each particular figure, to substitute for the general rules of distribution special rules of quantity and quality.

[331] As indicated in section 209, the special rules of Figure 1 follow immediately from the *dictum de omni et nullo*.

[332] Rule (2) provides against undistributed middle, and rule (1) against illicit major. We cannot have illicit minor, unless we have a universal conclusion with a particular premiss, and this also has been provided against.

Mr Johnson points out that the following symmetrical rules may be laid down for the correct distribution of terms in the different figures; and that these rules (three in each figure) taken together with the *rules of quality* are sufficient to ensure that *no* syllogistic rule is broken.

(i) To avoid undistributed middle: in Figure 1, If the minor is affirmative, the major must be universal; in Figure 4, If the major is affirmative, the minor must be universal; in Figure 2, One premiss must be negative; in Figure 3, One premiss must be universal. (The last of these rules is of course superfluous if the corollaries contained in section 200 are supposed given.)

(ii) To avoid illicit major: in Figures 1 and 3, If the conclusion is negative, the major must be negative and, therefore, the minor affirmative; in Figures 2 and 4, If the conclusion is negative, the major must be universal.

(iii) To avoid illicit minor: in Figures 1 and 2, If the minor is particular, the conclusion must be particular; in Figures 3 and 4, If the minor is affirmative, the conclusion must be particular. (The first of these two rules is again superfluous as a special rule if the corollaries are supposed given.)

The above rules are substantially identical with those given in the text.

$P - M$
$S - M$
―
$S - P$;

and its special rules (which the reader is recommended to deduce from the general rules of the syllogism for himself) are,—

(1) *One premiss must be negative*;
(2) *The major premiss must be universal.*

The application of these rules again leaves six moods, namely, *AEE, AEO, AOO, EAE, EAO, EIO.*

Recourse cannot now he had directly to the *dictum de omni et nullo* in order to shew positively that these moods are legitimate. It may, however, be shewn in each case that the cogency of the reasoning is self-evident. The older logicians did not adopt this course; their method was to shew that, by the aid of immediate inferences, each mood could be reduced to such a form that the *dictum* did apply directly to it. The doctrine of reduction resulting from the adoption of this method will be discussed in the following chapter.

The special rules and the legitimate moods of Figure 3.

The position of the terms in this figure is shewn thus,—

$M - P$
$M - S$
―
$S - P$;

and its special rules are,—

(1) *The minor must be affirmative*;
(2) *The conclusion must be particular.*

Proceeding as before, we are left with six valid moods, namely, *AAI, AII, EAO, EIO, IAI, OAO.*

The special rules and the legitimate moods of Figure 4.

The position of the terms in this figure is shewn thus,—

$P - M$
$M - S$
―
$S - P$;

and the following may be given as its special rules,—

(1) *If the major is affirmative, the minor must be universal*;

(2) *If either premiss is negative, the major must be universal*;
(3) *If the minor is affirmative, the conclusion must be particular.*[333]

The result of the application of these rules is again six valid moods, namely, *AAI, AEE, AEO, EAO, EIO, IAI*.

Our final conclusion then is that there are 24 valid moods, namely, six in each figure.

In Figure 1, *AAA, AAI, EAE, EAO, AII, EIO*.
In Figure 2, *EAE, EAO, AEE, AEO, EIO, AOO*.
In Figure 3, *AAI, IAI, AII, EAO, OAO, EIO*.
In Figure 4, *AAI, AEE, AEO, EAO, IAI, EIO*.

245. *Weakened Conclusions and Subaltern Moods.*—When from premisses that would have justified a universal conclusion we content ourselves with inferring a particular (as, for example, in the syllogism *All M is P, All S is M*, therefore, *Some S is P*), we are said to have a *weakened conclusion*, and the syllogism is said to be a *weakened syllogism* or to be in a *subaltern mood* (because the conclusion might be obtained by subaltern inference[334] from the conclusion of the corresponding unweakened mood).

In treating the syllogism on the traditional lines it is assumed that *S, M, P* all represent existing classes. Subaltern inference is, therefore, a valid process.

In the preceding section it has been shown that in each figure there are six moods which do not offend against any of the syllogistic rules: so that in all there are 24 distinct valid moods. Five of these, however, have weakened conclusions; and, since we are not likely to be satisfied with a particular conclusion when the corresponding universal can be obtained from the same premisses, these moods are of no practical importance. Accordingly when the moods of the various figures are enumerated (as in the mnemonic verses) they are usually omitted. Still, their recognition gives a completeness to the theory of the syllogism, which it cannot otherwise possess. There is also a symmetry in the result of their recognition as yielding exactly six legitimate moods in each figure.[335]

The subaltern moods are,—

In Figure 1, *AAI, EAO*;
In Figure 2, *EAO, AEO*;
In Figure 4, *AEO*.

It is obvious that there can be no weakened conclusion in Figure 3, since in no case is it possible to infer more than a particular conclusion in this figure.

AAI in Figure 4 is sometimes spoken of as a subaltern mood. But this is a mistake. With the premisses *All P is M, All M is S*, the conclusion *Some S is P* is certainly in one sense weaker than the premisses would warrant since the universal conclusion *All P is S* might have

---

[333] The special rules of the fourth figure are variously stated. They are given in the above form in the *Port Royal Logic*, pp. 202, 203. See, also, section 255.

[334] In treating the syllogism on the traditional lines it is assumed that *S, M, P* all represent existing classes. Subaltern inference is, therefore, a valid process.

[335] It has been remarked that 19 being a prime number at once suggests incompleteness or artificiality in the common enumeration.

been inferred. But *All P is S* is not the universal corresponding to *Some S is P*. The subjects of these two propositions are different; and we infer all that we possibly can about *S* when we say that *some S is P*. In other words, regarded as a mood of Figure 4, this mood is not a subaltern. *AAI* in Figure 4 is thus differentiated from *AAI* in Figure 1, and its inclusion in the mnemonic verses justified.

246. *Strengthened Syllogisms.*—If in a syllogism the same conclusion can still be obtained although for one of the premisses we substitute its subaltern, the syllogism is said to be a *strengthened syllogism*. A strengthened syllogism is thus a syllogism with an unnecessarily strengthened premiss.[336]

For example, the conclusion of the syllogism—

	All M is P,
	All M is S,
therefore,	Some S is P,

could equally be obtained from the premisses *All M is P, Some M is S*; or from the premisses *Some M is P, All M is S*.

By trial we may find that *every syllogism in which there are two universal premisses with a particular conclusion is a strengthened syllogism, with the single exception of AEO in the fourth figure.*[337]

In a full enumeration there are two strengthened syllogisms in each figure:—

In Figure 1, *AAI, EAO*;
In Figure 2, *EAO, AEO*;
In Figure 3, *AAI, EAO*;
In Figure 4, *AAI, EAO*.

It will be observed that in Figures 1 and 2, a syllogism having a strengthened premiss may also be regarded as a syllogism having a weakened conclusion, and *vice versâ*; but that in Figures 3 and 4, the contrary holds in both cases. The only syllogism with a weakened conclusion in either of these figures is *AEO* in Figure 4; and in this mood no conclusion is obtainable if either of the premisses is replaced by its subaltern.

If syllogisms containing either a strengthened premiss or a weakened conclusion are omitted, we are left with 15 valid moods, namely, 4 in each of the first three Figures and 3 in Figure 4.

247. *The peculiarities and uses of each of the four figures of the syllogism.*[338]—Figure 1. In this figure it is possible to prove conclusions of all the forms A, E, I, O; and it is the *only* figure in which a universal affirmative conclusion can be proved. This alone makes it by far the most useful and important of the syllogistic figures. All deductive science, the object of which is to establish universal affirmatives, tends to work in *AAA* in this figure.

Another point to notice is that only in this figure is it the case that both the subject of the conclusion is subject in the premisses, and the predicate of the conclusion predicate in the

---

[336] Compare De Morgan, *Formal Logic*, pp. 91, 130. De Morgan calls a syllogism *fundamental*, when neither of its premisses is stronger than is necessary to produce the conclusion (*Formal Logic*, p. 77).
[337] A general proof of this proposition will be given in section 351.
[338] On the distinctive characteristics of the different figures, see also sections 269 to 271.

premisses; in Figure 2 the predicate of the conclusion is subject in the major premiss; in Figure 3 the subject of the conclusion is predicate in the minor premiss; and in Figure 4 there is a double inversion.[339] This no doubt partly accounts for the fact that a reasoning expressed in Figure 1 so often seems more natural than the same reasoning expressed in any other figure.[340]

Figure 2. In this figure, only negatives can be proved; and therefore it is chiefly used for purposes of disproof. For example, *Every real natural poem is naïve*; *those poems of Ossian which Macpherson pretended to discover are not naïve* (*but sentimental*); *hence they are not real natural poems* (Ueberweg, *System of Logic*, § 113). It has been called the *exclusive* figure; because by means of it we may go on excluding various suppositions as to the nature of something under investigation, whose real character we wish to ascertain (a process called *abscissio infiniti*). For example, *Such and such an order has such and such properties*, *This plant has not those properties*; therefore, *It does not belong to that order*. A syllogism of this kind may be repeated with a number of different orders till the enquiry is so narrowed down that the place of the plant is easily determined. Whately (*Elements of Logic*, p. 92) gives an example from the diagnosis of a disease.

Figure 3. In this figure, only particulars can be proved. It is frequently useful when we wish to take objection to a universal proposition laid down by an opponent by establishing an instance in which such universal proposition does not hold good.

It is the natural figure when the middle term is a singular term, especially if the other terms are general. It has been already shown that if one and only one term of an affirmative proposition is singular, that term is almost necessarily the subject. For example, such a reasoning as *Socrates is wise*, *Socrates is a philosopher*, therefore, *Some philosophers are wise*, can only with great awkwardness be expressed in any figure other than Figure 3.

Figure 4. This figure is seldom used, and some logicians have altogether refused to recognise it. We shall return to a discussion of it subsequently. See section 262.

Lambert in his *Neues Organon* expresses the uses of the different syllogistic figures as follows: "The first figure is suited to the discovery or proof of the properties of a thing; the second to the discovery or proof of the distinctions between things; the third to the discovery or proof of instances and exceptions; the fourth to the discovery or exclusion of the different species of a genus."

EXERCISES

248. Why is *IE* an inadmissible, while *EI* is an admissible, mood in every figure of the syllogism? [L.]

249. What moods are good in the first figure and faulty in the second, and *vice versâ*? Why are they excluded in one figure and not in the other? [O.]

250. (i) Shew that *O* cannot stand as premiss in Figure 1, as major in Figure 2, as minor in Figure 3, as premiss in Figure 4.

---

[339] The double inversion in Figure 4 is one of the reasons given by Thomson for rejecting that figure altogether. Compare section 262.
[340] Compare Solly, *Syllabus of Logic*, pp. 130 to 132.

(ii) Shew that it is impossible to have the conclusion in *A* in any figure but the first. What fallacies would be committed if there were such a conclusion to a reasoning in any other figure? [C.]

251. Two valid syllogisms in the same figure have the same major, middle, and minor terms, and their major premisses are subcontraries; determine—without reference to the mnemonic verses—what the syllogisms must be. [K.]

252. Prove, by general reasoning, that any mood valid both in Figure 2 and in Figure 3 is valid also in Figure 1 and in Figure 4. [C.]

253. Shew, without individual reference to the different figures, that *EAO* is a strengthened syllogism in every figure, and that *AAI* is a strengthened syllogism whenever it is valid. [K.]

254. Shew, by general reasoning, that every valid syllogism in which the middle term is twice distributed contains a strengthened premiss. Does it follow that it must have also a weakened conclusion? [K.]

255. Shew that the following *two* rules would suffice as the special rules for the fourth figure: (i) The conclusion and major cannot have the same form unless it be particular affirmative; (ii) The conclusion and minor cannot have the same form unless it be universal negative. [J.]

Chapter 17

THE REDUCTION OF SYLLOGISMS

256. *The Problem of Reduction.*—By *reduction* is meant a process whereby the reasoning contained in a given syllogism is expressed in some other mood or figure. Unless an explicit statement is made to the contrary, reduction is supposed to be to Figure 1.

The following syllogism in Figure 3 may be taken as an example:

	All M is P,
	Some M is S,
therefore,	*Some S is P.*

It will be seen that by simply converting the minor premiss, we have precisely the same reasoning in Figure 1.

This is an example of *direct* or *ostensive* reduction.

257. *Indirect Reduction.*—A proposition is established *indirectly* when its contradictory is proved false; and this is effected if it can be shewn that a consequence of the truth of its contradictory would be self-contradiction.

The method of indirect proof is in several cases adopted by Euclid; and it may be employed in the reduction of syllogisms from one mood to another. Thus, *AOO* in Figure 2 is usually reduced in this manner. The argument may be stated as follows:—

From the premisses,—

	All P is M,
	Some S is not M,
it follows that	*Some S is not P*;

for if this conclusion is not true, then, by the law of excluded middle, its contradictory (namely, *All S is P*) must be so; and, the premisses being given true, the three following propositions must all be true, namely,

All P is M,
Some S is not M,
All S is P.

But combining the first and the third of these we have a syllogism in Figure 1, namely,

	All P is M,
	All S is P,
yielding the conclusion	All S is M.

Some S is not M and *All S is M* are, therefore, true together; but, by the law of contradiction, this is absurd, since they are contradictories.

Hence it has been shown that the consequence of supposing *Some S is not P* false is a self-contradiction; and we may accordingly infer that it is true.

It will be observed that the only syllogism made use of in the above argument is in Figure 1; and the process may, therefore, be regarded as a reduction of the reasoning to Figure 1.

This method of reduction is called *Reductio ad impossibile*, or *Reductio per impossibile*,[341] or *Deductio ad impossibile*, or *Deductio ad absurdum*. It is the only way of reducing *AOO* in Figure 2 or *OAO* in Figure 3 to Figure 1, unless negative terms are used (as in obversion and contraposition); and it was adopted by the old writers in consequence of their objection to negative terms.

It will be shewn later on in this chapter that by employing the method of indirect reduction systematically we can bring out with great clearness the relation between the different moods and figures of the syllogism.

258. *The mnemonic lines Barbara, Celarent, &c.*—The mnemonic hexameter verses (which are spoken of by De Morgan as "the magic words by which the different moods have been denoted for many centuries, words which I take to be more full of meaning than any that ever were made") are usually given as follows:

*Barbără, Cēlārent, Dărĭi, Fĕrĭŏ*que prioris:
Cēsărĕ, Cāmēstres, Festīnŏ, Bărōcŏ, secundae:
Tertia, *Dāraptī, Dĭsămis, Dātīsĭ, Fĕlapton,*
Bōcardō, Fērīsŏn, habet: Quarta insuper addit
Brāmantip, Cămĕnes, Dĭmăris, Fēsāpŏ, Frĕsīson.

Each valid mood in every figure, unless it be a subaltern mood, is here represented by a separate word; and in the case of a mood in any of the so-called imperfect figures (i.e., Figures 2, 3, 4), the mnemonic gives full information for its reduction to Figure 1, the so-called perfect figure.

The only meaningless letters are *b* (not initial), *d* (not initial), *l, n, r, t*; the signification of the remainder is as follows:—

The *vowels* give the quality and quantity of the propositions of which the syllogism is composed; and, therefore, really give the syllogism itself, if the figure is also known. Thus, *Camenes* in Figure 4 represents the syllogism—

	All P is M,
	No M is S,
therefore,	No S is P.

---

[341] Compare Mansel's *Aldrich*, pp. 88, 89.

The *initial letters* in the case of Figures 2, 3, 4 shew to which of the moods of Figure 1 the given mood is to be reduced, namely, to that which has the same initial letter. The letters B, C, D, F were chosen for the moods of Figure 1 as being the first four consonants in the alphabet.

Thus, *Camestres* is reduced to *Celarent*,—

	All P is M,	\ /	No M is S,
	No S is M,	/ \	All P is M,
therefore,	No S is P.	therefore,	No P is S,
		therefore,	No S is P.[342]

s (in the middle of a word) indicates that in the process of reduction the preceding proposition is to be simply converted. Thus, in reducing *Camestres* to *Celarent*, as shewn above, the minor premiss is simply converted.

s (at the end of a word) shews that the conclusion of the *new* syllogism has to be simply converted in order that the given conclusion may be obtained. This again is illustrated in the reduction of *Camestres*. The final *s* does not affect the conclusion of *Camestres* itself, but the conclusion of *Celarent* to which it is reduced.[343]

p (in the middle of a word) signifies that the preceding proposition is to be converted *per accidens*; as, for example, in the reduction of *Darapti* to *Darii*,—

	All M is P,		All M is P,
	All M is S,		Some S is M,
therefore,	Some S is P.	therefore,	Some S is P.

p (at the end of a word[344]) implies that the conclusion *obtained by reduction* is to be converted *per accidens*. Thus, in *Bramantip*, the *p* does not relate to the I conclusion of the mood itself;[345] it really relates to the A conclusion of the syllogism in *Barbara* which is given by reduction. Thus,—

---

[342] The *order* of inference in this and in other reductions might be made clear by the use of arrows, representing inference, as follows:

All P is M,	\ ↗	No M is S,
No S is M,	/ ↘	All P is M,
		↓
No S is P.	←	No P is S,

[343] This peculiarity in the signification of *s* and *p* when they are *final* letters is sometimes overlooked. The point to be noted is that the conclusion of the syllogism originally given is not, like the original premisses, a datum from which we set out, but a result that we have to reach. It follows that the conclusion to be manipulated, if any, must be the conclusion of the syllogism obtained by reduction, not the conclusion of the original syllogism. This is clearly shewn in the case of *Camestres* by the method adopted in the last preceding note to illustrate the reduction of *Camestres* to *Celarent*. The reduction of *Disamis, Bramantip, Camenes, Dimaris* to Figure 1 might be illustrated similarly.

[344] See the last preceding note.

[345] Compare, however, Hamilton, *Logic*, I. p. 264, and Spalding, *Logic*, pp. 230, 1.

	All P is M,	\\ /	*All M is S,*
	All M is S,	/ \\	*All P is M,*
therefore,	*Some S is P.*	therefore,	*All P is S,*
		therefore,	*Some S is P.*

m indicates that in reduction the premisses have to be transposed (*metathesis praemissarum*); as just shewn in the case of *Bramantip*, and also in the case of *Camestres*.

c signifies that the mood is to be reduced *indirectly* (i.e., by *reductio per impossibile* in the manner shewn in the preceding section); and the position of the letter indicates that in this process of indirect reduction the first step is to omit the premiss preceding it, i.e., the other premiss is to be combined with the contradictory of the conclusion (*conversio syllogismi*, or *ductio per contradictoriam propositionem sive per impossibile*), The letter *c* is by some writers replaced by *k*, *Baroko* and *Bokardo* being given as the mnemonics, instead of *Baroco* and *Bocardo*.

The following lines are sometimes added to the verses given above, in order to meet the case of the subaltern moods:—

Quinque Subalterni, totidem Generalibus orti,
Nomen habent nullum, nec, si bene colligis, usum.[346]

259. *The direct reduction of Baroco and Bocardo.*—These moods may be reduced directly to the first figure by the aid of obversion and contraposition as follows.[347]

---

[346] The mnemonics have been written in various forms. Those given above are from Aldrich, and they are the ones that are in general use in England. Wallis in his *Institutio Logicae* (1687) gives for the fourth figure, *Balani, Cadere, Digami, Fegano, Fedibo*. P. van Musschenbroek in his *Institutiones Logicae* (1748) gives *Barbari, Calentes, Dibatis, Fespamo, Fresisom*. This variety of forms for the moods of Figure 4 is no doubt due to the fact that the recognition of this figure at all was quite exceptional until comparatively recently. Compare sections 262, 263.
According to Ueberweg (*Logic*, § 118) the mnemonics run,—
  Barbara, Celarent primae, *Darii Ferio*que.
  Cesare, Camestres, Festino, Baroco secundae.
  Tertia grande sonans recitat *Darapti, Felapton,*
  Disamis, Datisi, Bocardo, Ferison. Quartae
  Sunt *Bamalip, Calemes, Dimatis, Fesapo, Fresison*.
Ueberweg gives *Camestros* and *Calemos* for the weakened moods of *Camestres* and *Calemes*. This is not, however, quite accurate. The mnemonics should be *Camestrop* and *Calemop*.
Professor Carveth Read (*Logic*, pp. 126, 7) suggests an ingenious modification of the verses, so as to make each mnemonic immediately suggest the figure to which the corresponding mood belongs, at the same time abolishing all the unmeaning letters. He takes *l* as the sign of the first figure, *n* of the second, *r* of the third, and *t* of the fourth. The lines (to be scanned, says Professor Read, discreetly) then run
  *Ballala, Celallel, Dalii, Felio*que prioris.
  Cesane, Camesnes, Fesinon, Banoco secundae.
  Tertia *Darapri, Drisamis, Darisi, Ferapro,*
  Bocaro, Ferisor habet. Quanta insuper addit
  Bamatip, Cametes, Dimatis, Fesapto, Fesistot.
Professor Mackenzie suggests that, if this plan is adopted, it would be better to take *r* for the first figure (*figura recta*, the straightforward figure), *n* for the second figure (*figura negativa*), *t* for the third figure (*figura tertia* or *particularis*), and *l* for the fourth figure (*figura laeva*, the left-handed figure). Compare also Mrs Ladd Franklin, *Studies in Logic*, Johns Hopkins University, p. 40.

[347] Another method is to reduce *Baroco* and *Bocardo* by the process of ἔκθεσις to other moods of Figures 2 and 3, and thence to Figure 1. Ueberweg writes, "*Baroco* may also be referred to *Camestres* when those (some) *S* of which the minor premiss is true are placed under a special notion and denoted by *S'*. Then the conclusion must hold good universally of *S'*, and consequently particularly of *S*. Aristotle calls such a procedure ἔκθεσις"

Baroco:—

	All P is M,
	Some S is not M,
therefore,	Some S is not P,

is reducible to *Ferio* by the contraposition of the major premiss and the obversion of the minor, thus,—

	No not-M is P,
	Some S is not-M,
therefore,	Some S is not P.

Faksoko has been suggested as a mnemonic for this method of reduction, *k* denoting obversion, so that *ks* demotes obversion followed by conversion (i.e., contraposition).

Whately's mnemonic *Fakoro* (*Elements of Logic*, p. 97) does not indicate the obversion of the minor premiss (*r* being with him an unmeaning letter).

Bocardo:—

	Some M is not P,
	All M is S,
therefore,	Some S is not P,

is reducible to *Darii* by the contraposition of the major premiss and the transposition of the premisses, thus,—

	All M is S,
	Some not-P is M,
therefore,	Some not-P is S.

Some not-P is S is not indeed our original conclusion, but the latter can be obtained from it by conversion followed by obversion. This method of reduction may be indicated by *Doksamosk* (which again is obviously preferable to *Dokamo*, suggested by Whately, since the latter would make it appear as if we immediately obtained the original conclusion in *Darii*.)

260. *Extension of the Doctrine of Reduction.*—The doctrine of reduction may be extended, and it can be shewn not merely that any syllogism may be reduced to Figure 1, but

---

(*Logic*, § 113). As regards *Bocardo*, "Aristotle remarks that this mood may be proved without apagogical procedure (*reductio ad impossibile*) by the ἐκθέσθαι or λαμβάνειν of that part of the middle notion which is true of the major premiss. If we denote this part by *N*, then we get the premisses; *NeP*; *NaS*: from which follows (in *Felapton*) *SoP*; which was to be proved" (§ 115). The procedure is, however, rather more complicated than appears in the above statements. In the case of *Baroco* (*PaM, SoM, ∴ SoP*), let the *S*'s which are not *M* (of which by hypothesis there are some) be denoted by *X*; then we have *PaM, XeM, ∴ XeP* (*Camestres*); but *XaS*, and hence we have further *XeP, XaS, ∴ SoP* (*Felapton*). In the case of *Bocardo* (*MoP, MaS, ∴ SoP*), let the *M*'s which are not *P* (of which by hypothesis there are some) be denoted by *N*; then we have *MaS, NaM, ∴ NaS* (*Barbara*); and hence *NeP, NaS, ∴ SoP* (*Felapton*). The argument in both cases suggests questions connected with the existential import of propositions; but the consideration of such questions must for the present be deferred.

also that it may be reduced to any given mood (not being a subaltern mood) of that figure.[348] This position will obviously be established if we can shew that *Barbara, Celarent, Darii,* and *Ferio* are mutually reducible to one another.

Barbara may be reduced to *Celarent* by the obversion of the major premiss and also of the new conclusion thereby obtained. Thus, using arrows, as in the note on page 320,

All M is P,	→	No M is not-P,
All S is M,	→	All S is M,
		↓
All S is P.	←	No S is not-P.

Conversely, *Celarent* is reducible to *Barbara*; and in a similar manner, by obversion of major premiss and conclusion, *Darii* and *Ferio* are reducible to one another.

It will now suffice if we can shew that *Barbara* and *Darii* are mutually reducible to one another. Clearly the only method possible here is the indirect method.

Take *Barbara*,

	MaP,
	SaM,
	—
∴	SaP;

for, if not, then we have *SoP*; and *MaP, SaM, SoP* must be true together. From *SoP* by first obverting and then converting (and denoting *not-P* by *P'*) we get *P'iS*, and combining this with *SaM* we have the following syllogism in *Darii*,—

	SaM,
	P'iS,
	—
∴	P'iM.

P'iM by conversion and obversion becomes *MoP*; and therefore *MaP* and *MoP* are true together; but this is impossible, since they are contradictories. Therefore, *SoP* cannot be true, i.e., the truth of *SaP* is established.

Similarly, *Darii* may be indirectly reduced to *Barbara*.[349]

	MaP,	(i)
	SiM,	(ii)
	—	
∴	SiP.	(iii)

---

[348] Compare, further, sections 284, 285.
[349] It has been maintained, that this reduction is unnecessary, and that, to all intents and purposes, *Darii* is *Barbara*, since the "some S" in the minor is, and is known to be, the *same some* as in the conclusion. Compare section 269.

The contradictory of (iii) is *SeP*, from which we obtain *PaS'*. Combining with (i), we have—

	PaS',	
	MaP,	
	—	
∴	*MaS'*	in *Barbara*.

But from this conclusion we may obtain *SeM*, which is the contradictory of (ii).

261. Is Reduction an essential part of the Doctrine of the Syllogism?—According to the original theory of reduction, the object of the process is to be sure that the conclusion is a valid inference from the premises. The validity of a syllogism in Figure 1 may be directly tested by reference to the *dictum de omni et nullo*: but this dictum has no direct application to syllogisms in the remaining three figures. Thus, Whately says, "As it is on the *dictum de omni et nullo* that all reasoning *ultimately* depends, so all arguments may be in one way or other brought into some one of the four moods in the first figure: and a syllogism is, in that case, said to be *reduced*" (*Elements of Logic*, p. 93). Professor Fowler puts the same position somewhat more guardedly, "As we have adopted no canon for the 2nd, 3rd, and 4th figures, we have as yet no positive proof that the six moods remaining in each of those figures are valid: we merely know that they do not offend against any of the syllogistic rules. But if we can *reduce* them, i.e., bring them back to the first figure, by shewing that they are only different statements of its moods, or in other words, that precisely the same conclusions can be obtained from equivalent premises in the first figure, their validity will be proved beyond question" (*Deductive Logic*, p. 97).

Reduction is, on the other hand, regarded by some logicians as both *unnecessary* and *unnatural*. It is, in the first place, said to be *unnecessary*, on the ground that the *dictum de omni et nullo* has no claim to be regarded as the paramount law for all valid inference.[350] In sections 270 to 272 it will be shown that dicta can be formulated for the other figures, which may be regarded as making them independent of the first, and putting them on a level with it. It may also be maintained that in any mood the validity of a particular syllogism is as self-evident as that of the *dictum de omni et nullo* itself; and that, therefore, although axioms of syllogism are useful as generalisations of the syllogistic process, they are needless in order to establish the validity of any given syllogism. This view is indicated by Ueberweg.

Reduction is, in the second place, said to be *unnatural*, inasmuch as it often involves the substitution of an unnatural and indirect for a natural and direct predication. Figures 2 and 3 at any rate have their special uses, and certain reasonings fall naturally into these figures rather than into the first figure.[351]

The following example is given by Thomson (*Laws of Thought*, p. 174): "Thus, when it was desirable to shew by an example that zeal and activity did not always proceed from selfish motives, the natural course would be some such syllogism as the following. The Apostles sought no earthly reward, the Apostles were zealous in their work; therefore, some zealous persons seek not earthly reward." In reducing this syllogism to Figure 1, we have to

---

[350] Compare Thomson, *Laws of Thought*, p. 172.
[351] Compare a quotation from Lambert (*Neues Organon*, §§ 230, 231) given by Sir W. Hamilton (*Logic*, II. p. 438).

convert our minor into "Some zealous persons were Apostles," which is awkward and unnatural.

Take again this syllogism, "Every reasonable man wishes the Reform Bill to pass, I don't, therefore, I am not a reasonable man." Reduced in the regular way to *Celarent*, the major premiss becomes, "No person wishing the Reform Bill to pass is I," yielding the conclusion, "No reasonable man is I."

Further illustrations of this point will be found if we reduce to Figure 1, syllogisms with such premisses as the following:—All orchids have opposite leaves, This plant has not opposite leaves; Socrates is poor, Socrates is wise.

The above arguments justify the position that reduction is not a necessary part of the doctrine of the syllogism, so far as the establishment of the validity of the different moods is concerned.[352]

At the same time, no treatment of the syllogism can be regarded as scientific or complete until the *equivalence* between the moods in the different figures has been shewn; and for this purpose, as well as for its utility as a logical exercise, a full treatment of the problem of reduction should be retained.[353]

262. *The Fourth Figure.*—Figure 4 was not as such recognised by Aristotle; and its introduction having been attributed by Averroës to Galen, it is frequently spoken of as the *Galenian Figure*. It does not usually appear in works on Logic before the beginning of the eighteenth century, and even by modern logicians its use is sometimes condemned. Thus Bowen (*Logic*, p. 192) holds that "what is called the fourth figure is only the first with a converted conclusion; that is we do not actually reason in the fourth, but only in the first, and then if occasion requires, convert the conclusion of the first." This account of Figure 4 cannot, however, be accepted, since it will not apply to *Fesapo* or *Fresison*. For example, from the premisses of *Fesapo* (*No P is M* and *All M is S*) no conclusion whatever is obtainable in Figure 1.[354]

---

[352] Hamilton (*Logic*, I. p. 433) takes a curious position in regard to the doctrine of reduction. "The last three figures," he says, "are virtually identical with the first." This has been recognised by logicians, and hence "the tedious and disgusting rules of their reduction." But he himself goes further, and extinguishes these figures altogether, as being merely "accidental modifications of the first," and "the mutilated expressions of a complex mental process." A somewhat similar position is taken by Kant in his essay *On the Mistaken Subtilty of the Four Figures*. Kant's argument is virtually based on the two following propositions: (1) Reasonings in Figures 2, 3, 4 require to be implicitly, if not explicitly, reduced to Figure 1, in order that their validity may be apparent; for example, in *Cesare* we must have covertly performed the conversion of the major premiss in thought, since otherwise our premisses would not be conclusive; (2) No reasonings ever fall naturally into any of the moods of Figures 2, 3, 4, which are, therefore, a mere useless invention of logicians. On grounds already indicated, both these propositions must be regarded as erroneous. A further error seems to be involved in the following passage from the same essay of Kant's: "It cannot be denied that we can draw conclusions legitimately in all these figures. But it is incontestable that all except the first determine the conclusion only by a roundabout way, and by interpolated inferences, and that *the very same conclusion would follow from the same middle term in the first figure by pure and unmixed reasoning*." The latter part of this statement cannot be justified in such a case as that of *Baroco*.

[353] See, further, sections 266, 268.

[354] For the most part the critics of the fourth figure seem to identify it altogether with *Bramantip*. The following extract from Father Clarke's *Logic* (p. 337) will serve to illustrate the contumely to which this poor figure is sometimes subjected: "Ought we to retain it? If we do, it should be as a sort of syllogistic Helot, to shew how low the syllogism can fall when it neglects the laws on which all true reasoning is founded, and to exhibit it in the most degraded form which it can assume without being positively vicious. Is it capable of reformation? Not of reformation, but of extinction...... Where the same premisses in the first figure would prove a universal affirmative, this feeble caricature of it is content with a particular; where the first figure draws its conclusion naturally and in accordance with the forms into which human thought instinctively shapes itself, this perverted

Thomson's ground of rejection is that in the fourth figure the order of thought is wholly inverted, the subject of the conclusion having been a predicate in the premisses, and the predicate a subject. "Against this the mind rebels; and we can ascertain that the conclusion is only the converse of the real one, by proposing to ourselves similar sets of premisses, to which we shall always find ourselves supplying a conclusion so arranged that the syllogism is in the first figure, with the second premiss first" (*Laws of Thought*, p. 178). As regards the first part of this argument, Thomson himself points out that the same objection applies partially to Figures 2 and 3. It no doubt helps to explain why as a matter of fact reasonings in Figure 4 are not often met with;[355] but it affords no sufficient ground for altogether refusing to recognise this figure. The second part of Thomson's argument is, for a reason already stated, unsound. The conclusion, for example, of *Fresison* cannot be "the converse of the real conclusion," since (being an O proposition) it is not the converse of any other proposition whatsoever.

It is indeed impossible to treat the syllogism scientifically and completely without admitting in some form or other the moods of Figure 4. In an *à priori* separation of figures according to the position of the major and minor terms in the premisses, this figure necessarily appears, and it yields conclusions which are not directly obtainable from the same premisses in any other figure. It is not actually in frequent use, but reasonings may sometimes not unnaturally fall into it; for example, None of the Apostles were Greeks, Some Greeks are worthy of all honour, therefore, Some worthy of all honour are not Apostles.

263. *Indirect Moods.*—The earliest form in which the mnemonic verses appeared was as follows:—

Barbara, Celarent, Darii, Ferio, Baralipton,
Celantes, Dabitis, Fapesmo, Frisesomorum,
Cesare, Camestres, Festino, Baroco, Darapti,
Felapton, Disamis, Datisi, Bocardo, Ferison.[356]

Aristotle recognised only three figures: the first figure, which he considered the type of all syllogisms and which he called the perfect figure, the *dictum de omni et nullo* being directly applicable to it alone; and the second and third figures, which he called imperfect figures, since it was necessary to reduce them to the first figure, in order to obtain a test of their validity.

Before the fourth figure, however, was commonly recognised as such, its moods were recognised in another form, namely, as *indirect* moods of the first figure; and the above

---

abortion forces the mind to an awkward and clumsy process which rightly deserves to be called 'inordinate and violent.'" Father Clarke's own violence appears to be attributable mainly to the fact that Figure 4 was not, as such, recognised by Aristotle.

[355] The reasons why Figure 4, "with its premisses looking one way, and its conclusion another," is seldom used, are elaborated by Karslake, *Aids to the Study of Logic*, I. pp. 74, 5.

[356] First published in the *Summulae Logicales* of Petrus Hispanus, afterwards Pope John XXI., who died in 1277. The mnemonics occur in an earlier unpublished work of William Shyreswood, who died as Chancellor of Lincoln in 1249.

mnemonics—*Baralipton, Celantes, Dabitis, Fapesmo, Frisesomorum*—represent these moods so regarded.[357]

The conception of indirect moods may be best explained by starting from a definition of figure, which contains no reference to the distinction between major and minor terms, and which accordingly yields only three figures instead of four, namely: Figure 1, in which the middle term is subject in one of the premisses and predicate in the other; Figure 2, in which the middle term is predicate in both premisses; Figure 3, in which the middle term is subject in both premisses. The moods of Figure 1 may then be distinguished as direct or indirect according as the position of the terms in the conclusion is the same as their position in the premisses or the reverse.[358] Thus, with the premisses *MaP*, *SaM*, we have a direct conclusion *SaP*, and an indirect conclusion *PiS*. These are respectively *Barbara* and *Baralipton*. Similarly, *Celantes* corresponds to *Celarent*, and *Dabitis* to *Darii*. With the premisses *MeP*, *SiM*, we obtain the direct conclusion *SoP*, but nothing can be inferred of *P* in terms of *S*. There is, therefore, no indirect mood corresponding to *Ferio*. On the other hand, *Fapesmo* and *Frisesomorum* (the *Fesapo* and *Fresison* of the fourth figure) have no corresponding direct moods.

Clearly it is no more than a formal difference whether the five moods in question are recognised in the manner just indicated, or as constituting a distinct figure; but, on the whole, the latter alternative seems less likely to give rise to confusion.

The distinction between direct and indirect moods as above expressed is for obvious reasons confined to the first figure. It will be observed, however, that in the traditional names of the indirect moods of the first figure the minor premiss precedes the major, and if we seek to apply a distinction between direct and indirect moods in the case of the second and third figures, it can only be with reference to the conventional order of the premisses. Thus, in the second figure, taking the premisses *PeM*, *SaM*, we may infer either *SeP* or *PeS*, and if we call a syllogism direct or indirect according as the major premiss precedes the minor, or *vice versâ*, then *PeM*, *SaM*, *SeP* will be a direct mood, and *PeM*, *SaM*, *PeS* an indirect mood. The former of these syllogisms is *Cesare*, and the latter is *Camestres* with the premisses transposed.[359] Hence the latter will immediately become a direct mood by merely changing the order of the premisses; and the artificiality of the distinction is at once apparent. The

---

[357] From the 14th to the 17th century the mnemonics found in works on Logic usually give the moods of the fourth figure in this form, or else omit them altogether. Wallis (1687) recognises them in both forms, giving two sets of mnemonics.

[358] It follows that if we compare the conclusion of an indirect mood with the conclusion of the corresponding direct mood (where such correspondence exists), we shall find that the terms have changed places. Mansel's definition of an indirect mood as "one in which we do not infer the immediate conclusion, but its converse" (*Aldrich*, p. 78) must, however, be rejected for the reason that it cannot be applied to *Fapesmo* and *Frisesomorum*, which are indirect moods having no corresponding valid direct moods at all. In these we cannot be said to infer "the converse of the immediate conclusion," for there is no immediate conclusion. Mansel deals with these two moods very awkwardly. "*Fapesmo* and *Frisesomorum*," he remarks, "have negative minor premisses, and thus offend against a special rule of the first figure; but this is checked by a counterbalancing transgression. For by simply converting O, we alter the distribution of the terms, so as to avoid an illicit process." But the notion that we can counterbalance one violation of law by committing a second cannot be allowed. The truth of course is that, in the first place, the special rules of the first figure as ordinarily given do not apply to the indirect moods; and in the second place, the conclusion O is not obtained by conversion at all.

[359] Take, again, the premisses *MaP*, *MoS*. Here there is no direct conclusion, but only an indirect conclusion *PoS*. This, however, is merely *Bocardo* with the premisses transposed.

result will be found to be similar in other cases, and the distinction may, therefore, be rejected so far as Figures 2 and 3 are concerned.

264. *Further discussion of the process of Indirect Reduction.*—The discussion of the problem of reduction in the preceding pages has in the main followed the traditional lines. It is, however, desirable to treat the process of indirect reduction in a rather more independent and systematic manner. By doing so, we shall find that the process enables us to exhibit very clearly and symmetrically the relations between the first three figures, and also the distinctive functions of these figures.

The argument on which indirect reduction is based is one of which we have several times made use (e.g., in the proof of the second corollary adopted from De Morgan in section 200, and in certain of the proofs contained in section 202), namely, that if X and Y together prove Z, then X and the denial of Z must prove the denial of Y, and *vice versâ*.

The process may conveniently be exhibited as the contraposition of a hypothetical. Thus, from the proposition *X being given, if Y then Z* we may infer by contraposition *X being given, if not Z then not Y*; and we can equally pass back from the contrapositive to the original proposition.

Since the contradictory of the conclusion of a syllogism may be combined with *either* of the original premisses, it follows that every valid syllogism carries with it the validity of *two* other syllogisms. Hence all valid syllogisms must be capable of being arranged in sets of three which are mutually equivalent.

The three equivalent syllogisms may be symmetrically expressed as follows (where P and P', Q and Q', R and R' are respectively contradictories):

(i) premisses, P and Q; conclusion R';
(ii) premisses, Q and R; conclusion P';
(iii) premisses, R and P; conclusion Q'.

It must be understood that the order of the premisses in these syllogisms is not intended to indicate which is major and which minor.

265. *The Antilogism.*—Each of the three equivalent syllogisms just given involves further the formal incompatibility of the three propositions P, Q, R (compare section 214). Three propositions, containing three and only three terms, which are thus formally incompatible with one another, constitute what has been called by Mrs Ladd Franklin an *antilogism*.[360] Thus, the syllogism, "MaP, SaM, therefore, SaP," has for its equivalent antilogism, "MaP, SaM, SoP are three propositions that are formally incompatible with one another."

266. *Equivalence of the Moods of the first three Figures shewn by the Method of Indirect Reduction.*—If one of our three equivalent syllogisms is in one of the first three figures, then it can be shewn that the two others will be in the remaining two of these figures.

---

[360] See Baldwin's *Dictionary of Philosophy*, art. *Symbolic Logic*. It is shewn in this article that the whole of syllogistic reasoning may be summed up in the following antilogism, the symbolism of section 138 being made use of,—
$[(AB = 0)(bC = 0)(AC > 0)] = 0.$
The fifteen moods containing neither a strengthened premiss nor a weakened conclusion may, by the aid of conversions and obversions, be obtained from this antilogism according as the contradictory of one or other of the three incompatibles is taken as the conclusion.

Thus, let $P, Q, \therefore R'$ be in Figure 1, the minor premiss being stated first. It may then be written

| $S-M, M-P, \therefore (S-P)'$. | (1) |

The second syllogism becomes

| $M-P, S-P, \therefore (S-M)'$; | (2) |

and the third is

| $S-P, S-M, \therefore (M-P)'$. | (3) |

It will be seen that (2) is in Figure 2, and (3) in Figure 3.

Next, let $P, Q, \therefore R'$ be in Figure 2, the major premiss being stated first. We then have for our three syllogisms,—

$P-M, S-M, \therefore (S-P)'$;	(1)
$S-M, S-P, \therefore (P-M)'$;	(2)
$S-P, P-M, \therefore (S-M)'$.	(3)

Here (2) is in Figure 3, (3) in Figure 1.

Finally, let $P, Q, \therefore R'$ be in Figure 3, the major premiss being stated first. We have

$M-P, M-S, \therefore (S-P)'$;	(1)
$M-S, S-P, \therefore (M-P)'$;	(2)
$S-P, M-P, \therefore (M-S)'$.	(3)

Here (2) is in Figure 1, (3) in Figure 2.

Hence we see that, starting with a syllogism in any one of the first three figures (the minor premiss preceding the major in Figure 1, but following it in Figures 2 and 3), and taking the propositions in the above cyclic order, then the figures will always recur in the cyclic order 1, 2, 3.[361]

It follows that (as we already know to be the case) there must be an equal number of valid syllogisms in each of the first three figures, and that they may be arranged in sets of equivalent trios. These equivalent trios will be found to be as follows (sets containing strengthened premisses or weakened conclusions being enclosed in square brackets);

Barbara, Baroco, Bocardo;
[AAI, AEO, Felapton;]
Celarent, Festino, Disamis;
[EAO, EAO, Darapti;]
Darii, Camestres, Ferison;

---

[361] If we were to start with a syllogism in Figure 1, the major premiss being stated first, then the cyclic order of figures would be 1, 3, 2, and in Figures 2 and 3 the minor premiss would precede the major.

Ferio, Cesare, Datisi.

The corresponding antilogisms are AAO, [AAE,] EAI, [EAA,] AIE, EIA.[362]

267. *The Moods of Figure 4 in their relation to one another.*—We have seen that in the equivalent trios of syllogisms yielded by the process of indirect reduction we never have in any one trio more than one syllogism in Figure 1, or in Figure 2, or in Figure 3. Figure 4 is, however, self-contained in the sense that if we start with a syllogism in this figure, both the other syllogisms will be in the same figure. Proceeding as in the last section, we may shew this as follows, the major premiss being stated first:[363]

$P-M, M-S, \therefore (S-P)'$;	(1)
$M-S, S-P, \therefore (P-M)'$;	(2)
$S-P, P-M, \therefore (M-S)'$.	(3)

It follows that in Figure 4 the number of valid syllogisms must be some multiple of three. The number is, as we know, six. There are, therefore, two equivalent trios; and they will be found to be as follows:

[Bramantip, AEO, Fesapo;]
Camenes, Fresison, Dimaris.

The equivalent antilogisms are [AAE,] AEI. Comparing this result with that obtained in the preceding section, we see that the only valid antilogistic combinations are AAO and AEI, with the addition of AAE (in which one of the three propositions is unnecessarily strengthened).[364]

268. *Equivalence of the Special Rules of the First Three Figures.*—Let the following be a valid syllogism in Figure 1,—

(minor)		$S-M$,	(1)
(major)		$M-P$,	(2)
(conclusion)	$\therefore$	$(S-P)'$.	(3)

Then the corresponding valid syllogism in Figure 2 will be

(major)		$M-P$,	(2)
(minor)		$S-P$,	contradictory of (3)
(conclusion)	$\therefore$	$(S-M)'$;	contradictory of (1)

and the corresponding valid syllogism in Figure 3 will be

---

[362] The position of the terms in these antilogisms corresponds to that of Figure 1, the major premiss being stated first.
[363] It will be found that it comes to just the same thing if the minor premiss is stated first.
[364] This result might be inferred from the rules given in section 214.

(major)		$S-P$,	contradictory of (3)
(minor)		$S-M$,	(1)
(conclusion)	∴	$(M-P)'$.	contradictory of (2)

The special rules of Figure 1 are

| minor | affirmative, |
| major | universal, |

that is, (1) must be affirmative, (2) must be universal.

In Figure 2, (2) is the major, and the contradictory of (1) is the conclusion. Therefore, in Figure 2 we must have the rules,—

| major | universal, |
| conclusion | negative [and hence *one premiss negative*]. |

In Figure 3, (1) is the minor, and the contradictory of (2) is the conclusion. Therefore, in Figure 3 we must have the rules,—

| minor | affirmative, |
| conclusion | particular. |

Thus the special rules of Figures 2 and 3 are shewn to be deducible from the special rules of Figure 1. We might equally well start from the special rules of Figure 2 or of Figure 3 and deduce the rules of the two other figures.[365]

269. *Scheme of the Valid Moods of Figure* 1.—So far as the nature of the reasoning involved is concerned, there is practically no distinction between *Barbara* and *Darii*, or between *Celarent* and *Ferio*. For in each case, if S is the minor term, the S's referred to in the conclusion are precisely *the same S*'s as those referred to in the minor premiss.

Again, the only difference between *Barbara* and *Celarent*, or between *Darii* and *Ferio*, is that the universal rule which the minor premiss enables us to apply to a particular case is in *Barbara* and *Darii* a universal affirmation, while in *Celarent* and *Ferio* it is a universal denial.

We may, therefore, sum up all four moods in the following scheme:[366]

---

[365] The complete rules for the antilogisms of the first three figures, as given at the end of section 266, are (*a*) first proposition universal, (*b*) second proposition affirmative, (*c*) third proposition opposite in quality to the first, and (unless it is strengthened) opposite in quantity to the second. These rules replace all general rules.

[366] Compare C. S. Peirce in the *Johns Hopkins Studies in Logic*, p. 148, and Sigwart, *Logic*, i. p. 354. Sigwart gives the following formula:

	If anything is M it is P (or *is not P*),
	Certain subjects S are M,
therefore,	*They are P* (or *are not P*).

	All B is C (or is not C),	(Rule)
	All (or some) A is B,	(Case)
therefore,	All (or some) A is C (or is not C).	(Result)

This way of setting out the valid moods of Figure 1 shews clearly how they are all included under the *dictum de omni et nullo*.

270. *Scheme of the Valid Moods of Figure 2.*—Applying the principle of indirect reduction, we may immediately obtain from the scheme given in the last preceding section the following scheme, summing up the valid moods of Figure 2:[367]

	All B is C (or is not C),	(Rule)
	Some (or all) A is not C (or is C),	(Denial of Result)
therefore,	Some (or all) A is not B.	(Denial of Case)

This scheme may be expressed in the following dictum,—"If a certain attribute can be predicated, affirmatively or negatively, of every member of a class, any subject of which it cannot be so predicated does not belong to the class."[368] This dictum may, like the *dictum de omni et nullo*, claim to be axiomatic, and it is related to the valid syllogisms of Figure 2 just as the *dictum de omni et nullo* is related to the valid syllogisms of Figure 1.[369]

271. *Scheme of the Valid Moods of Figure* 3.—Dealing with Figure 3 in the same way as we have done with Figure 2, we get the following scheme, summing up the valid moods of that figure:

	Some (or all) A is not C (or is C),	(Denial of Result)
	All (or some) A is B,	(Case)
therefore,	Some B is not C (or is C).	(Denial of Rule)

---

[367] Sigwart's way of putting it (*Logic*, i. p. 354) is that in Figure 2, instead of inferring from ground to consequence, we infer from invalidity of consequence to invalidity of ground; and he gives the following scheme:

	If anything is P it is M (or is not M),
	Certain subjects S are not M (or are M),
therefore,	They are not P.

[368] The dictum for Figure 2, sometimes called the *dictum de diverso*, is expressed in the above form by Mansel (*Aldrich*, p. 86). It was given by Lambert in the form, "If one term is contained in, and another excluded from, a third term, they are mutually excluded." This is at least expressed loosely, since it would appear to warrant a universal conclusion, if any conclusion at all, in *Festino* and *Baroco*. Bailey (*Theory of Reasoning*, p. 71) gives the following pair of maxims for Figure 2,—"When the whole of a class possess a certain attribute, whatever does not possess the attribute does not belong to the class. When the whole of a class is excluded from the possession of an attribute, whatever possesses the attribute does not belong to the class."

[369] Lambert is usually regarded as the originator of the idea of framing dicta that shall be directly applicable to figures other than the first. Thomson, however, points out that it is an error to suppose that Lambert was the first to invent such dicta. "More than a century earlier, Keckermann saw that each figure had its own law and its own peculiar use, and stated them as accurately, if less concisely, than Lambert" (*Laws of Thought*, p. 173, note). Distinct principles for the second and third figures are laid down also in the *Port Royal Logic*, which was published in 1662.

It is not easy to express this scheme in a single self-evident maxim[370] Separate dicta of an axiomatic character may, however, be formulated for the affirmative and negative moods respectively of Figure 3, namely, "If two attributes can both be affirmed of a class, and one at least of them universally so, then these two attributes sometimes accompany each other," "If one attribute can be affirmed while another is denied of a class, either the affirmation or the denial being universal, then the former attribute is not always accompanied by the latter."[371]

272. *Dictum for Figure* 4.—The following *dictum*, called the *dictum de reciproco*, was formulated by Lambert for Figure 4:—"If no *M* is *B*, no *B* is this or that *M*; if *C* is (or is not) this or that *B*, there are *B*'s which are (or are not) *C*." The first part of this *dictum* is intended to apply to *Camenes*, and the second part to the remaining moods of the fourth figure; but the application can hardly in either case be regarded as self-evident. Several other axioms have been constructed for Figure 4; but they are, as a rule, little more than a bare enumeration of the valid moods of that figure, whilst at the same time they are less self-evident than these moods considered individually. The following axiom, however, suggested by Mr Johnson, is not open to these criticisms: "Three classes cannot be so related, that the first is wholly included in the second, the second wholly excluded from the third, and the third partly or wholly included in the first." This *dictum* affirms the validity of two antilogisms; in other words, it declares the mutual incompatibility of each of the following trios of propositions: *XaY, YeZ, ZiX*; *XaY, YeZ, ZaX*; and it will be found that these incompatibles yield the six valid moods of the fourth figure.[372]

EXERCISES

273. Reduce *Barbara* to *Bocardo*, *Bocardo* to *Baroco*, *Baroco* to *Barbara*. [K.]

274. Reduce *Ferio* to Figure 2, *Festino* to Figure 3, *Felapton* to Figure 4. [K.]

275. Reduce *Camestres* to *Datisi*. Why cannot *Camestres* be reduced either directly or indirectly to *Felapton*? Can *Felapton* be reduced to *Camestres*? [K.]

276. Assuming that in the first figure the major must be universal and the minor affirmative, shew by *reductio ad absurdum* that the conclusion in the second figure must be negative and in the third particular. [J.]

277. State the following argument in a syllogism of the third figure, and reduce it, both directly and indirectly, to the first:—Some things worthy of being known are not directly useful, for every truth is worthy of being known, while not every truth is directly useful. [M.]

278. State the figure and mood of the following syllogism; reduce it to the first figure; and examine whether there is anything unnatural in the argument as it stands:—

---

[370] Lambert gave the following *dictum de exemplo* for Figure 3:—"Two terms which contain a common part partly agree, or if one contains a part which the other does not, they partly differ." This maxim is open to exception. The proposition "If one term contains a part which another does not, they partly differ" applied to *MeP, MaS*, would appear to justify *PoS* just as much as *SoP*, or else to yield an alternative between these two. Mr Johnson gives a single formula for Figure 3, namely, "A statement may be applied to part of a class, if it applies wholly [or at least partly] to a set of objects that are at least partly [or wholly] included in that class." This is correct, but perhaps not very easy to grasp.

[371] These dicta (or dicta corresponding to them) are sometimes called respectively the *dictum de exemplo* and the *dictum de excepto*.

[372] Compare section 267.

None who dishonour the king can be true patriots; for a true patriot must respect the law, and none who respect the law would dishonour the king. [J.]

279. "Rejecting the fourth figure and the subaltern moods, we may say with Aristotle: A is proved only in one figure and one mood, E in two figures and three moods, I in two figures and four moods, O in three figures and six moods. For this reason, A is declared by Aristotle to be the most difficult proposition to establish, and the easiest to overthrow; O, the reverse." Discuss the fitness of these data to establish the conclusion. [K.]

280. Prove, from the general rules of the syllogism, that the number of possible moods, irrespective of difference of figure, is 11.

In the 19 moods of the mnemonic verses, only 10 out of the possible 11 moods are represented. Find the missing mood, and account for its absence from the verses. [L.]

281. Given

(1) the conclusion of a syllogism in the first figure,

(2) the minor premiss of a syllogism in the second figure,

(3) the major premiss of a syllogism in the third figure, examine in each case how far the quality and quantity of the two remaining propositions of the syllogism can be determined (it being given that the syllogism does not contain a strengthened premiss or a weakened conclusion).

Express the result, as far as possible, in general terms in each figure. [J.]

282. Find out in which of the valid syllogistic moods the combination of one premiss with the subcontrary of the conclusion would establish the subcontrary of the other premiss. [L.]

283. Construct a syllogism in accordance with each of the following two dicta:—

(1) Any object that is found to lack a property known to belong to all members of a class must be excluded from that class;

(2) If any objects that have been included in a class are found to lack a certain property, then that property cannot be predicated of all members of the class. Assign the mood and figure of each argument, and shew the relations between the above dicta and the *dictum de omni et nullo*. [L.]

284. Shew that any given mood may be directly reduced to any other mood, provided (1) that the latter contains neither a strengthened premiss nor a weakened conclusion, and (2) that if the conclusion of the former is universal, the conclusion of the latter is also universal [K.]

285. Shew that any given mood may be directly or indirectly reduced to any other mood, provided that the latter has not either a strengthened premiss or a weakened conclusion, unless the same is true of the former also. [K.]

286. Examine the following statement of De Morgan's:—"There are but six distinct syllogisms. All others are made from them by strengthening one of the premisses, or converting one or both of the premisses, where such conversion is allowable; or else by first making the conversion, and then strengthening one of the premisses." [K.]

287. Shew, by the aid of the process of indirect reduction, that the special rules for Figure 4 given in section 244 are mutually deducible from one another. [RR.]

Chapter 18

THE DIAGRAMMATIC REPRESENTATION OF SYLLOGISMS

288. *The application of the Eulerian diagrams to syllogistic reasonings.*—In shewing the application of the Eulerian diagrams to syllogistic reasonings we may begin with a syllogism in *Barbara*:

	All M is P,
	All S is M,
therefore,	All S is P.

The premisses must first be represented separately by means of the diagrams. Each yields two cases; thus,—

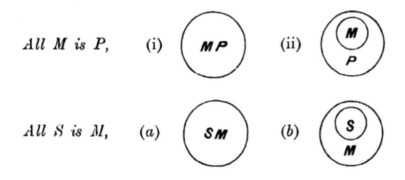

To obtain the conclusion, each of the cases yielded by the major premiss must now be combined with each of those yielded by the minor. This gives four combinations,[373] and whatever is true of *S* in terms of *P* in all of them is the conclusion required.

---

[373] These combinations afford a complete solution of the problem as to what class-relations between *S*, *M*, and *P* are compatible with the premisses; and similarly in other cases. The syllogistic conclusion is obtained by the elimination of *M*.

(i) and (a) yield

(i) and (b)

(ii) and (a)

(ii) and (b)

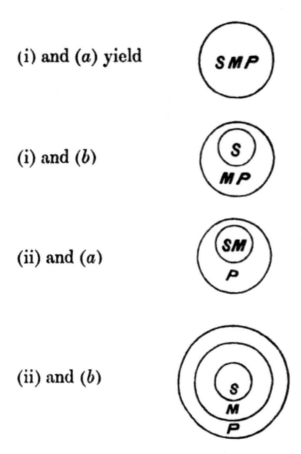

In each case S either coincides with P or is included within P; hence *all S is P* may be inferred from the given premisses.

Next, take a syllogism in *Bocardo*. The application of the diagrams is now more complicated. The premisses are

| Some M is not P, |
| All M is S. |

The major premiss yields three cases, namely,

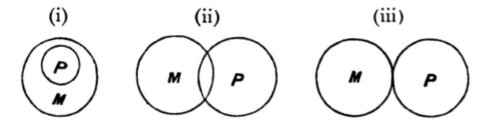

and the minor premiss two cases, namely,

The Diagrammatic Representation of Syllogisms   235

Taking them together we have six combinations, some of which themselves yield more than one case:—

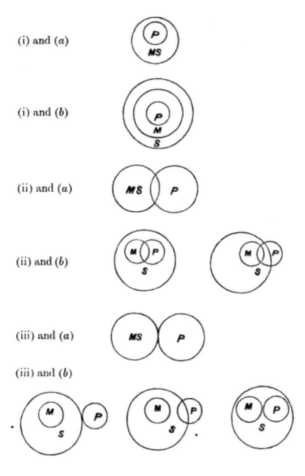

So far as *S* and *P* are concerned (*M* being left out of account) these nine cases are reducible to the following three:

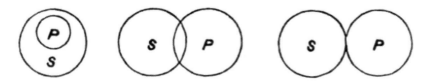

The conclusion, therefore, is *Some S is not P*.

It must be admitted that this is very complex, and that it would be a serious matter if in the first instance we had to work through all the different moods in this manner.[374] Still, for purposes of illustration, this very complexity has a certain advantage. It shews how many relations between three terms in respect of extension are left to us, even with two premisses given.

289. *The application of Lambert's diagrammatic scheme to syllogistic reasonings.*—As applied to syllogisms, Lambert's lines are much less cumbrous than Euler's circles. The main point to notice is that it is in general necessary that the line standing for the middle term should not be dotted over any part of its extent.[375] This condition can be satisfied by selecting the appropriate alternative form in the case of A, I, and O propositions, as given in section 127. As examples we may represent *Barbara, Baroco, Datisi,* and *Fresison* by Lambert's method.

Barbara :—

Baroco :—

Datisi :—

Fresison :—

---

[374] Ueberweg, however, takes the trouble to establish in this way the validity of the valid moods in the various figures. Thomson (*Laws of Thought*, pp. 189, 190) introduces comparative simplicity by the use of dotted lines. His diagrams are, however, incorrect.

[375] The following representation of *Barbara*,

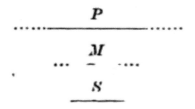

illustrates the kind of error that is likely to result if the above precaution is neglected. If this representation were correct we should be justified in inferring *Some P is not S* as well as *All S is P*.

The Diagrammatic Representation of Syllogisms 237

290. *The application of Dr Venn's diagrammatic scheme to syllogistic reasonings.*—Syllogisms in *Barbara*, *Camestres*, *Datisi*, and *Bocardo* may be taken in order to shew how Dr Venn's diagrams can be used to illustrate syllogistic reasonings.

The premisses of *Barbara*,

All M is P,
All S is M,

exclude certain compartments as shewn in the following diagram:

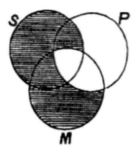

This yields at once the conclusion *All S is P*.
Similarly for *Camestres* we have the following:

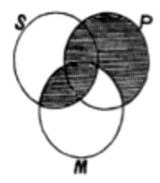

For *Datisi* we have

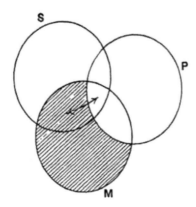

Bocardo yields

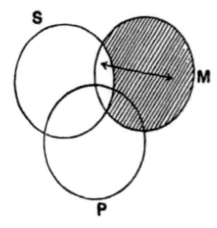

It will be remembered that this scheme is based upon a particular interpretation of propositions as regards their existential import. The student will find it useful to attempt to represent by Dr Venn's diagrams a mood containing a strengthened premiss, for example, *Darapti*.

EXERCISES

291. Represent *Celarent* by the aid of Euler's diagrams. Will the same set of diagrams serve for any other of the syllogistic moods? [K.]

292. Represent by means of the Eulerian diagrams the moods *Festino*, *Datisi*, and *Bramantip*. [K.]

293. Determine (i) by the aid of Euler's diagrams, (ii) by ordinary syllogistic methods, what is all that can be inferred about *S* and *P* in terms of one another from the following premisses, *Some M is P*, *Some M is not P*, *Some P is not M*, *Some S is not M*, *All M is S*. [K.]

294. Represent in Lambert's scheme the moods *Darii*, *Cesare*, *Darapti*, *Bocardo*, *Fesapo*. [K.]

295. Represent in Dr Venn's diagrammatic scheme the moods *Ferio*, *Cesare*, *Baroco*, *Dimaris*. [K.]

296. Shew (i) by means of Euler's diagrams, (ii) by means of Dr Venn's diagrams, that *IE* yields no conclusion in any figure. [K.]

297. Shew diagrammatically that no conclusion can be obtained from *IA* in Figure 1, from *AA* in Figure 2, from *AE* in Figure 3, from *AO* in Figure 4. [K.]

298. Determine, by the aid of Euler's diagrammatic scheme, all the relations that are *à priori* possible between three classes *S*, *M*, *P*. [K.]

299. Test the following argument (i) by Dr Venn's diagrammatic scheme, (ii) by ordinary syllogistic methods:

"All brave persons are well-disciplined; no patriots are mercenary; but some mercenary persons have been found to be brave, and not all patriots can be considered well-disciplined; it follows that some brave and well-disciplined persons have been both mercenary and unpatriotic, while others that have been patriotic and unmercenary were but ill-disciplined cowards." [C.]

300. Given *All X is Y or Z, All Y is Z or X, All Z is X or Y, All YZ is X, All ZX is Y, All XY is Z*, prove (*a*) by the aid of Dr Venn's diagrammatic scheme, (*b*) without the aid of diagrams, that *X, Y, Z* are coextensive. [RR.]

Chapter 19

CONDITIONAL AND HYPOTHETICAL SYLLOGISMS

301. *The Conditional Syllogism, the Hypothetical Syllogism, and the Hypothetico-Categorical Syllogism.*—The forms of reasoning in which conditional or hypothetical conclusions are inferred from two conditional or two hypothetical premisses are apparently overlooked by some logicians; at any rate, they frequently receive no distinct recognition, the term "hypothetical syllogism" being limited to the case in which one premiss only is hypothetical.

The following definitions may be given:

(1) A *conditional syllogism* is a reasoning consisting of two conditional premisses and a conditional conclusion;[376]

e.g.,	*If any A is C, it is D,*
	If any A is B, it is C,
therefore,	*If any A is B, it is D.*

(2) A *hypothetical syllogism* (or, more distinctively, a *pure hypothetical syllogism*) is a reasoning consisting of two hypothetical premisses and a hypothetical conclusion;

e.g.,—	*If Q is true, R is true,*
	If P is true, Q is true,
therefore,	*If P is true, R is true.*

(3) A *hypothetico-categorical syllogism* (or, as it may also be called, *a mixed hypothetical syllogism*) is a reasoning consisting of three propositions in which one of the premisses is hypothetical in form, while the other premiss and the conclusion are categorical;[377]

---

[376] To be quite exact, the condition should be added that the premisses and conclusion contain between them three and only three elements (corresponding to the terms of the categorical syllogism).
[377] It seems unnecessary to discuss separately the case in which a conditional premiss and a categorical premiss are combined: e.g., All selfish people are unhappy; If a child is spoilt, he is sure to be selfish; therefore, If a child is spoilt he will be unhappy. Such a syllogism as this is resolvable into an ordinary categorical syllogism by reducing the conditional premiss to the categorical form, "All spoilt children are selfish"; or it may be resolved into a conditional syllogism by transforming the categorical premiss into the corresponding conditional, "If anyone is selfish, he is sure to be unhappy." The following is another example: If water is salt it will not boil at

e.g.,—	If P is true, Q is true,
	P is true,
therefore,	Q is true.

This nomenclature, so far as concerns the distinction between the hypothetical and the hypothetico-categorical syllogism, is adopted by Spalding and Ueberweg. Sigwart uses the terms "pure hypothetical syllogism," and "mixed hypothetical syllogism." Some logicians (e.g., Fowler) give the name "hypothetical syllogism" to all the above forms of reasoning without distinction. Others (e.g., Jevons) define the hypothetical syllogism so as to include the last form only, the others not being recognised as distinct forms of reasoning at all. This view may be to some extent justified by the very close analogy that exists between the syllogism with two conditional or two hypothetical premisses and the categorical syllogism: but the difference in form is worth at least a brief discussion.

302. *Distinctions of Mood and Figure in the case of Conditional and Hypothetical Syllogisms.*—In the conditional, and in the hypothetical, syllogism, the antecedent of the conclusion is equivalent to the minor term of the categorical syllogism, the consequent of the conclusion to the major term, and the element which does not appear in the conclusion at all to the middle term. Distinctions of mood and figure may be recognised in precisely the same way as in the case of the categorical syllogism. Thus, the conditional syllogism given in the preceding section is in *Barbara*. The following are examples of other moods:

Festino,—	Never when E is F, is it the case that C is D,
	Sometimes when A is B, C is D,
therefore,	Sometimes when A is B, it is not the case that E is F.
Darapti,—	Whenever C is B, E is F,
	Whenever C is D, A is B,
therefore,	Sometimes when A is B, E is F.
Camenes,—	Whenever E is F, C is D,
	Never when C is D, is it the case that A is B,
therefore,	Never when A is B, is it the case that E is F.

In these three examples the form in which the propositions are expressed suggests an assertoric interpretation. On the modal interpretation, either of conditionals or of hypotheticals, the problematic proposition may be regarded as taking the place of the particular, and we shall then again have all the ordinary distinctions of mood and figure. We may illustrate from hypotheticals:

Darii,—	If Q is true, R is true,
	If P is true, Q may be true,
therefore,	If P is true, R may be true.
Baroco,—	If R is true, Q is true,
	If P is true, Q may be false,
therefore,	If P is true, R may be false.

212°; Sea water is salt; therefore, Sea water will not boil at 212°. Compare Mr F. B. Tarbell in *Mind*, 1883, p. 578. The hypothetico-categorical syllogism as above defined cannot be so summarily disposed of.

Disamis,—	*If Q is true, R may be true,*
	If Q is true, P is true,
therefore,	*If P is true, R may be true.*[378]
Camenes,—	*If R is true, Q is true,*
	If Q is true, P is not true,
therefore,	*If P is true, R is not true.*

303. *Fallacies in Hypothetical Syllogisms.*—On the mistaken supposition that a pure hypothetical proposition is equivalent to a categorical proposition in which both the subject and the predicate are singular terms, and therefore *ipso facto* distributed, it has been argued that the syllogistic rules relating to the distribution of terms have no application to hypothetical syllogisms; and that the only rules which need be considered in testing such syllogisms are those relating to quality, namely, the rule forbidding two negative premisses, and the rule insisting that a negative premiss and a negative conclusion must always be found together. But it is clearly an error to regard the consequent of a hypothetical proposition as equivalent to a singular term occurring as the predicate of a categorical proposition. An affirmative hypothetical is not simply convertible, and in respect of distribution, its consequent practically corresponds to the undistributed predicate of an affirmative categorical in which the terms are general. On the other hand, a negative hypothetical *is* simply convertible; and its consequent corresponds to the distributed predicate of a negative categorical. We may accordingly have fallacies in hypothetical syllogisms corresponding to (1) undistributed middle, (2) illicit major, (3) illicit minor. The following are examples of these fallacies respectively:—

(1) *If R then Q, If P then Q,* therefore, *If P then R;*
(2) *If Q then R, If P then not Q,* therefore, *If P then not R;*
(3) *If Q then R, If Q then P,* therefore, *If P then R.*

304. *The Reduction of Conditional and Hypothetical Syllogisms.*—Conditional and hypothetical syllogisms in Figures 2, 3, and 4 may be reduced to Figure 1 just as in the case of categorical syllogisms. Thus the conditional syllogism in *Camenes* given in section 302 may be reduced as follows to *Celarent:*

	Never when C is D, is it the case that A is B,
	Whenever E is F, C is D,
therefore,	*Never when E is F, is it the case that A is B,*
therefore,	*Never when A is B, is it the case that E is F.*

According to the ordinary rule as indicated in the mnemonic, the premisses have here been transposed, and the conclusion of the new syllogism is converted in order to obtain the original conclusion.

---

[378] The reader may possibly hesitate to admit the validity of this reasoning, although he feels no difficulty in regard to the validity of an ordinary categorical syllogism in *Disamis*. This apparent anomaly is connected with the problem of existential import. It will be shewn in section 342 that the validity of *Disamis* depends on our interpretation of propositions as regards their existential import, and we may perhaps not regard categoricals and hypotheticals as analogous in this respect.

Similarly the hypothetical syllogism in *Baroco* given in section 302 may be reduced as follows to *Ferio*:

	If Q is false, R is false,
	If P is true, Q may be false,
therefore,	*If P is true, R may be false.*

305. *The Moods of the Mixed Hypothetical Syllogism.*—It is usual to distinguish two moods of the mixed hypothetical syllogism, the *modus ponens* and the *modus tollens*.[379]

(1) In the *modus ponens* (also called the *constructive* hypothetical syllogism) the categorical premiss affirms the antecedent of the hypothetical premiss, thereby justifying as a conclusion the affirmation of its consequent. For example,

	If P is true then Q is true,
	P is true,
therefore,	*Q is true.*

(2) In the *modus tollens* (also called the *destructive* hypothetical syllogism) the categorical premiss denies the consequent of the hypothetical premiss, thereby justifying as a conclusion the denial of its antecedent. For example,

	If P is true then Q is true,
	Q is not true,
therefore,	*P is not true.*

These moods fall into line respectively with the first and second figures of the categorical syllogism. For we have seen that in Figure 1 we pass from ground to consequence, and in Figure 2 from denial of consequence to denial of ground.[380] It has, however, been shown in section 266 that to every syllogism in Figure 1 there corresponds not only a syllogism in Figure 2, but also a syllogism in Figure 3; and the question may therefore be asked what the mixed hypothetical syllogism yields that will fall into line with Figure 3. The answer is that, taking the place of Figure 3, we have a reasoning which consists in disproving a connection of ground and consequence by shewing that the supposed ground holds true but not the supposed consequence. This may be illustrated by writing down the two other reasonings corresponding to the ordinary *modus ponens*. We have

(1)	*If P, Q;*	(*a*)
	but *P*;	(*b*)
	∴ *Q*.	(*c*)
(2)	*If P, Q;*	(*a*)
	but *not Q*;	contradictory of (*c*)

---

[379] Ueberweg remarks that it would be more accurate to speak of the *modus ponens* as the *modus ponendo ponens*, and of the *modus tollens* as the *modus tollendo tollens* (*Logic*, p. 452).

[380] The mixed hypothetical syllogism may be reduced to the form of a pure hypothetical syllogism by writing the categorical *P is true* in the form *If anything is true, P is true*. If this is done, it will be seen from another point of view that the *modus ponens* may be regarded as belonging to Figure 1 and the *modus tollens* to Figure 2.

	∴ *not P*.	contradictory of (*b*)
(3)	*P*;	(*b*)
	but *not Q*;	contradictory of (*c*)
∴ *Q is not a necessary consequence of P*.		contradictory of (*a*)

If (1) is considered to be in Figure 1, then (2) is in Figure 2, and (3) in Figure 3. It is true that (3) departs too much from the ordinary type of the mixed hypothetical syllogism to justify us in calling it by that name. But it is a form of reasoning that may well receive definite recognition.

306. *Fallacies in Mixed Hypothetical Syllogisms.*—There are two principal fallacies that may be committed in arguing from a hypothetical major premiss:

(1) It is a fallacy to regard the affirmation of the consequent as justifying the affirmation of the antecedent. For example,

	If P is true then Q is true,
	Q is true,
therefore,	*P is true*.

(2) It is a fallacy to regard the denial of the antecedent as justifying the denial of the consequent. For example,

	If P is true then Q is true,
	P is not true,
therefore,	*Q is not true*.

These fallacies may be regarded as corresponding respectively to *undistributed middle* and *illicit major* in the case of categorical syllogisms.[381]

The results reached in this and the preceding section may be summed up in the following canon for the mixed hypothetical syllogism: Given a hypothetical premiss expressed affirmatively, then the affirmation of the antecedent justifies the affirmation of the consequent; and the denial of the consequent justifies the denial of the antecedent; but not conversely in either case.

307. *The Reduction of Mixed Hypothetical Syllogisms.*—Any case of the *modus tollens* may be reduced to the *modus ponens*, and *vice versâ*.

Thus,

	If P is true then Q is true,
	Q is not true,
therefore,	*P is not true*,

becomes, by contraposition of the hypothetical premiss,

---

[381] Given "If *P* and *only* if *P* then *Q*," then we may of course argue from *Q* to *P* or from *not-P* to *not-Q*; and no doubt in the case of ordinary hypotheticals it is often tacitly understood that the consequent is true *only* if the antecedent is true. This must, however, be expressly stated if the argument based upon it is to be formally valid.

	If Q is not true then P is not true,
	Q is not true,
therefore,	*P is not true;*

and this is the *modus ponens*.[382]

308. *Is the reasoning contained in the mixed hypothetical syllogism mediate or immediate?*[383]—Kant, Hamilton,[384] Bain, and others argue that inferences of the kind that we have just been considering are properly to be regarded not as mediate, but as immediate, inferences.

Now, taking the syllogism—

	If P is true then Q is true,
	but *P is true,*
therefore,	*Q is true,*

the conclusion is at any rate apparently obtained by a combination of two premisses, and the process is moreover one of elimination, namely, of the proposition *P is true*. Hence the burden of proof certainly lies with those who deny the claims of such an inference as this to be called mediate.

Bain (*Logic, Deduction*, p. 117) seems to argue that the so-called hypothetical syllogism is not really mediate inference, because it is "a pure instance of the law of consistency"; in other words, because "the conclusion is implied in what has already been stated." But is not this the case in all formal mediate inference? It cannot be maintained that the categorical syllogism is more than a pure instance of the law of consistency; or that the conclusion in such a syllogism is not implied in what has been already stated. But possibly Bain may mean that the conclusion is implied in the hypothetical premiss alone. Indeed he goes on to say, "'If the weather continues fine, we shall go into the country' is transformable into the equivalent form 'The weather continues fine, and so we shall go into the country.' Any person affirming the one, does not, in affirming the other, declare a new fact, but the same fact." Surely this is not intended to be understood literally. Take the following:—If war is declared, I must return home; If the sun moves round the earth, modern astronomy is a delusion. Are these respectively equivalent to the statements, War has been declared, and so I must return home; The sun moves round the earth, and so modern astronomy is a delusion? Besides, if the proposition *If P is true then Q is true* implies the truth of *P*, what becomes of the possible reasoning, "But *Q is not true*, therefore, *P is not true*"?

Further arguments that have been adduced on the same side are as follows:—

---

[382] A categorical syllogism in *Camestres* may similarly be reduced to *Celarent* without transposing the premisses. Thus, *All P is M, No S is M*, therefore, *No S is P*, becomes, by contraposition of the major and obversion of the minor premiss, *No not-M is P, All S is not-M*, therefore, *No S is P*.

[383] Similar arguments on both sides may be used in the case where a conditional premiss and a categorical premiss are combined.

[384] *Logic*, ii. p. 383. On page 378, however, Hamilton seems to take the other view.

Conditional and Hypothetical Syllogisms 247

(1) "There is no middle term in the so-called hypothetical syllogism."[385] The answer is that there is an element in the premises which does not appear in the conclusion, and that this corresponds to the middle term of the categorical syllogism.

(2) "In the so-called hypothetical syllogism, the minor and the conclusion indifferently change places."[386] This statement is erroneous. Taking the valid syllogism given at the commencement of this section and transposing the so-called minor and the conclusion, we have a fallacy.

(3) "The major in a so-called hypothetical syllogism consists of two propositions, the categorical major of two terms." This merely tells us that a hypothetical syllogism is not the same in form as a categorical syllogism, but seems to have no bearing on the question whether the so-called hypothetical syllogism is a case of mediate or of immediate inference.

Turning now to the other side of the question no satisfactory answers seem possible to the following arguments in favour of regarding the mixed hypothetical syllogism as a case of mediate inference. In any such syllogism, the two premises are quite distinct, neither can be inferred from the other, but both are necessary in order that the conclusion may be obtained. Again if we compare with it the inferences which are on all sides admitted to be immediate inferences from the hypothetical proposition, the difference between the two cases is apparent. From *If P is true then Q is true*, I can infer immediately *If Q is not true then P is not true*; but I require also to know that *Q is not true* in order to be able to infer that *P is not true*.

And whether the mixed hypothetical syllogism can or cannot be actually reduced to pure categorical form, it can at least be shown to be analogous to the ordinary categorical syllogism, which is admitted to be a case of mediate reasoning. Moreover there are distinct forms—the *modus ponens* and the *modus tollens*—which are analogous to distinct forms of the categorical syllogism; and fallacies in the mixed hypothetical syllogism correspond to certain fallacies in the categorical syllogism.

The argument in favour of regarding the *modus tollens*—*If P is true then Q is true, but Q is not true, therefore, P is not true*—as mediate inference is still more forcible; but of course the *modus ponens* and the *modus tollens* stand or fall together.[387]

Professor Croom Robertson (*Mind*, 1877, p. 264) has suggested an explanation as to the manner in which this controversy may have arisen. He distinguishes the *hypothetical* "if" from the *inferential* "if," the latter being equivalent to *since, seeing that, because*. No doubt by the aid of a certain accentuation the word "if" may be made to carry with it this force. Professor Robertson quotes a passage from *Clarissa Harlowe* in which the remark, "If you

---

[385] This is Kant's argument. A more plausible argument would be that there is no *minor* term. It will be found, however, that, in the reduction of the mixed hypothetical syllogism to the form of a pure hypothetical syllogism, something corresponding to a minor term has to be introduced. Compare note 2 on page 352.

[386] This argument is Hamilton's. He remarks that, in hypothetical syllogisms, "*the same proposition* is reciprocally medium or conclusion" (*Logic*, ii. p. 379). Dr Ray (*Deductive Logic*, Note C) holds that Hamilton is here wrongly interpreted; and that he meant no more than that with a hypothetical premiss *If A is B, C is D*, a relation between A and B may be either the other premiss (as in the *modus ponens*) or the conclusion (as in the *modus tollens*). Dr Ray is possibly right. But if so, Hamilton does not express himself clearly. For *A is B* (the premiss of the *modus ponens*) is certainly not *the same proposition* as *A is not B* (the conclusion of the *modus tollens*). It may be added that the argument in its new form is irrelevant. In the categorical syllogism we have something precisely analogous. For given a major premiss *All M is P*, a relation between *M* and *S* may be the minor premiss (in which case M will be the middle term), or it may be the conclusion (in which case *M* will be the major term). Compare the syllogisms: *All M is P, All S is M*, therefore, *All S is P*; *All M is P, No S is P*, therefore, *No S is M*.

[387] In section 316 it will be shewn further that the hypothetical syllogism and the disjunctive syllogism also stand or fall together.

have the value for my cousin that you say you have, you must needs think her worthy to be your wife," is explained by the speaker to mean, "*Since* you have &c." Using the word in this sense, the conclusion *C is D* certainly follows immediately from the bare statement *If A is B, C is is D*; or rather this statement itself affirms the conclusion. When, however, the word "if" carries with it this inferential implication, we cannot regard the proposition in which it occurs as merely hypothetical. We have rather a condensed mode of expression including two statements in one; it may indeed be argued that in the single statement thus interpreted we have a hypothetical syllogism expressed elliptically.[388]

EXERCISES

309. Shew how the *modus ponens* may be reduced to the *modus tollens*. [K.]

310. Test the following: "If all men were capable of perfection, some would have attained it; but none having done so, none are capable of it." [V.]

311. Examine technically the following argument:—

If you needed food, I would give you money; but as you do not care to work, you cannot need food; therefore, I will give you no money. [J.]

312. Shew what conclusion can be inferred from the premisses: He always stays in when it rains, but he often goes out when it is cold. [J.]

313. Construct conditional and hypothetical syllogisms in *Cesare, Bocardo, Dimaris* and reduce them to the first figure. [K.]

314. Name the mood and figure of the following, and shew that either one may be reduced to the other form:

(1)	If *R* is true, *Q* is true,
	If *P* is true, *Q* is not true,
therefore,	If *P* is true, *R* is not true;
(2)	If *Y* is true, *Z* is not true,
	If *Y* is true, *X* may be true,
therefore,	If *X* is true, *Z* need not be true.

[K.]

315. Let *X, Y, Z, P, Q, R* be six propositions.
Given (1) *If X is true, P is true*;
(2) *If Y is true, Q is true*;
(3) *If Z is true, R is true*;
(4) *Of X, Y, Z one at least is true*;
(5) *Of P, Q, R not more than one is true*;

prove syllogistically

(i) *If P is true, X is true*;
(ii) *If Q is true, Y is true*;

---

[388] Compare Mansel's *Aldrich*, p. 103.

(iii) *If R is true, Z is true;*
(iv) *Of P, Q, R, one at least is true;*
(v) *Of X, Y, Z, not more than one is true.* [K.]

Chapter 20

DISJUNCTIVE SYLLOGISMS

316. *The Disjunctive Syllogism.*—A *disjunctive* (or *alternative*) *syllogism* may be defined as a formal reasoning in which a categorical premiss is combined with a disjunctive (alternative) premiss so as to yield a conclusion which is either categorical or else disjunctive (alternative) with fewer alternants than are contained in the disjunctive premiss.[389]

For example,

	A is either B or C,
	A is not B,
therefore,	*A is C;*
	Either P or Q or R is true,
	P is not true,
therefore,	*Either Q or R is true.*

The categorical premiss in each of the above syllogisms *denies* one of the alternants of the alternative premiss, and the conclusion *affirms* the remaining alternant or alternants. Reasonings of this type are accordingly described as examples of the *modus tollendo ponens*.

It follows from the resolution of disjunctive propositions into conditionals or hypotheticals given in section 193 that (questions of modality being left on one side) the force of a disjunctive as a premiss in an argument is equivalent either to that of a conditional or to that of a hypothetical proposition.

---

[389] Archbishop Thomson's definition of the disjunctive syllogism—"An argument in which there is a disjunctive judgment" (*Laws of Thought*, p. 197)—must be regarded as too wide if, as is usually the case, an affirmative judgment with a disjunctive predicate is considered disjunctive. It would include such a syllogism as the following,—*B is either C or D, A is B,* therefore *A is either C or D.* The argument here in no way turns upon the alternation contained in the major premiss, and the reasoning may be regarded as an ordinary categorical syllogism in *Barbara*, the major term being complex.

Logicians have not, as a rule, given any distinctive recognition to arguments consisting of two disjunctive premisses and a disjunctive conclusion; and Mr Welton goes so far as to remark that "both premisses of a syllogism cannot be disjunctive since from two assertions as indefinite as disjunctive propositions necessarily are, nothing can be inferred" (*Logic*, p. 327). It is, however, clear that this is erroneous, if an argument consisting of two hypothetical premisses and a hypothetical conclusion is possible, and if a hypothetical can be reduced to the disjunctive form. As an example we may express in disjunctives the hypothetical syllogism given on page 348: *Either Q is not true or R is true, Either P is not true or Q is true,* therefore, *Either P is not true or R is true.* Here questions of modality are left on one side. They would not, however, in any case materially affect the argument.

Thus,

	Either A is B or C is D,
	A is not B,
therefore,	C is D;

may be resolved into the form

	If A is not B, C is D,
	A is not B,
therefore,	C is D;

or into the form

	If C is not D, A is B,
	A is not B,
therefore,	C is D.

A corollary from the above is that those who deny the character of mediate reasoning to the mixed hypothetical syllogism must also deny it to the disjunctive syllogism, or else must refuse to recognise the resolution of the disjunctive proposition into one or more hypotheticals.

In the above example it is not quite clear from the form of the major premiss whether we have a true hypothetical or a conditional. But in the following examples, which are added to illustrate the distinction, it is evident that the alternative propositions are equivalent to a true hypothetical and to a conditional respectively:

	Either all A's are B's or all A's are C's,
	This A is not B,
therefore,	All A's are C's;
	All A's are either B or C,
	This A is not B,
therefore,	This A is C.[390]

317. *The modus ponendo tollens.*—In addition to the *modus tollendo ponens*, some logicians recognise as valid a *modus ponendo tollens* in which the categorical premiss affirms one of the alternants of the disjunctive premiss, and the conclusion denies the other alternant or alternants. Thus,

---

[390] When the alternative major premiss is equivalent not to a true hypothetical but to a conditional (as in the second of the above examples), the syllogism may be reduced to pure categorical form (unless the categorical and conditional forms of proposition are in some way differentiated from one another). Thus,

	Every A which is not B is C,
	This A is an A which is not B,
therefore,	This A is C.

	A is either B or C,
	A is B,
therefore,	*A is not C*.

The argument here proceeds on the assumption that the alternants are mutually exclusive; but this, on the interpretation of alternative propositions adopted in section 191, is not necessarily the case. Hence the recognition or denial of the validity of the *modus ponendo tollens* in its ordinary form depends upon our interpretation of the alternative form of proposition.[391]

No doubt exclusiveness is often intended to be implied and is understood to be implied. For example, "He was either first or second in the race, He was second, therefore, He was not first." This reasoning would ordinarily be accepted as valid. But its validity really depends not on the expressed major premiss, but on the understood premiss, "No one can be both first and second in a race." The following reasoning is in fact equally valid with the one stated above, "He was second in the race, therefore, He was not first." The alternative premiss is, therefore, quite immaterial to the reasoning; we could do just as well without it, for the really vital premiss, "No one can be both first and second in a race," is true, and would be accepted as such, quite irrespective of the truth of the alternative proposition, "He was either first or second." In other cases the mutual exclusiveness of the alternants may be tacitly understood, although not obvious *à priori* as in the above example. But in no case can a special implication of this kind be recognised when we are dealing with purely symbolic forms. If we hold that the *modus ponendo tollens* as above stated is *formally* valid, we must be prepared to interpret the alternants as *in every case* mutually exclusive.

If, however, we take a major premiss which is disjunctive, not in the ordinary sense (in which disjunctive is equivalent to alternative), but in the more accurate sense explained in section 189, then we may have a formally valid reasoning which has every right to be described as a *modus ponendo tollens*. Thus,

	P and Q are not both true;
	but *P is true*;
therefore,	*Q is not true*.[392]

The following table of the *ponendo ponens*, &c., in their valid and invalid forms may be useful:

	Valid	*Invalid*
Ponendo Ponens	If *P* then *Q*, but *P*, ∴ *Q*.	If *P* then *Q*, but *Q*, ∴ *P*.
Tollendo Tollens	If *Q* then *P*,	If *Q* then *P*,

---

[391] It will be observed that, interpreting the alternants as not necessarily exclusive of one another, the *modus ponendo tollens* in the above form is equivalent to one of the fallacies in the mixed hypothetical syllogism mentioned in section 306.

[392] This is in the stricter sense a *disjunctive* syllogism, the *modus tollendo ponens* being an *alternative* syllogism. The reader must, however, be careful to remember that the latter is what is ordinarily meant by the disjunctive syllogism in logical text-books.

	but not P, ∴ not Q.	but not Q, ∴ not P.
Tollendo Ponens	Either P or Q, but not P, ∴ Q.	Not both P and Q, but not Q, ∴ P.
Ponendo Tollens	Not both P and Q, but P, ∴ not Q.	Either P or Q, but Q, ∴ not P.

The above valid forms are mutually reducible to one another and the same is true of the invalid forms.

318. *The Dilemma.*—The proper place of the dilemma amongst hypothetical and disjunctive arguments is difficult to determine, inasmuch as conflicting definitions are given by different logicians. The following definition may be taken as perhaps on the whole the most satisfactory:—A *dilemma* is a formal argument containing a premiss in which two or more hypotheticals are conjunctively affirmed, and a second premiss in which the antecedents of these hypotheticals are alternatively affirmed or their consequents alternatively denied.[393] These premisses are usually called the major and the minor respectively.[394]

Dilemmas are called *constructive* or *destructive* according as the minor premiss alternatively affirms the antecedents, or denies the consequents, of the major.[395]

Since it is a distinguishing characteristic of the dilemma that the minor should be alternative, it follows that the hypotheticals into which the major premiss of a *constructive dilemma* may be resolved must contain at least two distinct antecedents. They may, however, have a common consequent. The conclusion of the dilemma will then categorically affirm this consequent, and will correspond with it in form.[396] The dilemma itself is in this case called *simple*. If, on the other hand, the major premiss contains more than one consequent, the conclusion will necessarily be alternative, and the dilemma is called *complex*.

Similarly, in a *destructive dilemma* the hypotheticals into which the major can be resolved must have more than one consequent, but they may or may not have a common antecedent; and the dilemma will be *simple* or *complex* accordingly.

We have then four forms of dilemma as follows:

(i) The *simple constructive dilemma.*
  If A is B, E is F; and if C is D, E is F;

---

[393] In the strict use of the term, a *dilemma* implies only two alternants in the alternative premiss; if there are more than two alternants we have a *trilemma*, or a *tetralemma*, or a *polylemma*, as the case may be.

[394] This application of the terms *major* and *minor* is somewhat arbitrary. The *dilemmatic* force of the argument is indeed made more apparent by stating the alternative premiss (i.e., the so-called *minor* premiss) first.

[395] A further form of argument may be distinguished in which the alternation contained in the so-called minor premiss is affirmed only hypothetically, and in which, therefore, the conclusion also is hypothetical. For example,

	If A is B, E is F; and if C is D, E is F;
	If X is Y, either A is B or C is D;
therefore,	*If X is Y, E is F.*

This might be called the *hypothetical dilemma*. It admits of varieties corresponding to the varieties of the ordinary dilemma; but no detailed treatment of it seems called for.

[396] It will usually be a simple categorical; but see the following note.

but *Either A is B or C is D*;
therefore, *E is F*.
(ii) The *complex constructive dilemma*.
If A is B, E is F; and if C is D, G is H;
but *Either A is B or C is D*;
therefore, *Either E is F or G is H*.[397]
(iii) The *simple destructive dilemma*.
If A is B, C is D; and if A is B, E is F;
but *Either C is not D or E is not F*;
therefore, *A is not B*.
(iv) The *complex destructive dilemma*.
If A is B, E is F; and if C is D, G is H;
but *Either E is not F or G is not H*;
therefore, *Either A is not B or C is not D*.[398]

In the case of dilemmas, as in the case of mixed hypothetical syllogisms, the constructive form may be reduced to the destructive form, and *vice versâ*. All that has to be done is to contraposit the hypotheticals which constitute the major premiss. One example will suffice. Taking the simple constructive dilemma given above, and contrapositing the major, we have,—

If E is not F, A is not B; and if E is not F, C is not D;
but *Either A is B or C is D*;
therefore, *E is F*;

and this is a dilemma in the simple destructive form. The definition of the dilemma given above is practically identical with that given by Fowler (*Deductive Logic*, p. 116). Mansel (*Aldrich*, p. 108) defines the dilemma as "a syllogism having a conditional (hypothetical) major premiss *with more than one antecedent*, and a disjunctive minor." Equivalent definitions are given by Whately and Jevons. According to this view, while the constructive dilemma may be either simple or complex, the destructive dilemma must always be complex, since in the corresponding simple form (as in the example given on page 364) there is *only one antecedent* in the major. This exclusion seems arbitrary and is a ground for rejecting the definition in question. Whately, indeed, regards the name *dilemma* as necessarily implying *two antecedents*; but it should rather be regarded as implying *two alternatives*, either of which

---

[397] The following is a simple, not a complex, constructive dilemma:
If A is B, E is F or G is H; and if C is D, E is F or G is H;
but *Either A is B or C is D*;
therefore, *Either E is F or G is H*.
The hypotheticals which here constitute the major premiss have a common consequent; but since this is itself alternative, the conclusion appears in the alternative form. This case is analogous to the following,—*All M is P or Q, All S is M, therefore, All S is P or Q*,—where the conclusion of an intrinsically categorical syllogism also appears in the alternative form. Compare the note on page 359.
[398] The following is a simple, not a complex, destructive dilemma:
If both P and Q are true then X is true, and under the same hypothesis Y is true;
but *Either X or Y is not true*;
therefore, *Either P or Q is not true*.

being selected a conclusion follows that is unacceptable. Whately goes on to assert that the excluded form is merely a destructive hypothetical syllogism, similar to the following,

	If *A* is *B*, *C* is *D*;
	C is not *D*;
therefore,	*A* is not *B*.

But the two really differ precisely as the simple constructive dilemma given on page 364 differs from the constructive hypothetical syllogism,—

	If *A* is *B*, *E* is *F*;
	A is *B*;
therefore,	*E* is *F*.

Besides, it is clear that the form under discussion is not merely a destructive hypothetical syllogism such as has been already discussed, since the premiss which is combined with the hypothetical premiss is not categorical but alternative. The following definition is sometimes given:—"The dilemma (or trilemma or polylemma) is an argument in which a choice is allowed between two (or three or more) alternatives, but it is shewn that whichever alternative is taken the same conclusion follows." This definition, which no doubt gives point to the expression "the horns of a dilemma," includes the simple constructive dilemma and the simple destructive dilemma; but it does not allow that either of the complex dilemmas is properly so-called, since in each case we are left with the same number of alternants in the conclusion as are contained in the alternative premiss. On the other hand, it embraces forms that are excluded by both the preceding definitions; for example, the following reasoning—which should rather be classed simply as a destructive hypothetico-categorical syllogism—

	If *A* is, either *B* or *C* is;
	but *Neither B nor C is*;
therefore,	*A* is not.[399]

Jevons (*Elements of Logic*, p. 168) remarks that "dilemmatic arguments are more often fallacious than not, because it is seldom possible to find instances where two alternatives exhaust all the possible cases, unless indeed one of them be the simple negative of the other." In other words, many dilemmatic arguments will be found to contain a premiss involving a fallacy of incomplete alternation. It should, however, be observed that in strictness an argument is not itself to be called fallacious because it contains a false premiss.

EXERCISES

319. What can be inferred from the premisses, *Either A is B or C is D, Either C is not D or E is F*? Exhibit the reasoning (*a*) in the form of a hypothetical syllogism, (*b*) in the form of a dilemma. [K.]

---

[399] Compare Ueberweg, *Logic*, § 123.

320. Reduce the following argument, consisting of three disjunctive propositions, to the form of an ordinary categorical syllogism: *Everything is either M or P, Everything is either not S or not M,* therefore, *Everything is either P or not S.* [K.]

321. Discuss the logical conclusiveness of fatalistic reasoning like this:—If I am fated to be drowned now, there is no use in my struggling; if not, there is no need of it. But either I am fated to be drowned now or I am not; so that it is either useless or needless for me to struggle against it. [B.]

Chapter 21

IRREGULAR AND COMPOUND SYLLOGISMS

322. *The Enthymeme.*—By the enthymeme, Aristotle meant what has been called the "rhetorical syllogism" as opposed to the apodeictic, demonstrative, theoretical syllogism. The following is from Mansel's notes to *Aldrich* (pp. 209 to 211): "The enthymeme is defined by Aristotle, συλλογισμὸς ἐξ εἰκότων ἤ σημείων. The εἰκὸς and σημεῖων themselves are propositions; the former stating a *general probability*, the latter a *fact*, which is known to be an indication, more or less certain, of the truth of some further statement, whether of a single fact or of a general belief. The former is a proposition nearly, though not quite, *universal*; as 'Most men who envy hate': the latter is a *singular* proposition, which however is not regarded as a sign, except relatively to some other proposition, which it is supposed may be inferred from it. The εἰκός, when employed in an enthymeme, will form the *major premiss* of a syllogism such as the following:

	Most men who envy hate,
	This man envies,
therefore,	This man (probably) hates.

"The reasoning is logically faulty; for, the major premiss not being absolutely universal, the middle term is not distributed.

"The σημεῖων will form one premiss of a syllogism which may be in any of the three figures, as in the following examples:

Figure 1.	All ambitious men are liberal,
	Pittacus is ambitious,
therefore,	Pittacus is liberal.
Figure 2.	All ambitions men are liberal,
	Pittacus is liberal,
therefore,	Pittacus is ambitious.
Figure 3.	Pittacus is liberal,
	Pittacus is ambitious,
therefore,	All ambitious men are liberal.

"The syllogism in the first figure alone is logically valid. In the second, there is an undistributed middle term; in the third, an illicit process of the minor."[400]

An *enthymeme* is now usually defined as a syllogism incompletely stated, one of the premisses or the conclusion being understood but not expressed.[401] The arguments of everyday life are to a large extent enthymematic in this sense; and the same may be said of fallacious arguments, which are seldom completely stated, or their want of cogency would be more quickly recognised.

An enthymeme is said to be of the *first order* when the major premiss is suppressed; of the *second order* when the minor premiss is suppressed; and of the *third order* when the conclusion is suppressed.

Thus, "Balbus is avaricious, and therefore, he is unhappy," is an enthymeme of the first order; "All avaricious persons are unhappy, and therefore, Balbus is unhappy," is an enthymeme of the second order; "All avaricious persons are unhappy, and Balbus is avaricious," is an enthymeme of the third order.

323. *The Polysyllogism and the Epicheirema*.—A chain of syllogisms, that is, a series of syllogisms so linked together that the conclusion of one becomes a premiss of another, is called a *polysyllogism*. In a polysyllogism, any individual syllogism the conclusion of which becomes the premiss of a succeeding one is called a *prosyllogism*, any individual syllogism one of the premisses of which is the conclusion of a preceding syllogism is called an *episyllogism*. Thus,—

	All C is B,		
	All B is C,	}	prosyllogism,
therefore,	All B is D,		
but	All A is B,	}	episyllogism.
therefore,	All A is D,		

The same syllogism may of course be both an episyllogism and a prosyllogism, as would be the case with the above episyllogism if the chain were continued further.

A chain of reasoning[402] is said to be *progressive* (or *synthetic* or *episyllogistic*) when the progress is from prosyllogism to episyllogism. Here the premisses are first given, and we pass on by successive steps of inference to the ultimate conclusion which they yield. A chain of reasoning is, on the other hand, said to be *regressive* (or *analytic* or *prosyllogistic*) when the progress is from episyllogism to prosyllogism. Here the ultimate conclusion is first given and we pass back by successive steps of proof to the premisses on which it may be based.[403]

---

[400] On this subject the student may be referred to the remainder of the note from which the above extract is taken, and to Hamilton, *Discussions*, pp. 152 to 156. Compare also Karslake, *Aids to the Study of Logic*, Book II.

[401] This account of the enthymeme appears to have been originally based on the erroneous idea that the name signified the retention of one premiss *in the mind*, ἐν θυμῷ. Thus, in the *Port Royal Logic*, an enthymeme is described as "a syllogism perfect in the mind, but imperfect in the expression, since some one of the propositions is suppressed as too clear and too well known, and as being easily supplied by the mind of those to whom we speak" (p. 229). As regards the true origin of the name *enthymeme*, see Mansel's *Aldrich*, p. 218.

[402] The distinction which follows is ordinarily applied to chains of reasoning only; but the reader will observe that it admits of application to the case of the simple syllogism also.

[403] On the distinction between progressive and regressive arguments, see Ueberweg, *Logic*, § 124.

An *epicheirema* is a polysyllogism with one or more prosyllogisms briefly indicated only. That is, one or more of the syllogisms of which the polysyllogism is composed are enthymematic. The following is an example:

	All B is D, because it is C,
	All A is B,
therefore,	All A is D.[404]

324. *The Sorites.*—A *sorites* is a polysyllogism in which all the conclusions are omitted except the final one, the premisses being given in such an order that any two successive propositions contain a common term. Two forms of sorites are usually recognised, namely, the so-called *Aristotelian sorites* and the *Goclenian sorites*. In the former, the premiss stated first contains the subject of the conclusion, while the term common to any two successive premisses occurs first as predicate and then as subject; in the latter, the premiss stated first contains the predicate of the conclusion, while the term common to any two successive premisses occurs first as subject and then as predicate. The following are examples:

Aristotelian Sorites,—	All A is B,
	All B is C,
	All C is D,
	All D is E,
therefore,	All A is E.
Goclenian Sorites,—	All D is E,
	All C is D,
	All B is C,
	All A is B,
therefore,	All A is E.

It will be found that, in the case of the *Aristotelian* sorites, if the argument is drawn out in full, the first premiss and the suppressed conclusions all appear as *minor* premisses in successive syllogisms. Thus, the Aristotelian sorites given above may be analysed into the three following syllogisms,—

---

[404] A distinction has been drawn between *single* and *double* epicheiremas according as reasons are enthymematically given in support of *one* or *both* of the premisses of the ultimate syllogism. The example given in the text is a single epicheirema; the following is an example of a double epicheirema:

	All P is Y, because it is X;
	All S is P, because all M is P;
therefore,	All S is Y.

The epicheirema is sometimes defined as if it were essentially a *regressive chain* of reasoning. But this is hardly correct, if, as is usually the case, examples such as the above are given; for it is clear that in these examples the argument is only partly regressive.

(1)		*All B is C,*
		All A is B,
	therefore,	*All A is C;*
(2)		*All C is D,*
		All A is C,
	therefore,	*All A is D;*
(3)		*All D is E,*
		All A is D,
	therefore,	*All A is E.*

Here the premiss originally stated first is the minor premiss of (1), the conclusion of (1) is the minor premiss of (2), that of (2) the minor premiss of (3); and so it would go on if the number of propositions constituting the sorites were increased.

In the *Goclenian* sorites, the premisses are the same, but their order is reversed, and the result of this is that the premiss originally stated first and the suppressed conclusions become *major* premisses in successive syllogisms. Thus, the Goclenian sorites given above may be analysed into the three following syllogisms,—

(1)		*All D is E,*
		All C is D,
	therefore,	*All C is E;*
(2)		*All C is E,*
		All B is C,
	therefore,	*All B is E;*
(3)		*All B is E,*
		All A is B,
	therefore,	*All A is E.*

Here the premiss originally stated first is the major premiss of (1), the conclusion of (1) is the major premiss of (2); and so on.

The so-called Aristotelian sorites[405] is that to which the greater prominence is usually given; but it will be observed that the order of premisses in the Goclenian form is that which corresponds to the customary order of premisses in a simple syllogism.[406]

---

[405] This form of sorites ought not properly to be called *Aristotelian*; but it is generally so described in logical textbooks. The name *sorites* is not to be found in any logical treatise of Aristotle, though in one place he refers vaguely to the form of reasoning which the name is now employed to express. The distinct exposition of this form of reasoning is attributed to the Stoics, and it is designated *sorites* by Cicero; but it was not till much later that the name came into general use amongst logicians in this sense. The form of sorites called the Goclenian was first given by Professor Rudolf Goclenius of Marburg (1547 to 1628) in his *Isagoge in Organum Aristotelis*, 1598. Compare Hamilton, *Logic*, I. p. 375; and Ueberweg, *Logic*, § 125. It may be added that the term *sorites* (which is derived from σωρὸς, a heap) was used by ancient writers in a different sense, namely, to designate a particular sophism, based on the difficulty which is sometimes found in assigning an exact limit to a notion. "It was asked,—was a man bald who had so many thousand hairs; you answer, No: the antagonist goes on diminishing and diminishing the number, till either you admit that he who was not bald with a certain number of hairs, becomes bald when that complement is diminished by a single hair; or you go on denying him to be bald, until his head be hypothetically denuded." A similar puzzle is involved in the question,—On what day does a lamb become a sheep? Sorites in this sense is also called *sophisma polyzeteseos* or *fallacy of continuous questioning*. See Hamilton, *Logic*, i. p. 464.

A sorites may of course consist of conditional or hypothetical propositions; and it is not at all unusual to find propositions of these kinds combined in this manner. Theoretically a sorites might also consist of alternative propositions; but it is not likely that this combination would ever occur naturally.

325. *The Special Rules of the Sorites.*—The following special rules may be given for the ordinary Aristotelian sorites, as defined in the preceding section:—

(1) Only one premiss can be negative; and if one is negative, it must be the last.
(2) Only one premiss can be particular; and if one is particular, it must be the first.

Any Aristotelian sorites may be represented in skeleton form, the quantity and quality of the premisses being left undetermined, as follows:—

S	M_1
M_1,	M_2
M_2,	M_3
………	………
………	………
M_{n-2},	M_{n-1}
M_{n-1},	M_n
M_n,	P
—	—
S	P

(1) There cannot be more than one negative premiss, for if there were—since a negative premiss in any syllogism necessitates a negative conclusion—we should in analysing the sorites somewhere come upon a syllogism containing two negative premisses.

Again, if one premiss is negative, the final conclusion must be negative. Hence P must be distributed in the final conclusion. Therefore, it must be distributed in its premiss, i.e., the last premiss, which must accordingly be negative. If any premiss then is negative, this is the one.

(2) Since it has been shown that all the premisses, except the last, must be affirmative, it is clear that if any, except the first, were particular, we should somewhere commit the fallacy of undistributed middle.

The special rules of the Goclenian sorites, as defined in the preceding section, may be obtained by transposing "first" and "last" in the above.

326. *The possibility of a Sorites in a Figure other than the First.*—It will have been noticed that in our analysis both of the Aristotelian and of the Goclenian sorites all the resulting syllogisms are in Figure 1. Such sorites may accordingly be said to be themselves in Figure 1. The question arises whether a sorites is possible in any other figure.

The usual answer to this question is that the first or the last syllogism of a sorites may be in Figure 2 or 3 (e.g., in Figure 2 we may have *A is B, B is C, C is D, D is E, F is not E*, therefore, *A is not F*) but that it is impossible that all the steps should be in either of these

---

[406] The mistake is sometimes made of speaking of the Goclenian sorites as a regressive form of argument. It is clear, however, that in both forms of sorites we pass continuously from premisses to conclusions, not from conclusions to premisses.

figures.[407] "Every one," says Mill, "who understands the laws of the second and third figures (or even the general laws of the syllogism) can see that no more than one step in either of them is admissible in a sorites, and that it must either be the first or the last" (*Examination of Hamilton*, pp. 514, 5).

This treatment of the question seems, however, open to refutation by the simple method of constructing examples. Take, for instance, the following sorites:—

(i)		*Some S is not M_1,*
		All M_2 is M_1,
		All M_3 is M_2,
		All M_4 is M_3,
		All P is M_4,
	therefore,	*Some S is not P.*
(ii)		*Some M_4 is not P,*
		All M_4 is M_3,
		All M_3 is M_2,
		All M_2 is M_1,
		All M_1 is S,
	therefore,	*Some S is not P.*

Analysing the first of the above, and inserting the suppressed conclusions in square brackets, we have—

	Some S is not M_1,
	All M_2 is M_1,
[therefore,	*Some S is not M_2,]*
	All M_3 is M_2,
[therefore,	*Some S is not M_3,]*
	All M_4 is M_3,

---

[407] Sir William Hamilton indeed professes to give sorites in the second and third figures, which have, he says, been overlooked by other logicians (*Logic*, II. p. 403). It appears, however, that by a sorites in the second figure he means such a reasoning as the following,—*No B is A, No C is A, No D is A, No E is A, All F is A*, therefore, *No B, or C, or D, or E, is F*; and by a sorites in the third figure such as the following,—*A is B, A is C, A is D, A is E, A is F*, therefore, *Some B, and C, and D, and E, are F*. He does not himself give these examples; but that they are of the kind which he intends may be deduced from his not very lucid statement, "In second and third figures, there being no subordination of terms, the only sorites competent is that by repetition of the same middle. In first figure, there is a new middle term for every new progress of the sorites; in second and third, only one middle term for any number of extremes. In first figure, a syllogism only between every second term of the sorites, the intermediate term constituting the middle term. In the others, every two propositions of the common middle term form a syllogism." But it is clear that in the accepted sense of the term these are not sorites at all. In each case the conclusion is a mere summation of the conclusions of a number of syllogisms having a common premiss; in neither case is there any chain argument. Hamilton's own definition of the sorites, involved as it is, might have saved him from this error. He gives for his definition, "When, on the common principle of all reasoning,—that the part of a part is a part of the whole,—we do not stop at the second gradation, or at the part of the highest part, and conclude that part of the whole, but proceed to some indefinitely remoter part, as *D, E, F, G, H*, &c., which, on the general principle, we connect in the conclusion with its remotest whole,—this complex reasoning is called a *Chain-Syllogism* or *Sorites*" (*Logic*, I. p. 366). In connection with Hamilton's treatment of this question, Mill very justly remarks, "If Sir W. Hamilton had found in any other writer such a misuse of logical language as he is here guilty of, he would have roundly accused him of total ignorance of logical writers" (*Examination of Hamilton*, p. 515).

[therefore,	Some S is not M$_4$,]
	All P is M$_4$,
therefore,	Some S is not P.

This is the only resolution of the sorites possible unless the order of the premisses is transposed, and it will be seen that all the resulting syllogisms are in Figure 2 and in the mood *Baroco*. The sorites may accordingly be said to be in the same mood and figure. It is analogous to the Aristotelian sorites, the subject of the conclusion appearing in the premiss stated first, and the suppressed premisses being all *minors* in their respective syllogisms.

The corresponding analysis of (ii) yields the following:—

	Some M$_4$ is not P,
	All M$_4$ is M$_3$,
[therefore,	Some M$_3$ is not P,]
	All M$_3$ is M$_2$,
[therefore,	Some M$_2$ is not P,]
	All M$_2$ is M$_1$,
[therefore,	Some M$_1$ is not P,]
	All M$_1$ is S,
therefore,	Some S is not P.

These syllogisms are all in Figure 3 and in the mood *Bocardo*; and the sorites itself may be said to be in the same mood and figure. It is analogous to the Goclenian sorites, the predicate of the conclusion appearing in the premiss stated first, and the suppressed premisses being *majors* in their respective syllogisms.

It will be observed that the rules given in the preceding section have not been satisfied in either of the above sorites, the reason being that the rules in question correspond to the special rules of Figure 1, and do not apply unless the sorites is in that figure. For such sorites as are possible in Figures 2, 3, and 4, other rules might be framed corresponding to the special rules of these figures in the case of the simple syllogism.

It is not maintained that sorites in other figures than the first are likely to be met with in common use, but their construction is of some theoretical interest.[408]

---

[408] The examples given in the text have been purposely chosen so as to admit of only one analysis, which was not the case with the examples given in the first two editions of this work. The original examples were, however, perfectly valid, and further light may be thrown on the general question by a brief reply to certain criticisms passed upon those examples. The following was given for Figure 2 (the suppressed conclusions being inserted in square brackets), and it was said to be analogous to the Aristotelian sorites:—

	All A is B,
	No C is B,
[therefore,	No A is C],
	All D is C,
[therefore,	No A is D],
	All E is D,
therefore,	No A is E.

It has, to begin with, been objected that the above is Goclenian, and not Aristotelian, in form, "the subject of each premiss after the first being the predicate of the succeeding one." This overlooks the more fundamental characteristic of the Aristotelian sorites, that the first premiss and the suppressed conclusions are all *minors* in

327. *Ultra-total Distribution of the Middle Term.*—The ordinary syllogistic rule relating to the distribution of the middle term does not contemplate the recognition of any signs of quantity other than *all* and *some*; and if other signs are recognised, the rule must be modified. For example, the admission of the sign *most* yields the following valid reasoning, although the middle term is not distributed in either of the premisses:—

	Most M is P,
	Most M is S,
therefore,	Some S is P.

Interpreting *most* in the sense of *more than half*, it clearly follows from the above premisses that there must be some *M* which is both *S* and *P*. But we cannot say that in either premiss the term *M* is distributed.

In order to meet cases of this kind, Hamilton (*Logic*, II. p. 362) gives the following modification of the rule relating to the distribution of the middle term: "The quantifications of the middle term, whether as subject or predicate, taken together, must exceed the quantity of that term taken in its whole extent"; in other words, we must have an *ultra-total distribution* of the middle term in the two premisses taken together.

De Morgan (*Formal Logic*, p. 127) writes as follows: "It is said that in every syllogism the middle term must be universal in one of the premisses, in order that we may be sure that the affirmation or denial in the other premiss may be made of some or all of the things about which affirmation or denial has been made in the first. This law, as we shall see, is only a particular case of the truth: it is enough that the two premisses together affirm or deny of more than all the instances of the middle term. If there be a hundred boxes, into which a hundred *and one* articles of two different kinds are to be put, not more than one of each kind into any one box, some one box, if not more, will have two articles, one of each kind, put into it. The common doctrine has it, that an article of one particular kind must be put into every box, and then some one or more of another kind into one or more of the boxes, before it may be affirmed that one or more of different kinds are found together." De Morgan himself works the question out in detail in his treatment of *the numerically definite syllogism* (*Formal Logic*, pp. 141 to 170). The following may be taken as an example of numerically definite reasoning:—If 70 per cent of *M* are *P*, and 60 per cent are *S*, then at least 30 per cent. are both *S* and *P*.[409] The argument may be put as follows: On the average, of 100 *M*'s 70 are *P* and 60

---

their respective syllogisms. It has further been objected that the following analysis might serve in lieu of the one given above:—*AaB, CeB,* [∴ *CeA,*] *DaC,* [∴ *DeA*], *EaD,* ∴ *AeE*. No doubt this analysis is a possible one, but the objection to it is its heterogeneous character. The first premiss and the first suppressed conclusion are majors, while the last suppressed conclusion is a minor. Again, the first syllogism is in Figure 2, the second in Figure 1, and the third in Figure 4. It must be granted that what has been above called a heterogeneous analysis is in some cases the only one available, but it is better to adopt something more homogeneous where possible. If the first premiss of a sorites contains the subject, and the last the predicate, of the conclusion, then the last premiss is necessarily the major of the final syllogism; and hence the rule may be laid down that we can work out such a sorites homogeneously only by treating the first premiss and all the suppressed conclusions as minors, and all the remaining premisses as majors, in their respective syllogisms. A corresponding rule may be laid down if the first premiss contains the predicate, and the last the subject, of the conclusion.

It will be found that a sorites in Figure 4 cannot have more than a limited number of premisses. This point is raised in section 335.

[409] Using other letters, this is the example given by Mill, *Logic*, ii. 2, § 1, *note*, and quoted by Herbert Spencer, *Principles of Psychology*, II. p. 88. The more general problem of which the above is a special instance is as follows: Given that there are *n* *M*'s in existence, and that *a* *M*'s are *S* while *b* *M*'s are *P*, to determine what is

Irregular and Compound Syllogisms 267

are *S*; suppose that the 30 *M*'s which are not *P* are *S*, still 30 *S*'s are to be found in the remaining 70 *M*'s which are *P*'s; and this is the desired conclusion. Problems of this kind constitute a borderland between formal logic and algebra. Some further examples will be given in chapter 8 (section 345).

328. *The Quantification of the Predicate and the Syllogism.*—It will be convenient to consider briefly in this chapter the application of the doctrine of the quantification of the predicate to the syllogism; the result is the reverse of simplification.[410] The most important points that arise may be brought out by considering the validity of the following syllogisms: in Figure 1, UUU, IUη, AYI; in Figure 2, ηUO, AUA; in Figure 3, YAI. In the next section we will proceed more systematically, U and ω being left out of account.

(1) UUU in Figure 1 is valid:—

	All M is all P,
	All S is all M,
therefore,	*All S is all P*.

It will be observed that whenever one of the premisses is U, the conclusion may be obtained by substituting *S* or *P* (as the case may be) for *M* in the other premiss.

Without the use of quantified predicates, the above reasoning may be expressed by means of the two following syllogisms:

	All M is P,			*All M is S*,
	All S is M,			*All P is M*,
therefore,	*All S is P*;		therefore,	*All P is S*.

(2) IUη in Figure 1 is invalid, if *some* is used in its ordinary logical sense. The premisses are *Some M is some P* and *All S is all M*. We may, therefore, obtain the legitimate conclusion by substituting *S* for *M* in the major premiss. This yields *Some S is some P*.

If, however, *some* is here used in the sense of *some only*, *No S is some P* follows from *Some S is some P*, and the original syllogism is valid, although a negative conclusion is obtained from two affirmative premisses.

This syllogism is given as valid by Thomson (*Laws of Thought*, § 103); but apparently only through a misprint for IEη. In his scheme of valid syllogisms (thirty-six in each figure),

---

the least number of *S*'s that are also *P*'s. It is clear that we have no conclusion at all unless $a + b > n$, i.e., unless there is ultra-total distribution of the middle term. If this condition is satisfied, then supposing the $(n - b)$ *M*'s which are *not-P* are all of them found amongst the *MS*'s, there will still be some *MS*'s left which are *P*'s, namely, $a - (n - b)$. Hence the least number of *S*'s that are also *P*'s must be $a + b - n$.

[410] In connection with his doctrine of the quantification of the predicate, Hamilton distinguishes between the *figured syllogism* and the *unfigured syllogism*. In the *figured syllogism*, the distinction between subject and predicate is retained, as in the text. By a rigid quantification of the predicate, however, the distinction between subject and predicate may be dispensed with; and such being the case there is no ground left for distinction of figure (which depends upon the position of the middle term as subject or predicate in the premisses). This gives what Hamilton calls the *unfigured syllogism*. For example:—Any bashfulness and any praiseworthy are not equivalent, All modesty and some praiseworthy are equivalent, therefore, Any bashfulness and any modesty are not equivalent; All whales and some mammals are equal, All whales and some water animals are equal, therefore, Some mammals and some water animals are equal. A distinct canon for the unfigured syllogism is given by Hamilton as follows:—"In as far as two notions either both agree, or one agreeing the other does not, with a common third notion; in so far these notions do or do not agree with each other."

Thomson seems consistently to interpret *some* in its ordinary logical sense. Using the word in the sense of *some only*, several other syllogisms would be valid that he does not give as such.[411]

(3) AYI in Figure 1, *some* being used in its ordinary logical sense, is equivalent to AAI in Figure 3 in the ordinary syllogistic scheme, and is valid. But it is invalid if *some* is used in the sense of *some only*, for the conclusion now implies that *S* and *P* are partially excluded from each other as well as partially coincident, whereas this is not implied by the premisses. With this use of *some*, the correct conclusion can be expressed only by stating an alternative between *SuP*, *SaP*, *SyP*, and *SiP*. This case may serve to illustrate the complexities in which we should be involved if we were to attempt to use *some* consistently in the sense of *some only*.[412]

(4) ηUO in Figure 2 is valid:—

	No P is some M,
	All S is all M,
therefore,	*Some S is not any P.*

Without the use of quantified predicates, we can obtain the same conclusion in *Bocardo*, thus,—

	Some M is not P,
	All M is S,
therefore,	*Some S is not P.*

It will be observed that both (3) and (4) are strengthened syllogisms.

(5) AUA in Figure 2 runs as follows,—

	All P is some M,
	All S is all M,
therefore,	*All S is some P.*

Here we have neither undistributed middle nor illicit process of major or minor, nor is any rule of quality broken, and yet the syllogism is invalid.[413] Applying the rule given above that "whenever one of the premisses is U, the conclusion may be obtained by substituting *S* or *P* (as the case may be) for *M* in the other premiss," we find that the valid conclusion is *Some S is all P*. More generally, it follows from this rule of substitution that *if one premiss is* U *while in the other premiss the middle term is undistributed, then the term combined with the middle term in the* U *premiss must be undistributed in the conclusion*. This appears to be the one additional syllogistic rule required if we recognise U propositions in syllogistic reasonings.

---

[411] Compare section 144.
[412] Compare Monck, *Logic*, p. 154.
[413] We should have a corresponding case if we were to infer *No S is P* from the premisses given in the preceding example.

All danger of fallacy is avoided by breaking up the U proposition into two A propositions. In the case before us we have,—*All P is M, All M is S*; *All P is M, All S is M*. From the first of these pairs of premises we get the conclusion *All P is S*; in the second pair the middle term is undistributed, and therefore no conclusion is yielded at all.

(6) YAI in Figure 3 is valid:—

	Some M is all P,
	All M is some S,
therefore,	*Some S is some P.*

The conclusion is however weakened, since from the given premises we might infer *Some S is all P*.[414] It will be observed that when we quantify the predicate, the conclusion of a syllogism may be weakened in respect of its predicate as well as in respect of its subject. In the ordinary doctrine of the syllogism this is for obvious reasons not possible.

Without quantification of the predicate the above reasoning may be expressed in *Bramantip*, thus,

	All P is M,
	All M is S,
therefore,	*Some S is P.*

We could get the full conclusion, *All P is S*, in *Barbara*.

329. *Table of valid moods resulting from the recognition of* Y *and* η *in addition to* A, E, I, O.—If we adopt the sixfold schedule of propositions obtained by adding *Only S is P* (Y) and *Not only S is P* (η) to the ordinary fourfold schedule, as in section 150, every proposition is simply convertible, and, therefore, a valid mood in any figure is reducible to any other figure by the simple conversion of one or both of the premisses. Hence if the valid moods of any one figure are determined, those of the remaining figures may be immediately deduced therefrom.

It will be found that in each figure there are twelve valid moods, which are neither strengthened nor weakened. This result may be established by either of the two alternative methods which follow.

I. We may enquire what various combinations of premises will yield conclusions of the forms A, Y, E, I, O, η, respectively.

It will suffice, as we have already seen, to consider some one figure. We may, therefore, take Figure 1, so that the position of the terms will be—

M	*P*
S	*M*
———	
S	*P*

---

[414] Or, retaining the original conclusion, we might replace the major premiss by *Some M is some P*; hence, from another point of view, the syllogism may be regarded as strengthened.

(i) To prove *SaP*, both premisses must be affirmative; and, in order to avoid illicit minor, the minor premiss must be *SaM*. It follows that the major must be *MaP* or there would be undistributed middle. Hence AAA is the only valid mood yielding an A conclusion.

(ii) To prove *SyP*, both premisses must be affirmative; and, in order to avoid illicit major, the major premiss must be *MyP*. It follows that the minor must be *SyM*, in order to avoid undistributed middle. Hence YYY is the only valid mood yielding a Y conclusion.

(iii) To prove *SeP*, the major must be (1) *MeP* or (2) *MyP* or (3) *MoP* in order to avoid illicit major. If (1), the minor must be *SaM* or there would be either two negative premisses or illicit minor; if (2), it must be *SeM* or there would be undistributed middle or illicit minor; if (3), it must be affirmative and distribute both *S* and *M*, which is impossible. Hence EAE and YEE are the only valid moods yielding an E conclusion.

(iv) To prove *SiP*, both premisses must be affirmative, and since *SaM* would necessarily be a strengthened premiss, the minor must be (1) *SiM* or (2) *SyM*. If (1), the major must be *MaP* or there would be undistributed middle; and if (2), it must be *MiP* or there would be a strengthened premiss. Hence AII and IYI are the only valid (unstrengthened and unweakened) moods yielding an I conclusion.

(v) To prove *SoP*, the major must be (1) *MeP* or (2) *MyP* or (3) *MoP* or there would be illicit major. If (1), the minor must be *SiM* or there would be a strengthened premiss; if (2), it must be *SoM* or there would be either two affirmative premisses with a negative conclusion or undistributed middle or a strengthened premiss; and if (3), it must be *SyM* or there would be two negative premisses or undistributed middle. Hence EIO, YOO, OYO are the only valid (unstrengthened and unweakened) moods yielding an O conclusion.

(vi) To prove *SηP*, the minor must be (1) *SeM* or (2) *SaM* or (3) *SηM* or there would be illicit minor. If (1), the major must be *MiP* or there would be a strengthened premiss; if (2), the major must be *MηP* or there would be undistributed middle or two affirmative premisses with a negative conclusion or a strengthened premiss; and if (3), the major must be *MaP* or there would be undistributed middle or two negative premisses. Hence IEη, ηAη, Aηη are the only valid (unstrengthened and unweakened) moods yielding an η conclusion.

By converting one or both of the premisses we may at once deduce from the above a table of valid (unstrengthened and unweakened) moods for all four figures as follows:—

Figure 1.	Figure 2.	Figure 3.	Figure 4.
AAA	YAA	AYA	YYA
YYY	AYY	YAY	AAY
EAE	EAE	EYE	EYE
YEE	AEE	YEE	AEE
AII	YII	AII	YII
IYI	IYI	IAI	IAI
EIO	EIO	EIO	EIO
YOO	AOO	YηO	AηO
OYO	ηYO	OAO	ηAO
IEη	IEη	IEη	IEη
ηAη	OAη	ηYη	OYη
Aηη	Yηη	AOη	YOη

II. The above table may also be obtained by (1) taking all the combinations of premisses that are *à priori* possible, (2) establishing special rules for the particular figure selected, which (taken together with the rules of quality) will enable us to exclude the combinations of premisses which are either invalid or strengthened whatever the conclusion may be, (3) assigning the valid unweakened conclusion in the remaining cases.

The following are all possible combinations of premisses, valid and invalid:

AA (*b*)	YA	IA	EA (*b*)	OA	ηA(*b*) (*c*)
AY	YY (*a*)	IY (*a*)	EY	OY (*a*)	ηY
AI	YI (*a*)	II (*a*)	EI	OI (*a*)	ηI (*c*)
AE (*b*)	YE	IE	[EE] (*b*)	[OE]	[ηE] (*b*)
AO	YO (*a*)	IO (*a*)	[EO]	[OO] (*a*)	[ηO]
Aη (*b*) (*c*)	Yη	Iη (*c*)	[Eη] (*b*)	[Oη]	[ηη] (*b*) (*c*)

The combinations in square brackets are excluded by the rule that from two negative premisses nothing follows.

Taking the third figure, in which the middle term is subject in each premiss, and remembering that the subject is distributed in A, E, η and in these only, while the predicate is distributed in Y, E, O and in these only, the following special rules are obtainable:

(*a*) One premiss must be A, E, or η, or the middle term would not be distributed in either premiss;

(*b*) One premiss must be Y, I, or O, or the middle term would be distributed in both premisses, and there would hence be a strengthened premiss;

(*c*) If either premiss is negative, one of the premisses must be Y, E, or O, for otherwise (since the conclusion must be negative, distributing one of its terms) there would be illicit process either of major or minor.

These rules exclude the combinations of premisses marked respectively (*a*), (*b*), (*c*) above.

Assigning the valid unweakened conclusion in the case of each of the twelve combinations which remain, we have the following; AYA, AII, AOη, YAY, YEE, YηO, IAI, IEη, EYE, EIO, OAO, ηYη. From this, the table of valid (unstrengthened and unweakened) moods for all four figures may be expanded as before.

330. *Formal Inferences not reducible to ordinary Syllogisms.*[415]—The following is an example of what is usually called the argument *à fortiori*:

	B is greater than C,
	A is greater than B,
therefore,	A is greater than C.

As this stands, it is clearly not in the ordinary syllogistic form since it contains four terms; an attempt is, however, sometimes made to reduce it to ordinary syllogistic form as follows:

---

[415] Attempts to reduce *immediate* inferences to syllogistic form have been already considered in section 110. In the present section, non-syllogistic *mediate* inferences will be considered.

	B is greater than C,
therefore,	*Whatever is greater than B is greater than C,*
but	*A is greater than B,*
therefore,	*A is greater than C.*

With De Morgan, we may treat this as a mere evasion, or as a *petitio principii*. The principle of the argument *à fortiori* is really assumed in passing from *B is greater than C* to *Whatever is greater than B is greater than C*. It may indeed be admitted that by the above reduction the argument *à fortiori* is resolved into a syllogism together with an immediate inference. But this immediate inference is not one that can be justified so long as we recognise only such relations between terms or classes as are implied by the ordinary copula; and if anyone declined to admit the validity of the argument *à fortiori* he would decline to admit the validity of the step represented by the immediate inference.

The following attempted resolution[416] must be disposed of similarly:

Whatever is greater than a greater than C is greater than C,
A is greater than a greater than C,
therefore, *A is greater than C.*

At any rate, it is clear that this cannot be the whole of the reasoning, since *B* no longer appears in the premisses at all.

The point at issue may perhaps be most clearly indicated by saying that whilst the ordinary syllogism may be based upon the *dictum de omni et nullo*, the argument *à fortiori* cannot be made to rest entirely upon this axiom. A new principle is required and one which must be placed on a par with the *dictum de omni et nullo*, not in subordination to it. This new principle may be expressed in the form, *Whatever is greater than a second thing which is greater than a third thing is itself greater than that third thing.*

Mansel (*Aldrich*, pp. 199, 200) treats the argument *à fortiori* as an example of a *material consequence* on the ground that it depends upon "some understood proposition or propositions, connecting the terms, by the addition of which the mind is enabled to reduce the consequence to logical form." He would effect the reduction in one of the ways already referred to. This, however, begs the question that the syllogistic is the only *logical* form. As a matter of fact the cogency of the argument *à fortiori* is just as intuitively evident as that of a syllogism in *Barbara* itself. Why should no relation be regarded as *formal* unless it can be expressed by the word *is*? Touching on this case, De Morgan remarks that the formal logician has a right to confine himself to any part of his subject that he pleases; "but he has no right except the right of fallacy to call that part the whole" (*Syllabus*, p. 42).

There are an indefinite number of other arguments which for similar reasons cannot be reduced to syllogistic form. For example,—*A equals B, B equals C, therefore, A equals C*;[417] *X*

---

[416] Compare Mansel's *Aldrich*, p. 200.

[417] In regard to this argument De Morgan writes, "This is not an instance of common syllogism: the premisses are '*A is* an equal of *B*; *B is* an equal of *C*.' So far as common syllogism is concerned, that 'an equal of B' is as good for the argument as 'B' is a *material* accident of the meaning of 'equal.' The logicians accordingly, to reduce this to a common syllogism, state the effect of composition of relation in a major premiss, and declare that the case before them is an example of that composition in a minor premiss. As in, *A* is *an equal of an equal* (of *C*); Every *equal of an equal* is an *equal*; therefore, *A* is an *equal* of *C*. This I treat as a mere evasion. Among various sufficient answers this one is enough: *men do not think as above*. When *A* = *B*, *B* = *C*, is made

is a contemporary of Y, and Y of Z, therefore, X is a contemporary of Z; A is a brother of B, B is a brother of C, therefore, A is a brother of C; A is to the right of B, B is to the right of C, therefore, A is to the right of C; A is in tune with B, and B with C, therefore, A is in tune with C. All these arguments depend upon principles which may be placed on a par with the *dictum de omni et nullo*, and which are equally axiomatic in the particular systems to which they belong.

The claims that have been put forward on behalf of the syllogism as the exclusive form of all deductive reasoning must accordingly be rejected.

Such claims have been made, for example, by Whately. Syllogism, he says, is "the form to which *all* correct reasoning may be ultimately reduced" (*Logic*, p. 12). Again, he remarks, "An argument thus stated regularly and at full length is called a Syllogism; which, therefore, is evidently not a peculiar *kind of argument*, but only a peculiar *form* of expression, in which every argument may be stated" (*Logic*, p. 26).[418]

Spalding seems to have the same thing in view when he says,—"An inference, whose antecedent is constituted by more propositions than one, is a mediate inference. The simplest case, that in which the antecedent propositions are two, is the syllogism. The syllogism is the norm of all inferences whose antecedent is more complex; and all such inferences may, by those who think it worthwhile, be resolved into a series of syllogisms" (*Logic*, p. 158).

J. S. Mill endorses these claims. "All valid ratiocination," he observes, "all reasoning by which from general propositions previously admitted, other propositions equally or less general are inferred, may be exhibited in some of the above forms," i.e., the syllogistic moods (*Logic*, II. 2, § 1).

What is required in order to fill the logical gap created by the admission that the syllogism is *not* the norm of all valid formal inference has been called the *logic of relatives*.[419] The function of the logic of relatives is to take account of relations generally, and not "those merely which are indicated by the ordinary logical copula *is*" (Venn, *Symbolic Logic*, p. 400).[420] The line which this branch of logic may take, if it is ever fully worked out, is indicated by the following passage from De Morgan (*Syllabus*, pp. 30, 31):—"A *convertible* copula is one in which the copular relation exists between two names *both ways*: thus 'is fastened to,' 'is joined by a road with,' 'is equal to,' &c. are *convertible* copulae. If '*X* is equal to *Y*' then '*Y* is equal to *X*,' &c. A *transitive* copula is one in which the copular relation joins *X* with *Z* whenever it joins *X* with *Y* and *Y* with *Z*. Thus 'is fastened to' is usually understood as a transitive copula: '*X* is fastened to *Y*' and '*Y* is fastened to *Z*' give '*X* is fastened to *Z*.'" The student may further be referred to Venn, *Symbolic Logic*, pp. 399 to 404; and also to Mr Johnson's articles on *the Logical Calculus* in *Mind*, 1892, especially pp. 26 to 28 and 244 to 250.

---

to give $A = C$, the word *equals* is a *copula* in thought, and not a *notion attached to a predicate*. There are processes which are not those of common syllogism in the logician's major premiss above: but waiving this, logic is an analysis of the form of thought, possible and actual, and the logician has no right to declare that other than the actual is actual" (*Syllabus*, pp. 31, 2).

[418] Compare also Whately, *Logic*, pp. 24, 5, and 34.

[419] Compare pages 149 to 151.

[420] Ordinary formal logic is included under the logic of relatives interpreted in the widest sense, but only in a more generalised form than that in which it is customarily treated.

EXERCISES

331. Shew that if either of two given propositions will suffice to expand a given enthymeme of the first or second order into a valid syllogism, then the two propositions will be equivalent to each other, provided that neither of them constitutes a strengthened premiss.
[J.]

332. Given one premiss and the conclusion of a valid syllogism within what limits may the other premiss be determined? Shew that the problem is equally determinate with that in which we are given both the premisses and have to find the conclusion. In what cases is it absolutely determinate?
[K.]

333. Construct a valid sorites consisting of five propositions and having *Some A is not B* as its first premiss. Point out the mood and figure of each of the distinct syllogisms into which the sorites may be resolved.
[K.]

334. Discuss the character of the following sorites, in each case indicating how far more than one analysis is possible: (i) *Some D is E, All D is C, All C is B, All B is A*, therefore, *Some A is E*; (ii) *Some A is B, No C is B, All D is C, All E is D*, therefore, *Some A is not E*; (iii) *All E is D, All D is C, All C is B, All B is A*, therefore, *Some A is E*; (iv) *No D is E, Some D is C, All C is B, All B is A*, therefore, *Some A is not E*.
[K.]

335. Discuss the possibility of a sorites which is capable of being analysed so as to yield valid syllogisms all of which are in Figure 4. Determine the maximum number of propositions of which such a sorites can consist.
[K.]

336. Examine the validity of the following moods:

in Figure 1, UAU, YOO, EYO;
in Figure 2, AAA, AYY, UOω;
in Figure 3, YEE, OYO, AωO.
[C.]

337. Enquire in what figures, if any, the following moods are valid, noting cases in which the conclusion is weakened:—AUI; YAY; UOη; IUη; UEO.
[L.]

338. If *some* is used in the sense of "some, but not all," what can be inferred from the propositions *All M is some P, All M is some S*?
[K.]

339. Giving to *some* its ordinary logical meaning, shew that, in any syllogism expressed with quantified predicates, a premiss of the form U may always be regarded as a strengthened premiss unless the conclusion is also of the form U.
[K.]

340. Is it possible that there should be three propositions such that each in turn is deducible from the other two?
[V.]

341. Determine special rules for Figures 1, 2, and 4, corresponding to the special rules for Figure 3 given in section 329.
[K.]

Chapter 22

PROBLEMS ON THE SYLLOGISM

342. *Bearing of the existential interpretation of propositions upon the validity of syllogistic reasonings.*—We may as before take different suppositions with regard to the existential import of propositions, and proceed to consider how far the validity of the various syllogistic moods is affected by each in turn.

(1) *Let every proposition be interpreted as implying the existence both of its subject and of its predicate.*[421] In this case, the existence of the major, middle, and minor terms is in every case guaranteed by the premisses, and therefore no further assumption with regard to existence is required in order that the conclusion may be legitimately obtained.[422] We may regard the above supposition as that which is tacitly made in the ordinary doctrine of the syllogism.

(2) *Let every proposition be interpreted as implying the existence of its subject.* Under this supposition an affirmative proposition ensures the existence of its predicate also; but not so a negative proposition. It follows that any mood will be valid unless the minor term is in its premiss the predicate of a negative proposition. This cannot happen either in Figure 1 or in Figure 2, since in these figures the minor is always subject in its premiss; nor in Figure 3, since in this figure the minor premiss is always affirmative. In Figure 4, the only moods with a negative minor are *Camenes* and its weakened form AEO. Our conclusion then is that on the given supposition every ordinarily recognised mood is valid except these two.[423]

(3) *Let no proposition be interpreted as implying the existence either of its subject or of its predicate.* Taking S, M, P, as the minor, middle, and major terms respectively, the conclusion will imply that if there is any S there is some P or *not-P* (according as it is

---

[421] It will be observed that this is not quite the same as supposition (1) in section 156.

[422] If, however, we are to be allowed to proceed as in section 206 (where from *all P is M, all S is M*, we inferred *some not-S is not-P*) we must posit the existence not merely of the terms directly involved, but also of their contradictories.

[423] Reduction to Figure 1 appears to be affected by this supposition, since it makes the contraposition of A and the conversion of E in general invalid. The contraposition of A is involved in the direct reduction of *Baroco* (*Faksoko*). The process is, however, in this particular case valid, as the existence of *not-M* is given by the minor premiss. The conversion of E is involved in the reduction of *Cesare, Camestres,* and *Festino* from Figure 2; and of *Camenes, Fesapo,* and *Fresison* from Figure 4. Since, however, one premiss must be affirmative the existence of the middle term is thereby guaranteed, and hence the simple conversion of E in the second figure, and in the major of the fourth becomes valid. Also the conversion of the conclusion resulting from the reduction of *Camestres* is legitimate, since the original minor term is subject in its premiss. Hence *Camenes* (and its weakened form) are the only moods whose reduction is rendered illegitimate by the supposition under consideration. This result agrees with that reached in the text.

affirmative or negative). Will the premisses also imply this? If so, then the syllogism is valid; but not otherwise.

It has been shown in section 212 that a universal affirmative conclusion, *All S is P*, can be proved only by means of the premisses, *All M is P*, *All S is M*; and it is clear that these premisses themselves imply that if there is any *S* there is some *P*. On our present supposition, then, a syllogism is valid if its conclusion is universal affirmative.

Again, as shown in section 212, a universal negative conclusion, *No S is P*, can be proved only in the following ways:—

(i)	*No M is P* (or *No P is M*),
	All S is M,
	———
therefore,	*No S is P*;
(ii)	*All P is M*,
	No S is M (or *No M is S*),
	———
therefore,	*No S is P*.

In (i) the minor premiss implies that if *S* exists then *M* exists, and the major premiss that if *M* exists then *not-P* exists. In (ii) the minor premiss implies that if *S* exists then *not-M* exists, and the major premiss that if *not-M* exists then *not-P* exists (as shewn in section 158). Hence a syllogism is valid if its conclusion is universal negative.

Next, let the conclusion be particular. In Figure 1, the implication of the conclusion with regard to existence is contained in the premisses themselves, since the minor term is the subject of an affirmative minor premiss, and the middle term the subject of the major premiss. In Figure 2, we may consider the weakened moods disposed of in what has been already said with regard to universal conclusions; for under our present supposition subalternation is a valid process. The remaining moods with particular conclusions in this figure are *Festino* and *Baroco*. In the former, the minor premiss implies that if *S* exists then *M* exists, and the major that if *M* exists then *not-P* exists; in the latter, the minor premiss implies that if *S* exists then *not-M* exists, and the major that if *not-M* exists then *not-P* exists.

All the ordinarily recognised moods, then, of Figures 1 and 2 are valid. But it is otherwise with moods yielding a particular conclusion in Figures 3 and 4, with the single exception of the weakened form of *Camenes* (which is itself the only mood with a universal conclusion in these figures). Subalternation being a valid process, the legitimacy of the latter follows from the legitimacy of *Camenes* itself. But in all other cases in Figures 3 and 4, the minor term is the predicate of an affirmative minor premiss. Its existence, therefore, carries no further implication of existence with it in the premisses. It does so in the conclusion. Hence all the moods of Figures 3 and 4, with the exception of AEE and AEO in the latter figure, are invalid. Take, as an example, a syllogism in *Darapti*,—

	All M is P,
	All M is S,
	———
therefore,	*Some S is P*.

The conclusion implies that if S exists P exists; but consistently with the premisses, S may be existent while M and P are both non-existent. An implication is, therefore, contained in the conclusion which is not justified by the premisses.

Hence on the supposition that no proposition implies the existence either of its subject or of its predicate all the ordinarily recognised moods of Figures 1 and 2 are valid, but none of those of Figures 3 and 4 excepting *Camenes* and the weakened form of *Camenes*.[424]

(4) *Let particulars be interpreted as implying, but universals as not implying, the existence of their subjects.* The legitimacy of moods with universal conclusions may be established as in the preceding case. Taking moods with particular conclusions, it is obvious that they will be valid if the minor premiss is particular, having the minor term as its subject; or if the minor premiss is particular affirmative, whether the minor term is its subject or predicate. *Disamis*, *Bocardo*, and *Dimaris* are also valid, since the major premiss in each case guarantees the existence of M, and the minor implies that if M exists then S exists. The above will be found to cover all the valid moods in which one premiss is particular. There remain only the moods in which from two universals we infer a particular. It is clear that all these moods must be invalid, for their conclusions will imply the existence of the minor term, and this cannot be guaranteed by the premisses.[425]

On the supposition then that particulars imply, while universals do not imply, the existence of their subjects, the moods rendered invalid are all the weakened moods, together with *Darapti*, *Felapton*, *Bramantip*, and *Fesapo*,[426] each of which contains a strengthened premiss. More briefly, any ordinarily recognised mood is on this supposition valid, unless it contains either a strengthened premiss or a weakened conclusion.[427]

343. *Connection between the truth and falsity of premisses and conclusion in a valid syllogism.*—By saying that a syllogism is valid we mean that the truth of its conclusion follows from the truth of its premisses; and it is an immediate inference from this that if the conclusion is false one or both of the premisses must be false. The converse does not, however, hold good in either case. The truth of the premisses does not follow from the truth of the conclusion; nor does the falsity of the conclusion follow from the falsity of either or both of the premisses.

The above statements would probably be accepted as self-evident; still it is more satisfactory to give a formal proof of them, and such a proof is afforded by means of the three following theorems.[428]

(1) *Given a valid syllogism, then in no case will the combination of either premiss with the conclusion establish the other premiss.*

We have to shew that if one premiss and the conclusion of a valid syllogism are taken as a new pair of premisses they do not in any case suffice to establish the other premiss. Were it possible for them to do so, then the premiss given true would have to be affirmative,

---

[424] An express statement concerning existence may, however, render the rejected moods legitimate. If, for instance, the existence of the middle term is expressly given, then *Darapti* becomes valid.

[425] Hypothetical conclusions (of the form *If S exists then* &c.) will of course still be legitimate.

[426] It will be observed that the letter *p* occurs in the mnemonic for each of these moods, indicating that their reduction to Figure 1 involves *conversion per accidens*. On the supposition under discussion this process is invalid, and we may find here a confirmation of the above result.

[427] This result may be regarded as affording an additional argument in favour of the adoption of supposition (4).

[428] It is assumed throughout this section that our schedule of propositions does not include U. The theorems hold good, however, for the sixfold schedule, including Y and η, as well as for the ordinary fourfold schedule.

for if it were negative, the original conclusion would be negative, and combining these we should have two negative premisses which could yield no conclusion.

Also, the middle term would have to be distributed in the premiss given true. This is clear if it is not distributed in the other premiss; and since the other premiss is the conclusion of the new syllogism, if it is distributed there, it must also be distributed in the premiss given true or we should have an illicit process in the new syllogism.

Therefore, the premiss given true, being affirmative and distributing the middle term, cannot distribute the other term which it contains.[429] Neither therefore can this term be distributed in the original conclusion. But this is the term which will be the middle term of the new syllogism, and we shall consequently have undistributed middle.

Hence the truth of one premiss and the conclusion of a valid syllogism does not establish the truth of the other premiss; and *à fortiori* the truth of the conclusion cannot by itself establish the truth of both the premisses.[430]

(2) *The contradictories of the premisses of a valid syllogism will not in any case suffice to establish the contradictory of the original conclusion.*

The premisses of the original syllogism must be either (α) both affirmative, or (β) one affirmative and one negative.

In case (α), the contradictories of the original premisses will both be negative; and from two negatives nothing follows.

In case (β), the contradictories of the original premisses will be one negative and one affirmative; and if this combination yields any conclusion, it will be negative. But the original conclusion must also be negative, and therefore its contradictory will be affirmative.

In neither case then can we establish the contradictory of the original conclusion.[431]

(3) *One premiss and the contradictory of the other premiss of a valid syllogism will not in any case suffice to establish the contradictory of the original conclusion.*[432]

This follows at once from the first of the theorems established in this section. Let the premisses of a valid syllogism be P and Q, and the conclusion R, P and the contradictory of Q will not prove the contradictory of R; for if they did, it would follow that P and R would prove Q; but this has been shewn not to be the case.

We have now established by strictly formal reasoning Aristotle's dictum that although it is not possible syllogistically to get a false conclusion from true premisses, it is quite possible to get a true conclusion from false premisses.[433] In other words, the falsity of one or both of the premisses does not establish the falsity of the conclusion of a syllogism. The second of the above theorems deals with the case in which both the premisses are false; the third with that in which one only of the premisses is false.

---

[429] This statement, though not holding good for U, holds good for Y as well as A.
[430] Other methods of solution more or less distinct from the above might be given. A somewhat similar problem is discussed by Solly, *Syllabus of Logic*, pp. 123 to 126, 132 to 136. We have shewn that one premiss and the conclusion of a valid syllogism will never suffice to prove the other premiss, but it of course does not follow that they will never yield any conclusion at all; for a consideration of this question, see the following section.
[431] It is possible, however, that some conclusion may be obtainable. See section 359.
[432] It does not follow that one premiss and the contradictory of the other premiss of a valid syllogism will never yield any conclusion at all. See the following section.
[433] Hamilton (*Logic*, I. p. 450) considers the doctrine "that if the conclusion of a syllogism be true, the premisses may be either true or false, but that if the conclusion be false, one or both of the premisses must be false" to be extralogical, if it is not absolutely erroneous. He is clearly wrong, since the doctrine in question admits of a purely formal proof.

344. *Arguments from the truth of one premiss and the falsity of the other premiss in a valid syllogism, or from the falsity of one premiss to the truth of the conclusion, or from the truth of one premiss to the falsity of the conclusion.*—In this section we shall consider three problems, mutually involved in one another, which are in a manner related to the theorems contained in the preceding section. It has, for example, been shown that one premiss and the contradictory of the other premiss will not in any case suffice to establish the contradictory of the original conclusion; the object of the first of the following problems is to enquire in what cases they can establish any conclusion at all.

(i) *To find a pair of valid syllogisms having a common premiss, such that the remaining premiss of the one contradicts the remaining premiss of the other.*[434]

We have to find cases in which P and Q, P and Q' (the contradictory of Q) are the premisses of two valid syllogisms. In working out this problem and the problems that follow, it must be remembered that if two propositions are contradictories, they will differ in quality, and also in the distribution of their terms, so that any term distributed in either of them is undistributed in the other and *vice versâ*. We may, therefore, assume that Q is affirmative and Q' negative. Let P contain the terms X and Y, while Q and Q' contain the terms Y and Z, so that Y is the middle term, and X and Z the extreme terms, of each syllogism.

Since Q' is negative, P must be affirmative; and since Y must be undistributed either in Q or in Q', it must be distributed in P.

Hence $P = YaX$.

Q' must distribute Z: for the conclusion (being negative) must distribute one term, and X is undistributed in P. It follows that Z is undistributed in Q.

Hence $Q = YaZ$ or YiZ or ZiY;

$Q' = YoZ$ or YeZ or ZeY.

If the different possible combinations are worked out, it will be found that the following are the syllogisms satisfying the condition that if one premiss (that in black type) is retained, while the other is replaced by its contradictory, a conclusion is still obtainable:—

In Figure 1: AII;

In Figure 3: AAI, AAI, IAI, AII, EAO, OAO;

In Figure 4: IAI, EAO.

(ii) *To find a pair of valid syllogisms having a common conclusion, such that a premiss in the one contradicts a premiss in the other.*

Let Q and Q' (which we may assume to be respectively affirmative and negative) be the premisses in question, and P' the conclusion; also let Q and Q' contain the terms Y and Z, while P' contains the terms X and Z, so that Z is the middle term, and X and Y the extreme terms, of each syllogism.

It follows immediately that P' is negative; also that Y must be undistributed in P', since it is necessarily undistributed either in Q or in Q'.

Hence $P' = YoX$.

Since X is distributed in P' it must also be distributed in the premiss which is combined with Q'; and as this premiss must be affirmative, it cannot also distribute Z, which must therefore be distributed in Q' (and undistributed in Q).

---

[434] This problem was suggested by the following question of Mr O'Sullivan's, which puts the same problem in another form: Given that one premiss of a valid syllogism is false and the other true, determine generally in what cases a conclusion can be drawn from these data.

Hence $Q = YaZ$ or YiZ or ZiY;

$Q' = YoZ$ or YeZ or ZeY.

If the different possible combinations are worked out, it will be found that the following are the syllogisms satisfying the condition that the same conclusion is obtainable from another pair of premisses, of which one contradicts one of the original premisses (namely, that in black type):—

In Figure 1: EAO, EIO;
In Figure 2: EAO, AEO, EIO, AOO;
In Figure 3: EIO;
In Figure 4: AEO, EIO.

(iii) *To find a pair of valid syllogisms having a common premiss, such that the conclusion of one contradicts the conclusion of the other.*[435]

Let P be the common premiss, Q and Q' (respectively affirmative and negative) the contradictory conclusions; also let P contain the terms X and Y, while Q and Q' contain the terms Y and Z, so that X is the middle term, and Y and Z the extreme terms, of each syllogism.

Since Q is affirmative, P must be affirmative; and since either Q or Q' will distribute Y, P must distribute Y.

Hence $P = YaX$.

The premiss which, combined with P, proves Q must be affirmative and must distribute X; it cannot therefore distribute Z, and Z must accordingly be undistributed in Q (and distributed in Q').

Hence $Q = YaZ$ or YiZ or ZiY;

$Q' = YoZ$ or YeZ or ZeY.

If the different possible combinations are worked out, it will be found that the following are the syllogisms satisfying the condition that the contradictory of the conclusion is obtainable, although one of the premisses (that in black type) is retained:—

In Figure 1: AAA, AAI, EAE, EAO;
In Figure 2: EAE, EAO, AEE;
In Figure 4: AAI, AEE.[436]

The three sets of moods worked out above are mutually derivable from one another. Thus,

---

[435] This problem was suggested by the following question of Mr Panton's, which puts the same problem in another form: If the conclusion be substituted for a premiss in a valid mood, investigate the conditions which must be fulfilled in order that the new premisses should be legitimate.

[436] It will be observed that each of the above problems yields *nine* cases. Between them they cover all the 24 valid moods; but there are three moods (namely, *EAO* in Figures 1 and 2 and *AAI* in Figure 3) which occur twice over. The 15 unstrengthened and unweakened moods are equally distributed, namely, the four yielding *I* conclusions (together with *OAO*) falling under (i); the six yielding *O* conclusions (except *OAO*) under (ii); the five yielding *A* or *E* conclusions under (iii). All the moods of Figure 1 (except those with an *I* premiss) fall under (iii); all the moods of Figure 2 (except those with an *E* conclusion) under (ii); all the moods of Figure 3 (except the one not having an *A* premiss) under (i).

(i)		(ii)		(iii)
P and Q ∴ R	=	Q and R' ∴ P'	=	R' and P ∴ Q'
P and Q' ∴ T'	=	Q' and T ∴ P'	=	T and P ∴ Q

In this table (i) represents the possible cases in which, one premiss being retained, the other premiss may be replaced by its contradictory. We can then deduce (ii) the cases in which, the conclusion being retained, one premiss may be replaced by its contradictory; and (iii) the cases in which, one premiss being retained, the conclusion may be replaced by its contradictory. We might of course equally well start from (ii) or from (iii), and thence deduce the two others.

Comparing the first syllogism of (i) with the second syllogism of (iii) and *vice versâ*, we see further that (i) gives the cases in which, one premiss being retained, the conclusion may be replaced by the other premiss; and that (iii) gives the cases in which, one premiss being retained, the other premiss may be replaced by the conclusion.

The following is another method of stating and solving all three problems: *To determine in what cases it is possible to obtain two incompatible trios of propositions, each trio containing three and only three terms and each including a proposition which is identical with a proposition in the other and also a proposition which is the contradictory of a proposition in the other.*

Let the propositions be P, Q, R' and P, Q', T; and let P contain the terms X and Y; Q and Q' the terms Y and Z; R and T, the terms Z and X. Suppose Q to be affirmative, and Q' negative.

Then since one of each trio of propositions must be negative, and not more than one can be so (as shewn in section 214), P and T must be affirmative, and R' negative.

Again, since each of the terms X, Y, Z must be distributed once at least in each trio of propositions (as shewn in section 214), and since Y must be undistributed either in Q or in Q', Y must be distributed in P.

Hence $P = YaX$.

X, being undistributed in P, must be distributed in R' and T.

Hence $T = XaZ$.

Z, being undistributed in T, must be distributed in Q', and therefore undistributed in Q, and distributed in R'.

Hence $Q = YaZ$ or YiZ or ZiY;

$Q' = YoZ$ or YeZ or ZeY;

$R' = XeZ$ or ZeX.

We have then the following solution of our problem:—

YaZ, YaZ or YiZ or ZiY, XeZ or ZeX;
YaZ, YoZ or YeZ or ZeY, XaZ.

345. Numerical Moods of the Syllogism.[437]—The following are examples of numerical moods in the different figures of the syllogism:—

---

[437] This section was suggested by the following question of Mr Johnson's:—"Shew the validity of the following syllogisms: (i) All M's are P's, At least n S's are M's, therefore, At least n S's are P's; (ii) All P's are M's, Less than n S's are M's, therefore, Less than n S's are P's; (iii) Less than n M's are P's, At least n M's are S's,

Figure 1.	(i)	All M's are P's,
		At least n S's are M's,
therefore,		At least n S's are P's;
	(ii)	Less than n M's are P's,
		All S's are M's,
therefore,		Less than n S's are P's;
	(iii)	Less than n M's are P's,
		At least n S's are M's,
therefore,		Some S's are not P's;
Figure 2.	(iv)	All P's are M's,
		Less than n S's are M's,
therefore,		Less than n S's are P's;
	(v)	Less than n P's are M's,
		All S's are M's,
therefore,		Less than n S's are P's;
	(vi)	Less than n P's are M's,
		At least n S's are M's,
therefore,		Some S's are not P's;
Figure 3.	(vii)	Less than n M's are P's,
		At least n M's are S's,
therefore,		Some S's are not P's;
	(viii)	All M's are P's,
		At least n M's are S's,
therefore,		At least n S's are P's;
	(ix)	At least n M's are P's,
		All M's are S's,
therefore,		At least n S's are P's;
Figure 4.	(x)	At least n P's are M's,
		All M's are S's,
therefore,		At least n S's are P's;
	(xi)	All P's are M's,
		Less than n M's are S's,
therefore,		Less than n S's are P's;
	(xii)	Less than n P's are M's,
		At least n M's are S's,
therefore,		Some S's are not P's.

The above moods may be established as follows:—

(i) From *All M's are P's*, it follows that *Every S which is M is also P*, and since *At least n S's are M's*, it follows further that *At least n S's are P's*.

Denoting the major premiss of (i) by *A*, the minor by *B*, and the conclusion by *C*, we obtain immediately the following syllogisms:—

---

therefore, Some *S*'s are not *P*'s. Deduce from the above the ordinary non-numerical moods of the first three figures."

	A,		C',
	C',		B,
	—		—
∴	B';	∴	A';

and these are respectively equivalent to (iv) and (vii).

(v) is obtainable from (iv) by transposing the premisses and converting the conclusion;
(ii) from (v) by converting the major premiss;
(iii) from (vii) by converting the minor premiss;
(vi) from (iii) by converting the major premiss;
(viii) from (i) by converting the minor premiss;
(ix) from (viii) by transposing the premisses and converting the conclusion;
(x) from (i) by transposing the premisses and converting the conclusion;
(xi) from (iv) by converting the minor premiss;
(xii) from (vii) by converting the major premiss.

The ordinary non-numerical moods of the different figures may be deduced from the above results as follows:—

Figure 1. (i) Putting n = total number of *S*'s, we have *MaP, SaM,* ∴ *SaP,* that is, *Barbara*; and putting $n = 1$, we have *MaP, SiM,* ∴ *SiP,* that is, *Darii*.

(ii) Putting $n = 1$, *MeP, SaM,* ∴ *SeP* (*Celarent*).
(iii) Putting $n = 1$, *MeP, SiM,* ∴ *SoP* (*Ferio*).
AAI and *EAO* follow *à fortiori*.

Figure 2 (iv) Putting n = total number of *S*'s, *PaM, SoM,* ∴ *SoP* (*Baroco*); putting $n = 1$, *PaM, SeM,* ∴ *SeP* (*Camestres*).

(v) Putting $n = 1$, *PeM, SaM,* ∴ *SeP* (*Cesare*).
(vi) Putting $n = 1$, *PeM, SiM,* ∴ *SoP* (*Festino*).
AEO and *EAO* follow *à fortiori*.

Figure 3. (vii) Putting n = total number of *M*'s, *MoP, MaS,* ∴ *SoP* (*Bocardo*); putting $n = 1$, *MeP, MiS,* ∴ *SoP* (*Ferison*).

(viii) Putting $n = 1$, *MaP, MiS,* ∴ *SiP* (*Datisi*).
(ix) Putting $n = 1$, *MiP, MaS,* ∴ *SiP* (*Disamis*).
Darapti and *Felapton* follow *à fortiori*.
Figure 4. (x) Putting $n = 1$, *PiM, MaS,* ∴ *SiP* (*Dimaris*).
(xi) Putting $n = 1$, *PaM, MeS,* ∴ *SeP* (*Camenes*).
(xii) Putting $n = 1$, *PeM, MiS,* ∴ *SoP* (*Fresison*).
Bramantip, AEO, and *Fesapo* follow *à fortiori*.

EXERCISES

346. "*Whatever P and Q may stand for, we may shew à priori that some P is Q*. For *All PQ is Q* by the law of identity, and similarly *All PQ is P*; therefore, by a syllogism in *Darapti, Some P is Q*." How would you deal with this paradox? [K.]

A solution is afforded by the discussion contained in section 342; and this example seems to shew that the enquiry—how far assumptions with regard to existence are involved in syllogistic processes—is not irrelevant or unnecessary.

347. What conclusion can be drawn from the following propositions? The members of the board were all either bondholders or shareholders, but not both; and the bondholders, as it happened, were all on the board. [V.]

We may take as our premisses:

No member of the board is both a bondholder and a shareholder,
All bondholders are members of the board;
and these premisses yield a conclusion (in *Celarent*),
No bondholder is both a bondholder and a shareholder,
that is, No bondholder is a shareholder.

348. The following rules were drawn up for a club:—

(i) The financial committee shall be chosen from amongst the general committee; (ii) No one shall be a member both of the general and library committees, unless he be also on the financial committee; (iii) No member of the library committee shall be on the financial committee.

Is there anything self-contradictory or superfluous in these rules? [VENN, *Symbolic Logic*, p. 331.]

Let F = member of the financial committee,
G = member of the general committee,
L = member of the library committee.
The above rules may then be expressed symbolically as follows:—

(i) *All F is G*;
(ii) *If any L is G, that L is F*;
(iii) *No L is F*.

From (ii) and (iii) we obtain (iv) *No L is G*.
The rules may therefore be written in the form,

(1) *All F is G*,
(2) *No L is G*,
(3) *No L is F*.

But in this form (3) is deducible from (1) and (2).

Hence all that is contained in the rules as originally stated may be expressed by (1) and (2); that is, the rules as originally stated were partly superfluous, and they may be reduced to

(1) The financial committee shall be chosen from amongst the general committee;
(2) No one shall be a member both of the general and library committees.

If (ii) is interpreted as implying that there are some individuals who are on both the general and library committees, then it follows that (ii) and (iii) are inconsistent with each other.

349. Given that the middle term is distributed twice in the premisses of a syllogism, determine *directly* (i.e., without any reference to the mnemonic verses or the special rules of the figures) in what different moods it might possibly be.

The premisses must be either both affirmative, or one affirmative and one negative.

In the first case, both premisses being affirmative can distribute their subjects only. The middle term must, therefore, be the subject in each, and both must be universal. This limits us to the one syllogism,—

	All M is P,
	All M is S,
therefore,	*Some S is P.*

In the second case, one premiss being negative, the conclusion must be negative and will, therefore, distribute the major term. Hence, the major premiss must distribute the major term, and also (by hypothesis) the middle term. This condition can be fulfilled only by its being one or other of the following,—*No M is P* or *No P is M*. The major being negative, the minor must be affirmative, and in order to distribute the middle term must be *All M is S*.

In this case we get two syllogisms, namely,—

	No M is P,
	All M is S,
therefore,	*Some S is not P;*
	No P is M,
	All M is S,
therefore,	*Some S is not P.*

The given condition limits us, therefore, to three syllogisms (one affirmative and two negative); and by reference to the mnemonic verses we may identify these with *Darapti* and *Felapton* in Figure 3, and *Fesapo* in Figure 4.

350. If the major premiss and the conclusion of a valid syllogism agree in quantity, but differ in quality, find the mood and figure.

Since we cannot have a negative premiss with an affirmative conclusion, the major premiss must be affirmative and the conclusion negative. It follows immediately that, in order to avoid illicit major, the major premiss must be *All P is M* (where *M* is the middle term and *P* the major term). The conclusion, therefore, must be *No S is P* (*S* being the minor term); and this requires that, in order to avoid undistributed middle and illicit minor, the minor premiss should be *No S is M* or *No M is S*. Hence the syllogism is in *Camestres* or in *Camenes*.

351. Given a valid syllogism with two universal premisses and a particular conclusion, such that the same conclusion cannot be inferred, if for either of the premisses is substituted its subaltern, determine the mood and figure of the syllogism. [K.]

Let *S, M, P* be respectively the minor, middle, and major terms of the given syllogism. Then, since the conclusion is particular, it must be either *Some S is P* or *Some S is not P*.

First, if possible, let it be *Some S is P*.

The only term which need be distributed in the premisses is *M*. But since we have two universal premisses, *two* terms must be distributed in them as subjects.[438] One of these distributions must be superfluous; and it follows that for one of the premisses we may substitute its subaltern, and still get the same conclusion.

The conclusion cannot then be *Some S is P*.

Secondly, if possible, let the conclusion be *Some S is not P*.

If the subject of the minor premiss is *S*, we may clearly substitute its subaltern without affecting the conclusion. The subject of the minor premiss must therefore be *M*, which will thus be distributed in this premiss. *M* cannot also be distributed in the major, or else it is clear that its subaltern might be substituted for the minor and nevertheless the same conclusion inferred. The major premiss must, therefore, be affirmative with *M* for its predicate. This limits us to the syllogism—

	All P is M,
	No M is S,
therefore,	*Some S is not P*;

and this syllogism, which is AEO in Figure 4, does fulfil the given conditions, for it becomes invalid if either of the premisses is made particular.

The above amounts to a general proof of the proposition laid down in section 246:— *Every syllogism in which there are two universal premisses with a particular conclusion is a strengthened syllogism with the single exception of* AEO *In Figure 4*.

352. Given two valid syllogisms in the same figure in which the major, middle, and minor terms are respectively the same, shew, without reference to the mnemonic verses, that if the minor premisses are subcontraries, the conclusions will be identical. [K.]

The minor premiss of one of the syllogisms must be O, and the major premiss of this syllogism must, therefore, be A and the conclusion O. The middle and the major terms having then to be distributed in the premisses, this syllogism is determined, namely,—

	All P is M,
	Some S is not M,
therefore,	*Some S is not P*.

Since the other syllogism is to be in the same figure, its minor premiss must be *Some S is M*; the major must therefore be universal, and in order to distribute the middle term it must be negative. This syllogism therefore is also determined, namely,—

	No P is M,
	Some S is M,
therefore,	*Some S is not P*.

---

[438] We here include the case in which the middle term is itself twice distributed.

The conclusions of the two syllogisms are thus shewn to be identical.

353. Find out in which of the valid syllogisms the combination of one premiss with the subcontrary of the conclusion would establish the subcontrary of the other premiss. [J.]

In the original syllogism (α) let X (universal) and Y (particular) prove Z (particular), the minor, middle, and major terms being S M, and P, respectively. Then we are to have another syllogism (β) in which X and Z_1 (the sub-contrary of Z) prove Y_1 (the sub-contrary of Y). In β, S or P will be the middle term.

It is clear that only one term can be distributed in α if the conclusion is affirmative, and only two if the conclusion is negative. Hence S cannot be distributed in α, and it follows that it cannot be distributed in the premisses of β. The middle term of β must therefore be P, and as X must consequently contain P it must be the major premiss of α and Y the minor premiss.

Z must be either SiP or SoP. First, let $Z = SiP$. Then it is clear that $X = MaP$, $Z_1 = SoP$, $Y_1 = SoM$, $Y = SiM$. Secondly, let $Z = SoP$. Then $Z_1 = SiP$, $X = PaM$ or MeP or PeM (since it must distribute P), $Y_1 = SiM$ (if X is affirmative) or SoM (if X is negative), $Y = SoM$ or SiM accordingly.

Hence we have four syllogisms satisfying the required conditions as follows:—

MaP	MeP	PeM	PaM
SiM	SiM	SiM	SoM
—	—	—	—
SiP	SoP	SoP	SoP

It will be observed that these are all the moods of the first and second figures, in which one premiss is particular.

354. Is it possible that there should be a valid syllogism such that, each of the premisses being converted, a new syllogism is obtainable giving a conclusion in which the old major and minor terms have changed places? Prove the correctness of your answer by general reasoning, and if it is in the affirmative, determine the syllogism or syllogisms fulfilling the given conditions. [K.]

If such a syllogism be possible, it cannot have two affirmative premisses, or (since A can only be converted *per accidens*) we should have two particular premisses in the new syllogism.

Therefore, *the original syllogism must have one negative premiss*. This cannot be O, since O is inconvertible.

Therefore, *one premiss of the original syllogism must be* E.

First, let this be the major premiss. Then the minor premiss must be affirmative, and its converse (being a particular affirmative), will not distribute either of its terms. But this converse will be the *major* premiss of the new syllogism, which also must have a negative conclusion. We should then have illicit major in the new syllogism; and hence the above supposition will not give us the desired result.

Secondly, let the minor premiss of the original syllogism be E. The major premiss in order to distribute the old major term must be A, with the major term as subject. We get then the following, satisfying the given conditions:—

All P is M,
No M is S, or *No S is M*,
therefore, *No S is P*, or *Some S is not P*;

that is, we really have four syllogisms, such that both premisses being converted, thus,

No S is M, or *No M is S*,
Some M is P,

we have a new syllogism yielding a conclusion in which the old major and minor terms have changed places, namely, *Some P is not S*.

Symbolically,—

	PaM,				SeM,
	MeS,		or		MeS,
or	SeM,				MiP,
	—				—
∴	SeP			∴	PoS.
or	SoP				

If it be required to retain the *quantity* of the original conclusion, that conclusion must be *SoP*, in this case then we have only two syllogisms fulfilling the given conditions.

355. Shew that if the proportion of *B*'s out of the class *A* is greater than that out of the class *not-A*, then the proportion of *A*'s out of the class *B* will be greater than that out of the class *not-B*.[439] [J.]

Let the number of A's be denoted by $N(A)$, the number of AB's by $N(AB)$, &c.

Then, since *Every A is AB or Ab* (by the law of excluded middle) and *No A is both AB and Ab* (by the law of contradiction), it follows that

$N(A) = N(AB) + N(Ab)$.

We have to shew that

$$\frac{N(AB)}{N(B)} > \frac{N(Ab)}{N(b)}$$

follows from

$$\frac{N(AB)}{N(A)} > \frac{N(aB)}{N(a)}.$$

---

[439] This and the following problem cannot properly be called problems on the syllogism. They are given as examples in numerical logic.

This can be done by substituting

$N(AB) + N(Ab)$ for $N(A)$, &c.

Thus,

	$N(AB)$		$N(aB)$
	—	>	—,
	$N(A)$		$N(a)$
	$N(a)$		$N(A)$
∴	—	>	—,
	$N(aB)$		$N(AB)$
	$N(aB) + N(ab)$		$N(AB) + N(Ab)$
∴	—	>	—,
	$N(aB)$		$N(AB)$
	$N(ab)$		$N(Ab)$
∴	—	>	—,
	$N(aB)$		$N(AB)$
	$N(ab)$		$N(aB)$
∴	—	>	—,
	$N(Ab)$		$N(AB)$
	$N(Ab) + N(ab)$		$N(AB) + N(aB)$
∴	—	>	—,
	$N(Ab)$		$N(AB)$
	$N(b)$		$N(B)$
∴	—	>	—,
	$N(Ab)$		$N(AB)$
	$N(AB)$		$N(Ab)$
∴	—	>	—.
	$N(B)$		$N(b)$

356. Given the number (U) of objects in the Universe, and the number of objects in each of the classes $x_1, x_2, x_3, \ldots x_n$, shew that the least number of objects in the class ($x_1 x_2 x_3 \ldots x_n$)

$$= U - N(x_1) - N(x_2) - N(x_3) \ldots - N(x_n).$$

where $N(x_1)$ means the number of things which are *not* x_1; $N(x_2)$ means the number of things which are *not* x_2; &c. [J.]

Given $N(x_1)$, $N(x_2)$, &c., the number of objects in the class (x_1 or $x_2 \ldots$ or x_n) is greatest when no object belongs to any pair of the classes $x_1, x_2, \ldots$; and in this case it $= N(x_1) + N(x_2) \ldots + N(x_n)$.

Hence the least number in the contradictory class, $x_1 x_2 x_3 \ldots x_n$,

$$= U - N(x_1) - N(x_2) \ldots - N(x_n).$$

357. Prove that with three given propositions (of the forms *A*, *E*, *I*, *O*) it is never possible to construct more than one valid syllogism. [K.]

358. On the supposition that no proposition is interpreted as implying the existence either of its subject or of its predicate, find in what cases the reduction of syllogisms to Figure 1 is invalid. [K.]

359. Given a valid syllogism, determine the conditions under which the contradictories of the premisses will furnish premisses for another valid syllogism containing the same terms. How will the conclusions of the two syllogisms be related to one another? [K.]

360. Shew that the number of paupers who are blind males is equal to the excess, if any, of the sum of the whole number of blind persons, added to the whole number of male persons, added to the number of those who being paupers are neither blind nor males, above the sum of the whole number of paupers, added to the number of those who not being paupers are blind, and to the number of those who not being paupers are male. [Jevons, *Principles of Science*.]

361. Shew that, if *X* and *Y* are any two propositions containing a common term, then (*a*) *one* of the four combinations $XY, XY', X'Y, X'Y'$ will always form unstrengthened premisses for a valid syllogism; (*b*) either *only one* of the four combinations will do so; or, if two, the syllogisms so formed will be of the same mood. [RR.]

362. Two arguments whose premisses are mutually consistent but which contain sub-contrary conclusions are formed in the same figure with the same middle term. Find out directly from the general rules of syllogism what can be known with regard to the moods and figure of the two given arguments. [J.]

363. *Some M is not P, All S is all M.* What conclusion follows from the combination of these premisses?

Can you infer anything either about *S* in terms of *P* or about *P* in terms, of *S* from the knowledge that both the above propositions are false? [K.]

364. (i) *Either all M is all P or Some M is not P*; (ii) *Some S is not M.* What is all that can be inferred (*a*) about *S* in terms of *P*, (*b*) about *P* in terms of *S*, from the knowledge that both the above statements are false? [K.]

365. (*a*) "A good temper is proof of a good conscience, and the combination of these is proof of a good digestion, which again always produces one or the other." Shew that this is precisely equivalent to the following: "A good temper is proof of a good digestion, and a good digestion of a good conscience."

(*b*) Examine (by diagrams or otherwise) the following argument:—"*Patriotism* and *humanitarianism* must be either incompatible or inseparable; and though *family-affection* and *humanitarianism* are compatible, yet either may exist without the other; hence, *family affection* may exist without *patriotism*." Reduce the argument, if you can, to ordinary syllogistic form; and determine whether the premisses state anything more than is necessary to prove the conclusion. [J.]

366. "All scientific persons are willing to learn; all unscientific persons are credulous; therefore, some who are credulous are not willing to learn, and some who are willing to learn are not credulous."

Shew that the ordinary rules of immediate and mediate inference justify this reasoning; but that a certain assumption is involved in thus avoiding the apparent illicit process. Shew also that, accepting the validity of obversion and simple conversion, we have an analogous case in any inference of a particular from a universal, [J.]

367. An invalid syllogism of the second figure with a particular premiss is found to break the general rules of the syllogism in this respect only, that the middle term is undistributed. If the particular premiss is false and the other true, what do we know about the truth or falsity of the conclusion? [K.]

368. A syllogism is found to offend against none of the syllogistic rules except that with two affirmative premisses it has a negative conclusion. Determine the mood and figure of the syllogism. [K.]

369. Given two valid syllogisms in the same figure in which the major, middle, and minor terms are respectively the same, shew, without reference to the mnemonic verses, that if the minor premisses are contradictories, the conclusions will not be contradictories. [K.]

370. Find two syllogisms, having neither strengthened premisses nor weakened conclusions, and having M and N respectively as their middle terms, which satisfy the following conditions: (*a*) their conclusions are to be subcontraries; (*b*) their premisses are to prove that *Some M is N*, and to be consistent with the fact that *Some M is not N*. [J.]

371. Is it possible that there should be two syllogisms having a common premiss such that their conclusions, being combined as premisses in a new syllogism, may give a universal conclusion? If so, determine what the two syllogisms must be. [N.]

372. Three given propositions form the premisses and conclusion of a valid syllogism which is neither strengthened nor weakened. Shew that if two of the propositions are replaced by their contra-complementaries, the argument will still be valid, provided that the proposition remaining unaltered is either a universal premiss or a particular conclusion. [J.]

373. A certain proposition stands as *minor* premiss of a syllogism in the *second* figure whose *major* term is X. The same proposition stands also as *major* premiss of a syllogism in the *third* figure whose *minor* term is Y. If the given syllogisms are both formally and materially correct, shew how in every case we may conclude syllogistically that "some Y is not X" [J.]

374. Find out the valid syllogisms that may be constructed without using a universal premiss of the same quality as the conclusion.

Shew how these syllogisms may be directly reduced to one another; and represent diagrammatically the combined information that they yield, on the supposition that they have the same minor, middle, and major terms respectively. [J.]

375. Express the exact information contained in the two propositions, *All S is M, All M is P*, by means of (1) two propositions having S and *not-S* respectively as subjects; (2) two propositions having M and *not-M* respectively as subjects; (3) two propositions having P and *not-P* respectively as subjects. [K.]

Chapter 23

THE CHARACTERISTICS OF INFERENCE

376. *The Nature of Logical Inference.*—The question as to the nature and characteristics of inference, so far as its solution depends on the more or less arbitrary meaning that we choose to attach to the term "inference," is a merely verbal question. The controversies to which the question has given rise do not, however, depend mainly on verbal considerations; and the fact that they partly do so has increased rather than diminished the difficulties with which the problem is beset.

It will be generally agreed that inference involves a passage of thought from a given judgment or combination of judgments to some new judgment. This alone, however, is not sufficient to constitute inference in the logical sense. The formation of new judgments by the unconscious association of ideas is a psychological process which might be brought under the above description; but it is not what we mean by logical inference.

(1) It is, in the first place, an essential characteristic of logical inference that the passage of thought should be realised as such. The connection between the judgment or judgments from which we set out and the new judgment at which we arrive must be one of which we are, at any rate on reflection, explicitly conscious.

(2) But this again is not in itself sufficient. There must further be an apprehension that the passage of thought is one that is *valid*; there must, in other words, be a recognition that the acceptance of the judgment or judgments originally given constitutes a sufficient *ground* or *reason* for accepting the new judgment.

In logical inference, then, I do not merely pass from P to Q; I realise that I am doing so. And I apprehend further that the truth of P being granted, the truth of Q necessarily follows. For logical inference, in short, it is required that there should be a *logical* relation between a premiss or premisses and a conclusion, not merely a *psychological* relation between antecedents and consequents in a train of thought.

This distinction between the logical and the psychological may be briefly illustrated by reference to what are known as *acquired perceptions*. Psychologists are, for example, agreed that our perception of distance through the sense of sight or the sense of sound is not immediate, but acquired in the course of experience. Here then we have a case in which one perception generates another; but there is no conscious passing from premises to a conclusion, and nothing that can properly be called inference. Hence we must reject Mill's dictum that "a great part of what seems observation is really inference" (*Logic*, iv. 1, § 2), so far as the dictum is based—as to a large extent it is—on the position that a great part of our perceptions are acquired, not immediate. Here, as well as in connection with some of his other and more important logical doctrines, Mill is open to the charge of failing to distinguish between the *cause* of a belief and its *ground* or *reason*.

377. *The Paradox of Inference.*—The description of logical inference given in the preceding section leads up immediately to the fundamental difficulty which any discussion of the subject must inevitably bring to the forefront. We are in fact face to face with what has aptly been designated the "paradox of inference." On the one hand, we are to advance to something new; the conclusion of an inference must be different from the premisses, and hence must go beyond the premisses. On the other hand, the truth of the conclusion necessarily follows from the truth of the premisses, and the conclusion must therefore in some sense be contained in the premisses.

There may appear to be a contradiction here; and this view tends to be confirmed when it is found that the two characteristics of inference referred to are by different schools of logicians used in such a way as between them to deprive the category of inference of any content whatsoever.

On the one hand, by laying stress on the characteristic of novelty, we may be led to doubt whether formal inference of any description can properly be so called. For in all such inference the conclusion is implicitly contained in the premisses, and in uttering the premisses we have virtually committed ourselves to the conclusion. How then can we be said to make any advance to what is really new?

On the other hand, by laying stress on the characteristic of necessity, we may be led to doubt whether any inductive inference can properly be so called. For in such inference the falsity of the conclusion is not demonstrably inconsistent with the truth of the premisses. We may hold that if the premisses are true the conclusion *will be* true. But can we hold that it *must* be true, unless we also hold that in affirming the premisses we have virtually affirmed the conclusion too? And then we are back on the other horn of the dilemma.

This is not the place at which to discuss the difficulty from the point of view of inductive logic. We must, however, attempt a solution from the point of view of formal logic.

378. *The nature of the difference that there must be between premisses and conclusion in an inference.*—In order to find a solution of the difficulty, so far as formal inference is concerned, we must pursue our analysis further. We have said that the conclusion must be *different from* the premiss or premisses. But we have not yet asked what must be the nature of the difference or wherein it must consist; and it is on the answer to this question that everything turns.

If we consider two sentences we shall find that they may differ from one another from three distinct standpoints, representing three degrees of difference.

(1) In the first place, two sentences may differ from one another from the *verbal* standpoint only; that is to say, though different in the words of which they are made up, they may have the same meaning, and what the one is intended to convey to the mind may be precisely what the other is intended to convey. In this case, regarded as propositions and not as mere sentences, they cannot be said to be really different at all; for they do not represent different judgments.

This (to take an example from Jevons) applies to two such sentences as *Victoria is the Queen of England, Victoria is England's Queen*. It applies also to a statement expressed in a given language and the same statement translated into a second language, assuming that an absolutely literal translation is possible.

It has indeed been maintained by some writers that a difference of expression necessarily involves some difference of thought. But this at any rate appears not to be the case where one single word is substituted for another completely coincident with it both in denotation and in connotation (as thought by the speaker). Where one complex term is substituted for another (for example, *England's Queen* for *Queen of England*) there may no doubt be involved some change in the order of thought; but this does not necessitate any change of meaning in the thought considered as a whole. Again we ought perhaps not to say that the same proposition expressed in two different languages has absolutely the same mental equivalent, since a consciousness of the actual words of which a proposition consists may constitute part of its mental equivalent. But, as before, this makes no difference in the meaning that the proposition is intended to convey.

It should be added that when we have a judgment expressed in two different languages or in two different forms in the same language, there is (or may be) involved the further judgment that the two modes of expression are equivalent. A distinct issue is, however, here raised.[440]

It appears to me that there is here a failure to distinguish between two different points of view. We may no doubt draw an inference as to the equivalence of meaning of two terms or two expressions, where the whole argument is concerned with the meaning of terms or the force of expressions. Thus, to take (or, rather, adapt) another of Miss Jones's examples, we may readily admit that there is inference if a German argues that because the word *Valour is equivalent in meaning to the word Tapferkeit, and the word Bravery is also equivalent in meaning to the word Tapferkeit*, therefore, *the words Valour and Bravery are equivalent in meaning*. Again, a child or a foreigner may arrive by a process of inference at the equivalence of such forms as *Queen of England* and *England's Queen*. But in the syllogism given above the first premiss and the conclusion are statements of fact, while the second premiss is a statement as to modes of expression, its import being "The expression *Queen of England* is equivalent to the expression *England's Queen*." Hence there are more than three terms and we have not properly any syllogism at all. So far as there is inference in the case supposed, it will be something like the following,—"The form of words *Queen of England* is equivalent in meaning to the form of words *England's Queen*," therefore, "The judgment which is expressed in the form *Victoria is Queen of England* may also be expressed in the form *Victoria is England's Queen*." This is the inference, if any, that a foreigner studying the language would make; and it is very different from professing to pass from the judgment *Victoria is Queen of England* to the judgment *Victoria is England's Queen*.

(2) In the second place, we may have a difference which goes beyond mere difference of expression, and constitutes a difference in *subjective meaning*, though there may still be no difference from the objective standpoint. In this case we have two distinct propositions, not

---

[440] This issue is, I think, involved in an argument used by Miss Jones (in an article in *Mind*, April, 1898) in support of the doctrine that we have inference whenever we pass from a given proposition to another that is verbally different from it; for example, from *Victoria is Queen of England* to *Victoria is England's Queen*. The passage from one of these propositions to the other is, in Miss Jones's view, not indeed a formal immediate inference, but a syllogism in which an understood premiss has to be supplied: thus, *Victoria is Queen of England*, *The Queen of England is England's Queen*, therefore, *Victoria is England's Queen*. It may, Miss Jones adds, seem futile or even puerile to set out at length what everybody or nearly everybody knows without telling; but there may be cases (e.g., the case of a child or of a foreigner learning the English language) in which a reasoning of this kind has to be gone through.

merely two different sentences, and these propositions are the expressions of two different judgments.

This relation holds in my view between a proposition and its contrapositive; for example, between Euclid's twelfth axiom, "If a straight line meet two straight lines so as to make the two interior angles on the same side of it taken together less than two right angles, these straight lines, being continually produced, shall at length meet on that side on which are the angles that are less than two right angles," and the second part of the twenty-ninth proposition of his first book, "If a straight line fall on two parallel straight lines, it shall make the two interior angles on the same side together equal to two right angles." It cannot be said that in such a case as this we have any objective difference, any difference in the matter of fact asserted; but at the same time we hold that the two judgments to which expression is given are not to be regarded as identical *quâ* judgments.

To this distinction we shall return shortly from a more controversial point of view.

(3) In the third place, our sentences may differ not merely from the verbal and subjective standpoints, but also from the objective standpoint; they may affirm distinct matters of fact. As, for example, if one of them states that all potassium with which we have experimented takes fire when thrown on water, and the other that a piece of potassium with which we have not yet experimented will do the same.

Now in all three of these cases we have novelty, and the question to be decided is which of the three kinds of novelty is requisite in order that we may have inference. I hold the right answer to be that, for inference, *subjective* novelty is necessary and sufficient.

There is practically universal agreement that something more than mere difference of verbal expression is requisite for inference.[441]

Objective novelty is certainly sufficient, but is it requisite? It is affirmed to be so by writers of the school of Mill. This may of course be a mere question of definition; that is to say, inference may be defined *ab initio* in such a way as to require that the conclusion reached shall express some objective fact not contained in the data on which it is based. The matter being thus decided by definition, it follows without controversy that contraposition, syllogism, and other formal inferences (so called) are not properly to be spoken of as inferences at all. But there a good deal more than a mere question of definition involved. Those who demand objective novelty appear to hold that without it we cannot have more than mere verbal novelty. They overlook, or at any rate practically deny, the possibility of taking an intermediate course whereby we may have something more than verbal novelty, but something less than objective novelty.

Here then we have one form in which the point mainly at issue in regard to the nature of inference presents itself. Is it possible for two judgments to be different *quâ* judgments, although from the objective standpoint one of them states nothing that is not also stated by the other? Or, to put the question differently, can two judgments (or sets of judgments) be distinct as judgments although they are not logically independent, that is, although self-evident relations exist between them such that the truth of one of them involves the truth of the other?

I am ready to admit that it is no easy matter to draw a hard and fast line determining where mere verbal novelty ends and subjective novelty begins. Before attempting to deal with

---

[441] Miss Jones holds that verbal difference suffices; but this is only because she also holds, as we have seen, that we cannot have *mere* verbal difference, that is, difference of expression without difference of thought.

this difficulty, however, I will endeavour to shew that there undoubtedly are cases in which we have progress in thought without reaching anything that is objectively new.

Mill, after giving examples of so-called immediate inferences, says, "In all these cases there is not really any inference; there is in the conclusion no new truth, nothing but what was already asserted in the premisses, and obvious to whoever apprehends them" (*Logic*, ii. 1, § 2). Now it is certainly the case that in any formal inference the conclusion is implicitly contained in the premisses, and affirms no absolutely new fact. But it is one thing to say that a conclusion is virtually contained in certain premisses, and quite another to say that it is obvious to whoever apprehends the premisses. The identification of these two positions is one of the unfortunate consequences of taking simple conversion as the type of all immediate inference, and a single syllogism in *Barbara* as the type of all mediate formal inference. It may be difficult for anyone to apprehend that *no S is P* without at once apprehending that *no P is S*, or to apprehend the premisses of a syllogism in *Barbara* without at once apprehending the conclusion also. These cases will need discussion; but just now we are more concerned to point out that there are other formal inferences against which any similar charge of obviousness cannot be brought.

All the theorems of geometry are virtually contained in certain axioms and postulates, and if we can exhaustively enumerate the axioms there is in a sense no new geometrical fact left for us to assert. Yet no one would say that the whole of geometry is at once obvious to anyone who has clearly apprehended the axioms. We shall, however, deal with syllogistic inference more in detail in a later section. For the present we will in the main confine ourselves to immediate inferences.

In order to shew that the conclusion of an immediate inference is not always immediately obvious to anyone who clearly apprehends the given premiss, it may be pointed out that it is Euclid's practice to give independent proofs of contrapositives.[442] For example, the second part of Euclid I. 29 is the contrapositive of axiom 12. But it is impossible to suppose that if Euclid had regarded I. 29 as not really distinct from axiom 12, but merely as a repetition of that axiom in other words, he would have given an elaborate proof of it. The following are two other fairly simple examples of immediate inferences: *Where B is absent, either A and C are both present or A and D are both absent*, therefore, *Where C is absent, either B is present or D is absent*; *Where A is present, either B and C are both present, or C is present without D, or C is present without F, or H is present*, therefore, *Where C is absent, we never find H absent, A being present*.

In such cases as these, and they are comparatively simple ones of their kind, it cannot be maintained that the conclusion is at once obvious when the premiss is given. As a matter of fact, mistakes are not unfrequently made in immediate inferences of a still simpler and more elementary character.

379. *The Direct Import and the Implications of a Proposition.*—At this point a question may fairly be raised as to how we determine what is the explicit force of a given proposition, assuming the proposition to be clearly understood and fully grasped by the mind. This question is by no means easy to answer, and the difficulty which it presents is the source of the doubt which sometimes arises when we attempt to draw the line between immediate inferences and mere verbal transformations.

---

[442] See note 4 on page 136.

If immediate inferences are possible, we must be able to discriminate between the direct logical import (or *meaning*) of a proposition and its logical implications; and it must be possible to grasp fully the meaning without at the same time necessarily realising all the implications.[443] We may begin by distinguishing between (1) the content of the judgment actually present to our mind when we utter or accept a proposition in ordinary discourse or in ordinary reading; (2) the content of the judgment which on reflection we are able to regard as constituting the full logical *meaning* of the proposition; (3) the content of this judgment together with the content of other judgments which it logically implies.

(1) is a psychological product which may be, and usually is, logically imperfect; that is to say, it needs to be amplified if we are fully to realise the meaning of the proposition. Such amplification cannot be regarded as constituting inference. For, in making any inference, our starting point must be the proposition considered in its logical character. The inference comes in when we pass from (2) to (3). The question, however, arises as to how far the amplification is to extend if our object is to stop short at (2). In other words, where does *meaning* end and *implication* begin?

It has been pointed out at an earlier stage that in assigning to given combinations of words their logical import there is a certain element of arbitrariness. There is often a similar element of arbitrariness in formulating the fundamental axioms of a science, as well as in framing definitions. Thus, in geometry we cannot do without some special axiom relating to parallel straight lines, but we have some choice as to what the axiom shall be. Hence what is an axiom in one system may be a theorem in another, and *vice versâ*. Similarly, whether Q is to be regarded as part of the meaning of P, or as an inference from P, may be relative to the interpretation adopted of the schedule of propositions to which P belongs. Some illustrations of this point will be given shortly.

We have cited cases in which it appears clear that we have inference and not mere verbal transformation. But in most of these cases intermediate steps may be inserted; and if this is done to the fullest possible extent, the progress at each step may be so slight that it may not be at all easy to say wherein precisely the inference is to be found.

We must then proceed to consider the limiting cases in which there may be legitimate doubt as to whether we have inference or not. One of these cases is that of conversion. The question whether there is inference in conversion may be in itself, as Mr Bosanquet puts it, "a point of little interest" (*Essentials of Logic*, p. 141). Nevertheless, as a limiting case, it is not lightly to be put on one side when we are attempting to decide what fundamentally constitutes inference.

It appears to me that conversion is a process of inference if we are dealing with a schedule of propositions in which the predicative reading is adopted. In such a schedule the primary import of the various propositions involves a differentiation between subject and predicate, and to predicate P of S or to deny that P can be predicated of S is a different thing from predicating S of P or denying that S can be predicated of P. Moreover we may grasp the one relation without necessarily realising whether it does or does not involve the other. But in an equational system it is different. If two classes are affirmed to be identical it is merely a verbal question which is mentioned first, and we cannot consider that we have made any progress in thought when we merely alter the order in which they are named. It follows that

---

[443] Compare section 48.

we must consider that we have inference when we reduce a proposition expressed predicatively to the equational form.

In either schedule, contraposition (or a process analogous to contraposition) presents itself as an inference. In the one case, we have *All S is P, therefore, Anything that is not P is not S*; in the other case, $S = SP$, therefore, $P' = P'S'$.

Suppose again that we have an existential schedule, and that we start from the proposition $SP' = 0$ [*There is nothing that is S and at the same time not P*]. Here what corresponds to conversion is the passage to *Either PS > 0 or S = 0* [*There is something that is both P and S or else S is non-existent*]; and, what corresponds to contraposition is the passage to $P'S = 0$ [*There is nothing that is not P and at the same time S*]. Conversion, but not contraposition, now appears as a process of inference. It follows that there is inference when we pass to this schedule from either of the others, or *vice versâ*.

A further consequence to be drawn from the above considerations is that if propositions are given at random, inference may at the outset be required in order to adapt them to a given logical schedule, though as a rule this will not be necessary. This point has already been touched upon in section 48.

380. *Syllogisms and Immediate Inferences.*—In the above argument we have confined ourselves mainly to the consideration of immediate inferences. The same question in relation to the syllogism usually presents itself in a slightly different form, namely, whether every, syllogism involves a *petitio principii*; and we shall discuss it in this form in the following section. In the meantime, we may observe that if there is no such thing as immediate inference properly so called, then the claims of the syllogism to contain inference become very hard to maintain. For by the aid of immediate inferences the premisses of a syllogism can be combined into a single proposition, and the conclusion can then be obtained as an immediate inference from the combination.[444]

As an example, we may take a syllogism in *Barbara*:[445]

	All M is P,	(1)
	All S is M,	(2)
therefore,	*All S is P.*	

From (1),

	Everything is m or P,
therefore,	*Every S is m or P.*

Combining this with (2) we have
Every S is M, and also m or P; (3)
therefore, *Every S is MP* (since nothing can be *Mm*);
therefore, *Every S is P.*

---

[444] Compare section 207.
[445] In the argument that follows $m = not\text{-}M$, $s = not\text{-}S$.

All the above steps are immediate inferences, except the combination which yields (3). Hence, if we hold that syllogism is inference while so-called immediate inference is not, we must regard the whole of the inference as concentrated in the mere combination of two propositions into a single proposition; and this is hardly a position that can be accepted.

The given syllogism might also be reduced as follows:

From (1) it follows that *Everything is m or P*; (4)
and from (2) we get *Everything is s or M*. (5)
Combining (4) and (5), *Everything is (s or M) and (m or P)*;
therefore, *Everything is sm or sP or MP*;
therefore, *Every S is P*.

We may note in passing that if *elimination* is regarded as constituting the essence of inference, then in each of the above resolutions of the syllogism all the inference is concentrated in the last step, and this again seems paradoxical.

381. *The charge of Petitio Principii brought against Syllogistic Reasoning.*[446]—The objection to syllogistic reasoning that it necessarily involves *petitio principii* is of considerable antiquity. Thus Sextus Empiricus (*circa* 200 A.D.), one of the Later Skeptics, seeking to disprove the possibility of demonstration, urged, as one of his arguments, that every syllogism moves in a circle, since the major premiss, upon which the proof of the conclusion depends, requires in order that it may be itself established a complete enumeration of instances, amongst which the conclusion must itself be included.[447] The same objection to the syllogism is raised by many recent logicians, including Mill and his followers. "It must," says Mill, "be granted that in every syllogism, considered as an argument to prove the conclusion, there is a *petitio principii*" (*Logic*, ii. 3, § 2).

It may be said at the outset that the plausibility of the argument by which Mill seeks to justify this position depends a good deal upon a certain ambiguity that attaches to the phrase *petitio principii*. When the charge of *petitio principii* is brought against a reasoning, is it merely meant (1) that the premisses would not be true unless the conclusion also were true, or is it meant (2) that the conclusion is necessary for the proof of one of the premisses? It is clearly one thing to say that the premisses of a certain reasoning cannot be true unless the conclusion is true, and quite another to say that we cannot know the premisses to be true unless we previously know the conclusion to be so, or to say that the *proof* of the premisses necessitates that the conclusion shall have been already established. Only in the second of the above senses can *petitio principii* be regarded as a *fallacy*; and anyone who, seeking to prove that every syllogism is guilty of the *fallacy of petitio principii* merely shews that syllogistic reasoning involves *petitio principii* in the other sense, himself commits the fallacy of *ignoratio elenchi*.

In his systematic treatment of fallacies, Mill classifies *petitio principii* amongst fallacies of confusion, and quotes with approval Whately's definition: it is the fallacy "in which one of the premisses either is manifestly the same in sense with the conclusion, or is actually proved from it, or is such as the persons you are addressing are not likely to know, or to admit, except

---

[446] There is a very good discussion of this question in Venn's *Empirical Logic*, chapter 15. The reader may also be referred to Mansel's edition of *Aldrich*, note E, and to Lotze's *Logic*, §§ 98–100.

[447] Compare Ueberweg, *History of Philosophy* (English translation, i. p. 216).

as an inference from the conclusion" (*Logic*, v. 7, § 2 *n.*). This fallacy has been described as being a *fallacy of proof* rather than a *fallacy of inference*; that is to say, it arises when we ask how a given thesis is to be established, rather than when we ask what follows from a given hypothesis. We have to enquire whether every syllogism is open to the charge of *petitio principii* in this sense.

It is obvious that the answer to the question in the case of any particular syllogism depends upon the grounds on which the premisses are themselves affirmed; and we may begin by calling attention to certain cases in which the justice of the charge must be admitted, the conclusion of the syllogism being regarded as a thesis to be proved.

One case is when the major premiss is an analytic proposition.[448] For if M by *definition* includes P amongst its properties, I am not justified in saying of S that it is M unless I have already satisfied myself that it is P. The following is an example: All triangles have three sides; the figure ABC is a triangle; therefore, it has three sides.

A second obvious case of *circulus in probando* is where we seek to establish one of the premisses of a syllogism by means of another syllogism in which the ultimate conclusion itself appears as a premiss. For example,—*All M is P* (for *all S is P*, and *all M is S*); and *all S is M*; therefore, *all S is P*.

A third case, which for our immediate purpose is more important than either of the above, is where the major premiss is an enumerative universal, summing up a number of individual instances each one of which has been separately considered. For example, All the apostles were Jews; Peter was an apostle; therefore, Peter was a Jew. A universal proposition relating to a limited class, such as the apostles, is usually established by considering the members individually; and if the truth of a universal proposition could be established in this manner only, then the charge that syllogistic reasoning necessarily involves *petitio principii* would not admit of refutation. This appears to be assumed in the argument of Sextus Empiricus quoted above. It is also assumed in the following dilemma, which has been given as summing up Mill's doctrine: "If *all* the facts of the major premiss of any syllogism have been examined, the syllogism is needless; and if *some* of them have not been examined, it is a *petitio principii*. But either all have been examined or some have not. Therefore, the syllogism is either useless or fallacious," Mill's own argument may also be quoted: "We cannot be assured of the mortality of all men, unless we are already certain of the mortality of every individual man" (*Logic*, ii. 3, § 2).[449]

It cannot, however, for a moment be allowed that universal propositions admit of proof only by enumeration. Propositions that do admit of such proof are indeed generally speaking of little importance. The syllogism is chiefly of value inferentially where the major premiss is universal in the fullest and most unlimited sense, that is, unconditionally universal, expressing a general law dependent on qualitative relations. The true character and value of such a

---

[448] This case is noticed by Lotze, *Logic*, § 99.
[449] Bain (*Logic, Deduction*, p. 208) taking as an example the syllogism, "All men are mortal, All kings are men, therefore, All kings are mortal," asks "Supposing there were any doubt as to the conclusion that kings are mortal, by what right do we proclaim, in the major, that *all men* are mortal, kings included?" He then continues, "In order to say, 'All men are mortal,' we must have found in some other way that all kings and all people are mortal. So that the conclusion first contributes its quota to the major premiss, and then takes it back again." The reply to Bain's challenge is that if we are in doubt as to whether kings are mortal, we may resolve our doubt by shewing that kings belong to a class the mortality of which is admitted. The question then resolves itself into whether it is possible to establish the mortality of mankind in general without any explicit consideration of the particular case of kings.

premiss, though ordinarily written in the form *All S is P*, would be better brought out by the use of one of the forms *Any S is P*, *Whatever is S is also P*, *It is the nature of S to be P*, *If anything is S it is P*.[450]

The following may be noted as typical cases in which the grounds for accepting the truth of the premisses of a syllogism are quite independent of any explicit knowledge of the truth of the conclusion.

(1) The major premiss may itself be accepted as axiomatic, or it may be deducible (without the assistance of the conclusion) from more ultimate principles that are accepted as axiomatic. It has indeed been argued that a self-evident maxim cannot be used, or is at any rate superfluous, as a proof, because any conclusion that it might be employed to establish would be itself equally self-evident.[451] A consideration of ordinary geometrical proofs will, however, at once shew that this is not necessarily the case, and that by the aid of self-evident premisses conclusions may be reached that are certainly not themselves self-evident.

(2) The major premiss may be based on authority, or may be accepted on testimony; or it may be the expression of a civil law, or of a command, or of a rule of conduct;[452] and in none of these cases can it be in any degree grounded upon the conclusion.

(3) The major premiss may be an imperfect induction, based on evidence that does not include the conclusion. As an example, we may take the reasoning involved in testing the nature of a given substance in practical chemistry. In a reasoning of this kind our immediate starting point is general knowledge of the properties of chemical substances. This knowledge has been inductively obtained, but it is impossible that it should in the slightest degree depend on any antecedent acquaintance with the properties of the particular substance which is now to be investigated for the first time. Or, again, we may take astronomical inferences based on the law of universal gravitation. That law is an induction based on particular observations, but it implies an infinite number of facts that form no part of the evidence on which it is accepted as true; and many of these facts are in the first instance brought to our notice as inferences from the law, not as data leading up to it. If it is affirmed that, in cases such as these, the

---

[450] Sigwart holds that, in order properly to understand the value of the syllogism, we should take as our type the conditional (or, as he expresses it, the hypothetical), rather than the categorical, syllogism. We need, he says, but glance at any mathematical or physical text-book to assure ourselves that by far the greater number of propositions which are used as major premisses are hypothetical in nature, if not in expression. "Propositions such as 'two circles which intersect have no common centre' are hypothetical in nature; the proposition states the condition upon which the predicate is denied.... It is the same with the formulae of analytical mechanics; these and others of the same description are hypothetical judgments, and inferences are made in accordance with them by substituting definite values for the general symbols" (*Logic*, § 55). Sigwart perhaps attaches undue importance to the mere question of form. If our major premiss is unconditionally universal, and is understood to be so, it does not affect the character of the reasoning whether we adopt the categorical mode of expression or the conditional. Sigwart's reason for dwelling on the hypothetical force of the major premiss is to be found largely in the trivial nature of the examples that it has been customary to give of the purely categorical syllogism.

[451] Compare Bailey, *Theory of Reasoning*, p. 74.

[452] "We find," says Sigwart, "a wide field for our inferences in the application of general laws which have their origin in our will and are meant to regulate that will. In laying down a general rule of conduct, our will determines that there shall be a universally valid connection between certain conditions and certain modes of action. If we will the general law, it is logically necessary that we should will the particular actions prescribed by the law, if our will is to be constant and consistent, and valid for everyone who agrees in willing the general law. All penal codes in imposing a penalty of imprisonment for theft, of capital punishment for murder, lay down a series of hypothetical judgments which establish a universal connection between committing the crime and incurring the penalty. These judgments, moreover, may also be regarded as theoretical propositions in so far as they express the general obligation of the judge to give sentence in accordance with the law" (*Logic*, i. p. 337).

major premisses cannot legitimately be established independently of the conclusions syllogistically derived from them, then the validity of imperfect induction as a process of arriving at knowledge must be denied.

If asked to meet the argument contained in the preceding paragraph, Mill would doubtless refer to his doctrine of the function of the major premiss in a syllogism. The real proof of the conclusion of a syllogism, he would say, is to be found, not in the major premiss itself, but in the evidence on which the major premiss is based: the major premiss is nothing more than a memorandum of evidence from which the conclusion might be directly obtained: the intervention of the major premiss is often convenient, but it is not an essential link in the passage from the ultimate data to the conclusion. In reply, it may be said that there is at any rate a shifting of the ground here, and that Mill's doctrine, even if accepted, fails to justify the charge that every syllogism involves *petitio principii*; for it is admitted that the conclusion does not itself constitute any part of the data from which the major premiss is obtained. We must, however, go further and reject the doctrine on the ground that there are at any rate some cases in which the general law expressed by the major premiss is an absolutely necessary link in the argument. Thus, to take but one illustration, there are many consequences of the law of universal gravitation which it would be quite impossible to infer directly from the evidence lying behind that law without the intervention of the law itself.

Having regard then to instances such as those adduced above, we must reject the view that syllogistic reasoning essentially involves *petitio principii*, in the sense of *circulus in probando*. Any plausibility that the opposed view may possess depends upon some confusion between the statement that every syllogism is guilty of *petitio principii* in the above sense and the statement that in every syllogism the premisses presuppose the conclusion in the sense that they could not be true unless the conclusion were true.

The latter statement is applicable not only to syllogistic, but to all demonstrative, inference. The question may indeed be raised whether it is not applicable to all valid inference whatsoever. It is in fact one horn of the dilemma referred to in section 377.

At any rate it is a misuse of language to speak of a reasoning as involving *petitio principii* on this ground. By *petitio principii* is always understood a certain form of fallacy. But in making explicit what to begin with is merely implicit there is nothing that can by any stretch of language be termed fallacious. To say that all deductive science is nothing but a huge *petitio principii* is clearly an absurdity. The most that can be said is that in all demonstrative reasoning (so-called) there is really no inference from premisses but only the interpretation of premisses. So far as this is a mere question of language, it may suffice to note the paradoxical conclusions to which it leads; for example, that in the whole of Euclid there is no such thing as inference or proof. So far as it is not a mere question of language, it turns on points that we have already discussed, for instance, the possibility of there being an advance in knowledge subjectively considered although from the objective standpoint the conclusions reached contain nothing new. It is unnecessary to repeat the discussion with special reference to the syllogism.

Chapter 24

EXAMPLES OF ARGUMENTS AND FALLACIES

382. In how many different moods may the argument implied in the following proposition be stated?

"No one can maintain that all persecution is justifiable who admits that persecution is sometimes ineffective."

How would the formal correctness of the reasoning be affected by reading "deny" for "maintain"? [V.]

383. No one can maintain that all republics secure good government who bears in mind that good government is inconsistent with a licentious press.

What premisses must be supplied to express the above reasoning in *Ferio, Festino* and *Ferison* respectively? [V.]

384. Write the following arguments in syllogistic form, and reduce them to the first figure:—

(α) Falkland was a royalist and a patriot; therefore, some royalists were patriots.

(β) All who are punished should be responsible for their actions; therefore, if some lunatics are not responsible for their actions, they should not be punished.

(γ) All who have passed the Little-Go have a knowledge of Greek; hence *A.B.* cannot have passed the Little-Go, for he has no knowledge of Greek. [K.]

385. "It is impossible to maintain that the virtuous alone are happy, and at the same time that selfishness is compatible with happiness but incompatible with virtue."

State the above argument syllogistically in as many different moods as possible. [J.]

386. Give the technical name of the following argument:—Payment by results sounds extremely promising; but payment by results necessarily means payment for a minimum of knowledge; payment for a minimum of knowledge means teaching in view of a minimum of knowledge; teaching in view of a minimum of knowledge means bad teaching. [K.]

387. From P follows Q; and from R follows S; but Q and S cannot both be true; shew that P and R cannot both be true. [De Morgan.]

388. If (1) it is false that whenever X is found Y is found with it, and (2) not less untrue that X is sometimes found without the accompaniment of Z, are you justified in denying that (3) whenever Z is found there also you may be sure of finding Y? And, however this may be, can you in the same circumstances judge anything about Y in terms of Z? [R.]

389. Can the following arguments be reduced to syllogistic form?

(1) The sun is a thing insensible;
The Persians worship the sun;
Therefore, the Persians worship a thing insensible.

(2) The Divine law commands us to honour kings;
Louis XIV. is a king;
Therefore, the Divine law commands us to honour Louis XIV. [*Port Royal Logic.*]

390. Examine the following arguments; where they are valid, reduce them if you can to syllogistic form; and where they are invalid, explain the nature of the fallacy:—

(1) We ought to believe the Scripture;
Tradition is not Scripture;
Therefore, we ought not to believe tradition.

(2) Every good pastor is ready to give his life for his sheep;
Now, there are few pastors in the present day who are ready to give their lives for their sheep;
Therefore, there are in the present day few good pastors.

(3) Those only who are friends of God are happy;
Now, there are rich men who are not friends of God;
Therefore, there are rich men who are not happy.

(4) The duty of a Christian is not to praise those who commit criminal actions;
Now, those who engage in a duel commit a criminal action;
Therefore, it is the duty of a Christian not to praise those who engage in duels.

(5) The gospel promises salvation to Christians;
Some wicked men are Christians;
Therefore, the gospel promises salvation to wicked men.

(6) He who says that you are an animal speaks truly;
He who says that you are a goose says that you are an animal;
Therefore, he who says that you are a goose speaks truly.

(7) You are not what I am;
I am a man;
Therefore, you are not a man.

(8) We can only be happy in this world by abandoning ourselves to our passions, or by combating them;
If we abandon ourselves to them, this is an unhappy state, since it is disgraceful, and we could never be content with it;
If we combat them, this is also an unhappy state, since there is nothing more painful than that inward war which we are continually obliged to carry on with ourselves;
Therefore, we cannot have in this life true happiness.

(9) Either our soul perishes with the body, and thus, having no feelings, we shall be incapable of any evil; or if the soul survives the body, it will be more happy than it was in the body;
Therefore, death is not to be feared. [*Port Royal Logic.*]

391. Examine the following arguments:—

(1) "He that is of God heareth my words: ye therefore hear them not, because ye are not of God."

(2) All the fish that the net inclosed were an indiscriminate mixture of various kinds: those that were set aside and saved as valuable, were fish that the net inclosed: therefore, those that were set aside and saved as valuable, were an indiscriminate mixture of various kinds.

(3) Testimony is a kind of evidence which is very likely to be false: the evidence on which most men believe that there are pyramids in Egypt is testimony: therefore, the evidence on which most men believe that there are pyramids in Egypt is very likely to be false.

(4) If Paley's system is to be received, one who has no knowledge of a future state has no means of distinguishing virtue and vice: now one who has no means of distinguishing virtue and vice can commit no sin: therefore, if Paley's system is to be received, one who has no knowledge of a future state can commit no sin.

(5) If Abraham were justified, it must have been either by faith or by works: now he was not justified by faith (according to James), nor by works (according to Paul): therefore, Abraham was not justified.

(6) For those who are bent on cultivating their minds by diligent study, the incitement of academical honours is unnecessary; and it is ineffectual, for the idle, and such as are indifferent to mental improvement: therefore, the incitement of academical honours is either unnecessary or ineffectual.

(7) He who is most hungry eats most; he who eats least is most hungry: therefore, he who eats least eats most.

(8) A monopoly of the sugar-refining business is beneficial to sugar-refiners: and of the corn-trade to corn-growers: and of the silk-manufacture to silk-weavers, &c., &c.; and thus each class of men are benefited by some restrictions. Now all these classes of men make up the whole community: therefore, a system of restrictions is beneficial to the community. [Whately, *Logic*.]

392. The following are a few examples in which the reader can try his skill in detecting fallacies, determining the peculiar form of syllogisms, and supplying the suppressed premisses of enthymemes:

(1) None but those who are contented with their lot in life can justly be considered happy. But the truly wise man will always make himself contented with his lot in life, and, therefore, he may justly be considered happy.

(2) All intelligible propositions must be either true or false. The two propositions "Caesar is living still," and "Caesar is dead," are both intelligible propositions; therefore, they are both true, or both false.

(3) Many things are more difficult than to do nothing. Nothing is more difficult to do than to walk on one's head. Therefore, many things are more difficult than to walk on one's head.

(4) None but Whigs vote for Mr. B. All who vote for Mr. B. are ten-pound householders. Therefore, none but Whigs are ten-pound householders.

(5) If the Mosaic account of the cosmogony is strictly correct, the sun was not created till the fourth day. And if the sun was not created till the fourth day, it could not have been the cause of the alternation of day and night for the first three days. But either the word "day" is used in Scripture in a different sense to that in which it is commonly accepted now, or else the sun must have been the cause of the alternation of day and night for the first three days. Hence it follows that either the Mosaic account of the cosmogony is not strictly correct, or else the word "day" is used in Scripture in a different sense to that in which it is commonly accepted now.

(6) Suffering is a title to an excellent inheritance; for God chastens every son whom he receives.

(7) It will certainly rain, for the sky looks very black. [Solly, *Syllabus of Logic*.]

393. Examine the following arguments; so far as they are valid, reduce them to syllogistic form; and where they are invalid, explain the nature of the fallacy involved:—

(1) If you argue on a subject which you do not understand, you will prove yourself a fool; for this is a mistake that fools always make.

(2) It is not the case that any metals are compounds, and it is incorrect to say that every metal is heavy; it may, therefore, be inferred that some elements are not heavy, and also that some heavy substances are not elements.

(3) No young man is wise; for only experience can give wisdom, and experience comes only with age. [K.]

394. Examine technically the following argument:— Everyone is either well informed of the facts or already convinced on the subject; no one can be at the same time both already convinced on the subject and amenable to argument: hence it follows that only those who are well informed of the facts are amenable to argument. [J.]

395. Dr Johnson remarked that "a man who sold a penknife was not necessarily an ironmonger." Against what logical fallacy was this remark directed? [C.]

396. Examine the following arguments, pointing out any fallacies that they contain:

(*a*) The more correct the logic, the more certainly will the conclusion be wrong if the premisses are false. Therefore, where the premisses are wholly uncertain the best logician is the least safe guide.

(*b*) The spread of education among the lower orders will make them unfit for their work: for it has always had that effect on those among them who happen to have acquired it in previous times.

(*c*) This pamphlet contains seditious doctrines. The spread of seditious doctrines may be dangerous to the State. Therefore, this pamphlet must be suppressed. [C.]

397. Examine the following arguments:—

(1) A telescope with the eye-piece at one side of the tube is probably a reflector; Lord Rosse's telescope is a reflector; therefore, Lord Rosse's telescope probably has the eye-piece at one side of the tube.

(2) Good workmen do not complain of their tools; my pupils do not complain of their tools; therefore, my pupils are probably good workmen.

(3) If, on the one hand, the heathen, through want of better knowledge, cannot help breaking the Ten Commandments, then they do not stand condemned; if, on the other hand, they are condemned, it is for doing that which they well knew was wicked, and which they were well able to refrain from doing; therefore, whatever happens to them, justice is satisfied. [K.]

398. Discuss the nature of the reasoning contained, or apparently intended, in the following sentences:—

It is impossible to prove that persecution is justifiable if you cannot prove that some non-effective measures are justifiable; for no persecution has ever been effective.

This deed may be genuine though it is not stamped, for some unstamped deeds are genuine. [C.]

399. State the following arguments in logical form, and examine their validity:—

(1) Poetry must be either true or false: if the latter, it is misleading; if the former, it is disguised history, and savours of imposture as trying to pass itself off for more than it is. Some philosophers have therefore wisely excluded poetry from the ideal commonwealth.

(2) If we never find skins except as the teguments of animals, we may safely conclude that animals cannot exist without skins. If colour cannot exist by itself, it follows that neither can anything that is coloured exist without colour. So if language without thought is unreal, thought without language must also be so.

(3) Had an armistice been beneficial to France and Germany, it would have been agreed upon by those powers; but such has not been the case; it is plain therefore that an armistice would not have been advantageous to either of the belligerents.

(4) If we are marked to die, we are enow
To do our country loss: and, if to live,
The fewer men, the greater share of honour. [O.]

400. Examine logically the following arguments:—

(*a*) If truthfulness is never found save with scrupulousness, and if truthfulness is incompatible with stupidity, it follows that stupidity and scrupulousness can never be associated.

(*b*) You say that there is no rule without an exception. I answer that, in that case, what you have just said must have an exception, and so prove that you have contradicted yourself.

(*c*) Knowledge gives power; consequently, since power is desirable, knowledge is desirable. [L.]

401. Examine the following arguments, stating them in syllogistic form, and pointing out fallacies, if any:—

(*a*) Some who are truly wise are not learned; but the virtuous alone are truly wise; the learned, therefore, are not always virtuous.

(*b*) If all the accused were innocent, some at least would have been acquitted; we may infer, then, that none were innocent, since none have been acquitted.

(*c*) Every statement of fact deserves belief; many statements, not unworthy of belief, are asserted in a manner which is anything but strong; we may infer, therefore, that some statements not strongly asserted are statements of fact.

(*d*) That many persons who commit errors are blameworthy is proved by numerous instances in which the commission of errors arises from gross carelessness. [M.]

402. Examine technically the following arguments:—

(1) Those who hold that the insane should not be punished ought in consistency to admit also that they should not be threatened; for it is clearly unjust to punish anyone without previously threatening him.

(2) If he pleads that he did not steal the goods, why, I ask, did he hide them, as no thief ever fails to do?

(3) Knavery and folly always go together; so, knowing him to be a fool, I distrusted him.

(4) How can you deny that the infliction of pain is justifiable if punishment is sometimes justifiable and yet always involves pain?

(5) If I deny that poverty and virtue are inconsistent, and you deny that they are inseparable, we can at least agree that some poor are virtuous. [V.]

403. Detect the fallacy in the following argument:—

"A vacuum is impossible, for if there is nothing between two bodies they must touch."

[N.]

404. Consider the following argument:—

Granted that A is B, to prove that B is A. B (like everything else) is either A or not A. If B is not A then by our first premiss we have the syllogism—A is B, B is not A, therefore, A is not A, which is absurd. Hence it follows that B is A. [Professor Jastrow, in the *Journal of Education* February, 1897.]

405. Examine the following argument:—

It is impossible to prove that society can continue to exist without competition unless you can also prove that the absence of competition would not lead to the deterioration of individuals; for a society whose members deteriorate cannot long continue to exist. [M.]

406. Express the following propositions in their simplest logical form; examine their mutual consistency or inconsistency, and the validity of the final conclusion:— Some of Mr N's published views are new, and some true; in fact, they are all one or the other; and, though it cannot be maintained in general that a view that is not new is on that account necessarily not true, yet it can be confidently asserted that every possible false view on this subject was propounded by someone or other before Mr. N. wrote: from which it would appear that while it may or may not be that Mr. N.'s views are all new, it is certain that they are all true. [J.]

407. Examine technically the following arguments:—

(*a*)

"'Tis only the present that pains,

And the present will pass."

(*b*) All legislative restraint is either unjust or unnecessary; since, for the sake of a single man's interests, to restrain all the rest of the community is unjust, and to restrain the man himself is unnecessary.

(*c*) Only Conservatives—and not all of them—are Protectionists; only Liberals—and not all of them—are Home Rulers; but both parties contain supporters of women's franchise. Hence only Unionists—and not all of them—are Protectionists, while the supporters of women's franchise contain both Unionists and Free-traders.

(*d*) No school-boy can be expected to understand Constitutional History, and none but school-boys can be expected to remember dates; so that no one can be expected both to remember dates and to understand Constitutional History.

(*e*) To be wealthy is not to be healthy; not to be healthy is to be miserable; therefore, to be wealthy is to be miserable.

(*f*) Whatever any man desires is desirable; every man desires his own happiness; therefore, the happiness of every man is desirable. [J.]

408. Examine the validity of the following arguments:—

(1) I knew he was a Bohemian, for he was a good musician, and Bohemians are always good musicians.

(2) Bullies are always cowards, but not always liars; liars, therefore, are not always cowards.

(3) If all the soldiers had been English, they would not all have run away; but some did run away; and we may, therefore, infer that some of them at least were not English.

(4) None but the good are really to be envied; all truly wise men are good; therefore, all truly wise men are to be envied.

(5) You cannot affirm that all his acts were virtuous, for you deny that they were all praiseworthy, and you allow that nothing that is not praiseworthy is virtuous.

(6) Since the end of poetry is pleasure, that cannot be unpoetical with which all are pleased.

(7) *Most M is P, Most S is M*, therefore, *Some S is P*.

(8) Old Parr, healthy as the wild animals, attained to the age of 152 years; all men might be as healthy as the wild animals; therefore, all men might attain to the age of 152 years.

(9) It is quite absurd to say "I would rather not exist than be unhappy," for he who says "I will this, rather than that," chooses something. Non-existence, however, is no something, but nothing, and it is impossible to choose rationally when the object to be chosen is nothing.

(10) Because the quality of having warm red blood belongs to all known birds, it must be part of their specific nature; but unknown birds have the same specific nature as known birds; therefore, the quality of having warm red blood must belong to the unknown as well as the known birds, i.e., be a universal and essential property of the species. [K.]

APPENDIX A. THE DOCTRINE OF DIVISION

409. *Logical Division.*—The term *division*, as technically used in logic, may be defined as the setting forth of the smaller groups which are contained under the extension of a given term. It is also defined as the separation of a genus into its constituent species. These two definitions are practically equivalent to one another. *Division* is to be distinguished from the setting forth of the individual objects belonging to a species, which is technically described as *enumeration*.

In logical division, the larger class which is divided is called the *totum divisum*, the smaller classes into which it is divided being the *membra dividentia* (dividing members). By the ground or principle of division (*fundamentum sive principium divisionis*) is meant that attribute or characteristic of the *totum divisum* upon whose modifications the division is based. A given class may of course be divided in different ways according to the particular attribute or attributes whose variations are selected as differentiating its various species. Thus, having regard to the equality or inequality of the sides, triangles may be divided into equilateral, isosceles, and scalene; or, having regard to the size of the largest angle, into obtuse-angled, right-angled, and acute-angled. Again, propositions are divisible according to their truth or falsity, or according to their quantity, or their quality, and so on.

It is sometimes said that the principle of division must be present throughout the dividing members, though constantly varied. On the other hand, it is said that in division we invariably try to think of some attribute which is predicable of certain members of the group, but not of others. The former of these statements does not very well apply when we simply divide a class according to the presence or absence of some attribute (for example, candidates for the Civil Service into successful and unsuccessful) or when the attribute in question may be entirely wanting in some instances whilst present in varying degrees in other instances. In other words, given the attribute whose variations constitute our principle of division, we may have to recognise a limiting case in which it is altogether absent; thus, in dividing undergraduates according to their colleges, we may have to recognise a class of non-collegiate students. The second statement is always true when we simply contrast any given species with all the remaining species, and it may be considered adequate where we have division by contradictories. In other cases, however, it is inadequate; as, for instance, when we divide candidates who are successful in the Indian Civil Service Examination according to the province to which they are assigned.

410. *Physical Division, Metaphysical Division, and Verbal Division.*—Following the older logicians, we may distinguish division as defined in the preceding paragraph, that is, *logical division* in the strict sense, from other senses in which the term is used.

The division of an individual thing into its separate parts is called *physical division* or *physical definition* (Whately, *Logic*, p. 143) or *partition*; as, for example, if we divide a watch into case, hands, face, and works; or a book into leaves and binding. We have, on the other hand, a logical division if we divide watches into gold, silver, &c., or into English, Swiss, American, &c.; or if we divide books into folios, quartos, &c. Bain (*Logic*, II. p. 197) gives the analysis of a chemical compound as an instance of logical division. It is rather an instance of physical division. In logical division the *totum divisum* is always predicable of all the individuals belonging to each of the *membra dividentia*; for example, All men are animals, All squares are rectangles. But this is not the case in chemical analysis. We cannot say that oxygen is water, or that sulphur is vitriol, or that sodium is salt.

Distinct both from logical division and from physical division is the mental division of a thing into its separate qualities. This is called *metaphysical division*. We have an example when we enumerate the separate qualities of a watch, its size, accuracy, the material of which its case is composed, &c.; or when we specify the size of a book, its thickness, colour, the material of its binding, the quality of the paper of which its leaves are composed, and so on. A physical division can be actually made; a watch, for example, can be taken to pieces. A metaphysical division, on the other hand, is only possible mentally. It should be added that the metaphysical division of individual objects may be made the basis of a logical division of the class to which they belong.

One further kind of division may be noticed, namely, the division of an ambiguous or equivocal term into its several significations. This is called *verbal division* (Clarke, *Logic*, p. 331) or *distinction* (Mansel's *Aldrich*, p. 37). For example, we have to distinguish between a watch in the sense of a vigil, in the sense of a guard, and in the sense of a time-piece.

411. *Rules of Logical Division.*—The fundamental rules of logical division are (1) that the members of the division shall be mutually exclusive; and (2) that collectively they shall be exactly coextensive with the class that is divided. Thus if the class X is correctly divided into XA, XB, XC, the following propositions must hold good, namely, *No XA is B or C, No XB is C or A, No XC is A or B, Every X is A or B or C.*

The two following rules are generally added: (3) Each distinct act of division should proceed throughout upon one and the same basis or principle; (4) If the division involves more than one step, it should proceed gradually and continuously from the highest genus to the lowest species, that is to say, it should not pass suddenly from a high genus to a low species.

It may be objected that (1) and (2) ought not in a strict sense to be described as *rules*, but rather as constituting between them a precise statement of what is implied when we speak of a logical division. They become rules, however, in the sense that a professed logical division which fails to satisfy either of them implies relations between the members of the division which do not as a matter of fact hold good. Rules (3) and (4) are of a different character. They are rules in the sense that they must be complied with if a division is to have practical utility.

Rule (3) is not intended to condemn the processes of *sub-division* and *co-division*. Having made a division upon one principle, we may proceed to subdivide the classes thus arrived at in accordance with another principle, and so on indefinitely. A scientific classification will always consist of a hierarchy of classes thus obtained. There is again no reason why the same class should not for different purposes be divided in accordance with two or more different principles, so long as these are kept distinct from one another, and the members of the different resulting divisions not confused together.

It has been said that a breach of rule (1) necessarily involves a breach of rule (3), since there cannot be any overlapping of classes so long as a division proceeds correctly upon a single principle. This does not, however, always hold good unless we interpret the word "correctly" as implying that precautions are taken to avoid any overlapping, which of course begs the question. Thus, if we divide triangles into those which have (*a*) a right angle, (*b*) an obtuse angle, (*c*) an acute angle, we may be said to proceed upon one principle, and yet the resulting classes are not mutually exclusive. It may, again, be argued that the classes equilateral triangle, isosceles triangle, scalene triangle (which result from a division based upon a single principle) are not mutually exclusive, since all equilateral triangles are isosceles.

This argument can only be met by saying that, in the first case, we are not proceeding upon any clear principle unless we make our division into triangles whose *largest* angle is an obtuse angle, a right angle, or an acute angle, respectively; nor unless, in the second case, our principle is the *maximum* number of sides that are equal to one another, so that an isosceles triangle is defined as a triangle that has two and only two sides equal. Any overlapping of classes is then in each case provided against; but only, it may be argued, because special precautions have been taken to attain this end. By the adoption of similar precautions, a division which proceeds "correctly" upon a single principle will also be exhaustive.

Looking at the question from the other side we may note that a division which satisfies both rule (1) and rule (2) may nevertheless be a cross-division; for it may happen that two different principles of division yield coincident results. For example, an isosceles triangle being defined as a triangle that has two and only two sides equal, there is a cross-division, but no overlapping of classes, or omission of any class contained in the *totum divisum*, if we divide triangles into scalene, isosceles, and equiangular; or if we divide plants into acotyledons, monocotyledons, and exogens.

As regards rule (4), it is to be observed that a division which proceeds *per saltum* will usually be much less effective than one in which the intermediate steps are filled in. The worst violation of this rule occurs when the division is *disparate*, that is, when "one of the classes into which we divide is an immediate and proximate class, while others are mediate and remote" (Clarke, *Logic*, p. 242); as, for example, if we divide animals into invertebrates, fishes, amphibians, reptiles, birds, elephants, horses, dogs, &c.

Another rule of division is sometimes added, namely, that "none of the dividing members must be equal in extent to the divided whole" (Clarke, *Logic*, p. 236). When this rule is broken, the division is said to become null and void, because one of the sub-divisions contains no members. From the formal point of view, however, the observance of this rule can hardly be insisted upon. We need not regard a division as necessarily implying the actual occurrence of all its members in the universe of discourse; and the rule in question would deprive the logician of the right to employ the powerful method of division by contradictories. It may be a different matter when we are considering scientific classification from the material standpoint.

412. *Division by Dichotomy.*—Division by dichotomy or, as it is sometimes called more distinctively, *dichotomy by contradiction* is the division of a class simply with reference to the presence or absence of a given attribute or set of attributes; as, for example, when X is divided into *XA* and *Xa* (where $a = \text{not-}A$). An illustration is afforded by the Tree of Porphyry or Ramean Tree, in which Substances are first divided into Corporeal Substances (Bodies) and Incorporeal Substances, Bodies being then divided into Animate Bodies (Living Beings) and Inanimate Bodies, Living Beings being next divided into Sensitive Living Beings (Animals) and Insensitive Living Beings, and Animals being in their turn divided into Rational Animals (Men) and Irrational Animals. At each step in this scheme we proceed by taking contradictories. It was in praise of dichotomal division that Jeremy Bentham, who is here quoted with approval by Jevons (*Principles of Science*, 30, § 12), spoke of "the matchless beauty of the Ramean Tree." When this method is employed we ensure formally that the members of our division shall be mutually exclusive and collectively exhaustive. For, by the law of contradiction, *No X is both A and a*; and, by the law of excluded middle, *Every X is either A or a*.

It is pointed out by Spalding (*Logic*, p. 146) and by Jevons (*Principles of Science*, 30, § 9) that all logically perfect division is ultimately reducible to dichotomy, usually with the implication that some of the sub-classes which are *à priori* possible are not as a matter of fact to be found in the universe of discourse. Thus, if we take the class *X* and divide it into *XA* and *XB* we imply that in the class *X*, *A* and *B* are never found either both present or both absent. Hence the division is equivalent to the following dichotomal division:—

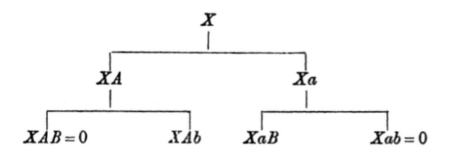

Any other division, however complicated in its character, may be reduced to dichotomy in a similar way. This is interesting and important and brings out the value of dichotomy as a method of testing divisions. It must be understood, however, that in speaking of all division as ultimately reducible to dichotomy, it is not intended to imply that dichotomy usually represents our actual procedure in making divisions. Each sub-class is usually arrived at immediately by reference to some positive modification of the *fundamentum divisionis*; and the different sub-classes are co-ordinate with one another. Consider, for example, the division of conic sections into parabolas, hyperbolas, ellipses, circles, and pairs of straight lines. It must be added that from the material standpoint, pure division by dichotomy is of little scientific value, because of the indefinite character of the sub-classes which are determined negatively.

413. *The place of the Doctrine of Division in Logic.*—The doctrine of division, as treated by the older logicians, receives little recognition by some modern writers on two very different grounds: (1) by Mill, taking the material standpoint, it is regarded as too purely formal, and hence is merged in the doctrine of scientific classification; (2) by some writers belonging to the conceptualist school, e.g., Mansel, it is rejected as not being sufficiently formal.

(1) It is true that the rules of logical division lead us a very little way in practical science. They give certain conditions which must be complied with; but they neither help us towards making good divisions, nor provide us with a test which is capable of being formally applied. Leaving dichotomy on one side, we cannot, without the aid of material knowledge, even determine whether the members of a given division are mutually exclusive and collectively exhaustive. When, however, we avowedly pass beyond purely formal considerations and take up a material standpoint, then the doctrine of division should rightly give place to a doctrine of classification, which is not content with such rules as those laid down above, but seeks to indicate the principles that should serve as a guide in the classification of objects scientifically.

In regard to the use of the terms *division* and *classification*, Miss Jones draws a distinction which is of value and to which it might be well systematically to adhere. "Division and classification are the same thing looked at from different points of view; any table presenting a division presents also a classification. A division starts with unity and differentiates it; a classification starts with multiplicity, and reduces it to unity, or at least to system" (*Elements of Logic*, p. 123).

(2) It remains to be considered how far any treatment of division whatever can properly fall under the consideration of formal logic. From this point of view division is usually contrasted with definition. The latter of these—using the phraseology of the conceptualist logicians—expounds the intension of a concept; the former expounds its extension. But the intension of a concept is said to be far more intrinsic to it than its extension. Given a concept its intension is necessarily given; but knowledge of its extension, such as may serve to determine its division, will require a fresh appeal to the subject-matter. "Division," says Mansel, "is not, like definition, a mental analysis of *given* materials: the specific difference must be *added* to the given attributes of the genus; and to gain this additional material, it is necessary to go out of the act of thought, to seek for new empirical data" (*Prolegomena Logica*, p. 192). For example, the division of members of the University of Cambridge into those *in statu pupillari* and members of the Senate could not be obtained without something more being given than the mere conception of a member of the University. Moreover, unless we proceed by contradictories, we cannot, when we have got our division, formally determine whether it complies with our rules or not.

The above position may be accepted, if an exception is made for division by dichotomy. Mansel, however, and some other logicians will not even allow that division by dichotomy is a formal process; and here they lay themselves open to criticism. The grounds on which their view is based are twofold:—(i) It is not sufficient that the genus to be divided be given; the principle of division must be given also. "Even in the case of dichotomy by contradiction the principle of division must be given, as an addition to the attributes comprehended in the concept, before the logician can take a single step" (*Prolegomena Logica*, p. 207). "The division of *A* into *B* and *not-B* is not strictly formal; for the dividing attribute, not being part of the comprehension of *A*, has to be sought for out of the mere act of thought, after *A* has been given" (Mansel's *Aldrich*, p. 38). (ii) We cannot tell *à priori* that both the sub-classes obtained by dichotomy really exist. How, for example, can we divide *A* into *B* and *not-B* when for anything we know to the contrary all *A* may be *B*? "Logically, the division of animal into mortal and immortal is as good as that into rational and irrational" (Mansel's *Aldrich*, p. 38). Both these arguments are summed up in the following quotation from Mr Monck: "It is alleged indeed that Logic enables us to divide all the *B*'s into the *B*'s which are *C*'s and the

B's which are not C's...... But Logic does not supply us with the term C and after we have obtained this term there are two cases in which the proposed division fails, namely, where all the B's are C's and where none of them are so. In either of these events the class B remains as whole and undivided as before; and whether they have occurred or not cannot be ascertained by Logic. This Division by Dichotomy, as it is called, is as much outside the province of Logic as any other kind of division" (*Logic*, p. 174).

As regards the first of the above arguments, there is no reason why the principle of division (A) should not be assumed given as well as the *totum divisum* (X). The question is whether we can then formally divide X into XA and Xa. The fact that A must be given as well as X does not prevent the possibility of formal division by dichotomy, any more than the fact that the conclusion of a syllogism is not contained in one premiss alone prevents the syllogism from being a formal process.

The force of the second argument depends upon the implication that all the sub-classes obtained as the result of a division necessarily exist in the universe of discourse. If this implication is granted, then dichotomy is certainly not a formal process; but why need we assume the existence of all the sub-classes obtained by dichotomy? Without such an assumption, our division may not have much practical utility, but its formal validity will remain unaffected. We have only to make it clear that we are dividing the *extension* of a term, not its *denotation*, in the sense in which extension and denotation have been already distinguished.[453] This is in keeping with the general standpoint of formal logic, which can deal with classes without regarding their existence as necessarily guaranteed in any assigned universe of discourse. If we are not allowed to apply the principle of excluded middle in formal logic and say *Every X is A or a*, until we know that there actually exist both XA's and Xa's, we shall be exceedingly hampered, and can make but little progress, especially in the treatment of complex inferences. Some schemes of symbolic logic (e.g., Jevons's) depend essentially and explicitly upon an antecedent scheme of dichotomal division.

We may then regard division by dichotomy as a formal process, but only on the understanding (1) that the principle of division is given as well as the genus to be divided; (2) that the division is not assumed to be more than hypothetical so far as concerns the existence of the resulting sub-classes in any assigned universe of discourse.

---

[453] See section 21.

APPENDIX B. THE THREE FUNDAMENTAL LAWS OF THOUGHT

414. *The three Laws of Thought.*—The so-called fundamental laws of thought (the law of identity, the law of contradiction, and the law of excluded middle) are to be regarded as the foundation of all reasoning in the sense that consecutive thought and coherent argument are impossible unless they are taken for granted. The function which they thus perform is, however, negative rather than positive. Whilst constituting necessary postulates, apart from which our thought would become chaotic, they do not by themselves advance us on our way. On the one hand, we cannot without their support proceed a step in reasoning; on the other hand, if we were to rely on their aid alone, thought would immediately come to a standstill.

This is at any rate the view taken of the three laws in the exposition that follows. It is true that many logicians have ascribed to them functions of a more positive character, and—starting from the position that they are the fundamental assumptions of logic—have gone on to regard them as the basis upon which alone all logical doctrine, at any rate in its more formal aspect, can be established. The attempt to justify this view has necessitated reading into the laws much more meaning than they can properly be made to contain, and their interpretation has in consequence become highly complex and even confused.

At the outset the question arises whether the laws are to be regarded as referring to terms (or concepts) or to judgments. My own view is that, in all three cases, the latter reference is the more fundamental, but that a reference of the former kind is involved secondarily. This I shall endeavour to bring out in dealing with the laws individually. The distinction is one to which considerable importance is rightly attached by Sigwart.

The question of the mutual relations between the three laws may be briefly touched upon before we proceed to consider the laws separately and in detail; it is not, however, a question that can be disposed of until a later stage. The main point to which attention may conveniently be called at once is that it is only in relation to the other laws that the full force of each of them can be brought out. The laws of identity and contradiction may be regarded as positive and negative statements of the same principle, namely, the unambiguity of the act of judgment; and the laws of contradiction and excluded middle are supplementary to one another in so far as between them they express the nature of negation. At the same time, an endeavour will be made to establish the independence of the laws in the sense that they cannot be deduced one from another.

415. *The Law of Identity.*—Following Sigwart, I think it most convenient to interpret this law as expressing the unambiguity of the act of judgment. Truth is something fixed and invariable. In the words of Mr. Bradley, "Once true always true, once false always false. Truth is not only independent of me, but it does not depend upon change and chance. No alteration in space or time, no possible difference of any event or context, can make truth falsehood. If that which I say is really true, then it stands for ever" (*Logic*, p. 133).[454] Hence, since a judgment is the expression of truth, the content of a judgment is fixed and invariable; and only when our judgments are so regarded can our thoughts and reasonings be valid. It is in this sense that the law of identity is a fundamental principle of logic (which is the science of valid thought and reasoning); for it is clear that if for a given judgment we were allowed—when it suited us—to substitute another, or if the content of a given judgment could be regarded as now this and now something else, all thought would become chaotic and reasoning would be a sham. Of the validity of no single step of reasoning could we be sure, since as we took the step the content of the original judgment might change, and on this ground it would be open to anyone to admit the original judgment and at the same time deny the inference attempted to be drawn from it.

It may be said that, as thus interpreted, the law of identity merely states that we cannot both affirm a judgment and deny it, and that this is what is expressed in the law of contradiction. There is force in this, to the extent that the laws of identity and contradiction may be regarded as expressing the positive and negative aspects of the same principle. It is, as Sigwart has said, only through the rejection of simultaneous affirmation and negation that we become conscious of the unambiguity of the act of judgment. At the same time, the positive formulation of the principle in the form of the law of identity—apart from its negative formulation in the form of the law of contradiction—is justifiable and helpful.

The unambiguity of the act of judgment may be expressed somewhat differently (and its positive aspect, as distinct from what is expressed by the law of contradiction, may thereby be made more clear) by saying that the repetition of a judgment neither adds to nor alters its force. On this basis we may perhaps justify the passage of thought which consists in the repetition, not of a complete judgment, but of part of its content only. In other words, we may thus justify formal reasoning, so far as it involves mere elimination; and in the majority of formal reasonings elimination is involved, though it may be questioned whether mere elimination from a single proposition (as in passing from *All S is MP* to *All S is P*) is by itself entitled to the name of reasoning at all.

Mill gives an enunciation of the law of identity which must be distinguished from the above: "Whatever is true in one form of words is true in every other form of words which conveys the same meaning" (*Examination of Sir William Hamilton's Philosophy*, p. 466). This is a postulate which it is necessary to make in connection with the use of language as an instrument of thought. So long as the judgment expressed is the same, the form of expression which we give to it is immaterial; and, since in logical doctrine we cannot explicitly recognise more than a limited number of distinct propositional forms, we have to claim to be allowed to substitute for any non-recognised form that recognised form which expresses the same judgment. Mill's postulate, however, goes beyond the law of identity regarded as expressing

---

[454] Compare what has been already said in section 50 about the universality of judgments. In particular, the bearing of Mr Bosanquet's distinction between the time *of* predication and the time *in* predication must be borne in mind. When we say that the truth affirmed in any judgment is independent of time, we mean the time *of* predication, and we assume that the judgment is fully expressed: in order that it may be fully expressed, the time *in* predication, if any, must be made explicit.

the unambiguity of the act of judgment, and it cannot be regarded as equally fundamental. It is sometimes given as the justification of immediate inferences: to this point we shall return.

We may now turn to the law of identity in the form in which it is more ordinarily stated, namely, *A is A, Everything is what it is*. This form is open to criticism if regarded as professing to give information with regard to objects. In another sense, however, it may be taken to express an unambiguity of terms or concepts which is involved in the unambiguity of the act of judgment. For it is clear that unless in any given process of thought or reasoning our terms or concepts have a fixed signification and reference, the unambiguity of the act of judgment cannot be realised. We have here the secondary reference to terms or concepts which is contained in all the laws of thought in addition to their primary reference to judgments.

As the repetition of a judgment neither adds to nor alters its force, so we may say the same of terms (or concepts), meaning thereby that to refer to anything as both A and A is the same thing as to refer to it simply as A. This yields Boole's fundamental equation $x^2 = x$ (which itself admits of a twofold interpretation according as x stands for a term or a proposition).

The reasons why we should not interpret the formula *A is A* as expressing a judgment respecting the object A have to be considered. The fundamental difficulty is that this so-called judgment is, if interpreted literally, not thinkable at all. For all actual thought implies difference of some kind. Whenever we think of anything, it is as distinguished from something else, or as having properties in common with other things, or at any rate as itself existing at different times. Hence in no case can we think pure identity.

There are two ways of avoiding this difficulty.

(*a*) We may say that what is intended by identity is not pure identity, but exact likeness in some assigned respect or respects, the likeness sometimes amounting, so far at any rate as our apprehension is concerned, to indistinguishableness except in the property of occupying different portions of space (as, for example, in the case of a number of pins or bullets of the same make and size). On this interpretation, the law of identity may be regarded as equivalent to Jevons's principle of the Substitution of Similars—"Whatever is true of a thing is true of its like"—or to the axiom that "Things that are equal to the same thing are equal to one another." Mansel indeed explicitly gives this axiom as equivalent to the law of identity.

It seems clear, however, on reflection that it is a misnomer to speak of these principles as laws of *identity*, and that at any rate they cannot be adequately expressed by the bare formula *A is A*. Nor can any analogous interpretation be given to the laws of contradiction and excluded middle. We must, therefore, reject this interpretation of the law of identity regarded as one of the three traditional laws of thought.

(*b*) We may attempt to evade the difficulty by explaining that by identity we mean continuous identity, as when I say "This pen is the same as the one with which I was writing yesterday." Here there is no longer pure identity, since there is a difference of time.

If, adopting this interpretation, we mean by the law of identity that what is true of anything at a given time is true of it at other times also, we have no self-evident law, but a fallacy. For the properties of objects are not constant. In other words, the possession by an object of any given property is not, like the truth of a judgment (fully expressed), independent of time.

We must then by the law of identity, as thus interpreted, mean to assert not any identity of properties, but the identity of the subject of properties amidst all the changes that may take place in the properties themselves. This may be regarded as a theory as to the nature of individuality and continuous identity in the midst of change, and is of great importance in its proper place. But it cannot properly stand as one of the traditional laws of thought which constitute the foundation of logical doctrine.

416. *The Law of Contradiction.*—The principle of contradiction is best regarded as expressing one aspect of the relation between contradictory judgments, namely, that they cannot both be true. The essential characteristic of a judgment is that it claims to be true. But we cannot declare anything to be true without implicitly declaring something else to be false. All affirmation implies denial; and we cannot clearly grasp the import of any given judgment unless we understand precisely what it denies.

The relation between a judgment and its denial is made explicit by the law of contradiction and the law of excluded middle, the first of which declares that two contradictory judgments cannot both be true, and the second that they cannot both be false.

It is clear that the law of contradiction, as thus interpreted, does not carry us very far, and that it cannot fulfil the function, which Hamilton assigned to it, of serving as the principle of all logical negation. It serves, however, to express the significance of negation, and at the same time to set forth (from a different point of view from that taken by the law of identity) a fundamental postulate which must be granted if our processes of thought and reasoning are to be valid. For validity of thought and reasoning demand that false judgments shall be refuted; and only by the help of the law of contradiction is any such refutation possible. The refutation requires that another judgment contradictory of the first shall be established; but this would go for nothing, if two contradictories could be true together.

The law of contradiction thus takes its place by the side of the law of identity as a first principle of dialectic and reasoning: not indeed advancing us on our way, but serving as a postulate, without which it would not even be possible for us to make a start.

We may pass to a consideration of the formula *A is not not-A*, by which the law of contradiction is more usually expressed. Here, as Sigwart points out, we have no longer an expression of a relation between two judgments, but an affirmation that in a given judgment the predicate must not contradict the subject; and inasmuch as denial and contradiction have primarily no meaning except in relation to judgments, this interpretation of the principle of contradiction can at any rate not be regarded as equally fundamental with that which we have previously given. At the same time, it is clear that if any *A* were *not-A*, then, understanding *not-A* to denote whatever does not belong to the class *A*, we should have two contradictory judgments, for we should be able to assert of something both that it belonged to the class *A* and that it did not belong to the class *A*.

The formula *A is not not-A* need not, therefore, be rejected, if its secondary character is recognised.

Mill's attitude towards the law of contradiction involves an apparent inconsistency. He begins by regarding it as a mode of defining negation.[455] It is, he says, a mere identical proposition that if the negative be true, the affirmative must be false; for the negative asserts nothing but the falsity of the affirmative, and has no other sense or meaning whatever. He goes on, however, both in the *Logic* and in the *Examination of Sir William Hamilton's Philosophy*, to speak of the law as a generalisation from experience. He finds its original foundation in the fact that belief and disbelief are two different mental states, excluding one

---

[455] *Logic*, ii. 7 § 5.

another, this being a fact which we obtain by the simplest observation of our own minds. We observe, moreover, that light and darkness, sound and silence, equality and inequality, in short any positive phenomenon whatever and its negative, are distinct phenomena, pointedly contrasted, and the one always absent when the other is present. From all these facts the law of contradiction is, in Mill's opinion, a generalisation.

Two distinct points appear to be involved in this argument. As regards the reference to belief and disbelief, we must agree that the foundation of the law of contradiction is to be found in the nature of judgment. The essential characteristic of a judgment is that it claims to be true, and the affirmation of a truth implies by its very nature a denial. It is, however, difficult to see where any generalisation comes in here.

The other point that Mill raises, namely, the fact that all our knowledge is of contrasts is a generalisation which is ordinarily known as the psychological law of relativity. The fact, however, that we cannot apprehend light except as distinguished from darkness, sound except as distinguished from silence, etc., cannot be regarded as equivalent to the law of contradiction. What that law asserts is, as Mill himself puts it, that "the same proposition cannot be both false and true."

Boole maintains that "the axiom of metaphysicians which is termed the principle of contradiction, and which affirms that it is impossible for anything to possess a quality and at the same time not to possess it, is a consequence of the fundamental law of thought, whose expression is $x^2 = x$." The law of contradiction is expressed in Boole's system in the form $x(1 - x) = 0$, where x may stand either for the truth of a judgment or for a term; and it is of course clear that $x(1 - x) = 0$ follows from $x^2 = x$. It will, however, be observed that the converse also holds good, so that the question as to which of the two laws is really the more fundamental remains open to discussion. Apart from this, any attempt to deduce the law of contradiction from any other principle whatsoever is open to the fundamental objection that unless the law of contradiction is accepted as a postulate no single step in reasoning is possible: for as soon as it is open to us to affirm a judgment and at the same time to deny it, it is *à fortiori* open to us to affirm a judgment and to deny any inference that may be drawn from it. To the question of the interdependence of the laws of thought we shall return.

It has been denied that the law of contradiction is a necessary law of thought, on the ground that not only do we often meet with self-contradiction, but that sometimes people have even boasted of holding contradictory opinions.[456] If, however, the law of contradiction is to be rejected, it must be shewn not merely that we sometimes contradict ourselves, but that we do so with perfect clearness of thought, and that we do not thereby stultify ourselves.

The mere fact of our holding contradictory opinions goes for nothing so long as the self-contradiction is not realised by us. In such cases it may be assumed that one or other of the contradictory doctrines will be given up as soon as the contradiction between them is made manifest. If the truth of both is still maintained, it will probably be found that there is some reservation—as, for example, by means of a distinction between different kinds of truth, one doctrine being held to be true literally and the other in some poetical or allegorical sense—whereby consistency is restored at the expense of ambiguity and want of clearness. Apart from some explanation of this kind, the problem of accounting for the way in which some of us appear to hold inconsistent beliefs is one for the psychologist rather than the logician. The ultimate explanation must be sought in confusion of thought, or lack of intellectual sincerity,

---

[456] Compare Bain, *Logic, Deduction*, p. 223.

or in these two causes combined. From a logical point of view to rest in an unresolved contradiction is to stultify ourselves and to confess failure.

417. *The Sophism of "The Liar."*—The sophism known as Ψευδόμενος or *The Liar* has been thought by some writers to present an exception to the universal applicability of the law of contradiction.[457]

"Epimenides, the Cretan, says that all Cretans are liars. He is, therefore, himself a liar. Hence what he says is not true, and the Cretans are not liars. But if so, his statement may be accepted, and they are liars. And so on, *ad infinitum*."

The solution is simple if we interpret the statement of Epimenides to mean merely that Cretans usually speak falsehood. Let his assertion then be understood in a stricter sense than this, and as meaning that Cretans are always in all things liars, that no assertion made by a Cretan is ever by any chance true.

Again the solution is simple if we merely suppose the assertion false. Epimenides here speaks falsely, but Cretans frequently or sometimes speak the truth. We are obviously confusing the contradictory with the contrary if we pass from the position that it is not true that Cretans are always in all things liars to the position that what a Cretan says must therefore be true.

The sophism is a little more puzzling if we begin by assuming it to be true that Cretans never speak the truth. Such an assumption contains no self-contradiction, and there is therefore nothing to prevent our taking it as our starting-point. This being so, let Epimenides make his assertion. Because it is true, here is a Cretan who has spoken the truth, and therefore it is false. Its own truth proves its own falsity. But, again, because it is true, Epimenides cannot be speaking the truth, and therefore it is false. Once more its own truth proves its own falsity.

The argument may also be put as follows. Assume it to be true that Cretans are always in all things liars, and then let Epimenides, the Cretan, make this assertion. Either he speaks truly or he speaks falsely. But if he speaks truly, it thereby follows that he speaks falsely; whilst, on the other hand, if he speaks falsely, he merely affords additional evidence of the truth of what he says.

The problem offering itself for solution is how an apparently valid argument can thus yield as its result nothing but a bare contradiction. The explanation is that we have commenced with premises that are implicitly contradictory, and that our subsequent reasoning has fulfilled its proper function in making the contradiction explicit. There is nothing self-contradictory in assuming that Cretans never speak the truth; but having commenced with this assumption, we cannot without implicit contradiction suppose a Cretan to make the assertion. In other words, the two premisses—Cretans are always in all things liars; and Epimenides, the Cretan, said so—cannot be true together.

418. *The Law of Excluded Middle.*—The law of excluded middle supplements the law of contradiction in explaining the nature of the relation between two contradictory judgments. The law of contradiction tells us that, of two contradictory judgments one or other must be false, the truth of either implying the falsity of the other; the law of excluded middle tells us that of two contradictory judgments one or other must be true, the falsity of either implying the truth of the other. It is only by the aid of the two laws combined that the meaning of negation can be fully expressed.

---

[457] Compare Ueberweg, *Logic*, p. 245.

Sigwart regards the law of excluded middle as a derivative principle dependent upon the principle of contradiction and another principle which he designates the *principle of twofold* (or *double*) *negation*. He observes that to interpret the nature of negation completely we must add to the principle of contradiction the further principle that the negation of the negation is affirmative, that to deny a negation is equivalent to affirming the same predicate of the same subject. To this further principle he gives the name of double negation; and it is, he says, only because the denial of the negation is the affirmation itself that there is no medium between affirmation and negation.

The deduction is as follows. Let $X = A$ *is B*, and $\overline{X} = A$ *is not B*. The principle of contradiction tells us that of the two judgments X and $\overline{X}$, one is necessarily false. It follows that one is necessarily true. For if I deny X then by so doing I maintain $\overline{X}$, while if I deny $\overline{X}$ then (by the principle of double negation) I maintain X. Therefore, the denial of both is equivalent to the affirmation of both, that is, it involves a contradiction. Hence there is no middle statement between affirmation and negation.

In criticism of the above it may be questioned whether the bare law of contradiction justifies us in passing explicitly from the denial of $\overline{X}$ to the affirmation of X. Sigwart's own statement of the principle of contradiction is that X and $\overline{X}$ cannot be true together. This enables us to pass from the affirmation of X to the denial of $\overline{X}$, or from the affirmation of $\overline{X}$ to the denial of X; but nothing more. There appears, moreover, to be a want of symmetry in Sigwart's treatment of the matter. He makes the law of contradiction yield (1) affirmation of X is denial of $\overline{X}$, (2) affirmation of $\overline{X}$ is denial of X, (3) denial of X is affirmation of $\overline{X}$; while the principle of double negation yields only (4) denial of $\overline{X}$ is affirmation of X.

All four of these relations are required in order that the nature of contradiction may be fully expressed; but unless we sum up all four in a single statement, it seems better to express (1) and (2) by means of the principle of contradiction, and (3) and (4) by means of a second principle, whether we call the latter by the name of the principle of excluded middle or by any other name. It will be observed that we can express (1) and (2) together in the form *Not both X and $\overline{X}$*, and (3) and (4) together in the form *Either X or $\overline{X}$*.

Sigwart's principle of double negation thus appears to express one-half of what is ordinarily expressed by means of the law of excluded middle; and its separate recognition may be regarded as unnecessary. I agree with Sigwart, however, in holding that the law of excluded middle does no more than help to unfold the meaning of negation.

It is not necessary to occupy space in discussing the relation of the formula *Every A is B or not-B* to the principle of excluded middle as above described. This formula expresses a secondary relation between so-called contradictory terms which follows from the corresponding, but more fundamental, relation between contradictory judgments.

For what is ordinarily known as the law of excluded middle, Jevons proposes the name *law of duality*.[458] This he does on the ground that the law in question asserts that at every step there are two possible alternatives, and hence gives to all the formulae of reasoning a dual character. The law of duality occupies an important position in Jevons's system of formal logic, which is based on the repeated application of the principle of dichotomal division. It may, however, be questioned whether, as thus employed, the law of duality ought not to include the law of contradiction as well as the law of excluded middle. It is as important at each stage that the alternatives are exclusive as that they are exhaustive.

---

[458] *Principles of Science*, 1, § 3.

419. *Grounds on which the absolute universality and necessity of the law of excluded middle have been denied.*—The universal applicability of the law of excluded middle has been more frequently denied than that of either of the two laws previously discussed. The denial usually depends upon a confusion between contradictory opposition and contrary opposition. It is said, for example, that there is a mean between *greater* and *less*. This is true; but the law of excluded middle does not exclude the possibility of such a mean. That law does not tell us that a given quantity must be either greater or less than another given quantity; it only tells us that it must be either greater or not greater.

Closely connected with this is the case where our inability (through lack of the requisite knowledge or power of discernment) to decide in favour of either of two contradictory alternatives is supposed to yield a third alternative; as, for example, where to the two alternatives "guilty" and "not guilty" is added the third alternative "not proven." "Guilty" and "not guilty," considered purely in relation to the supposed culprit, are true contradictories, and they admit of no mean. But "proved to be guilty" and "proved to be not guilty" are contraries, not contradictories; and it is here that the third alternative "not proven" comes in.

Some difficulty may also arise from ambiguity or uncertainty in the use of language. Thus it may perhaps be said that a prisoner may be neither "guilty" nor "not guilty," but "partially guilty." By "guilty," however, we must understand either "entirely guilty" or "guilty in any degree"; and whichever of these meanings we adopt the difficulty is resolved.

We may deal similarly with the question whether an action occupying a finite interval of time for its completion has or has not taken place when it is actually proceeding; for example, whether a battle has or has not been fought when it is half through, or whether the sun has or has not risen when half its circumference is above the horizon.

The difficulties which arise in such cases as these are really verbal difficulties.

Other difficulties arising from uncertainty as to the precise range of application of terms are partly verbal and partly dependent upon our imperfect powers of discrimination. We may perhaps hesitate to say of a given colour whether it is "blue" or "green," and therefore whether it is "blue" or "not blue." If, however, by means of the spectrum or otherwise we are able to determine quite precisely what we mean by "blue," the difficulty is obviated.

Mill remarks, on a different ground from any of the above, that the principle of excluded middle is not true unless with a large qualification. "A proposition must be either true or false, *provided* that the predicate be one which can in any intelligible sense be attributed to the subject. 'Abracadabra is a second intention' is neither true nor false. Between the true and the false there is a third possibility, the unmeaning" (*Logic*, ii. 7, § 5).

The reply to this is that the law of excluded middle applies only to propositions properly so-called, that is, to propositions regarded as the verbal expressions of judgments, a condition which clearly is not satisfied by a sentence (falsely called a proposition) which is unmeaning. If we define a proposition as the verbal expression of a judgment, then an "unmeaning proposition"—a mere fortuitous jumble of words that conveys nothing to the mind—is in reality a contradiction in terms.

By an "unmeaning proposition" in the above argument we have understood a so-called proposition which has no meaning for the person who utters it or for anyone else. To a given individual a statement made by someone else may be unmeaning because he does not understand the force of the terms employed; but this in no way affects the principle that the statement will as a matter of fact be either true or false.

Whilst, however, every judgment must be either true or false, it is quite possible that unsuitable questions may be put, the correct answers to which will be negative, but will be felt to be barren and insignificant because anyone who understands the meaning of the terms employed will recognise at once that the predicate cannot in any intelligible sense be attributed to the subject.[459]

Is virtue circular? This question is felt to be absurd; but it is not unmeaning. By saying that anything is circular we mean that it has some figure and that its figure is circular. If, therefore, the question of circularity is raised in connection with something that is immaterial, and therefore has no figure at all, the answer must be in the negative.[460]

This point may perhaps hardly seem worth raising. It helps, however, to explain how Mill is led to his denial of the universal applicability of the law of excluded middle. In his criticism of Hamilton's doctrine of *noumena* the question is raised whether matter in itself has a minimum of divisibility or is infinitely divisible. Mill's answer is that although we appear here to have contradictory alternatives, both may have to be rejected, since divisibility may not be predicable at all of matter in itself. In other words, the proposition that matter in itself has a minimum of divisibility is neither true nor false, but unmeaning.

It is to be observed, however, that "having a minimum of divisibility" and "being infinitely divisible" are not contradictories except within the sphere of the divisible. If a wider point of view be taken, the contradictory of "having a minimum of divisibility" must be expressed simply in the form "not having a minimum of divisibility," the latter including the case of "infinite divisibility," and also that of "the absolute inapplicability of the attribute of divisibility."

420. *Are the Laws of Thought also Laws of Things?*—On the view taken of the laws of thought in the preceding pages, the question whether these laws are also laws of things must be regarded as somewhat misleading. We have described the laws as postulates which are fundamental in all valid thought and reasoning, and we have regarded them as concerned essentially with judgments. Our results may be very briefly summarised as follows.

The truth affirmed in any judgment, when fully expressed, is independent of time and context. It is accordingly not open to us to accept a judgment at one stage of an argument or course of reasoning and reject it at another. This unambiguity of the fact of judgment is declared by the law of identity, and again by the law of contradiction, the one looking at the question from the positive, and, the other from the negative, point of view. Again, all judgment involves both affirmation and denial; and the force of any judgment is not fully grasped by us until we realise clearly what it denies as well as what it affirms. The law of contradiction, in conjunction with the law of excluded middle, has the function of making explicit what we mean by denial. The three laws may be expressed by these formulae: *I affirm what I affirm, and deny what I deny*; *If I make any affirmation, I thereby deny its contradictory*; *If I make any denial, I thereby affirm its contradictory*.

It follows that we cannot make any progress in material knowledge except in subordination to these laws. But at the same time they do not directly advance our knowledge of things. They are distinctly laws relating to judgments, and not directly to the things about which we judge.

---

[459] Compare section 85.
[460] Compare Bradley, *Principles of Logic*, p. 145. Mr Bradley puts the question, "When a predicate is really known *not* to be 'one which can in any intelligible sense be attributed to the subject,' is not that itself ground enough for denial?"

No doubt when it is said that the laws of thought are also laws of things, the laws are contemplated in what we have regarded as their secondary forms: *A is A*; *A is not not-A*; *Everything is A or not-A*. But even so it is difficult to give them any meaning regarded as real propositions. By "*A*" we mean "*A*" neither more nor less; and by "*not-A*" we mean "*that which is not A but includes everything else*." The laws do not profess to give any material knowledge, and their validity is in no way dependent upon material conditions.

The question raised in this section has in substance been already dealt with in rather more detail in special connection with the law of identity.

421. *Mutual Relations of the three Laws of Thought.*—If the validity of the ordinary processes of immediate inference is granted, it can be shown that the three laws of thought mutually involve one another.

Starting from the hypothetical proposition,

| If A is true then C is true | (i), |

we obtain as its (true) disjunctive equivalent,

| *It cannot be that A is true and C is not true* | (ii), |

and as its alternative equivalent,

| *Either C is true or A is not true* | (iii). |

If now for *C*, we write *A* we have the following set of equivalent propositions:

If A is true, it is true;
It cannot be that A is both true and not true;
A is either true or not true;

and these are expressions of the law of identity, the law of contradiction, and the law of excluded middle respectively.

It has been already shewn in section 108 that a similar result is obtainable if we write *S* for *P* in the following trio of equivalent propositions:

Every S is P;
Nothing is both S and not P;
Everything is P or not S.

These results indicate the close relations that exist between the three laws. But it is a mistake to suppose that we can regard one only of them as fundamental and the two others as deducible from this one. For the laws of thought stand at the foundation of all proof, and they must be postulated in order that the equivalences above assumed may themselves be shown to be valid.

422. *The Laws of Thought in relation to Immediate Inferences.*—Granting that the laws of thought stand at the foundation of all proof, it is a further question what inferences, if any, can be shown to be valid by their aid alone.

Hamilton claims that the law of identity is the principle of all logical affirmation, the law of contradiction of all logical negation, and the law of excluded middle of all logical disjunction. By logical affirmation we may here understand affirmation which can be based on purely formal considerations without reference to the matter of thought, and we may interpret logical negation and logical disjunction similarly. The three laws of thought are accordingly held by Hamilton to justify what we have elsewhere called formal propositions, according as they are affirmative, negative, or disjunctive respectively. The division into affirmative, negative, and disjunctive is, however, of the nature of a cross division; and the question arises where we are to place formal hypotheticals such as the following:—*If it is true that whatever is S is P, then it is true that whatever is not P is not S*; *If it is true that all S is M and that all M is P, then it is true that all S is P.* Apparently, since they are affirmative, they are to be brought under the law of identity; and inasmuch as the principle of any formal inference whatsoever may be expressed in a formal proposition similar in character to the above propositions, we find that Hamilton practically lays down the doctrine that in the three laws of thought (if not in the law of identity alone) we have a sufficient foundation upon which to base all logical inference.

This doctrine may, in the first place, be briefly considered with special reference to immediate inferences.

It may be granted that the process of obversion can be based exclusively on the laws of contradiction and excluded middle. From *All S is P* we pass to *No S is not-P* by the law of contradiction; and from *No S is P* we pass to *All S is not-P* by the law of excluded middle.

But it is a different matter when we pass to the consideration of the processes of conversion and contraposition; and it will be found that attempts to base these processes exclusively on the three laws of thought usually resolve themselves either into bare assertions or else into practical denials that conversion and contraposition are processes of inference at all.

De Morgan observes, "When any writer attempts to shew *how* the perception of convertibility '*A* is *B* gives *B* is *A*' follows from the principles of identity, difference, and excluded middle, I shall be able to judge of the process; as it is, I find that others do not go beyond the simple assertion, and that I myself can detect the *petitio principii* in every one of my own attempts" (*Syllabus of Logic*, p. 47).

The test that I should be disposed to apply to any attempted proof of the validity of the process of conversion is to ask wherein the principle involved in the proof makes manifest the inconvertibility of an O proposition, and the illegitimacy of the simple conversion of A. It is clear that we have no right to assume that any self-evident principles that we may call to our aid[461] are equivalent to the law of identity.

The following attempt to establish the conversion of A and of I by means of the law of identity may be taken as an example: "Every affirmative proposition may be considered as asserting that there are certain things which possess the attributes connoted both by the

---

[461] For example,—If one class is wholly or partially contained in a second, then the second is at least partially contained in the first; If one class is wholly excluded from a second, then the second is wholly excluded from the first.

subject and the predicate—the class *SP*. Hence the principle of identity justifies the conversion of an affirmative proposition. For if there are *S*'s which possess the attribute *P*, the principle of identity necessitates that some of the objects which possess that attribute are *S*'s." The law of identity is referred to here, but we may fairly ask in what form that law really comes in. Does the argument amount to more than that as thus analysed the validity of the conversion in question is self-evident?[462] Might we not for the words "the principle of identity necessitates" substitute the words "it is self-evident"?[463]

No doubt if immediate inferences are no more than verbal transformations, then they can all be based on the principle of identity as interpreted by Mill, namely, on the principle that whatever is true in one form of words is true in any other form of words having the same meaning. But if conversion (or any other form of immediate inference) is more than mere verbal transformation, the equivalence of the convertend and the converse is just what we have to shew; they are not merely two different forms of words having the same meaning.

423. *The Laws of Thought and Mediate Inferences.*—Mansel expresses the view that syllogistic reasoning—and indeed all formal reasoning whatsoever—can be based exclusively on the laws of identity, contradiction, and excluded middle. The principle of identity is, he says, immediately applicable to affirmative moods in any figure, and the principle of contradiction to negatives.[464] His proof of this position consists in quantifying the predicates of the propositions constituting the syllogism, and then making use—for affirmatives—of the axiom that "what is given as identical with the whole or a part of any concept, must be identical with the whole or a part of that which is identical with the same concept," and—for negatives—of the axiom that "some or all *S*, being given as identical with all or some *M*, is distinct from every part of that which is distinct from all *M*."

These formulae, however, go distinctly beyond the laws of identity and contradiction as ordinarily stated. They may indeed be regarded as equivalent to the *dictum de omni et nullo*, adapted so as to be applicable to syllogisms made up of propositions with quantified predicates; and if it is assumed that the dictum is only another form of stating the laws of identity and contradiction then the question needs no further discussion. Only in this case we must no longer express the law of identity either in the form "What is true is true," or in the form "*A* is *A*"; nor the law of contradiction either in the form "If a judgment is true, its contradictory is not true," or in the form "*A* is not not-*A*." The laws as thus formulated cannot be regarded as adequate expressions of the axiom upon which syllogistic reasoning proceeds. They do not bring out the function of the middle term which is the characteristic feature of the syllogism, nor could the rules of the syllogism be deduced from them.

Of course syllogistic reasoning, like all other reasoning, presupposes the laws of thought, and in the process of indirect reduction, which occupies a not unimportant place in the doctrine of the syllogism, these laws come in explicitly.

It is not necessary to consider in detail formal inferences belonging to the logic of relatives, e.g., *B is greater than C, A is greater than B*, therefore, *A is greater than C*. Here we require the principle that whatever is greater than anything that is greater than a third thing is itself greater than the third thing; and it would be still more difficult than in the case of the *dictum de omni et nullo* to evolve this principle immediately out of the three laws of thought.

---

[462] In so far as the argument is intended to amount to more than this, it contains a *petitio principii*.
[463] Compare, further, the discussion of the legitimacy of conversion in section 99.
[464] *Prolegomena Logica*, p. 222.

APPENDIX C. A GENERALIZATION OF LOGICAL PROCESSES IN THEIR APPLICATION TO COMPLEX PROPOSITIONS[465]

THE COMBINATION OF TERMS

424. *Complex Terms.*—A *simple term* may be defined as a term which does not consist of a combination of other terms. We denote a simple term by a single letter; for example, *A*, *P*, *X*. The combination of simple terms yields a *complex term*; and the combination may be either *conjunctive* or *alternative*.

A complex term resulting from the conjunctive combination of other terms may be called a *conjunctive term*, and it will be found convenient to denote such a term by the simple juxtaposition of the other terms involved.[466] This kind of combination is sometimes called *determination*; and we may speak of the elements combined in a conjunctive term as the *determinants* of that term. Thus, *A* and *B* are the determinants of the conjunctive term *AB*.

A complex term resulting from the alternative combination of other terms may be called an *alternative term*; and we may speak of the elements combined in such a term as the *alternants* of that term. Thus, *A* and *B* are the alternants of the alternative term *A or B*.[467]

In the following pages, in accordance with the view indicated in section 191, the alternants in an alternative term are not regarded as necessarily exclusive of one another (except of course where they are formal contradictories). Thus, if we speak of anything as being *A or B* we do not intend to exclude the possibility of its being both *A and B*. In other words, *A or B* does not exclude *AB*.

It is necessary at this point to consider briefly the logical signification of the words *and*, *or*. In the predicate of a proposition their signification is clear; they indicate conjunctive and alternative combination respectively; for example, *P is Q and R*, *P is Q or R*. But when they occur in the subject of a proposition there is in each case an ambiguity to which attention must be called.

---

[465] The following pages deal with problems that have ordinarily been relegated to symbolic logic. They do not, however, treat of symbolic logic directly, if that term is understood in its ordinary sense, namely, as designating that branch of the science in which symbols of *operation* are used. Of course in a broad sense all formal logic is symbolic.

[466] The conjunctive combination of terms is in symbolic logic usually represented by the sign of *multiplication*.

[467] The alternative combination of terms is in symbolic logic usually represented by the sign of *addition*.

Thus, there would be a gain in brevity if we could write a proposition with an alternative term as subject in the form *P or Q is R*. This last expression would, however, more naturally be interpreted to mean *P is R or Q is R*, the force of the *or* being understood, not as yielding a single categorical proposition with an alternative subject-term, but as a brief mode of connecting alternatively two propositions with a common predicate. Hence, when we intend the former, the more definite mode of statement, *Whatever is either P or Q is R*, or *Anything that is either P or Q is R*, should be adopted.

There is also ambiguity in the form *P and Q is R*. This would naturally be interpreted, not as a single categorical proposition with a conjunctive subject-term (*PQ is R*), but as a brief mode of connecting conjunctively two propositions with a common predicate, namely, *P is R and Q is R*. In order, therefore, to express unambiguously a proposition with a conjunctive subject-term, it will be well either to adopt the method of simple juxtaposition without any connecting word as, for example, *PQ is R*, or else to employ one of the more cumbrous forms, *Whatever is both P and Q is R*, or *Anything that is both P and Q is R*.[468]

425. *Order of Combination in Complex Terms.*—The order of combination in a complex term is indifferent whether the combination be conjunctive or alternative.[469]

Thus, *AB* and *BA* have the same signification. It comes to the same thing whether out of the class *A* we select the *B*'s or out of the class *B* we select the *A*'s.

Again, *A or B* and *B or A* have the same signification. It is a matter of indifference whether we form a class by adding the *B*'s to the *A*'s or by adding the *A*'s to the *B*'s.

426. *The Opposition of Complex Terms.*—However complex a term may be, the criterion of contradictory opposition given in section 40 must still apply: "A pair of contradictory terms are so related that between them they exhaust the entire universe to which reference is made, whilst in that universe there is no individual of which both can be affirmed at the same time." In what follows it will be found convenient to denote the contradictory of any simple term by the corresponding small letter. Thus for *not-A* we may write *a*, and for *not-B* we may write *b*.

Now whatever is not *AB* must be either *a* or *b*, whilst nothing that is *AB* can be either *a* or *b*. Hence

$$\begin{cases} AB, \\ a \text{ or } b, \end{cases}$$

constitute a pair of contradictories. Similarly,

$$\begin{cases} A \text{ or } B, \\ ab, \end{cases}$$

---

[468] It will be observed that both in this case and in the case of *or*, we get rid of the ambiguity by making the words occur in the predicate of a subordinate sentence. Mr Johnson expresses the substance of the last three paragraphs in the text by pointing out that "common speech adopts the convention: *Subjects are externally synthesised and predicates are internally synthesised*" (*Mind*, 1892, p. 239). In other words, *and* and *or* occurring in a predicate are understood as expressing a conjunctive or an alternative *term*; but occurring in a subject they are understood as expressing a conjunctive or an alternative *proposition*.

[469] This is sometimes spoken of as the law of *commutativeness*. Compare Boole, *Laws of Thought*, p. 31, and Jevons, *Principles of Science*, 2, § 8.

are a pair of contradictories. And the same will hold good if *A* and *B* stand for terms which are already themselves complex (although relatively simple as compared with *AB* or *A or B*).

If, then, two terms are conjunctively combined into a complex term (of which they will constitute the determinants), the contradictory of this complex term is found by alternatively combining the contradictories of the two determinants. And, conversely, if two terms are alternatively combined into a complex term (of which they will constitute the alternants), the contradictory of this complex term is found conjunctively combining the contradictories of the two alternants.

In each case, we substitute for the relatively simple terms involved their contradictories, and (as the case may be) change conjunctive combination into alternative combination, or alternative combination into conjunctive combination.

But whatever degree of complexity a term may reach, it will consist of a series of conjunctive and alternative combinations; and it may be successively resolved into the combination of pairs of relatively simple terms till it is at last shewn to result from the combination of absolutely simple terms. For example,—*ABC or DE or FG* results from the alternative combination of *ABC or DE* with *FG*; *ABC or DE* results from the alternative combination of *ABC* with *DE*; *FG* results from the conjunctive combination of *F* with *G*; and *ABC, DE* may be resolved similarly.

Hence the successive application of the above rule, for finding the contradictory of a complex term where we are dealing with a single pair of determinants or alternants, will result in our ultimately substituting for each simple term involved its contradictory, and reversing the nature of their combination throughout.[470] We may, therefore, lay down the following rule for obtaining the contradictory of any complex term: *Replace each constituent simple term by its contradictory and throughout substitute conjunctive combination for alternative combination* and vice versâ.[471] This rule is of simple application, and it is of fundamental importance in the treatment of complex propositions adopted in the following pages.

Thus, the contradictory of *A or BC*

is *a and (b or c)*,
i.e., *ab or ac*;

and the contradictory of *ABC or ABD* is (*a or b or c*) *and* (*a or b or d*), which, by the aid of rules presently to be given, is reducible to the form *a or b or cd*.

It is possible for two complex terms to be formally *inconsistent* or *repugnant* without being true contradictories. This will be the case if they contain contradictory determinants without between them exhausting the universe of discourse. The terms *AB* and *bC* afford an example: nothing can be both *AB* and *bC* (for, if this were so, something would be both *B* and

---

[470] Thus, taking the term *ABC or DE or FG*, and in the first instance denoting the contradictory of a complex term by a bar drawn across it, we have successively,—

	ABC or DE or FG
=	ABC (DE or FG)
=	(AB or c) DE . FG
=	(a or b or c) (d or e) (f or g).

[471] Compare Schröder, *Der Operationskreis des Logikkalkuls*, p. 18.

not-B), but we cannot say *à priori* that everything is either *AB* or *bC* (since something may be *Abc*, which is neither *AB* nor *bC*).

427. *Duality of Formal Equivalences in the case of Complex Terms.*—It will be shown in the following sections that certain complex terms are formally equivalent to other complex terms or to simple terms (for example, *A or aB = A or B*, *A or AB = A*); and it is important to notice at the outset that such formal equivalences always go in pairs. For if two terms are equivalent, their contradictories must also be equivalent; and hence, applying the rule for obtaining contradictories given in the preceding section, we are enabled to formulate the simple law that *to every formal equivalence there corresponds another formal equivalence in which conjunctive combination is throughout substituted for alternative combination and* vice versâ.[472] This law may be more precisely established as follows:—A formal equivalence that holds good for any given set of terms must equally hold good for any other set of terms; and, therefore, whatever holds good for the terms *A*, *B*, &c. must hold good for their contradictories *a*, *b*, &c. Hence, given any equivalence, we may first replace each simple term by its contradictory, and then take the contradictory of each side of the equivalence. The result of this double transformation will be that we shall obtain another equivalence in which every conjunctive combination has been replaced by an alternative combination, and conversely, while the term-symbols involved have remained unchanged. This proves what was required.

The application of the above law will be fully illustrated in the sections that immediately follow.

428. *Laws of Distribution.*—In order to combine a simple term conjunctively with an alternative term, we must conjunctively combine it with every alternant of the alternative.[473] *A and (B or C)*[474] denotes whatever is *A* and at the same time either *B* or *C*, and hence is equivalent to *AB or AC*. It follows that in order to combine two alternative terms conjunctively, we must conjunctively combine every alternant of the one with every alternant of the other. Thus, *(A or B)(C or D)* denotes whatever is either *A* or *B* and at the same time either *C* or *D*, and is equivalent to *AC or AD or BC or BD*.[475]

We have then

A(B or C) = AB or AC,

and applying the law of duality of formal equivalences given in the preceding section, we have at once another equivalence, namely,

A or BC = (A or B)(A or C).[476]

---

[472] This is pointed out by Schröder, *Der Operationskreis des Logikkalkuls*, p. 3. The two equivalences which are thus mutually deducible the one from the other may be said to be *reciprocal*.
[473] Compare Jevons, *Principles of Science*, 5, § 7.
[474] In such a case as this the use of brackets is necessary in order to avoid ambiguity. Thus, *A and B or C* might mean *AB or C*, or as above *AB or AC*.
[475] Whether or not we introduce algebraic symbols into logic, there is here a very close analogy with algebraic multiplication which cannot be disguised.
[476] This equivalence might also be established independently by the aid of certain of the equivalences given in the following sections.

Appendix C. A Generalization of Logical Processes... 335

These two equivalences are called by Schröder the *Laws of Distribution*.[477] They are of the greatest importance in the manipulation and simplification of complex terms.

429. *Laws of Tautology.*—The following rules may be laid down for the omission of superfluous terms from a complex term:

(*a*) *The repetition of any given determinant is superfluous.*

Out of the class *A* to select the *A*'s is a process that leaves us just where we began. In other words, what is both *A* and *A* is identical with what is *A*. Thus, such terms as *AA*, *ABB*, are tautologous; the former merely denotes the class *A*, and the latter the class *AB*. Hence the above rule, which is called by Jevons the *Law of Simplicity*.[478]

(*b*) *The repetition of any given alternant is superfluous.*

To say that anything is *A* or *A* is equivalent to saying simply that it is *A*. Hence such terms as *A* or *A*, *A* or *BC* or *BC*, are tautologous; and we have the above rule, which is called by Jevons the *Law of Unity*.[479]

It will be seen by reference to the rule given in section 427 that the Law of Simplicity (*AA* = *A*) and the Law of Unity (*A* or *A* = *A*) are reciprocal; that is, the former is deducible from the latter and *vice versâ*. For the only difference between them is that conjunctive combination in the one is replaced by alternative combination in the other.[480]

430. *Laws of Development and Reduction.*—Important formal equivalences are yielded by the laws of contradiction and excluded middle.

By the law of contradiction a term containing contradictory determinants (for example, *Bb*) cannot represent any existing class. Hence *A* or *Bb* is equivalent to *A* simply; in other words, the *conjunctive combination of contradictories* may be indifferently introduced or omitted as an *alternant*.

Again, by the law of excluded middle a term containing contradictory alternants (for example, *B* or *b*) represents the entire universe of discourse. Hence *A* (*B* or *b*) is equivalent to *A* simply; in other words, the *alternative combination of contradictories* may be indifferently introduced or omitted as a *determinant*.

It will be observed that the above equivalences, namely,

A or *Bb* = *A*,
A (*B* or *b*) = *A*,

are reciprocal.

Applying further the Laws of Distribution given in section 428 we have the following:

A = *A* or *Bb* = (*A* or *B*) (*A* or *b*),
A = *A* (*B* or *b*) = *AB* or *Ab*.

---

[477] *Der Operationskreis des Logikkalkuls*, pp. 9, 10.
[478] See *Pure Logic*, § 42; and *Principles of Science*, 2, § 8. The corresponding equation $x^2 = x$ is in Boole's system fundamental; see *Laws of Thought*, p. 31.
[479] See *Pure Logic*, § 69; and *Principles of Science*, 5, § 4.
[480] It may assist the reader in following the reasoning in section 427 if we work through this particular case independently. If *AA* = *A*, then *aa* = *a*, for whatever is formally valid in the case of *A* must also be formally valid in the case of any other term. But if two terms are equivalent their contradictories must be equivalent. Hence from *aa* = *a*, it follows that *A* or *A* = *A*. And it is clear that we might pass similarly from *A* or *A* = *A* to *AA* = *A*.

These may be taken as formulae for the *development* and the *reduction* of terms. Thus, the substitution of (*A or B*) (*A or b*) for *A* may be called the *development of a term by means of the law of contradiction*; and the substitution of *AB or Ab* for *A* the *development of a term by means of the law of excluded middle*. In both the above cases the term *A* is developed with reference to the term *B*. Similarly by developing *A* with reference to *B* and *C*, we should have (*A or B or C*) (*A or B or c*) (*A or b or C*) (*A or B or c*) if we make use of the law of contradiction, or *ABC or ABc or AbC or Abc* if we make use of the law of excluded middle. Development by means of the law of excluded middle is the more useful of the two processes in the manipulation of complex terms, and it may be understood that this is meant when the development of a term is spoken of without further qualification.

Conversely, the process of passing from (*A or B*) (*A or b*) to *A*, or from *AB or Ab* to *A*, may be called the *reduction of a term* by means of the law of contradiction or the law of excluded middle, as the case may be.

Following Jevons, we may speak of an alternative term of the type *AB or Ab* as a dual term, and of the substitution of *A* for *AB or Ab* as the *reduction of a dual term*.[481]

431. *Laws of Absorption.*—It may be shown that any alternant which is merely a subdivision of another alternant may be indifferently introduced or omitted from a complex term. Thus, *AB* being a subdivision of *A*, the terms *A or AB* and *A* are equivalent. This rule (which is called by Schröder the *Law of Absorption*[482]) may be established as follows: By the development of *A* with reference to *B*, *A or AB* becomes *AB or Ab or AB*; but, by the law of unity, this is equivalent to *AB or Ab*; and by reduction this is equivalent to *A*.

Applying the rule given in section 427 we obtain a second law of absorption, namely, *A* (*A or B*) = *A*, which is the reciprocal of the first law of absorption, *A or AB* = *A*.

432. *Laws of Exclusion and Inclusion.*—The contradictory of any alternant in a complex term may be indifferently introduced or omitted as a determinant of any other alternant; that is to say, the terms *A or aB* and *A or B* are equivalent. This may be established as follows: By the law of absorption *A or aB* is equivalent to *A or AB or aB*, and by reduction this yields *A or B*. The above equivalence may be called the *Law of Exclusion* on the ground that by passing from *A or B* to *A or aB* we make the alternants mutually exclusive.

The reciprocal equivalence *A* (*a or B*) = *AB* may be expressed as follows: The contradictory of any determinant in a complex term may be indifferently introduced or omitted as an alternant of any other determinant. This equivalence may be called the *Law of Inclusion* on the ground that by passing from *AB* to *A* (*a or B*) we make the determinants collectively inclusive of the entire universe of discourse.

433. *Summary of Formal Equivalences of Complex Terms.*—The following is a summary of the formal equivalences contained in the five preceding sections (those that are bracketed together being in each case related to one another reciprocally in the manner indicated in section 427):—

---

[481] *Pure Logic*, § 103. The conjunctive term (*A or B*) (*A or b*) may also be spoken of as a dual term, and its reduction to *A* as the reduction of a dual term.
[482] *Der Operationskreis des Logikkalkuls*, p. 12. This Law of Absorption is equivalent to one of Boole's "Methods of Abbreviation" (*Laws of Thought*, p. 130). Compare, also, Jevons, *Pure Logic*, § 70.

(1)	$A(B \text{ or } C) = AB \text{ or } AC$,	}	*Laws of Distribution*;
(2)	$A \text{ or } BC = (A \text{ or } B)(A \text{ or } C)$,	}	
(3)	$AA = A$,	}	*Laws of Tautology* (*Law of Simplicity*
(4)	$A \text{ or } A = A$,	}	*and Law of Unity*);
(5)	$A = A \text{ or } Bb = (A \text{ or } B)(A \text{ or } b)$,	}	*Laws of Development and Reduction*;
(6)	$A = A(B \text{ or } b) = AB \text{ or } Ab$,	}	
(7)	$A \text{ or } AB = A$,	}	*Laws of Absorption*;
(8)	$A(A \text{ or } B) = A$,	}	
(9)	$A \text{ or } B = A \text{ or } aB$,	}	*Law of Exclusion and Law of Inclusion.*
(10)	$AB = A(a \text{ or } B)$,	}	

434. *The Conjunctive Combination of Alternative Terms.*—The first law of distribution gives the general rule for the conjunctive combination of alternatives. But with a view to such combination special attention may be called (i) to the second law of distribution, namely, (*A or B*) (*A or C*) = *A or BC*; and (ii) to the equivalence (*A or B*) (*AC or D*) = *AC or AD or BD*, which may be established as follows: By the first law of distribution (*A or B*) (*AC or D*) is equivalent to *AAC or ABC or AD or BD*; but by the law of simplicity *AAC = AC*, and by the law of absorption *AC or ABC = AC*; hence our original term is equivalent to *AC or AD or BD*, which was to be proved.

From the above equivalences we obtain the two following practical rules which are of great assistance in simplifying the process of conjunctively combining alternatives:

(1) If two alternatives which are to be conjunctively combined have an alternant in common, this alternant may be at once written down as one alternant of the result, and we need not go through the form of combining it with any of the remaining alternants of either alternative;

(2) If two alternatives are to be conjunctively combined and an alternant of one is a subdivision of an alternant of the other, then the former alternant may be at once written down as one alternant of the result, and we need not go through the form of combining it with the remaining alternants of the other alternative.[483]

EXERCISES

435. Simplify the following terms: (i) *AD or acD*; (ii) *Ad or Ae or aB or aC or aE or bC or bd or bE or be or cd or ce*. [K.]

(i) By rule (1) in section 433, *AD or acD* is equivalent to (*A or ac*) *D*; and this by rule (9) is equivalent to (*A or c*) *D*; which again by rule (1) is equivalent to *AD or cD*.[484]

(ii) The dual term *bE or be* may be reduced to *b*, and hence *Ad or Ae or aB or aC or aE or bC or bd or bE or be or cd or ce = Ad or Ae or aB or aC or aE or b or bC or bd or cd or ce*. By section 433, rule (7), we may now omit all alternants in which *b* occurs as a determinant, and by rule (9), *B* may be omitted wherever it occurs as a determinant; accordingly our term is reduced to *Ad or Ae or a or aC or aE or b or cd or ce*. Since *a* is now

---

[483] These rules are equivalent to Boole's second Method of Abbreviation (*Laws of Thought*, p. 131).
[484] We might also proceed as follows: *AD or acD = AD or AcD or acD* [by rule (7)] = *AD or cD* [by rule (5)].

an alternant, a further application of the same rules leaves us with *a or b or cd or ce or d or e*; and this is immediately reducible to *a or b or d or e*.

436. Shew that *BC or bD or CD* is equivalent to *BC or bD*. [K.]

437. Give the contradictories of the following terms in their simplest forms as series of alternants:—*AB or BC or CD*; *AB or bC or cD*; *ABC or aBc*; *ABcD or Abcde or aBCDe or BCde*. [K.]

438. Simplify the following terms:

(1) *Ab or aC or BCd or Bc or bD or CD*;

(2) *ACD or Ac or Ad or aB or bCD*;

(3) *aBC or aBe or aCD or aDe or AcD or abD or bcD or aDE or cDE*;

(4) *(A or b) (A or c) (a or B) (a or C) (b or C)*. [K.]

439. Prove the following equivalences:

(1) *AB or AC or BC or aB or abc or C = a or B or C*;

(2) *aBC or aBd or acd or ABd or Acd or abd or aCd or BCd or bcd = aBC or ad or Bd or cd*;

(3) *Pqr or pQs or pq or prs or qrs or pS or qR = p or q*. [K.]

COMPLEX PROPOSITIONS AND COMPOUND PROPOSITIONS

440. *Complex Propositions.*—A *complex proposition* may be defined as a proposition which has a complex term either for its subject or its predicate. The ordinary distinctions of quantity and quality may be applied to complex propositions; thus *All AB is C or D* is a universal affirmative complex proposition. *Some AB is not EF* is a particular negative complex proposition. In the following pages propositions written in the indefinite form will be interpreted as universal, so that *AB is CD* will be understood to mean that *all AB is CD*. It is to be added that in dealing with complex propositions we interpret particulars as implying, but universals as not implying, the existence of their subjects in the universe of discourse.

441. *The Opposition of Complex Propositions.*—The opposition of complex terms has been already dealt with, and the opposition of complex propositions in itself presents no special difficulty. It must, however, be borne in mind that as we interpret particulars as implying the existence of their subjects, but universals as not doing so, we have the following divergences from the ordinary doctrine of opposition: (1) we cannot infer I from A, or O from E; (2) A and E are not necessarily inconsistent with each other; (3) I and O may both be false at the same time. The ordinary doctrine of *contradictory opposition* remains unaffected. The following are examples of contradictory propositions: *All X is both A and B*, *Some X is not both A and B*; *Some X is Y and at the same time either P or Q or R*, *No X is Y and at the same time either P or Q or R*.

442. *Compound Propositions.*[485]—A *compound proposition* may be defined as a proposition which consists in a combination of other propositions. The combination may be either conjunctive (i.e., when two or more propositions are affirmed to be true together) or alternative (i.e., when an alternative is given between two or more propositions); for example,

---

[485] Compare section 55.

All AB is C and some P is not either Q or R is a compound conjunctive proposition; *Either all AB is C or some P is not either Q or R* is a compound alternative proposition. Propositions conjunctively combined may be spoken of as *determinants* of the resulting compound proposition; and propositions alternatively combined may be spoken of as *alternants* of the resulting compound proposition. In what follows, both conjunctive and alternative propositions are interpreted as being assertoric.

Only two types of compound propositions are here recognised, the *conjunctive* and the *alternative*. Pure hypothetical propositions are compound, but (except in so far as we interpret hypotheticals and alternatives differently in respect of modality) they are equivalent to alternative propositions, and may be regarded as constituting one mode of expressing an alternative synthesis. Thus (taking x and y as symbols representing propositions, and $\bar{x}$ and $\bar{y}$ as their contradictories) the hypothetical proposition *If $\bar{x}$ then y* expresses an alternative between x and y and is, therefore, equivalent to the alternative proposition x or y. Combinations of the true disjunctive type (for example, *not both x and y*) may also be regarded as a mode of expressing an alternative synthesis; thus, the true disjunctive proposition just given is equivalent to the alternative proposition $\bar{x}$ or $\bar{y}$.[486]

Mr Johnson shews that any ordinary proposition with a general term as subject may be regarded as a compound proposition resulting from the conjunctive or alternative combination of singular (molecular) propositions, with a common predication, but different subjects. Let $S_1, S_2, \ldots S_\infty$ represent a number of different individual subjects; and let S represent the aggregate collection of individuals $S_1, S_2, \ldots S_\infty$. Then

S_1 and S_2, and $S_3 \ldots$ and S_∞ = *Every S*;
S_1 or S_2, or $S_3 \ldots\ldots$ or S_∞ = *Some S*.

"Thus we arrive at the common logical forms, *Every S is P*, *Some S is P*. The former is an abbreviation for a *determinative*, the latter for an *alternative*, synthesis of molecular propositions."[487]

In other words,

Every S is P = S_1 is P and S_2 is P and S_3 is $P \ldots$ and S_∞ is P;
Some S is P = S_1 is P or S_2 is P or S_3 is $P \ldots$ or S_∞ is P.

443. *The Opposition of Compound propositions.*—The rule for obtaining the contradictory of a complex term given in section 426 may be applied also to compound propositions. Thus, the contradictory of a compound proposition is obtained by replacing the

---

[486] The above may seem to imply that an alternative synthesis may be expressed in a greater number of ways than a conjunctive synthesis. This, however, is not the case. It has been shewn that an alternative synthesis may be expressed by a hypothetical or by the denial of a conjunctive (that is, by a true disjunctive). But corresponding to this, a conjunctive synthesis may be expressed by the denial of a hypothetical or by the denial of an alternative. Thus, representing the denial of a proposition by a bar drawn across it, we have
$xy = \bar{x}$ or $\bar{y} = $ *If* $x, \bar{y}$;
$\overline{xy} = x$ or $y = \overline{If\, x, y}$.
[487] *Mind*, 1892, p. 25. Mr Johnson of course recognises that a quantified subject-term (*all S*) is not usually a mere enumeration of individuals first apprehended and named. But he points out that "however the aggregate of things, to which the universal name applies, is mentally reached, the propositional force for purposes of inference or synthesis in general is the same" (p. 28).

constituent propositions by their contradictories and everywhere changing the manner of their combination, that is to say, substituting conjunctive combination for alternative and *vice versâ*.[488] The following are examples: *All A is B and some P is Q* has for its contradictory *Either some A is not B or no P is Q*; *Either some A is both B and C, or all B is either C or both D and E* has for its contradictory *No A is both B and C, and some B is not either C or both D and E*.

It follows, as in section 427, that there is a duality of formal equivalences in the case of compound propositions, each equivalence yielding a reciprocal equivalence in which conjunctive combination is throughout substituted for alternative combination and *vice versâ*.

444. *Formal Equivalences of Compound Propositions.*—The laws relating to the conjunctive or alternative synthesis of propositions are practically identical with those relating to the conjunctive or alternative combination of terms; and we have accordingly the following propositional equivalences corresponding to the equivalences of terms given in section 433. The symbols here stand for *propositions*, not terms; and *negation* is represented by a *bar* over the proposition denied.

(1)	$x(y \text{ or } z) = xy \text{ or } xz$,	}	*Laws of Distribution*;
(2)	$x \text{ or } yz = (x \text{ or } y)(x \text{ or } z)$,	}	
(3)	$xx = x$,	}	*Laws of Tautology* (*Law of Simplicity and Law of Unity*);
(4)	$x \text{ or } x = x$,	}	
(5)	$x = x \text{ or } yy = (x \text{ or } y)(x \text{ or } y)$,	}	*Laws of Development and Reduction*;
(6)	$x = x(y \text{ or } y) = xy \text{ or } xy$,	}	
(7)	$x \text{ or } xy = x$,	}	*Laws of Absorption*;
(8)	$x(x \text{ or } y) = x$	}	
(9)	$x \text{ or } y = x \text{ or } xy$,	}	*Law of Exclusion and Law of Inclusion.*
(10)	$xy = x(x \text{ or } y)$,[489]	}	

---

[488] It has been shewn in the preceding section that the words *all* and *some* are abbreviations of conjunctive and alternative synthesis respectively. Hence the rule that, in the ordinarily recognised propositional forms, contradictories differ in quantity as well as in quality is itself only a particular application of the general law here laid down.

[489] It is not maintained that all the above laws are ultimate or even independent of one another. The synthesis of propositions is admirably worked out by Mr Johnson in his articles on *the Logical Calculus* (*Mind*, 1892). He gives *five independent laws* which are necessary and sufficient for propositional synthesis. These laws are briefly enumerated below; for a more complete exposition the reader must be referred to Mr Johnson's own treatment of them.

(i) *The Commutative Law*: The order of pure synthesis is indifferent ($xy = yx$).

(ii) *The Associative Law*: The mode of grouping in pure synthesis is indifferent ($xy \cdot z = x \cdot yz$).

(iii) *The Law of Tautology*: The mere repetition of a proposition does not in any way add to or alter its force ($xx = x$).

(iv) *The Law of Reciprocity*: The denial of the denial of a proposition is equivalent to its affirmation ($\bar{\bar{x}} = x$). "In this principle are included the so-called Laws of Contradiction and Excluded Middle, *viz.*, 'If x, then not not-x', and 'If not not-x, then x'."

(v) *The Law of Dichotomy*: The denial of any proposition is equivalent to the denial of its conjunction with any other proposition together with the denial of its conjunction with the contradictory of that other proposition ($\bar{x} = \overline{xy}\, \overline{x\bar{y}}$). "This is a further extension of the Law of Excluded Middle, when applied to the combination of propositions with one another. The denial that x is conjoined with y combined with the denial that x is conjoined with *not-y* is equivalent to the denial of x absolutely. For, if x were true, it must be conjoined either with y or with *not-y*. This law, which (it must be admitted) looks at first a little complicated, is the special instrument of the logical calculus. By its means we may always resolve a proposition into two determinants, or conversely we may compound certain pairs of determinants into a single proposition."

445. *The Simplification of Complex Propositions.*—The terms of a complex proposition may often be simplified by means of the rules given in the preceding chapter, and the force of the assertion will remain unaffected. For the further simplification of complex propositions the following rules may be added:

(1) *In a universal negative or a particular affirmative proposition any determinant of the subject may be indifferently introduced or omitted as a determinant of the predicate and* vice versâ.

To say that *No AB is AC* is the same as to say that *No AB is C*, or that *No B is AC*. For to say that *No AB is AC* is the same thing as to deny that anything is *ABAC*; but, as shewn in section 429, the repetition of the determinant *A* is superfluous, and the statement may therefore be reduced to the denial that anything is *ABC*. And this may equally well be expressed by saying *No AB is C*, or *No B is AC*.[490]

Again, *Some AB is AC* may be shown to be equivalent to *Some AB is C*, or to *Some B is AC*; for it simply affirms that something is *ABAC*, and the proof follows as above.

(2) *In a universal affirmative or a particular proposition any determinant of the subject may be indifferently introduced or omitted as a determinant of any alternant of the predicate.*

All A is AB may obviously be resolved into the two propositions *All A is A, All A is B*.[491] But the former of these is a merely identical proposition and gives no information. *All A is AB* is, therefore, equivalent to the simple proposition *All A is B*. Similarly, *All AB is AC or DE* is equivalent to *All AB is C or DE*.

Again, *Some A is not AB* affirms that *Some A is a or b*;[492] but by the law of contradiction *No A is a*; therefore, *Some A is not B*, and obviously we can also pass back from this proposition to the one from which we started. Similarly, *Some AB is not either AC or DE* is equivalent to *Some AB is not either C or DE*.

(3) *In a universal affirmative or a particular negative proposition any alternant of the predicate may be indifferently introduced or omitted as an alternant of the subject.*

If *All A is B or C*, then by the law of identity it follows that *Whatever is A or B is B or C*; it is also obvious that we can pass back from this to the original proposition.

Again, if *Some A or B is not either B or C*, then since by the law of identity *All B is B* it follows that *Some A is not either B or C*; and it is also obvious that we can pass back from this to the original proposition.

(4) *In a universal affirmative or a particular mgative proposition the contradictory of any determinant of the subject may be indifferently introduced or omitted as an alternant of the predicate, and* vice versâ.

By this rule the three following propositions are affirmed to be equivalent to one another: *All AB is a or C; All B is a or C; All AB is C*; and also the three following: *Some AB is not either a or C; Some B is not either a or C; Some AB is not C*.

The rule follows directly from rule (1) by aid of the process of obversion (see chapter 3).

(5) *In a universal negative or a particular affirmative proposition the contradictory of any determinant of the subject may be indifferently introduced or omitted as an alternant of the predicate.*

---

[490] See also the sections in the following chapter relating to the conversion of propositions.
[491] The resolution of complex propositions into a combination of relatively simple ones will be considered further in the following section.
[492] The process of obversion will be considered in detail in chapter 3.

By this rule the two following propositions are affirmed to be equivalent to one another: *No AB is a or C*; *No AB is C*; and also the two following: *Some AB is a or C*; *Some AB is C*.

The rule follows directly from rule (2) by obversion.

(6) *In a universal negative or a particular affirmative proposition the contradictory of any determinant of the predicate may be indifferently introduced or omitted as an alternant of the subject.*

This rule follows from rule (3) by obversion.

446. *The Resolution of Universal Complex Propositions into Equivalent Compound Propositions.*—We may enquire how far complex propositions are immediately resolvable into a conjunctive or alternative combination of relatively simple propositions. Universal propositions will be considered in this section, and particulars in the next.

Universal Affirmatives. Universal affirmative complex propositions may be immediately resolved into a conjunction of relatively simple ones, so far as there is alternative combination in the subject or conjunctive combination in the predicate. Thus,

(1) *Whatever is P or Q is R = All P is R and all Q is R*;
(2) *All P is QR = All P is Q and all P is R.*

Universal Negatives. Universal negative complex propositions may be immediately resolved into a conjunction of relatively simple ones, so far as there is alternative combination either in the subject or in the predicate. Thus,

(3) *Nothing that is P or Q is R = No P is R and no Q is R*;
(4) *No P is either Q or R = No P is Q and no P is R.*

So far as there is conjunctive combination in the subject or alternative combination in the predicate of universal affirmative propositions, or conjunctive combination either in the subject or in the predicate of universal negative propositions, they cannot be *immediately*[493] resolved into either a conjunctive or an alternative combination of simpler propositions. It may, however, be added that propositions falling into this latter category are immediately *implied by* certain compound alternatives. Thus,

(i) *All PQ is R* is implied by *All P is R or all Q is R*;
(ii) *All P is Q or R* is implied by *All P is Q or all P is R*;
(iii) *No PQ is R* is implied by *No P is R or no Q is R*;
(iv) *No P is QR* is implied by *No P is Q or no P is R.*

447. *The Resolution of Particular Complex Propositions into Equivalent Compound Propositions.*—Particular complex propositions cannot be resolved into compound conjunctives, but they may under certain conditions be immediately resolved into equivalent *compound alternative propositions* in which the alternants are relatively simple. This is the case so far as there is alternative combination in the subject or conjunctive combination in the

---

[493] It will be shewn subsequently that even in these cases universal complex propositions may be resolved into a conjunction of relatively simpler ones by the aid of certain immediate inferences.

predicate of a particular negative, or alternative combination either in the subject or in the predicate of a particular affirmative. Thus,

(1) *Some P or Q is not R = Some P is not R or some Q is not R*;
(2) *Some P is not QR = Some P is not Q or some P is not R*;
(3) *Some P or Q is R = Some P is R or some Q is R*;
(4) *Some P is Q or R = Some P is Q or some P is R*.

Particular complex propositions cannot be immediately resolved into compound propositions (either conjunctive or alternative) so far as there is conjunctive combination in the subject or alternative combination in the predicate if the proposition is negative, or so far as there is conjunctive combination either in the subject or in the predicate if the proposition is affirmative. In these cases, however, the complex proposition *implies* a compound conjunctive proposition, though we cannot pass back from the latter to the former. Thus,

(i) *Some PQ is not R* implies *Some P is not R and Some Q is not R*;
(ii) *Some P is not either Q or R* implies *Some P is not Q and some P is not R*;
(iii) *Some PQ is R* implies *Some P is R and some Q is R*;
(iv) *Some P is QR* implies *Some P is Q and some P is R*.

It must be particularly noticed that, although in these cases the compound proposition can be inferred from the complex proposition, still the two are not equivalent. For example, from *Some P is Q and some P is R* it does not follow that *Some P is QR*, for we cannot be sure that the same *P*'s are referred to in the two cases.

All the results of this section follow from those of the preceding section by the application of the rule of contradiction to the propositions themselves and the rule of contraposition to the relations of implication between them.

448. *The Omission of Terms from a Complex Proposition.*—From the two preceding sections we may obtain immediately the following rules for inferring from a given proposition another proposition in which certain terms contained in the original proposition are omitted:

(1) *Any determinant may be omitted from an undistributed term*;[494]
(2) *Any alternant may be omitted from a distributed term.*[495]

For example,—

Whatever is A or B is CD, therefore, *All A is C*;
Some AB is CD, therefore, *Some A is C*;
Nothing that is A or B is C or D, therefore, *No A is C*;
Some AB is not either C or D, therefore, *Some A is not C*.

---

[494] The subject of a particular or the predicate of an affirmative proposition.
[495] The subject of a universal or the predicate of a negative proposition.

The above rules may also be justified independently, as will be shewn in the following section. The results which they yield must be distinguished from those obtained in section 445. In the cases discussed in that section, the terms omitted were superfluous in the sense that their omission left us with propositions equivalent to our original propositions; but in the above inferences we cannot pass back from conclusion to premiss. From *Some A is C*, for example, we cannot infer that *Some AB is C*.

449. *The Introduction of Terms into a Complex Proposition.*—Corresponding to the rules laid down in the preceding section we have also the following:

(1) *Any determinant may be introduced into a distributed term*;
(2) *Any alternant may be introduced into an undistributed term.*

These rules, and also the rules given in the preceding section, may be established by the aid of the following axioms: *What is true of all (distributively) is true of every part*; *What is true of part of a part is true of a part of the larger whole.*

When we add a determinant to a term, or remove an alternant, we usually diminish, and at any rate do not increase, the extension of the term; when, on the other hand, we add an alternant, or remove a determinant, we usually increase, and at any rate do not diminish, its extension. Hence it follows that if a term is distributed we may add a determinant or remove an alternant, whilst if a term is undistributed we may add an alternant or remove a determinant. Thus,

All A is CD, therefore, *All AB is C*;
No A is C, therefore, *No AB is CD*;
Some AB is C, therefore, *Some A is C or D*;
Some AB is not either C or D, therefore, *Some A is not C.*

From the above rules taken in connection with the rules given in section 445 we may obtain the following corollaries:

(3) *In universal affirmatives, any determinant may be introduced into the predicate, if it is also introduced into the subject; and any alternant may be introduced into the subject if it is also introduced into the predicate.*

Given *All A is C*, then *All AB is C* by rule (1) above; and from this we obtain *All AB is BC* by rule (2) of section 445.

Again, given *All A is C*, then *All A is B or C*; and therefore, by rule (3) of section 445, *Whatever is A or B is B or C.*

(4) *In universal negatives any alternant may be introduced into subject or predicate, if its contradictory is introduced into the other term as a determinant.*

Given *No A is C*, then *No AB is C*; and, therefore, by rule (5) of section 445, *No AB is b or C.*

Again, given *No A is C*, then *No A is BC*; and, therefore, by rule (6) of section 445, *No A or b is BC.*

In none of the inferences considered in this section is it possible to pass back from the conclusion to the original proposition.

450. *Interpretation of Anomalous Forms.*—It will be found that propositions which apparently involve a contradiction in terms and are thus in direct contravention of the fundamental laws of thought—for example, *No AB is B*, *All Ab is B*—sometimes result from the manipulation of complex propositions. In interpreting such propositions as these, a distinction must be drawn between universals and particulars, at any rate if particulars are interpreted as implying, while universals are not interpreted as implying, the existence of their subjects.

It can be shown that a universal proposition of the form *No AB is B* or *All Ab is B* must be interpreted as implying the non-existence in the universe of discourse of the subject of the proposition. For a universal negative denies the existence of anything that comes under both its subject and its predicate; thus, *No AB is B* denies the existence of *ABB*, that is, it denies the existence of *AB*. Again, a universal affirmative denies the existence of anything that comes under its subject without also coming under its predicate; thus, *All Ab is B* denies the existence of anything that is *Ab* and at the same time *not-B*, that is, *b*; but *Ab* is *Ab* and also *b*, and hence the existence of *Ab* is denied.

Since the existence of its subject is held to be part of the implication of a particular proposition, the above interpretation is obviously inapplicable in the case of particulars. Hence if a proposition of the form *Some Ab is B* is obtained, we are thrown back on the alternative that there is some inconsistency in the premisses; either some one individual premiss is self-contradictory, or the premisses are inconsistent with one another.

EXERCISES

451. Shew that if *No A is bc or Cd*, then *No A is bd*. [K.]

452. Give the contradictory of each of the following propositions:—(1) Flowering plants are either endogens or exogens, but not both; (2) Flowering plants are vascular, and either endogens or exogens, but not both. [M.]

453. Simplify the following propositions:—

(1) *All AB is BC or be or CD or cE or DE*;
(2) *Nothing that is either PQ or PR is Pqr or pQs or pq or prs or qrs or pS or qR.*   [K.]

IMMEDIATE INFERENCES FROM COMPLEX PROPOSITIONS

454. *The Obversion of Complex Propositions*—The doctrine of obversion is immediately applicable to complex propositions; and no modification of the definition of obversion already given is necessary. From any given proposition we may infer a new one by changing its quality and taking as a new predicate the contradictory of the original predicate. The proposition thus obtained is called the obverse of the original proposition.

The only difficulty connected with the obversion of complex propositions consists in finding the contradictory of a complex term; but a simple rule for performing this process has been given in section 426:—*Replace all the simple terms invoked by their contradictories, and throughout substitute alternative combination for conjunctive and* vice versâ.

Applying this rule to *AB or ab*, we have *(a or b)* and *(A or B)*, that is, *Aa or Ab or aB or Bb*; but since the alternants *Aa* and *Bb* involve self-contradiction, they may by rule (5) of section 433 be omitted. The obverse, therefore, of *All X is AB or ab* is *No X is Ab or aB*.

As additional examples we may find the obverse of the following propositions: (1) *All A is BC or DE*; (2) *No A is BcE or BCF*; (3) *Some A is not either B or bcDEf or bcdEF*.

(1) *All A is BC or DE* yields *No A is (b or c) and at the same time (d or e)*, or, by the reduction of the predicate to a series of alternants, *No A is bd or be or cd or ce*.

(2) *No A is BcE or BCF*. Here the contradictory of the predicate is *(b or C or e) and (b or c or f)*, which yields *b or Cc or Cf or ce or ef*. *Cc* may be omitted by rule (5) of section 433; also *ef* by rule (7), since *ef* is either *Cef* or *cef*. Hence the required obverse is *All A is b or Cf or ce*.

(3) *Some A is not either B or bcDEf or bcdEF*. The obverse is *Some A is b and (B or C or d or e or F) and (B or C or D or e or f)*; and by the application of the rules summarised in section 433 this will be found to be equivalent to *Some A is bC or bDF or bdf or be*.

455. *The Conversion of Complex Propositions.*—Generalising, we may say that we have a process of conversion whenever from a given proposition we infer a new one in which any term that appeared in the predicate of the original proposition now appears in the subject, or vice versâ.

Thus the inference from *No A is BC* to *No B is AC* is of the nature of conversion. The process may be simply analysed as follows:—

No A is both B and C,
therefore, *Nothing is at the same time A, B, and C*,
therefore, *No B is both A and C*.

The reasoning may also be resolved into a series of ordinary conversions:—

No A is BC,
therefore (by conversion), *No BC is A*,
that is, *within the sphere of C, no B is A*,
therefore (by conversion), *within the sphere of C, no A is B*,
that is, *No AC is B*,
therefore (by conversion), *No B is AC*.

Or, it may be treated thus,

No A is BC,
therefore, by section 445, rule (1), *No AC is BC*,
therefore, also by section 445, rule (1), *No AC is B*,
therefore (by conversion), *No B is AC*.

Similarly it may be shewn that from *Some A is BC* we may infer *Some B is AC*.

Hence we obtain the following rule: *In a universal negative or a particular affirmative proposition any determinant of the subject may be transferred to the predicate or* vice versâ *without affecting the force of the assertion.*

We have just shewn how from *No A is BC.* We may obtain by conversion *No B is AC.* Similarly, we may infer

No C is AB,
No AB is C,
No AC is B,
No BC is A.

The proposition may also be written in the form: *There is no ABC,* or, *Nothing is at the same time A, B, and C.*

The last of these is a specially useful form to which to bring universal negatives for the purpose of logical manipulation.

In the same way from *Some A is BC or BD* we may infer

Some AB is C or D,
Some AC or AD is B,
Some B is AC or AD,
Some C or D is AB,
Some BC or BD is A,
Something is ABC or ABD.

There is no inference by conversion from a universal affirmative or from a particular negative.

456. *The Contraposition of Complex Propositions.*—According to our original definition of contraposition, we contraposit a proposition when we infer from it a new proposition having the contradictory of the old predicate for its subject. Adopting this definition, the contrapositive of *All A is B or C* is *All bc is a.*

The process can be applied to universal affirmatives and to particular negatives. By obversion, conversion, and then again obversion, it is clear that in each of these cases we may obtain a legitimate contrapositive by *taking as a new subject the contradictory of the old predicate, and as a new predicate the contradictory of the old subject, the proposition retaining its original quality.* For example: *All A is BC*, therefore, *Whatever is b or c is a*; *Some A is not either B or C*, therefore, *Some bc is not a.*

The above may be called the full contrapositive of a complex proposition. It should be observed that any proposition and its full contrapositive are equivalent to each other; we can pass back from the full contrapositive to the original proposition.

In dealing with complex propositions, however, it is convenient to give to the term contraposition an extended meaning. We may say that we have *a process of contraposition when from a given proposition we infer a new one in which the contradictory of any term that appeared in the predicate of the original proposition now appears in the subject, or the contradictory of any term that appeared in the subject of the original proposition now appears in the predicate.*

Three operations may be distinguished all of which are included under the above definition, and all of which leave us with a full equivalent of the original proposition, so that there is no loss of logical power.

(1) The operation of obtaining the full contrapositive of a given proposition, as above described and defined.[496]

(2) An operation which may be described as *the generalisation of the subject of a proposition by the addition of one or more alternants in the predicate*. Thus, from *All AB is C* we may infer *All A is b or C*; from *Some AB is not either C or D* we may infer *Some A is not either b or C or D*.

For inferences of this type the following general rule may be given: *Any determinant may be dropped from the subject of a universal affirmative or a particular negative proposition, if its contradictory is at the same time added as an alternant in the predicate*.

This rule may be established as follows: Given *All AB is C* (or *Some AB is not C*)—and these may be taken, so far as the rule in question is concerned, as types of universal affirmatives and particular negatives respectively—we have by obversion *No AB is c* (or *Some AB is c*), and thence, by the rule for conversion given in section 455, *No A is Bc* (or *Some A is Bc*); then again obverting we have *All A is either b or C* (or *Some A is not either b or C*), the required result.

It will be observed that, as stated at the outset, these operations leave us with a proposition that is equivalent to our original proposition. There is, therefore, no loss of logical power.

By the application of the above rule with regard to all the explicit determinants of the subject any universal affirmative proposition may be brought to the form *Everything is X_1 or X_2 ... or X_n*; and it will be found that by means of this transformation, complex inferences are in many cases materially simplified.

(3) An operation which may be described as *the particularisation of the subject of a proposition by the omission of one or more alternants in the predicate*. Thus, from *All A is B or C* we may infer *All Ab is C*; from *Some A is not either B or C* we may infer *Some Ab is not C*.

For inferences of this type the following general rule may be given: *Any alternant may be dropped from the predicate of a universal affirmative or a particular negative proposition, if its contradictory is at the same time introduced as a determinant of the subject*.[497]

This rule is the converse of that given under the preceding head; and it follows from the fact that the application of that rule leaves us with an equivalent proposition.

---

[496] In some cases we may desire to drop part of the information given by the complete contrapositive. Thus, from *All A is BC or E* may infer *Whatever is be or ce is a*; but in a given application it may be sufficient for us to know that *All be is a*.

[497] The application of this rule again leaves us with a proposition equivalent to our original proposition. The following rule, which may be regarded as a corollary from the above rule, or which may be arrived at independently, does not necessarily leave us with an equivalent: *If a new determinant is introduced into the subject of a universal affirmative proposition* (see section 449) *every alternant in the predicate which contains the contradictory of the determinant may be omitted*. Thus, from *Whatever is A or B is C or DX or Ex*, we may infer *Whatever is AX or BX is C or D*.

The application of this rule may sometimes result in the disappearance of all the alternants from the predicate; and the meaning of such a result is that we now have a non-existent subject.

Thus, given *All P is ABCD or Abcd or aBCd*, if we particularise the subject by making it *PbC*, we find that all the alternants in the predicate disappear. The interpretation is that the class *PbC* is non-existent, that is, *No P is bC*; a conclusion which might of course have been obtained directly from the given proposition.

The following may be taken as typical examples of the different operations included above under the name contraposition:—

All AB is CD or de;	
therefore,	(1) *Anything that is either cD or dE is a or b*;
	(2) *All A is b or CD or de*;
	(3) *Whatever is ABD or ABE is CD.*
Combinations of the second and third operations give	
Anything that is Ac or Ad is b or de;	
Anything that is BD or BE is a or CD;	
&c.	

In all the above cases one or more terms disappear from the subject or the predicate of the original proposition, and are replaced by their contradictories in the predicate or the subject accordingly. Only in the full contrapositive, however, is every term thus transposed.

The importance of contraposition as we are now dealing with it in connection with complex propositions is that by its means, *given a universal affirmative proposition of any complexity, we may obtain separate information with regard to any term that appears in the subject, or with regard to the contradictory of any term that appears in the predicate, or with regard to any combination of such terms.*

Thus, given *All AB is C or De*, by the process described as the generalisation of the subject we have *All A is b or C or De*, *All B is a or C or De*, *Everything is a or b or C or De*; the particularisation of the subject yields *All ABc is De*, *Whatever is ABd or ABE is C*, &c.; and by the combination of these processes we have *All Ac is b or De*, &c.

Again, the full contrapositive of the original proposition is *Whatever is cd or cE is a or b*; from which we have *All c is a or b or De*, *Whatever is d or E is a or b or C*, &c.

457. *Summary of the results obtainable by Obversion, Conversion, and Contraposition.*— The following is a summary of the results obtainable by the aid of the processes discussed in the three preceding sections:

(1) By *obversion* any proposition may be changed from the affirmative to the negative form, or *vice versâ*.

For example, *All AB is CD or EF*, therefore, *No AB is ce or cf or de or df*; *Some P is not QR*, therefore, *Some P is either q or r*.

(2) By the *conversion* of a universal negative proposition separate information may be obtained with regard to any term that appears either in the subject or in the predicate, or with regard to any combination of these terms.

For example, from *No AB is CD or EF* we may infer *No A is BCD or BEF*, *No C is ABD or ABEF*, *No BD is AC or AEF*, etc.

Also by conversion any universal negative proposition may be reduced to the following: *Nothing is either X_1 or X_2 ... or X_n.*

For example, the above proposition is equivalent to the following: *Nothing is either ABCD or ABEF*.

(3) By the *conversion* of a particular affirmative proposition separate information may be obtained with regard to any determinant of the subject or of the predicate, or with regard to any combination of such determinants.

For example, from *Some AB or AC is DE or DF* we may infer *Some A is BDE or BDF or CDE or CDF*, *Some D is ABE or ABF or ACE or ACF*, *Some AD is BE or BF or CE or CF*, etc.

Also by conversion any particular affirmative proposition may be reduced to the form *Something is either X_1 or X_2 ... or X_n*.

For example, the above proposition is equivalent to the following: *Something is either ABDE or ABDF or ACDE or ACDF*.

(4) By the *contraposition* of a universal affirmative proposition separate information may be obtained with regard to any term that appears in the subject, or with regard to the contradictory of any term that appears in the predicate, or with regard to any combination of these terms.

For example, from *All AB is CD or EF* we may infer *All A is b or CD or EF*, *All c is a or b or EF*, *All Be is a or CD*, *All ce is a or b*, *All Adf is b*, &c.

Also by contraposition any universal affirmative proposition may be reduced to the form *Everything is either X_1 or X_2 ... or X_n*.

For example, the above proposition is equivalent to the following: *Everything is a or b or CD or EF*.

(5) By the contraposition of a particular negative proposition separate information may be obtained with regard to any determinant of the subject or with regard to the contradictory of any alternant of the predicate or with regard to any combination of these.

For example, from *Some AB or AC is not either D or EF* we may infer *Some A is not either bc or D or EF*, *Some d is not either a or bc or EF*, *Some Ae or Af is not either bc or D*, &c.

Also by contraposition any particular negative proposition may be reduced to the form *Something is not either X_1 or X_2 ... or X_n*.

For example, the above proposition is equivalent to the following: *Something is not either a or bc or D or EF*.

EXERCISES

458. No citizen is at once a voter, a householder, and a lodger; nor is there any citizen who is none of the three.

Every citizen is either a voter but not a householder, or a householder and not a lodger, or a lodger without a vote.

Are these statements precisely equivalent? [V.]

In may be shown that each of these statements is the logical obverse of the other. They are, therefore, precisely equivalent.

Let	V = voter,	v = not voter;
	H = householder,	h = not householder;
	L = lodger,	l = not lodger.

The first of the given statements is *No citizen is VHL or vhl*; therefore (by obversion), *Every citizen is either v or h or l and is also either V or H or L*; therefore (combining these possibilities), *Every citizen is either Hv or Lv or Vh or Lh or Vl or Hl.*

But (by the law of excluded middle), *Hv is either HLv or Hlv*; therefore, *Hv is Lv or Hl*. Similarly, *Lh is Vh or Lv*; and *Vl is Hl or Vh*.

Therefore, *Every citizen is Vh or Hl or Lv*, which is the second of the given statements.

Again, starting from this second statement, it follows (by obversion) that *No citizen is at the same time v or H, h or L, l or V*; therefore, *No citizen is vh or vL or HL, and at the same time l or V*; therefore, *No citizen is vhl or VHL*, which brings us back to the first of the given statements.

459. Given "All *D* that is either *B* or *C* is *A*," shew that "Everything that is not-*A* is either not-*B* and not-*C* or else it is not-*D*." [De Morgan.]

This example and those given in section 466 are adapted from De Morgan, *Syllabus*, p. 42. They are also given by Jevons, *Studies*, p. 241, in connection with his Equational Logic. They are all simple exercises in contraposition.

We have *What is either BD or CD is A*; therefore, *All a is (b or d) and (c or d)*; therefore, *All a is bc or d*.

460. Infer all that you possibly can by way of contraposition or otherwise, from the assertion, *All A that is neither B nor C is X*. [R.]

The given proposition may be thrown into the form

Everything is either a or B or C or X;

and it is seen to be symmetrical with regard to the terms *a*, *B*, *C*, *X*, and therefore with regard to the terms *A*, *b*, *c*, *x*. We are sure then that anything that is true of *A* is true *mutatis mutandis* of *b*, *c*, and *x*, that anything that is true of *Ab* is true *mutatis mutandis* of any pair of the terms, and similarly for combinations three and three together.

We have at once the four symmetrical propositions:

All A is B or C or X;	(1)
All b is a or C or X;	(2)
All c is a or B or X;	(3)
All X is a or B or C.	(4)

Then from (1) by particularisation of the subject:

All Ab is C or X; (i)

with the five corresponding propositions;

All Ac is B or X;	(ii)
All Ax is B or C;	(iii)
All bc is a or X;	(iv)
All bx is a or C;	(v)
All cx is a or B.	(vi)

By a repetition of the same process, we have

All Abc is X (which is the original proposition over again);		(α)
and corresponding to this:	All Abx is C;	(β)
	All Acx is B;	(γ)
	All bcx is a.	(δ)

It will be observed that the following are pairs of full contrapositives;—(1) (δ), (2) (γ), (3) (β), (4) (α), (i) (vi), (ii) (v), (iii) (iv).

A further series of propositions may be obtained by obverting all the above; and as there has been no loss of logical power in any of the processes employed we have in all thirty propositions that are equivalent to one another.

461. If *AB* is either *Cd* or *cDe*, and also either *eF* or *H*, and if the same is true of *BH*, what do we know of that which is *E*? [K.]

Whatever is AB or BH is (Cd or cDe) and (eF or H);
therefore, *Whatever is AB or BH is CdeF or cDeF or CdH or cDeH;*
therefore, *Whatever is ABE or BHE is CdH;*
therefore, *All E is ah or b or CdH.*

462. Given *A is BC or BDE or BDF*, infer descriptions of the terms *Ace, Acf, ABcD.*
[Jevons, *Studies*, pp. 237, 238.]

In accordance with rules already laid down, we have immediately—
Ace is BDF;
Acf is BDE;
ABcD is E or F.

463. Find the obverse of each of the following propositions:—
(1) *Nothing is A, B, or C;*
(2) *All A is Bc or bD;*
(3) *No Ab is CDEf or Cd or cDf or cdE;*
(4) *No A is BCD or Bcd;*
(5) *Some A is not either bcd or Cd or cD.* [K.]

464. Shew that the two following propositions are equivalent to each other:—*No A is B or CD or CE or EF; All A is bCde or bcEf or bce.* [K.]

465. Contraposit the proposition, *All A that is neither B nor C is both X and Y.* [L.]

466. Find the full contrapositive of each of the following propositions:
(1) *Whatever is B or CD or CE is A;*
(2) *Whatever is either B or C and at the same time either D or E is A;*
(3) *Whatever is A or BC and at the same time either D or EF is X;*
(4) *All A is either BC or BD.* [De Morgan.]

467. Find the full contrapositive of each of the following propositions:—
All A is BCDe or bcDe;
Some AB is not either CD or cDE or de;

Whatever is AB or bC is aCd or Acd;

Where A is present along with either B or C, D is present and C absent or D and E are both absent;

Some ABC or abc is not either DEF or def. [K.]

468. What information can you obtain about *Af, Be, c, D*, from the proposition *All AB is CD or EF*? [M.]

469. Establish the following: Where *B* is absent, either *A* and *C* are both present or *A* and *D* are both absent; therefore, where *C* is absent, either *B* is present or *D* is absent. [K.]

470. Establish the following: Where *A* is present, either *B* and *C* are both present or *C* is present *D* being absent or *C* is present *F* being absent or *H* is present; therefore, where *C* is absent, *A* cannot be present *H* being absent. [K.]

471. Given that *Whatever is PQ or AP is bCD or abdE or aBCdE or Abcd*, shew that (1) *All abP is CD or dE or q*; (2) *All DP is bC or aq*; (3) *Whatever is B or Cd or cD is a or p*; (4) *All B is C or p or aq*; (5) *All AB is p*; (6) *If ae is c or d it is p or q*; (7) *If BP is c or D or e it is aq*. [K.]

472. Bring the following propositions to the form *Everything is either X_1 or X_2 ... or X_n*:—

Whatever is Ac or ab or aC is bdf or deF;

Nothing that is A and at the same time either B or C is D or dE. [K.]

473. Shew that the results in section 447 follow from those in section 446 by the rules of contradiction and contraposition. [K.]

THE COMBINATION OF COMPLEX PROPOSITIONS

474. *The Problem of combining Complex Propositions.*—Two or more complex propositions given in simple combination, either conjunctive or alternative, constitute a compound proposition. Hence the problem of dealing with a combination of complex propositions so as to obtain from them a single equivalent complex proposition, which is the problem to be considered in the present chapter, is identical with that of passing from a compound proposition to an equivalent complex proposition; and it is, therefore, the converse of the problem which was partially discussed in sections 446, 447. The latter problem, namely, that of passing from a complex to an equivalent compound proposition, will be further discussed in chapter 6.

475. *The Conjunctive Combination of Universal Affirmatives.*—We may here distinguish two cases according as the propositions to be combined have or have not the same subject.

(1) *Universal affirmatives having the same subject.*

All X is P_1 or P_2 ...... or P_m,
All X is Q_1 or Q_2 ...... or Q_n,

may for our present purpose be taken as types of universal affirmative propositions having the same subject. By conjunctively combining their predicates, thus,

All X is (P_1 or P_2 ... or P_m) and also (Q_1 or Q_2 ... or Q_n),

that is, *All X is P_1Q_1 or P_1Q_2 ... or P_1Q_n
or P_2Q_1 or P_2Q_2 ... or P_2Q_n
or ......
......
or P_mQ_1 or P_mQ_2 ... or P_mQ_n,*

we may obtain a new proposition which is equivalent to the conjunctive combination of the two original propositions; it sums up all the information which they jointly contain, and we can pass back from it to them.

In almost all cases of the conjunctive combination of terms there are numerous opportunities of simplification; and, after a little practice, the student will find it unnecessary to write out all the alternants of the new predicate in full. The following are examples:—

(i)	*All X is AB or bce,*
	All X is aBC or DE;
therefore,	*All X is ABDE.*

It will be found that all the other combinations in the predicate contain contradictories.

(ii)	*All X is A or Bc or D,*
	All X is aB or Bc or Cd;
therefore,	*All X is ACd or aBD or Bc.*
(iii)	*Everything is A or bd or cE,*
	Everything is AC or aBe or d;
therefore,	*Everything is AC or Ad or bd or cdE.*

(2) *Universal affirmatives having different subjects.*

Given the conjunctive combination of two universal affirmative propositions with different subjects, a new complex proposition may be obtained by conjunctively combining both their subjects and their predicates. Thus, if *All X is P_1 or P_2* and *All Y is Q_1 or Q_2*, it follows that *All XY is P_1Q_1 or P_1Q_2 or P_2Q_1 or P_2Q_2*. But in this case the new proposition obtained is not equivalent to the conjunctive combination of the original propositions; and we cannot pass back from it to them.

A single complex proposition which sums up all the information contained in the original propositions may, however, be obtained by first reducing each of them to the form *Everything is X_1 or X_2 ... or X_n*, and then conjunctively combining their predicates.

476. *The Conjunctive Combination of Universal Negatives.*—Here again we may distinguish two cases according as the propositions to be combined have or have not the same subject.

(1) *Universal negatives having the same subject*

No X is P_1 or P_2 ...... or P_m,
No X is Q_1 or Q_2 ...... or Q_n,

may for our present purpose be taken as types of universal negative propositions having the same subject. Given these two propositions in conjunctive combination, a new complex proposition may be obtained by alternatively combining their predicates. Thus,

No X is P_1 or P_2 ...... or P_m or Q_1 or Q_2 ...... or Q_n.

This new proposition is equivalent to the two original propositions taken together, so that we can pass back from it to them. The process of combining the predicates is again likely to give opportunities of simplification. The following are examples:

(i)	No X is either aB or aC or aE or bC or bE,
	No X is either Ad or Ae or bd or be or cd or ce;
	therefore, No X is either a or b or d or e.[498]
(ii)	Nothing is aBC or aBe or aCD or aDe,
	Nothing is AcD or abD or aDE or bcD or cDE;
	therefore, Nothing is aBC or aBe or aD or cD.

(2) *Universal negatives having different subjects.*

Given the conjunctive combination of two universal negative propositions with different subjects a new complex proposition may be obtained by conjunctively combining their subjects and alternatively combining their predicates. Thus, if *No X is P_1 or P_2* and *No Y is Q_1, or Q_2*, it follows that *No XY is P_1 or P_2 or Q_1 or Q_2*. In this case the inferred proposition is not equivalent to the premises; and we cannot pass back from it to them.

A single complex proposition which sums up all the information contained in the original propositions may, however, be obtained by first reducing each of them to the form *Nothing is X_1, or X_2 ... or X_n*, and then alternatively combining their predicates.

477. *The Conjunctive Combination of Universals with Particulars of the same Quality.—* We may here consider, first, affirmatives, and then, negatives.

(1) *Affirmatives*. From the conjunctive combination of a universal affirmative and a particular affirmative having the same subject, a new particular affirmative proposition may be obtained by conjunctively combining their predicates. If *All X is P_1 or P_2* and *Some X is Q_1 or Q_2*, it follows that *Some X is P_1Q_1 or P_1Q_2 or P_2Q_1 or P_2Q_2*. Here the particular premiss affirms the existence of X and of either XQ_1 or XQ_2; and the universal premiss implies that if X exists then either XP_1 or XP_2 exists.

We can pass back from the conclusion to the particular premiss, but not to the universal premiss. The conclusion is, therefore, not equivalent to the two premises taken together.

A new complex proposition cannot be directly obtained from the conjunctive combination of a universal affirmative and a particular affirmative having different subjects. The propositions may, however, be reduced respectively to the forms *Everything is P_1 or P_2 ... or P_m, Something is Q_1 or Q_2 ... or Q_n*, and their predicates may then be conjunctively combined in accordance with the above rule.

(2) *Negatives*. From the conjunctive combination of a universal negative and a particular negative having the same subject, a new particular negative proposition may be obtained by the alternative combination of their predicates. If *No X is either P_1 or P_2* and *Some X is not*

---

[498] Compare section 435.

either Q_1 or Q_2 it follows that *Some X is not either P_1 or P_2 or Q_1 or Q_2*. The validity of this process is obvious since the particular premiss affirms the existence of *X*. By obversion it can also be exhibited as a corollary from the rule given above in regard to affirmatives. We can again pass back from the conclusion to the particular premiss, but not to the universal premiss.

With regard to the conjunctive combination of universal negatives and particular negatives having different subjects, the remarks made concerning affirmatives apply *mutatis mutandis*.

478. *The Conjunctive Combination of Affirmatives with Negatives.*—By first obverting one of the propositions, the conjunctive combination of an affirmative with a negative may be made to yield a new complex proposition in accordance with the rules given in the preceding sections. For example,

(1)	*All X is A or B*,
	No X is aC,
	therefore, *All X is A or Bc*;
(2)	*Everything is P or Q*,
	Nothing is Pq or pR,
	therefore, *Nothing is pR or q*;
(3)	*All X is AB or bce*,
	Some X is not either aBC or DE,
	therefore, *Some X is ABd or ABe or bce*.

479. *The Conjunctive Combination of Particulars with Particulars.*—Particulars cannot to any purpose be conjunctively combined with particulars so as to yield a new complex proposition. It is true that from *Some X is P_1 or P_2 and some X is Q_1 or Q_2*, we can pass to *Some X is P_1 or P_2 or Q_1 or Q_2*. But this is a mere weakening of the information given by either of the premisses singly; and by the rule that *an alternant may at any time be introduced into an undistributed term* (section 449), it could equally well be inferred from either premiss taken by itself. Again from *Some X is not either P_1 or P_2 and some X is not either Q_1 or Q_2* we can pass to *Some X is not either P_1Q_1 or P_1Q_2 or P_2Q_1 or P_2Q_2*. But similar remarks again apply, since we have already found that *a determinant may at any time be introduced into a distributed term*.

480. *The Alternative Combination of Universal Propositions.*—Given a number of universal propositions as alternants in a compound alternative proposition we cannot obtain a single equivalent complex proposition. From the compound proposition *Either all A is P_1 or P_2 or all A is Q_1 or Q_2* we can indeed infer *All A is P_1 or P_2 or Q_1 or Q_2*; but we cannot pass back from this to the original proposition.[499]

481. *The Alternative Combination of Particular Propositions.*—It follows from the equivalences shewn in section 447 that a compound alternative proposition in which all the alternants are particular can be reduced to the form of a single complex proposition. If all the alternants of the compound proposition have the same subject and are all affirmative, their predicates must be alternatively combined in the complex proposition; if they all have the same subject and are all negative, their predicates must be conjunctively combined in the

---

[499] Compare section 446.

complex proposition. If the alternants have different subjects, they must all be reduced to the form *Something is ...* before their predicates are combined; if they differ in quality, recourse must be had to the process of obversion. It is unnecessary to discuss these different cases in detail, but the following may be taken as examples:

(i)	*Some X is P or some X is Q = Some X is P or Q*;
(ii)	*Some X is not P or some X is not Q = Some X is not PQ*;
(iii)	*Some X is P or some Y is Q = Something is XP or YQ*;
(iv)	*Some X is P or some Y is not Q = Something is XP or Yq.*

482. *The Alternative Combination of Particulars with Universals.*—From a compound alternative proposition in which some of the alternants are particular and some universal, we can infer a particular complex proposition; but in this case we cannot pass back from the complex proposition to the compound proposition. The following are examples:

| (1) | *All A is P or some A is Q*, therefore, *Something is a or P or Q*;[500] |
| (2) | *All A is P or some B is not Q*, therefore, *Something is a or Bq or P.* |

EXERCISES

483. Reduce the propositions *All P is Q, No Q is R* to such a form that the universe of discourse appears as the subject of each of them; and then combine the propositions into a single complex proposition. How is your result related to the ordinary syllogistic conclusion *No P is R*? [K.]

484. Combine the following propositions into a single equivalent complex proposition: *All X is either A or b; No X is either AC or acD or CD; All a is B or x.* [K.]

485. Every voter is both a ratepayer and an occupier, or not a ratepayer at all; If any voter who pays rates is an occupier, then he is on the list; No voter on the list is both a ratepayer and an occupier.
Examine the results of combining these three statements. [V.]

486. Every *A* is *BC* except when it is *D*; everything which is not *A* is *D*; what is both *C* and *D* is *B*; and every *D* is *C*. What can be determined from these premises as to the contents of our universe of discourse? [M.]

INFERENCES FROM COMBINATIONS OF COMPLEX PROPOSITIONS

487. *Conditions under which a universal proposition affords information in regard to any given term.*—The problem to be solved in order to determine these conditions may be formulated as follows: *Given any universal proposition, and any term X, to discriminate*

---

[500] We cannot infer *Some A is P or Q*, since this implies the existence of *A*, whereas the non-existence of *A* is compatible with the premiss.

between the cases in which the proposition does and those in which it does not afford information with regard to this term.

In the first place, it is clear that if the proposition is to afford information in regard to any term whatever it must be non-formal. If it is negative, let it by obversion be made affirmative. Then it may be written in the form

Whatever is A_1A_2 ... or B_1B_2 ... or &c. is P_1P_2 ... or Q_1Q_2 ... or &c.,

where A_1, B_1, P_1, Q_1, &c. are all simple terms.[501]

As shewn in section 446, this may be resolved into the independent propositions:—

All A_1A_2 ... is P_1P_2 ... or Q_1Q_2 ... or &c.;
All B_1B_2 ... is P_1P_2 ... or Q_1Q_2 ... or &c.;
&c. &c. &c.;

in none of which is there any alternation in the subject.

These propositions may be dealt with separately, and if any one of them affords information with regard to X, then the original proposition does so.

We have then to consider a proposition of the form

All A_1A_2 ... A_n is P_1P_2 ... or Q_1Q_2 ... or &c.;

and this proposition may by contraposition be reduced to the form

Everything is a_1 or a_2 ... or a_n or P_1P_2 ... or Q_1Q_2 ... or &c.;

from which may be inferred

All X is a_1 or a_2 ... or a_n or P_1P_2 ... or Q_1Q_2 ... or &c.

Any alternant in the predicate of this proposition which contains x may clearly be omitted.

If all the alternants contain x, then the information afforded with regard to X is that it is non-existent.

If some alternants are left, then the proposition will afford information concerning X unless, when the predicate has been simplified to the fullest possible extent,[502] one of the alternants is itself X uncombined with any other term, in which case it is clear that we are left with a merely formal proposition.

Now one of these alternants will be X in the following cases, and only in these cases:—

First, If one of the alternants in the predicate of the original proposition, when reduced to the affirmative form, is X.

---

[501] So that both subject and predicate consist of a series of alternants which themselves contain only simple determinants; that is, there is no alternant of the form (*A or B*)(*C or D*).

[502] All superfluous terms being omitted, but the predicate still consisting of a series of alternants which themselves contain only simple determinants.

Secondly, If any set of alternants in the predicate of the original proposition, when reduced to the affirmative form, constitutes a development of *X*, since any development (for example, *AX* or *aX*, *ABX* or *AbX* or *aBX* or *abX*) is equivalent to *X* simply.[503]

Thirdly, If one of the alternants in the predicate of the original proposition, when reduced to the affirmative form, contains *X* in combination solely with some determinant that is also a determinant of the subject or the contradictory of some other alternant of the predicate; since in either of these cases such alternant is equivalent to *X* simply.[504]

Fourthly, If one of the determinants of the subject is *x*; since in that case we shall after contraposition have *X* as one of the alternants of the predicate.

The above may be summed up in the following proposition:—Any non-formal universal proposition will afford information with regard to any term *X*, unless, after it has been brought to the affirmative form, (1) one of the alternants of the predicate is *X*, or (2) any set of alternants in the predicate constitutes a development of *X*, or (3) any alternant of the predicate contains *X* in combination solely with some determinant that is also a determinant of the subject or the contradictory of some other alternant of the predicate, or (4) *x* is a determinant of the subject.

If, after the proposition has been reduced to the affirmative form, all superfluous terms are omitted in accordance with the rules given in chapters 1 and 2, then the criterion becomes more simple:—Any non-formal universal proposition will afford information with regard to any term *X*, unless (after it has been brought to the affirmative form and its predicate has been so simplified that it contains no superfluous terms) *X* is itself an alternant of the predicate or *x* is a determinant of the subject.[505]

If instead of *X* we have a complex term *XYZ*, then no determinant of this term must appear by itself as an alternant of the predicate, and there must be at least one alternant in the subject which does not contain as a determinant the contradictory of any determinant of this complex term; i.e., no alternant in the predicate must be *X*, *Y*, or *Z*, or any combination of these, and some alternant of the subject must contain neither *x*, *y*, nor *z*.

The above criterion is of simple application.

488. *Information jointly afforded by a series of universal propositions with regard to any given term.*—The great majority of direct problems[506] involving complex propositions may be brought under the general form, *Given any number of universal propositions involving any number of terms, to determine what is all the information that they jointly afford with regard to any given term or combination of terms.* If the student turns to Boole, Jevons, or Venn, he will find that this problem is treated by them as the central problem of symbolic logic.[507]

---

[503] See section 430.

[504] By section 445, rule (2), *All AB is AX or D* is equivalent to *All AB is X or D*; and by the law of exclusion (section 432) *A or aX* is equivalent to *A or X*.

[505] It may be added that every universal proposition, unless it be purely formal, will afford information *either with regard to X or with regard to x*. For if both *X* and *x* appear as alternants of the predicate, or as determinants of the subject of a universal affirmative proposition, then the proposition will necessarily be formal.

[506] Inverse problems will be discussed in the following chapter.

[507] "Boole," says Jevons, "first put forth the problem of Logical Science in its complete generality:—*Given certain logical premisses or conditions, to determine the description of any class of objects under those conditions.* Such was the general problem of which the ancient logic had solved but a few isolated cases—the nineteen moods of the syllogism, the sorites, the dilemma, the disjunctive syllogism, and a few other forms. Boole shewed incontestably that it was possible, by the aid of a system of mathematical signs, to deduce the conclusions of all these ancient modes of reasoning, and an indefinite number of other conclusions. Any conclusion, in short, that it was possible to deduce from any set of premisses or conditions, however numerous

A general method of solution is as follows:—

Let X be the term concerning which information is desired. Find what information each proposition gives separately with regard to X, thus obtaining a new set of propositions of the form *All X is P_1 or P_2 ... or P_n*.

This is always possible by the aid of the rules for obversion and contraposition given in chapter 3. By the aid of the rule given in the preceding section those propositions which do not afford any information at all with regard to X may at once be left out of account.

Next let the propositions thus obtained be combined in the manner indicated in section 475. This will give the desired solution.

If information is desired with regard to several terms, it will be convenient to bring all the propositions to the form

Everything is P_1 or P_2 ... or P_n;

and to combine them at once, thus summing up in a single proposition all the information given by the separate propositions taken together. From this proposition all that is known concerning X may immediately be deduced by omitting every alternant that contains x, all that is known concerning Y by omitting every alternant that contains y, and so on.

The method may be varied by bringing the propositions to the form

No X is Q_1 or Q_2 ... or Q_n,

or to the form

Nothing is Q_1 or Q_2 ... or Q_n,

then combining them as in section 476, and (if an affirmative solution is desired) finally obverting the result. It will depend on the form of the original propositions whether this variation is desirable.[508]

In an equational system of symbolic logic, a solution with regard to any term X generally involves a partial solution with regard to x also. In the employment of the above methods, x must be found separately. It may be added that the complete solutions for X and x sum up between them the whole of the information given by the original data; in other words, they are, taken together, equivalent to the given premisses.[509]

The following may be taken as a simple example of the first of the above methods. It is adapted from Boole (*Laws of Thought*, p. 118).

"Given 1st, that wherever the properties A and B are combined, either the property C, or the property D, is present also, but they are not jointly present; 2nd, that wherever the

---

and complicated, could be calculated by his method" (*Philosophical Transactions*, 1870). Compare also *Principles of Science*, 6, § 5.

[508] This second method is analogous to that which is usually employed by Dr Venn in his *Symbolic Logic*. Both methods bear a certain resemblance to Jevons's Indirect Method; but neither of them is identical with that method.

[509] Having determined that *All X is P* and that *All x is q*, we may by contraposition bring the latter proposition to the form *All Q is X*, and it may then be found that P and Q have some alternants in common. These alternants are the terms which (in Boole's system) are taken in their whole extent in the equation giving X; and the solution thus obtained is closely analogous to that given by any equational system of symbolic logic.

properties *B* and *C* are combined, the properties *A* and *D* are either both present with them, or both absent; 3rd, that wherever the properties *A* and *B* are both absent, the properties *C* and *D* are both absent also; and *vice versâ*, where the properties *C* and *D* are both absent, *A* and *B* are both absent also. Find what can be inferred from the presence of A with regard to the presence or absence of *B*, *C*, and *D*."

The premisses may be written as follows: (1) *All AB is Cd or cD*; (2) *All BC is AD or ad*; (3) *All ab is cd*; (4) *All cd is ab*.

Then,	from (1),	*All A is b or Cd or cD*;
	and from (2),	*All A is b or c or D*;
therefore	(by combining these),	*All A is b or cD*;

(3) gives no information regarding *A* (see the preceding section);

but by (4),	*All A is C or D*;
therefore,	*All A is bC or bD or cD*;

and, since *bD* is by development either *bCD* or *bcD* this becomes

All A is bC or cD.

This solves the problem as set. Proceeding also to determine *a*, we find that (1) gives no information with regard to this term; but by (2), *All a is b or c or d*; and by (3), *All a is B or cd*; therefore, *All a is Bc or Bd or cd*. Again by (4), *All a is b or C or D*. Therefore, *All a is BCd or BcD or bcd*; and by contraposition, *Whatever is Bcd or bC or bD or CD is A*.[510]

489. *The Problem of Elimination.*—By *elimination* in logic is meant the omission of certain elements from a proposition or set of propositions with the object of expressing more directly and concisely the connection between the elements which remain. An example of the process is afforded by the ordinary categorical syllogism, where the so-called *middle term* is eliminated. Thus, given the premisses *All M is P*, *All S is M*, we may infer *All S is MP*; but if we desire to know the relation between *S* and *P* independently of *M* we are content with the less precise but sufficient statement *All S is P*; in other words, we eliminate *M*.

Elimination has been considered by some writers to be absolutely essential to logical reasoning. It is not, however, necessarily involved either in the process of contraposition or in the process discussed in the preceding section; and if formal inferences are recognised at all, the name of inference certainly cannot be denied to these processes. We must, therefore, refuse to regard elimination as of the essence of reasoning, although it may usually be involved therein.[511]

490. *Elimination from Universal Affirmations.*—Any universal affirmative proposition (or, by combination, any set of universal affirmative propositions) involving the term *X* and its contradictory *x* may by contraposition be reduced to the form *Everything is PX or Qx or R*,

---

[510] Taking into account the result arrived at above with regard to *A*, it will be seen that this may be resolved into *Whatever is bC or bD is A* and *Nothing is BCD or Bcd*. These two propositions taken together with the solution for *A* are equivalent to the original premisses.

[511] Compare sections 207, 208.

where *P, Q, R* are themselves simple or complex terms not involving *X* or *x*; and since by the rule given in section 448 a determinant may at any time be omitted from an undistributed term, we may eliminate *X* (and *x*) from this proposition by simply omitting them, and reducing the proposition to the form *Everything is P or Q or R*.[512]

We must, however, here admit the possibility of *P, Q, R* being of the forms *A or a, Aa*. These are equivalent respectively to the *entire universe of discourse* and to *nothing*. Thus, if *P* is of the form *A or a*, and *Q* is of the form *Aa*, our proposition will before elimination more naturally be written *Everything is X or R*; if *Q* is of the form *A or a*, and *R* of the form *Aa*, it will more naturally be written *Everything is PX or x*. It follows that if either *P* or *Q* is of the form *A or a* (that is, if either *P* or *Q* is equivalent to the entire universe of discourse), the proposition resulting from elimination will not afford any real information, since it is always true *à priori* that *Everything is A or a or &c*. Thus we are unable to eliminate *X* from such a proposition as *All A is X or BC*.

The following may be given as an example of elimination from universal affirmatives.

Let it be required to eliminate *X* (together with *x*) from the propositions *All P is XQ or xR, Whatever is X or R is p or XQR*. Combining these propositions, we have *Everything is XQR or p*; therefore, by elimination, *Everything is QR or p* that is, *All P is QR*. It will be observed that *P* (together with *p*) cannot be eliminated from the above propositions.

491. *Elimination from Universal Negatives.*—Any universal negative proposition (or, by combination, any set of universal negative propositions) containing the term *X* and its contradictory *x* may by conversion be reduced to the form *Nothing is PX or Qx or R*, where *P, Q, R* are themselves simple or complex terms not involving either *X* or *x*. Here we might, in accordance with the rule given in section 448, simply omit the alternants *PX, Qx*, leaving us with the proposition *Nothing is R*. This, however, is but part of the information obtainable by the elimination of *X*. We have also *No X is P*, and *No Q is x*, that is, *All Q is X*; whence by a syllogism in *Celarent* we may infer *No Q is P*. The full result of the elimination is, therefore, given by the proposition *Nothing is PQ or R*.[513]

Another method by which the same result may be obtained is as follows: By developing the first alternant with reference to *Q* and the second with reference to *P*, *Nothing is PX or Qx or R* becomes *Nothing is PQX or PqX or PQx or pQx or R*. But *PQX or PQx* is reducible to *PQ*, and on omitting *PqX* and *pQx*, we have *Nothing is PQ or R*.

It is interesting to observe that the above rule for elimination from negatives is equivalent to Boole's famous rule for elimination. In order to eliminate *X* from the equation $F(X) = 0$, he gives the formula $F(1) F(0) = 0$. Now any equation containing *X* can be brought to the form $AX + Bx + C = 0$, where A, B, C are independent of X. Applying Boole's rule we have $(A + C)(B + C) = 0$, that is, $AB + C = 0$; and this is precisely equivalent to the rule given in the text.

The following is an example: Let it be required to eliminate *X* from the propositions *No P is Xq or xr, No X or R is xP or Pq or Pr*. Combining these propositions we have *Nothing is*

---

[512] We might also proceed as follows: Solve for *X* and for *x*, as in section 488, so that we have *All X is A, All x is B*, where *A* and *B* are simple or complex terms not involving either *X* or *x*. Then, since *Everything is X or x*, we shall have *Everything is A or B*, and this will be a proposition containing neither *X* nor *x*.

[513] Compare Mrs Ladd Franklin's Essay on *The Algebra of Logic* (*Studies in Logic by Members of the Johns Hopkins University*). The same conclusion may be deduced by obversion from the result obtained in the preceding section. *Nothing is PX or Qx or R* becomes by obversion *Everything is prX or qrx*. Therefore, by the elimination of *X*, *Everything is pr or qr*; and this proposition becomes by obversion *Nothing is PQ or R*.

XPq or *XPr* or *xP* or *PqR*; therefore, by elimination in accordance with the above rule, *Nothing is Pq or Pr*, that is, *No P is q or r*.

492. *Elimination from Particular Affirmatives.*—Any particular affirmative proposition involving the term *X* may by conversion be reduced to the form *Something is either PX or Qx or R*, where *P, Q, R* are independent of *X* and *x*. We may here immediately apply the rule given in section 448 that a determinant may at any time be omitted from an undistributed term; and the result of eliminating *X* is accordingly *Something is either P or Q or R*.[514]

493. *Elimination from Particular Negatives.*—Any particular negative proposition involving the term may by contraposition be reduced to the form *Something is not either PX or Qx or R*. By the development of the first alternant with reference to *Q* and that of the second alternant with reference to *P*, this proposition becomes *Something is not either PQX or PqX or PQx or pQx or R*. But *PQX or PQx* is reducible to *PQ* and the alternants *PqX, pQx* may by the rule given in section 448 be omitted. Hence we get the proposition *Something is not either PQ or R*, from which *X* has been eliminated.[515]

494. *Order of procedure in the process of elimination.*—Schröder (*Der Operationskreis des Logikkalkuls*, p. 23) points out that first to eliminate and then combine is not the same thing as first to combine and then eliminate. For, *as a rule, if a term X is eliminated from several isolated propositions the combined results give less information than is afforded by first combining the given propositions and then effecting the required elimination.*

There are indeed many cases in which we cannot eliminate at all unless we first combine the given propositions. This is of course obvious in syllogisms; and we have a similar case if we take the premisses *Everything is A or X*, *Everything is B or x*. We cannot eliminate *X* from either of these propositions taken by itself, since in each of them *X* (or *x*) appears as an isolated alternant. But by combination we have *Everything is Ax or BX*; and this by the elimination of *X* becomes *Everything is A or B*.[516]

There are other cases in which elimination from the separate propositions is possible, but where this order of procedure leads to a weakened conclusion. Take the propositions *Everything is AX or Bx*, *Everything is CX or Dx*. By first eliminating *X* and then combining, we have *Everything is AC or AD or BC or BD*. But by first combining and then eliminating *X* our conclusion becomes *Everything is AC or BD*, which gives more information than is afforded by the previous conclusion.

EXERCISES

495. Suppose that an analysis of the properties of a particular class of substances has led to the following general conclusions, namely:

---

[514] Thus the rule for elimination from particular affirmatives is practically identical with the rule for elimination from universal affirmatives.

[515] Thus the rule for elimination from particular negatives is practically identical with the rule for elimination from universal negatives. The same rule may be deduced by obversion from the result obtained in the preceding section. *Something is not either PX or Qx or R*; therefore, *Something is either prX or qrx or pqr*; therefore, *Something is either pr or qr*; therefore, *Something is not either PQ or R*.

[516] Working with negatives we get the same result. Taking the propositions *Nothing is ax*, *Nothing is bX*, separately, we cannot eliminate *X* from either of them. But combining them in the proposition *Nothing is ax or bX*, we are able to infer *Nothing is ab*.

1st, That wherever the properties A and B are combined, either the property C, or the property D, is present also; but they are not jointly present;

2nd, That wherever the properties B and C are combined, the properties A and D are either both present with them, or both absent;

3rd, That wherever the properties A and B are both absent, the properties C and D are both absent also; and *vice versâ*, where the properties C and D are both absent, A and B are both absent also.

Shew that wherever the property A is present, the properties B and C are not both present; also that wherever B is absent while C is present, A is present.

[Boole, *Laws of Thought*, pp. 118 to 120; compare also Venn, *Symbolic Logic*, pp. 276 to 278.]

A solution of this problem has already been given in section 488. We may also proceed as follows. The premisses are:

All AB is Cd or cD,	(i)
All BC is AD or ad,	(ii)
All ab is cd,	(iii)
All cd is ab.	(iv)
By (i), *No AB is CD*, therefore, *No A is BCD*.	(1)
By (ii), *No BC is Ad*, therefore, *No A is BCd*.	(2)

Combining (1) and (2), it follows immediately that *No A is BC*.

Boole also shews that *All bC is A*. This is a partial contrapositive of (iii). We have so far not required to make use of (iv) at all.

496. Given the same premisses as in the preceding section, prove that:—

(1) Wherever the property C is found, either the property A or the property B will be found with it, but not both of them together;

(2) If the property B is absent, either A and C will be jointly present, or C will be absent;

(3) If A and C are jointly present, B will be absent. [Boole, *Laws of Thought*, p. 129.]

First, By (i), *All C is a or b or d*; by (ii), *All C is a or b or D*; therefore, *All C is a or b*.	
Also, by (iii), *All C is A or B*;	
therefore, *All C is Ab or aB*.	(1)
Secondly, By (iii). *All b is A or c*,	
therefore, by section 432, *All b is AC or c*.	(2)
Thirdly, from (1) it follows immediately that	
All AC is b.	(3)

The given premisses may all be summed up in the proposition: *Everything is AbC or AbD or $aBCd$ or $abcd$ or BcD*. From this, the above special results and others follow immediately.

497. Given that *everything is either Q or R*, and that *all R is Q, unless it is not P*, prove that *all P is Q*. [K.]

The premisses may be written as follows: (1) *All r is Q*, (2) *All PR is Q*.

By (1), *All Pr is Q*, and by (2), *All PR is Q*; but *All P is Pr or PR*; therefore, *All P is Q*.

498. Where *A* is present, *B* and *C* are either both present at once or absent at once; and where *C* is present, *A* is present. Describe the class *not-B* under these conditions. [Jevons, *Studies*, p. 204.]

The premises are (1) *All A is BC or bc*, (2) *All C is A*.

By (1) *All b is a or c*, and by (2) *All b is A or c*, therefore, *All b is c*.

499. It is known of certain things that (1) where the quality *A* is, *B* is not; (2) where *B* is, and only where *B* is, *C* and *D* are. Derive from these conditions a description of the class of things in which *A* is not present, but *C* is. [Jevons, *Studies*, p. 200.]

The premises are: (1) *All A is b*; (2) *All B is CD*; (3) *All CD is B*.

No information regarding *aC* is given by (1). But by (2), *All aC is b or D*; and by (3), *All aC is B or d*.

Therefore, *All aC is BD or bd*.

500. Taking the same premises as in the previous section, draw descriptions of the classes *Ac*, *ab*, and *cD*. [Jevons, *Studies*, p. 244.]

By (1), *Everything is a or b*, and by (2), *Everything is b or CD*. Therefore, *Everything is aCD or b*; and by (3), *Everything is B or c or d*. Therefore, *Everything is aBCD or bc or bd*.

Hence we infer immediately *All Ac is b*, *All ab is c or d*, *All cD is b*.

501. There is a certain class of things from which *A* picks out the '*X* that is *E*, and the *Y* that is not *Z*,' and *B* picks out from the remainder 'the *Z* which is *Y* and the *X* that is not *Y*.' It is then found that nothing is left but the class '*Z* which is not *X*.' The whole of this class is however left. What can be determined about the class originally? [Venn, *Symbolic Logic*, pp. 267, 8.]

The chief difficulty in this problem c

All W is XZ or Yz or YZ or Xy or xZ,	
that is, *All W is X or Y or Z*;	(1)
All xZ is W;	(2)
No xZ is WXZ or WYz or WYZ or WXy,	
that is, *No xZ is WYZ*.	(3)

We may now proceed as follows:—By (1), *All W is X or Y or Z*; and by (3), *All W is X or y or z*. Therefore, *All W is X or Yz or yZ*. (2) affords no information regarding the class *W*, except that everything that is *Z* but not *X* is contained within it.

502. (1) If a nation has natural resources, and a good government, it will be prosperous. (2) If it has natural resources without a good government, or a good government without natural resources, it will be contented, but not prosperous. (3) If it has neither natural resources nor a good government it will be neither contented nor prosperous.

Shew that these statements may be reduced to two propositions of the form of Hamilton's U. [O'S]

Let a nation with natural resources be denoted by *R*, a nation with a good government by *G*, a prosperous nation by *P*, and a contented nation by *C*. Then the given statements may be expressed as follows:—(1) *All RG is P*; (2) *All Rg or rG is Cp*; (3) *All rg is cp*.

By contraposition, (2) may be resolved into the two propositions, *All cp is RG or rg*, *All P is RG or rg*. But by (1) *No cp is RG*; and by (3) *No P is rg*. Hence the two propositions into which (2) was resolved may be reduced to the form, *All cp is rg*, *All P is RG*.

The three original statements are accordingly equivalent to the two U propositions *All RG is all P, All rg is all cp*.

503. Let the observation of a class of natural productions be supposed to have led to the following general results.

1st. That in whichsoever of these productions the properties A and C are missing, the property E is found, together with one of the properties B and D, but not with both.

2nd. That wherever the properties A and D are found while E is missing, the properties B and C will either both be found, or both be missing.

3rd. That wherever the property A is found in conjunction with either B or E, or both of them, there either the property C or the property D will be found, but not both of them. And conversely, wherever the property C or D is found singly, there the property A will be found in conjunction with either B or E or both of them.

Shew that it follows that *In whatever substances the property A is found, there will also be found either the property C or the property D, but not both, or else the properties B, C, and E will all be wanting*. And conversely, *Where either the property C or the property D is found singly or the properties B. C, and D are together missing, there the property A will be found*. Shew also that *If the property A is absent and C present, D is present*.

[Boole, *Laws of Thought*, pp. 146–148. Venn, *Symbolic Logic*, pp. 280, 281. *Johns Hopkins Studies in Logic*, pp. 57, 58, 82, 83.]

The premisses are as follows:—

1st,	*All ac is BdE or bDE*;	(i)
2nd,	*All Ade is BC or bc*;	(ii)
3rd,	*Whatever is AB or AE is Cd or cD*;	(iii)
	Whatever is Cd or cD is AB or AE.	(iv)

We are required to prove:—

All A is Cd or cD or bcd;	(α)
All Cd is A;	(β)
All cD is A;	(γ)
All bcd is A;	(δ)
All aC is D.	(ε)

First, By (iii), *All A is Cd or cD or bc*. But by (ii), *All Abe is c or d*; and by (iv), *All Abe is CD or cd*; therefore, *All Abe is cd*. Hence, *All A is Cd or cD or bcd*. (α)

Secondly, (β) and (γ) follow immediately from (iv).

Thirdly, from (i), we have directly, *No ac is bd*; therefore (by conversion), *No bcd is a*; therefore, *All bcd is A*. (δ)

Lastly, by (iv), *All Cd is A*; therefore, by contraposition, *All aC is D*. (ε)

We may obtain a complete solution so far as A is concerned as follows:

By (ii),[517] *All A is BC or bc or d or E*;

---

[517] No information whatever with regard to A is given by (i), since a appears as a determinant of the subject. See section 487.

by (iii), *All is be or Cd or cD*;

therefore, *All A is Cd or cDE or bcD or bce or bde*;

by (iv). *All A is B or E or CD or cd*;

therefore, *All A is cDE or bcde or BCd or CdE*.

This includes the partial solution with regard to *A*,—*All A is Cd or cD or bcd*. Boole contents himself with this because he has started with the intention of eliminating *E* from his conclusion.

We may now solve for *a*. (ii) and (iii) give no information with regard to this term. But by (i), *All a is BdE or bDE or C*; and by (iv), *All a is CD or cd*. Therefore, *All a is BcdE or CD*. And this yields by contraposition, *Whatever is bc or Cd or cD or ce is A*.

504. Given the same premises as in the preceding section, shew that,—

1st. *If the property B be present in one of the productions, either the properties A, C, and D are all absent, or some one alone of them is absent. And conversely, if they are all absent it may be concluded that the property B is present.*

2nd. *If A and C are both present or both absent, D will be absent, quite independently of the presence or absence of B.* [Boole, *Laws of Thought*, p. 149.]

We may proceed here by combining all the given premises in the manner indicated in section 475. From the result thus obtained the above conclusions as well as those contained in the preceding section will immediately follow.

By (iii), *Everything is a or be or Cd or cD*;

and by (iv). *Everything is AB or AE or CD or cd*;

therefore, *Everything is ABCd or ABcD or ACdE or AcDE or aCD or acd or bCDe or bcde*;

therefore by (i), *Everything is ABCd or ABcD or Abcde or ACdE or AcDE or aBcdE or aCD or bCDe*;

therefore by (ii), *Everything is ABCd or Abcde or ACdE or AcDE or aBcdE or aCD*.   (v)

Hence, *All B is ACd or AcDE or acdE or aCD*;

All acd is BE;
All AC is Bd or dE;
All ac is BdE.

Eliminating *E* from each of the above we have the results arrived at by Boole.

Eliminating both *A* and *E* from (v) we have

Everything is BCd or bcd or Cd or cD or Bcd or CD;

that is *Everything is C or D or cd*, which is an identity. This is equivalent to Boole's conclusion that "there is no independent relation among the properties *B*, *C*, and *D*" (*Laws of Thought*, p. 148).

Any further results that may be desired are obtainable immediately from (v).

505. Given $XY = A$, $YZ = C$, find XZ in terms of *A* and *C*.

[Venn, *Symbolic Logic*, pp. 279, 310–312. *Johns Hopkins Studies in Logic*, pp. 53, 54.]

The premises may be written as follows:

Everything is AXY or ax or ay;	(1)
Everything is CYZ or cy or cx.	(2)

By (1), *All XZ is AY or ay*, and by (2), *All XZ is CY or cy*; therefore, *All XZ is ACY or acy*. Hence, eliminating *Y*, *All XZ is AC or ac*.

This solves the problem as set. But in order to get a complete solution equivalent to that which would be obtained by Boole, the following may be added: Solving as above for *x* or *z*, and eliminating *Y*, we have *All that is either x or z is AcXz or aCxZ or ac*. Whence, by contraposition, *Whatever is AC or Ax or AZ or CX or Cz is XZ*. In other words, *Whatever is AC or AZ or CX is XZ*; and *Nothing is Ax or Cz*.

506. Shew the equivalence between the three following systems of propositions: (1) *All Ab is cd*; *All aB is Ce*; *All D is E*; (2) *All A is B or c or D*; *All BE is A*; *All Be is Ad or Cd*; *All bD is aE*; (3) *Whatever is A or e is B or d*; *All a is bE or bd or BCe*; *All bC is a*; *All D is E*.

[K.]

By obversion, the first set of propositions become *No Ab is C or D*; *No aB is c or E*; *No D is e*; and these propositions are combined in the statement, *Nothing is either AbC or AbD or aBc or aBE or De*. (1)

By obverting and combining the second set of propositions, we have *Nothing is AbCd or aBE or aBce or BDe or AbD or bDe*. (2)

But *AbCd or AbD* is equivalent to *AbC or AbD*; *aBE or aBce* to *aBE or aBc*; *BDe or bDe* to *De*. Hence (1) and (2) are equivalent.

Again, by obverting and combining the third set of propositions, we have *Nothing is AbD or bDe or aBc or aBE or abDe or acDe or AbC or De*. (3)

But since *bDe*, *abDe*, *acDe* are all subdivisions of *De*, (3) immediately resolves itself into (1).

507. From the premisses (1) *No Ax is cd or cy*, (2) *No BX is cde or cey*, (3) *No ab is cdx or cEx*, (4) *No A or B or C is xy*, deduce a proposition containing neither *X* nor *Y*. [*Johns Hopkins Studies*, p. 53.]

By (2), *No X is Bcde*, and by (1) and (3), *No x is Acd or abcd or abcE*; therefore, by section 491, *No Acd or abcd or abcE is Bcde*; therefore, *No Acd is Be*. It will be observed that since *Y* does not appear in the premisses, *y* can be eliminated only by omitting all the terms containing it.

508. The members of a scientific society are divided into three sections, which are denoted by *A*, *B*, *C*. Every member must join one, at least, of these sections, subject to the following conditions: (1) any one who is a member of *A* but not of *B*, of *B* but not of *C*, or of *C* but not of *A*, may deliver a lecture to the members if he has paid his subscription, but otherwise not; (2) one who is a member of *A* but not of *C*, of *C* but not of *A*, or of *B* but not of *A*, may exhibit an experiment to the members if he has paid his subscription, but otherwise not; but (3) every member must either deliver a lecture or perform an experiment annually before the other members. Find the least addition to these rules which will compel every member to pay his subscription or forfeit his membership. [*Johns Hopkins Studies*, p. 54.]

Let *A* = member of section *A*, &c.; *X* = one who gives a lecture; *Y* = one who performs an experiment; *Z* = one who has paid his subscription.

The premisses are

(1) *All Ab or aC or Bc is x or Z*;
(2) *All Ac or aB or aC is y or Z*;
(3) *Every member is X or Y*;
(4) *Every member is A or B or C*.

The problem is to find what is the least addition to these rules which will result in the conclusion that *Every member is Z*.

By (1), *All z is either x or else (a or B) (A or c) (b or C)*;
therefore, *All z is x or ABC or abc*.
Similarly, by (2), *All z is y or AC or abc*;
therefore, *All z is xy or xAC or ABC or abc*.
By (3), *All z is X or Y*;
therefore, *All z is XABC or Xabc or xYAC or YABC or Yabc*.
By (4), *All z is A or B or C*;
therefore, *All z is XABC or xYAC or YABC*;
but *All YABC is either XYABC or xYABC*;
therefore, *All z is XABC or xYAC*.

Hence, we gain the desired result if we add to the premisses, *No z is XABC or xYAC*. The required rule is therefore as follows: *No one who has not paid his subscription may join all three sections and deliver a lecture, nor may he join A and C and exhibit an experiment without delivering a lecture.*

509. What may be inferred independently of *X* and *Y* from the premisses: (1) *Either some A that is X is not Y, or all D is both X and Y*; (2) *Either some Y is both B and X, or all X is either not Y or C and not B*? [*Johns Hopkins Studies*, p. 85.]

The premisses may be written as follows: (1) *Either something is AXy, or everything is XY or d*; (2) *Either something is BXY, or everything is x or y or bC*.

By combining these premisses as in chapter 4, *Either something is AXy and something is BXY, or something is AXy and everything is x or y or bC, or something is BXY and everything is XY or d, or everything is bCXY or bCd or dx or dy*.[518]

Therefore, eliminating *X* and *Y* (see sections 490 and 492), *Either something is A and something is B, or something is A, or something is B, or everything is bC or d*; and by combining the first three alternants as in section 481, this becomes

Either something is A or B or everything is bC or d.

This conclusion may also be expressed in the form

If everything is ab, then every c is d.

510. Six children, *A, B, C, D, E, F* are required to obey the following rules: (1) on Monday and Tuesday no four can go out together; (2) on Thursday, Friday, and Saturday no three can stay in together; (3) on Tuesday, Wednesday, and Saturday, if *B* and *C* are together, then *A, B, E,* and *F* must be together; (4) on Monday and Saturday *B* cannot go out unless either *D*, or *A, C,* and *E* stay at home. *A* and *B* are first to decide what they will do, and *C* makes his decision before *D, E,* and *F*. Find (α) when *C* must go out, (β) when he must stay in, and (γ) when he may do as he pleases. [*Johns Hopkins Studies*, p. 58.]

Let *A* = case in which *A* goes out, *a* = that in which he stays in, &c.

---

[518] We cannot, if we are to be left with an equivalent proposition, express the first three of these alternants in a non-compound form. See sections 477, 479.

Then the premises are as follows:
(1) On Monday and Tuesday,—*three at least must stay in*;
(2) On Thursday, Friday, and Saturday,—*no three can stay in together*;
(3) On Tuesday, Wednesday, and Saturday,—*Every case is ABEF or abef or Bc or bC*;
(4) On Monday and Saturday,—*Every case is ace or b or d*.

In order to solve the problem, we must combine the possibilities for each day, then eliminate D, E, and F, and find in what ways the movements of A and B determine those of C.

(i) On Monday,—we have *Every case is ace or b or d*, combined with the condition that three at least must stay in. One alternant therefore is *def* without further condition, and it follows that we can determine no independent relation between A, B, and C.

Hence *on Monday C may do as he pleases*.

(ii) On Tuesday,—we have *Every case is ABEF or abef or Bc or bC*, combined with the condition that three at least must stay in. Therefore, *Every case is abef or Bc or bC*;[519] and eliminating D, E, and F, *Every case is ab or Bc or bC*.

Hence it follows that *on Tuesday (α) if A goes out while B stays in, C must go out, and (β) if B goes out, C must stay in*.

(iii) On Wednesday,—*Every case is ABEF or abef or Bc or bC*; or, eliminating D, E, and F, *Every case is AB or ab or Bc or bC*. Therefore, *All Ab is C* and *All aB is c*.

Hence *on Wednesday (α) if A goes out while B stays in, C must go out, and (β) if A stays in while B goes out, C must stay in*.

(iv) On Thursday and Friday,—the only condition is that no three can stay in together.

Hence *on Thursday and Friday if A and B both stay in, C must go out*.

(v) On Saturday,—*Every case is ABEF or abef or Bc or bC*; also *Every case is ace or b or d*. Combining these premises, *Every case is ABdEF or abef or aBce or Bcd or bC*. But we have the further condition that no three can stay in together. Therefore, *Every case is ABdEF or ABcdEF or AbCDE or AbCDF or AbCEF or bCDEF*. Therefore, eliminating D, E, and F, *Every case is AB or bC*.

Hence *on Saturday if B stays in, C must go out*.

511. Given (1) *All P is QR*, (2) *All p is qr*; shew that (3) *All Q is PR*, (4) *All R is PQ*. [K.]

512. Eliminate R from the propositions *All R is P or pq, All q is Pr or R, All qR is P*. [K.]

513. Shew the equivalence between the following sets of propositions:—(1) *a is BC; b is AC; C is Ab or aB*; (2) *a is BC; B is Ac or aC; c is AB*; (3) *A is Bc or bC; b is AC; c is AB*.

[K.]

514. Say by inspection, stating your reasons, which of the following propositions give information concerning A, aB, b, bCd, respectively: *All Ab is bCd or c; All bd is A or bC or abc; Whatever is a or B is c or D; Whatever is Ab or bc is bD or cD or e; Everything is A or ab or Bc or Cd*.

[K.]

---

[519] The two alternants *Bc* and *bC* might here be made more determinate, thus, *aBcd or aBce or aBcf or Bcde or Bcdf or Bcef* and *abCd or abCe or abCf or bCde or bCdf or bCef*. But since we know that we are going on immediately to eliminate *d*, *e*, and *f*, it is obvious, even without writing them out in full, that these more determinate expressions will at once be reduced again to *Bc* and *bC* simply.

515. Determine the conditions under which a particular proposition affords information in regard to any given term. [K.]

516. It is known of certain things that the quality A is always accompanied by C and D, but never by B; and further, that the qualities C and D never occur together, except in conjunction with A. What can we infer about C? [M.]

517. Given that everything that is Q but not S is either both P and or neither P nor R and that neither R nor S is both P and Q, shew that no P is Q. [K.]

518. Where C is present, A, B, and D are all present; where D is present, A, B, and C are either all three present or all three absent. Shew that when either A or B is present, C and D are either both present or both absent. How much of the given information is superfluous so far as the desired conclusion is concerned? [K.]

519. Given (i) *All Pqr is ST*; (ii) *Q and R are always present or absent together*; (iii) *All QRS is PT or pt*; (iv) *All QRs is Pt*; (v) *All pqrS is T*; then it follows that (1) *All Pq is rST*; (2) *All Ps is QRt*; (3) *All pQ is RSt*; (4) *All pT is qr*; (5) *All Qs is PRt*; (6) *All QT is PRS*; (7) *All qS is rT*; (8) *All qs is pr*; (9) *All qt is prs*; (10) *All sT is pqr*. [K.]

520. What can be determined about P in terms of Q and R from the premisses *All P is Q or X, Some P is not RX*? [K.]

521. Given that all honest men are happy, and that all dishonest men are unwise; and assuming that honest and dishonest, happy and unhappy, wise and unwise, are pairs of logical contradictories; what is all that can be inferred about men who are happy, unhappy, wise, unwise, respectively? [K.]

522. If thriftlessness and poverty are inseparable, and virtue and misery are incompatible, and if thrift be a virtue, can any relation be proved to exist between misery and poverty? If moreover all thriftless people are either virtuous or not miserable, what follows? [V.]

523. At a certain examination, all the candidates who were entered for Latin were also entered for either Greek, French, or German, but not for more than one of these languages; all the candidates who were not entered for German were entered for two at least of the other languages; no candidate who was entered for both Greek and French was entered for German, but all candidates who were entered for neither Greek nor French were entered for Latin. Shew that all the candidates were entered for two of the four languages, but none for more than two. [K.]

524. (1) Wherever there is smoke there is also fire or light; (2) Wherever there is light and smoke there is also fire; (3) There is no fire without either smoke or light.

Given the truth of the above propositions, what is all that you can infer with regard to (i) circumstances where there is smoke; (ii) circumstances where there is not smoke; (iii) circumstances where there is not light? [W.]

525. In a certain warehouse, when the articles offered are antique, they are costly, and at the same time either beautiful or grotesque, but not both. When they are both modern and grotesque, they are neither beautiful nor costly. Everything which is not beautiful is offered at a low price, and nothing cheap is beautiful. What can we assert (1) about the antique, and (2) about the grotesque articles? [M.]

526. Shew that the following sets of propositions are equivalent to one another:—

(1) *All a is b or c*; *All b is aCd*; *All c is aB*; *All D is c*.
(2) *All A is BC*; *All b is aC*; *All C is ABd or abd*.

(3) *All A is B*; *All B is A or c*; *All c is aB*; *All D is c*.
(4) *All b is aC*; *All A is C*; *All C is d*; *All aC is b*.
(5) *All c is aB*; *All D is aB*; *All A is B*; *All aB is c*.
(6) *All A is BC*; *All BC is A*; *All D is Bc*; *All b is C*. [K.]

527. Shew that a certain set of four properties must be found somewhere together, if the following facts are known: "Everything that has the first property or is without the last has the two others; and if everything that has both the first and last has one or other but not both of the two others, then something that has the first two must be without the last two." [J.]

528. Given the propositions: (i) all material goods are external; (ii) no internal (= non-external) goods are dispropriable; (iii) all dispropriable goods are appropriable; (iv) no collective goods are appropriable or immaterial (= non-material); what is all that we can infer about (*a*) appropriable goods, (*b*) immaterial goods? [J.]

529. Eliminate *X* and *Y* from the following propositions: *All aX is BcY or bcy*; *No AX is BY*; *All AB is Y*; *No ABCD is xY*. Shew also that it follows from these propositions that *All XY is Ab or aBc*. [K.]

530. Given (1) *All A is Bc or bC*, (2) *All B is DE or de*, (3) *All C is De*; shew that (i) *All A is BcDE or Bcde or bCDe*, (ii) *All BcD is E*, (iii) *All abd is c*, (iv) *All cd is ab or Be*, (v) *All bCD is e*. [Jevons, *Pure Logic*, § 160.]

531. Given (1) *All aB is c or D*, (2) *All BE is DF or cdF*, (3) *All C is aB or BE or D*, (4) *All bD is e or F*, (5) *All bf is a or C or DE*, (6) *All bcdE is Af or aF*, (7) *All A is B or CDEf or cDf or cdE*; shew that (i) *All A is B*, (ii) *All C is D*, (iii) *All E is F*. [K.]

532. Shew the equivalence between the two following sets of propositions: [K.]

(1)	*All A is BC or BE or CE or D*;
	All B is ACDE or ACde or cdE;
	All C is AB or AE or aD;
	All D is ABCE or Ace or aC;
	All E is AC or aCB or Bc.
(2)	*All a is BcdE or bcde or bD*;
	All b is a or ce or dE;
	All c is AbDe or abde or BdE;
	All d is abce or BcE or Be or bE;
	All e is ab or bc or d.

533. Given

(1)	*All bc is DE or Df or hk*,
(2)	*All C is aB or DEFG or BFH*,
(3)	*All Bcd is eL or hk*,
(4)	*All Acf is d*,
(5)	*All k is BC or Cd or Cf or H*,
(6)	*All ABCDEFG is H or K*,
(7)	*All DEFGH is B*,
(8)	*All ABl is f or h*,

(9)	All ADFKl is H,
(10)	All ADEFH is B or C or G or L;

show that *All A is L*   .[K.]

THE INVERSE PROBLEM

534. *Nature of the Inverse Problem.*—By the *inverse problem* is here meant a certain problem so-called by Jevons. Its nature will be indicated by the following extracts, which are from the *Principles of Science* and the *Studies in Deductive Logic* respectively.

"In the Indirect process of Inference we found that from certain propositions we could infallibly determine the combinations of terms agreeing with those premisses. The inductive problem is just the inverse. Having given certain combinations of terms, we need to ascertain the propositions with which they are consistent, and from which they may have proceeded. Now if the reader contemplates the following combinations,—

ABC	abC
aBC	abc,

he will probably remember at once that they belong to the premisses $A = AB$, $B = BC$. If not, he will require a few trials before he meets with the right answer, and every trial will consist in assuming certain laws and observing whether the deduced results agree with the data. To test the facility with which he can solve this inductive problem, let him casually strike out any of the possible combinations involving three terms, and say what laws the remaining combinations obey. Let him say, for instance, what laws are embodied in the combinations,—

ABC	aBC
Abc	abC

"The difficulty becomes much greater when more terms enter into the combinations. It would be no easy matter to point out the complete conditions fulfilled in the combinations,—

ACe
aBCe
aBcdE
abCe
abcE.

After some trouble the reader may discover that the principal laws are $C = e$, and $A = Ae$; but he would hardly discover the remaining law, namely that $BD = BDe$" (*Principles of Science*, 1st ed., vol. I., p. 144; 2nd ed., p. 125).

"The inverse problem is always tentative, and consists in inventing laws, and trying whether their results agree with those before us" (*Studies in Deductive Logic*, p. 252).

The problem may preferably be stated as follows:—

Given a complex proposition of the form
Everything is $P_1P_2 \ldots$ or $Q_1Q_2 \ldots$ or $\ldots$,

to find a set of propositions not involving any alternative combination of terms, which shall together be equivalent to it.[520]

It may be observed that Jevons does not definitely exclude alternative terms in his solutions of inverse problems, though he generally seeks to avoid them. The problem cannot, however, be defined with accuracy unless such terms are explicitly excluded.

The inverse problem is in a sense indeterminate, for we may find a number of sets of propositions, not involving any alternative combination of terms, which are precisely equivalent in logical force, and hence any inverse problem may admit of a number of solutions. But it is not necessary to have recourse to a series of guesses in order to solve any inverse problem, nor need the method of solution be described as wholly tentative. Several systematic methods of solution applicable to any inverse problem are formulated in the following sections. Since, however, more solutions than one are possible, some of which are simpler than others, the process may be regarded as more or less tentative in so far as we seek to obtain the most satisfactory solution.

The following may be taken as our criterion of simplicity. Comparing two equivalent sets of propositions, not involving any alternative combination of terms, that set may be regarded as the simpler which contains the smaller number of propositions. If each set contains the same number of propositions, then we may count the number of terms involved in their subjects and predicates taken together, and regard that one as the simpler which involves the fewer terms.

535. *A General Solution of the Inverse Problem.*—Let us suppose, then, that we are given a complex proposition involving alternative combination, and that we are to find a set of propositions, not involving alternative combination, which shall together be equivalent to it.

The data may be written in the form

Everything is P or Q or S or T or &c.,

where *P, Q,* &c., are themselves complex terms involving conjunctive, but not alternative, combination.[521]

By contraposition one or more of these complex terms may be brought over from the predicate into the subject, so that we have

Whatever is not either P or S or &c. is Q or T or &c.

---

[520] The problem may also be stated as follows:—*Given a universal affirmative complex proposition containing alternative terms to find an equivalent compound conjunctive proposition all the determinants of which are affirmative and free from alternative terms.*

[521] The proposition in its original form may admit of simplification in accordance with the rules laid down in chapter 1. It will generally speaking be found advantageous to have recourse to such simplification before proceeding further with the solution.

The selection of certain terms for transposition in this way is arbitrary (and it is here that the indeterminateness of the problem becomes apparent); but it will generally be found best to take two or three which have as many common determinants as possible.

What is not either P or S or &c. is Q or T or &c.

will, when the subject is written in the affirmative form, be immediately resolvable into a series of propositions, which taken together give all the information originally given.[522] Any of these propositions which still involve alternative combination may be dealt with in the same way, until no alternative combination remains.

We shall now be left with a set of propositions which will satisfy the required conditions. The possibility of various simplifications has, however, to be considered. Thus, it will be necessary to make sure that each of the propositions is itself expressed in its simplest form;[523] and to observe whether any two or more of the propositions admit of a simple recombination.[524] It may also be found that some of the propositions can be altogether omitted, inasmuch as they add nothing to the information jointly afforded by the remainder; or that, considered in their relation to the remaining propositions, they may, at any rate, be simplified by the omission of one or more of the terms which they contain.[525] When these simplifications have been carried as far as is possible we shall have our final solution.[526]

The solution may, if we wish, be verified by recombining into a single complex proposition the propositions that have been obtained, an operation by which we shall arrive again at a series of alternants substantially identical with those originally given us. Such verification is, however, not essential to the validity of our process, which, if it has been correctly performed, contains no possible source of error.

The following examples will serve to illustrate the above method.

I. For our first example we may take one of those chosen by Jevons in the extract quoted in the preceding section.

Given the proposition, *Everything is either ABC or Abc or aBC or abC*, we are to find a set of propositions not involving alternative combination which shall be equivalent to it.

By the reduction of *aBC or abC* to *aC*, followed by contraposition, we have *What is neither ABC nor Abc is aC*; therefore, *What is a or Bc or bC is aC*; and this may be resolved into the three propositions:—

	All a is C,
	Bc is non-existent,
	All bC is a.

---

[522] See section 446.
[523] For example, *All AB is BC* may be reduced to *All AB is C*.
[524] For example, *All ac is d* and *All Bc is d* may be combined into *All cD is Ab*.
[525] Thus, for the propositions *All AB is CD* and *All Ab is C* we may substitute the propositions *All AB is D* and *All A is C*.
[526] It may be observed that it is no part of our object to obtain a set of propositions which are mutually independent. As a matter of fact, it will generally be found that the maximum simplification involves the repetition of some items of information. Thus, in the example given in the preceding note the propositions *All AB is CD* and *All Ab is C* are quite independent of one another; but the proposition *All A is C* renders superfluous part of the information given by the proposition *All AB is D*.

Bc is non-existent is reducible to *All B is C*; and this proposition and *All a is C* may be combined into *All c is Ab*.

Hence we have for our solution the two propositions:—

{	All c is Ab,
	All bC is a.

It will be found that by the recombination of these propositions we regain the original proposition.

II. We may next take the more complex example contained in the same extract from Jevons.

The given alternants are *ACe, aBCe, aBcdE, abCe, abcE*; and by the reduction of dual terms, they become *aBcdE, abcE, Ce*. Therefore, *What is not aBcdE or abcE is Ce*; and this proposition may be resolved into the four propositions:—

{	All A is Ce;	(1)
	All BD is Ce;	(2)
	All C is e;	(3)
	All e is C.	(4)

But since by (3) *All C is e*, (1) may be reduced to *All A is C*; and this proposition may be combined with (4) yielding *All c is aE*. Also by (3), (2) may be reduced to *All BD is C*.

Hence our solution becomes

{	All BD is C,
	All C is e,
	All c is aE.

This solution may be shewn to be equivalent to the solution given by Jevons himself.

III. The following problem is from Jevons, *Principles of Science*, 2nd ed., p. 127 (Problem v).

The given alternants are *ABCD, ABCd, ABcd, AbCD, AbcD, aBCD, aBcD, aBcd, abCd*.

By the reduction of duals these alternants may be written as follows: *ABC or ABcd or AbD or aBCD or aBc or abCd*.

Therefore, by contraposition, *Whatever is not ABC or AbD or aBc is ABcd or aBCD or abCd*.

But *Whatever is not ABC or AbD or aBc* is equivalent to *Whatever is ABc or aBC or ab or bd*. Hence we have for our solution the following set of propositions:

(1) All ABc is d,	(2) All aBC is D,
(3) All ab is Cd,	(4) All bd is a.[527]

This is equivalent to the solution given by Jevons, *Studies*, p. 256.

---

[527] We first obtain *All bd is aC*; but since by (3) *All abd is C*, this may be reduced to *All bd is a*.

Appendix C. A Generalization of Logical Processes... 377

IV. The following example is also from Jevons, *Principles of Science*, 2nd edition, p. 127 (Problem viii). In his *Studies*, p. 256, he speaks of the solution as *unknown*. A fairly simple solution may, however, be obtained by the application of the general rule formulated in this section.

The given alternants are *ABCDE, ABCDe, ABCde, ABcde, AbCDE, AbcdE, Abcde, aBCDe, aBCde, aBcDe, abCDe, abCdE, abcDe, abcdE*.

By the reduction of duals these alternants may be written: *ABCe or ABcde or Abcd or ACDE or aBCde or abdE or aDe*.

Therefore, by contraposition, *Whatever is not either ABCe or ABcde or Abcd or abdE or aDe is ACDE or aBCde*.

But it will be found that, by the application of the ordinary rule for obtaining the contradictory of a given term, *Whatever is not either ABCe or ABcde or Abcd or abdE or aDe* is equivalent to *Whatever is AbC or ade or BE or AcD or DE*.

Hence our proposition is resolvable into the following:

(i)	*All AbC is DE*;
(ii)	*All ade is BC*;
(iii)	*All BE is ACD*;
(iv)	*AcD is non-existent*;
(v)	*All DE is AC*.

But by (v) *All BE is AC or d*; therefore, (iii) may be reduced to *All BE is D*. Again by (iv), *All DE is a or C*; therefore, (v) may be reduced to *All DE is A*.

Hence we have the following as our final solution:—

| (1) *All AbC is DE*; |
| (2) *All ade is BC*; |
| (3) *All BE is D*; |
| (4) *All cD is a*; |
| (5) *All DE is A*. |

536. *Another Method of Solution of the Inverse Problem.*—Another method of solving the inverse problem, suggested to me by Dr Venn, is to write down the original complex proposition in the negative form, i.e., to obvert it, before resolving it. It has been already shown that a negative proposition with an alternative predicate may be immediately broken up into a set of simpler propositions.

In some cases, especially where the number of destroyed combinations as compared with those that are saved is small this plan is of easier application than that given in the preceding section.

To illustrate this method we may take two or three of the examples already discussed.

I. *Everything is ABC or Abc or aBC or abC*;

therefore, by obversion, *Nothing is AbC or ac or Bc*;

and this proposition is at once resolvable into

{	*All Ab is c,*
	All c is Ab.[528]

II. *Everything is ACe or aBCe or aBcdE or abCe or abcE*; therefore, by obversion, *Nothing is Ac or BcD or CE or ce.*

This proposition may be successively resolved as follows:

{	*No c is A or e,*
	No E is C,
	No BD is c.
{	*All c is aE,*
	All E is c,
	All BD is C.

III. *Everything is ABCD or ABCd or ABcd or AbCD or AbcD or aBCD or aBcD or aBcd or abCd*; therefore, by obversion, *Nothing is ABcD or Abd or aBCd or abc or abD*; and this proposition may be successively resolved as follows:

{	*No ABc is D*;
	No bd is A;
	No aBC is d;
	No ab is c or D.
{	*All ABc is d*;
	All bd is a;
	All aBC is D;
	All ab is Cd.

It is rather interesting to find that notwithstanding the indeterminateness of the problem we obtain by independent methods the same result in each of the above cases.

537. *A Third Method of Solution of the Inverse Problem.*—The following is a third independent method of solution of the inverse problem, and it is in some cases easier of application than either of the two preceding methods.

532 Any proposition of the form

Everything is ……

may be resolved into the two propositions:

{	*All A is ……*
	All a is ……

which taken together are equivalent to it; similarly *All A is ……* may be resolved into the two *All AB is ……, All Ab is ……* and it is clear that by taking pairs of contradictories in this way we may resolve any given complex proposition into a set of propositions containing no alternative terms. Redundancies must of course as before be as far as possible avoided.

[528] The equivalence between this and our former solution is immediately obvious. Equationally it would be written *Ab* = *c*.

Appendix C. A Generalization of Logical Processes... 379

To illustrate this method we may again take the first three examples given in section 535.

I. *Everything is ABC or Abc or aBC or abC* may be resolved successively as follows:

{	All C is AB or aB or ab;
	All c is Ab.
{	All bC is a;[529]
	All c is Ab.

II. *Everything is ACe or aBCe or aBcdE or abCe or abcE* may be resolved successively as follows:

{	All C is Ae or aBe or abe;
	All c is aBdE or abE.
{	All C is e;
	All c is aE;
	All c is Bd or b.
{	All C is e;
	All c is aE;
	All Bc is d.

III. *Everything is ABCD or ABCd or ABcd or AbCD or AbcD or aBCD or aBcD or aBcd or abCd* may be resolved successively as follows:

{	All B is ACD or ACd or Acd or aCD or acD or acd;
	All b is ACD or AcD or aCd.
{	All B is AC or aD or cd;
	All b is AD or aCd. 533
{	All BC is A or aD;
	All Bc is aD or d;
	All Ab is D;
	All ab is Cd.
{	All BCd is A;
	All ABc is d;
	All Ab is D;
	All ab is Cd.

The above solutions are practically the same as those obtained in the two preceding sections.

538. *Mr Johnson's Notation for the Solution of Logical Problems.*—In his articles on *the Logical Calculus* Mr Johnson proposes a notation by the aid of which the solution of inverse problems may be facilitated. It consists in representing *conjunctive* combination by *horizontal* juxtaposition, and *alternative* combination by *vertical* juxtaposition. A bar—drawn

---

[529] Taking *BC* as our subject we have *All BC is A or a*, and since this is a merely formal proposition, it may be omitted.

horizontally or vertically—serves the purpose of a bracket where necessary. Thus, $\genfrac{}{}{0pt}{}{AB}{CD}$ represents AB or CD; $\begin{array}{c|c} A & B \\ \hline C & D \end{array}$ represents (*A or C*) *and* (*B or D*). These two forms are of course not equivalent to each other. But *if contradictories are placed in a pair of diagonally opposite corners*, then the combination is the same in whichever way we read it. Thus, $\genfrac{}{}{0pt}{}{AB}{Ca}$ represents AB or aC; $\begin{array}{c|c} A & B \\ \hline C & a \end{array}$ represents (*A or C*) *and* (*a or B*). But these are equivalent to each other; for (*A or C*) *and* (*a or B*) is equivalent to *AB or aC or BC*, and—since *BC* by development is *ABC or aBC*—this is equivalent to *AB or aC*. Mr Johnson continues as follows:—"By adopting the plan of placing successive letter-symbols in opposite corners we may solve the *inverse problem* with surprising ease. The method of solution closely resembles the third of those adopted by Dr Keynes, and it was this that suggested mine. I will, therefore, illustrate by taking Dr Keynes's three examples which are the following:—

I. $\displaystyle \frac{\overline{\dfrac{ABC}{Abc}}}{\overline{\dfrac{aBC}{abC}}} = \frac{\overline{\dfrac{BC}{aC}}}{\overline{Abc}} = \frac{C}{Ab} \Bigg| \genfrac{}{}{0pt}{}{B}{a} \atop c$

Here the columns or determinants may be read off:—
(*C or Ab*) *and* (*B or a or c*) = (*If c, then Ab*) *and* (*If AC, then B*).

II. $\displaystyle \frac{\overline{\dfrac{ACe}{aBCe}}}{\overline{\dfrac{aBcdE}{abCe}}} = \frac{\overline{\dfrac{Ce}{abcE}}}{\overline{acdE}} = \frac{C}{aE\begin{array}{c|c}b\\d\end{array}}\Bigg|\genfrac{}{}{0pt}{}{e}{c}$

This is read: (*If c, then aE*) *and* (*If BD, then C*) *and* (*If C, then e*).

III. $\displaystyle \frac{\overline{\dfrac{ABC}{BCD}}}{\overline{\dfrac{aBc}{Bcd}}} = \ldots$
$\overline{AbD}$
$\overline{abCd}$

$B \quad \begin{array}{c|c} A & D \\ \hline Cd & a \end{array} \quad \begin{array}{c|c} C & A \\ \hline \begin{array}{c}a\\d\end{array} & c \\ \hline & b \end{array}$

That is: (*If ab, then Cd*) *and* (*If bd, then a*) *and* (*If ABD, then C*) *and* (*If BCd, then A*). In this last problem, we first place *B* and *b* opposite; then for the *B* alternants, we place *C* and *c* opposite, and for the *b* alternants *A* and *a*. To get the simplest result, we should aim at dividing the columns into as equal divisions as possible.

The notation thus explained enables us to solve any problems in a simple manner. The expression in its final form may be read equally well in columns or in rows, i.e., as a determinative or as an alternative synthesis. Of course, a precisely similar process may be used, if we started with determinatively given or mixed data" (*Mind*, 1892, p. 351).

539. *The Inverse Problem and Schröder's Law of Reciprocal Equivalences.*—The inverse problem may also be solved, though somewhat laboriously, by the aid of the reciprocal relation between the laws of distribution given in section 428, this reciprocal relation depending upon the law that to every equivalence there corresponds another equivalence in which conjunctive combination is throughout substituted for alternative combination and *vice versâ*. Thus, by the first law of distribution, (A or B) and (C or D) = AC or AD or BC or BD, and hence follows the corresponding equivalence AB or CD = (A or C) and (A or D) and (B or C) and (B or D). In this way any inverse problem may be practically resolved into the more familiar problem of conjunctively combining a series of alternative terms.[530]

Taking as an example the first problem given in section 535, we may proceed as follows: (A or B or C) and (A or b or c) and (a or B or C) and (a or b or C) = (A or Bc or bC) and (a or C) = AC or aBc or bC. Therefore, we have the corresponding equivalence ABC or Abc or aBC or abC = (A or C) and (a or B or c) and (b or C). Hence the proposition *Everything is ABC or Abc or aBC or abC* may be resolved into the three propositions, *Everything is A or C, Everything is a or B or c, Everything is b or C*; and we have for our solution of the inverse problem: *All c is A, All bC is a, All c is b*; or, combining the first and last of these propositions, *All c is Ab, All bC is a*.

Similarly, the second problem in section 535 may be solved as follows:—(A or C or e) (a or B or C or e) (a or B or c or d or E) (a or b or C or e) (a or b or c or E) = aC or bCd or CE or ce. Hence the corresponding equivalence ACe or aBCe or aBcdE or abCe or abcE = (a or C) (b or C or d) (C or E) (c or e); and we have for our solution of the inverse problem, *All A is C, All BD is C, All c is E, All C is e*; or, combining the first and third of these propositions, *All c is aE, All BD is C, All C is e*.

EXERCISES

540. Find propositions that leave only the following combinations, *ABCD, ABcD, AbCd, aBCd, abcd*. [Jevons, *Studies*, p. 254.]

Jevons gives this as the most difficult of his series of inverse problems involving four terms. It may be solved as follows:—

Everything is ABCD or ABcD or AbCd or aBCd or abcd; therefore, by contraposition and the reduction of dual terms, *Whatever is not either AbCd or aBCd is ABD or abcd*.

Therefore, *Whatever is AB or ab or c or D is ABD or abcd*; and this is resolvable into the four following propositions:

---

[530] It will be observed that the inverse problem involves the transformation of a logical expression consisting of a series of alternants into an equivalent expression consisting of a series of determinants. Schröder's Law of Reciprocity shews that the process required for this transformation is practically the same as that by which an expression consisting of a series of determinants is transformed into an equivalent expression consisting of a series of alternants.

$$\left\{\begin{array}{l}\text{All } AB \text{ is } D, (1)\\ \text{All } ab \text{ is } cd, (2)\\ \text{All } c \text{ is } ABD \text{ or } abd, (3)\\ \text{All } D \text{ is } AB. (4)\end{array}\right.$$

Since by (4) *All D is AB*, and by (2) *All ab is d*, (3) may be reduced to *All c is D or ab*, and therefore to *All cd is ab*. Also, by (4) *All ab is d*, and hence (2) may be reduced to *All ab is c*.

Our set of propositions may therefore be expressed as follows:—

$$\left\{\begin{array}{l}\text{All } AB \text{ is } D,\\ \text{All } ab \text{ is } c,\\ \text{All } cd \text{ is } ab,\\ \text{All } D \text{ is } AB.^{531}\end{array}\right.$$

541. Resolve the proposition *Everything is ABCDeF or ABcDEf or AbCDEF or AbCDeF or AbcDeF or aBCDEf or aBcDEf or abCDeF or abCdeF or abcDef or abcdef* into a conjunction of relatively simple propositions.

[Jevons, *Principles of Science*, 2nd ed., p. 127 (Problem x.)]

The following is a solution:—

| (1) *All A is D*; |
| (2) *All ABC is e*; |
| (3) *All aF is bCe*; |
| (4) *All Bf is DE*; |
| (5) *All bf is ace*; |
| (6) *All cF is be*. |

This is somewhat less complex than the solution by Dr John Hopkinson given in Jevons, *Studies in Deductive Logic*, p. 256, namely:—

(i)	*All d is ab*;
(ii)	*All b is AF or ae*;
(iii)	*All Af is BcDE*;
(iv)	*All E is Bf or AbCDF*;
(v)	*All Be is ACDF*;
(vi)	*All abc is ef*;
(vii)	*All abef is c*.

542. How many and what non-disjunctive propositions are equivalent to the statement that "What is either *Ab* or *bC* is *Cd* or *cD*, and *vice versâ*"? [Jevons, *Studies*, p. 246.]

The given statement is at once resolvable into the four following propositions:

---

[531] Restoring the second of these propositions to the form *All ab is cd*, and writing the propositions equationally, the solution may be expressed in a still simpler form, namely, $AB = D$, $ab = cd$.

Appendix C. A Generalization of Logical Processes... 383

		All Ab is Cd or cD,	(i)
		All bC is Cd or cD,	(ii)
		All Cd is Ab or bC,	(iii)
		All cD is Ab or bC.	(iv)
(i) may be resolved into		All Abc is D,	(v)
		All AbD is c.	(vi)

But (vi) is inferable from (ii); and observing some other obvious simplifications we obtain immediately the following solution:

| (1) *All Abc is D*; |
| (2) *All bC is d*; |
| (3) *All Cd is b*; |
| (4) *All cD is Ab.* |

543. Shew the equivalence between the two sets of propositions given in section 541.
[K.]

544. Find which of the following propositions may be omitted without affecting the information given by the propositions as a whole: *All Ab is cDE*; *All Ac is bDE*; *All Ad is BCe*; *All Ae is BCd*; *No aE is B or C*; *No B is c*; *All Bd is ACe*; *No bD is C or e*; *No bE is Ad or C*; *All C is B*; *All Cd is ABe*; *All cD is bE*; *All cE is AbD or ab*; *All de is ABC or abc*. [K.]

545. Resolve each of the following complex propositions into a conjunction of propositions not containing any alternative combination of terms:

(1) *Everything is ABCD or AbCd or aBcD or abcd*;

(2) *Everything is AbCD or AbCd or Abcd or aBcd or abCD or abCd or abcd*;

(3) *Everything is AbcDE or aBCd or aBCE or aBcd or aBde or abCe or abce or abDe or abde or BcdE or bCDe*;

(4) *Everything is ABCE or ABcd or ABcE or ABde or Abcd or abCE or abcE or abdE or abde or BCde*;

(5) *Everything is ABCDE or ABCdE or ABcDE or ABcDe or ABcde or AbCdE or Abcde or aBCDE or aBCde or abCDE or abcDe*;

(6) *Everything is ABDe or ABDF or AcDe or Acef or aBDe or aBDF or abCD or abCd or abcD or abcd or aCDE or aCDe or aCdE or aCde or acDe or aDEF or aDEf or aDeF or aDef or BcDF or bceF or bcef*;

(7) *Everything is AbdE or Abef or AbF or Acdef or aBDF or abCF or aCdE or ade or bCDe or bCdf or bDEF*;

(8) *Everything is ABCEf or Abe or aBCdf or aBcdE or aBcdeF or abef or bceF.* [K.]

546. Express the following proposition in as small a number as you can of propositions in which no alternative combination of terms occurs: *Everything is ABCDe or ABCdE or ABcDe or AbCdE or AbCde or aBCdE or aBcDE or aBcde or aBcdE or abCde or abCdE.* [J.]

547. Solve the fourth problem given in section 535, (α) by the method described in section 536, (β) by that described in section 537. [K.]

548. Solve the problem given in section 540 and also the fourth problem given in section 535 by aid of the notation described in section 538. [K.]

549. Solve the third and fourth problems given in section 535 by the method described in section 539. [K.]

550. Shew that any universal complex proposition may be resolved into a set of propositions in which no conjunctive combination of terms occurs. [K.]

INDEX

A

abstract character, 42, 43, 45
abstract names, 7, 9, 10, 22
acquired perceptions, 293
ad absurdum, 97, 216, 230
added determinants, 95
addition, iv, xi, xiii, xx, 9, 12, 19, 21, 44, 45, 52, 96, 135, 136, 182, 184, 199, 227, 252, 269, 272, 317, 321, 331, 348, 368, 369
aequipollence, 85, 197
affirmative proposition, 55, 59, 60, 82, 104, 107, 121, 123, 126, 129, 135, 140, 154, 192, 196, 200, 212, 275, 329, 341, 342, 343, 347, 348, 349, 350, 353, 354, 355, 359, 361, 363
Aldrich, 28, 69, 73, 83, 86, 96, 97, 182, 216, 218, 224, 229, 248, 255, 259, 260, 272, 300, 314, 317
alleged reciprocal character, 176
alternant, 251, 252, 334, 335, 336, 337, 338, 341, 342, 343, 344, 348, 350, 356, 358, 359, 360, 362, 363, 370
alternative combination of terms, 331, 340, 374, 383
alternative terms, 180, 334, 337, 374, 378, 381
ambiguous middle, 191
ambiguous term, 37
analytic propositions, 28, 29
antecedent, 75, 95, 127, 163, 164, 165, 166, 167, 168, 169, 171, 172, 174, 175, 176, 242, 244, 245, 254, 255, 273, 302, 318
antilogism, 225
argument *à fortiori*, 271, 272
Aristotelian Sorites, 261, 262, 263, 265
Aristotle, 83, 86, 97, 199, 218, 222, 223, 231, 259, 262, 278

B

Baroco and Bocardo, 218
Benecke, E. C., 13
Bentham, Jeremy, 316
Boethius, 86
Boole, xiii, xv, 127, 139, 199, 321, 323, 332, 335, 336, 337, 359, 360, 362, 364, 366, 367, 368

C

Carroll, Lewis, 144, 177
categorical propositions, v, 56, 66, 69, 75, 81, 85, 86, 87, 93, 120, 122, 125, 128, 139, 144, 152, 155, 162, 165, 175
categorical syllogism, 133, 189, 190, 191, 241, 242, 243, 244, 245, 246, 247, 251, 255, 257, 302, 361
change of relation, 95, 169
classification, 12, 49, 50, 56, 64, 74, 120, 127, 182, 184, 314, 315, 316, 317
co-division, 314
collective names, 6, 7
combination, 41, 44, 45, 51, 56, 58, 87, 101, 110, 116, 140, 143, 144, 159, 168, 169, 171, 180, 181, 231, 246, 263, 277, 278, 287, 290, 293, 299, 300, 331, 332, 333, 334, 335, 337, 338, 339, 340, 341, 342, 343, 346, 349, 350, 353, 354, 355, 356, 357, 359, 361, 362, 363, 374, 375, 379, 381
combination of complex propositions, 353
complementary propositions, 85, 91, 105, 110, 205
complex conception, 95
complex constructive dilemma, 255
complex destructive dilemma, 255
complex propositions, vi, vii, 153, 157, 182, 331, 333, 338, 341, 342, 343, 345, 346, 347, 349, 353, 357, 359, 383

complex terms, 13, 36, 331, 332, 333, 334, 335, 336, 362, 374
composition, 7, 51, 96, 272
compound judgments, 50, 51, 52, 56, 163
compound propositions, 74, 175, 338, 339, 340, 342, 343
comprehension, xi, 11, 13, 14, 16, 17, 18, 19, 20, 21, 22, 23, 24, 26, 117, 121, 123, 130, 317
concept, 3, 4, 14, 33, 34, 35, 61, 317, 330
concrete names, 8, 10
conditional propositions, 152, 163, 165, 167, 169
conditional syllogism, 241, 242, 243
conditionals, 164, 165, 166, 167, 168, 169, 170, 172, 173, 176, 178, 179, 184, 242, 251
conjunctive combination of terms, 331, 354, 384
connotation, xi, 4, 6, 11, 12, 13, 14, 15, 16, 17, 18, 19, 20, 22, 23, 24, 25, 26, 27, 28, 29, 30, 37, 117, 118, 119, 120, 121, 122, 123, 125, 126, 130, 167, 295
connotative mode of interpreting propositions, 122
connotative names, 21, 22, 25, 34
consequent, 156, 163, 164, 165, 167, 169, 171, 172, 174, 175, 176, 242, 243, 244, 245, 254, 255
constructive dilemma, 254, 255
constructive hypothetical syllogism, 244, 256
continuous questioning, 262
contra-complementary propositions, 85, 105
contradiction in terms, 29, 75, 326, 345
contradictory opposition, 69, 70, 71, 326, 332, 338
contradictory propositions, 71, 104, 338
contradictory terms, 34, 35, 152, 325, 332
contraposition, 83, 85, 86, 87, 89, 97, 98, 99, 116, 137, 147, 148, 149, 157, 169, 174, 175, 196, 197, 216, 218, 219, 225, 245, 246, 275, 296, 299, 329, 343, 347, 349, 350, 351, 353, 358, 359, 360, 361, 363, 365, 366, 367, 368, 374, 375, 376, 377, 381
contraposition *per accidens*, 87, 149
contrapositive, 86, 87, 90, 98, 99, 105, 112, 116, 137, 147, 148, 169, 174, 175, 177, 178, 225, 296, 297, 347, 348, 349, 352, 364
contrary opposition, 69, 72, 73, 131, 326
contrary propositions, 36
contrary terms, 36
contraversion, 85, 86
conventional, 12, 13, 14, 15, 16, 21, 43, 224
conventional intension, 13, 14, 21
converse, 81, 82, 83, 86, 87, 90, 96, 98, 99, 116, 131, 135, 137, 147, 148, 169, 175, 202, 223, 224, 277, 287, 323, 330, 348, 353
converse relation, 96
conversion, 81, 82, 83, 84, 86, 87, 88, 89, 90, 96, 97, 99, 104, 116, 119, 130, 131, 135, 137, 143, 147, 148, 149, 157, 169, 174, 175, 176, 194, 219, 220, 222, 224, 231, 275, 277, 298, 299, 329, 330, 341, 346, 347, 348, 349, 350, 362, 363, 366
conversion by contraposition, 86
conversion by limitation, 83
conversion by negation, 86
conversion of propositions, 84, 104, 130, 341
conversion *per accidens*, 81, 82, 83, 84, 104, 149, 277
convertend, 81, 82, 83, 330
convertible copula, 273
copula, 27, 28, 57, 59, 83, 90, 96, 101, 126, 272, 273
correlative name, 37

D

Deductio ad impossibile, 216
definition, vii, 6, 9, 10, 11, 13, 14, 17, 18, 19, 20, 21, 22, 23, 24, 28, 30, 36, 42, 59, 69, 72, 73, 75, 86, 87, 89, 91, 168, 173, 193, 224, 251, 254, 255, 256, 264, 296, 300, 301, 317, 345, 347, 348
definition by type, 18
denial, 35, 36, 50, 51, 52, 54, 56, 57, 63, 66, 72, 73, 75, 76, 77, 135, 136, 142, 143, 144, 151, 155, 156, 159, 160, 162, 168, 171, 172, 193, 194, 196, 225, 228, 229, 230, 244, 245, 253, 266, 322, 323, 325, 326, 327, 339, 340, 341
denotation, 4, 11, 13, 14, 15, 16, 17, 18, 19, 20, 21, 22, 23, 25, 26, 34, 117, 118, 119, 120, 122, 123, 125, 126, 130, 180, 295, 318
Der Operationskreis des Logikkalkuls, 333, 334, 335, 336, 363
destructive dilemma, 254, 255
destructive hypothetical syllogism, 244, 256
determinant, 95, 335, 336, 337, 341, 342, 343, 344, 347, 348, 349, 350, 356, 359, 362, 363, 366
determination, 125, 207, 331
diagrammatic representation, v, vi, 101, 112, 114, 233
diagrammatic scheme, 101, 102, 106, 108, 236, 237, 238, 239
diagrams, ix, xiii, 84, 101, 102, 103, 104, 105, 106, 107, 108, 110, 111, 112, 113, 114, 116, 121, 132, 134, 180, 191, 192, 233, 234, 236, 237, 238, 239, 290
dichotomy, 315, 316, 317, 318, 340
dictum, 4, 122, 145, 199, 200, 201, 202, 208, 209, 221, 223, 229, 230, 231, 272, 273, 278, 293, 330
dilemma, 254, 255, 256, 294, 301, 303, 359
direct reduction, 218, 275
direct reduction of *Baroco* and *Bocardo*, 218
disjunctive syllogism, vi, 247, 251, 252, 253, 359
distinction, ix, xi, xviii, 4, 5, 6, 7, 8, 9, 11, 14, 15, 16, 23, 27, 28, 29, 30, 31, 34, 35, 37, 42, 44, 46, 47,

49, 50, 51, 52, 53, 54, 56, 59, 60, 61, 62, 63, 64, 65, 73, 76, 86, 87, 89, 96, 117, 118, 119, 121, 122, 126, 130, 132, 140, 141, 145, 160, 163, 165, 166, 167, 168, 170, 179, 199, 224, 228, 242, 252, 260, 261, 267, 293, 296, 314, 317, 319, 320, 323, 345

distribution of terms in a proposition, 60
distributive use of names, 7
division, vi, ix, 7, 8, 9, 27, 29, 34, 41, 50, 51, 52, 56, 57, 58, 64, 65, 112, 169, 182, 313, 314, 315, 316, 317, 318, 325, 329
division according to quantity, 56
division and classification, 317
division by dichotomy, 315, 316, 317, 318
doctrine of modality, 53
doctrine of opposition, 70, 72, 104, 149, 152, 157, 158, 338
doctrine of reduction, 209, 219, 222
doctrine of the quantification of the predicate, 59, 119, 129, 130, 131, 267
duality of formal equivalences, 340

E

education, 308, 310
elimination, 93, 131, 176, 177, 199, 233, 246, 300, 320, 361, 362, 363
empirical, 7, 14, 16, 24, 28, 36, 59, 61, 105, 118, 119, 154, 300, 317
empirically universal propositions, 165
enthymeme, 259, 260, 274
enumeration, 19, 24, 28, 61, 62, 154, 210, 211, 230, 300, 301, 313, 339
epicheirema, 260, 261
episyllogism, 260
equivalent propositions, 72, 74, 82, 83, 91, 92, 93, 328
equivocal term, 314
euclid, 87, 215, 296, 297, 303
eversion, 81
exclusive figure, 212
exclusive proposition, 135
exemplification, 17, 18, 19, 20, 21, 22, 24, 26, 117, 122
existential import, v, vii, ix, xi, 55, 95, 139, 140, 141, 142, 143, 144, 145, 146, 147, 149, 151, 152, 153, 157, 158, 160, 161, 162, 166, 168, 194, 219, 238, 243, 275
existential import of propositions, vii, ix, xi, 95, 141, 147, 149, 157, 161, 219, 275
existential propositions, 91, 143, 145, 150
exponible proposition, 64, 131
extensive definition, 17, 18, 19, 20, 21, 22, 28, 117

F

fallacy, xx, 7, 29, 73, 82, 91, 95, 96, 117, 131, 175, 191, 192, 194, 195, 200, 245, 247, 256, 262, 263, 269, 272, 300, 303, 306, 308, 309, 321
few, xv, 24, 64, 66, 78, 143, 181, 306, 307, 359, 373
figures of the syllogism, 207, 211, 216, 281
folk-lore, 141
form and matter, xviii
form of a proposition, 196
formal and material, 73
formal contradictories, 36, 331
formal equivalences, 334, 335, 336, 340
formal logic, vii, xi, xiii, xvii, xviii, xix, 29, 55, 62, 64, 81, 85, 96, 98, 105, 118, 119, 128, 139, 141, 142, 144, 145, 193, 194, 211, 266, 272, 273, 294, 317, 318, 325, 331
formal obversion, 85
formal propositions, v, 27, 29, 329
formulation, xx, 44, 45, 46, 49, 50, 55, 58, 143, 192, 320
fourth figure, 120, 210, 211, 213, 218, 222, 223, 224, 230, 231
fundamental postulate of logic, 129

G

Galenian Figure, 222
Game of Logic, 144
general names, 5, 6, 7, 8, 11, 16, 21, 25, 117
general propositions, 7, 73, 273
Goclenian Sorites, 261, 262, 263, 265
Greek mythology, 141
Green, T. H., 22, 30
grounds of denial, 77

H

Hamilton, Sir W., 221, 264
Hamiltonian scheme of propositions, 136
hypothetical dilemma, 254
hypothetical propositions, v, vii, xi, 56, 163, 170, 172, 174, 175, 263, 339
hypothetical syllogism, vi, 241, 242, 243, 244, 246, 247, 248, 251, 256
hypotheticals, 51, 56, 163, 164, 165, 170, 171, 172, 173, 174, 175, 176, 178, 179, 183, 184, 242, 243, 245, 251, 252, 254, 255, 329, 339
hypothetico-categorical syllogism, 241, 242, 256

I

illicit major, 192, 194, 202, 203, 208, 243, 245, 270, 285, 287
immediate inferences, v, xiii, 74, 81, 82, 83, 90, 94, 95, 97, 105, 114, 116, 137, 147, 148, 149, 153, 157, 162, 169, 174, 175, 198, 209, 247, 271, 297, 298, 299, 300, 321, 329, 330, 342, 345
imperfect figures, 216, 223
import of propositions, 4, 9, 43, 45, 71, 157, 158, 160
indefinite proposition, 65
independent propositions, 136, 358
indesignate proposition, 65
indirect moods, 223, 224
indirect reduction, vii, 195, 215, 216, 218, 225, 227, 229, 231, 330
individual name, 5
individual proposition, 63, 102
inequality, xviii, 102, 127, 313, 323
inference, vi, vii, 35, 43, 45, 53, 54, 70, 81, 82, 83, 84, 85, 86, 87, 88, 89, 93, 95, 96, 97, 98, 99, 104, 108, 132, 145, 148, 150, 157, 158, 161, 162, 169, 170, 171, 172, 174, 176, 196, 198, 199, 210, 217, 221, 246, 247, 260, 272, 273, 277, 290, 293, 294, 295, 296, 297, 298, 299, 300, 301, 303, 320, 323, 328, 329, 330, 339, 346, 347, 361, 373
infinitation, 85
infinite proposition, 66
Institutiones Logicae, 218
integration, 132
intensive definition, 17, 18, 19, 20, 21, 22, 24, 30
interpretation, ix, xix, 13, 19, 29, 42, 43, 44, 45, 46, 55, 64, 69, 73, 95, 101, 110, 118, 119, 120, 121, 122, 123, 127, 129, 131, 132, 133, 134, 136, 140, 141, 142, 143, 145, 149, 154, 156, 157, 158, 166, 167, 168, 169, 170, 171, 174, 175, 180, 181, 182, 183, 184, 238, 242, 243, 253, 275, 298, 303, 319, 321, 322, 345, 348
inverse, xiii, 19, 20, 21, 89, 90, 91, 99, 111, 116, 137, 359, 373, 374, 377, 378, 379, 381
inverse problem, xiii, 359, 373, 374, 377, 378, 379, 381
invertend, 89

J

Johnson, W. E., vii, ix, xi, xv, 43, 163
judgment, xvii, xix, xx, 3, 26, 29, 30, 33, 35, 41, 42, 43, 46, 47, 48, 49, 50, 51, 52, 53, 54, 55, 56, 61, 62, 65, 66, 75, 76, 77, 78, 79, 81, 82, 97, 120, 125, 128, 129, 130, 132, 134, 135, 139, 149, 160, 161, 164, 165, 166, 169, 170, 176, 177, 181, 182, 184, 251, 293, 295, 298, 319, 320, 321, 322, 323, 326, 327, 330
judgments of necessity, 55

K

Kant, 50, 53, 56, 57, 64, 65, 222, 246, 247
Karslake, 223, 260

L

language, xviii, xix, 3, 4, 11, 14, 15, 35, 41, 42, 43, 62, 95, 129, 130, 131, 143, 154, 181, 182, 195, 264, 294, 295, 303, 309, 320, 326
language as the instrument of thought, xix, 11
law of commutativeness, 332
law of contradiction, 94, 97, 98, 216, 288, 316, 319, 320, 322, 323, 324, 325, 327, 328, 329, 330, 335, 336, 341
law of duality, 325, 334
law of excluded middle, 35, 94, 98, 144, 145, 147, 148, 161, 215, 288, 316, 319, 322, 324, 325, 326, 327, 328, 329, 335, 336, 351
law of exclusion, 359
law of identity, 94, 95, 98, 127, 284, 319, 320, 321, 322, 327, 328, 329, 330, 341
law of relativity, 36, 37, 152, 323
law of simplicity, 337
law of unity, 336
laws of distribution, 381
laws of thought, vii, xix, 94, 319, 321, 322, 323, 327, 328, 329, 330, 345
legitimacy of the process, 84
liar, 73, 324
limitative proposition, 65
limited identities, 126, 127
limiting cases, 298
logic, v, vii, xiii, xv, xvii, xviii, xix, xx, xxi, 3, 4, 5, 7, 9, 10, 13, 14, 15, 16, 18, 19, 21, 22, 23, 24, 25, 28, 29, 30, 31, 33, 34, 35, 36, 37, 41, 42, 43, 45, 46, 47, 50, 51, 53, 55, 59, 61, 62, 63, 65, 69, 71, 76, 77, 78, 81, 82, 83, 84, 85, 86, 87, 89, 96, 97, 98, 101, 103, 105, 118, 119, 120, 125, 129, 130, 131, 132, 133, 134, 135, 136, 139, 141, 142, 143, 144, 148, 150, 151, 153, 157, 159, 163, 166, 167, 169, 172, 176, 179, 181, 184, 196, 197, 198, 199, 211, 212, 217, 218, 219, 221, 222, 223, 224, 228, 229, 244, 246, 247, 251, 255, 256, 260, 262, 264, 266, 268, 273, 278, 288, 293, 294, 297, 298, 300, 301, 302, 307, 308, 313, 314, 315, 316, 317, 318, 319, 320, 322, 323, 324, 326, 327, 330, 331, 334,

335, 336, 351, 359, 361, 362, 366, 367, 372, 373, 374, 382
logic of relatives, xviii, 37, 96, 273, 330
logic of terms, 4, 5
logical concepts, 14
logical division, 130, 182, 313, 314, 317
logical doctrine, 3, 4, 15, 128, 136, 140, 141, 142, 147, 294, 319, 320, 322
logical signification, 139, 331
logical unit, 3, 4

modality, vii, 43, 48, 50, 52, 53, 54, 55, 56, 57, 67, 97, 146, 172, 251, 339
modality of judgments, 48, 52
moods of the fourth figure, 224, 230
moods of the syllogism, 359
moral universality, 65
multiple quantification, 56, 65, 172
multiplication, 331, 334
Musschenbroek, P. van, 218
mutual relations, ix, 47, 91, 319, 328

M

Mackenzie, J. S., vii
major premiss, 190, 193, 196, 199, 200, 202, 203, 204, 207, 208, 209, 212, 213, 219, 220, 222, 224, 226, 227, 231, 233, 234, 245, 247, 251, 252, 253, 254, 255, 259, 260, 262, 267, 269, 270, 272, 276, 277, 282, 283, 285, 286, 287, 291, 300, 301, 302, 303
major term, 120, 189, 190, 192, 193, 199, 200, 201, 202, 203, 204, 205, 208, 242, 247, 251, 275, 285, 286, 287, 291
material consequence, 96, 272
material contradictories, 36
material contrariety, 73
material obversion, 85
meaning and implication, 44
mediate inferences, 97, 271, 330
metaphysical, xx, 14, 41, 47, 65, 314
metaphysical division, 314
metaphysical universality, 65
metathesis praemissarum, 218
middle term, 120, 189, 190, 191, 192, 193, 194, 195, 198, 199, 200, 201, 203, 208, 212, 213, 222, 224, 236, 242, 247, 259, 264, 266, 267, 268, 269, 271, 275, 276, 277, 278, 279, 280, 285, 286, 287, 290, 291, 330, 361
Mill, J. S., 273
minor premiss, 190, 193, 196, 197, 199, 200, 201, 202, 203, 204, 208, 212, 215, 217, 218, 219, 224, 226, 227, 228, 231, 234, 246, 247, 254, 260, 261, 262, 270, 272, 275, 276, 277, 283, 285, 286, 287, 291
minor term, 120, 189, 190, 192, 195, 199, 201, 203, 204, 205, 207, 213, 223, 224, 228, 242, 247, 275, 276, 277, 285, 286, 287, 288, 291
mixed hypothetical syllogism, 241, 242, 244, 245, 246, 247, 252, 253, 255
mnemonic verses, 210, 211, 213, 223, 231, 285, 286, 291
modal consequence, 97
modal propositions, 74, 152, 160, 168, 183

N

names, ix, 3, 4, 5, 6, 7, 8, 9, 10, 11, 13, 14, 15, 18, 21, 22, 23, 24, 25, 26, 28, 30, 33, 34, 35, 36, 37, 54, 85, 117, 140, 224, 273
nature, ix, xvii, xviii, xix, 5, 6, 27, 29, 42, 43, 45, 47, 50, 54, 59, 66, 70, 71, 72, 74, 75, 77, 78, 82, 99, 105, 122, 139, 140, 142, 147, 154, 156, 157, 159, 165, 176, 181, 184, 212, 228, 293, 294, 296, 302, 306, 308, 311, 319, 322, 323, 324, 325, 329, 333, 346, 373
nature of inference, 296
nature of significant denial, 43, 66, 70, 77
negative judgments, 4
negative names, v, vii, 4, 33, 34
negative premisses, 132, 192, 193, 194, 196, 197, 202, 203, 207, 243, 263, 270, 271, 278
negative propositions, 27, 60, 83, 93, 104, 155, 342, 355, 362
negative terms, 66, 87, 93, 94, 102, 111, 114, 169, 216
nominalist treatment of logic, xix
numerical moods, 281, 282, 283
numerically definite propositions, 56, 64, 73
numerically definite syllogism, 266

O

objective, xvii, xviii, 4, 12, 13, 14, 15, 16, 37, 43, 46, 47, 48, 50, 52, 53, 54, 55, 121, 139, 142, 295, 296, 303
objective extension, 15
objective intension, 13, 14
objective reference, xvii, xviii, 4, 14, 46, 47, 139
obverse, 85, 86, 89, 90, 99, 137, 148, 345, 346, 350, 352
obversion, 35, 85, 86, 87, 88, 89, 90, 93, 98, 99, 147, 148, 149, 152, 157, 175, 194, 196, 197, 216, 218, 219, 220, 246, 290, 329, 341, 342, 345, 347, 348, 349, 351, 356, 357, 358, 360, 362, 363, 368, 377, 378

obvertend, 85
octagon of opposition, 92, 93
 of *Baroco* and *Bocardo*, 218
opposition, v, 33, 69, 70, 73, 74, 76, 77, 78, 91, 104, 133, 137, 148, 149, 151, 152, 162, 167, 168, 170, 172, 173, 332, 338, 339
opposition of complex terms, 338
opposition of propositions, 104, 152
ostensive reduction, 215

P

paradox, 284, 294
partial identities, 126, 135
particular propositions, xi, 47, 62, 64, 93, 110, 127, 145, 156, 158, 356
partition, 314
parts in intension, 19
peculiarities and uses, 211
Peirce, C. S., 228
perfect figure, 216, 223
permutation, 85
petitio principii, 28, 272, 299, 300, 301, 303, 329, 330
petrus hispanus, 86, 193, 223
physical definition, 314
physical division, 314
plurative propositions, 64
polylemma, 254, 256
polysyllogism, 260, 261
Pope John XXI, 193, 223
port royal logic, xv, 65, 72, 197, 210, 229, 260, 306
positive name, 34, 35
postulate of logic, 45
predicate of a proposition, 59, 82, 93, 101, 119, 121, 130, 135, 150, 331
predicative mode of interpretation, 120, 121
predicative mode of interpreting propositions, 119
principle of double negation, 325
problematic judgments, 53
proper names, 6, 7, 8, 13, 14, 21, 22, 23, 24, 25, 26, 28, 31
proposition ω, 136
propositional forms, xix, 29, 42, 43, 45, 49, 55, 56, 81, 86, 94, 101, 102, 107, 110, 115, 123, 128, 130, 131, 132, 133, 134, 136, 142, 153, 154, 166, 173, 183, 197, 320, 340
propositions, v, vii, ix, xiii, xviii, xix, 3, 4, 5, 6, 7, 9, 10, 15, 27, 28, 29, 31, 33, 35, 39, 41, 42, 43, 44, 45, 46, 47, 48, 49, 52, 53, 55, 56, 57, 59, 60, 61, 62, 63, 64, 65, 66, 67, 69, 70, 71, 72, 73, 74, 75, 76, 78, 79, 81, 82, 83, 84, 85, 87, 88, 90, 91, 93, 94, 96, 97, 98, 99, 100, 101, 102, 103, 104, 105, 106, 108, 110, 111, 114, 116, 117, 118, 119, 120, 121, 122, 123, 126, 127, 128, 129, 131, 132, 133, 134, 135, 136, 137, 139, 140, 141, 142, 143, 144, 145, 146, 147, 148, 149, 150, 151, 152, 153, 154, 155, 156, 158, 159, 160, 161, 162, 163, 164, 165, 166, 167, 168, 169, 170, 171, 172, 173, 174, 175, 176, 177, 178, 179, 180, 181, 182, 183, 184, 185, 189, 190, 191, 193, 194, 196, 197, 199, 200, 201, 202, 204, 208, 211, 215, 216, 222, 225, 226, 227, 230, 231, 236, 238, 241, 242, 243, 247, 248, 251, 252, 253, 257, 259, 260, 261, 262, 263, 264, 268, 269, 272, 273, 274, 275, 277, 279, 281, 284, 290, 291, 294, 295, 298, 299, 300, 301, 302, 307, 310, 313, 314, 326, 329, 330, 332, 338, 339, 340, 341, 342, 343, 344, 345, 346, 351, 352, 353, 354, 355, 356, 357, 358, 359, 360, 361, 362, 363, 365, 366, 368, 370, 371, 372, 373, 374, 375, 376, 377, 378, 381, 382, 383, 384
propositions in extension and intension, ix, 82
prosyllogism, 260
psychology, xvii, xix, xx, 4, 5, 41, 47, 91, 144, 266

Q

quantification of the predicate, 49, 121, 129, 130, 131, 137, 267, 269

R

ramean tree, 316
real propositions, 27, 28, 29, 121, 122, 144, 328
reciprocal equivalences, 381
reduction of dual terms, 376, 381
reduction of syllogisms, 215, 290
reference to time, 47, 65, 139
reference to time in judgments, 47
regressive argument, 260
relation, xix, xx, 4, 6, 8, 9, 11, 19, 20, 21, 36, 37, 47, 48, 50, 51, 52, 53, 56, 61, 62, 63, 69, 70, 72, 74, 76, 79, 91, 93, 94, 96, 100, 101, 102, 103, 105, 116, 117, 118, 119, 120, 121, 122, 123, 126, 128, 130, 131, 133, 135, 144, 152, 157, 158, 160, 161, 163, 165, 166, 168, 170, 171, 173, 175, 176, 178, 179, 184, 189, 190, 199, 216, 227, 247, 272, 273, 293, 296, 298, 299, 319, 322, 324, 325, 326, 329, 361, 367, 370, 371, 375, 381
relative names, v, 33, 36, 37
Rogers, R. A. P., xv, 196
Ross, G. R. T., 182

S

Schröder, 333, 334, 335, 336, 363, 381
secondary opposition, 73
secondary quantification, 65, 73
self-contradiction, 133, 215, 216, 323, 324, 346
Sextus Empiricus, 300, 301
sign, 28, 57, 60, 62, 126, 218, 259, 266, 331
Sigwart, vii, 14, 18, 29, 33, 34, 35, 47, 51, 53, 61, 76, 82, 87, 153, 169, 172, 228, 229, 242, 302, 319, 320, 322, 325
simple constructive dilemma, 254, 255, 256
simple contraposition, 87, 90, 149, 157, 158
simple conversion, 82, 83, 84, 90, 98, 130, 149, 157, 158, 176, 269, 275, 290, 297, 329
simple destructive dilemma, 255, 256
simple identities, 126, 127, 135
simple term, 36, 81, 89, 152, 167, 331, 332, 333, 334, 346, 358
simplification, 103, 130, 135, 267, 335, 341, 354, 355, 374, 375
singular names, 5, 6, 8, 21, 22, 23, 25
singular propositions, 63, 65, 73, 135, 162
Solly, xv, 212, 278, 308
Sorites, 261, 262, 263, 264
special rules, 200, 207, 208, 209, 210, 213, 224, 227, 228, 231, 263, 265, 271, 274, 285
square of opposition, 69, 70, 72, 73, 74, 75, 79, 91, 95, 147, 168, 173
strengthened syllogism, 211, 213, 268, 286
Studies in Logic by Members of the Johns Hopkins University, 362
subaltern moods, 210, 218, 231
subaltern opposition, 69
sub-complementary propositions, 85, 105
subcontrary opposition, 69
sub-division, 314, 315
subject of a proposition, 4, 28, 118, 119, 130, 331, 348
subjective, xvii, 11, 12, 13, 14, 15, 16, 20, 22, 23, 24, 29, 30, 37, 43, 46, 48, 52, 53, 54, 56, 121, 295, 296
subjective distinctions of modality, 53
subjective extension, 15, 16, 20
subjective intension, 11, 13, 14, 15, 22, 23, 24, 29, 30, 121
substantial terms, 5, 7
Syllabus of Logic, 87, 212, 278, 308, 329
syllogism, vi, xiii, 20, 28, 31, 63, 64, 97, 98, 103, 107, 120, 122, 130, 131, 132, 135, 172, 189, 190, 191, 192, 193, 194, 195, 196, 197, 198, 199, 200, 201, 202, 203, 204, 205, 207, 208, 209, 210, 211, 212, 213, 215, 216, 217, 219, 220, 221, 222, 223, 224, 225, 226, 227, 230, 231, 233, 234, 241, 242, 243, 244, 246, 247, 251, 252, 253, 255, 259, 260, 261, 262, 263, 264, 265, 266, 267, 268, 269, 272, 273, 274, 275, 276, 277, 278, 279, 280, 281, 284, 285, 286, 287, 288, 290, 291, 295, 296, 297, 299, 300, 301, 302, 303, 310, 318, 330, 362
syllogisms with two singular premisses, 198
syllogistic reasonings, 105, 233, 236, 237, 268, 275
syllogistic rules, 197, 198, 202, 203, 207, 210, 221, 243, 291
symbol of equality, 125, 127
symbolic logic, xiii, 101, 103, 107, 108, 121, 127, 128, 132, 139, 145, 149, 153, 154, 155, 156, 225, 273, 284, 318, 331, 359, 360, 364, 365, 366, 367
synthesis of propositions, 180, 340
synthetic proposition, 29, 31

T

tables of equivalent propositions, ix
Tarbell, F. B., 242
tertii adjacentis, 57
traditional scheme, 43, 49, 50, 56, 57, 58, 60, 62, 66, 73, 81, 117
traditional scheme of propositions, 43, 49, 57, 58, 60, 81, 117
transitive copula, 273
transversion, 81, 95, 170
trilemma, 254, 256
two types, 179, 339
types of logical equations, 126

U

ultra-total distribution, 266, 267
ultra-total distribution of the middle term, 266, 267
unconditionally universal propositions, 165
undistributed middle, 20, 192, 194, 195, 197, 202, 203, 208, 243, 245, 260, 263, 268, 270, 278, 285
unfigured syllogism, 267
universal judgments, 61, 62, 78, 79
universal propositions, 60, 63, 93, 127, 142, 145, 151, 157, 158, 161, 301, 342, 356, 359
universality, 35, 43, 47, 65, 320, 326
universality of judgments, 320
universe, 5, 12, 15, 16, 18, 19, 20, 22, 26, 34, 35, 36, 46, 81, 89, 94, 105, 111, 112, 113, 114, 115, 139, 140, 141, 142, 143, 144, 149, 150, 151, 152, 153, 155, 156, 157, 161, 162, 289, 315, 316, 318, 332, 333, 335, 336, 338, 345, 357, 362
universe of attributes, 16

V

validity of the process, 35, 329
various suppositions, 144, 147, 149, 212
Venn, J., xv
verbal disputes, 27
verbal division, 314
verbal propositions, ix, 27, 28, 30

W

weakened conclusion, 210, 211, 213, 225, 226, 231, 277, 291, 363
weakened syllogism, 210
weaker premiss, 192

ἔ

ἔκθεσις, 83, 218

Related Nova Publications

Foreign Language Teaching and Learning: New Research

Editor: Terrell Welch

Series: Languages and Linguistics

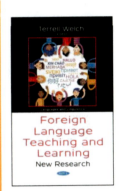

Book Description: *Foreign Language Teaching and Learning: New Research* begins by examining whether, and to what extent, the three types of linguistico-cultural expressions (proverbs, idioms and sayings) of Nepali translated into English would be intelligible to native English speakers and non-native English speakers outside of Nepal.

Hardcover ISBN: 978-1-53615-530-3
Retail Price: $195

The Linguistics of Vocabulary

Editor: Christine Hansen

Series: Languages and Linguistics

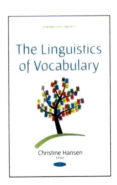

Book Description: In this compilation, the authors open with an analysis of the formation of philosophical terminology in the history of Early-Modern Ukrainian culture; specifically, two philosophical concepts—dobro and blaho (добро and благо)—are the focus here.

Softcover ISBN: 978-1-53613-860-3
Retail Price: $82

To see a complete list of Nova publications, please visit our website at www.novapublishers.com

Related Nova Publications

THE LANGUAGE OF PEDAGOGY TODAY: WHAT ARE THE NEW TEACHING CHALLENGES?

AUTHOR: Rebecca Soler Costa

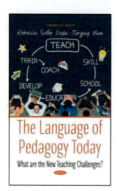

SERIES: Languages and Linguistics

BOOK DESCRIPTION: In the field of pedagogy, there are different publications about the processes of didactic interaction in the classroom. However, there are no scientific works that reflect an analysis showing the terms and expressions this language of specialty has in the conformation of its lexicon.

HARDCOVER ISBN: 978-1-53613-129-1
RETAIL PRICE: $160

TEACHING AND LEARNING ENGLISH FOR ACADEMIC PURPOSES: CURRENT RESEARCH AND PRACTICES

EDITORS: Lap Tuen Wong and Wai Lam Heidi Wong

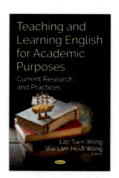

SERIES: Languages and Linguistics

BOOK DESCRIPTION: This book explores the teaching and learning of English academic discourse in an international perspective so that readers can gain a comprehensive and in-depth understanding of how EAP education is practised in different parts of the world.

HARDCOVER ISBN: 978-1-53612-814-7
RETAIL PRICE: $230

To see a complete list of Nova publications, please visit our website at www.novapublishers.com